PHILOSOPHY
AND THE
AMERICAN SCHOOL

An Introduction to the Philosophy of Education
Second Edition

Van Cleve Morris
University of Illinois at Chicago Circle

Young Pai
University of Missouri—Kansas City

UNIVERSITY
PRESS OF
AMERICA

Lanham • New York • London

Reprinted in 1994 by
University Press of America®, Inc.
4720 Boston Way
Lanham, Maryland 20706

3 Henrietta Street
London WC2E 8LU England

Originally published and copyrighted in 1976 by
Houghton Mifflin Company.
Copyright 1961 by Van Cleve Morris.
Reprinted by arrangement.

Library of Congress Cataloging-in-Publication Data

Morris, Van Cleve.
Philosophy and the American school : an introduction to the
philosophy of education / Van Cleve Morris, Young Pai. — 2nd ed.
p.   cm.
Reprint. Previously published: Boston : Houghton Mifflin, © 1976.
Includes bibliographical references and index.
1. Education—Philosophy.   I. Pai, Young.   II. Title.
LB885.M67P45   1993   370'.1—dc20   93–4902 CIP

ISBN 0–8191–9005–5 (pbk. : alk. paper)

 The paper used in this publication meets the minimum requirements of
American National Standard for Information Sciences—Permanence
of Paper for Printed Library Materials, ANSI Z39.48–1984.

Contents

A Critical Estimate *Philosophical foundations, Methodological behaviorism, The technology of teaching, Behavioral objectives and performance-based instruction, Accountability in education*
Conclusion

Figures

Preface

The American people invented public education. And for all of our other uncertainties and anxieties about the general state of things on our bicentennial we still harbor a quiet faith in formal schooling. We march in protest over bussing, we argue incessantly over why Johnny and Jane can't read, we systematically turn down bond issues and school referendums, we even listen attentively to arguments for "deschooling" America. But through it all, and in spite of our continuing uneasiness about the way schools are run these days, we still exhibit an unshaken attachment to the idea of free-of-charge, publicly supported, available-to-all schooling for our children.

Our attachment to the idea is firm, but our conception of what the school should be doing for our youngsters is troubled and in doubt. The design of the curriculum, the mode of instruction, indeed, the overall aims of education are still matters of fierce debate throughout the nation's 25,000 school districts.

It is in these hours of discussion and argument that the study of educational theory becomes directly relevant to educational decision making. When individuals disagree, it is imperative that they at least know what all of their options are and what possibilities lie at the other end of each alternative way of thinking. The examination of these options and alternatives is the chief business of the discipline of philosophy. This book proposes to introduce you, the reader, to the study of philosophy and to how that study can illuminate your understanding of education.

There are a number of ways in which educational philosophy can be studied. We, the authors, have chosen the route that might be designated the "philosophy-to-models" approach and we explain this approach in the following way:

Philosophy   All philosophy deals essentially with three major questions: What is real? What is true? What is good? Sooner or later all philosophical discussion ends up under one of these three categories. In the technical language of the philosopher, these categories are called *metaphysics*, *epistemology*, and *axiology*, respectively. Before anyone can think intelligently about educational philosophy, he or she must acquire a working knowledge of these three questions—what they involve, how the discipline of philosophy deals with them, and how they relate to educational theory. Accordingly, after a brief introductory Part One, we have devoted the first portion of this book to these three questions. Part Two takes up the question, What is real?; Part Three the question, What is true?; and Part Four the question, What is good?

Each of these parts is composed of a triad of chapters. The first chapter in the triad attempts to show what the title question involves, what its philosophical dimensions are. The second chapter examines how the question is dealt with by five major philosophic schools of thought: Idealism, Realism, Neo-Thomism, Experimentalism, and Existentialism. The final chapter in each triad explains how these five ways of dealing with the question relate to educational theory.

Models The first four parts of the book carry us to Chapter 10 and represent the philosophic base from which all educational philosophers must work. We now wish to use this analytical material in the examination, in Part Five, of three models of education, three general strategies for American education currently argued for by three more or less distinct groups of educational theorists and practitioners.

The first of these models we have chosen to call "Education as Behavior Engineering," a point of view holding to the mechanistic, behavioristic conception of humanity and advocating the shaping of human behavior through reinforcement (Chapter 11). The second of these models we label "Education as Self-Actualization," an outlook embracing the subjective, humanistic view of humanity and emphasizing the awakening of the person's inner self and its directive powers (Chapter 12). The third and final model, "Education and Cultural Pluralism," identifies with the contemporary persuasion in the social sciences that humanity is, in the end, a cultural artifact, both shaping and shaped by its surrounding environment and that each individual's education must be a full and variegated interaction with all surrounding value systems and life styles (Chapter 13).

In the exploration of these three models of education, we shall have occasion to employ the analytical material developed in the first ten chapters. In addition, we attempt to describe how these models work in concrete practice in contemporary schools. Finally, we offer a critical estimate of their long-range value in the ever-developing directions of American education.

In preparing this volume, we have tried to keep in mind that philosophy, defined literally, is "love of wisdom"—not wisdom itself, we must remember, but *love of* wisdom. As such, philosophy is one of humanity's oldest pursuits. It is also one of its most precarious. For philosophy is what people turn to when they are not sure of themselves, when they are confused and in doubt. Philosophy's attraction as a human enterprise, therefore, always teeters on the balance of whether or not it can help people in the passage from perplexity to clarity in what they are about.

Being a precarious undertaking, philosophy provides no assurances that it can successfully carry us to educational truth. We do not pretend therefore to hold out to any reader the prospect of a settled and certain philosophy of education upon completing this book. We offer the reader only an awareness of what is involved in the philosophic enterprise as it relates to the understanding and evaluation of contemporary movements in educational thinking.

Finally, may we make public our appreciation for the contribution of a small company of individuals who assisted with the preparation of this revision:

Catherine F. Morris, for her helpful comments and criticisms on the entire manuscript.

Charles Tesconi, for helpful assistance in bibliographical updating in Parts One through Four.

Martha Bunch and David Jensen for their comments on Part Five and Mike Spear for his bibliographic work.

Rosemary Mikolajewski and Pauline Sells for their skills at the typewriter and paste pot in putting this manuscript into shape for composition.

In undertaking this revision, we believe we have created an essentially new book, utilizing much of the analytic material of the original, but turning that material to a new and currently more significant use.

Van Cleve Morris

Young Pai

Philosophy and the
American School

PART ONE

The Task of
Educational
Philosophy

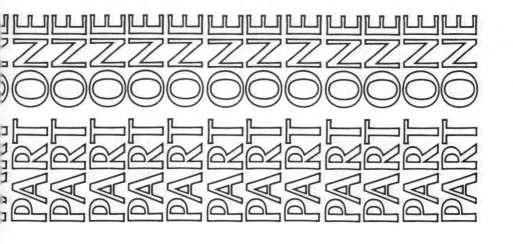

1

How Philosophy Works

Theory and Practice

Why Study Theory?

Beliefs have consequences. What we *think* influences what we *do*. Philosophy is the study of how we acquire our beliefs. This book centers on the connection between our beliefs and how we teach the young.

When we say that beliefs have consequences in conduct, we mean that we eventually reveal the ideas that develop in our heads in what we say or how we act in daily life. If, while getting dressed in the morning, the thought rolls around in your head that it might rain, you are likely to take your umbrella. As long as people thought the world was flat, they never sailed very far from shore. In an earlier day, many teachers believed that each child was born with a will that must be "broken" and reshaped along adult lines. Under the auspices of this belief, teaching included the periodic beating of children with a stick.

The word *theory* refers to a set of beliefs for which there is some, but not completely supporting, evidence. In the case of the "flat earth" and "fallen soul" notions, we have supplanted these "theories" with new theories of the cosmos and of Man. So theories can turn out to be incorrect, or at least faulty, in predicting what will happen or in justifying our actions. When that occurs, we try to develop better theories. There seems to be some drive in us to explain why things happen the way they do; we are theory-prone.

The connection between theory and practice, however, is a lot more complicated. Not only do we want to know *why* things happen but, more important, we want to know how to *make* things happen to our own advantage. The theory of the internal combustion engine was worked out largely under the stimulus of the need for a cheap source of power for human locomotion. The psychoanalytic theory of personality was developed out of a need to treat serious mental illness. There is, therefore, a vital linkage between a theory and the use to which we wish to put it.[1] This relationship turns out to be a two-way street.

How Theory and Practice Serve Each Other

Throughout history a distinction has been drawn between so-called men of action and men of thought. Presumably the same distinction can be drawn between "societies of action" and "societies of thought." American society certainly belongs in the former category. We pride ourselves on being "action-oriented"; we "get things done." We build great cities, big bridges, continental superhighways, enormous navies, globe-girdling air forces, spaceships to the moon. We produce refrigerators, automobiles, stereos, breakfast food, and cigarettes in wild profusion. In spite of the obvious damage we are doing to our environment and the ever-higher piles of garbage we are creating, we press on with this orgy of productive activity. We *do* things. And we scoff a bit at "societies of thought"—China, Tibet, ancient Greece—where people find reward in thoughtful reflection. We are even a bit dubious of Western Europe for its loving attention to the intellectual tradition. And, finally, we visit this doubt and suspicion on our own intellectuals, whom we condescendingly tolerate as necessary "freaks" of society.

No wonder that, of the two, practice rides higher than theory in most of what we do in America. If there is a discrepancy between theory and practice it is usually theory that is wrong. We say, "That's all right in theory but it won't work in practice," or "That looks good on paper but it isn't practical," meaning thereby that the practical is the more trustworthy of the two and should serve as the yardstick for measuring theory.

It is true, of course, that practice does just this: it checks and verifies theory. When the social psychologist develops, say, a "sociocultural theory of the self-concept," wherein the "self-concept" is the product of a youngster's constant contact and interaction with community, family, and entire social environment, then the teacher can check the value of this theory by putting it to work in group procedures in the classroom to see how boys and girls grow in self-understanding in direct contact with their peers. Or when the Progressive educator develops a theoretical idea like the "child-centered concept," for instance, the teacher can try it out in the classroom to see if it works. What is found will condition the teacher's view of the concept.

But theory fulfills this same function with regard to practice; it "checks" and judges practice. When we find ourselves, in the heat of annoyance, punishing children in school through the use of piercing ridicule, we ask ourselves if this is right in light of our beliefs about the dignity of the

[1] For other examples of theory controlling practice, see V. C. Morris, "Movable Furniture and a Theory of Man," *Educational Theory* 8, no. 3 (July 1957): 187–193.

human person. In this instance, our *theory* of human worth in a democratic order is the test of the legitimacy of our *practice* of imposing harsh or cruel punishment on children. Or when women are denied equal pay for equal work or their way to career advancement is subtly blocked just because they are women, we measure this practice against our theory of social justice. And what we discover when we make these tests against theory will condition our judgment of the practice we have called into question.

Always, whether we realize it or not, we are in the process of testing our beliefs through our conduct and our conduct through our beliefs. It is not so much that a particular practice specifies a particular theory, or that a theory, on paper, specifies a particular practice. It is, rather, that theory and practice *criticize* one another; they *check* and *warrant* one another. And since it is through a continuous course of criticism that we find our way to a higher order of activity—in running governments, in practicing medicine, in teaching the young—it is imperative to address ourselves, sooner or later, to the matter of fundamental theory.

THEORY AND PHILOSOPHY

Every important human activity can be shown to have a basis in theory, a unifying idea of what it is all about, what it is trying to do, and how it operates in human experience. Physicists have their atomic theory. They can't actually see atoms or tell what they are made of. But they can make guesses (which is an informal term for "hypotheses") and if these guesses help to explain or "rationalize" a large number of phenomena that they *can* observe, then physicists say they have a tenable theory of atoms. Or musicians have their contrapuntal theory. If sound is controlled by certain rules of composition, it will produce certain effects upon the eardrum. When this "eardrum effect" is shown to be associated with a set of ideas as to how music is built, then musicians say they have a theory of counterpoint.

So likewise in education there is a claim to theory, to the possibility of setting down general ideas that will explain and rationalize the various phenomena occurring in the educational enterprise. And, generally speaking, the larger the range of phenomena accounted for, the better the theory. We might say, for instance, that one theory of learning is that of *conditioning*, habituating the youngster to certain responses when given certain stimuli.[2] When youngsters learn the multiplication tables they are doing just this—artificially building automatic reactions to problems posed either orally or on paper. This, then, is certainly one theory of learning.

But can "conditioning" be considered a general theory of *all* kinds of learning? Does it successfully explain what goes on when a child learns the duties of citizenship in civics class, or the appreciation of great music in

2 This theory will be examined in depth in Chapter 11.

music class, or the difference between right and wrong wherever? Are learning citizenship, aesthetic response, and moral judgment a matter of habit conditioning? If yes, then we can arrange the educational situation accordingly; if no, we must state precisely how large a sphere of learning the "habit-formation" theory covers and go in search of other theories to cover the remaining areas of education. We may, for instance, identify other theories that help us understand other kinds of learning: learning as "disciplining the mind," learning as "the absorption of factual knowledge," learning as "problem solving," learning as "the development of the intuitive powers," learning as "conformity to the Will of God." We continue in search of theories until we feel we have exhausted all the areas of human learning.

The trouble with extended theory building, however, is that some theories may be found to be incompatible with others. So we attempt to organize the theories themselves into a meta-theory, which, in turn, seeks to harmonize, integrate, rationalize, and explain all the different conceptions we have built up to this point. In addition, a meta-theory, a theory of theories, provides us with the criteria by which we can evaluate the adequacy (comprehensiveness, consistency, and coherence) of various theories. It is this activity that we call philosophy.

Educational philosophers seek the single formula by which all human learning can be understood and managed. In this, they are principally engaged in the process of unification, in the endeavor to comprehend all that goes on in the educative process under a master set of consistent ideas, so that if problems come up for which ready answers are not available they can look to their theory for guides to practical action.

It is in this sense that a good theory is the most practical thing a person can have. A teacher who teaches by impulse, like an aviator who flies "by the seat of his pants," may conceivably teach well; but when unexpected situations arise the teacher's actions are likely to be flustered and thin. With a well-thought-out theory or philosophy of education we know what we are doing and why.

The practical reason for philosophizing can therefore be put very simply: to be able to explain our educational behavior, to be able to defend a position with respect to the management of learning. In these days of the so-called client revolution, there is a greater openness to the criticisms of learners and their parents about the school's work. If a parent challenges the teacher's conduct, the teacher wants to be in a position to explain what he or she is doing and why. A sound philosophy of education, therefore, is the solid base for what might be called intellectual accountability. It is the structure upon which one can provide a rational answer to the question, "Why do you teach that way?"

Teachers are not only accountable to their clients—students and their parents. They are also accountable to their profession. It is when our practical conduct becomes more and more rational, that is, increasingly subject to critical theory, that we say it becomes more and more professional in character. Truly professional teachers temper and redirect native impulse with the rational theory of their craft. It is this that the study of philosophy can help to supply.

The Philosophical Dimensions of Education

Education is a complicated business, especially in modern civilizations. One way of simplifying it is to separate its basic elements and to let those elements define the area of discourse.

One of the things educational philosophers are interested in, for instance, is the *individual human being* who shows up for instruction. Just what kind of creature is this? What can a person become? What is the potential of a human being? What, in short, is the nature of human nature, on which all education eventually works?

The philosopher is also interested in *society*, in "man-in-groups." What is a society? How does it work? What is the individual's relationship to it? Does the school stand in some special way between the individual and society?

The philosopher is also interested in the *cosmos*. What kind of universe do we live in? What possibilities does it provide? What prospects does it hold out for us? What, in short, is the meaning of life? And can this meaning find expression in our school program?

These are the kinds of problems that philosophers study. A closer look at these questions may be helpful in getting your mind in gear philosophically and suggesting what this book is all about.

EDUCATION AND HUMAN NATURE

Every educator wants to know what human beings are and what they might be. The anthropologists have told us that Man is a curious biped who *makes* things—tools, instruments, machines. He is *homo faber*. This being the case, it is held that education should be organized around this "making," *technological* tendency. We know also, however, that people can talk and write; they can live in a world of their own, a world of symbols. Man is *homo symbolicum*. Therefore education should also be organized around this *symbol-using* tendency.

But the educator needs to know more than this, for *making* and *symbol-using* can be used for very different ends. Taken together the technological and symbolic traits constitute Man's ability to build "culture." [3] Over the course of time, people have built many different cultures, each with its own

---

[3] Culture may be defined as all of the man-made parts of our environment—tools, institutions, ideas.

peculiar set of beliefs and practices. Hence, when we go in search of a common element of human nature on which to build an educational program, we are confronted by a multitude of possibilities.

Some of these possibilities are to be found within our own culture here in the United States. For instance, some people claim that human beings are by nature acquisitive and aggressive. People who talk like this are usually staunch defenders of capitalism as an economic system and believe that the school should encourage individual effort and the competitive spirit, with each child pitted against the others to motivate learning. Other people contend that capitalism brings out our least attractive qualities, and that, on the contrary, human beings are by nature loving, helpful, and cooperative. These people usually think that the school should teach cooperative effort and mutual assistance, with the youngsters associated together in a common enterprise.

Which of these groups is right about schoolroom procedure will depend, of course, on which is right about the nature of Man. Is Man basically competitive and aggressive, as the capitalists say? Or is he basically cooperative and generous, as the Judeo-Christian ethic has claimed? Or neither? It would be extremely helpful to get a definitive answer to this.

The social psychologists generally hold that human beings are really both competitive and cooperative, and that whichever trait the surrounding culture encourages will be the more prominent. Hence, Man's basic nature is to adopt the patterns of life about him. There are a multitude of these patterns, as we have noted, but what is constant appears to be Man's ability to learn any pattern of culture that is set before him. The plasticity of the psychosocial organism called Man is such that the daughter of Chinese parents raised from birth in an American home would become as thoroughly American in character as her American foster brother; and an American boy raised in China would become as thoroughly Chinese as any of his Chinese playmates.

What this signifies is that the general features of human character are social in origin: they arise out of the child's environment. It is theoretically possible, therefore, to modify and change certain aspects of human character through the control of an individual's experience. (See Chapter 11.) And since education is a specialized form of controlled experience, it is important for educators to remember that what children experience in the school they will learn. We are beginning to appreciate the fact that children who go to dingy, dirty schools, for instance, will grow up with different tastes in architecture, art, and interior design from those of children who go to bright, colorful, attractive schools; or that youngsters who are taught by teachers who make reading assignments a routine chore develop attitudes toward books different from the attitudes of those students for whom reading is made to seem an adventure into unknown and interesting places.

But does the fact that people are the product of their culture make them passive recipients of it? Certainly, they are, if only potentially, active contributors to it. Since cultures have been built, there must have been a creative element somewhere in the human material. It is this so-called creative tendency—of the original thinker, the poetic dreamer, the scientific inventor—that we have come to think the school should foster and nurture. We know that these abilities exist in some individuals. But are they, like other traits, themselves the product of social experience in a culture, or are they spontaneous and unique in each individual? In either case, can they actually be artificially excited and released in a deliberate program of education? Can a teacher teach creativity to a youngster? (See Chapter 12.)

Out of these creative insights and spontaneous beginnings, a rich variety of individual value systems and lifestyles has been generated. Many of them have withstood the sweet seduction of the "melting pot" and have evolved, over the years, into vibrant and powerful subcultures in the American system. Individually and collectively, these subcultures—Jewish, Irish, Polish, black, Chicano, Indian—are now recognized as competitors with and challenges to the dominant culture. Of the many cultures now extant in America, which should we make accessible to the child in school? If we present them all, which should we recommend? If none is to be recommended over any other, what does the school do when the values of one subculture collide with the values of another? (See Chapter 13.)

These and other open questions concerning the possibilities of human raw material obviously play a central role in developing a philosophy of education, for the powers we assign to the human material necessarily set limits to what we consider a person's role to be, in society and in cosmos.

EDUCATION AND SOCIETY

The School as Reproductive Agent   Every American, of all the millions now living, will someday die. We know this. If it were not for continuous regeneration of this group through sexual reproduction, we should certainly someday pass into extinction as a society. But we also know that each of these individuals will take to the grave the complex aggregate of behavior patterns and beliefs that we speak of as "the American way of life." And all the new individuals who are procreated and introduced into our number must be taught this "way," so to speak, "from scratch." They are not equipped with it at birth. And, if the society did not provide some method of social and psychological procreation, we might conceivably survive as a physical group, but we should certainly perish as an integrated society with beliefs, values, and ways of living.

In uncomplicated, nonliterate societies this social procreation of new individuals and generations occurs in the normal course of growing up and in apprenticing the young to the ways and thoughts of their elders. But, as civilization advances, the gap between young and old tends to widen; the growing-up, life-apprenticeship process is not efficient enough to equip the young with all they must know and understand in order to reach full adult maturity. At this point in their historical evolution, societies recognize the need for a formal and deliberate agency to take over this work, to concentrate and intensify the growing-up process, and to regulate it according to the developing necessities of any given social system.[4]

It is out of this social need for continuity that we get schools. Seen in this light, schools are not just places of convenience for the benefit of individuals—to expand their knowledge, to sate their intellectual curiosity, to prepare them for better, higher-paying jobs, or to give them an enriched form of social life. On the contrary, the schools' *first* function is to sustain and perpetuate a cherished pattern of living and to guarantee more surely that the society of which they are the instruments shall continue to prosper.

Viewed in this way, education is certainly the most important single function of a society. Not even the function of government outranks it, for while government may maintain order and tranquillity and fight off external enemies for short-run survival, there will eventually remain nothing to govern if the society does not see to it that each new generation is inducted into its lifeways. So we can begin to see that education is not only a social institution of primary magnitude but quite obviously the vital core function on which all else ultimately depends. It is imperative, therefore, for educators and educational philosophers to develop a theory of society, to understand what a society is trying to be and do, and then to translate that social self-image into a working educational program.

The School and Social Change   What makes this philosophic task so difficult is that modern societies—ours in particular—do not stand still long enough for the philosophic surveyor to get a good plot. By the time a generation of scholars and thinkers arrive at the working ethos of the American way, write their books and articles explaining this ethos, render their findings to the encyclopedists and applicators who themselves write books and manuals, who in turn convey their work to the textbook writers and teachers of teachers, who then transmit these ideas to teachers, and they to boys and girls—by the time all this has transpired, the fast-changing American ethos has found a thousand new interpretations, sufficient to make it appear almost a different way of life.

[4] See John Dewey, *Democracy and Education* (New York: Macmillan, 1916), chap. 1. When Dewey first developed this thesis, it seemed to most of his followers an illuminating but merely academic point, difficult to argue except in the abstract. They had no way of anticipating that this phenomenon would be illustrated and given vivid expression in totalitarian societies later in the century. The schools of the Soviet Union and the People's Republic of China are today living examples of the use of education as a tool of social survival. These schools have been taken over by their central governments as instruments of the state to bring Soviet and Chinese youth, by carefully planned steps, into conformity with the political objectives of their ruling leaders.

Examples of this "educational lag" are almost too numerous to mention. As a sample, consider the following:

—In the last generation, relations between the sexes have been revolutionized. Virginity is no longer a serious expectation by either party. Premarital sexual intercourse has replaced sexual continence. Prohibitions against premarital cohabitation have disappeared, and coed dorms and experimental "marriages" are common features of contemporary life. Victorian prudery and restraint have been completely put to rout.

—Since World War II, the "work ethic" so dear to the Puritan tradition has suffered massive deterioration. Coffee breaks have lengthened, the three-martini lunch has become commonplace, and the one-month vacation has reached into virtually every sector of the labor force.

—Over the last quarter century, America has become so successful at producing goods and services that it has converted itself into a "fun culture"; the *Playboy* mentality and what one periodical refers to as the pleasure machines (stereos, sports cars, sophisticated camping equipment, and house-yachts on wheels) have become a standard medium of self-expression, not only for the young but for all ages. Now, just as the "fun culture" is almost literally at full throttle, we suddenly find ourselves in collision with the energy crisis. We had been psychologically converted to an economy of abundance. What new form of Puritan self-denial awaits us as we turn once again to an economy of scarcity?

—Within the short lifetime of most of the people reading this book, the American polity has adopted violence as an increasingly acceptable form of human behavior. Far from being classified as obscene by the censors, murder and mayhem are celebrated in our motion pictures and on television as just another way for people to deal with their world. Gun-control legislation is virtually impossible to obtain in contemporary politics. Mugging, rape, gang "rumbles," and indiscriminate homicide have become everyday features of urban living. Finally, mass violence against helpless people has become standard practice by our national government in its foreign policy. American society now stands before the world as one of the most violent in history.

But the educational question we must ask is this: Has the public school been responding to these major shifts in public conduct, or has it tried to remain detached from them? Any observer would have to report that the latter is more nearly the case. The school has not discussed, let alone evaluated, these sharp turns in public outlook. It has seemed, through its curriculum and instruction, to be deliberately silent about the moral texture of contemporary American behavior. The world moves by, and as social practices and beliefs are wrenched into new shapes, boys and girls go on learning much that is neither true nor false but merely irrelevant to the world they can expect to live in.[5]

The school, therefore, at least in its present mode of organization, appears to be insufficiently connected to the life around it. In its contemporary conception, the school suffers from a kind of "cultural isolation." This situation raises a basic problem for the social philosophers of education: Supposing that this gap between school and life could be closed, what then should the role of the school be in a period like the one in which we live—one of social and cultural transition? There are at least four distinct positions that philosophers can take on this question.

1. They can lay down the premise that social change is completely irrelevant to the educational process. This view, usually taken by that group we shall come to know as the Neo-Thomists, holds that though the school is maintained by society it is not necessarily a *social* institution in the literal sense. Its social function, if you want to call it that, is to *transcend* society, to deal in the absolute principles and changeless values on which societies depend, whether they undergo change or not. Thus, in this view, a school betrays its true function if it turns away from eternal truth in favor of a shifting subject matter that has to be reshaped every September into a "modern, up-to-date" curriculum. For this reason, educators should, as the Neo-Thomist sees it, disregard social change and fix their attention on those First Principles or Eternal Verities that by definition never change and that every child must learn in order to grow up properly.

2. Advocates of the second position do not regard social change as an irrelevancy but consider it a phenomenon that the school should try to obstruct or, at least, reduce to manageable form for youngsters in school. From this outlook, which we shall later see is compatible with the social thinking of Idealists and Realists, the school is viewed as a conservationist agency, compiling and preserving knowledge, reducing it to study-able form for youngsters, adding to and correcting it year by year as new things

[5] The failure of the school in this regard may help to explain its apparent impotence on a more modest but related enterprise, that of equalizing the achievement of all youngsters by raising the slowest and most disadvantaged through special compensatory efforts. It used to be argued that the public school, since it touched virtually everybody, was democracy's Great Equalizer. But serious challenges have been raised to this claim by major studies during the late 1960s and early 1970s. In the well-known Coleman Report [James S. Coleman et al., *Equality of Educational Opportunity* (Washington: U.S. Department of Health, Education, and Welfare, National Center for Educational Statistics, 1966)] the overall conclusion of the investigators was that the financial support and educational quality of any given educational program makes very little difference in the ultimate development of the child, the primary variable being the environment in which the child spends most of his time, that is, his home and neighborhood. In a follow-up examination of some of Coleman's raw data, Christopher Jencks [Christopher Jencks, *Inequality: A Reassessment of the Effect of Family and Schooling in America* (New York: Harper & Row, Harper Colophon Books, 1972)] concluded that schools, of whatever quality, count for very little in the overall results of human maturation, the primary counters being social-class origins, desire, and luck.

are discovered, but not troubling youngsters with the turbulent and changing character of this knowledge as it is put to use in modern life. People have accumulated a great deal of important information about their world in the course of time. They write it down in books and encyclopedias, and teachers help young people learn it in school as preparation for intelligent living. The learning process, in this view, would be unwholesomely disturbed and disrupted if children were overly exposed to the changing character of their world before they acquired the accumulated knowledge of those who had come before them. Thus the school's job is to conserve knowledge, be its curator and caretaker, and dispense it to the young with the emphasis always on its reliable and enduring character. The school should not participate in social change. It should instead stand aside and equip the young with firm and stable knowledge with which they can figure out what is going on in the outside world.

3. These two positions strike Experimentalists as both timid and unwise. Social change, they say, is but an everyday phenomenon that reveals the changing character of the universe itself. The universe isn't finished yet— it is "becoming." And societies reflect this becoming-ness, revising and altering their beliefs and outlooks as they move along through social history. If the school is to serve society, it must acquaint young people with change as a prime ingredient of the lives they are to lead. This is the way, claim the Experimentalists, that the school truly serves society. We shall see later that the Experimentalists also hold that acquiring knowledge for its own sake is not what schools are for. Rather, schools exist to help boys and girls learn how to think, how to use their intelligence in solving problems. This world is full of problems, and our continual solving of them— under differing conditions and circumstances and with differing goals in mind—inevitably produces changes in it. Knowledge is to be acquired to be *used*, not just to be possessed in one's head. So, according to the Experimentalists the school should take an active role in social change. In fact, the school should try to simulate the wider society by rendering itself a miniature replica of a problem-filled world. By learning how to solve problems, boys and girls not only acquire knowledge but learn how to cope with a changing world.

4. The logical extension of this view is one associated with a special branch of Experimentalism called Reconstructionism. As the name implies, this school of thought holds that schools should take the lead in reconstructing our social order. Social change, in this view, is not just an earthly symptom of a "becoming" universe; it is the very vehicle of human progress and fulfillment. Furthermore, social change is getting out of hand, and if things are not managed properly we shall all be atomic cinders before we can do anything about it. However, according to the Reconstructionists, we now know that human beings have the equipment—intellectual, technological, moral—to take charge of change, to gain control of its dynamic processes, and to turn it to their own account. If it were not for

this, say these individuals, we should all be at the mercy of the forces that seem, in our time, to be carrying us, as on a huge ocean wave, to ultimate destruction on the rocks of our own stupidity. Out of a sense of urgency, then, if not for the more noble motive of achieving full use of our human powers, the Reconstructionists advise us to turn the school into the central headquarters for deliberate social planning and directed social change.

These four views, then, specify different functions for the school to perform in and for its environing social system. Since they help us distinguish between educational ideologies, it may be useful to indicate graphically how they are related. Figure 1 represents a time line from past to present to future. When we consider social history as a movement of human groups, through the time dimension, from past to future, we are forced to recognize that no single instant can be called The Present. Instead, we must consider the present to be the general region of the recent past, the present instant, and the immediately emergent future. Now if we can think of Western social life, particularly in a highly dynamic America, as moving along this time line, we may then consider the different roles the school might play as a social institution.

As we have already indicated, the Neo-Thomist holds that social change and historical movements are quite irrelevant to the work of the school. They are not genuinely real aspects of reality, but only surface characteristics of our temporal existence. Therefore, the school should be removed from and set above the chaotic conditions of humanity and focused upon eternal qualities as the proper intellectual and moral environment for the young.

Idealism and Realism, while differing in content, nevertheless join forces in their views on this question. Since they are essentially *conservationist* theories, their idea of the school is of a repository of the Western tradition, where knowledge can be accumulated, organized, and systematically disseminated to the young. Because the process of organization takes some

Figure 1   *Historical Time Line*

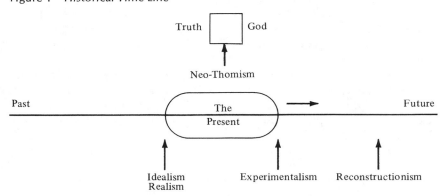

time, there is an inevitable lag between a new discovery and its incorporation into the books and encyclopedias. Therefore, we place the Idealist-Realist school at the "trailing edge" of the present, where it can best operate to integrate new knowledge into the curriculum and delay the assimilation of uncertain new ideas until such time as they have won wide acceptance.

The Experimentalist camp would consider the "growing" or "forward" edge of the present to be a more advantageous and exciting place for learning to go on. It is in the solving of real and genuine problems of life today, in the criticism and evaluation of contemporary knowledge, that youngsters truly grow. For this reason, the school must get into the thick of social life, not insulating youngsters from the dynamics of progress by exposing them only to the settled and agreed upon, but having them share, in increasingly sophisticated degrees, in the total life of the community.

The Reconstructionist, carrying this view to its logical limit, would have the school adopt an admittedly Utopian doctrine by which the dream we have of the future would be actively described and worked for in the school program. The Utopian future, then, would serve as the rallying focus for the Reconstructionist's curriculum, and this school would energetically nurture in the young a sense of social direction.

Another educational philosophy, Existentialism, which we shall also consider, has not yet developed much in the way of social theories. For this reason it will be difficult to assign any position on this question to this new philosophy. We have said enough, though, to suggest the *type* of question that educational philosophers raise when they consider the school as a social institution and the kinds of theoretical distinctions that we can draw between different philosophies.

EDUCATION AND THE COSMOS

The Meaning of Life   The most troublesome and yet most abiding question in philosophy is the question concerning the overall meaning of life. What are we doing here? What is the purpose of Man? What is a human life for? If there is a design in nature or a developing purpose in the universe, it is not unreasonable to suspect that the human race is playing out some role in it.

Cosmologists have recently excited anew our interest in this question. They are individuals who study the physical universe—earth, planets, stars, galaxies, matter, energy, and celestial motion. With their telescopes, spectroscopes, and complex mathematics, they are telling us that there is every likelihood that star systems like our own inhabit the heavens in the order of several millions.[6] Biochemists and physiologists, with their increasing

---

[6] For an exciting adventure into these probabilities, see Fred Hoyle, *The Nature of the Universe* (New York: Harper, 1950).

understanding of life processes, tell us that when the chemical ingredients for living tissue are present the likelihood is great that life forms will emerge and start evolving.[7] From all this work we are left with the distinct and apparently reliable impression that intelligences other than our own quite probably inhabit the outer reaches and that we are perhaps not so special in this universe.

When we consider these reports and these conclusions, we begin to wonder just what this planet we inhabit is all about, what its place is in the total cosmos, and what we as its passengers are supposed to be doing here.[8] Theology, of course, views these ultimate questions as its special province, but philosophy also seeks answers to them. And educational philosophers are or should be especially interested in them for the simple reason that if some reliable answers can be given as to the end and purpose of Man we shall be well on our way to understanding the kind of education he should have. If it is felt that there is a given design and structure to the cosmos one might conclude that our principal function is to discover this design and find our place in it. This conclusion would seem to call for an education to assist our adjustment to a given reality. Others might decide otherwise: that this cosmos is not yet finished and our role is to make it over—to the degree of which we are capable—into something closer to what it ought to be. This outlook would seem to call for an education that would awaken our creative and productive energies. A sizable amount of educational dispute in our time can be traced to the many aspects of this "cosmological" question.

Man or God Closely related to these considerations, of course, is the companion question of whether education is principally Man-centered or God-centered. If it is Man-centered, then education should encourage the open and curious mind to inquire into and challenge any idea it chooses, trusting that "truth will out" in the end. If education, on the other hand, is essentially God-centered, then there will be certain subject matters that the child must learn of necessity, that lie beyond the reach of question and individual judgment. Since they are authored by God, not Man, they do not have to be investigated or discussed, only learned in and for themselves.

You can readily see that here is a region where a great deal of educational dispute originates, for knowledge and truth are the "stock in trade"

[7] See Harlow Shapley, *Of Stars and Men* (Boston: Beacon, 1958), and also J. H. Rush, *The Dawn of Life* (New York: Hanover House, 1958).

[8] C. S. Lewis, for instance, raises the question of what would happen were we, in our forthcoming space travels, to run into an "unfallen race," a race of creatures who never suffered as have we the misfortunes of a wayward Adam, who, through a momentary lapse of judgment, got us off on the wrong foot with God. Suppose these creatures are, unlike us, completely in step with God and have no understanding whatsoever of what good and evil are all about. Aside from the trauma such a discovery would surely set in motion, what effect might this have on our moral training of the young?

of schools. Where knowledge and truth come from, then, God or man, bears directly on how this basic "commodity" is retailed in the school.

The Ultimate Moral Nature of Education   Finally it is necessary to connect what has been said with the essentially moral quality of all education. When we use the word *moral* in this context we do not have in mind the usual problems of moral conduct—stealing, lying, adultery, and so on—but the wider, all-inclusive meaning of all moral judgment: making decisions that represent what we want from life and what we want young people to become. Education, ultimately and fundamentally, is the process of deliberately attempting to make of the young something that if left to themselves they would not become.

If this is true, then it is clear that every deliberate system of education must make some fundamental decisions concerning both the type of society it prefers and means to bring about, and the consequent type of individual it values and means to produce. As John Childs has said:

> A school is organized whenever a human group begins to become conscious of its own experience, and desires to select from the totality of its beliefs and practices certain things which it is concerned to preserve and foster by reproducing them in the lives of its young.[9]
>
> . . . A manifestation of preference for certain patterns of living as opposed to others is therefore inherent in every program of deliberate education.[10]
>
> . . . As we introduce the young to the various aspects of human experience —familial, economic, scientific, technological, political, religious, artistic— we inevitably encourage attitudes and habits of response in and to these affairs. In order to encourage, we must also discourage; in order to foster, we must also hinder; in order to emphasize the significant, we must identify the nonsignificant; and, finally, in order to select and focus attention on certain subject matters of life, we have to reject and ignore other subject matters.[11]

The preferences and values that educators must perforce exhibit likewise reveal the kind of cosmos they think we live in or the kind of cosmos they think we *want* to live in. Professor Childs would prefer the "human order" as the final universe he would want to talk about. Moral judgments, he says, find their final validations in social experience. To say, as Professor Childs does, that education is a moral undertaking is simply to say that deliberate education involves choices that make a difference in the individual and social lives of human beings.

Other theorists prefer to think the moral character of education extends

[9] John L. Childs, *Education and Morals* (New York: Appleton-Century-Crofts, 1950), p. 6. Reprinted by permission of Prentice-Hall, Inc., Englewood Cliffs, N.J.
[10] Ibid., p. 7.
[11] Ibid., p. 19.

beyond the human into the transhuman or supernatural. Here, they say, is the origin of all morality, all rightness and wrongness. Hence, education is a moral undertaking in the sense that it attempts to divine the absolute goods of the supernatural and translate them into ideal images of individual and society.

In either case, education can be seen to be far more of a value-judgment enterprise than most of us think. For as we go to school and learn, we are actually being inducted into a system of moral and ethical decisions that have, for the most part, already been made. We in America grow up to value economic free enterprise; making money and accumulating consumer goods; social status, position, and power; sex; staying young; and personal self-fulfillment. These are, in a sense, all types of prepared moral judgments, ready and waiting for us as we grow up to adulthood.

All educators are therefore concerned not alone with facts and ideas and concepts. They are, whether they know it or not, confronted also by goods, preferences, desires, and "shoulds" that the surrounding culture continually forces on the attention of their students. Selection from this total catalogue of values eventually reveals the kind of world that educators believe *ought to be*. This kind of world they endeavor to realize through educating the young.

The Philosophic Task

THE SUBJECT MATTER OF PHILOSOPHY

When the philosopher begins work, the dominant occupational trait is to start asking questions. Questions, as a matter of fact, constitute the raw materials of this trade; philosophy is the study of questions, rather than the study of answers. The preceding section has indicated the general dimensions of education—individual, social, cosmic—within which the philosopher asks these questions.

What the philosopher is primarily concerned with, however, is asking the *right* questions. By *right* we mean relevant and meaningful. The philosopher's job is to ask the kinds of questions that are relevant to the subject under study, the kinds of questions we really want to get answered rather than merely muse over, the kinds of questions whose answers make a real difference in how we live and work. As this book illustrates, asking the right questions is not as easy as it may look.

One way to study educational philosophy is to take up one philosophical question at a time, first examining the many points of view that different schools take on it and then indicating the type of educational practice it seems to call for. With this analytical background, we are then in a position to examine and evaluate the several educational movements at large in contemporary America. The study of these movements is the purpose of

Part Five of this book. But before we arrive at that point, we must take up the fundamental questions of philosophy itself and show how they underlie the problems encountered by educators in the schools.

THE THREE BASIC QUESTIONS OF PHILOSOPHY

All philosophy asks three basic questions. The first of these is simply, What is real? This seems straightforward enough. It may sound, to the newcomer to philosophy, even a little too naive and simple a question for grown men and women to spend their time on. But, as we shall see, it is a very prickly problem, and it directly concerns education because the school needs to base its program upon fact and reality rather than upon fancy and illusion. A curriculum that announces the existence of gremlins and affirms the authenticity of giants in the earth is more than erroneous; it is downright pernicious. We shall wish to see, therefore, how the real, as against the fictional or illusory, is to be understood. In more homely language, we shall want to know what the world is made of. This branch of philosophy is formally known as *metaphysics*,[12] the study of what is real. Metaphysics is closely allied with *ontology*, the study of existence or being. In essence, ontology is the study of the tiny infinitive *to be*. We shall take up these questions in Part Two, which follows, considering first the problem itself, then examining different answers to the problem, and finally considering the influence these various answers have upon the educational process.

The second problem of philosophy can be simply stated as, What is true? It has direct kinship with the first problem, in that we want to know, first of all, how certain we can be of the statements we make about reality. Certainly we must have confidence in this knowledge before we go on to develop other knowledge. In reverse fashion, our knowledge actually depends on what reality makes possible. The real world, that is, must include the *ability to know* if we are to undertake the knowing process at all. All of these considerations come under the heading of *epistemology*, the study of knowledge or how we know things. We shall consider this in Part Three, looking first at the problem itself, then at a number of views of it, and finally at its relevance for education.

The third and final problem of philosophy consists of asking, What is good? In formal discourse, this is customarily divided into two divisions, the question of *ethics* (What is right conduct?) and the question of *aesthetics* (What is beautiful?). In both instances, we are dealing not so much with reality or with truth but with *value*. These matters are known under the larger term *axiology*, the study of value. We shall take this up in Part Four, with the customary trio of topics: the question, the several answers, and the educational implications.

---

[12] *Meta* from the Greek, meaning "beyond" the physics; it was simply the "appendix" or last section of Aristotle's book on physics, for which he could find no better name.

Philosophy and Its Uses

Education has always had its fads and gimmicks, perhaps more so today than ever before. But out of the welter of recommendations the teacher faces today, one can discern several emerging educational positions. Each appears to have a philosophical base and to have finally arrived at that point where we can call it a "school of thought." In Part Five, we shall select for special study three contemporary movements in education: Education as Behavior Engineering, Education as Self-Actualization, and Education and Cultural Pluralism. We shall examine these schools of thought now making the rounds in professional circles and test their validity in light of the philosophical grounds on which they rest. In this examination, you will begin to see how the analytical material in Parts Two, Three, and Four can help in understanding and evaluating the ideas put forward by advocates of these three positions.

Each chapter in the book is followed by a short bibliography. These entries indicate only a sampling of the references you might conceivably consult, but they are among the first you should go to if you are curious about any given area and want to expand your understanding of it. One way to quicken your curiosity and expand your understanding both at the same time is to engage in some "do-it-yourself" philosophizing. There is perhaps no more effective channel to keener perception in philosophy than a serious confrontation of theoretical questions that you recognize as relevant to your own life and work. You are encouraged therefore to indulge in this activity. Preferably you should not rely on the questions provided at the close of each chapter, but they are offered here to help you get started.

Questions

1. How would you define the relationship between theory and practice? Take, for instance, a field other than education—politics, agriculture, the game of bridge, architecture, interior design, football—and try to explain the function of both theory and practice in these activities. Is the relationship the same as in education?

2. In your own schooling, what would be a good example of "educational lag"— something you were taught in school that turned out to be *not* "the way it is"? Why do you think you were taught that?

3. Social change can be measured in three dimensions: the technological (e.g., invention of the automobile, radio, television, rocketry to outer space), the social (e.g., social inventions such as the labor union, suburbia, "the organization man,"), and the moral (e.g., changing attitudes toward such matters as sex, divorce, God). What should the school's policy be with respect to these different sectors of change—to stand above them, to ignore them, to report them, to help produce them?

Further Reading

Brameld, T. *Philosophies of Education in Cultural Perspective*. New York: Dryden, 1955. The social and cultural setting of education is definitely portrayed in this book. Especially in Chapters 1 and 2 you will find the purpose—indeed, the urgency—of the study of educational philosophy in our time. Brameld, as the leading spokesman for Reconstructionism, has developed this outlook more fully and more forcefully in a companion volume, *Toward a Reconstructed Philosophy of Education* (New York: Dryden, 1955).

Childs, John L. *Education and Morals*. New York: Appleton-Century-Crofts, 1950. In his preface, Childs writes that "devotion to the ideals of democracy in no way bars us from making a deliberate effort to nurture the young" in particular and specified ways. Selecting these ways is the basically moral task of the educator, and a study of philosophy is the prelude to the effective discharge of this task. Chapters 1 and 2 examine this theme in powerful and convincing language.

Dewey, John. *Democracy and Education*. New York: Macmillan, 1916. Perhaps the most frequently quoted statement of Dewey's, at least by educational theorists, is his famous dictum that ". . . philosophy may be defined as the general theory of education." Certainly no other author has shown so vital a connection between these two branches of human endeavor. You will find this dictum and the compelling elaboration of it in Chapter 24.

Feinberg, Walter. *Reason and Rhetoric—The Intellectual Foundations of Twentieth-Century Liberal Educational Policy*. New York: Wiley, 1975. In a wide-swinging, analytical treatise on the American liberal and the liberal's favorite institution, the school, Feinberg provides a persuasive argument for the view that schooling grows out of a body of thinking that is peculiarly indigenous to the American mind. Chapter 1, "From a Philosophy of Man to a Science of Management," is especially appropriate for the newcomer to educational philosophy.

Gray, J. Glenn. *The Promise of Wisdom*. New York: J. B. Lippincott, 1968. Although the entire volume is devoted to the function of philosophy in illuminating educational problems, Part 1 on "A Definition of Education" is as good a place as any to see how philosophy and education intersect.

Greene, Maxine. *Teacher as Stranger*. Belmont, Calif.: Wadsworth, 1973. In the rich and elegant writing of this educational philosopher, we learn in Chapter 1 of the joys and heartbreaks of "Doing Philosophy and Building a World." As Greene says, philosophy is probing, inquiring, questioning what surrounds us—always an uncomfortable, but in the end rewarding, enterprise.

Gutek, Gerald Lee. *Philosophical Alternatives in Education*. Columbus, Ohio: Merrill, 1974. Chapter 1, "Philosophy and Education," presents to the newcomer in educational theory a greeting, "Welcome to the teaching profession, but before entering, first consider the many ways that systematic philosophy bears on classroom instruction." Gutek's brief epilogue closing the volume also provides a glimpse of what the study of educational philosophy can yield to the aspiring teacher.

Morris, Van Cleve. *Modern Movements in Educational Philosophy.* Boston: Houghton Mifflin, 1969. In the Preface, Morris offers an invitation to the study of educational philosophy. This is followed in Chapter 1 by *Time* magazine and Professor Isaiah Berlin answering the question, "What's the use of philosophy?"

Scheffler, Israel. *Reason and Teaching.* New York: Bobbs-Merrill, 1973. In Chapter 2 ("Philosophy of Education and the New Activism"), Chapter 3 ("Philosophy and the Curriculum"), and Chapter 6 ("Philosophical Models of Teaching") Professor Scheffler examines the linkage between the study of philosophy and what goes on in schools—teaching, learning, maturing.

Smith, Philip G. *Philosophy of Education, Introductory Studies.* New York: Harper & Row, 1964. In his first three chapters, Smith invites the reader to examine three questions: What is philosophy?, What is education?, and What is philosophy of education? In these explorations, the student is shown the outlines of educational theory and how it shapes and controls school practice.

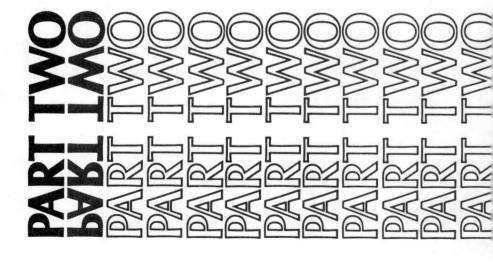

PART TWO

Metaphysics: What is Real?

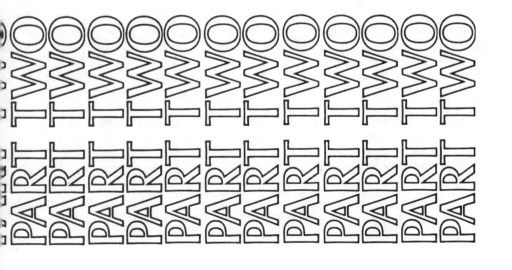

2
Metaphysics:
The Question of Reality

What Is?

THE PROBLEM

If philosophy is essentially a set of problems, the very first we must tackle is the problem of reality: What is the world "made of"? To many a reader, this will sound like the most fatuous of questions. Why should we waste our time arguing about the nature and character of a world that is so obviously clear to us day by day? It is just this kind of nonsense, some say, that brings philosophy into so much disrepute in the modern world, where people who disregard such ridiculous "ivory-towered" questions go blissfully and ignorantly ahead into their world and make it do what they want it to do.

The fatuity of our question, if any, is exceeded only by the fatuity of the above hypothetical response. The fact is that we moderns have succeeded in our bold technological exploits by taking seriously the important question of the nature of the world, not by ignoring it. Perhaps the classic examples of this are the atom bomb and its successor, the thermonuclear bomb, which stand as a kind of symbol of our mighty supremacy over nature. These amazing devices became possible only when we changed our metaphysics, that is, changed our theories of what the world, at its most fundamental and basic level, consists of.

After the early Greeks had spent a great deal of time and energy speculating on the relative merits of earth, air, fire, and water as the prime ingredients of reality, Democritus came up with the suggestion that perhaps the world is not made of any "natural essence"[1] but of tiny pieces—build-

---

[1] The Pythagoreans believed that all four of these were aspects of reality, bound together and unified under the fifth essence or "quintessence," of which the heavenly bodies were composed. This quintessence, sometimes designated as "ether," represented the *undergirding quality* of all the lesser essences—an idea that is very close to Aristotle's notion of Pure Form (see Chapter 3).

ing blocks of the universe—that could be arranged in an almost unlimited variety of combinations. These tiny pieces came to be referred to as *atoms,* a word from the Greek that means indivisible. Hence, the tiniest piece of matter, the piece that finally resisted any attempt to split or cut it, would eventually be discovered to be the ultimate unit of physical reality.

Atomic physics, then, originated with the Greeks, in the sense that the search for the basic building blocks of the universe began with their original setting of the problem. This search has continued down to our own time, and much research in physics has sought to locate the final "piece of matter." It was presumed by many nineteenth- and early twentieth-century physicists that the atom would probably be spherical in shape, and that matter, ultimately, would be discovered to be made up of an infinity of tiny particles resembling marbles or billiard balls in shape.

The twentieth century yielded information that the atom is actually constructed of still smaller particles—electrons, which revolve around a nucleus or "sun" much as the planets revolve about their sun. More recently, we learned that the nucleus itself is composed of still tinier pieces of matter—neutrons and protons—and these of still tinier ones.

But physicists soon began to ask themselves where all this research was leading. Was it possible, they began to wonder, to plumb the depths of matter to locate the truly fundamental particle of matter, the absolutely indivisible unit of reality? They had, of course, by this time gone far beyond the reach of their own eyesight or even of the most powerful microscopes. Instead, they had to content themselves with theoretical models of atomic particles, which they used to describe the *behavior* of atoms. At this point they began to realize that, in truth, it is the behavior of matter, as well as its structure, that represents what they were really interested in. Furthermore, as research delved further down into the family of particles, it became more evident that some nuclear force would be required to hold the particles in place and to account for their motions and behaviors. Soon the motions and behaviors themselves attracted as much attention as the particles. In fact, the particles came more and more to be understood as points or poles of energy, as well as tiny pieces of something. This led to the rise of modern physics, which considers matter as "constructed" of what the physicist sometimes calls "congealed energy" as well as little "marbles." Energy and matter, in short, are merely two forms of the same thing.

With this fundamental revision of thinking, there obviously came a thoroughgoing revolution in the meaning of physics, a new alignment of procedures and experimental design. In fact, there were whole new problems that would never have occurred to Democritean atomic physicists, with their exclusively "marble" theory of matter. One of these problems, of course, concerned the possibilities of releasing some of the energy trapped in the atom. The experimental results of this research are by now familiar to us all. But these results would never have been possible, never even dreamed of, if we had not first arrived at a thoroughly unorthodox, novel, and radically different view of the nature of matter itself.

The point is that we must attend to the problem of reality precisely because our conception of reality controls the very questions we ask of our world. And without questions, we obviously cannot have the answers out of which we may eventually build our bodies of knowledge and subject-matter disciplines. Put another way, the curriculum of the school—its scope and content—derives directly from what Man has come to know and value in this universe. What he has come to know—the sum total of his knowl-edge—is the product of curiosities he develops about his world and inquiries he makes of it in the course of his experience. These curiosities, these in-quiries, quite obviously are controlled by what people think their world is like and what questions and inquiries are relevant to it. Hence our ultimate preoccupation in educational theory is with the most primary of all philo-sophic problems: metaphysics, the study of ultimate reality.

The close companion of metaphysics, as we said in Chapter 1, is the dis-cipline of ontology. The two terms are almost equivalent in meaning. There is only a subtle difference: Whereas metaphysics is concerned with the nature of *reality*, ontology is the study of the nature of *existence* (or what it means for anything *to be*). Since that which is real is presumed to exist and that which exists is necessarily real, we need not quibble over the fine dis-tinctions between the two concepts. At least for the present treatment, the two will operationally refer to the same area of concern.

The Study of Metaphysics: Differing Views

It should be said at this point that serious preoccupation with metaphysics is scorned by a sizable segment of the community of educational philos-ophers. These individuals consider metaphysics an area of inquiry that yields little or no fruit for the simple reason that questions asked here can never be answered, at least not with any finality or assurance. Hence, they insist, other questions that yield more readily to human intelligence should receive our attention.

Some individuals, for instance, consider reality a kind of "given" quality or "ground" of the human situation. We are unable to discuss the nature and character of this ground because we can never truly know it; there is nothing against which we can see it. It is, as they say, a "surd," i.e., basically irrational or a-rational, possibly even transrational, or beyond the reach of human mentality, and hence not subject to intelligent study.

You should not get the idea, however, that this view, which we shall see is associated for the most part with the Experimentalists and a group known as the Analysts, is taken with a kind of highhanded disregard of metaphysical considerations. On the contrary, it is taken only after the ontological and metaphysical problem has been explored and found to be unyielding to inquiry.

For this reason, no student of educational theory can safely take this position without examining the metaphysical field itself. Furthermore, educational philosophers are not unanimous on this point by any means. Many of them believe that the metaphysical question is a genuine problem, that it deserves our study, and that we must go ahead and make the most of what is admittedly a very difficult task. Reality, from this standpoint, cannot be dismissed as unfathomable. On the contrary, the meaning of reality, the very meaning of existence—that of the cosmos at large or that of our own selves—constantly clamors for explanation. To make a steady intellectual attack on this question—even if it has not yet appeared to yield any very substantial results—is certainly better than to give up in the face of difficulty.

THE INFINITIVE "TO BE"

It comes as something of an unsettling discovery to realize that the most impenetrable verb in our language is perhaps the shortest and certainly the most common one—the infinitive *to be*. We say very casually, "I am an American," or "The apple is a fruit." We thus simply use the verb *to be* to identify something as belonging to a class of things. But when it is not used to identify a thing as belonging to a kind, the verb *to be* takes on an altogether different meaning. Consider, for instance, the statement, "I am," or "I exist." We sometimes affirm our own existence by referring to the fact that we were born; our existence is measured from the moment of a physical event. But this doesn't help too much. What exactly does it mean to say "I am"? Does it mean that I am present in the world in a three-dimensional kind of way, that I am taking up space? Or is the spatial quality of my being relatively unimportant and the presence of my psychic, inner "self" the genuine meaning of my existence? If this, then can we say we exist as selves at the moment of conception, or at the moment of birth, or at any other moment? When, indeed, does selfhood first begin? Is it gradual and evolutionary, or is it sudden and instantaneous? In either case, the meaning of our existence is not clear.

The case of the apple's existence presents other difficulties, even though it lies outside of us and is presumably free of any complications of selfhood. For when we say, "The apple is," do we mean that it is present in the world in a spatial way, occupying cubic territory in the cosmos? If this, how does one ascertain the occupation of such territory? The answer, quite simply, is through our senses. But, then, if there are no sensations of the apple, does it exist?

Finally, there is the question whether things that do not yield to our senses—the idea of loyalty, say, or the notion of time, or a thing like "democracy"—do or do not exist. If we hold that they exist, then quite obviously the use of perception as a criterion—the judgment of the senses —is not enough to affirm the existence of anything.

Perhaps, as some say, things that are said to exist actually exist in different ways. There are different classifications, as it were, of existence.

Apples may exist in one way; feelings like hunger, for instance, may exist in another; ideas like love or Communism exist in another; and perhaps human selves in yet another.

REALITY AND APPEARANCE

We can take a closer look at this problem of the varieties of *to be* if we consider briefly some specific varieties of metaphysical *procedure*. The first of these is used in distinguishing what is genuinely real and existential from that which only appears to be real and existential. (As noted above, we are considering the two terms, *real* and *existential*, as more or less interchangeable.) Our senses tell us that a stick is straight before we thrust it into the water; but when part of it is in the water our senses tell us it is bent. We retrieve it, and the first report is repeated. By such direct confrontation of competing perceptual reports we can make our selection of which is more "really" real, assigning the other to the limbo of "appearance" only.

But what are we to do with differing perceptual reports that do not directly confront one another? For instance, the floor on which I stand, to me, seems a rather straightforward kind of existent—it is a flat surface of a particular color that supports my weight. To a chemist, however, it is no such thing. Rather, it is a body of hydrocarbons associated in a particular way and subject to certain kinds of environmental conditions, such as heat and cold, wet and dry, and oxidation. To a physicist it is still different: It consists of atoms, electrons, and other forms of physical energy, which make my floor actually a jumping hotbed of atomic motion. That I can stand on such a thing is rather a wonder to me.

But the point is that the floor presents its existence in a variety of ways, and, what is more, all of these dimensions of existence seem plausible and acceptable, in varying degrees, to the chemist, to the physicist, and to me. Which, though, is most real? Which of these three "appearances" of the floor (there are many others) most closely approximates reality? Quite obviously, we are not prepared to say; the experience of the three of us points to different existential qualities. The floor, indeed, may be said to be existing in different modes.

We move from this rather simplified example of competitive perceptual reports to a slightly more sophisticated problem in which the perceptual reports are the same but are interpreted differently by different individuals. We are all familiar with the difficulty of securing the same description of an event—an accident or a catastrophe, let us say—from half a dozen independent observers. No chemists or physicists here, just idle onlookers. Why can't they "see" the same thing? But, more important, in the variety of reports, which one describes what really happened? How is one who was not a witness—a judge, say—to decide which report is the most accurate duplicate of the real quality of the event?

Quite obviously, this failing in the human perceptual system is a very real limitation in the field of jurisprudence. It is also troublesome in education. In the field of history, for instance, it is commonplace to say that different historians see the past differently. One would think that the past is the past, and that is that. Why then can't we all get together and write one final, objective, and true history of the entire world? We could then chop this up into smaller segments—chapters, topics, assignments—and hand it out to all the children of the world for their study in school. Unfortunately, history doesn't seem to work this way. History in and of itself may occur in a brute kind of way, but we never know about this. All we ever know about history is what the historians—either formal scholars or informal storytellers—tell about it. It must always be filtered through a human mind, and every human mind has its peculiar opacities and translucencies concerning the meaning of human events.

But suppose all witnesses to a catastrophe or all historians of a specific event in the past happened to agree on the explicit description of the catastrophe or the meaning and significance of the event. Would this be a warrant for us to say that the real quality of the happening had finally been revealed? If we say yes, then what we really mean is that reality can be ascertained through an "opinion poll" technique. If all the returns agree, then we have a picture of the actual existent—the thing or event. But suppose one of a hundred reporters disagreed with the ninety-nine others. Does this invalidate the testimony of the ninety-nine? What about 51 percent versus 49 percent?

These questions, simple and rudimentary as they are, illustrate the extreme difficulty of locating ultimate reality except through the clouded medium of appearance. How we consider this matter makes a difference in educational work precisely because our assurance must reside in the thing that we are teaching. We must feel confident that it is a representation of the real world that we and our students inhabit. If teachers ignore the implicit warning of such metaphysical considerations, they may consider their subject matter certain knowledge and feel they can afford to be dogmatic in their teaching and insist that their charges learn it without too much question. But if, on the other hand, they recognize the unreliability of human perception and observation, they may be more inclined to remain open on the matter, permitting discussion and the weighing of evidence, if appropriate, in the learning situation.

EXISTENTS AND SYMBOLS

Another procedural difficulty in the field of metaphysics concerns the manner or mode of existence exercised by physical things, which we perceive through our senses, compared to that exercised by the symbols we invent to stand for these things and the ideas and concepts concerning things that we "manufacture" in our minds and think about. Take this book you are now reading. Our senses tell us that it is in existence here in our hands. But consider the peculiar little series of marks we put on paper—B O O K—and the noise we make with our mouths from these marks to designate the thing we hold in our hand.

Certainly these marks on paper exist in a perceptual sense; we can see them there. And the noise we make exists because we hear it. But what we see and hear is not what is important. What is important is that something has been introduced into our experience that is *not* the book itself or merely a visual image or a sound but something that stands for the book and makes possible our "having" the book in our experience even when the perceptual book is removed. We have entered, as it were, a new kind of reality, a reality that transcends the perceptual, five-sense world that we customarily inhabit.

This "world of symbols" happens to be the most important "reality" that a human being occupies because symbols have the marvelous capacity to represent *all other kinds of reality* that our experience provides. Symbols can stand for things we perceive with our senses; they can stand for feelings inside ourselves; they can stand for ideas we think about in our heads; they can stand for fictional existents (ghosts, gremlins) and the most nebulous qualities of our experience. In short, they can open up to us the full range of our existing as no other vehicle can.

It is the power to symbolize, incidentally, that is now considered the essential distinguishing feature that separates humanity from the rest of nature. For a long time, it was thought that humanity stood above nature—most specifically the animal kingdom, of which it otherwise was a part—by virtue of its unique possession of reason. Thus the Greeks spoke of people as "rational animals," thinking that this definition clarified the matter. It has turned out, however, that if the word "rational" means "intelligent," then animals share, if in a lower degree, the ability to exercise intelligence and reason upon problems in their own experience. So we have been forced to give up this unique distinction, even though we are admittedly far superior to animals in what is termed "intelligent behavior." We have turned once again to the problem of locating a distinction of *kind* rather than mere *degree* to separate us from animals, and the most recent hypothesis is that the use of symbols constitutes such a distinction.

If this hypothesis turns out to be correct[2] then we can say that the world

---

[2] The issue is complicated because of the similarity, in the formal study of semantics, between *symbols* and *signs*. Signs—noises, gestures, visual images, calling for some specific behavior—fall within the powers of many animals. In this sense, animals can communicate with one another by means of a "sign" language. Symbols—noises, gestures, visual images which merely represent other sectors of experience—appear to be beyond the powers even of the highest primates. There is some doubt about this, however, and in the case of some very complicated and sophisticated experimental "problem-solving" situations [see R. Linton, *The Study of Man* (New York: Appleton-Century, 1936), pp. 65–66, or D. O. Hebb, *A Textbook of Psychology* (Philadelphia: Saunders, 1958), pp. 133–134], chimpanzees appear to be attaching symbolic significance to poker chips which they collect for later use in a food-dispensing machine. For a thorough discussion of the problem of symbolism, see Suzanne K. Langer, *Philosophy in a New Key* (Cambridge: Harvard University Press, 1942).

of symbols is the exclusive property of humanity. But this does not answer our ontological question: Do symbols exist? And, if so, do they exist in the same way in which that for which they stand exists?

This discussion may appear to be getting quite far afield from the study of educational theory. But actually we are dealing with a very vital question in education—the role of symbols in the educational program. As we have seen, symbols and their manipulation are the medium through which human beings, most particularly youngsters in school, come into an acquaintance with their world. But historically there have been numerous instances in which the medium of symbols began to take on an educational value of its own and the understanding to which symbolic manipulation should eventually lead was considered secondary. The most familiar example of this is the obsession of educators down through the ages with the study of language. Language is but a catalogue of symbols through which ideas and information are passed among human beings. But the study of language, not as means but as end in itself, is an old story in Man's efforts to educate himself. So rigid did this attitude become that in England and colonial America of the seventeenth and eighteenth centuries the very name for secondary education was *Latin grammar school*. The study of grammar was undertaken and made a central and almost exclusive part of a youngster's life for the avowed reason that the mastery of symbols in and for themselves was the mark of the truly educated person. To this day the single most important measure of the educated individual is the degree of mastery of one's own tongue. Content with this point of view, modern American educators allot more time to the study of English than to any other subject.

In the field of mathematics the situation is often repeated. Symbols—numbers—are properly tools for understanding mathematical ideas. But so much is made of mastering these sysbols that they are eventually taken to be educational ends in their own right. And boys and girls continue in their study of mathematics—into logarithms, quadratic equations, and calculus—far beyond the point where mathematics represents the *medium* through which they are to come to understand their world. They continue beyond this point because mathematics is thought to be valuable in its own right, whether useful or not, simply because it is symbolic in character.

We can say that educators who permit this to happen reveal their ontological classification of *symbols*; that is, they elevate symbols to a higher existential rank than the things for which they stand. Other educators, more favorable to *things*—concrete perceptions of the environment—reveal their ontological leanings by espousing direct, unmediated experience for the young. Demonstrations in the classroom, object lessons concerning a physical thing brought into the school, or field trips outside the school to learn of places firsthand are all specific examples of this tendency. The point is that whatever teachers believe about the relative ontological status of symbols and their referents will show up in their educational theory and practice. What appears to be a remote and esoteric consideration is actually a significant determinant of how we operate schools.

THING AND PROCESS

Another procedural problem in metaphysics concerns the relative emphasis we place upon the "thing" nature of reality as against its dynamic, "process" character. We referred above to the fact that twentieth-century physicists came to see the atom as a constellation of *behaviors* rather than a structural *thing*. This was partially due to the dead-end results of their "thing"-oriented inquiries. But it was also due to a new realization that the *behavior* of matter is of vastly greater significance to humanity than knowledge of how matter is built. Of course, in order to ask behavioral questions of atoms one must have some theory of their structure. But, increasingly, structure has come to be considered principally a means to the more vital end of comprehending the dynamic *processes* going on in the subatom. The transfer of physicists' concern from matter to energy reveals keener interest in the dynamic as against the structurally static.

This points up a much wider philosophic problem—namely, whether the rest of us should make similar shifts in our outlook. In the study of biology, for instance, the emphasis before Darwin in the nineteenth century was upon structure—the physiologist and the anatomist were seeking to comprehend the structure of living tissue. Words like *protoplasm* and *cell* and *organ* all suggested the structural approach. But Darwin introduced the concept of evolutionary process, and today biologists are not so much interested in how living tissue is built as they are in how it behaves. According to this approach *function* rises to a new prominence, and words like *digestion, maturation,* and *metabolism* become the verbal counters in biological inquiry. The study of medicine, that special branch of physiology dealing with functional disorders, concerns itself almost entirely with the *processes* going on in the human body.

What has been happening in the physical sciences has also, in a lesser way, turned up in the social sciences. The shift in emphasis is perhaps not so clear-cut, but it is nonetheless evident. Our social sciences used to consist only of history (the study of statically arranged sequences in human events), political science (the study of the structure of political institutions), and economics (the study of the structure of wealth-generating systems). But social scientists have gradually adopted a whole new family of disciplines—sociology, social psychology, anthropology—which turn from *structure* to examine *conduct* in human affairs. So thoroughly has this transition taken place that we now call these the *behavioral* sciences. Even the science of psychology, orginally the off-shoot of physiology and neurology, now concerns itself principally with human *behavior*.

Now the significance of all these changes in emphasis is simply that we may be altering our metaphysical outlook, our concept of reality, in favor of a changing, "becoming," evolving cosmos as against a stationary, static cosmos of pure being. Aristotle, of course, could see change taking place in his experience—nature is full of it—and certain features of his metaphysics appear to reflect a dynamic, world-in-motion point of view. But when he is all done explaining, it is clear that Aristotle believed change to be only a superficial characteristic of an underlying reality of things or "essences" that does not change. (The study of process, in our modern understanding of the term, would not have occurred to him, because essences, by definition, were static existents which "stood existentially still" in the Greek cosmos.) Indeed, it is still the popular theological view of reality that the universe was created in an instant and that, though it exhibits change and motion, it is basically in a state of indestructible "being." Except for Anaximander and Heraclitus in the sixth and fifth centuries B.C., men never very seriously considered the metaphysics of constant process until just recently—within the last hundred years or so, in which the scientific revolution has reached a climax. And since the dialectic between the static and dynamic theories of reality contributes so much to our understanding of the educational process, we shall wish, in Chapter 3, to study these competing views carefully.

Not the least of the educational referents of this discussion is the question whether youngsters in school should be introduced to a static world, where facts and formulas describe how things really are and always will be for all eternity, or, instead, to a changing, dynamic world, where facts and formulas are modified from one age to another and where only the *methods* and *procedures* of solving problems are necessary. The issue is considerably more complicated than this, but this will indicate its metaphysical significance and its educational relevance.

PURPOSE AND PURPOSELESSNESS

One final element in the study of metaphysics centers on the problem of purpose. Purpose, of course, is familiar enough in our day-to-day lives. We all have purposes, either short-range and immediate, like buying groceries, or long-range and strategic, like raising a family or building a career. Purpose is so much with us, as a matter of fact, that we often are inclined to wonder whether nature itself or the cosmos at large is endowed with purpose. Nature seems to present to us the raw materials out of which we could possibly infer some purpose. It is characterized by change. Without observable change in condition or status, there is no question of purpose. It is difficult to conceive that a stone possesses purpose.

But whenever change is present, there is always the question as to whether movement from one condition to another condition is prompted by some underlying or inherent purpose in the process itself. For instance, does a caterpillar purposefully set about becoming a moth? We usually do not use the word *purpose* in this way. But how about this: Does *nature* set about purposefully to change caterpillar into moth?

On a somewhat more sophisticated level, we can ask whether nature, by its constant system of replenishing itself through reproduction, actually is expressing the underlying purpose of life. Nature, in this light, may be said to be sustaining itself through its "purposeful" movement toward more and more life. The only trouble with this hypothesis is that death is quite as much a part of nature as is life, and it would be difficult to demonstrate one tendency as more purposeful than the other.

At a still more sophisticated level, the matter of transhuman purpose is often met in the field of philosophy and religion. The cosmos itself evidences qualities of change. Do these changes actually represent symptoms of a developing purpose in the universe? Is there a cosmic will—the Will of God, perhaps—which is unfolding before our eyes? If so, how do we establish the truth and accuracy of such a cosmic will? Are we once again driven to a kind of opinion-polling technique to find out what purpose is being expressed? These are legitimate questions to ask because many different religions have developed many different and even contradictory ideas of the presumably unitary "Will of God." Some hold that God will soon bring human life to a close, either because he did not mean for us to be permanent residents here and he has other plans, or because he has become disenchanted with our conduct since Adam. Others hold that God supports us, benignly forgetting all our sins if we are satisfactorily penitent. Still others say that God supports and "elects" a few of us but damns the rest of us. Still others say that God's Will was simply to create the world and set it in motion; by his own choice, he no longer influences it.

As we shall see in Chapters 11 and 12, our fundamental stance concerning the purposiveness (or nonpurposiveness) of the universe often influences the ways in which we think about people, their nature and behavior, as well as the ends and means of their education. To expand the context of that discussion, we might look at the matter in a slightly different way: We are uncertain not only about purposiveness *as such* as a quality of the universe but more immediately about what such a purpose might be, presuming there is one. Reduced to its simplest form, this issue can be compressed within the question, Is the universe friendly to humanity? Is it, as it were, "on our side"? Here we enter perhaps the most difficult realm of metaphysics, the subjective, anthropocentric judgment of the "attitude" of the cosmos toward the human race. Most religions, almost by definition, resolve this problem in the affirmative: The cosmos in some mysterious way looks after our ultimate wants. Certainly, this is one of the universal appeals of religion—its capacity to provide a home for the human spirit, a final anchorage for our bewildered navigation toward ultimate meaning in life.

But this tendency is also found in philosophy. Almost every recorded philosophy down through the ages, with the possible exception of Schopenhauer's "will-is-evil" idea, Nietzsche's "God-is-dead" outlook, and the more recent "God-is-irrelevant" doctrine of the atheistic wing of Existentialism, has ended up with a metaphysics that is either friendly to human aspiration or, at the very least, sufficiently neutral to provide the ground for aspiration. No theory of the cosmos has ever come around to the view that the universe is actually working against us. No view of this kind would be popular; there is too much built-in optimism in the human soul.

We must be cautious, therefore, in evaluating various metaphysical theories, for philosophers in general, like human beings individually, are tempted to let "the wish become father to the thought." And educators particularly must guard against this, for they must not deceive children into thinking that the world into which they are being inducted is more hospitable to their needs and requirements than it actually is. How hospitable it actually is, of course, is an open question. Different philosophies have taken different views. And consequently they lead to different programs of education. Some philosophies hold that the universe contains within itself the moral road signs which, if heeded, will lead us to the Good Life. School programs built on this premise mean to instruct boys and girls in what these signs say and how one is to follow them. Other philosophies, on the other hand, say either that there are no road signs at all or that what signs there are have been put there by the human community itself, to be changed and altered as the situation requires. The school program based on this point of view would lay a much heavier responsibility upon boys and girls not only to develop their own interpretation of the signs that are in place but also to locate the intersections in human experience where new or different signs are needed. The most urgent example of this is in the field of sexual behavior, where the established codes of conduct seem less and less relevant to modern life. Because this is so sensitive an area of human concern, and because we have not put up the new signposts, teachers in the schools prefer to remain silent on the whole matter, leaving children to find their own way. Whether this is or is not an ethical moral posture for the educator to assume will depend finally on the metaphysics we choose to believe in.

What Isn't?

But now that we have examined the dimensions of the question, "What is?," we are compelled to turn briefly to its opposite: "What isn't?" We have already intimated the scope of this problem by indirection, but we must confront it directly to assign its relevance to the educative process.

What was said earlier about the impenetrability of the infiinitive *to be* can now be seen as the problem of distinguishing the real, existential world from what is illusory, fictional, or simply nonexistent. Put another way, it is the problem of drawing a boundary line between what is real and what is not. If, as we pointed out, there is possibly a different mode for different existents—for physical things, for symbols, for ideas, for human selves—then we should wish to establish the specific standards to distinguish these existents from other candidates in the same category or mode that do not truly exist. If this book, a physical thing, exists, then how about the candidacy of a gremlin for existential status? If we conclude that a gremlin is really only an idea in our minds of a contrary little elf who commands an army of "bugs" that inhabit untried machinery, then what do we do with the idea of "careless workmanship" or "improper design," either of which seems to us a more plausible explanation for our technological setbacks? For these are but ideas also, and as symbolic referents they can claim no more existential status than the referent of the symbol "gremlin."

Clearly, the test in this case is our empirical judgment of what went wrong. As soon as we can lay it to our own errors, then we dismiss "gremlin" as a satisfactory explanation and hence from the realm of true existence. But where empirical testing does not pertain, as it does not and cannot in the field of religion, for instance, what are we to do with such transempirical (beyond-experience) ideas as Satan or "heavenly angel" or Holy Ghost? Some educational theorists would even place the idea of "selfhood" in this trans- or at least nonempirical category. But the educational question is simply whether boys and girls can be introduced to such concepts as if they stood for actual, bona fide constituents of genuine reality. The secular school, it is true, has chosen to remove whatever might be classified as *mysterious* from its subject matter. Mystery, except as a game or for motivational purposes, has no place in the public school program. But there are many educators who insist that mystery is a part of life and therefore ought not and must not be quarantined, like a disease, at a distance from the maturing and developing child.

On a much more prosaic level, we may point to the field of mathematics. Mathematics is, of course, a contrived system of symbols that refer to nothing in our experience; there are no twos and threes in nature. But we accept the reality of mathematical symbols without question and we make quite a business of teaching them to the young. Mathematics even invents purely imaginary numbers such as $\sqrt{-3}$ and makes good use of them in the development of mathematical skill.

In all these ways, the world of unreality constantly makes overtures in our direction, asking to be let in to the scholastic world of the child. And yet there are as well the overtures of the mystics, the astrologers, the religious fanatics, and the crackpots. Educators certainly should have a metaphysical yardstick to determine which shall pass.

At its most sophisticated level, the problem of "What isn't?" terminates in the logical predicament of what to do with "nothingness." Consider this book, the shoes you have on, your own person. Now consider that all of these lose their existence, they pass out of being. Finally, extend this to every existent in the cosmos, whether it be physical, symbolic, or whatever. What do we have? We have complete nothingness. But the fact that we can assign a symbol—*nothing*—to this circumstance (a symbol, moreover, that seems to have meaning) and the fact that we can conceptualize this "state of affairs" or this "thing" called *nothing* and work it into our language and experience might seem to qualify "nothingness" for existential status. Even if nothingness does not exist physically, it certainly stands as fully in our minds as any other similar symbolic quality, e.g., everything, cosmos, eternity. And if it gains entry as symbol, we are obligated to pay as much attention to it as to any other.

We come, then, to the ridiculous paradox of being required to say that "*Nothing* is a something," or, in the technical language of philosophers, "Nonbeing must be considered a special instance or mode of Being." We cannot easily indicate the relevance of this technical philosophical problem to education. It is pointed out here only to reveal how troublesome our world can really become if we take seriously our desire to comprehend it intelligently.

What Might Be?

Lying metaphysically somewhere between what *is* and what *is not* is the logical no man's land of *possibility*. To sense the proportions of this problem, we need only point to two concepts. If we refer to a "square circle," we are obviously not talking about what *might* be; we are talking in contradictions and therefore of what simply *cannot* be. There is no possibility of a square circle coming into existence. But if we speak of a gold mountain on the outskirts of Albuquerque, we are quite obviously speaking of what is metaphysically possible. There doesn't happen to be a solid gold hillock anywhere in the vicinity of Albuquerque, nor is there one anywhere in the world, to anyone's knowledge. But, even though it is geologically out of the question, from a purely logical and ontological standpoint we must insist that a gold mountain occupies the realm of the possible.

Now what are we to do with "possibility" in human affairs? To be more philosophically practical, what should we do with the possibility of genuine world government, with the possibility of a world order of Christian love, with the possibility of fatal overpopulation of the earth? Do these represent actual existents in our experience—are they somehow in place in the order of things, so that we can speak of them intelligibly? Or are they really only the logically extreme extensions of particular attributes of our social experience? Are they like the idea of "infinity" in mathematics and logic, which is logically *possible* (not contradictory) but, by definition, practically out of reach? If so, do these possibilities, like "infinity," lie within or outside of the existential world?

It matters educationally how one goes at a question of this sort, for we are permitted to dismiss from scholastic concern whatever does not enjoy existential status. Placing world government, for instance, outside the realm of the possible into the realm of the impossible (nonbeing) is to say that we need not—in fact, *must* not—point to it and draw attention to it as an authentic if only potential aspect of the future lives of our boys and girls in the schools. This practice would be, in this view, outright deceit. On the other hand, if world government is considered capable of existence even if only potentially, we are licensed to proceed with our examination of it, especially if its possibility is of transcendent concern to human affairs. We must, of course, make it clear to boys and girls that it is only possibility, nothing more. Whether people choose to work for it is another matter. But at least it is *able to be worked for,* in this view, which is quite different from the contrary view, which postulates that it (world government) is an impossibility and *cannot be intelligently worked for* in the political occupations of people.

This brings us finally to the crucial linkage between this matter of possibility and education. To refer again to the section on Purpose, we may now say that purposes are empty if they do not refer to what is actually *possible* in the metaphysical frame of the cosmos. In this sense, all purposes —human or natural or divine—must somehow be contingent upon what is deemed possible. And if what is possible is constantly hedged in either by a kind of overriding skepticism of human powers or by a view of the universe as a place where the lines of human direction are already laid down and specified (as in the Catholic religion or Marxist ideology, to cite a couple of examples), then it is clear that the educative process must be more dogmatic and doctrinaire, more unyielding in outlook, and more rigidly specific in terms of subject matter.

If, on the other hand, the range of possibilities in the cosmos is considered as practically without limit, and if, moreover, these possibilities are taken to be the occasion for authentic human purposing, then the school program will point them out to youngsters, will excite their interest in testing to see which possibilities should be aspired to, and will attempt to show the young how these finally can be reached. A school program of this sort will obviously exhibit greater flexibility in what it thinks important in the experience of the child and will place greater stress on the curious and inquisitive tendencies of the young.

Conclusion

So we come finally to the technical questions of metaphysics: What truly occupies the realm of the real? What really exists? These questions are beset, as we have seen, by several procedural hazards. But they are also confounded by the difficulty of assigning strict criteria by which we can separate that which is real and genuinely existential from that which definitely is not, and, in turn, each of these from that which is existentially possible.

As children are gradually inducted into the world of adults it is inevitable that their minds will increasingly take up the metaphysical question. Their first metaphysical problem occurs perhaps with the issue of Santa

Claus. As adults, we are piqued and amused by the intellectual awakenings that begin to stir in the five- or six-year-old mind. We forget, though, that metaphysical problems of greater complexity continue to arise in the child's mind throughout the years of development. And even after we reach adulthood we are wrong if we think there is no more to ask of our metaphysics. For if we mean to take life seriously—not glumly or morbidly, but earnestly and seriously—and if we mean to teach the young as competently as we can, we must continue the metaphysical quest into those higher questions of God and the human spirit. Not only will examination of these questions help us recognize the metaphysical stirrings in the life of the young, but it will, as this chapter has attempted to show, control and govern the quality and character of the educative process itself.

As we move now, in Chapter 3, to a consideration of several metaphysical theories, it is important to keep in mind that metaphysicians are unable to prove the correctness of their positions. That explains in part why we have so many competing notions of how the universe is constructed. Most contemporary metaphysicians are aware of this limitation and are willing to accept it. What they assert is that *their* particular way of arranging the world and its contents is their *recommendation* of how we *ought* to look at the matter because of the benefits that flow from a particular formulation. They are, in effect, saying that a particular metaphysics or ontological frame, although not finally verifiable in experience, is a conceptual scheme that facilitates our understanding of the remainder of experience and of the workings of the world as we encounter it day by day. In a very literal sense, the educational stategies put forward in Chapters 11, 12, and 13 are founded on different conceptual schemes. These conceptual schemes, as we shall see, do have consequences in our conduct.

In any event, the metaphysicians representing different philosophical persuasions are inviting us to consider the advantages of looking at the world their way. We turn now to these several alternatives.

Questions

1. How would you define the infinitive *to be*?

2. How many different kinds of beings can you name? We have mentioned physical things, symbols, ideas, human selves. Are there any others? In what ways, if any, do all these *exist* differently?

3. Of all the things that make up reality, are there any that are more important than the others? That is, is there a kind of rank-order of existents (beings)? How would you go about defending your list?

4. What difference in metaphysical outlook would you expect from teachers of different subjects? For instance, would teachers of the physical sciences, the social sciences, the languages, and the humanities necessarily have different views of what ultimate reality is exclusively or primarily made up of?

5. How would you handle the metaphysical problem of Santa Claus with a young child?

6. In preparation for Chapter 3, set down a brief statement of what you believe to be the character of ultimate reality.

Further Reading

Brubacher, John. *Modern Philosophies of Education*, 2d ed. New York: McGraw-Hill, 1950. In Chapter 2 Brubacher discusses the "generic traits of existence" as they are seen by various philosophies: Is reality changing or changeless? Are reality and appearance two different things? Is the world evolving novelly or has everything been planned out in advance? Is there a boundary to time (or space)? What is eternity? An excellent opener for a study of metaphysics.

Dewey, John. *Experience and Nature*. Chicago: Open Court, 1926. This is Dewey's magnum opus on what passes for metaphysics. Dewey was never too much concerned with metaphysical questions, because of their opacity when handled in open forum, where all questions, Dewey thought, should be threshed out. But in this book he attempts a "metaphysic of experience." (Give special attention to Chapter 2.)

Hook, Sidney. "The Quest for Being." *Journal of Philosophy*, 50, no. 24 (November 19, 1953): 709–731. In this article Professor Hook summarizes the many philosophical attempts to define Being. Then, in rather technical language, he goes on to declare these attempts futile. He believes with Dewey that Being is simply one of those *infinity* words (like *everything, the world*, etc.) we use to represent the ground of discourse. We can't really say anything about it; we merely assume it, usually unconsciously.

Hoyle, Fred. *The Nature of the Universe*. New York: Harper, 1950. For a startlingly novel and refreshingly anti-Genesis theory of creation, read cosmology according to Hoyle. The universe was not born in a thunderous cataclysm eons ago, says he. It is being "born" all the time, with the "continuous creation" of atoms of hydrogen, the virgin element. If so, is reality then at root merely "variations" on the hydrogen "theme"?

Phenix, Philip H. *Philosophy of Education*. New York: Henry Holt, 1958. In a book of essays (completely free of footnotes, by the way, in order not to distract from the ideas themselves) Phenix devotes one essay (Chapter 28) to "the ultimate nature of things," discussing substance and process, structure and function, things and events, essence and existence, mind and matter, nature and supernature. He follows this with a chapter on "cosmic process."

White, Morton G. *Toward Reunion in Philosophy*. Cambridge: Harvard University Press, 1956. The plan of the present book was inspired, for the most part, by White's discussion in this volume of the three major questions in philosophy: the metaphysical, the epistemological, and the axiological. For an advanced consideration of these areas in so-called pure or academic philosophy (as contrasted with educational philosophy), this is the place to go. In Chapters 1 through 6 White asks and reviews the answers to the question, "What is?"

3

Comparative Metaphysics

It is admittedly a long way, both logically and psychologically, from the concerns of ultimate reality to teaching young Joey Doakes in, say, eighth-grade social studies. But eventually, as we shall see more explicitly in Chapters 11, 12, and 13, the way we handle Joey and the material we wish him to know reveals our idea of what we think the world is like. The task of educational philosophy, among other things, is not so much to justify one metaphysics over another, nor, as a consequence, to justify one teaching practice over another, but quite modestly to try to build a connection in thinking between our ideas of basic reality and our day-to-day procedures in the classroom.

While the possibility of this linkage was examined in Chapter 2, it is now necessary to come more directly to the business of particular metaphysical positions and their implied specifications as to the manner in which boys and girls learn and teachers teach. In order to do this systematically, we will take up in turn five such positions: Idealism, Realism, Neo-Thomism, Experimentalism, and Existentialism, establishing the main concepts of each and pointing to their educational significance. The history of philosophic thinking is not, of course, quite so neat as we are to present it here. These systems (and the many others) were not established and then put in place as distinct and disparate theories of life. Instead, they grew and developed, like everything else, out of the conditions of the human situation at the time. As such, they represent what different people, living in different places and times, believed to be significant and important in their experience. Viewing these separate theories in this light, we must not expect them to be mutually exclusive in every respect—that is, to be distinct theories that are entirely different from one another. Rather, they are "magnetic poles" of emphasis, around which certain beliefs are collected and made systematically intelligible. This means that some of the theories we separate for the convenience of study and analysis will often be seen to have a kinship with one another. Or, attacking problems in human experience from different sectors, they will arrive at conclusions that are quite similar, even though expressed in different language. Just to give a brief example, we can point to the idea of "soul" in theological writings as being intellectually close to the idea of "self," particularly as the "self" is defined by Idealists. And when both the theologian and the Idealist philosopher, in the development of their notions of "soul" and "self," construe the idea of "will" in the same way, we should not be too surprised.

With this forewarning not to take these five sections as idea-tight compartments but as regions on the spectrum of ideas, we may begin to see how different metaphysical theories come into being by the way in which they point to and emphasize different characteristics of human experience.

Idealism: A World of Mind

PLATO'S CAVE

The quickest and most efficient way of coming to understand Idealist metaphysics is to go directly to the forefather of all Idealists—Plato. In *The Republic*, his major treatise on the ideal state, Plato has given us the famous Allegory of the Cave.[1] Imagine, he suggests, a group of people sitting in a dark cave chained down in such a way that they can look in only one direction, toward the expanse of wall on one side of the cave. Several yards behind them is an open fire providing light, and between the fire and where they are sitting is a raised runway along which figures move, casting their shadows upon the wall. The individuals, chained so that they face the wall, cannot see the fire or the figures, but only the shadows. Now, if we imagine them confined to this position for their entire lives, we must expect them to consider the shadows as real, genuinely existent beings. Not knowing anything else, having no three-dimensional beings to use for comparison, these prisoners in the cave would come to believe that what they saw before them represented true reality.

Now imagine that they are unchained and can turn around to see the fire and the figures that have occasioned the shadows. Certainly, says Plato, they would readjust their conception of reality, altering it to fit the new perceptual data that their eyes are now able to collect. Moving about the cave, they begin to get a sense of the three-dimensional character of their environment. They conclude by thinking that they had been fooled all along and that now they truly know what reality is.

But then imagine that they are led from the cave into the blinding brilliance of a noonday sun outside. Wouldn't they, asks Plato, be struck dumb by the complete impossibility of it? Wouldn't they turn away in

[1] Plato, *The Republic*, trans. Francis Cornford (New York: Oxford University Press, 1958), bk. 7, steph. 514–518.

complete bewilderment, not wishing to see the real truth of their world? Wouldn't they gradually retreat to their cave, preferring its more manageable environment to the fantastically incredible world of space and sunlight?

Well, then, suggests the allegory, here we humans are in our own cave —the world as we see it with our five senses. It looks real enough: rocks and trees and birds and people. But it is actually only a world of images, three-dimensional "shadows" of another, more genuinely real world, a world of *pure ideas*, standing "behind" this world we see and hear and touch. And this realm of pure ideas or "pure mind" is so absolute in its perfection, so superlatively complete in every way, as to possess an intensity beyond the reach of the human mind. Like the sun that blinds our eyes, the "Absolute Mind" completely overwhelms our feeble intellects; and we turn away from it, as we turn our eyes from the sun, bedazzled and "injured" by our attempt to perceive it. And so, preferring a more manageable and comfortable existence, even if less genuinely real, we retreat to our "cave," the world of sense perception, permitting our intellects only occasional and fleeting glimpses of ultimate reality.[2]

Figure 2 may help you visualize this "two-world" concept of Plato's. Everything we see in our experience—trees, chairs, books, circles, people— is only a limited and imperfect expression of an underlying idea. Every tree we see is different, but there is an *Idea* of tree-ness which they all share. Chairs we can see and sit in; but what is *really* real is not this chair or that, but the *Idea* of "chair," the idea that actually supports and sustains all the individual objects we call chairs; for without this idea no chair could come into being for us to use. Likewise, people can draw circles, but only imperfect ones; a perfect circle is only an idea in our minds that we try to copy. It is the Idea of circularity that is truly and genuinely real, for it is eternal and unchanging.

We can draw an analogy with identical trinkets in a toy store—let us say a shelfful of cast models of the Empire State Building. Each of these toy models is slightly different, showing imperfections of one kind or another. But they all came from the same mold. And it is the mold that gave them form and meaning. Thus the mold is the authentic reality. The several models are only limited expressions of the "idea" of the model contained in the mold. In like fashion, everything we see and perceive in this world is but a transient and fleeting replica or "shadow" of eternal qualities—what Plato called "Ideas"—and it is the world of these "Ideas" that constitutes ultimate and absolute reality.

It is from Plato's conception of ultimate Ideas that we get the word *Idealism*. Technically, it should read *Idea-ism*, a metaphysics of ideas.

---

[2] Like the yogi who finds supreme happiness in worshipping his deity by staring at the sun, Man can find his highest being by "staring" at eternal and universal ideas, by pointing his mind toward the Absolute. Thus, to Plato, the highest form of human existence was the life of pure contemplation.

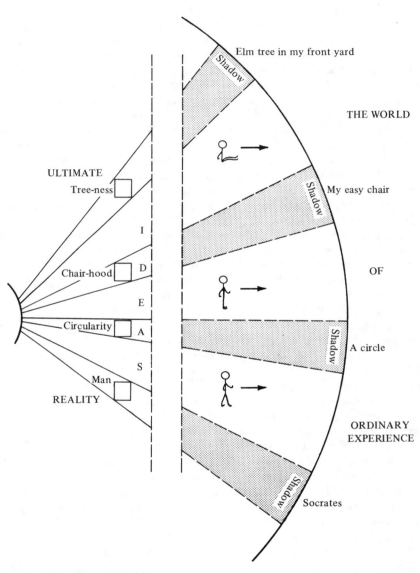

Figure 2   Plato's Two Worlds

Plato was not talking about ideals in the sense of valued ends or goals to reach. He referred only to ideas and to the fact that ideas in their ultimate form are the "figures" behind us that cast their "shadows" (in the form of things we experience in our world) on the walls of our cave. The *l* in *Idealism* is inserted only for the sake of euphony.

THE APPARENT AND THE REAL

In Idealism, therefore, we need to divide all reality into two major divisions: the apparent and the real. The "apparent" realm is our day-to-day experience as mortals. This is the region of change, of coming and going, of being born, growing, aging, and dying; it is the realm of imperfection, irregularity, and disorder; finally, it is the world of trouble and suffering, evil and sin. The "real" world, fortunately, is not like this. It is the home of the mind, the realm of ideas; it is therefore the home of eternal qualities, of permanence, of regularity, of order, of absolute truth and value.

Of the two, quite obviously, the idea-l is of higher rank. Not only is it distinct from the world we know directly, but it stands existentially higher. This is because perfection reigns there. Perfect things are those things that do not change; they don't have to. What conceivably could they change to? Since eternal ideas do not change, they represent a perfect order. This fundamental value judgment—that that which is of the mind is of higher rank than that which is of the world of things—is so deeply embedded into Western culture's thinking processes that it is almost never challenged. The Greek philosophers more than 2,000 years ago formalized and announced this doctrine, and we have believed ever since that that which is removed from this world and eternal is somehow of higher existential status than the world we experience, that is, the world of change, of growth, of problems and purposes.

We see this bias most tenaciously held to, incidentally, in the field of education. To this day, in most high schools, the subject matter of ideas— literature, for example—is considered by most people to be of higher rank and greater importance than the subject matter of physical things—auto mechanics, for example. Throughout the curriculum there is a kind of established hierarchy of subjects. Toward the top of this hierarchy are the subjects whose content consists of ideas and concepts. These subject matters are, generally speaking, given and settled: mathematics, the languages, and history. In the middle of the list are the sciences, which, though they search for certainty and permanent truth, never seem to reach it because all science by definition is inextricably embedded in the physical world of indeterminacy and change. Finally, at the bottom, are the technical and manual subjects—home economics, wood shop, arts and crafts, and driver education—which are relatively less concerned with the theoretical and conceptual, stressing primarily tactics and techniques.

At the college level the Idealist bias is even more obvious. The liberal arts are thought to provide substance for reflection and the liberation of the mind. Necessarily such studies are found among the subjects that are theoretical, abstract, and symbolic in character and that rely on a great deal of book learning. Anything that is seen to be occupationally useful or applicable to preparation for a profession or a calling is immediately relegated to nonliberal-arts status such as "premed," "prelaw," or "professional training." Thus whatever is too closely related to the world of action, of change, of making a livelihood, is held of lower rank than that which is relatively abstract (in the best sense of that term) and more remote and insulated from ordinary affairs.

THE WORLD AS IDEA

The Idealists, then, begin their systematic thinking with the fundamental view that ultimate reality is of the nature of mind. There are different varieties of Idealism, and the metaphysics of Idea is expressed in different ways. But it is enough at this point to establish the root position from which these varying interpretations have historically developed.

Hegel, for instance, went beyond Plato and added the *dynamic* interpretation of Idealism. All reality, said Hegel, is the surging and moving contest between opposites: night and day, cold and hot, up and down, life and death. This "contest of opposites" represents the so-called dialectic of nature, a dialectic re-enacted in human nature also. Ordinary human thought is possible only by virtue of contending ideas competing for attention in our consciousness: love and hate, justice and injustice, individual and society, order and chaos. Indeed, thought Hegel, each of Plato's Ideas has its own antithesis. Hence, Plato's Ideal realm is not just an eternal residence for static ideas, but a moving, flowing stream of conscious intelligence at work in the world. It is, as it were, an Absolute Mind thinking out its world.

Technically, Hegel used the thesis-antithesis-synthesis triad to explain what he meant by this. Every *thesis* (e.g., man is an end in himself) can be set against its *antithesis* (e.g., man cannot be merely an end to himself —he must also live for others). This confrontation of opposites produces a resolution of the issue, or *synthesis* (e.g., man fulfills his true end by serving others). The synthesis then becomes a new thesis, to be counterposed with a new antithesis, which, in turn, yields a new synthesis, ad infinitum. (See Figure 3.)

This, said Hegel, is the way in which history, for example, can be understood. Concrete events in the past are only particular expressions of much larger and longer-range movements and trends. The American Revolution resulted from a collision of the "thesis" of old-world monarchic authoritarianism and the "antithesis" of colonial libertarianism. The issue was joined and the "synthesis" of the American republic was the result. But almost immediately this synthesis became a new thesis, with Hamilton's Federal-

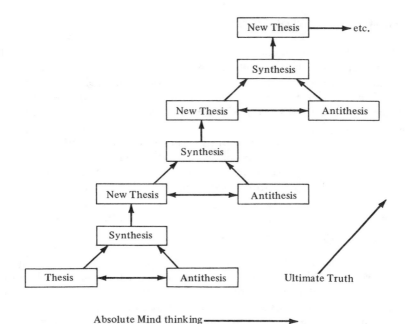

Figure 3   *Hegel's Dialectic*

ists representing a new antithesis. The synthesis eventually came to be the system lying somewhere between Hamiltonianism and Jeffersonianism.

But then this became a new thesis, to be contested by Jacksonianism later in the century. The dialectic continued, to find a new expression in the Civil War. This war subsequently produced a new set of circumstances which themselves were seen to be in need of change and reform. On and on it goes, but through it all, thought Hegel, a Cosmic Idea is trying to express itself in the historic events of people and societies. This Cosmic Idea is Ultimate Reality, or at least a segment of it, seeking expression in the world of physical reality and constant change. It is, as it were, an idea that is being thought by Absolute Mind, which led Hegel to say that "history is God thinking." God thinks out his plans and purposes through the instumentality of human history. He tries things out, waits for the results, weighs the pros and cons (the dialectic), and then tries new combinations (syntheses) to see if they will work even better.

Throughout the process, Ultimate Reality can be glimpsed from time to time by the limited intellectual perceptions of people; sages and prophets, scholars and poets, artists and theologians—all make a business of this attempt to peer into the Absolute. It is as if all people were straining to have the experience reported by Handel after composing *The Messiah* in the concentrated space of twenty-four days in 1741: "I did think I did see all Heaven before me, and the Great God Himself."

Realism: A World of Things

If Plato is the Father of Idealism, we can point to his pupil Aristotle as the Father of Realism. The name Realism may strike some kind of ironic note for you. Is Realism, you ask, the only "realistic" philosophy? Does it somehow have a corner on reality, an authentic insight into what is truly real? The answer, generally speaking, must be no. We give the name Realism to those theories that find in the world of physical things, and in our perceptions and experiences of those things, the basis for an understanding of what is truly real. Realists do not, as Plato did, feel the necessity to flee to some realm of nonsensory qualities to find out what is genuinely real. With this in mind, we can begin to understand more in detail what the Realist metaphysics is.

ARISTOTLE'S BAREHANDED INTERPRETATION

Aristotle stands at the base of this intellectual structure by virtue both of the supreme simplicity of his approach to the metaphysical problem and of his extravagant genius in providing an answer to it—an answer, incidentally, that has shaped the Western mind for over 2,000 years and which, in many respects, is still dominant today. Working without microscope or telescope, ignorant of atomic or nuclear physics and concepts of heredity and biological evolution, Aristotle stood barehanded before an awesome cosmos and asked himself the simple question, What do I see? His answer was the same as any individual's would be: I see earth beneath my feet. I see objects—trees, birds, people, houses, a multitude of things—before my eyes. I see sun and moon and stars high in the heavens.

Now what, to ask the first question, do all these things have in common? What, that is, can we say of all of them taken together? First, they all seem to be made of something, some stuff that serves as a raw material. We shall call this Matter. Everything, without exception, can be said to be composed of Matter.

But we notice more. We notice that these things can be distinguished one from another. The Matter of which they are made is arranged in different ways, taking on one form in a stone, another in a blade of grass, another in people, still another in sun and moon. Each thing in its own way is different from the next thing. This difference is occasioned by the particular form or design that the basic stuff, Matter, has assumed in each thing. We shall call this the Principle of Form.

THE FORM-MATTER HYPOTHESIS

Taking these perceptions, Aristotle then exhibited the magnificence of his genius by putting them together into what he called the Form-Matter

Hypothesis. We can notice, he said, that looking downward we see the nearest thing to Prime Matter, the earth beneath our feet. This Matter is inchoate, apparently in its virgin state, just there in a brute kind of way and possessing only the minimum of Form. But as we lift our eyes, moving physically upward, we begin to see more and more of the distinguishing element in things. We see plants of different sorts, animals of different kinds; we see people. We notice also that people stand vertically erect and that, as Plato pointed out, as we move physically upward in Man from genitals and viscera, the locus of purely animal functions, to heart and breast, the locus of the higher virtues of courage and valor, to head, the locus of the highest virtues of reason and thought, we can see a gradual reduction of the principle of Matter (Body) and a gradual increase in the Principle of Form (Mind). Finally, as we leave Man and cast our eyes upward into the heavens, we see even less Matter, only points of light moving in regularly patterned and mathematically precise ways, which to Aristotle represented a more nearly pure expression of the Principle of Form.

What we can actually see and perceive in our own experience Aristotle then put into a logical system. Matter, standing at the base of all things, became for him the Principle of Potentiality: Matter can become any thing; it can be shaped and organized into any kind of being; and without it no *thing* is possible. However, Matter cannot achieve thinghood alone. By itself, it is nothing; to become anything it requires the stamp of Form. That is, Matter has to assume the shape and form of some particular thing before it can actualize its potentiality. Hence, to Aristotle, Form was the Principle of Actuality. Each Principle—Matter and Form—must be considered logically separate; they are two different concepts. But they are never found separately in our experience; necessarily, they are always found associated in the things that constitute the cosmos.

We can visualize this Aristotelian system by means of a pyramidal arrangement of ideas. (See Figure 4.) At the base of the metaphysical pyramid is Matter, representing pure possibility. Alone it is nothing, but it serves as the ingredient of potentiality, from which all things are made. As we rise in the pyramid, we see Matter assuming more and more Form (more varieties of distinguishable entities, more complex organizations of Matter in living organisms, and more evidence of immaterial qualities, such as sensation, thought, and, eventually, pure contemplation). As we rise in this system, the operations of order, pattern, regularity and perfection—in short, the attributes of Mind and Reason— become increasingly noticeable, until ultimately there emerges Pure Mind, Absolute Reason, or, as Aristotle called it, Pure Form. As human beings, we can never hope to know or understand this apex of the pyramid; but we can, by logical extension, comprehend its role: It is the Principle of Reason, "knowing and ruling all the categories of nature. [Here is] the

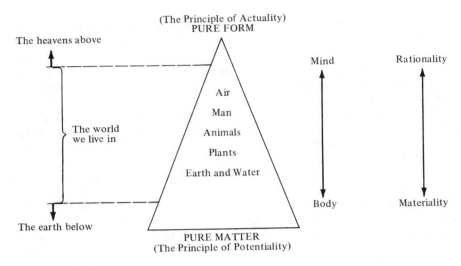

Figure 4   Aristotle's Form-Matter Hypothesis

great First Cause, the Prime Mover, the Absolute Knower, independent of the world, but acting upon it and endowing it with movement, development, order, and reason." [3] It is as if an enormous metaphysical magnet—the magnet of Actuality—were drawing all lesser potentialities toward it.

PLATO AND ARISTOTLE

By this stroke of genius, therefore, Aristotle put back together a world that Plato had rent asunder. There are not two separate realities, one of ideas and another of sense, with one higher than the other, as Plato said. There is only one reality, a hierarchy of things stretching in both directions between the ground of potentiality and the pinnacle of actuality. We ourselves stand somewhere in the middle of the metaphysical spectrum, sharing through our bodies in the materiality of things but participating through our minds—at a very modest level, to be sure—in the rationality of Pure Form. Though we cannot ever directly know Pure Form, because of its infinite distance from us along the dimension of reality, we must logically recognize that it is truly there, governing all things and endowing the cosmos with rational meaning.

Through the master stroke of the Form-Matter Hypothesis Aristotle helped to redirect the attention of Greek metaphysics to the world we

[3] Edward H. Reisner, "Philosophy and Science in the Western World: A Historical Overview," Chapter 1 in *Philosophies of Education*, Forty-first Yearbook of the National Society for the Study of Education, ed. N. B. Henry, Part 1 (Chicago: the Society, 1942), p. 12.

actually live in. What to Plato was an illusory world of shadows (which he dismissed in favor of a real world of Ideas) became for Aristotle the real world itself: hence, the simple designation of Realism for the view that the world we experience is not some dim copy of reality but indeed the real thing.

At this point it is necessary to make clear something that will be increasingly bothersome in the chapters ahead: Sometimes philosophers' theories get worked over by succeeding generations of thinkers and are thus extended and improved. This is the case with Neo-Thomism, which has perpetuated Aristotelian metaphysics and extended it to a more sophisticated level of analysis. We shall take up the metaphysics of Neo-Thomism in the next section. At other times, however, a theorist's ideas are taken only as points of departure. Succeeding generations carry them so far along the road of intellectual development as to turn the original ideas into whole new theories, even while expressing their indebtedness to those ideas which theirs no longer resemble. In a manner of speaking, this is what has happened to Realism. Over the last 2,000 years Realism has come to take on quite a different meaning in people's minds. It is to this modern version we now turn.

SCIENTIFIC REALISM

What Aristotle fundamentally did for metaphysics, as we saw above, was to direct attention to the world we actually experience, turning away from the tendency to concoct other worlds presumably more real than the one we wake up to every day. With the actual, three-dimensional world confronting us, what can we say about it in a metaphysical way? Without complicating the issue with the Form-Matter theory, we can return to the simple, primitive approach that Aristotle used. Using this method we can say, first of all, that the world is made up of (among other things) matter. This matter is constantly undergoing changes—physical, chemical, biological. It is more turbulent in structure than Aristotle thought—the molecules, electrons, neutrinos, and other particles of which it is composed are themselves in motion; but it is matter nonetheless. So the scientific realist has chosen to describe the physical world as "matter in motion."

Now, this motion of matter is the great concern of scientists. They try in experimental situations to observe the many changes in the position and state of matter so as to make certain generalizations. When they get hold of a generalization that encompasses a fairly wide range of observed phenomena they call it a "law." And if repeated experiments and the passage of years continue to confirm their findings, the original generalization is taken to be a "Law of Nature" (Newton's Law of Gravitation, for instance).

The Realist is of the view that the physical world we live in is the basic reality and that its component elements all move and behave according to fixed natural laws. We do not know all these laws, but we discover them year by year through the instrumentality of science. For this reason the Realist likens the cosmos to an enormous machine. A good analogue is the internal-combustion engine in an automobile. When it is running, physical and chemical changes are taking place constantly inside it. Levers, wheels, gears, electrical impulses, explosions, and the rushing of various gases here and there all combine to present what would be to uninformed spectators a most delirious and bewildering confusion. But if our visitors chose to stay awhile and chart and plot the movements and changes they witnessed, they would soon begin to generalize on what they saw and even arrive at certain "laws" apparently controlling the movements of the engine.

What are human beings, then, say the Realist, but tiny spectators of an enormous machine, the cosmos? They stand before it as fleas before an electronic computer, but with one advantage: intelligence. Gradually, piece by piece, they can come to a wider and fuller understanding of their world. And this is possible because this world, like any machine, is not a haphazard, fortuitous collection of atoms and molecules, but a structure built according to plan and endowed (as is the automobile engine) with predetermined and necessary movements. The task of the scientist, then, is literally *dis-covery*, taking the "cover" from a cosmos already in operation and quite independent of human understanding of it.

Human beings are the spectators of a running machine. When their observations become purposeful and controlled, then in that measure people become scientific.[4] When regularities are observed in this machine —in living organisms, in chemical changes, in physical phenomena—and when the scientist can set them down in unequivocal language, then we say science has made another discovery.

In the extended interpretations of this metaphysics it is asserted further that the objective machine of reality controls affairs even beyond the physical sciences. In human affairs, as in atomic affairs, there is a Rule of Law that is built directly into nature. When John Locke spoke of "the natural rights of man" he was talking about human rights that are embedded within the very texture of reality. And when Jefferson asserted that rights are "inalienable" he meant that alienating them is not unlike defying a law of nature. When Adam Smith spoke of "economic law" he was referring to the laws that he discovered operating in human nature but lying beyond the reach of human control, except through direct interference. What he did, of course, was to lay down an economic theory that would have us submit to these necessities of nature, thereby maximizing the welfare of all. Finally, in the field of ethics, some theistic variants of Realism hold to a *moral* law that operates in nature. Fundamentalist Protestant theology may be said to contain a good deal of this element. These

---

[4] This conception of what it means to be scientific is quite at variance with the view held by the Experimentalists, whose metaphysical position—both an outgrowth of and a departure from Realist metaphysics—we shall examine later in the chapter.

laws of conduct and judgment—the Decalogue, for instance—control our lives absolutely. They can no more be violated than the law of gravity.

As we shall see in Chapter 11, this metaphysical point of view, with some minor adjustments, supports the educational theories of behavior engineering. As a chief spokesman for this approach to teaching and learning, B. F. Skinner holds that human beings are natural, biological mechanisms whose behavior can be plotted, predicted, and controlled in much the same manner as that of rats or pigeons.

You will begin to notice the frequency with which the words "nature" and "natural" intrude into discussions of Realism. All varieties of naturalism—all the theories holding that nature is at the center of things—are blood kin of Realism, for they all posit a reality that can be witnessed, at least in part, through our own human experience, and they all hold to a fixed, orderly, and regular process that is the ground for human knowing.

This, then, is the Realist metaphysics, a world of things in motion, an enormous mechanism endowed with pattern, order, and harmonious movement.

Neo-Thomism: A World of Being

Neo-Thomism is named for St. Thomas Aquinas, the famed "Angelic Doctor" of the thirteenth-century Schoolmen. It is *Neo* in the sense that St. Thomas's view of the cosmos has been updated to the twentieth century, made compatible with science, and yet held consistent and true to the original insights formulated by this master metaphysician 700 years ago. In order to understand the "Neo" variety, we must obviously understand St. Thomas first. And to do this we must retreat still further, to the origins of his thought in Aristotle.

ARISTOTLE REVISITED

In the preceding section we saw that Aristotle's metaphysics, because it directed attention to this world of things, gave rise to views that are generally subsumed under the heading of Realism. We want now to single out another feature of Aristotelian thought—the logical union of potentiality and actuality—and to show how St. Thomas advanced this to a higher level of interpretation.

You will recall that for Aristotle Matter was the Principle of Potentiality: capable of becoming nothing by itself, yet persisting as the basic stuff out of which all things are made. Form, the actualizing force, when joined with Matter brought material substance into the status of a recognizable "thing." Hence, Form was considered the Principle of Actuality. Now, when a thing is produced from the union of Form and Matter, we witness another logical phenomenon. This thing can be differentiated and distinguished from all other things; that is, it assumes a quality and character all its own. It gathers to itself an absolute identity. This identity Aristotle called *essence*. So when Aristotle asked himself what all things have in common, when he inquired what could be said of all things he saw in his world, he could respond very simply that they all represented one or another coming together of Form and Matter. They all possessed an essence. The essence of any thing is its basic "what-ness" (what the technical philosopher sometimes calls *quiddity*, from the Latin *quid—what*). And it is this root what-ness of things that Aristotle sought in his metaphysics.

One of the simplest illustrations of this concept lies in the question, What is Man? The answer: Man is a rational animal. Within the predicate of this sentence, according to Greek philosophy, is the fundamental what-ness of a human being. Aristotle's "essence," it may be noted, was an improvement on Plato's "idea" precisely because it included the familiar ingredients of our own experience. It brought reality much more within reach, so to speak. That is, whereas Plato divided all things into two worlds—the one ideal, and therefore real, the other sensory, shadowlike, and therefore unreal—Aristotle connected everything together and showed that Ideas (Forms) joined with sensory "shadows" (Matter) in a logical way: not two worlds, one of them out of reach, but one world, distributed along a logical continuum and eventually knowable by reason.

St. Augustine and the Christian Message

Something like 1,500 years elapsed between Aristotle's primary insights and St. Thomas's adaptation of them into a more refined metaphysics. During much of this time Aristotle's thought was unknown to most of Europe. His works had been lost and forgotten and his ideas had passed from currency. Moreover, in the meantime Jesus had come to the world. Whatever people might have remembered of Aristotle's complicated thinking would very likely have been forgotten under the compelling appeal of the simple but spectacular Christian message.

St. Augustine, for example, writing as early as the fifth century, had probably never heard of Aristotle. The first in a long line of systematic Christian theologians, Augustine attempted to organize Jesus' message into an ordered religious philosophy. The world that he saw was quite a different place from Aristotle's; it was a cosmos of compassion and love as well as truth and reason. Speaking metaphysically, the matter-of-fact, objective, and mathematically neat cosmic designs of Plato and Aristotle gave way to a world with a person—the Godhead—in it to make it all credible. There was no warmth, no "personality" to Plato's and Aristotle's world. It was just there, exacting of people a compliance of necessity rather than duty. To Augustine, however, who was perhaps fortunate in not having had this metaphysical tradition to build upon, the world was a place of warmth and love, a place where people are not merely "rational animals" but spiritual creatures—creations of a divinely inspired act, possessing a direct linkage to the Absolute.

Down through the centuries, St. Augustine's vision seemed adequate enough as the intellectual rationale for Christianity. But in the tenth century some long-lost manuscripts of Aristotle were found. Avicenna in the tenth century and Averroës in the twelfth century (two Arabian physicians and philosophers) rediscovered Aristotle for the world. As they worked along, translating and interpreting these writings, it soon became evident that Aristotle's God-less metaphysics was incompatible with—indeed, downright hostile to—the Christian Church. But the more that people came to understand Aristotle, the more the logic and beauty of his thinking took hold of the Western mind. Finally it became obvious that a rapprochement between the two must be found. This task eventually fell to St. Thomas Aquinas.

With St. Thomas to Higher Ground

It was possible, thought St. Thomas, to have a world of both mathematical symmetry and God's love at the same time. Though he began by accepting the major outlines of Aristotelian metaphysics, he was primarily fascinated by the notion of Potentiality and Actuality. He proposed to show how this concept could be advanced to a new and higher level of intellectual analysis.

In its simplest terms, the problem once again reverted to the question posed by Aristotle: What is it we can say of everything in the world? What do all things hold in common? We have seen that Aristotle's answer was that every *thing* has its own peculiar what-ness, or essence. But, said St. Thomas, this is not the most fundamental answer one can give. I am, he said, not so much interested in *what* things are as I am in the fact *that* they are! How is it that things even exist? The problem of "essence" is really a secondary problem. Our inquiry into *what* things are will have to wait on our understanding of what it means for things *to exist*. The root ingredient of all things is existence—the act of *be-ing*.[5]

With this master leap St. Thomas, in a manner of speaking, mounted Aristotle's intellectual shoulders. Caught within the curiosities of "essence," Aristotle never reached the more primary question of "existence." But he provided the logical structure for St. Thomas's work on it, that is, the companion Principles of Potentiality and Actuality. (See Figure 5.)

---

[5] In his famous little essay *On Being and Essence*, St. Thomas says, "Every essence or quiddity can be understood without anything being known of its existing. I can know what a man or a phoenix is and still be ignorant whether it exists in reality. From this it is clear that the act of existing is other than essence or quiddity, unless, perhaps, there is a being whose quiddity is its very act of existing." [St. Thomas Aquinas, *On Being and Essence* (Toronto: The Pontifical Institute of Medieval Studies, 1949), p. 46.] As we shall see in a few paragraphs, it turns out that there is indeed such a being.

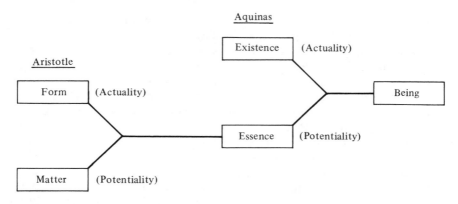

Figure 5 *St. Thomas's Adaptation of Aristotle's Potentiality and Actuality Principles*

Essence, to St. Thomas, was the Principle of Potentiality. Essences, by themselves, are nothing; they require the act of existing before they actualize themselves. There can be, let us say, the essence of Man—"rational animal." But without the act of existence this essence remains in the limbo of possibility only. Like Matter in Aristotelian thinking, the essence of Man would continue to be just essence, nothing more. But when joined with Existence, the Principle of Actuality, the essence of Man completes itself. Real human beings, complete with existence and essence, come into being.

In like manner, Existence, the Principle of Actuality, depends on Essence. That is, Existence must have some "stuff" to endow with being. Like Form in Aristotle's system, it requires an object on which to lay its powers, and this object is Essence. Existence, like Aristotelian Form, is pure principle, and as principle it is metaphysically of higher rank than Essence. Just as Form outranks Matter as the higher principle in Aristotle's thought, so does Existence outrank Essence as the higher principle in Aquinas's.

Now, if we press further with the Aristotelian analogue, we can see, says St. Thomas, a hierarchy not only of Matter and Form but the ultimate hierarchy of Essence and Existence. There are, as it were, different categories of existence, in which essences exercise the act of "to be" in different degrees. Just as Aristotle held that some Matter possessed more Form than other Matter, so Aquinas tells us that some essences possess more existence than other essences. This is because all beings are contingent: They depend for their existence on something else. They are not responsible for their own being. But they are dependent in varying degrees. Though some essences in receiving the act of "to be" actually receive more *being* than other essences, they are all, said Aquinas, limited expressions of the Principle of Existence. But the limitations themselves are distributed in an uneven and hierarchical fashion. Thus a stone, for instance, is the most contingent of all beings. It represents an essence existing, but it claims the least responsibility for its own being. On up the scale to plants, animals, and people, we see an increasing participation in the act of existing, an increasing share in the responsibility for one's own being. It is as if the limitations on existing are gradually removed, and a higher and higher expression of being is attained.

Even human beings, though, are not completely responsible for their own being, not free of limitation. Higher in rank still are the angels, who are, among other things, relieved of the limitations imposed by corporeal existence. Finally, at the top of the hierarchy is Pure Being, the Being in whom the Principle of Existence reaches its absolute expression. Here, Essence and Existence are no longer divided; they are one. For it is the *essence* of this Being *to exist*. At last, the ultimate source of all existence is reached. We can designate this pinnacle with the name "Being" (using the capital *B*). It is not a principle, or a concept, or an idea, or a notion. It is above all these, for it is an immediate apprehension by the human intellect relying upon nothing in our sensory experience for intelligibility.

So, asks St. Thomas, where are we? We are at God. We have arrived at the Godhead via the intellectual route. For God and Being are one and the same. What our faith has already given us, our reason now confirms. For God is the source and origin of all being, the ultimate union of "what-ness" and "is-ness," whose very essence is simply *to be*. When Moses called up to God and asked his name, the reply was, "I am who am."

The Neo-Thomist

Since St. Thomas, of course, the world has witnessed the arrival of a whole new intellectual way of life—the Way of Science. To the Neo-Thomist, however, science is but a new and rather spectacular exploitation of a relatively limited sector of the logical system, the sector dealing with Aristotelian essences. One of the primary approaches to the comprehension of essence is the observation of what the Thomist calls the attributes and properties of things. The function of science is to organize its observations methodically and systematically so that the properties of things can lead us to an understanding of their inner essence. So science is not so much a new world of the mind as it is a new method of understanding the inner "what-ness" of our universe.

Moreover, science increasingly deals with process and movement—in biology, physics, cosmology. This movement, this dynamic quality of the cosmos, is but a confirmation of the "becoming-ness" of the Potentiality-Actuality Principle. Things move and change and "become" in our experience, not only upward from Matter to Form but also upward from lower to higher expressions of being. Science deals with the cosmos at the Aristotelian level of essence. By the limitations of its own methods, science simply cannot reach into the genuinely metaphysical problems of being. Science really has nothing to say about these matters, and never will.

TELEOLOGY

The single most important concept in Neo-Thomist ontology for education is, of course, the Potentiality-Actuality Principle. An idea such as this is called teleological. By *teleology* the philosopher refers to any belief which holds that the universe as a whole or Man within it is moving toward some prescribed culmination or destiny. The most primitive types of teleology hold either that the world is coming to an end or that it is evolving toward an ultimate union with God. The latter type is characteristic of most systematic religions, especially in regard to human destiny. The underlying idea of every teleology is that the *end* is implicit in the *process*, that the end point of the process is either known or knowable before it is reached, and, furthermore, that the process itself can be understood only in terms of its end point.

Thomism posits a process whose destined fulfillment is Absolute Being; hence we speak of Thomism as a teleological doctrine. Plato's Idealism was a static doctrine of two worlds not proceeding to any end but merely existing; hence teleology could not be ascribed to Plato. Hegel's Idealism, however (see pages 48–49), represents a dialectical movement to an ever higher order of synthesis. It is presumed in Hegel that there is an absolute synthesis toward which all dialectic propends. Metaphorically, we might speak of such a synthesis as the state in which God, having thought out all his ideas through history, now sits back in sweet and final repose. In this light, Hegelian Idealism may be called teleological.

In the case of Realism, Realistic mechanism (see pages 50–55) may or may not be teleological. If the "machine" is "going somewhere," if its motions and changes are oriented toward a predestined outcome, then it is teleologic. If, however, the "machine" is just running, without terminal orientation, then it is not teleologic. It is this latter brand of Realism that serves as the jumping-off place for Experimentalist metaphysics, which we shall take up in the next section.

The main virtue of teleological systems of metaphysics in educational thinking is their claim to greater certainty as to what human beings are tending to become, and hence as to how we learn and grow in the fulfillment of this necessary destiny. Or, put another way, if we know the end of the adult human being, then we know the end of the child. And if we know the end of the child, it is a much simpler matter to decide what that child should be taught and how to go about doing it. In the absence of such ultimate knowledge, say the teleologists, education—or any other significant human activity—is chaotic and aimless.

A well-known theory advanced by philosopher Mortimer Alder holds that people, by nature, tend toward their fulfillment as "rational animals" in much the same manner that kernels of corn when planted tend to become fully grown corn plants. The "end" of the kernels is already written into their structure. So likewise, the end of human beings is given in their rational nature; their "end" is the attainment of Reason. This theory leads quite appropriately to both a curricular program of studies providing mental discipline and a methodology of teaching emphasizing the exercise of the child's rational faculties. Or human fulfilment might be held to be ultimate union with God. Under the aegis of this doctrine, a school curriculum should contain studies, exercises, and rituals designed to assist individuals toward this union. Both of these positions grow directly out of the *a priori* [6] definition of the end of Man, and both of these views, it may be noted, are firmly rooted in Aristotelian and Thomistic thinking.

The primary difficulty with teleologies, however, is the problem of agreeing upon the foreordained end. We must be absolutely certain that we have selected the true end; otherwise we risk working at cross-purposes with the specific fulfillment of Man that the cosmos truly intends. But whether the human intellect is capable of fathoming the ultimate questions of the cosmos is still, to put it mildly, an open question. The fact that there are today so many competing views of "the true end of Man"—just as there are multiple and competing theologies—would seem to call for the greatest diligence in considering the whole matter. More fundamentally troublesome is the fact that every closed-end teleological system has the ultimate effect of compromising human freedom—the freedom for human beings to control their own evolution along paths of their own choosing. Generally speaking, the open-end, nonteleologic outlook of science leaves people this privilege. Teleologies, almost by definition, tend to hedge it in. But these problems we must leave until later.

We turn now to two open-end metaphysical theories: Experimentalism and Existentialism.

Experimentalism: A World of Experience

Experimentalism, as a formal and systematic philosophy, is less than a hundred years old—a youngster as philosophies go. Following upon so illustrious a history of philosophic thinking, it has found itself concerned primarily with the negative side of fundamental thought, that is with denying and standing opposed to earlier views. While the twentieth century has

[6] The term *a priori*, an important one in philosophy, will occur frequently in this book. It refers literally to that which is prior, that which is antecedent, that which is already given. Thus, an *a priori* definition of the end of Man is a definition that was prior to and therefore independent of human beings' actual coming into the world. Teleologies generally hold to *a priori* principles; that is, they hold that the end of a process is already given before the process itself takes place.

seen Experimentalism move to somewhat more positive ground, it is imperative that we first understand what this philosophy rejects before we see what it affirms.

One of the ways to do this is to return to Plato's Cave (see pp. 44–47). Like it or not, says the Experimentalist, the cave is all we have. The world we live in—the world of sensation, of change, of growth and death, of joy and misfortune, of trouble and misery, of problems and their solutions—is the only world we can intelligently manage in human discourse. The difficulty with all other worlds, says the Experimentalist, is that there are so many of them. The Platonist has his realm of Ideas, the Aristotelian has his Pure Form, the theologian has his Heaven, the mystic has his "inner sanctum of the soul," and the crackpot or lunatic his own, very special idea of the Ultimate. Which of these interpretations of the "other," presumably more real or higher world are we to accept?

Other worlds may be fine for idle dreaming; they may serve as the stuff of vision and imagination; they may even help us see what we want to do and be in this life, what we want to make of our temporal circumstances here on this earth. But they are so unreliable and so variable in content as to be almost completely unmanageable in human thought. What is more, these "other worlds" are contaminated by a strange bias: They are always seen to be not only separate and removed from the world we actually live in but also *better than* this world. But, in the strictest interpretation of metaphysics, there is no necessary reason why this world we live our days in should be thought inferior to true reality. Perhaps, says the Experimentalist, true reality is something like what we have right here in front of us—oak trees and doorknobs, mothers-in-law and ice cream, sunsets and war, love and hurricanes. The whole thing, just as we experience it, is the way it *really* is.

We saw in the previous section that Realism in its nonteleological frame (i.e., having no culminating end point) may be considered the general region in which Experimentalist metaphysics has developed. The world just as we find it, the world of mechanical regularity and also of unmechanical unpredictability, is the world that the Experimentalist starts with. John Childs, a leading contemporary Experimentalist, has put the issue this way:

> . . . the divisions between the natural and the supernatural, the real and the ideal, reality and appearance, subject and object, mind and body, thought and activity, all seem to many to be obviously natural dualisms. Our moral bias also makes it "natural" to believe that in the last analysis the good is the permanent and real, while the evil is transient and illusory. Thus it comes also to be a matter of mere "common sense" to perceive that confusion, ambiguity, uncertainty, and indeterminateness have their exclusive locus in man, and that nature is without any such irregularities, for nature is an orderly, fixed, and rational system. In other words, it becomes "natural" for us to think that things actually are not what they are experienced to be. Experience is good enough for managing everyday affairs, but

if we desire to get a description of things as they really are, we must resort to something other than the common things of ordinary experience.

At this point the experimentalist enters his objection. He asserts unqualifiedly that experience is all that we have or can ever hope to have. It is "the ultimate universe of discourse." In more homely language, "it is anything that anybody can talk about." As such it has the first word and the last word. Experience "sets our problems," and it "tests our solutions." Hence, if human experience cannot give us an adequate account of realities, then man has no possibility of gaining such an account.[7]

NAIVE REALISM

The position Childs takes in this passage is a variant of what is called Naive Realism.[8] Naiveté can be damaging in social situations but in metaphysics it can be the greatest of virtues. In this context, it simply refers to an artless, guileless, and uncomplicated straightforwardness in telling the truth about what one sees in the world. What troubles Experimentalists so much is the tendency among other philosophers—most particularly Platonists, Aristotelians, and Thomists—to elaborate and sophisticate their primary conceptions with a superstructure of metaphysical presumption. In each of these positions, what is directly experienced in ordinary affairs has been extracted, extended, elaborated, and finally worked up into a systematic blueprint for all reality, a reality that nobody ever meets. When the Experimentalists refer to experience as the ultimate ground of human discourse, they mean simply that experience—ordinary human experience, day by day—is where all thinking begins, and we must return constantly to ordinary experience to see if what we say of our world is actually true. We may invent ideas in our heads—whole metaphysics, as we have seen—that go beyond the primary data of our experience. But we do so, say the Experimentalists, at the great peril of concocting false doctrines—doctrines that, precisely because they are imagined or intellectually "spun out" rather than directly experienced, cannot be checked for accuracy by other people.

For all its trouble and cussedness, this reality we wake up to every morning has one spectacular advantage over all other realities: It is open to the public—that is, whatever one may claim to see here can be looked for by another; it can be "checked out." And if it fails to check out over repeated trials, then we can afford to forget it. If repeated trials confirm it, then we seek to work it into our previous knowledge. But the nobility of this metaphysics is its *public* character. There is no exclusiveness, no "country club" of saints and prophets who will explain to the rest of us how our world is built and what kinds of things it makes possible.

[7] John L. Childs, *Education and the Philosophy of Experimentalism* (New York: Century, 1931), pp. 50–51 (in Chapter 3, "Has Experimentalism a Metaphysics?"). By permission of Appleton-Century-Crofts.

[8] For the purposes of this analysis Naive Realism will be defined as the view that reality is simply what we experience it to be.

EXPERIENCE

With this initial overview in mind, we must now begin to refine the meaning of this idea. The key word is, of course, *experience*. But we must be cautious not to place too narrow an interpretation on it. It is not restricted to just the experience of our senses. It includes all that people do and think and feel. It includes quiet reflection as well as active doing, "feeling" as well as knowing, speculating as well as seeing and touching. What it does *not* include is a transformation of these quite ordinary experiences into the transempirical (beyond-experience) components of reality, which are intellectually out of reach and supposedly of higher metaphysical rank than the experiences themselves.

Figure 6 (see page 66), an adaptation of the Platonic Cave idea in Figure 2 (see page 46), will help us visualize the Experimentalist position. We will take our world as we find it, heartache and happiness together. Call it a "cave" if you will; it becomes whatever you make it. The world-as-cave is for the faint of heart, those who think this world is not enough, who believe that they deserve better than this and expect to find it "outside" somewhere. The experimentalists are much more positive of mind. They find this world quite enough for the fulfillment of human purposes. Besides, what lies beyond is unknowable. We need assert neither that such a transempirical realm *does exist* nor that it *does not*. We are unable to say anything about it because we can never know it, and we cannot know it because we cannot experience it.

What we most definitely *do* experience is this world, and it is in this world, the Experimentalists maintain, that Reality is to be found. As we have noted, the Realist's world—the objective entity, the "mobile thing," the machine "out there" waiting to be found out about by human spectators —is very close to Experimentalist thinking. But even this, insist the Experimentalists, is saying too much, going too far beyond our primary data. For, say the Experimentalists, the designation we give to this "mobile thing," what we say it is, is itself the product of our experience of "it." "It" (the real world), therefore, cannot be certainly known. "It" must always be understood through the medium of human experience. What we say is true of the real world is only what our experience indicates is plausible to say about it.

So, therefore, not only is the transempirical realm out of reach and unknowable, but the real world of the Realist is out of reach—just barely, but nevertheless quite necessarily, out of reach—and ultimately unknowable. We are forced, say the Experimentalists, to tear away the rind of all outer realities—the realities that come to us through traditional system-building and those that point to a physical reality we can directly perceive—and retreat to the virgin stuff of reality: *human experience in its raw form.*

This is never very easy to do. To most of us the world of the Realist is so clearly out there. We can see it, and it seems to persist and exist without our aid. Common sense dictates that the real world must exist in its own right. But the Experimentalists are adamant. The real world, when all is said and done, they say, is what human beings say it is, and we have nothing to go on except this thing called experience.

The "real" world, we are reminded, used to be flat; it also used to be at the center of the universe; before Darwin it was a closed cycle of organic forms. Today the "real" world is quite a different place. It is round, now but a minor planet in a speck of the universe, and evolving in all kinds of ways. If the real world is so existentially "out there," why do we have so much difficulty in locating it? But, you may say, we find out new things about it all the time. We can make mistakes about reality, but we correct them with closer inquiry. To which the Experimentalists return to their ultimate position: It is our *inquiry*, they say, rather than the "real" world, that is the author of genuine and authentic reality. And *inquiry* is but a name for systemized and regulated experience. In short, our *conception* of reality, resulting from careful inquiry, is as close to reality as we can ever hope to get. Let us call it reality and be done.

TRANSACTION

The technical name the Experimentalists give to this process of inquiry is *transaction*, a word first applied to philosophy by John Dewey (see Figure 6). Controlled experience, said Dewey, is in the nature of a "trans-action," a two-way movement of phenomena between ourselves and this reality we can never know directly. We do things to the world, we act upon it, and then it responds, it acts upon us. We dam a stream and nature "answers back" with water power. We bring together two masses of uranium and nature replies with an explosion. We educate a child and nature responds with certain changes in behavior. In Dewey's language, we *do* things to the world, and then we undergo the consequences. Gradually, humanity comes to associate its doing with the consequences; this is what we call "intelligence." As we civilize ourselves—as we come to see more and more sophisticated connections between our doing and our undergoing (the consequences provided by the response of our reality)—we grow in intelligence. The development of this power to see connections between what we do and what we undergo is, to the Experimentalists, what education is all about. It is to these concerns that we shall turn in Chapter 4.

We may summarize Experimentalist metaphysics by saying that if we must have metaphysics, let us name it Experience. Experimentalists, however, do not as a rule concern themselves with metaphysics. They are, as theorists, much more interested in the problems of knowing and conduct, the branches of theory we shall cover later in the chapters on epistemology and axiology. Experimentalism declines engagement in metaphysical conversation on the grounds of the private and therefore highly variable character of metaphysical conceptions. An Experimentalist would be in-

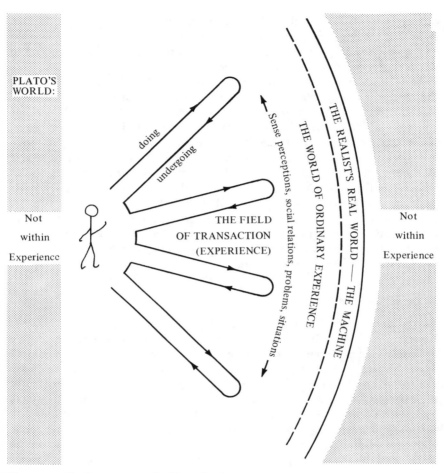

Figure 6   The Experimentalist Metaphysics

clined to the view that one person's metaphysics is as good as another's. Furthermore, the Experimentalist contends, Reality is not something one can talk about. Either it is a kind of "given" (Dewey called it a "taken") assumption we all make about our world but do not discuss or it is, as the Experimentalist sometimes says, a "surd"—analogous to an irrational number in mathematics ($\sqrt{3}$ or pi), which is rationally *approachable* but not rationally *soluble*. Reality never "comes out even." Its final closure, that is, our final understanding of it, always seems to elude the human intellect.

Therefore, says the Experimentalist, let us turn our minds and energies to more dependable ground. Let us turn to the next best thing, the ground of experience. For it is in experience that human lives are actually lived, and it is by experience that we determine both what "reality" requires of us and what this "reality" makes possible. Since we can never really know "it," let us turn to the study of how to *manage* "it."

PROCESS

Our discussion points to one final reason why Experimentalists are not overly fascinated with metaphysical concerns. Their metaphysics, unlike the traditional theories, is a metaphysics of *process* rather than of a substantive "something." Idealists, Realists, and Thomists all, for the most part, view reality as a *thing*—either material or immaterial. *Reality*, according to these outlooks, is a name we give to a substantive. It is a *noun*. But to an Experimentalist, reality is a process: Experience. And as process Experience is better likened to an activity, a moving, flowing event, than to a substantive thing. Reality is more like a *verb*.

It is very difficult to discuss reality-as-verb with language that has, for more than 2,000 years, been shaped to the notion of reality-as-noun. The very structure of our sentences—subjects and predicates—directs our thought. We state a subject, a substantive of some kind, and then we attach a predicate, a description or action of the subject. But when we utter the subject—the substantive—we are actually *assuming* the existential status of it, nothing more. And our predicates are merely appendages of these existentially tenuous assumptions called subjects.

To traditional philosophies, reality is all subject.[9] To Experimentalism it is all predicate. Western languages, for the most part, give greater emphasis to and are controlled by subjects. If we could invent a language oriented more to predicates, we could, say the Experimentalists, then begin to engage in intelligent discourse on the subject of metaphysics. Until then we shall speak with nouns that have the quality of verbs, e.g., *doing, undergoing, action, transaction,* and, the most important of all to educators, *problem solving.* These kinds of nouns are about as close as we can get to reality, our language being what it is.

Taken all together, they describe what we call experience, the dynamic, "trans-actional" ebb and flow of human living. This ebb and flow of doing and undergoing has no particular pattern or rhythm to it, and a great deal of it is unreflective, that is, it passes us by without our thinking about it. As Dewey put it, experience is simply "had." But we can introduce pattern and rhythm into experience by becoming reflective, by taking special pains to *do* under controlled conditions and then to *undergo* with our eyes open, so that we can report what happens. This is what we call "science." It is also what we call "inquiry." In its most general form, it is what we call reflective thinking. And it is reflective thinking that Experimentalists mean to develop in human beings in the schools.

[9] The Thomists would argue this, saying that in their "being" (substantive) and "to be" (verb) they have found the ultimate union of subject and predicate.

The principal feature of this metaphysics, as we have said, is its "open-end" quality—reality can change! And so it does, down through the ages, because humanity's experience changes. It is also noteworthy as a metaphysics because it is oriented toward human beings. The ancient Greek dictum, "Man is the measure of all things," is here reaffirmed in an almost literal sense. As a metaphysics it is important to educators because of its lack of interest, as we have seen, in the "substantive world" that allegedly contains objective truth that can be mined out, refined into encyclopedias and books, and then retailed portion by portion to the minds of the young. Instead, Experimentalism posits a world of process, where there are no pre-established truths, where inquiry (truth *seeking*) and thinking (intelligence in *action*) and problem solving are emphasized. Teaching and learning will obviously take on a different flavor and quality within this paradigm. We shall see how in Chapter 4.

Existentialism: A World of Existing

If Experimentalism is philosophically adolescent, Existentialism is downright infantile, since it is, for the most part, a twentieth-century product. Its intellectual ancestry is usually traced to Sören Kierkegaard, a complicated and troubled Danish philosopher who lived and wrote in the first half of the 1800s. But elaboration and interpretation of his views has come only recently. None of his works was translated into English until this century, and most of the theoretical work in this philosophical camp has been done by European writers who are still living.

The relative recency of Existentialism as a philosophic outlook may be expected to limit its usefulness as the base for an educational theory. For the most part, Existentialists have addressed themselves principally to metaphysical questions, not yet having taken up examination of the areas of more direct concern to educational thinkers. Furthermore, Existentialism's primary concern with the individual has led to a neglect of that whole band of modern questions we designate as *social*—politics, institutional life, and social order. Since education, in our time, has come to be so thoroughly social in outlook and practice, Existentialism has not had much to say about it. Therefore, while we may be permitted a glimpse of its basic metaphysics, we are on our own when it comes to developing its implications for educational doctrine.

EXISTENCE PRECEDES ESSENCE

There are many places to begin understanding Existentialist metaphysics, but perhaps we have already touched on the best place in another connection—Aristotelian essence and Thomistic existence. We can, say the Existentialists, develop all kinds of interesting theories concerning essence and existence in the universe at large. But when we come to human beings we are stumped. Traditional philosophies have always assumed the priority in time of the essence of Man over his existence. That is, we look upon God, for instance, as a superartificer—a maker and creator of things. When he made human beings, he had the *idea of Man* in mind before actually creating him. Just as a carpenter holds the *idea* of a table in his mind before he fabricates the table from wood, so has our Creator worked from a prior design (essence) in bringing us into being (existence). Even without the metaphor of the master artificer, most philosophies hold to the notion that Man is a *something*; he can be defined. He is a something understandable in terms of a basic idea. In Platonic terms, the customary position is that even if there were no people on earth there would still be the Idea of Man.

Existentialism begins by turning this priority upside down: In Man, existence precedes essence. We first are; then we attempt to define ourselves. Human beings are the great contingency; their essence is not given. Their very specialness lies in their "ungivenness." In the colorful and figurative language of the Existentialists, we have been "thrown into existence." Not knowing whence we came, we wake up to discover ourselves here. And once we discover ourselves in existence, we commence the long slow journey to find our essence. As we travel, as we perform this and that activity, make this and that choice, prefer this, reject that, we are actually engaged in the process of defining ourselves, of providing the essence for which we search.

This idea is not altogether farfetched. All children, as they grow up, eventually reach the point in life—usually around the age of puberty—when they recognize for the first time that they are individuals, distinct personalities in the world. Around this age they enjoy a spectacular insight, and each one declares, "It's me. I'm a person. I'm here!" For a while, they revel in this new finding. But then they gradually awaken to what it really means: Each individual, for the first time in life, is responsible for himself or herself. Usually youngsters will recoil at the magnitude of this responsibility. After a severe remonstrance from their parents, perhaps, they will try to divest themselves of individual responsibility by saying, "I didn't ask to be born!"

This remark, for all its poignant insolence, is perhaps the most absurd and irrational statement a human being can utter. It is the crowning achievement in human irrelevancy. For the magnificent irony is that, whether we ask to be born or not, here we are! Here we are, in place in the world, existing, and therefore responsible once and for all for our thought and conduct. There is, as it were, no retreat. Even those who choose total retreat—taking their own lives—have, by that act, chosen and thus "cast their vote" on the essence of Man. Once we pass that moment in life—what might be called the Existential Moment—we wake up to discover ourselves, quite without any say in the matter, here in the world, committed to existence and confronted by the absolute necessity of choice.

FROM EXISTENCE TO CHOICE

Now if the biological rule of "Ontogeny recapitulates phylogeny" [10] applies also to psychological phenomena, we can say that what we experience individually is but a reproduction of what the race has experienced. Human beings, according to this view, have gradually awakened to their existence as people. They have found themselves here in the world faced with the task of finding out who they are. The earliest prehistoric peoples, like children, did not know who they were; they didn't even know *that* they were. They wandered about their environment, cleverer than other organisms, to be sure, but essentially innocent of their basic "*is*-ness."

Greek civilization might be likened to the Existential Moment in human history. People awoke to Truth, they awoke to Value. In short, they awoke to themselves, to the idea that human life matters, that some ways of living it may be judged better than others, and that humanity has no one to turn to, save itself, to find this better way. We rightly speak of the Greeks as the first society to become deliberately self-conscious. They stand at the head-waters of Western civilization because they were the first to recognize the necessity of choice among competing alternatives in thought and conduct.

But no sooner had this awakening occurred—to continue with our allegory—than people began crying, "I didn't ask to be born!" Plato and Aristotle tried to remove an individual's responsibility for choice and re-locate it in a logical system of rational necessity. The Christians relocated it in a God watching over and taking charge of all. St. Thomas relocated it in Being. Then the Realistic Naturalists said, "Follow nature; let nature be responsible." Today the Experimentalists say, "Look to the scientific method." And since this last method is a public procedure of thought and criticism, we are advised also to "look to the community," especially when involved in a social or moral problem.

The Existentialists balk at all this. In every instance, they say, people have been separated from their basic humanity, that is, their circumstance of ultimate choice. They have been relieved of responsibility for themselves as individuals. But the fact is that a person is still confronted by choice. After all, one must decide which agency—Reason, God, Being, Nature, or Science—should be called on for relief. And this is an ultimate choice, for which each individual must take responsibility.

Thus, says the Existentialist, the ultimate and final Reality resides within the self of the individual human person. (This idea is developed further in Chapter 12.) At the very core of the human being there operates the power of choice. And it is this power of choice, operating within the necessary medium of responsibility, that sets us off as human beings, that

---

[10] Translation: The growth sequence of the individual organism retraces the developmental sequence of the species. Man, starting as animal on all fours, stands up on hind legs, develops speech, makes tools, builds cultures, learns writing, acquires history, reasons. A baby first crawls on all fours, stands, walks, speaks, manipulates and constructs, learns to write, acquires a sense of time, begins to reason.

decides not only what is true but what criteria shall be used to determine truth, what standards shall be used in choosing between competing criteria, and what judgments shall be employed in deciding on the standards, ad infinitum. Human choice is the ultimate court of judgment both in morals and in practical judgment. It rules between competing practical judgments, as it rules between competing choices of moral action. But it also rules on what moralities shall be used in making judgments, and what meta-moralities shall be used in deciding which morality is best, ad infinitum. Ultimately, when all the sham of Reason and Nature and Science have been stripped away, there stand you and I, our choosing selves naked before a cosmos of alternatives, trying to plot our human way through it and thus to give substance and essence to the Idea of Man.

In this admittedly rhetorical way, Existentialism reclaims the final responsibility for individuals to decide for themselves who and what they are, and, by extension, what their reality is. If Experimentalism has given modern expression to the idea that "Man is the measure of all things," then Existentialism can be said to have carried this dictum to its final and absolute fulfillment. Indeed, Existentialism means to elevate this principle to a central position in its metaphysical superstructure, changing it from a somewhat wistful and provocative observation into an absolute moral imperative.

SELF IN A WORLD OF CHOICE

To an Existentialist, then, *Reality* is even more elusive a concept than it is to the Experimentalists. The Existentialist might be willing to go along with the Experimentalist in asserting the primacy of experience. But experience is always individual experience, the "human reality," to cite a favorite expression of Jean Paul Sartre. It is always individual selves reporting on what they see and find. More technically, the doing-and-undergoing nexus is all very neat and pretty. But doing is always authored by an individual human person, and undergoing is always "had" by an individual human person. And whatever can be made in the way of a connection between doing and undergoing is, by necessity, the private operation of each separate individual. Science can point out plausible connections, but unless people individually accept those connections science turns into merely another "debating society."

Hence, Reality in Existentialist language is "self-operating- in-cosmos-of-choice" or simply "self-choosing." There is a sly double-entendre here. For not only is the self choosing, but it is choosing *itself*. That is, it is choosing its own definition, with every choice casting a ballot as to what a human being is, what it is for in this world, and what a human life is intended to be in this existence. It is through the lives we live, say the Existentialists, that we fashion the *essence* of Man. Our existence is given; we wake up to it. Our essence is what is in question; it becomes our project. And having such a noble project is the exclusive privilege of humanity. No other creature can manufacture its own essence. It is difficult work, to be sure, and down through the ages humanity has tried to escape the heaviness of the awesome responsibility. But it is ours whether we choose to accept it or not. This is the towering irony of the human predicament.

THE "OPEN END"

We may now note that Existentialism, like Experimentalism, is characterized by what we have called "open-endedness." In fact, the quality of contingency, the element of nothing given beforehand, nothing prescribed, nothing necessary, is even more pronounced here. For in Experimentalism we always had science to retreat to, or, in the case of a troublesome public question, the community. No such shelters can be found in Existentialism. The sky is open. But generally speaking these two philosophies stand opposed to the first three principally on this count: that they posit to reality no absolute or necessary qualities standing outside of and independent of human knowing. In these two philosophies reality is, in one way or another, man-made. As contradictory as this may be to your sense of common sense (to be purposefully redundant), it is this "reality is man-made" orientation that has given us so many new ideas in the modern world, not only in education but also in science, politics, and even religion.

Whether new ideas—in metaphysics or anywhere else—are really better than old ones is perhaps, as the Existentialist would certainly say, for each person to decide. But biding this troublesome issue for a time, we must now see how the five metaphysical positions make their impact on differing educational theories. To this we turn in Chapter 4.

Questions

1. In attempting to organize in your mind what this chapter is all about, try now to give a general definition of the word *metaphysics*. Then look it up in the unabridged dictionary to see how close you have come. Would each of the five positions described conform to your definition? What changes, if any, would each one require? Is it possible to get a commonly acceptable definition for this word?

2. Most traditional views of metaphysics hold that that which does not change is more "real" than that which does. Give some examples of this. What views do you hold on this question?

3. Some of the antonyms for "real" are "unreal," "apparent," "illusory," "ersatz," "phony," "artificial." Which of these is (or are) best suited for discussion in metaphysics? Why?

4. Descartes in the seventeenth century "solved" the metaphysical puzzle, to his own satisfaction at least, by doubting the reality and existence of everything

—except one thing: his own doubting. So his famous *Cogito, ergo sum* (I think, therefore I am) became for him the absolute starting point for all metaphysical thinking. What would each of our five positions have to say about this? Would Descartes fit into any of them?

5. Can you recall your experiencing of an Existential Moment? If so, what provoked its occurrence?

Further Reading

Idealism

Du Noüy, Lecomte. *Human Destiny*. New York: Longmans, Green, 1947. (Also New York: New American Library, Signet Books, 1947.) In this compelling and highly readable volume. Du Noüy first dismisses the mechanistic metaphysics of the Realists by showing that some intelligence outside the realm of chance is at work in the world. Then he develops the idea that Man, having reached the summit in *physiological* evolution, will now participate more actively in this macro-intelligence by embarking in a "Second Chapter of Genesis," that is, *psychological* evolution, that will eventually culminate in our union with God. This theory of human destiny he labels *Telefinalism*.

Plato. *The Republic*. Translated by Francis Cornford. New York: Oxford University Press, 1958. In Book 7 you will find the full dialogue on the Allegory of the Cave—Plato at his most persuasive.

Realism

Montague, William P. *The Ways of Things*. New York: Prentice-Hall, 1940. In two early chapters, (Part 1, Chapters 4 and 5) on the metaphysics of macrocosm and microcosm Montague works over, in semitechnical fashion, the metaphysical outlooks of Dualism, Positivism, Idealism, and Materialism. Then in a later essay (Part 2, Chapter 7) he gives us a sketch of modern Einsteinian physics and its philosophic import.

Wild, John. *Introduction to Realistic Philosophy*. New York: Harper, 1948. In Chapters 13 through 16 Wild explains the Realist's "Evolving World" by drawing attention to Change and describing how Change gets "caused," the substantive Cosmos that is doing the changing, and, finally, the First Cause.

Neo-Thomism

Maritain, Jacques. *Existence and the Existent*. Translated by L. Galantière and G. B. Phelan. New York: Belgrave, 1948. Maritain explains the difference between the original (St. Thomas's) existentialism and the newer and, to him, corrupted brand of Existentialism. Then he goes on to elaborate what he calls the "Intuition of Being" and the various existents it encompasses.

————. *A Preface to Metaphysics*. New York: Sheed and Ward, 1948. Seven lectures by the greatest twentieth-century Thomist on the central concept in Thomistic philosophy, Being—what it is, how we can think about it, and why the "First Principles" the Neo-Thomist advocates are necessarily attached to it.

Experimentalism

Dewey, John. *Experience and Nature.* Chicago: Open Court, 1926. In Chapter 1 the most famous (to some, notorious) Experimentalist lays down the ground rules for metaphysical thinking. Then, especially in Chapters 2, 8, and 10, he develops what for want of a better term we can call an Experimentalist metaphysics.

Hook, Sidney. *The Metaphysics of Pragmatism.* Chicago: Open Court, 1927. The year after Dewey published *Experience and Nature* his student Sidney Hook attempted (and largely succeeded in) a more precise and thorough statement of the Experimentalist position.

Morris, Van Cleve. "An Experimentalist on Being." *The Modern Schoolman*, 35, no. 2 (January 1958): 125–133. The author attempts to state what an Experimentalist, if driven into a corner, would say about Being. Using Thomistic and Aristotelian language, this essay points to a "procedural" or "event-ual" (rather than "substantive") definition of Being.

Existentialism

Harper, Ralph. *Existentialism: A Theory of Man.* Cambridge: Harvard University Press, 1948. An exposition of the Existentialist position, with special emphasis on the number one fact: the *existence* of man.

Vandenberg, Donald. *Being and Education: An Essay in Existential Phenomenology.* Englewood Cliffs, N.J.: Prentice-Hall, 1971. Professor Vandenberg, in a relatively abstruse but highly perceptive book, has collected and augmented some of his earlier articles and focused them on the central Existential concept of Being. Primarily a treatise on phenomenology, this book explores the growth of the individual's awareness of self and of the world as a prelude to learning and knowing.

4

Comparative Metaphysics and the Educative Process

The Problem of Application

Discussions in philosophy such as the ones in the preceding chapters are necessarily oversimplifications of the complex and chaotic jumble of ideas that have been thought by human beings down through time. What we tried to do in Chapter 3 was to single out for special study and analysis those ideas that relate to the fundamental views of the world and the nature of ultimate reality as they have been formulated in five major philosophic outlooks. You are reminded again that these views are not so neatly disparate as we have been forced to make them appear here. Our object is simply to separate ideas for the purpose of analysis and understanding.

The present chapter attempts another kind of analysis, that of showing how the various metaphysics lead to different conceptions of the educative process. Later, in Part Five, we employ this analytical material in examining and evaluating three philosophical models of education now current among educational theorists. Through these applications, we will have a chance to demonstrate how philosophies and theories help us understand concrete educational practice in the day-to-day work of the school. When you reach these later chapters, you may wish to return to the present chapter (and also to Chapters 7 and 10) to illuminate further the educational interpretation of these models.

It should be said that a sizable number of thinkers in the field of educational philosophy object to the pretension of showing logical linkages between fundamental outlooks and patterns for teaching and learning. The claim is made that, in the strictest terms of modern logic, it is not possible to proceed from a statement of basic point of view ("Ultimate reality is such and such. . . .") to a statement of educational prescription ("Such a metaphysics leads to a curriculum of such and such. . . ."). It is not possible to say that if the world *is* "built" in such-and-such a way then education *should be* arranged in such-and-such a fashion. We cannot proceed from a statement of description (an "is" statement) to a statement of prescription (an "ought" or "should" statement).[1]

There is a counterview, however, that holds that when linkages are drawn between philosophy and educational doctrine no hard and fast logical products are intended. We are, when we do this, merely attempting to draw the most reasonable inferences we can from philosophic positions. We start with philosophies and then extend them into their practical, situational *implications*, seeking to show what they point to, what they *mean operationally*.[2] If what we wind up with is a collection of indistinguishable doctrines—if they mean operationally the same thing—then we would conclude that the philosophies themselves are indistinguishable. But if we wind up with doctrines that are *distinguishable*, we can point to this or that educational idea or practice as being associated with a given philosophic outlook. According to this position, if we are unable to refer to larger philosophical views in order to draw distinctions between educational doctrines and to use these distinctions in understanding and controlling educational practice, then we have to conclude that all philosophy is irrelevant to the guidance and control of practice, not only in the field of education but also in politics, social life, religion, and every other sector of human experience.

While some people believe this, it is not the view taken here. The whole thesis of this book is that differences in philosophical outlook have something to do with the way teachers teach boys and girls in the classroom. We know, as a matter of fact, that teaching and learning are carried on in different ways in different schools in the United States. These differences in practice are due not merely to temperamental variations in teachers' personalities nor merely to environmental variations in regional outlooks. At bottom, they are ideological differences. As we shall see in Chapters 11, 12, and 13, they spring from the differences people hold toward questions concerning Man and universe. If there is no hard and fast *logical* connection, there most certainly is a psychological connection between philosophy and practice.[3] Empirically, there is a connection between what teachers believe

[1] For a fuller treatment of this important point, see Edward H. Reisner, "Philosophy and Science in the Western World: A Historical Overview," p. 32, and Mortimer J. Adler, "In Defense of the Philosophy of Education," pp. 230–235, both in *Philosophies of Education*, Forty-first Yearbook of the National Society for the Study of Education, ed. N. B. Henry (Chicago: the Society, 1942). See also Sidney Hook, "The Scope of Philosophy of Education," *Harvard Educational Review* 26, no. 2 (Spring 1956): 145–148.

[2] For a fuller development of this view see Joe R. Burnett, "Some Observations on the Logical Implications of Philosophic Theory for Educational Theory and Practice," *Proceedings of the Fourteenth Annual Meeting of the Philosophy of Education Society* (Lawrence, Kansas: University of Kansas Press, 1958), pp. 51–57. See also C. I. Stevenson, "The Scientist's Role and the Aims of Education," *Harvard Educational Review* 24, no. 4 (1954): 231–238.

[3] For a convincing demonstration of this point, see Hobert Burns, "The Logic of the 'Educational Implication,'" *Proceedings of the Sixteenth Annual Meeting of the Philosophy of Education Society* (Lawrence, Kansas: University of Kansas Press, 1960), pp. 49–55.

and how they act, whether there should be or not. What teachers say will tell you something of what to expect if you walk into their classrooms and watch them teach. Conversely, how they teach will tell you something of what to expect in their conversation over the coffee cups in the teachers' room. It is these connections that this book is all about.

The World the Learner Lives In

When children go to school, they enter into an environment that is, for better or worse, different from what they experience elsewhere. They are, first of all, placed in a situation of close association with others of their own age—more of them, really, than any one of them would come to know outside of the school. Also, their lives begin to take on a quality of formality and regimentation that is not characteristic at home. And, generally speaking, they deal from morning to afternoon with subject matters that are not typical of their out-of-school hours. In all of these ways, the environment of the school is an artificial one; that is, it is deliberately distinct from and (it is hoped) an improvement on the aimless and willy-nilly experience of the "natural" child growing up on his or her own. In this sense, the school is an intentionally contrived living situation where growth can be more effectively and efficiently provoked and directed.

Perhaps the most significant factor in the youngsters' new world is the existence of a small group of adults—the teachers—who have taken on the task of managing their lives. It is these individuals who establish the circumstances to which they are expected to adjust and who create this environment in which the difficult and delicate process called learning is intended to take place. It goes without saying that the tone and structure of this world is necessarily conditioned by the life outlooks of the adults. In most of us, teachers as well as others, these outlooks may not be linguistically expressible on short notice. Trying to write a term paper on one's "philosophy of life" or preparing, say, a professional credo in less than 200 words for the inside cover of a P.T.A. pamphlet is a rather difficult undertaking.

But these outlooks reside within us nevertheless. They exist perhaps at the subconscious level in our nervous systems. Most people, for instance, can tap this store of belief on occasion for a philosophic attitude on a particular situation that arises in their life. In a very real way, this kind of subconscious philosophy moves within all of us, and it eventually serves to establish the "psychological climate" that we attempt to arrange for the young to live in during their hours in school.

Since these outlooks which control the quality of the school's environment find their base in the metaphysics we carry around with us, it is necessary and fitting that we examine briefly how the different metaphysical theories view the educative process in its most general setting.

THE LEARNER AND IDEAS

The Idealist is, of course, principally oriented to ideas. What the world itself was to Plato or Hegel, the school attempts to recreate in miniature, so to speak, for the child: Though there must be desks, and blackboards and recess periods and lunch hours and bells that ring to move us from this place to that, the essence of a school is its *ideational* quality, its function as a vehicle for the things of the mind. An Idealist school, then, attempts to create for the young an environment of "mind." It will, as we saw in Chapter 2, show special interest in the principal medium through which Mind operates: symbols. For it is through symbols—not only in language, but in mathematics and the arts also—that the human mind transacts its business.

THE LEARNER AND THINGS

The Idealist's kind of school is a little too vague and intangible for Realists. They want things they can feel and see and measure. Their world is a *thing*, as we have seen in Chapter 3, and they wish to introduce the child to this enormous and complicated thing in as systematic and direct a way as they can. Ideas, as ideas, will come in their time. We must first start to expose youngsters to physical reality—the regular, orderly, and systematic natural reality that they inhabit. The school should attempt to recreate this kind of world in the experience of the child, and in so doing become, through its own procedures, as systematic and orderly and fully regulated as administrators and teachers can make it. Copying "Nature," the school will provide a time for everything, a place for everything. Its procedures will be systematic and prescribed, and the routine of the learner will simulate a smooth-running, "clockwork" sequence of learning activities. Orderliness in thinking grows out of orderliness in living.

THE LEARNER AND BEING

Neo-Thomists understand all this and go along with most of both Idealist and Realist views. But they see no reason to select either "mind" or "thing" as the primary attribute of the cosmos: the world is both. What ties them together is the important thing. And what is it? Recalling the Potentiality-Actuality Principle (Chapter 3), we can say that this unifying force is *Being*, which is identical with *God*.

Neo-Thomists now explain that this Absolute Pinnacle (Being and/or God) is accessible through two routes. Quite obviously, one of these routes is Faith, dramatized historically by Mosaic Revelation (see page 59) and practiced in the Roman Catholic religion. But we now see that we can reach this same eminence by a second route: Reason. The human mind can not only entertain "ideas" and perceive "things" but it can work its way to

Absolute Truth, and in the attainment of Absolute Truth it can "see" pure Being. Reason now confirms and backs up what Faith has revealed.

Herein lies a distinction we must now make: Neo-Thomism is today made up of two divisions or "wings"—the Ecclesiastical Wing and the Lay Wing. The Ecclesiastical Wing, which in contemporary educational thinking is represented principally by the Roman Catholic Church and its educational agents, finds its chief source of educational ideas in a somewhat literal use of St. Thomas's philosophic and religious writings; it is therefore the least "Neo" of the modern Thomists. This wing is, of course, committed to both Reason and Faith, but its prescription for the "psychological climate" of the school is more nearly associated with the latter. Boys and girls should grow and learn within the warming environment of God's love.

The Lay Wing, on the other hand, has developed a much more purely rationalistic point of view, seizing upon the simple grandeur of Aristotelian logic and on St. Thomas's exhibition of the power of this logic in his rational demonstrations of the existence of God (see pages 57–59). The rallying point for Lay Neo-Thomists is Truth, spelled with a capital T and signifying a body of Absolute or Eternal Verities existing at the pinnacle of this world of "mind" and "thing." We do not have to introduce any theistic element into this Absolute, say the Lay representatives; it stands on Reason alone, without the assistance of Faith.

This realm of the Absolute is accessible to the human mind by special training and effort. The young should be provided an environment in their schools that will show them the existence of this realm of Truth, while making it clear that it is accessible only after careful and arduous training of the mind. The mental processes must be sharpened before Absolute Truth comes within reach. The climate of the school should be such as to awaken the young to the love of Truth, *in and for itself*, and to quicken and motivate the young to begin the rigorous task of attaining it.

In summary, what both wings of Neo-Thomism would provide for the child is an environment of ultimate certainty. In the case of the Ecclesiastical Wing, it is a certainty of the existence of God and the absolute assurance of his love. In the case of the Lay Wing, it is a certainty of Truth, a final culmination of our limited exercise of the faculty of Reason in an Ultimate Truth that stands steady for ever and ever—Man's ultimate mooring to the cosmos.

The Learner and Experience

The Experimentalists have not been too tactful, in decades past, in the skepticism, scorn, and even contempt they have shown for the Neo-Thomist position. Of course, since we in America have affirmed the principle of the separation of church and state and made our schools nonsectarian and secular (concerned with things of *this* world only), religious and theistic educational doctrines are considered out of bounds for use in the public schools. Experimentalism, therefore, which has turned secularism into a primary item of belief (see pages 61–68), would not be expected to have much in common with the Ecclesiastical Wing of Neo-Thomism.

But the Lay Wing thereof is another matter. For the Lay Neo-Thomists insist that, while God may not belong in the public school, Truth most certainly does, and their program is offered as supremely suited to the public schools. Consequently Experimentalism has confronted an earnest and persuasive opponent in recent years in the public debate over what the philosophy of American education should be. The controversy has raged over the spirit and climate of the school, over what truth is, and, figuratively, over the question whether *truth* should or should not be spelled with a capital *T*.

The capital *T*, it turns out, makes quite a bit of difference. The Experimentalist, you will recall, rejects all transempirical (beyond-experience) features of so-called reality. Reality is what our experience in this world says it is; hence, we can take our experience itself for ultimate reality, since it is the source of all our problems and the ground for all our thinking and knowing. If we are to spell *truth* with a capital *T*, say the Experimentalists, we are turning it into a transempirical component of reality. No one has ever genuinely experienced Absolute Truth. Truth, upper or lower case, must earn its way in the marketplace of human experience: If a statement is a candidate for becoming an Absolute Truth, it must first be returned to concrete day-to-day affairs to see if it works—to see if it is true. And when we make this test we merely affirm the criterial priority of our concrete experience over whatever our minds may tell us is true. Hence, says the Experimentalist, the environment of the school should be of ongoing experience, a living circumstance, in which ideas and truths are tested in action. Young people should be constantly reminded that truth is not something that is attained and clutched for its own sake. Truth is sought and reached because it can be *used* in our lives. "Knowledge for Use" (as we shall see in the section on epistemology) is the educational aim of the Experimentalists. As such, it indicates the kind of environment they mean to create in the school.

The Learner and Choice

Existentialists, bewildered by all this elaborate system building and the consequent argument over whose system is best, ask us to return, quite simply and guilelessly, to the individual human being. Here, they maintain, is where it all gets settled eventually, within the "choosing mechanism" of every person. And since it is never possible to force a choice on anyone, not even if the choice is offered as "scientifically true," there is a certain futility to all this argument over what kind of environment to create and sustain in the school. The environment of the child should be one of complete and absolute freedom, a freedom where selfhood can operate without hindrance. We should not impose upon a youngster any environment whatsoever—neither Mind, nor Things, nor God, nor Truth, nor Experience lived with and among other human beings. In every case, say the Existentialists, the prearranged environment tends, just by its presence, to favor certain choices over others. And to "rig" the choices, even in the slightest degree, is to intrude upon the autonomy of the human self.

Each individual will have to decide what role ideas and things and God and Absolute Truth play in the cosmos (see Chapter 12). Even the function of other people—the milieu of social experience the Experimentalist talks about—must be decided by the individual. Democratic group decision may be an improvement on dogmatic, authoritarian decision, but it is still inferior to an even more basic level of action—individual decision. Indeed, says the Existentialist, Experimentalism has fooled us with its apparent hospitality to individuality, for it eventually winds up putting all of us in the social collective. There is no tyranny so insidious, we are reminded, as the tyranny of "other people."

The environment of the school, then, should be as completely unspecified as it is possible to make it. The educators' task is to place at the disposal of the young as many different "climates" as they can conceive of: the autocratic and the democratic, the religious and the atheistic, the doctrinaire and the open-ended, the teacher-dominated and the pupil-dominated, the ordered and the anarchic. From these "climates" the youngster's own selfhood will create its own climate: It will select out of this endless continuum of possible human experiences what it considers relevant to its fulfillment as a unique and ultimate human self. When we choose for the child, says the Existentialist, by giving prior design and tone to the environment in the school, by that much we diminish the child as a human being.

The Curriculum of the Learner

Now that the youngsters are in school, what should they learn? What, in short, should the content of experience in school consist of? The problem of curriculum is complicated by a confusion in educational circles as to the meaning of the word. Stemming from the Latin, *curriculum* literally means a "race course," or a course of studies though which one "runs" to reach the end, an end presumably of full knowledge, keen insight, and mature citizenship. Generally speaking, we still use the word in this sense, even though there are a multitude of curriculums or courses of study that individuals can, as we say, pursue.

The confusion lies, rather, within the nature and quality of the "studies" that make up the course. On the one hand, they can be considered substantive *bodies of information*, organized in advance and set out before the learner to be learned, like English literature or plane geometry. On the other hand, they can be considered *experiences that the learner is to have*, dynamic, ongoing events deliberately contrived to take place in the life of the student, like experimentation in the laboratory or field trips to the courthouse or a project in raising pigs. In Chapter 2 we took note of the shift from "thing" to "process" thinking. In Chapter 3 we expanded on this idea by distinguishing between the "substantive" ("subject") metaphysical tendencies in Idealism, Realism, and Neo-Thomism[4] and the "predicate," "action" ("verblike") metaphysical tendencies in the more modern philosophies of Experimentalism and Existentialism. We can now make these running distinctions even more explicit by pointing to associate variations in conceptions of the curriculum.

Generally speaking, we can say that "substantive" metaphysics will lean in the direction of substantive subject matters, those subject matters best characterized by the word *content*, while "verbal" metaphysics will lean in the direction of "verbal," "process" subject matters, those subject matters best characterized by the word *experiences*. (Indeed, we might logically rename the latter "verb matters" or "predicate matters," if we were to celebrate the shift in emphasis that these curricular patterns often express.)

The Subject Matter of Symbol and Idea

From our study of metaphysics we could expect to find an Idealist curriculum principally interested in and concerned with subject matters of the mind, that is, studies whose content consists of *ideas*. We are forewarned, of course, that in a sense all education—indeed, all experience—is mental or ideational in character. But we speak here principally of those branches of knowledge that are concerned with the development and exploration of ideas in and for themselves. Perhaps the most appropriate example of this is the field of literature. Literature is, by definition, concerned with "letters," with symbols. It is through these "letters" that we convey human feeling and insight. In their most advanced form, in the works of the literary giants, "feeling and insight" are sufficiently removed from the immediate, day-to-day world to enable them to endure as valid from one age to another. Lucretius, Cervantes, and Shakespeare are just as provocative today as they ever were, and this is due principally to the fact that they are dealing with permanent and enduring ideas of the human condition and not with this or that passing expression of it.

A subject matter with which the Idealist is even more closely associated is history. Through history, it is thought, the individual can begin to discern the total meaning of life—not so much by the study of so many battles or presidential administrations as by trying to catch the underlying

---

[4] As noted earlier, some features of Neo-Thomist metaphysics would require a qualification of this placement of it among the "substantive" metaphysics. Nevertheless, Neo-Thomism represents a "closed-system" metaphysics, along with Idealism and Realism. In this sense, at least, it is "substantive" in quality.

currents of human affairs, trying to sense the *meaning* of history through the careful connection of one event with another, one movement with another, one epoch with another. Here, it is thought, may lie the most fruitful territory for finding Man's true role in the cosmos. Every historian who proceeds beyond mere data will inevitably come upon the larger question, "What does it all mean?" *What*, a Hegelian might ask, is trying to express itself through the ongoing ebb and flow of human affairs? If we could somehow fathom the dynamic essence of the past, the master formula of historical movement, we would be in a position to understand more completely the "idea" of the cosmos, that is, what it ultimately means.

Although they are not all classifiable as Idealists, many historical scholars and philosophers have attempted just this sort of grand distillation of human events. Plato himself, in *The Republic*, sought to condense all the meaning of humanity's political life into the concept of Justice. Out of this analysis he sought to build the ideal political state. Much later Tolstoi, in *The Kingdom of God Is Within You*, saw in history a grand rhythm from the animal or pagan epoch to the human or social epoch to the finally emergent universal and divine epoch, into which we are now very gradually passing. Lecomte du Noüy, in his *Human Destiny*, has spun out a fascinatingly elaborate idea that the evolutionary force of the cosmos, having spent itself in the inorganic (cosmological) and organic (Darwinian, biological) sectors of the cosmos, will now come to a halt in those areas and shift to the psychological. The earth has finished evolving and human beings, as animals, have arrived at the limit of their physiological development. But psychologically they are just beginning to evolve. Their intelligence is now sufficient to control their biological evolution: Through nutrition and genetics, they can theoretically guide the biological development of the species along any course they may select. Or they may, with nuclear energy, bring it to a halt. But these are only small beginnings, for true fulfillment as Man lies not in physiology but in psychology. And, says Du Noüy, humanity will now embark upon its final adventure to find final union with God.

Hegel, as we have seen, maintains that the central feature of history is dialectic, the continuing rhythm of the contest between opposites. Marx, building upon this theory in *Das Kapital*, explains that in human terms this struggle is fundamentally an economic one, between those who control and those who do not control the means of production. In agrarian epochs this struggle is kept relatively quiescent, but in industrial, technological periods it reaches proportions beyond the control of the ruling classes. There follow economic upheaval and revolution, and (through some mysterious political alchemy Marx never convincingly demonstrates) the struggle, the dialectic, is brought to a halt in the supreme synthesis of a classless society. Aside from the utter illogic of the view that a fundamentally dialectical human world can culminate in its exact opposite, a fundamentally *un*dialectical human society, Marxism still fascinates us as a supreme example of a "theory of history" attempting to reveal the inner meaning of human existence.

From all these (and many other) examples[5] we can testify to the continuing interest human beings have exhibited in the questions of the basic "lesson of history": Where have we come from? And where are we headed? These, to the Idealist, are the central questions in life; and so they should become the central focus of the curriculum of the school. Though the educator will not be unmindful of science and geography and all the rest, these subjects should play a secondary role to subject matters that awaken us to the basic *ideas* of the cosmos. At the college level, we call such subjects the *humanities*: literature, art, philosophy, religion, intellectual history. The Idealists have no monopoly on this segment of the curriculum, as we shall see, but that is not the point. The important thing is to see that Idealist metaphysics signifies an abiding interest in the study of the things of the mind.

THE SUBJECT MATTER OF THE PHYSICAL WORLD

To a Realist the humanities seem vague and indefinite. In their worst form they border on mysticism, a kind of transcendental set of generalities that, because they are so general, cannot even be "right" or "wrong"—merely "interesting." We can never come directly to grips with them, and so, the Realist is likely to say, perhaps we had better leave them to the theologians and philosophers to reflect on. For educational purposes they are too indefinite.

In their best form, the basic ideas of the cosmos are represented by the laws of nature. If this is what we are talking about, says the Realist, then perhaps we can get somewhere. But the laws of nature are not learned in literature and history. They are learned by the direct study of nature, which we have come to associate with the subject matters of science: biology, zoology, botany, geology, chemistry, physics, astronomy, and their many subdivisions. These subject matters are definite and specific. One doesn't have to guess about things or speculate on the meaning of the material. It is either right or wrong.

Mathematics, as the language of quantity, is the symbol system we use in studying the physical world of nature. So it will be necessary for the child to master mathematics in order to grow into a mature understanding of the world. Mathematics, moreover, is the very epitome of order and

[5] We should point also to more recent contributions: Toynbee's thesis of the "life (and death) cycles" of civilizations, which in his earlier work seemed "open-ended" and humanly controllable, but more recently are seen by him to be directed by some kind of cosmic force; George S. Counts's thesis of "cultural transition," from nomadic to agrarian to technological to collective social life; and David Riesman's thesis of the "characterological shift," from tradition-directed to inner-directed to other-directed to autonomous Man.

precision, two of the basic features of the "world-as-machine" meta-physics. Mathematics may be abstract, but it certainly is not vague. *Vague* and *abstract* are *not* synonyms. What mathematics does is to render symbolic the absolute precision and regularity of the cosmos we live in. As symbology it should be attractive to Idealists as well, but as the medium of discourse for work in the sciences it is an essential in the Realist curriculum.

Generally speaking, then, we can point to mathematics and the natural sciences as the central feature of the Realist educational program. Mathematics serves as the symbolic tool for this program in somewhat the same way that language is the symbolic tool for study in an Idealist curriculum. Whereas the Idealist will stress reading, writing, and spelling (the "Language Arts") as the "basic tool subjects," the Realist will be inclined to stress arithmetic, algebra, geometry, and trigonometry (what we might designate as the "Measurement Arts") as tool subjects. At the risk of oversimplifying things, we might also note that the Idealist is primarily interested in *qualities* in the universe and in *qualitative* or *normative* subject matter, whereas the Realist is primarily interested in *quantities* in the universe and in *quantitative* and *mensural* subject matter.

Insofar as the subject matters beyond the natural sciences can be rendered quantitative, the Realist will embrace these also. Perhaps the most generalized dictum of the Realist position was made by the famous psychologist E. L. Thorndike when he said, "Whatever exists exists in some amount." He was talking, at the time, about mental factors of intelligence, and in defense of his efforts to measure intelligence he insisted that if a thing called intelligence exists at all it must exist in a quantitative sense. That is, it must exist in such a way that a person can measure it. Out of this prior assumption he proceeded, along with others, to develop quantitative measuring instruments—intelligence tests—to assess the relative presence or absence of what had always been thought too indefinite to measure. The quantitative interpretation of *mind* has now been carried so far that it is thought possible to express intelligence by means of a number: the intelligence quotient, literally a quotient, computed from a fraction whose numerator is the *mental age* (in months) and whose denominator is the *chronological age* (in months) of the individual. In order to get rid of the untidy decimal places, we multiply the result by 100.

Well, one may say, if *mind* can be treated in so purely and precisely a mathematical way as this, then presumably everything else can also. For what is more immaterial than mind? If immaterial mind can be measured, then we can go ahead and measure other things as well. This is the true significance of Thorndike's dictum.

To this end the social sciences have been pushing forward in the measurement of other immaterial factors, most notably that "thing" we call *behavior*. In the field of psychology, for instance, we attempt to isolate "units" of behavior just as the physicist isolates units of energy or heat.

Having started out with the study of rats in a maze, the psychologist moves on to more complicated forms of observable reactions to specific stimuli: the behavior of a child deprived of love at home, the reactions of an adolescent to group pressures, the "attitude structure" of an adult as revealed by the responses on a questionnaire. For all of these cases, units of behavior have been isolated for measurement and analysis. When properly observed and noted they can be plotted on a scale.

Another example is the field of economics. We can measure not only the familiar dollars and cents or the productive output of a factory but also a society's whole "economic behavior" of buying, selling, bargaining, and so forth. The impact of an advertisement on our spending habits, for instance, can be ultimately reduced to units of economic behavior, which then can be manipulated, analyzed, and studied for the extraction of regularities of human conduct.[6] Just as we study atoms and molecules to see what they do under specifiable conditions, so can we study human beings as "social molecules" in motion in society. And we can, it is thought, derive from these studies certain "laws of behavior" (the law of supply and demand in economics, for example), which, if found regular and consistent, can assume the status of *natural* law. Those behaviors, for instance, that we designate by the term "human nature" are presumably regulated by laws outside ourselves. These laws control human beings everywhere.

Taken to its extreme limit, this Realist tendency would make of the social sciences the study of mechanical forces, represented by environmental stimuli that come to bear upon the human beings and *make* them do what they do. A determinism in human conduct, much like the cause-and-effect determinism that Newtonian physics has held operates in the physical world, is the major postulate. Not all Realists, of course, take such an extreme position. Only the Behaviorists, as we shall see in Chapter 11, have carried Newtonian naturalism to its ultimate limit. But the spirit of Realism is revealed by this search for regularity and predictability in human as well as nonhuman affairs. And, returning to our curricular problem, insofar as the social sciences point to and magnify this aspect of their subject matter, they will find a welcome place in the Realist educational program.

Whether all things that exist exist in some amount is still an open question, however. In the humanities (the special interest of the Idealist) we can point to love and friendship and freedom and beauty—all "things" that exist in our lives. But do they exist *in some amount*? Can we reduce them

---

[6] One of the most interesting developments along these lines—both exciting and frightening—is the recent union of Sigmund Freud and Adam Smith: subliminal advertising. In these experiments, "imperceptible" images are flashed rapidly on a movie or TV screen—"*Eat*," for instance, after which theater popcorn sales are said to increase, or "*Chilly*," after which a rustling of putting on of coats is observed. One wiseacre, sensing the Victorian possibilities of this, suggests that we continually flash on outdoor movie screens, "*Abjure Fleshly Wants*," for the better control of the morals of young lovers in their parked automobiles.

to measurable units that we can plot on a curve? Most of us would be inclined to say no: to measure such things is to spoil them. Once you "touch" them you destroy them. Partly because of their immunity and resistance to measurement, the Realists find it difficult to work such subject matters into their educational thinking. As *people* they may feel these qualities, but as *educators* they are inclined to the view that these qualities are too vague and indefinite to be taught.

The Subject Matter of the Spirit and the Intellect

The Neo-Thomist's orientation concerning the content of the school program is both more specific and more logically sophisticated than that of the Idealist or the Realist. It is more specific, even if bifurcated, in that both the Ecclesiastical and the Lay divisions of this philosophy have clear ideas of what educational content can best reveal to the young the type of world they must come to know.

The Ecclesiastical Neo-Thomist can be expected to include religious and liturgical material in the school program. The Holy Scriptures, the Catechism, and the explanatory materials on Christian doctrine and dogma necessarily play a large and significant role in the curricular organization of Catholic parochial schools, where Ecclesiastical Neo-Thomism is most fully realized. In the literature courses, for example, wherever theistic works can be studied with profit, they will take precedence over purely secular works. Indeed, until just recently in these schools, some secular works were not only passed over but actively avoided. The *Index*, a list of books considered potentially corruptive of young Catholic minds, used to be a standard fixture of Catholic parochial education. Updated periodically, it specified works that youngsters were not, at risk of ecclesiastical penalty, ever to come in contact with, except with the express permission of the priest.[7] If the young are to be introduced to the true world of the divine spirit, ran the argument, they must be sheltered from statements that blaspheme that world. This brand of educational censorship has gradually been found unworkable, especially in the United States. Accordingly, in a Monitum of the Church published on June 14, 1966, it was announced that the *Index* was "no longer binding in conscience," and its use in Catholic schools has been discontinued.

No such censorship has ever operated in the Lay Wing of Neo-Thomism. In fact, a militancy of freedom, a freedom to think and speak and write on any subject, is more in keeping with the Neo-Thomist outside the theological restrictions of the Catholic Church. One of the best advocates

---

[7] For instance, Edward Gibbon's *The History of the Decline and Fall of the Roman Empire*, Victor Hugo's *Les Misérables*, Blaise Pascal's *Pensées*, Jean Jacques Rousseau's *Émile* and *Du Contrat Social*, all of George Sand's love stories, and all the works of Jean Paul Sartre, André Gide, Anatole France, Giovanni Gentile, David Hume, and Émile Zola.

of Lay Neo-Thomism, Robert M. Hutchins, has consistently championed the absolute necessity in a democratic community for scholastic and academic freedom for both teacher and student. But despite this emphasis on freedom, it is mandatory that we provide students with subject-matter content that will make them equal to the task that academic freedom places upon them. In short, we must train their minds to think, for without a trained and sharpened intellect no amount of freedom will produce an intelligent and educated person.

The Lay Neo-Thomist, then, is more inclined to lean in the direction of the disciplinary subject matters, subject matters that attempt to reveal the Absolute Truths of the cosmos and also toughen the mind to the arduous task of reaching such truths. Traditionally effective in this office have been the various branches of mathematics. Mathematics may be, as the Realist insists, the "language" of the sciences. But it is much more than that. It is the nearest approach human beings have made to Pure Reason, uncontaminated by the irregularities and indeterminacies of ordinary day-to-day affairs. Mathematics is, indeed, so disconnected from ordinary experience as to be *trans*natural, somehow removed from and ruling over the physical world. There are, we are reminded, no twos or sevens in nature. There are no binomial theorems or equilateral triangles lying around in a natural state for us to pick up and examine for closer study. Not at all. These things are purely rational dimensions of the cosmos that force themselves into our consciousness because they are *in* and *of* the world of Absolutes. Our minds "think" them because they *must*, just as our eyes *must* see light, our ears *must* perceive sound, our bodies *must* feel temperature. There is an inevitability of rational structure that the mind cannot permanently deny; it is the rational structure with which the very cosmos itself is endowed. Mathematics happens to be the closest human approximation to this structure. It gives us the "counters" and the rational procedures for moving systematically toward Absolute Truth.

We shall have occasion to examine the disciplinary function of such studies as mathematics when we come to the epistemological question in Part Three, which follows. It is enough to say here that if ultimate reality is represented best by the idea of Absolute Truth, we must provide youngsters with the mental equipment to reach it. Subject matter, then, has two jobs: to explain the world to the student (the metaphysical function) and to train the intellect to understand the world (the psychological or, more generally, the epistemological function). Fortunately, according to Neo-Thomism, studies like algebra and geometry discharge both of these functions. They not only epitomize Absolute Truth (the central metaphysical principle of Neo-Thomism) but also assist the mind in developing the powers to grasp it.

Of somewhat less precision but of coordinate importance are foreign languages. Languages are not so absolutely systematic as mathematics;

their syntactical rules are subject to exception dependent on usage. But, generally speaking, languages in their design and structure reflect the immanent order that inhabits the human mind. Like mathematics, language arises without any perceptual counterpart in nature; that is, nature does not contain symbols. Symbols must be created and, once created, organized and codified into syntactical systems and grammars—a task the human mind has performed without any prompting or insistence from nature. Languages simply arise. And the reason for this, according to Neo-Thomist theorizing, is the rational necessity for the mind to lay its powers of organization upon its raw materials, symbols.

Languages do, of course, differ. Their grammars are not all organized in the same way, nor are they all equally systematic. Latin and Greek, for instance, which are perhaps the most rigorously systematic, stand at the top of the list of linguistic studies in Neo-Thomist educational thinking. The modern languages of English, French, and German are less grammatically precise (especially English), and so they are of secondary importance in Neo-Thomist curriculums.[8]

Other subject matters will of course be studied in Neo-Thomist programs, but their value will be distributed along a curricular scale according to the degree in which order and system inhabit their content. The natural sciences reveal some of this; the social sciences, somewhat less. The humanities possess perhaps the least of all.

THE SUBJECT MATTER OF SOCIAL EXPERIENCE

It is now necessary to pass over to a newer philosophy, which looks upon the curriculum of the school in quite a different light. In the first place, as we have noted, Experimentalism holds to a metaphysics of process, a world that is not "sitting still out there" in a state of "being" waiting to be found out about, but rather a world in a dynamic process of becoming. It is what William James called "the universe with the lid off."

In order for boys and girls to reach an awareness of this kind of cosmos, the Experimentalist holds, it is necessary to provide a similar tone and quality to their studies in the school. The curriculum should consist not of a given set of facts or ideas or bodies of knowledge set out in advance to be mastered, but rather of a series of experiences in which the evolutionary

---

[8] Some philologists hold that it was, in fact, the inflexibility of Latin and Greek that caused their demise, making them now "dead" languages. The modern languages, most notably English, while less orderly and more linguistically chaotic, are, by that very factor, less rule-ridden and more flexible in providing symbolic expression for the variegated and expanding types of experiences human beings have. In English—especially the American variety—the coining of new words and the taking of liberties with grammatical form are going on constantly. Latin, it is now believed, could never serve adequately as the vehicle for modern technological and organizational life; it is too linguistically "tight." It has become defunct because of the very virtue for which the Neo-Thomist wishes to sustain it in the program of the school.

and "becoming" quality of our world is represented in the microcosm of the classroom. No truths about the world we live in, says the Experimentalist, not even the most rigorously achieved scientific truths, are ever absolutely and forever true; they are always subject to change. And this is because the final metaphysical reference point is human experience, which is a moving, flowing event. We must therefore engage in a perpetual revising and correcting of our knowledge as we continue to make sense out of our experience. For this reason, knowledge cannot be set out in so many compartments for the student to master. Such an arrangement would give students the impression that the world the curriculum tells them about is static and fixed. But the world is not like that, says the Experimentalist, and the curriculum in its office as intermediary and liaison agent between reality and the learner must therefore assume the same characteristics as the reality it represents, that is, the characteristics of "becoming," of dynamic movement, of process.

Once we have this principle in mind, we can proceed into the more specific curricular preferences of the Experimentalist position. Obviously, if we must begin with schools as they are, we must begin with the familiar subject-matter curriculums most schools still maintain. The less militant among Experimentalists might be satisfied simply to emphasize those subject matters that are most "procedural" in character and de-emphasize those subject matters that are most "substantive" in character. In this case the social studies might be singled out as most representative of the type of thing the Experimentalist has in mind. The social studies are the closest to the unsettled and indeterminate features of the cosmos. This is because they have to do with human beings and with the institutional structures human beings invent to organize their life. With the possible exception of the arts, the social studies are the least systematic, settled, and "given" among the subjects taught in today's schools. Because they are the closest approximation in contemporary curricular practice of the "open-endedness" of the Experimentalist metaphysical persuasion, they should be elevated to a position of primary importance in the life of the young.

The impact of Experimentalism in twentieth-century America has certainly borne this out. Most of the major changes in curricular structure in our schools have taken place in the social studies division of the schools' work. New courses in Citizenship, Social Living, and Problems of American Democracy have been established to take over from systematic, chronological history the task of educating the young in their social heritage. The study of the past—especially the distant past—says the Experimentalist, inclines the child too much to the "substantive" features of human life. The past is just "there," in a brute kind of way, irretrievable and existentially static. All one can do with history is to learn it; nothing can be done *about* it. The prime reason we study history, the Experimentalist reminds us, is to comprehend and manage the present. We must start our social learning in the present and work into historical materials when and as (but only when and as) they will assist us in understanding the present.[9] This is what history is for. Too often, says the Experimentalist, we insist that the child learn history for the same reason Mallory gave for climbing Mount Everest: simply because "it is there." This motivation may seem plausible enough for the adventurous spirit of a Himalayan mountain climber, but it is not much of an educational principle. The purpose of gaining knowledge, as we shall see in Experimentalist epistemology, is to help us live better. There is too little time for the luxury of scholastic endeavor solely because knowledge exists.

Our "Minimum" Experimentalists, in rounding out their curriculum, might simply say that the more substantive subject matters should be expected to hold a lesser position in the hierarchy of studies. Latin, for instance, will probably have to go. For some students it might be valuable, but its static quality—its "deadness" and consequent lack of utility in modern social life—makes it too expensive a "frill" for most schools to maintain. The sciences will, of course, be emphasized, not so much for the scientific knowledge already accumulated but for an understanding of the way in which scientists work, how they inquire into their subject, and what traits of mind they exhibit as scientists—that is, scientific *process* or *method*. This, to the Experimentalist, is the necessary emphasis in chemistry, biology, or physics: not so much a valence table to be committed to memory, but how chemists contrived the valence table, how new elements are added to it all the time, and how chemists decide where in the table each new element should go.

We must consider also a much more authentic strain of Experimentalist theory: the problem-solving curriculum. The more resolute Experimentalists, since they consider fundamentally wrongheaded the "subject-matter-set-out-to-be-learned" approach to learning, would favor scrapping the whole traditional curriculum. If we are really serious about inducting the young into a "cosmos of process," then working with the old order and compromising with a basically static substantive curriculum will only weaken our efforts and blunt the force of our argument. We must rid ourselves, they say, of the fundamental notion that learning goes on in compartments, that learning is essentially the mastery of preordered materials, organized and systematized into study-able form and set, like so much pastry, before the learner.

Learning is essentially growing. And growing, in Experimentalist language, means the increase of intelligence in the management of life. This in turn means the expansion of reflective thinking and the consequent application of thought to action in the wide reach of affairs we honor with the name "human." If we are to produce growth effectively we must turn

---

[9] The logical limit of this tendency is reached in what now goes by the name of historical "revisionism," in which history is actually rewritten (revised) to fit present insights. An episode in the past is recast into the form it would take and the evaluation it would receive if it were occurring today.

the whole learning process, as traditionally conceived, upside down! That is, we must start with the affairs of life, wherever we may meet them, and let those affairs dictate what should be learned and known in order to manage them properly. Hence the entire curriculum will be inverted from *subject matter* intended to be applied later to life situations to the *life situations* themselves that provoke the kinds of learning in or between subject-matter areas that intelligent living calls for. The most convenient and available paradigm for this is, once again, the social studies course called "Problems of American Democracy." In this type of learning situation we begin, without apology, with real-life problems: crime, divorce, juvenile delinquency, racism, and so on. Teacher and pupil combine their forces in studying, understanding, and proposing solutions for these problems. In the process they need information—the police functions of government, court procedure, the psychological basis for aberrant behavior, the nature of prejudice. On and on one could go, says the Experimentalist, delineating the outward extensions of knowledge and skill— reading, writing, computing, comparing, judging—which the thorough study of real-life problems will call into play in the school.

We shall examine this procedure more carefully in the section on epistemology, for it should be apparent by now that the Experimentalist curriculum is primarily an epistemological (How do we know?) problem, rather than metaphysical (What is real?) problem. The complete reconstruction of fundamental principle—from substance to process—has altered fundamentally what we mean by the phrase "the curriculum of the school." At the very least, to use familiar language, Experimentalists may describe their curriculum as a series of problems to be solved rather than a set of subjects to be learned. But even their series of problems is not specified in advance. It will grow out of the interests and needs of the young. That is, the problems will grow directly out of ultimate reality— the *experience* of human beings.

In the Experimentalist school, therefore, we are likely to find the so-called project method in full flower. Boys and girls study botany to learn the best type of grass to plant in the schoolyard; adolescents study nutrition and physiology to understand the dangers of drug abuse; college students put out a literary magazine as part of their course in literary criticism: These are the situations out of which genuine growth emerges. These types of experiences—properly motivated, joined to the real concerns of the young, and carried to full and meaningful termination—are the prime ingredients of the Experimentalist curriculum.

THE SUBJECT MATTER OF CHOICE

As we have noted earlier (see page 16), Existentialism, as a still developing philosophy, has not yet taken up what we might classify as the mundane, nonmetaphysical problems of organized social life—politics, social organization, institutional education. The problem of a curriculum, therefore, that is a specific and tactical branch of institutional education, has not yet come under discussion in Existentialist literature. It may be too early, in fact, to venture anything definitive in the way of a curricular program for this body of theory. What we must be content with is a presumed (and therefore potentially presumptuous) extension of Existentialist metaphysical doctrine into the more proximate area of learning experiences in the school, hoping of course that as little violence as possible is done to what one or another Existentialist may conceive to be the authentic message of this challenging point of view.

Essentially, we may approach the task in somewhat the same way we approached Experimentalism. That is, given the prevailing subject-centered curriculum of the school, with which everyone is directly familiar, what might the Existentialists point to in such a curriculum as its most important features, as far as their metaphysical outlook is concerned? We should recall that the Existentialists have found unconvincing the metaphysical views that either the physical world of things or the Platonic world of transcendental ideas represents ultimate reality. And although St. Thomas, on account of his metaphysical establishment of the absolute ultimacy of "Being," can, in a manner of speaking, be considered the first existentialist, still the modern Existentialist finds Neo-Thomism wanting because it assigns absolute existence to an external God or Cosmos rather than to the inner self of Man, where existence actually originates. Existence "originates" in the inner self of Man because it is here that the primal cognition of the idea first occurs. Both the microcosmic individual and the macrocosmic human race utter the expression "I am" before they have anything to say about the existence of nature, other people, God, Truth, or the cosmos at large. Therefore, Man first *is*; then he undertakes the task of determining *what* he is. But beyond this—and this is our present point—the individual human being is the *first thing that is*.

Now carrying forward these purely metaphysical notions, the Existentialists must necessarily proclaim, with an understandable firmness, the ultimate primacy of the individual self. They must also, therefore, turn away from the Experimentalists' notion of experience as the ground of reality. For experience itself is secondary; it necessarily has to *follow*, not precede, the initial cognition that "I am." Here I find myself, "thrown" into existence, an existence of indeterminate qualities. I may, if I choose, decide that this existence is an existence of "experience," as the Experimentalists say, but I must *choose* this. It isn't just there, forced on me.[10] I choose it. I create it. Therefore, I first *am*; then I specify the nature of my "am-ness": the experiential ground of existing.

What this means in more prosaic language is that the final court to

---

[10] The Experimentalist might be inclined to say that it *is* forced on you. No matter what you choose you are still "experiencing." Hence, experience is the ultimate ground.

which all questions must be brought—even the most transcendental and metaphysical questions—is the human self. Experience, as the Experimentalists use the term, is merely a convenience we employ to denote the region in which we choose to exist. It is only a thin "surface" area, where human selves congregate and communicate with one another. But beneath the surface they exist ultimately as autonomous human selves.

From all this we may tentatively suggest that the Existentialists consider the Experimentalist school too superficial, too involved with group process, too concerned with sharing and communication. In fact, in its more extravagant form, the Experimentalist school has become so enraptured of "group dynamics" and "sharing" and "communication" that it has lost the individual. Johnny becomes so enmeshed in the "group," and the teacher and the class become so interested in "togetherness" in and for itself, that Johnny—with his own private self, unique and absolute—is forgotten as the unit that makes it all possible. For it is within Johnny's own selfhood, not in the group, that things are seen to be true or untrue, right or wrong, relevant or irrelevant. Before any group can function, there must be individual selves to make choices.

Therefore, to follow our line of argument, the individual self in its function as "choice-maker" must somehow be "set in the eye" of the entire educative process. To this end, we should search out those sectors of the school program where the individual comes into the greatest prominence, for wherever in the school program the individual private judgments of the child come most actively into play is the likely center of greater Existentialist interest.

Among the most promising candidates for this preferential position are the arts: music, painting, poetry, creative writing. Probably the field of painting is the best case in point. Certainly here the individual is most at liberty, at least nowadays, to exert the power of ultimate choice, to expose to public view private notions of what his or her world is all about, without intimidation or fear of rebuke. There is a kind of finality to a piece of art. There it is for all to see, uncompromisable, immodifiable, not subject to refinement—as is the case with an idea or concept—by further discussion. Perhaps the symbolism or "message" of a painting can be clarified with words, but this is only symptomatic of its failure *as* a painting. A painting is the inner life of a human being laid bare. Its value or authenticity does not depend on group discussion or democratic process.[11] It is simply *there*, inserted once and for all into our lives. As such, it represents, along with the other art forms, the nearest approach to what is ultimately real in this world: the selfhood of a single human person.

Already in our school programs we are witnessing this approach in the

---

[11] Here again the Experimentalist would demur. As we shall see in the section on axiology, the Experimentalist holds that works of art are ultimately tested for their aesthetic quality in the same way that ideas and beliefs are tested, that is, in the marketplace of public judgment.

field of art. Boys and girls, especially in the elementary schools, paint, model clay, and construct mobiles that do not rely on prearranged concepts or inherited forms that they are expected to follow. Rather, the children are deliberately left as free as possible to explore the realm of color, shape, relationship, and form to find there what they want to say about the world they live in. No judgments are required on their work. Their designs and creations simply stand as a public expression of private feeling.

There is more to this, incidentally, than mere Freudian catharsis. Nondirective art teaching may have this function, too, of course, but the Existentialists are not primarily interested in psychic regurgitation of old experiences for the sake of inner cleansing of the subconscious. They are, rather, interested in the guileless, uncomplicated, and "unsocialized" release of human feeling, old *or* new, and in the integration of these authentic feelings into our developing conception of Man.

There is every likelihood that as Existentialism becomes more and more explicit about its educational views (as we shall see in Chapter 12), it will turn in the general direction of the arts as the most provocative vehicle for its ontological and metaphysical message.[12] One would expect that as the subjectivity of the learner finds increased elbowroom for action in this area, the Existentialist would then explore similar possibilities in, perhaps, the social sciences. Although the social sciences are, almost by definition, studies of group behavior, they must ultimately be seen as studies in human motivation. And since motivation is fundamentally not social but individual, it may be possible to evoke Existentialist tendencies in young people in their study of such topics as the disparities in male and female viewpoints on family life and marital affairs, divergent political parties and their appeal to the emotions, the differences in political ideology between East and West and the resulting conflict in cultures, the collisions between value systems such as materialism and intellectualism, and the strife born of competing religions in their attempt to commandeer the human mind for the service of God. Certainly wherever these fields of inquiry call for moral judgment—and, of course, they often do—then Existentialist educational theory may have much to contribute to their curricular role in the life of the school.

The Real Man

To sum up the discussion and to restate in more specific terms the linkage between metaphysics and the work of the school, we have only to summarize what each of these curriculums aims to perform in the life of the growing person. We can do this best by drawing attention to what shall be

---

12 For a more detailed examination of this position, see Van Cleve Morris and I. L. de Francesco, "Modern Art and the Modern School," *The Clearing House* 32, no. 2 (October 1957): 67–71.

spoken of here as "Paradigmatic Man," the image of the most genuinely *real* (in the metaphysical sense) person that can serve as the educational model in the school. Every philosophy, once its metaphysics is elaborated and "in place," will necessarily seek to locate Man in some important and prominent position in its scheme of things. To this end, every philosophically oriented school program will seek to realize its purpose by working with every child for the development of the full and "compleat" self. It does not matter, at this stage, whether human material as we know it is capable of fulfilling all the aspirations that various philosophies have for it; this is for the educational tactician—the teacher in the classroom—to determine and report back. What we are concerned with here is simply the kind of person—the paradigmatic "Perfect Man"—each philosophy means to have emerge under the curricular influence of the school.

Idealists quite understandably, are likely to have in mind a "man of arts and letters," an individual facile in the intellectual heritage of the human race. They are going to be interested, of course, in how well this person lives and moves in the practical world of meeting time schedules, earning a living, and getting things done, but these are and must be subordinate to the life of the mind which they will wish this person to consider his home. A life among books is both the *idea* life and the *ideal* life. The life of the mind is not only metaphysically required by the character of ultimate reality but morally good in its own right as the best life to lead.

The Realist would be expected to have in mind a more precise and practically oriented person as the model to follow. Paradigmatically, such an individual might be summarized as "the master of the machine of nature," provided, of course, that we understand the word *machine* in its widest context. Generically we conjure up the image of the "man of action," an individual who studies the world for principles, regularities, and laws and then turns these understandings into programs for doing things. Such persons will probably be more regulated in their personal lives than the other types; they will systematize their work and perhaps even their play to harmonize with the essentially systematic character of the world about them. Efficiency and economy are both inherent attributes of Nature. The more we can imitate these characteristics in our own lives, the more fully human we shall become.

When we arrive at Neo-Thomism we are, as previously noted, faced with two patterns of personality development: the spiritual (Ecclesiastical Wing) and the rationalistic (Lay Wing). Quite obviously, the person of reverent spirit before the awesome God of Absolute Being will serve as the model for a Roman Catholic parochial school. As the highest expression of one's limited existence, a fully developed sense of duty—to family, to Church, to God—represents for this wing the attributes of the model person. The Lay Neo-Thomist, less concerned with theological qualities and interested principally in the intellect, would set before us the model of the highly trained mind, sharpened to a keen edge of intuition of First

Principles and Absolute Truth. We could expect such individuals to consider their first business to be the training of their intellect, the disciplining of their mental processes by the most rigorous logic. Only in this way can human beings rise to the fullest expression of their unique role as rational creatures.

Experimentalism withdraws from all these high-minded and traditional images of the perfect individual and asserts simply that the world of the twentieth century requires trained *intelligence*. *Intelligence*, to employ a term quite different from *intellect* (at least, as the latter is used by Neo-Thomists), is the name given to the bringing of thought *to bear upon action*, that is, the function of mind in guiding conduct. In this light, then, our model person is a reflective do-er, a person whose humanity is measured by the intelligence of outward behavior. In digested language, we can say that these people are the supreme "problem solvers," scientifically oriented to the continuing task of confronting and resolving the problematic situations with which this life is filled. Since problem solving can best be carried on in concert with others, we may expect the Experimentalist Man to be effective in group endeavor, socially attuned to the motivations and capacities of others, and able to lead or follow, as the dynamics of group process require.

There is a kind of "infinity" to the Existentialist conception of self so final and absolute as to prejudice in advance any "definition" we might draw up of the Perfect Man. One of Existentialism's central tenets is that the Idea of Man is not yet finished. We help make this Idea with our lives, with our choices. The highest form of human existence would therefore be the repudiation of any so-called Paradigm. Human beings are not done defining themselves. How, therefore, can we say what they ought to be? However, if we see individuals who are awake to their personal existence, who know that they *are*, and who feel the heavy burden and enormous challenge of their individual "is-ness" in an earnest and serious concern with the life choices they must make day by day as their contribution to the "meaning of Man," then we may suspect the presence of Existentialists in our midst.

Questions

1. How would each of the five metaphysical theories react to the curriculum of the high school you attended? What changes would each one make in order to bring it into line with its basic outlook?
2. The most widely known college-level curriculum is what is generally called "the liberal arts." Although this curriculum customarily covers much more than the arts, it reveals a number of metaphysical biases. Explain what these are.
3. What would each of the metaphysical doctrines think of the following recent additions to the high school program: Driver Training, Distributive Education, Computer Math, Space Physics, Logic, 100 Great Books?

4. This chapter mentioned the shift from "substantive" to "process" thinking in philosophy and education. Can you cite any examples outside these fields that are symptomatic of the shift?
5. Attend the next meeting of the board of education in your city. Prepare a report indicating the metaphysics of the members of the board based on their remarks in board debate and their subsequent votes in taking action.
6. From what they say and write, what metaphysical preferences are revealed by (a) the editorial writer of your local newspaper, (b) the most vehement critic of public education you can think of, (c) the instructor of this course? How can you tell? Do you think every individual should be required to announce a personal metaphysical outlook before discussing education?

Further Reading

Idealism

Butler, J. D. *Idealism in Education.* New York, Harper & Row, 1966. In this small volume Professor Butler explores the history of Idealism, provides a synopsis of its major views, and draws from these the outlines of "Idealism as a Philosophy of Education."

Frankena, William K. *Three Historical Philosophies of Education.* Chicago: Scott, Foresman, 1965. In Chapter 3, "Kant's Philosophy of Education," the author works from Kant's philosophic thought to his views on the nature of educational theory and the "five jobs of education."

Realism

Brameld, T. *Philosophies of Education in Cultural Perspective.* New York: Dryden, 1955. In Chapter 8 you will find a discussion of the Essentialist "pattern of educational beliefs," an excellent summary of what Realism and Idealism have to say about educational theory as regards concepts of learning, the design of the curriculum, and the role of the school in society.

Brubacher, John. *Modern Philosophies of Education,* 2d ed. New York: McGraw-Hill, 1950. In Chapter 2 you will find a splendid review of the metaphysical problems—appearance and reality, change and the changeless, the novel and the primordial, the individual and the universal, time and eternity—and how these bear on educational theory.

Neo-Thomism

Adler, Mortimer J. "In Defense of the Philosophy of Education," Chapter 5 in *Philosophies of Education,* Forty-first Yearbook of the National Society for the Study of Education, ed. N. B. Henry, Part I. Chicago: the Society, 1942. Adler here defends what he considers not *a* but *the* (the only) philosophy of education. In grand syllogistic fashion he claims that since philosophy deals with truth and since by definition several different theories or philosophies cannot be true at the same time, therefore there can only be one true philosophy. And he tells us about it here, with thumping emphasis on the First Principles.

Greeley, Andrew M., and Peter H. Rossi. *The Education of Catholic Americans.* Chicago: Aldine, 1966. Chapter 1 on "The Nature of the Problem" and Chapter 3 on "Religious Consequences of Catholic Education" examine the contemporary character of educational programs built on Thomistic principles.

Redden, J. D., and F. A. Ryan. *A Catholic Philosophy of Education*, rev. ed. Milwaukee: Bruce, 1956. Book 1 of this volume states and applies the modern Thomist position to various topics: science, the intellect, morals, aesthetics, physical education. Chapter 11, on philosophy and the curriculum, discusses the content of the Catholic educational program, but Chapter 1 provides a better view of the linkage between metaphysics and education.

Experimentalism

Bayles, Ernest E. *Pragmatism in Education.* New York: Harper & Row, 1966. Professor Bayles takes us from "relativity taken seriously" through truth, value, existence, and culture to educational purpose and program. In conversational prose, the author provides lots of examples of Experimentalism in action.

Dewey, John. *Democracy and Education.* New York: Macmillan, 1916. In Chapters 11, 14, 16, and 17 the real meaning of a "metaphysics of experience" is brought forth in educational terms. Here Dewey explains the "experience concept" as it relates to human thinking. Then, after discussing the nature of subject matter, he proceeds to show the application of the concept in such fields as history, geography, and science.

Existentialism

Buber, Martin. *I and Thou.* New York: Scribner's, 1970. More than any other Existentialist thinker, Buber has examined the medium of communication between two human persons. His insights reveal the fragile fabric of the human encounter and how the encounter can be made to enlarge both teacher and learner in the educational experience.

Harper, Ralph. "Significance of Existence and Recognition for Education," Chapter 7 in *Modern Philosophies and Education*, Fifty-fourth Yearbook of the National Society for the Study of Education, ed. N. B. Henry, Part I. Chicago: the Society, 1955. In this powerful and illuminating chapter Harper points to the loss of recognition in modern "mass" Man. The "metaphysics of the ultimate self" can here be seen in its educational setting, as the author discusses educational aims, the curriculum, the school and society, and the school and the individual. The chapter is followed by a short essay by Professor Robert Ulich of Harvard, a sympathetic critic of Existentialism.

Lesnoff-Caravaglia, Gari. *Education as Existential Possibility.* New York: Philosophical Library, 1972. In this volume the author compares and contrasts the philosophical views of Italy's chief exponent of Existentialism, Nicola Abbagnano, with those of Jean Paul Sartre and Martin Heidegger. Abbagnano turns from the nihilistic and anguished themes of other European thinkers and instead stresses Man's faith in himself and his hope for a fuller future.

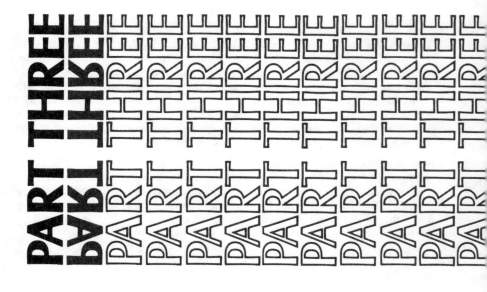

PART THREE

Epistemology:
What is True?

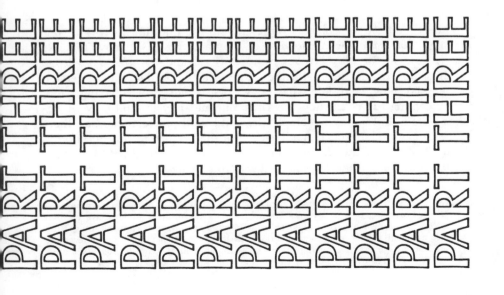

5

Epistemology: The Question of Truth and Knowledge

Knowledge and the School

We come now to our second major set of problems in the study of philosophy, those that cluster about the seminal question, What is true? Our first consideration, comprising Part Two, had to do with the metaphysical question, What is real? We must turn now to the more immediate concern of determining what precisely we can *say* about that which is real. That is, we need to pay attention to what we say about reality as well as what we assume reality to be. As we pass into this second set of problems, we come much closer to the concrete work of the school, namely, saying things about (describing and explaining) the world to neophyte inhabitants of it.

This second set of problems represents all the questions we have concerning *knowledge:* how knowing takes place, how we know that we know, how we decide between competing "candidates" for knowledge (what to do, for instance, with the Biblical versus the Darwinian version of Genesis), how we decide what knowledge is most worth having,[1] and, finally coming full circle, how we *know* our metaphysics and how we become certain that our own metaphysics is the really correct one. Can there be, really, more than one metaphysics? We shall return to this question in the final section of the chapter. But here we are concerned with the problem of knowing—what is designated *epistemology.*

---

[1] This is also an axiological (value) question, with referents in Part Four. Knowing is one thing; ordering our "knowings" in a hierarchy is another. At least we can say here that axiological ordering of knowledge cannot get under way until some alternatives are available from which to choose. In the present instance, our understanding of knowledge making must provide us with what knowledge is *possible* before we can engage in knowledge judging to decide what knowledge is *worthiest.*

KNOWLEDGE AS THE SCHOOL'S "STOCK IN TRADE"

One of the principal tasks of the school is to transmit to each generation the heritage of the race, to equip the young with as much as possible of what humanity has come to know about the world it lives in. To use a somewhat questionable simile, the school can be likened to a store whose stock in trade is knowledge. Knowledge of all types lines its shelves, and its principal task is to retail this knowledge to each wave of customers, each succeeding generation. But as an epistemological retail establishment it has two fundamental problems. One concerns the authenticity and accuracy of the stock itself. Can we have confidence that all of the items on the "shelf of knowledge" are really true? In order to be sure, we must inquire into how these things were first found out. If we have confidence in such-and-such a method of finding something out, then we can return to the "store," tag the "merchandise" as authentic, and proceed to retail it as true.

Epistemology is a problem, and thus occupies the philosopher, because there are several alternative ways of knowing, and some of them are held to be better than others. What is more, the way in which something is found out and, hence, *known* tells us something about how much trust we can put in it, or at least the manner in which we shall use the item of knowledge. Say, for instance, that we are told by a voodoo artist or palm reader that we are scheduled to encounter, in the unspecified future, a misfortune of some kind causing great hardship and inconvenience. We should certainly treat this bit of information quite differently from the information that, upon investigation of the garage mechanic, our automobile engine at some unspecified time in the future is expected to break down due to a developing weakness in a crankshaft bearing.

In the latter instance we confront empirical information resulting from data gathered by a trained observer. In the former instance we confront mystical knowledge that is—because it is occult—beyond the reach of our criticism or judgment. We tend to place more trust in one than in the other, and if we are professional educators we tend to include the latter type and exclude the former type of knowledge in shaping the school's curricular program.

How we know, then, has much to tell us about the authenticity and trustworthiness of our "stock" of curricular knowledge, and, to return to our retail establishment, our judgment of an item on the shelf rests only partially on seeing it on a page of a book or even hearing it firsthand from an authority. It rests ultimately on the manner in which the item of information was originally gathered in and added to the sum of human knowledge.

Our second concern in the epistemological retail establishment concerns the "customers": How do they come to know things? If we understood how knowing-in-general takes place, perhaps we could get a better idea of how boys' and girls' knowing in the classroom takes place. Especially would this be true if we could discover a similarity between the knowing process of the research scholar, standing at the frontier of knowledge and probing the unknown, and the knowing process of youngsters standing at their own "frontier" and being taken by their teacher in successive stages into wider and wider spheres of thought and action.

To raise this question at all is to intimate that different philosophic schools have different positions on it, some holding that the way discoverers learn new things is essentially different from the way youngsters learn things in school. Others hold, on the other hand, that there is a generic identity of procedure in the two cases and that the "level of sophistication" is the only factor that needs to be varied as we proceed up the educational ladder. We shall take up this question in Chapter 7.

To summarize, then, epistemology takes as its range of discourse those problems relating to the nature of knowledge and the character of the procedures we use to attain it. Since this study bears directly on the dependability of knowledge and the propriety of various methods of reaching warrantable truth, it stands at the very base of the entire educative process. It is every philosopher's obligation—and that of every student of philosophy—to comprehend the epistemological dimension of philosophic thinking (the topic of the present chapter), to appreciate the variety of epistemologies presently available (Chapter 6), and to recognize their significance in controlling the educative process (Chapter 7).

The Dimensions of Knowing

THE INTELLIGIBILITY OF THE COSMOS

In taking hold of the epistemological problem, we can find no better starting place than the metaphysical concerns we have just left behind. And we can put the question without complication: Whatever reality is, can it be known? Or, to say it another way, with longer words, is intelligibility one of the attributes of the real world? This is, as we shall see later, something of a circular question. But at this stage we are asking for a fundamental ground rule to be agreed on before the epistemological expedition can set out—namely, that knowing, in and of itself as an occurrence in the cosmos, is *possible*. Its possibility is contingent in part upon the psychology of human beings, most evidently revealed in the varieties of knowing to be discussed below. But the possibility of knowing is also contingent upon whether the cosmos will "cooperate," whether its very structure or character permits or supports this thing we call knowing.

To raise this question is to imply that the answer to it is, in a manner of speaking, "open." And to say that it is "open" is to suggest that a hornets' nest of troubles awaits us as we try to answer it. This unfortunately is precisely the predicament we find ourselves in. For if the answer is no, we are stopped dead in our tracks; we are prevented from advancing to any knowledge whatsoever, except perhaps a set of fancies and fantasies we are able to concoct in our own minds. If, on the other hand, the answer is yes, then we are obligated to go on to specify the *kinds* of knowledge that ultimate reality is prepared to yield. It should be obvious that the kinds of knowledge reality makes possible will depend on our conceptions of reality: the kinds of knowledge available to us will vary from metaphysic to metaphysic.

Idealism, for instance, will accept the possibility of perceptual knowledge but will hold that reality is prepared to yield a more genuine knowledge—the knowledge of ideas existing behind the sensory screen—if we but take the trouble to find it out. Realism will hold to a reality that offers only sensory knowledge; out of such knowledge we can expect to extract relations and associations *among* things but certainly not ideas *behind* things. (As we shall see in Chapter 11, the central role of sensory knowledge is an essential requirement of behavior engineering.) Neo-Thomism will not only accept the possibility of sensory knowledge but will go on to show that the powers of the intellect are such that we can find our way to absolute truth (Lay Thomism) or that the human spiritual powers are occasionally receptive to revealed knowledge from God (Ecclesiastical Thomism). Experimentalism, holding the "transactional" metaphysics that it does, will center its attention on the possibility of empirical knowledge, based in sensory experience but reflectively fashioned into "working truths" that are tested in action. Finally, Existentialism, not yet inclined to deal with epistemological matters in philosophically customary ways and basing its metaphysics in sheer existence, might be willing to say that all these types of knowledge *have occurred* historically, although none of them has any metaphysical base other than ultimate human choice; even to decide among competing epistemologies is itself a choice. (This idea is developed further in Chapter 12.)

"Truth" or "truth"

For better or worse, we can say here that almost all philosophies (certainly those presented in this book) hold to some kind of position that makes knowledge metaphysically (not necessarily psychologically)[2] possible and that serves to justify the generalized statement, "The cosmos is fundamentally intelligible," even though—we are warned—the precise definition of *cosmos* and *intelligible* in this statement may require elaborate

[2] We must continue to make this distinction, because to say that such-and-such type of knowledge is metaphysically available to us is not to say that human beings, as knowing creatures, are capable of knowing such knowledge. As the Existentialist Karl Jaspers once put it epigrammatically. "It is thinkable that there should be something unthinkable." Most philosophies, however, assume some equivalence between the knowledge the universe makes possible and that which the human mind can take hold of—another instance, incidentally, of the propensity to egocentrism of the human race in constructing a reality "in its own image," that is, a cosmos built along lines compatible with human powers and purposes. Metaphysically speaking, there is no defensible warrant for this.

qualification. Forsaking for the moment, however, the more technical points of philosophy, we now have at least a working base on which to build, namely, the metaphysical *possibility* of knowledge. We are now in a position to ask some things *about* the knowledge that our "reality" makes available.

Is this knowledge, for instance, presented to us in such a way that we are *obligated* to believe it? That is to say, are there some items of knowledge that are not only seen by people as true but that are always and eternally true in every century and for all time, and universally true in all societies and in all places? Is there, to use our customary linguistic shorthand, such a thing as *absolute* truth, absolutely true without qualification of any kind? If this kind of knowledge is contained in the universe, then it would certainly be to our advantage to find it out, for it would obviously be of great help in finding our way in a troubled world. And, of course, it would be ideal material to place in the curriculum of the school, for it would not have to be tampered with or modified every five years in a "curriculum revision" project.

The great difficulty with this type of truth (often spelled with a capital T: *Truth*) is that people are, generally speaking, not agreed on what it is. There might be considerable agreement that the statement "The internal angles of a triangle equal 180 degrees" is an absolute truth.[3] But in the social sphere when, let us say, the political status of people is up for consideration, there is precious little agreement among people or societies on what truths control political arrangements. When Jefferson said in the Declaration that "all men are created equal" (or, to render it in more secular terms, "all people are equal") he sought to elevate this principle to an absolute status by claiming that it was "self-evident." But its presumed self-evidence is somewhat gratuitous. Indeed, as any careful chronicler could demonstrate, the history of humanity has been one long, episodic exhibit of the "self-evidence" of its opposite. And even among contemporary societies there prevails a disturbing lack of unanimity on this question. When Jefferson composed this phrase he was referring, of course, not to physical or intellectual equality but to equality before the law. But since laws are made by people rather than by some cosmic legislature, we are forced to reduce and rephrase Jefferson thus: "All men are equal before man-made institutions." Even this statement might require considerable going over before being acceptable to world sentiment. But the point of all this is merely to demonstrate that what claims to be absolute may quickly be seen, according to some philosophies, to require a libraryful of adequately grounded reservations and qualifications. And only one reservation is required to repeal the absoluteness of a statement.

In the moral sphere, which is treated in detail in Part Four, the

---

[3] Even this, believe it or not, is open to challenge. In non-Euclidean geometry it does not hold. And even in Euclidean geometry it is held to be a "tautology," a statement whose predicate merely contains one of the definitions of the subject and which, therefore, says no more than "A = A," and tells us nothing new.

question of absolutes is still more precarious. If, let us say, questions of sexual behavior are up for discussion, there is little agreement among people on how life should properly be lived. And the irony of it all is that the sexual sphere is one of those areas of social thought in which every society thinks itself to have found something closely approximating absolute truth. A more confounding irony is that it is in the social and moral regions of living—not the geometrical and mathematical—that we are most in need of absolutes, that is, sure moorings to the cosmos. But it is precisely in these areas that absolutes are so difficult to come by.

For these (and many other, more complicated) reasons, the notion of Absolute Truth, for all its attractive qualities in educational concerns, has lost some of its sheen in modern secular thought. We are driven back, say the secularists, upon the finite limitations of human knowing and are required to settle for "truth" with a lower-case *t*—that is, truths that are *thought* to be eternal and absolute but that are always open to substantial qualification or to change and repeal.

Vicarious and Direct Knowing

Moving gradually away from our metaphysical base of epistemological operations, we must now ask a series of questions concerning the *human* "dimensions" of knowing. The first of these has to do with a distinction between "knowing by acquaintance" and "knowing by description." Knowing by acquaintance consists in having a direct and immediate awareness of some feature of our environment—what we had for breakfast, the personality quirks of our friends and associates, the meaning of free enterprise in American economics. But we are not limited to direct knowledge. We can as well know *about* things that we never directly experience but that are described to us—what the "boss" had for breakfast, the personality quirks of the president of the United States, and the meaning of "freedom" in the Soviet Union. Now, although this distinction may border on the innocuously obvious, it has important ramifications in understanding the knowing process and, ultimately, in managing the learning process.

Our problem comes to immediate focus in considering epistemological circumstances of the "how-to-do-something" variety. Suppose a father wants to teach his daughter to drive an automobile. He begins by the "descriptive" approach of having her read a book on the subject. Then he proceeds to explain it to her, perhaps embellishing the discourse with appropriate gestures. Then he proceeds to demonstrate by getting into the vehicle and letting her watch him drive, all the while providing a running verbal commentary on what he is doing and why. Suppose this reading and listening and watching is kept up for a period of, say, six months, to the point that the daughter is completely knowledgeable about driving a car. Question: Does she or does she not know how to drive a car?

The usual course to follow in answering this question is to let her try it and *see* if she knows. But whether or not she is successful in the trial, the epistemological question remains: Did she know before she tried it? The reason this is a troublesome issue is precisely that in most knowing and learning situations we must operate in what is here spoken of as the "vicarious" region of action—reading books, listening to people, observing processes under way. Especially in education is this vicariousness of experience carried to its extended limit, for a school is deliberately removed from life. It is thought that an ordered presentation of learning material through the written and audible symbol, together with some limited "spectator" experience, will produce genuine knowing and hence genuine learning.

To change our example and thereby point to the significance of this issue: Can children learn democratic behavior by reading books and doing scrapbook projects in civics class? We are not teaching someone to operate a machine; we are teaching youngsters what democracy means, what a democratic way of life—social, political, personal—is all about, what feelings and attitudes are necessary to democratic patterns of living. In a general way we are teaching them *how* to live democratically. Can we, to ask our question again, manage to do this through the manipulation of symbols in their experience (words and numbers, both written and oral)?

Upon confronting this question we are seldom badgered by a similar impatience to "let them try it." How are they to try it? Practically speaking, they cannot "try it" until they grow up. So we give them a paper-and-pencil test, reduce their answers to scores, and record a number or letter on a report card to designate how much they now *know*. The society at large, however, is only incidentally interested in paper-and-pencil knowledge. It is looking for attitudes, feelings, behavior patterns. And it expects that these are developed in some meaningful way in the civics classroom—which deals almost exclusively in "knowledge by description."

The whole set of relationships between thought and action is thus brought into play in epistemology and in education. And the position and function of these two ingredients of human experience will noticeably alter as we move from one epistemology to another.

Subjective and Objective Knowledge

Closely related to the preceding problem is that of the nature of the knowing process. Again we can get right at the difficulty by asking the question, is knowledge something that comes to us from the "outside"—is it inserted into our minds and nervous systems somewhat in the way iron ore is dumped into a ship? Or do we, as knowers, contribute something in this engagement of ourselves with the world in such a way as to be partially responsible for the knowledge that ends up in our being and eventually flows into our behavior? Or do we, to consider a third alternative, actually exist as "pure" *subjects* and thereby become the manufacturers of truth rather than either the recipients of it or the participants, along with the real world, in its identification and use? That is, do we introduce *into* reality whatever meaning and truth and knowledge we then say it already contains?

From our previous study of metaphysics, it should be evident that different philosophies will take a different stand on this matter. For if reality is essentially "out there" waiting to be found out about, then we may consider knowledge as a commodity that enters from the outside and is then worked into our mental equipment, our personalities, and our day-to-day conduct. If our metaphysics is of a "transactional" sort, we shall incline toward the second position, namely, that we *know* things by receiving impressions from reality, which we then turn into guesses or hypotheses of what is true, which we then verify by acting them out "on" reality to see how they work. If, finally, our metaphysics is a kind of "in-here" subjectivism, we shall lean in the direction of the third alternative—an epistemology of ultimate human authorship of the truths and values that are said to exist in this universe but that exist only on sufferance of our saying that they do.

While the educational implications of this question are to be more thoroughly examined in Chapter 7, it might be helpful at this point to note that the first of the above positions tends to be held by mathematicians, physical and natural scientists, and historians. In these areas, a body of factual content can be identified as quite independent of what human beings think of it. The second position, on the other hand, tends to be more compatible with the thinking in the social and behavioral sciences, in which a body of empirical and conceptualized knowledge constantly requires rechecking and reinterpretation. The human knower is trying to *know himself*, albeit in groups; and in knowing himself, the individual must be both subject *and* object. The third position above, the "Man-creates-truth" view, is more likely to be held in the humanities— the arts, literature, and those subjects dealing with moral questions and ethical interpretations—where individual human judgment (although not necessarily *behavior*) is permitted the greatest latitude of expression.

That is why, to add to our aside here, the Realists (and, with some qualification, the Idealists) will do the bulk of their educational thinking in the sciences and objective history; why the Experimentalists feel more at home when they are dealing with social studies and the human sciences; and why the Existentialists remain relatively silent on physics and sociology and dwell instead on those humanistic matters relating to feeling and commitment, especially those having to do with moral decision.[4]

[4] Do not be misled into thinking that the several philosophies, in holding to a given view on the "subjective-objective" question, would restrict their curriculum to any one of the three divisions mentioned. Instead, each attempts to show how its epistemological view can be applied to *all* studies in the school. Since a given curricular area yields more readily to their epistemological position, it is used primarily to *exemplify* how things should be managed elsewhere in the school's work.

The *A Priori* and the *A Posteriori*

We now sum up by pointing to a final and perhaps decisive epistem-ological consideration: the logical and chronological locus of genuine knowledge. To come right to the point, is true knowledge *prior* to or *posterior* to human experience? Can a truth be said to be in hand before it is introduced into human concerns, or must it wait upon its involvement in life's affairs to attain whatever sort of "truth-fulness" we say that it enjoys? This may be recognized as a generalized and somewhat more sophisticated restatement of the difficulties encountered in the previous sections.

When we speak of *a priori* knowledge we designate that which is known and knowable in and of itself. The ratio existing between the diam-eter and the circumference of a circle—*pi*—may be said to be prior to our knowledge of it. This relationship is inherent in the characteristics of circles; it is a truth antecedent to any human attempt to know it. There-fore, once this relationship is seen as inherent to circles, we are not obli-gated to test it out in our experience every time we confront a circle.

But the relation existing between one circle and another circle is not given. That one circle is above, or larger than, or in a different plane from a second circle requires human experience for verification. Whatever knowledge we attain, therefore, is *a posteriori*; it is posterior to the onset of human awareness of it.

Traditional philosophies have always regarded *a priori* knowledge as superior to *a posteriori* knowledge. For one thing, being prior, it is thought to represent the real world; it has a metaphysical status; it is woven into the very texture of reality. If reality is fixed and permanent, these philos-ophies hold, then *a priori* truths are fixed and permanent. They are eternal, outside of time, and hence absolute. (See the earlier section on absolute versus relative truth.) For this same reason, *a priori* knowledge enjoys another advantage: It is free of contamination by human knowers, with all their emotions, opinions, and interpretations. One cannot have opin-ions about *a priori* knowledge. It is simply true.

A posteriori knowledge, on the other hand, resting as it does in human experience, is subject to all the ills and frailties of the knowing mechanism of the individual. Such truths must suffer the same infirmities suffered by human beings, with their clouded perception and limited abilities of com-prehension. Such knowledge, therefore, is always in some measure un-reliable, impermanent, corrigible.

For this reason, the traditional philosophies have given *a priori* knowl-edge—especially as it is found in mathematics and geometry—the "inside track" in education, leaving *a posteriori* knowledge (in general, we can call all scientific knowledge *a posteriori*) a subordinate position in the curriculum. Neo-Thomism, as we shall see in the next chapter, is partic-ularly partial to this view.

The newer philosophies, most especially Experimentalism, tend to invert this, claiming that all knowledge, sooner or later, must be tested in experience. There is a suggestion that *a priori* knowledge actually does not exist, that as soon as knowledge is *had* by some human knower it has entered the zone of experience and is therefore *a posteriori*. The mathematical computation of *pi* (3.1416), for instance, did not come into our knowledge until some human being somewhere became curious about that relationship, worked it out, checked and rechecked it, and finally accepted it as true. The fact that the relationship is true of all circles was itself established in experience.

In every case, then, the quest for knowledge originates in human beings' curiosity about their world, and whatever claims to be knowledge must first have satisfied some human knowers somewhere as being relative to and contingent upon their experience.

In a further elaboration of this point, the Logical Positivists and Analysts have shown that *a priori* knowledge is tautological and definitional. That is, propositions of this kind simply restate what is already assumed. To say that the relation *pi* is an inherent characteristic of all circles is simply to say that this is one of the things we mean by the term *circle*. We have said nothing new, really. We have merely elaborated upon the *meaning* of the object in our experience. It is much like saying that roundness is a characteristic of all circles.

We shall consider the Analyst's thesis in more detail in a brief section at the close of Chapter 6.

Although there are other, more complex "dimensions" to the epistemological problem, these will suffice to indicate the type of considerations in understanding the knowing process that have direct relevance to the educational task. We now turn to the different ways of knowing that are pointed to by various epistemologists and that provide the foundation for the various educational theories.

The Varieties of Knowing

SENSE DATA

Every philosophy must come to terms at the outset of its epistemology with the most immediate of all types of knowledge, the knowledge to which we have access through our five senses. There is no convincing way to gainsay the authenticity of such knowledge, at least as it seems to be experienced by individual human beings. When I walk outdoors and see snow falling, feel the dry chill of a wintry day, hear the rumble of the train in the distance, smell the exhaust of nearby industries, and taste the chocolate bar I'm munching, I am knowing things. There are, to be sure, many refinements that can and should be made on this kind of knowledge; the "seeing" of the outdoor thermometer sharpens my knowledge of the "feeling" of cold. And many psychological studies in sensory perception —in the field of optics, in the determination of space relations, in auditory acuity—have revealed that our sensory apparatus is far less reliable a knowing instrument than we may think it is. Even so common a thing as reporting an event, whether over the backyard fence, in a newspaper dispatch, or before a court of law, is fraught with unnumbered hazards of error in relating what actually happened. The persistence of unsubstantiated rumor, letters of correction to the editor, and widely divergent testimony on the witness stand all suggest that human knowing via the senses is considerably less dependable than we individually think our own sensory knowing to be.

But the presence of sensory data cannot be denied. We cannot escape their impact on our beings. If we are alive and awake, we are engaging in sensory perception all the time, and our senses cannot be shut off, except temporarily in slumber. This inexorability of sensation suggests, at the outset, that our epistemology must somehow take account of the fact that we are existentially "plugged in" to nature, that we cannot entertain ideas or notions that contradict the sensory truths we feel ourselves capable of apprehending directly, and, therefore, that sensation, as undependable as it may be, must somehow stand at the center of whatever knowing theory we choose to concoct.

As a matter of philosophical fact, the primacy of sensory knowledge is recognized in most, if not all, philosophical positions, at least in the sense that it is the *starting place* for all knowing. But the trouble with sensory knowledge is precisely what we have already alluded to, its lack of dependability. Furthermore, it does not account for all or even a very large share of what we seem to feel is the range of human knowing. It is only a partial and limited type of knowledge, one that we share with the rest of the animal kingdom.[5]

Sensory knowledge is therefore insufficient on at least two counts: undependability and incompleteness. These two deficiencies provoke us into further inquiry, for epistemologists are in the business not merely of recording types of knowing but of exhausting, without remainder, *all* the channels of epistemological activity people are capable of and of evaluating and criticizing those channels for their comparative effectiveness in coming to genuine truth. Consequently we must proceed to other possibilities.

COMMON SENSE

The first extension we can make in this undertaking is in the direction of the other sentient creatures who possess with us, it appears, the same sensory equipment. The great advantage of human beings over all other animals is our ability to reduce our sensory experience to symbols, that is,

---

[5] Indeed, while the totality of our sensory apparatus is perhaps of higher competence than that of any other single organism, there are many animals that can outstrip us in any one of the five senses—eagles in sight, dogs in hearing and smell, and so on.

to noises, gestures, and designs made on surfaces. This makes it possible not only to share sensations—which animals cannot do—but, what is more important, to check the accuracy and authenticity of our sensations with others—which animals cannot do either.

Immediately this can be seen as a very great epistemological convenience, for it helps us discard what is untrue or at least less true and fasten upon that which is more true and hence more dependable in organizing and managing our lives. If I cannot detect the odor of toxic ozone in a closed room but ten others do detect it, I am likely to readjust my understanding of the situation in their favor and get out of there. But even in considerably less urgent circumstances I am still inclined to discount my own sensations if there is a sufficient weight of reports from others that I am either missing something or perceiving the "wrong" thing. So extensive is this tendency that it has become something of a socially recognized epistemological axiom: "Fifty million Frenchmen can't be wrong!" And in modern scientific sociology and anthropology this willingness to yield to the "common sense," the generally held sense perceptions of the community, is taken as a basic concept in understanding political and moral behavior.[6]

The primary difficulty with this "common-sense" way to true knowledge is that it rests ultimately upon individual sensations. It is therefore theoretically subject to the same kind of error that any individual is subject to in his perceptions. A majority vote of a group's individual sensations is not, after all, a genuine guarantee that real truth has been achieved, especially if the sensations are fleeting and incomplete. The ten people *could* be wrong about the ozone; their sensation might be due merely to a superexotic perfume on one of the women. And 50 million Frenchmen *can* be wrong, just as wrong as 70 million Nazi Fascists or 100 million Soviet Communists or 200 million Americans.

What we must do, therefore, in the epistemological enterprise, is to search further for more creditable and dependable ways of knowing, against which to check both individual sensations and common sensations. The most widely applicable of these meta-methods in our time is science, which attempts to control sensory experiences in such a way that the sensory reports will be confined to a limited set of circumstances, reduced to objective measures, and codifiable within a rigorous system of specific (even if tentative) conclusions. But before we take up this epistemological tack, we must examine other possibilities.

---

[6] An important psychological experiment along these lines was conducted at the Laboratory of Social Relations at Harvard University and reported in Solomon E. Asch, "Opinions and Social Pressure," *Scientific American*, November 1955, p. 3. In this study all the subjects but one were instructed to give erroneous reports of their perceptions of various geometric shapes—relative lengths of lines, relative sizes of cubes or circles, etc. Then the experimenters measured how long it took for the lone individual to repudiate his own senses (!) and agree to go along with the group's judgment. The fact that almost every test subject eventually did yield tells us a great deal about modern individuals.

LOGIC

To the classical logicians the difficulty with sensory knowledge is that it stops short of true knowledge. We forget, they say, that the intellect is already "in place" before sense data are received, and the intellect has the capacity to extend the process of knowing by utilizing sensory information in a purely nonsensory and wholly mental progression to a new kind of truth. This capacity is customarily exemplified by the use of the syllogism, a series of statements that proceeds from the base of experience to the intellectual apprehension of truths that sensory experience cannot yield. Consider the familiar syllogism:

> All men are mortal.
> Socrates is a man.
> Therefore, Socrates is mortal.

In order to assert the first statement (the major premise) we need only generalize from our sensory data concerning the mortality of the individual. Certainly not one single sensory datum has yet been collected to disprove it. So we assert it is true that "All men are mortal." The second statement (the minor premise) is based completely on sense data. We experience the entity of Socrates and assign the word *man* to him. Now, by purely intellectual means we proceed to the third statement, "Socrates is mortal." This truth, so long as Socrates lives, cannot be verified through sensation. It is a truth *based* in sensation but not verified there. Hence it is an item of knowledge to be added to what we have already gathered in through our senses.

It is the position of those who hold to the possibility of logical knowledge that this same procedure can be applied to many other areas of knowing. Whenever we can assert certain things about our world and can arrange these assertions in specifically definable ways, we can then proceed to genuinely new knowledge. This knowledge can then be systematized and, just like sensory knowledge, arranged in different subject matters and included in the content of the educative process. The most obvious example of this is seen in the field of mathematics, most notably geometry, where certain truths are not immediately known but, rather, *derived* from proof. (For a refutation of this position, see the section on the Analytic Movement at the close of Chapter 6.)

SELF-EVIDENCE AND INTUITION

Closely related to the logical position is the view that the human intellect is capable not only of *building up* truths from the raw materials of experience but of *apprehending* certain truths directly and immediately, with no recourse whatsoever to experience. It is capable, say the proponents of this position, of taking hold of certain ideas and recognizing them, on a purely intellectual basis, as true. These truths are true in and of themselves and come by their truth in a state of supreme independence of ordinary human experience.

Perhaps the most common examples of this type of truth can be found in geometry and mathematics. When we assert that "two things equal to the same thing are equal to each other," we are not reporting observations from previous experience nor are we setting up a hypothesis to be tested later in some experiment. We are, rather, making a statement whose truth lies wholly in a mental apprehension by the intellect. It is simply true, and the intellect needs no assistance whatsoever—either from the senses or from mathematical demonstration—to assert it.

We speak of such truths as "self-evident," as containing their own verification. We shall wish to take a much closer look at this kind of knowing in Chapter 6, especially in the examination of Thomistic epistemology; but the above example is sufficient at this point to suggest the general nature of immediately apprehensible intellectual knowledge.

The point at which the intellect makes this final leap to new truth is spoken of in Aristotelian epistemology as *intuition*. Among moderns the word *intuition* has a faintly mystical, somewhat magical quality. In popular parlance we speak of "woman's intuition," by which we mean to suggest a knowing power beyond all reasonable description. But in formal epistemology intuition must be taken more seriously, since it refers to a kind of knowing whereby a person's rational faculty takes hold of an idea and sees it to be true necessarily.

Nowhere is this injunction to seriousness more binding than in religious and theological thought, where "intuitions" are being had and reported all the time. Probably every human being, at one time or another, has had the feeling of seeing something that no one else has ever seen. We must somehow take account of that "inner fire" of conscience, of the artist's awakening to a new feeling that demands expression, of an idea seen excitedly for the first time. Finally, there are mystical intuitions that claim to have revealed God himself touching us directly.

The major difficulty with knowledge of this variety, especially the last, is that it originates and must live out its entire existence in a circumstance of supreme privacy. There is no way to get at these truths save through individual subjective experience, one individual at a time. These feelings and insights are exceedingly difficult to communicate to other people; they lose much of their integrity "in translation," striking us as delusory, fanciful, or, at the very most, merely interesting ruminations of the "inner person." They do not, according to many epistemologies, contribute much to the hard and rigorous business of human knowing.

The problem they present is perhaps most vividly illustrated when we are forced to deal with the "crackpot" or religious fanatic, an individual who, it is presumed, has as many qualifications for and as much right to have intuitions as the reasonable person. In the intermediate zone we might place the "guru" or the "prophet." Where, indeed, are we to draw the line between the fanatic's intuitions and those of the benign but erroneous prophet, or between the erroneous prophet and the true prophet, the individual we speak of as the "statesman" or the "person with vision"?

There is no sure way, of course, except to wait and see how things turn out. And when we do this we are relegating intuitions to the "humiliating" criterion of empirical testing. It is to this method of knowing that we now turn.

SCIENCE

Science is a term that conjures up in the modern mind a host of associations having to do with laboratories, jet airplanes, and rockets to the moon. It designates, in one of its meanings, a tremendous body of knowledge that we have put to use in our lives to control disease, to fashion machines, and to produce a lavish profusion of consumer products all the way from "Scarlet Rage" lipstick to I.B.M. computers. But in the epistemological sense science is considered not so much a body of knowledge as a *method of knowing*. It is the *method* of science that is of such profound importance to modern society, rather than the knowledge it produces or the technology which that knowledge makes possible. And the *method* of science lies principally in the testing of ideas in what is metaphorically referred to as the "crucible of experience."

Given sensory experience, human beings seem capable of seeing relationships, associations, and connections among the various sectors of their sensory world. They then attempt to identify and assert those relations as items of knowledge about their world. A primitive hunter may come to the view that wild game is more plentiful in the open valley than in the jungle thicket, but only on cloudy days. Or the physiologist may have a hunch that cigarette smokers fall victim to cancer more often than non-smokers. But in either case we are dealing only with hunch or guess or, in the scientific lexicon, *hypothesis*. We do not yet really *know*. Even intuition is admissible at this point, as long as we treat it as simply a *candidate* for truth rather than a matter of settled fact.

What must follow is a rigorous testing of the hunch or intuition to see if it is really true. And we do this by organizing a more refined and controlled interval of "experience," customarily spoken of as an "experiment," in which the relevant conditions of the problem are systematically ordered and taken account of in the experimental procedure. If hunters pretended to a scientific approach, they would begin counting the animals in both valley and thicket on both cloudy and sunny days. Their tabulations would soon lead them, if they were thorough and persistent enough, to a more accurate and dependable generalization concerning the availability of their food supply. Physiologists, likewise, entering upon a fantastically more complex problem, are essentially under the same obligation —to begin counting the cigarettes smoked, the cancer cases showing up in the hospital, and the cancer cells detectable in the diseased bodies. Only through this procedure can they arrive at anything that they would accept as physiological knowledge. The handling of intuition is perhaps more involved, but if the intuition is such as to yield to empirical treatment, which, as noted above, is not always the case, then the same procedure would be expected. If a so-called parapsychologist holds that human beings have a "sixth" or "extrasensory" sense that enables them to control an external event such as coin-flipping, it is theoretically possible to design an experiment in which the truth of this hypothesis may be tested.

Although our contemporary conception of the word *science* (as the above implies) is closely tied up with the formal process of framing and testing hypotheses in a controlled experiment, some investigators prefer a purely descriptive definition. B. F. Skinner, for example, views science as a process of merely describing our observations and summarizing them without testing hypotheses, drawing inferences, or constructing theories. This view of science leads to a different kind of knowledge and directs us more immediately to practical measures to take in daily life. We see this view of science developed more fully in Chapter 11.

We may summarize all this by saying that scientific epistemology insists on staying outside the interior workings of an assumed intellect, sticking to the region of open and public observation. There is no pretention, as we shall see in more detail in Chapter 6, that this procedure will lead to absolute truth. Whatever is found out, and therefore *known*, is to be held only temporarily and tentatively, until such time as the conclusions are modified or overturned. Since all scientific truth is at the mercy of observed phenomena and of the procedure by which those phenomena are reported and tabulated, any change in the phenomena or the reports must eventuate in altered conclusions.

CHOICE

Perhaps not an epistemological method at all, but only a strategic feature of all knowing, is the matter of ultimate choice. We include choice here primarily in anticipation of the epistemological considerations associated most directly with Existentialism.

The fittest approach may be to go back to the nonreferability of all human reports in the knowing process. At the base of all these procedures described in the previous sections is an individual "I" making certain assertions about experience. In the case of sense experience, I am the one who avers that the industrial exhaust "stinks." In the case of common sense, I am the one who asserts what the common sense of the community happens to be on a political question. In logic, I am the one who accepts the credibility of the statement "All men are mortal" and the credibility of a linkage between this and a similar pronouncement concerning Socrates; I have to "string along," as it were, step by logical step, in order for the logician to make any headway. And to "string along" I must make ultimate, if only minuscule, choices along the way in order for the knowing process to terminate in anything.

In the case of self-evidence and intuition, the situation is perhaps most concretely illustrated. For I am most certainly the active agent in asserting what is and what is not genuinely self-evident, and in the case of intuitions I am quite obviously the ultimate author of them. No one else can have intuitions for me.

But even in the case of the scientific method, which presumably transcends and "covers" all subjectivism, we are beset by the same problem. The scientist is, after all, dependent upon what human beings report concerning phenomena. To refine and order the circumstances in which phenomena are permitted to occur does not in any way change the situation with respect to the reporting of them; the reports must still be made by individuals relating their personal assessments, even if rigorous and disciplined, of the phenomenal situation as they see it. This epistemological caveat may appear somewhat labored when applied to the physical sciences—in counting the animals in a valley or the tar content of cigarettes. Can there really be significant dispute in such reporting? But the caveat assumes crucial importance in the social sciences and the humanistic studies, where human assessment of a situation is open to considerably greater variation. For instance, the Platonic "justice" of capital punishment is still, to put it mildly, an open question.

To speak, then, of the "nonreferability" of human choices is simply to make clear that at some point in every epistemological enterprise decisions have to be made that cannot be referred any further: the epistemological "buck" cannot be passed. I must take a stand—on how many animals I see or on whether the gas chamber is or is not morally right. And no particular stand is absolutely *required* of me, for if certain stands *were* required, in an absolute sense, then there would be no epistemological problem at all. We should all just yield to what *had* to be said about this or that sensory experience, this or that logical progression, this or that phenomenal situation.

Nothing *has* to be said about *anything*, really. Epistemology, and indeed philosophy itself, has assumed the importance it has because of the "open-endedness" of human knowing, and, therefore, the unspecified character of the content of our knowledge.

Epistemology and Metaphysics

We may now address ourselves to the inherently circular character of all epistemological ventures. While this may be a somewhat unhappy note on which to close this discussion, we need to make ourselves aware of it if we wish to be honest in the philosophical enterprise.

Our predicament can be gotten at directly by noting that *nonrefer-*

ability is characteristic not only of procedural decisions in our epistemology but of the very base of the procedure itself, the metaphysics we start out with. I am not absolutely required to accept *any* metaphysics. I am free to choose. I am at liberty to select from a goodly number of theories the metaphysics I wish to have as my epistemological foundation. The only thing I can do is to draw attention to certain features of my world that seem to me to be more *real* than others. And I pursue the examination of these features so as to back up my metaphysical choice.

Temperament, whether we like it or not, has a great deal to do with this. If I am a bookish sort of fellow, happiest when manipulating ideas, I am likely to lean in the direction of a mentalistic or "idea-filled" metaphysics. If I enjoy working with machinery I am likely to favor a mechanistic metaphysics. Of course, my metaphysics may have some feedback effect on my temperament, but, as the Idealist Herman Horne once put it, "We probably live our way into a system of thinking rather than think our way into a pattern of living."

At any rate, when it comes to selecting a metaphysics I am very much on my own. The only systematic thing I can do—if I do not want to trust my temperament—is to look more closely at those features of my world that I claim are most real to see *why* it is I claim that they *are* most real. How do I know that they *are* real? How do I know that ideas are more real than things, or things more real than ideas, or "experience" more real than either?

When I ask this question, I am really asking how do I *know*. And so I am back in my old difficulty, epistemology!

To generalize this, we may say that an epistemology makes sense only if it appears compatible with a basic metaphysics. For the many reasons discussed in this chapter, any method of knowing must somehow be supported and made possible by a previously held metaphysics. But, in like manner, a metaphysics cannot be set in place without making statements about reality. Since these statements signify some knowledge we have of reality, they immediately reveal a previously held epistemology. Thus, ultimately, our metaphysics is contingent upon our epistemology.

So we are, as it were, "trapped." Once engaged in the philosophical enterprise, we become committed to this or that circle of theory. But this is not so hopeless as it sounds. For one of the functions of philosophy, as stressed in Chapter 1, is to unify all our disparate thoughts into a master formula by which not only education but all the activities of life can be intelligently carried on. Each epistemology, then, may be expected to attempt to reach out and pull into its circle *all* the items of experience that human beings are said to have, to "colonize" all beachheads and frontiers of human existence, and to "imperialize" all human thought and action under its own intellectual hegemony. As you may already suspect, this is not an easy task. How it is attempted we shall now examine in Chapter 6.

Questions

1. Take each of the following statements and analyze the epistemological problem it poses:

   "I just know we're going to have a war with China."
   "Know thyself."
   "You can be *sure* if it's Westinghouse."
   "Know, think, do! God will follow you!"
   "He's all right, once you get to know him."

2. A distinction is often made between "knowing what" and "knowing how." Which of the several varieties of knowing is most closely associated with these two terms?

3. Some educators say we have had enough of "know-what" and "know-how." What we need is a little "know-*why*." What epistemological difficulties are likely to be encountered in knowing "why"?

4. Take a thorough look at the *Encyclopædia Britannica* and the *Encyclopedia of the Social Sciences*. These two encyclopedias (literally, from the Greek, "circle of knowledge") contain what we may designate as knowledge. Is the type of knowledge contained in the two different in any way? How?

5. A proposal was once made to the United Nations Educational, Scientific, and Cultural Organization (UNESCO) to sponsor and finance an international group of historians to write an authoritative, once-for-all world history, which could then be translated into every language and used in all the schools of the world. If you were selected to manage this project, what epistemological problems would you anticipate?

Further Reading

Brennan, Joseph G. *The Meaning of Philosophy*. New York: Harper, 1953. In a survey of "the problems of philosophy," Brennan devotes Part 2 to "Problems of Knowledge" and in successive chapters considers truth and certainty, our knowledge of the world outside us, and methods of knowledge. These three chapters, thorough and at the same time eminently readable, explain the problematic character of knowledge and knowing.

Bruner, Jerome. *On Knowing: Essays for the Left Hand*. Cambridge: Harvard University Press, 1962. A sequel to *The Process of Education*, this little volume seeks out the affective (left hand) as against the purely cognitive (right hand) dimensions of learning.

Grene, Marjorie. *The Knower and the Known*. New York: Basic Books, 1966. The book jacket provides a capsule annotation: "Marjorie Grene maintains that modern philosophy, held captive by the 'objectivism' of science, has been unable to develop an adequate theory of knowledge as a venture of living individuals. . . ." She proceeds to develop this argument, basing much of her thesis on the work of Michael Polanyi, who published the landmark work, *Personal Knowledge*, eight years earlier.

Phenix, Philip. *Philosophy of Education*. New York: Henry Holt, 1958. In Chapter 17, on "Knowledge," Phenix considers: contrasting aspects of knowledge, knowledge as subjective and objective, the sources of knowledge, and finally, the organization of knowledge into "knowable" categories.

Polanyi, Michael. *Personal Knowledge*. Chicago: University of Chicago Press, 1958. In a major epistemological work and one of the few by a physical scientist, Professor Polanyi sums up his career of reflection and inquiry by examining "the nature and justification of scientific knowledge in particular and of knowledge in general." His aim, he says, is a "Post-Critical [post-scientific] Philosophy."

Roszak, Theodore. *The Making of a Counter Culture*. Garden City, N.Y.: Doubleday, 1968. In Chapter 7, "The Myth of Objective Consciousness," the author lays down the proposition that modern, scientific knowledge is just as infected by human bias as any religion or political ideology.

Ryle, Gilbert. "Knowing How and Knowing That," a selection from the author's *The Concept of Mind* (London: Hutchinson University Library, 1949), in I. Scheffler, ed. *Philosophy and Education*. Boston: Allyn and Bacon, 1958. In drawing the distinction between the "how" and the "what," Ryle penetrates to the core of the modern epistemological problem: the role of scientific, operational knowledge in a residual intellectualist tradition that insists that there are some absolute truths that the mind grasps before it starts to "think."

Scheffler, Israel. *Conditions of Knowledge: An Introduction to Epistemology and Education*. Chicago: Scott, Foresman, 1965. Scheffler explores three philosophies of knowledge and then relates their different views to teaching, to knowledge and truth, and finally to belief and skill.

Stroll, Avrum, ed. *Epistemology: New Essays in the Theory of Knowledge*. New York: Harper & Row, 1967. Here, in a technical discussion aimed at an advanced audience, Professor Stroll and his colleagues open up some of the theory questions concerning knowledge: the role of sensation, knowing that we know, the privacy of experience, the existence of other minds.

Comparative Epistemologies

As we noted in Chapter 5, knowing has become a "problem" because there are several ways of engaging in it. And these several ways of knowing compete for attention among thoughtful people and attempt to establish themselves as the most dependable or the most fully authenticated procedure to follow if one seeks genuinely true knowledge. Since most of us —especially educators—*are* interested in true knowledge, we must pay careful attention to the competition in epistemology and to the relative claims for this or that epistemological procedure. We are under this obligation not only from the standpoint of authenticating our own day-by-day knowledge but, perhaps more important, from the standpoint of authenticating the procedures we follow in the educative function in managing the knowing process of boys and girls. This, after all, is where our epistemology is put to work, where it is tested in the real affairs of life, and where it does or does not "pay off."

As we proceed through these various epistemological theories, therefore, you should attempt in your study to anticipate the discussion in Chapter 7—namely, how each theory can be applied to the educational situation, the kinds of learning each makes possible, and those sectors of the school's curriculum to which each is most relevant. As in the discussion of metaphysics, we are not concerned here with engaging in polemics or in arguing a case for this or that way of knowing. We are involved, rather, in an exposure to and, it is hoped, an understanding of the various epistemological alternatives open to us in the work of educating the young.

Idealism: Truth as Idea

THE ABSOLUTE MIND

Since the Idealist's metaphysics is composed principally of mental "stuff," of ideas existing in a purely mental realm, we may suspect at the outset that an epistemology to match would hold knowing to be principally an enterprise in mentally grasping ideas and concepts. This turns out to be the case. To return briefly to the metaphysical discussion in Chapter 3 (see Figure 2, page 46), we may say that human beings are but prisoners in a three-dimensional "cave," a world of physical dimension and physical sensation. But the genuinely real world lies somewhere beyond all this. Knowing, then, is not merely "sensing" something. Knowing is, rather, taking hold of the *idea* of something and retaining it in the mind.

For example, I may have sense experience of many trees during the course of a day: the already cited elm tree in my front yard, the maple trees lining the avenue, the pear tree on the campus. But I truly know these objects in my experience only when I understand what they all have in common—what it is, in short, that makes them trees rather than something else. To put it more explicitly, I genuinely *know* them when I know the *idea* of "tree," the Idea that stands "behind" all trees and that they individually, but imperfectly, express.

Now if we were to collect all such Platonic Ideas—Tree-ness, Chairhood, Circularity, Man, Sparrowness, Doorknob-hood, Love, Democracy, Frog-hood, and all the rest—if, that is, we were to conceive of the absolute sum total of *all* Ideas, we would have in hand what might be designated the Platonic conception of absolute and ultimate reality. But ideas, by themselves, are only fictions; they require a mind to think them. And so, in later developments in Idealism, it has been held that there exists an Absolute Mind that is constantly thinking these thoughts and ideas. Indeed, to Hegel, it was the thinking of these ideas by the Universal Mind that explained their existential status: "History is God thinking."

The concept of the Absolute Mind is not so mystical as it may seem on the surface. In our own experience we know that some minds are "larger" than others; that is, some individuals can know more, have a wider grasp of the affairs of the world, see more deeply into life's problems, than others. In Platonic terms, they are able to penetrate the sensory screen to the Idea World beyond much better than their less-gifted fellows. Now, if we were merely to extend this ideational power to its logical limit, we should be able to imagine a Mind that exists wholly and completely beyond the sensory screen, that has no thoughts save those that are resident in the Universal and Idea-l realm, and that by these same tokens, is completely free of the error and passion that becloud human knowing.

Microcosm and Macrocosm

Epistemology in the Idealist setting, therefore, is primarily a description of how the human mind, with all its limitations, can be brought into communication with the Absolute Mind. In order to understand the circumstances in which this problem is met, Idealists customarily bring to mind the bipolar concept of microcosm and macrocosm. The simplest analogue is perhaps the microcosm of the physicist's atom and the macrocosm of the astronomer's solar system. As Chapter 2 noted, atomic particles are thought to revolve about their nucleus somewhat in the fashion that the planets orbit about the sun. Consequently we speak of the atom as a microcosm—a miniature replica—of the solar system.

Now, analogically, we may say somewhat the same thing of the human mind and the Absolute Mind. All the qualities of the Absolute Mind are present in our own; the qualities are simply found in more limited form. Therefore, our limited human minds are theoretically capable of communicating with and sharing in the Absolute Mind; they are made of the same "stuff," so to speak. Our minds, to return to the first metaphor, *participate* in the cosmic activity of thought in somewhat the same fashion that an atom participates in the solar system. There is a fantastically wide gap separating the two, to be sure, but this gap is not one of kind but of degree. The human mind and the Absolute Mind are fundamentally *en rapport*, even at the great "psychological" distance by which they are separated, by virtue of the fact that they are constructed of the same type of "material."

At the outset, then, Idealist epistemology posits a fundamental compatibility between a knowable reality and a capable knower. With these two "polar" points the epistemological problem is narrowed to the task of showing how they are brought into communication. Before we pass directly to this matter, however, it may be helpful to examine another aspect of the microcosm-macrocosm nexus: the dimension of selfhood.

THE ABSOLUTE SELF

What has already been said of the Absolute Mind may now be translated into similar designations concerning an entity that is at once more precise and more nebulous than the concept "mind"—the human *self*. When Descartes began his philosophizing he decided to start with the field of ontology and he began by doubting the existence of everything. Everything that had, previous to his time, been placed in some kind of existential category he systematically chose to doubt the existence of. He went down the list: things, ideas, Ideas, spirit, God, everything. Everything is to be doubted! Except one thing: my doubting. I cannot doubt my doubting; simply by doubting it I affirm it. I am therefore forced to begin, ontologically speaking, with my own doubts, my own thoughts. There is no escape. *Cogito, ergo sum:* I think, therefore I am. What proceeds from this Descartes built into a philosophic system. But at the root of it all stands this entity, the "I" in the *cogito*, which somehow is required to serve as the point of origin for all thinking, all ontologizing, and hence all knowing.

For want of a better term we may designate this entity as the *self*. The concept of the self has been a subject of ardent philosophic discourse through the ages, largely because it is almost impossible to define. As a symbol-concept it is almost as unyielding to definition as the Thomist term

Being or the ontological infinitive *to be*. We come perhaps as close as anything to it with our common, everyday word *person*. To think of a *person* as providing the vehicle for what we call *personality* takes us even closer to the idea of the self. And the *person* is what the Idealist sometimes calls the "self-conscious center of experience."

Beyond these few notions, however, it is difficult to set down precisely what selfhood consists in. We are blocked, as it were, from making any high-styled analysis of it.[1] But there is, nevertheless, a kind of nagging necessity to affirm the reality of the self, if not for other human beings then at least for our own individual being. I must somehow affirm the identity of my own experience. I can somehow point to something in myself which seems, to me at least, to be something more than the accretions of past experience, for, as the Existentialists are at great pains to point out (see pages 68–71), I am ultimately capable of *renouncing* my prior experience and adopting new and unconditioned forms of behavior. My selfhood is not locked into some determined system; indeed, the whole idea of "self" (as in *self-control, self-discipline*, etc.) contains the root notion of some kind of autonomy.[2]

The Idealist, then, must make a primary affirmation of his own selfhood and of selfhood as a real quality in the world. Now, let us suppose there is a concentric progression of selfhood similar to the logical extension of "mind" discussed above. In Figure 7 we graphically represent the possibility of enlarging our concept of self. At the center is the ordinary human being, conscious of himself, of other things in his reality, and of other selves. As he grows and matures he expands the reach of his selfhood, claiming larger and larger territory in knowing, understanding, feeling. He has more and more experiences, learns more and more, assumes deeper and more sensitive responses to the world about him. We say he has matured. But even among the so-called mature, there are some whose "selfhoods" may be said to encompass more than others. They are more knowledgeable about the the world, they understand more, they feel more keenly the beauties and tragedies of life, they reach out more readily to absorb the experiences of other people. Certainly an Albert Schweitzer or a Martin Luther King, Jr., possessed a "larger self" than I do. In this sense, then, we may be permitted the license of saying that some human beings are "larger selves" than others, and, to generalize further, that selfhood as an existential quality is capable of expansion and enlargement.

If we are willing to grant this bit of logical metaphorizing we can proceed ultimately to the logical possibility of a self whose reach is ultimate,

[1] An earlier social psychology has, to be sure, attempted to prove that selfhood is but the empirical product of social experience, being built up over the years from the results of countless conditionings. See W. H. Kilpatrick, *Selfhood and Civilization* (New York: Teachers College Bureau of Publications, 1941). But this whole proof begs the question of the origin of that "center" of thought and will that performs the assimilation and integration of the conditionings.

[2] Some individuals dismiss all this as "mere subjectivism." An Idealist might respond: If this be subjectivism, make the most of it! Subjectivism is precisely what we're talking about. Subjectivism is a real quality, existentially present in the real world.

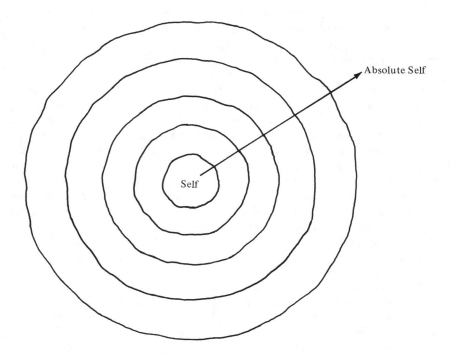

Absolute Self

Self

Figure 7   The Microcosmic-Macrocosmic Self

whose knowledge is complete, whose empathic powers know no bounds: the Absolute Self. Theologically, this is recognizable as the Omnipotent Person—God. God, in most theologies, has the qualities of a *person* that are elevated to their unlimited and absolute level.[3] But to introduce theology at this point would only deflect us from the genuine Idealist position, for God is not absolutely necessary to Idealist metaphysics or epistemology. All we need affirm at this point is the Absolute Self, which, like the Absolute Mind, serves as the ultimate ground in which we human beings participate.

This may seem a somewhat mystical approach to epistemology, and in

[3] John Locke, while not an Idealist in the Platonic sense, expressed it very well. In a section on the "Idea of God" in his famous *Essay Concerning Human Understanding,* he says: ". . . having, from what we experiment in ourselves, got the ideas of existence and duration, of knowledge and power, of pleasure and happiness, and of several other qualities and powers which it is better to have than to be without; when we would frame an idea the most suitable we can to the Supreme Being, we enlarge every one of these with our idea of infinity; and so, putting them together, make our complex idea of God. For that the mind has such a power of enlarging some of its ideas, received from sensation and reflection, has been already showed." (Chicago: Gateway Editions, 1956, p. 111. The *Essay* was first published in 1690, and the selection quoted is drawn from Book 2, Chapter 23.)

a sense it is. For in Idealist epistemology we are concerned not only with providing linkages of communication between mind and Absolute Mind but also—and this is a somewhat more sophisticated notion—with providing a medium of contact between the microcosmic *self* and the macrocosmic *Absolute Self*.

THE EMERGENT SELF

The Idealist epistemology may now be seen to involve something more than merely bringing a limited mind into contact with an absolute one: It involves as well the provocation and nurture of an emerging personality in the human being. This, it goes without saying, includes not only intellectual activities but moral, aesthetic, and emotional aspects of growth as well. And here is where Idealist epistemology becomes most vague and mystical. We are dealing with a quality—selfhood—that we have already indicated is largely beyond definition and analysis, and yet we say that this quality of selfhood can somehow be made to grow and expand under the special ministrations of the school.

It is a temptation at this point to dismiss the Idealist attention to selfhood as a benign but essentially misdirected exercise in poetic license: Selfhood is too vague a concept and its development too vague an epistemology to get us anywhere in the shaping of our educational ideas. This is a formidable temptation, except for the fact that we somehow subjectively feel that there is some warrant to the Idealist claim here—namely, that our own schooling, especially at the college or university level in a liberal institution, say, did indeed have an "enlarging" effect on us. We somehow feel "in our bones" that we are fuller human beings—more knowledgeable, more intensely aware of the world, more sensitive to its beauties and values—for having been immersed for four years in the liberal tradition. As ill-defined and nebulous as this feeling is, there seems to be some authenticity to it.

MIND, SELF, AND KNOWING

One of the things that the Idealist is prepared to say at this point is that individuals may discover the Universal Mind and Self—in microcosm, to be sure—in their own thoughts and feelings. I can look within, as it were, and find a tiny replica of the Ultimate Mind. One of the vital keynotes, therefore, of Idealist epistemology is *introspection,* the looking inside ourselves for what is genuinely real and true. Plato sounded this keynote beautifully in his doctrine of contemplation.

> True knowledge comes only from the spiritual world of eternal and changeless ideas, and this knowledge is innate in the immortal soul, which has dwelt in the spiritual world before being incased in the mortal body. Knowledge is thus acquired, not by sense experience, but by a process of

reminiscence, by which the intellect remembers what it knew before its association with an imperfect body. To remember perfectly, the intellect must rigorously close the windows of the body to the external world and open only the windows of the intellect, so that it may look upon and contemplate eternal truth. Intellectual discipline of the strictest kind, achieved by means of mathematics and philosophy, is the only true road to knowledge.[4]

It is, therefore, as if we were compelled to shut our eyes and ears to the sensations of this world and to see, almost literally "in our mind's eye," the truths of an ideational and spiritual reality. It was this idea that led Plato to the view that learning is essentially a process of "remembering," of "recognition"—literally *re-cognition*, or cognizing again. Our senses give us only the surface of things. We must deliberately turn from them in order to *know again* what the mind, because it participates in the Absolute, already knows.

To speak thus is to suggest that we can never know the world directly, that is, by looking at it. We must have a theory of knowledge that explains how it is that we achieve true knowledge through some more dependable means than mere sensation. While the Realists, as we shall see in the next section, are willing to settle for sensation, the Idealists require a more elaborate if somewhat less precise theory. They call it the "Coherence Theory of Knowledge." [5]

Immanuel Kant, in his systematic works, spoke of percepts (the data we receive through the senses) and concepts (the ideas that arise in our minds). Is there a linkage between these? asked Kant. Most certainly, he said. For concepts depend upon percepts for the raw data of thought; and percepts must terminate in concepts, else they are merely physical impulses impinging upon bodily tissue. As Kant put it: "Concept without percept is empty. Percept without concept is blind." We may say simply that the mind requires the "fuel" that the senses can deliver it in the way of sense perceptions. The mind needs to have something to work on, and the five senses are its "tentacle receptors" in the knowable world. Without these tentacles the mind would be isolated, an empty vacuum with nothing to do, no sense data to assimilate and organize, no impressions to test or evaluate—indeed, no thoughts to think whatsoever.

There is, then, a very vital role for sense perception to play in Idealist epistemology. But note one important feature of this epistemology: *It presupposes the existence of the mind itself.* We shall see that in other epistemologies the mind is thought to depend for its very existence upon sense data, or, a more generalized term for the same thing, "experience." But in Idealism the mind is held to be pre-existent to all sensing and all experi-

---

[4] R. F. Butts, *A Cultural History of Western Education*, 2d ed. (New York: McGraw-Hill, 1955). p. 49.

[5] For a technical discussion of this theory, see "Coherence as the Nature of Truth," in Brand Blanshard, *The Nature of Thought* (London: Allen & Unwin, 1939), pp. 261–297. Also helpful is "Coherence as an Account of the Nature of the World," in A. C. Ewing, *Idealism: A Critical Survey* (London: Methuen, 1961), pp. 228–236.

encing. It is, therefore, the ultimate explainer of what happens to it and hence the ultimate explainer of the world.[6]

As ultimate explainer of the world and itself, the mind enjoys a metaphysical autonomy that puts it at the very center of all epistemological activity. And this is precisely the point of entry for what we have termed "coherence." The mind's task is to receive data from many different sources, to assimilate them, to arrange them in some systematic order, to associate them with other sense data received earlier or in other circumstances, and, finally, to establish coherence among them. When this point is reached—depending on the degree of coherence among empirical reports —the mind can be said to have attained truth.

I can, for instance, in examining a piece of unknown mineral material feel its hardness, see its color, heft it, smell it, hear the sound a geologist's hammer makes on it, maybe even taste it. If all these reports seem to hang together and confirm my previous experience, I say I have in my hand a piece of coal. Or, in a less material setting, I may read Locke, Jefferson, and Rousseau and then study the French Revolution and the American Revolution, and then read Adam Smith, and then study the Civil War and World War I and World War II. I may then have it dawn on me that there was a big idea trying to be expressed in all of these events and writings. I say I have my hands (my mind) on the Idea of Freedom. This idea is revealed to our perceptions in this phrase, in that book, in this battle, in that war, in this public utterance, in that Declaration. And finally we take hold of the idea and it is ours, not in tiny pieces, like our perceptions, but whole and complete in our minds.

The mind therefore is in its epistemological office the organizer and systemizer of sense data. The sensory environment may provide the basic data for thought, the so-called stimulants to conceptualization, but it is the mind that does the knowing. And it performs this function through seeing relationships, finding connections between one impression and another, and finally arriving at a defensible conception of truth. Our minds proceed by getting successive "plots" on our position, by taking this and that "reading" of the situation, this and that "sighting" of landmarks. Then, by a process of organization and comparison, we assess "where" we are, what our existence is all about. It is as if, to employ a nautical metaphor, we are

---

[6] It is in this vein the Idealist often succeeds in dismissing the Realist's view that physical matter, rather than Idea, is the fundamental "stuff" of reality—most particularly, the view that the mind must be seen as a physicochemical organ functioning according to physical laws: ". . . the very notion of the mind as a function of the brain or of the living organism is itself one of the conceptions held of mind. The mind that can formulate such a conception to describe and explain itself is more than the conception it formulates." [H. H. Horne in *Philosophies of Education*, Forty-first Yearbook of the National Society for the Study of Education, ed. N. B. Henry (Chicago: the Society, 1942), Part I, p. 145.]

The counterview, of course, would insist that even the mind's view of *itself* is a physicochemical reaction made possible by "chemicals in motion" in the brain. Obviously, physiologists and psychologists could keep up this intellectual Ping-Pong ad infinitum.

"triangulating" our way through the sensory (and thus the metaphysically inferior) world heading for the ultimate harbor of the Absolute Mind. In Brand Blanshard's phrase, "Truth is the approximation of thought to reality. It is thought on its way home."

Realism: Truth as Observable Fact

NATURAL LAW

As we intimated earlier, every philosophy must present to thinking people a view of life and thought that can be seen to accord with common sense. Philosophical doctrine that repeatedly repudiates what we call common sense has never proved to be long-lived. That is not to say, however, that common sense cannot be improved upon, only that it must be accounted for and adjusted to in the day-by-day operations of philosophy.

It is to the fundamentals of common sense that Realism would have us turn for the foundation blocks of our epistemology—a common sense uncomplicated by mystical, otherworldly realms of Ideas or transcendent Persons or Selves. In Plato's terms, Realists are content to live in the so-called cave. They find reality there, and so there it is that they engage in their epistemological activity, the activity of knowing. But let us, says the Realist, be done with the metaphor of the "cave" forthwith! The mere metaphor is compromising. Here the world is, in all its ontological existentiality. It is not some kind of shadow of a presumably more real world, as the Idealist would say. No, the world we see *is* the real world. Epistemologically, we come at it without mystery; we come at it with our senses. And since this world is knowable—because it provides the occasion for sense perceptions—we engage in epistemological activity with some assurance that we are getting at the real thing, and not some illusion.

Reality is not an Absolute Mind thinking thoughts or an Infinite Self of which we are microcosms. Reality just *is*, without regard to human plans or purposes. It is, one might say, epistemologically neutral. To render it anthropomorphically, we might say that reality is "out there waiting to be known"; metaphysically, it is simply "there," awaiting the onset of epistemological activity toward it. If anything can be called a common-sense view of the metaphysics–epistemology relationship, certainly this can.

We know further, says the Realist, that this reality—which we can just as well now speak of as "Nature"—contains certain regularities: Water runs downhill, the sun comes up regularly in a certain sector of the sky, seeds placed in the earth will sprout and grow. If we look more carefully we can see that water runs downhill, for example, according to a regular pattern, a pattern that never varies given a certain set of circumstances. There is, as it were, a law of downhill-running-water. And there is an associate set of laws of sun-rising-in-the-East and corn-kernels-tossed-on-the-ground.

In these and myriad other ways, the real world we encounter every day contains regularities and patterns of structure and motion that represent its epistemological fascination for us. It exists, yes. It exists in a wonderful way—according to a vast plan—and it moves and evolves according to an even vaster plan, the plan of Natural Law. This Plan of Nature is the object of our epistemological enterprise.

By way of anticipating the discussion in Chapter 11 (where the Realist's epistemology is seen to support a Behaviorist approach to education) it may be well to articulate the views of David Hume, an eighteenth-century Scottish philosopher whose analysis of knowledge and knowing is still surprisingly apt in today's philosophical discussions.

For Hume, our ideas (that is, our knowledge) concerning matters of fact (reality) always originate in sense perceptions or in inferences based on them. When we encounter the ordinary world, we need not posit any metaphysical, unseen entities or principles to account for it. The knowledge-getting activity may proceed without building a case for how such activity is metaphysically possible.

Now, if we wish to check the truth of our ideas about matters of fact, we simply trace the ideas back to their sources to see if they come from immediate sense data or inferences based on them. If an idea cannot claim such a genealogy, then it cannot tell us anything about reality. For example, in analyzing the notion of causation, we find that nothing in our experience actually tells us that some kind of "power" or "necessary connection" is at work. All that our experience reveals is a constant conjunction between cause and effect. Thus, the phrase "A causes B" means no more than "If A, then B," and our ideas about the mysterious relationship between cause and effect are revealed as myth.

Causation is a central element in any Stimulus-Response, Reinforcement pedagogy. And, as we shall see in Chapter 11, B. F. Skinner holds to the "constant conjunction" view of causation, which has far-reaching implications in education.

THE "SPECTATOR THEORY"

The Realists, unlike the Idealists, are not concerned with where the Plan of Nature came from, or Who (in the sense of an Absolute Mind) conceived it. They are concerned with simply *what* the Plan is. Their epistemology focuses on the straightforward though arduous task of looking at the world and describing what it is and how it works. The epistemology (refer to Chapter 5, pages 111–113) can be rendered in philosophical shorthand thus: A person knows by being *a spectator of a world-as-machine*. In this sentence, the word *spectator* refers not just to eyesight but to all the five senses; the word *machine* metaphorically signifies that the object of our knowing is a physical thing in motion, controlled by built-in laws that it can be made to reveal.

To the Realists, then the epistemological problem boils down to what we might call "organized spectating," taking pains to "spectate" carefully and rigorously, checking our results, and, if our observations are systematic enough, coming up with generalizations, principles, and laws that tell us how our world is built and how it works. This may be readily recognized as the common-sense understanding of the word *science;* and it is in this uncomplicated meaning of science that Realists locate the basis of their epistemology.[7] This meaning of science, incidentally, extends beyond the physical sciences into social and political affairs. As pointed out in the discussion of Realist metaphysics in Chapter 3, there may be said to be a "natural law" of human affairs embedded within the very texture of Nature, as the classical economists were so fond of saying. And while moral and ethical matters are further afield, there is a sense in which Realists can speak of a moral law at work in the cosmos. There is, so to speak, a moral, good-and-bad dimension to the texture of Nature as well as an epistemological, true-and-false dimension. We shall examine this point more thoroughly in the sections dealing with Realism in Part Four on Axiology.

It may be noted that Realist epistemology shares some of the tendencies and interests of Idealism. The concept of Natural Law, for instance, is conceptually very proximate to Universal Mind. But these two ideas are different and distinct, and it is not just a profitless splitting of hairs to take note of the difference at this point: Idealism's ultimate and primary principle is Mind—Mind-in-Ultimate—that by its transcendent operations makes Nature, and therefore Natural Law, possible. Nature, in short, is the expression of a *prior* Mind. Realism's ultimate and primary principle, on the other hand, is Nature—a Nature-in-Ultimate—which by its existential motions and energies makes individual brains and nervous systems possible and therefore makes individual minds, and therefore Absolute Mind, possible. Mind, in short, is the expression of a *prior* Nature.

Perhaps an even more subtle point of contact relates directly to the so-called spectator epistemology. This theory of knowing, so evidently applicable to Realism, is likewise characteristic of Idealism—that is, if we are willing to allow the metaphor a bit more poetic leeway. That is to say, we can call Idealism a spectator theory in the sense that the inner mind does the "spectating." Our everyday phrase, "to see with the mind's eye," is an accurate if homely expression of how the Idealist views the spectator qualities of the knowing process.

---

[7] It should be noted at this point that the word *science* has become something of an epistemological troublemaker because it has taken on two rather distinct meanings: first, *a body of knowledge*, and, second, *a method of knowing*. By and large, the Realists are more interested in the knowledge than the method, whereas the Experimentalists, as we shall see later in this chapter, have become so interested in the method as to turn it into a systematic logic in its own right, a logic so imperial, they say, as to be epistemologically applicable to *all* knowing.

This is not an idle point, for it is crucial to understand that both Idealism and Realism are *objective* doctrines, at least insofar as they are treated in this book.[8] When we say *objective* we refer to the "out-there-ness" of the metaphysics of both schools of thought. Idealism's "out-there-ness" is the Universal Mind, with which the individual, microcosmic mind has contact. Realism's "out-there-ness" is the real physical world. The point is that both metaphysics are objective; and, therefore, both epistemologies view the knowing process principally as a bridge between the individual human being engaged in the knowing process (the subject) and the "out-there" world to be known (the object).

To restate the significance of this Principle of Objectivity,[9] we can say with the Realist that Nature seems to exhibit certain patterns of structure and regularities of performance that are occasionally refined into Law; that these Laws can be known and utilized to guide our conduct and to control what would otherwise be a pesky and arbitrary environment; but that in the "controlling" we are actually adjusting to and cooperating with an antecedent Nature whose ways must be known and followed in order for us to turn them to human account. When General Motors initiates its engineering activity upon Mesabi iron ore with the general aim of producing a Chevrolet, it must work upon the ore in ways consistent with what the ore can do. It cannot treat the ore as if it were something else. Hence, environmental "control" is only a sophisticated, anthropocentric euphemism for human adjustment to a prior and necessary natural state. We "operate" *on* nature by "cooperating" *with* it.

PURE THEORY

The Realist, then, is epistemologically concerned primarily with the business of discovering—literally *dis-covering*, removing the cover from—a pre-existent and existentially independent reality and thereby gaining knowledge of it. Another way of looking at this is to attend to what the Realist considers the highest kind of knowledge, Pure Theory. Here, again, we are not dealing with any esoteric or mysterious epistemological activity but, rather, with a commonplace of everyday life, namely, the theoretical knowledge that rationalizes practical understanding of life's daily affairs, from nuclear physics to child care. This theory is the epistemological "distillate" of countless observations of the real world. As such, it is "continuous" with the real world, both *in* and *of* it—not dispatched, as in the case of Idealism, to some other region of reality. The

---

[8] There is a position spoken of as "subjective" or "personalistic" Idealism; this, however, is not discussed herein. In these pages, we are treating Idealism in the Hegelian sense of the term, i.e., an Idealism holding to a Universal Mind at work in the world.

[9] Also developed as the Principle of Independence (the world is existentially independent of the knower) in F. S. Breed, "Education and the Realistic Outlook," in *Philosophies of Education*, Part I, pp. 104–105.

wave theory of light or the Freudian theory of neurosis is ultimately built up, says the Realist, out of concrete observations of what goes on in the sense world.

And we would not be wrong if we were to take this last statement quite literally. Knowing, to the Realist, is founded ultimately in sense perception. Gathering up those perceptions, organizing them, and rendering them systematic comprises the epistemological process. Here, once again, the value of common sense is recognized. For not only are our metaphysics and epistemology consistent with the common sense of the "man in the street," but epistemological *use* is made of common sense, literally the *common sensations* of human beings, in arriving at a genuine and dependable knowledge of the world. The Idealist's notion of "Coherence," says the Realist, is all well and good; but the seeing of coherence is primarily a private activity of the individual mind, rather than a public process of several minds acting in concert to validate their beliefs. Common sense is just what it says it is: a commonly held sensation of the way things are. As such, common sense is the first leg of the journey to "pure knowledge."

The second leg, of course, is the criticism of common sense, the extension of our common sensations into more rigorous and controlled "spectating" circumstances, and the sophistication of our common sensations into more generalized and more refined truths. Finally, if our investigations succeed, we are in a position to state generalized laws and principles that represent the way nature ultimately behaves, the kind of knowledge the Realist designates as Pure Theory.

This refining process goes on all the time in the physical sciences. For example, we make a distinction between "pure" research and "applied" research in physics. Studies having to do with the structure of the sun or with the so-called parity principle of matter may be thought of as "pure" problems,[10] whereas studies of space-vehicle navigation, which depend on but essentially *apply* the findings of the "pure" scientist, are spoken of as "applied" problems.

Pure Theory is sometimes thought of as the highest form of knowledge; scholars seek it not to *use* it but simply to *know* it. Knowing is its own reward. If a use can be found for such knowledge, so much the better, but ultimate use is not the justification for finding it out. *Knowing* it is the primary motivation. Of course, it is important to point out that so-called pure knowledge still depends on the observations of a human being. In studying the sun we are still required to peer through telescopes, analyze photographs, measure temperatures on spectrographs, read dials and

---

[10] The use of the word *pure* in this context reveals an interesting bias of the modern mind that runs all the way back to the Greeks. An idea or theory for which there is no immediate use or application is considered valuable in its own right, whereas an idea or theory having to do with some practical matter is "contaminated" by association with everyday circumstance—hence, of an inferior epistemological rank! A Platonism of two worlds—one practical and inferior, the other ideal and superior—may be said to account for this peculiar wrinkle in Western thought.

meters. We have not, in any absolute way, transcended the world of physical action, the Realist reminds us.

Here we must pause to remind ourselves of a subtle but important distinction in Realist theory. The *object* of our knowing, that is, the real world existing "out there," does not depend for its existence on any epistemological activity we engage in toward it. But the *content* of our knowledge-claims does depend for its existence on our epistemological activity. The structure of the sun is as it is; we are not going to change it in any way by knowing it. But our knowledge of the structure of the sun is subject to error, because it is ultimately contingent upon our ways of knowing. Pure Theory is the name we give to knowledge when it comes into conformity with and correspondence to the existential world as it really is.

THE CORRESPONDENCE THEORY

We may now examine the central proposition in Realist epistemology: the Theory of Correspondence. We are not, to review, concerned with the problem of bringing the finite mind into communication with an Infinite Mind, as the Idealist epistemologist would say, but rather with the essentially simple, straightforward, and uncomplicated problem of seeing to it that our statements about the world we live in do in fact correspond to the way things really are. This, as guileless as it may sound, is all there is to Realist epistemology.

It turns out, of course, that this is a bigger order than it may appear to the uninitiated epistemologist, and even Realists are not inclined to make light of the problem. Their position is that the epistemological enterprise, while difficult, is not in any way mysterious or mystical. It is open and public, because it is carried on in an open reality, a reality that, to be sure, does not give up its secrets easily but that nevertheless is not hostile to giving them up. This reality gives up its truth when we "come and get it." And we say we really possess it when our ideas correspond to the way things truly are.

There are three modes by which this "purchase" of truth may be understood in Realist terms. The first is the simple and omnipresent sense mode, that is, knowing things by direct sensing of them in our waking moments. So simple and immediate is this procedure that many Realists consider it unnecessary to contrive an epistemological theory to account for it.[11] Human beings are, after all, animals. They share with animals a nervous system and sensory network that possess the power (1) to gather in stimuli from the physical environment, (2) to organize those stimuli into what may be called a kind of immediate knowledge, and (3) to allow those stimuli to terminate in overt behavior—what is spoken of in the psychologist's lexicon as "response." Response to stimuli is but the overt sign of

---

[11] J. S. Brubacher, *Modern Philosophies of Education* (New York: McGraw-Hill, 1950), p. 77.

an inner knowledge held somehow in suspension in the nervous system and employed in the direction of conduct. In teaching the multiplication tables or typewriting, we rely almost exclusively on this kind of immediate (unmediated) mode of knowing. The behavior engineers, discussed in Chapter 11, have built virtually their entire argument on what they claim is the absolutely central role of stimulus-response phenomena in human conduct.

The second mode is the scientific. As noted above, we know things in varying degrees, less or more thoroughly. Science, to the Realist, is a procedure for looking more deeply into the nature of things and how they work by rigorously regulating the perceptive process and systematizing the reporting of what is observed. When we study geography, for instance, we do not merely step outside and look around at the local topography. Rather, we dig beneath the surface of things; we explore more adventurously the nooks and crannies of geographic reality. Similarly, when we study history we are not content just to read the newspapers of the period under view. Rather, we make a systematic comparison of the events of that period with what preceded and what came after it, in order to discern, if possible, any linkages that would make our knowledge more sophisticated and mature. It is in this sense of wider and deeper *investigation* that the Realist understands the word *science*, and it is this mode which activates the greatest part of Realist knowing.

The third mode of arriving at truth, more complicated and recondite than the other two, is not often emphasized in contemporary Realism but is nevertheless native to it. It may be labeled the "epistemology of essences." We referred in Chapter 3 (see page 53) to the fact that Aristotelianism has historically culminated in two somewhat divergent metaphysics: modern scientific Realism (here under discussion) and Neo-Thomism. Though they are divergent, these world views share enough to make it possible for them to come to terms with each other on epistemological matters. The matter of "essences" happens to be a common interest of both these doctrines.

To get right to the point, the Correspondence Theory comes to full application when we can say that the *idea* in our minds corresponds perfectly with the *thing* being known. And the *idea of the thing* is what is called "essence," the underlying, constituent, and central element that makes the thing what it is and not something else. Knowing, in the most mature mode, is to have a complete understanding of *what* things are. This interest in "what-ness," this central concern with the *quiddity* of the world, is seen as thoroughly consistent and harmonious with the metaphysics of the Realists, who considers reality to be a substantive something or collection of "somethings." It is this *quiddity* of the world that is the ultimate epistemological goal of Realist knowing.

Realists, however, do not customarily concern themselves with this type of knowing, leaving its elaboration to the similar but essentially more complicated epistemology of the Lay and Ecclesiastical Thomists, to which we now turn.

Neo-Thomism: Truth as Reason and Intuition

Metaphysical Underpinnings

As is true of any epistemology, that of the Neo-Thomist may best be approached by understanding first the metaphysical ground in which the knowing process is carried on. If we know what kind of reality we are dealing with, we are in a much better position to describe the procedure by which we can come to true knowledge of it. So, to refer to Chapter 3 briefly, we may remind ourselves that, like the Realist, the Neo-Thomist is dealing with only one world (rather than the Idealist's two) and that what we see and perceive is genuinely real. However, according to the Neo-Thomist, this world we see is characterized by *logical* as well as existential features, most notably Matter and Form, which stand as logical constructs in Aristotelian thought. Matter is the principle of potentiality and Form the principle of actuality.

As St. Thomas reworked Aristotelian logic, he demoted Essence (the union of Matter-and-Form) to the principle of potentiality and placed a new, and *ultimate*, logical construct—Existence—in the position of the principle of actuality. When essence and existence come together, there results a "being." This is the final thing one can say about anything: that it *is*.

In both Aristotelian and Thomistic thought, we must remember, the potentiality-actuality nexus is uppermost, leading finally in Aristotle's system to Pure Form and in St. Thomas's system to Being or God. Also, whatever epistemology may be derived from this plan must recognize that reality is *logically* put together. That is, reality is necessarily, not capriciously or fortuitously, just the way it happens to be. Therefore, our epistemological activity is directed toward a fixed metaphysical object. To put it in plainer language, what it is we are trying to know is existentially permanent and unchanging and logically ordered and regulated. Reality is there, logically precise and necessary, and our epistemological attack on it will in no way upset its logical order. This Neo-Thomist reality is exceedingly difficult to understand, to be sure, but once it is understood, in this or that degree, we may say that we have put our minds upon genuine truth.

So certain of this are the Neo-Thomists that they speak of truth with a capital *T*: Truth. In the end, they say, what we are after and what we can actually attain is a kind of knowledge that is permanent and absolute because it is a logical apprehension of a reality that is permanent and absolute. Moreover, since reality itself is a *logical system* as well as a collection of either ideas (Idealism) or things (Realism), and since our minds are capable of logical thought now, we are as it were already in epistemological touch with reality. We are "tuned in," one might say, to the wavelength of ultimate reality. And as we gather signals, we become increasingly knowledgeable about our world. With these preliminaries out of the way, then, how does Neo-Thomist epistemology work out?

THE INTELLECT

Fortunately, the epistemological enterprise may be begun without too much difficulty, for, according to the Neo-Thomist, the human mind naturally tends to know. As Mortimer Adler puts it, "The human mind naturally tends to learn, to acquire knowledge, just as the earth naturally tends to support vegetation." [12] In dealing with a more complex point about the axiological or "value" dimension of knowing ("To know is good"), Adler confirms the above view:

> In the case of the intellect itself, which, as a power of knowing, naturally tends toward the possession of truth as its perfection, the habit of knowledge is good by reason of conformity to the natural tendency of the cognitive power, and the habit of error is bad by reason of violation of that tendency. If the intellect were indifferently a power of knowing and not-knowing, possession of truth and possession of error would be indifferently good as actualizations of the cognitive power.[13, 14]

So the epistemological expedition can set out without any special prodding. Human beings already lean toward knowledge. We are disposed here only to show how that leaning is translated into forward epistemological motion.

SELF-EVIDENCE AND INTUITION

To say that the mind is naturally oriented to reality by virtue of its logical structure is to say that the mind—or, more precisely, the intellect—can take hold of certain truths in and by itself. It can, in the language of the Neo-Thomist, *intuit* truth. To understand this concept of intuition, it is necessary to point to two kinds of truth characteristic of Aristotelian thought: synthetic or "evident" truth and analytic or "self-evident" truth. Synthetic truth is the garden-variety type of knowledge with which science deals. If I say that the distance between New York and Chicago is so many miles, I am uttering a synthetic truth, synthetic in the sense that the predicate of a proposition is not contained in the subject. Evidence is

---

[12] "In Defense of the Philosophy of Education," in *Philosophies of Education*, Part I, p. 211.

[13] Ibid., p. 243.

[14] A logical demurrer may be entered here in the following form: If we posit a *natural tendency*, then we must rule out *free choice*. If the mind naturally tends to know then it "cannot help it" if it knows. How, then, can knowing be called a good when it is, in a sense, "forced" on the mind? How can anything be good that is the product of a necessary and built-in characteristic? In modern ethical theory, especially in Experimentalism and Existentialism, good is the result of free and undetermined choice. We shall take up these matters in more detail in Part Four.

required. But if I say that two things equal to the same thing are equal to each other, I am uttering an analytic truth—the kind of statement whose predicate is analyzed out of the subject and which therefore does not have to be tested out in action. There is no need for me to draw two lines each equal to a third and then measure them to see if they are equal. My intellect tells me this is true: I intuit it as true.

At the base of both kinds of truth, the Neo-Thomist will readily admit, lies sense experience. Both synthetic and analytic knowing originate and have their impetus in the ground of ordinary perceiving. Certainly sense data are needed in the New York-Chicago statement. And in the second statement one must have a background of experience in order to understand the terms *two, thing, equal,* etc. But here the similarity between synthetic and analytic truth ends, for in the latter category experience is not necessary to establish the truth of the statement. Its truth is an immediate apprehension of the intellect.

Self-evidence, then, is the key to a whole range of truth that is not accessible through science. And to the Neo-Thomist this kind of truth is far superior to scientific truth precisely because it stands above the changeable weather of day-to-day experience and the resultant storms of controversy in the empirical world. Scientific knowledge, says the Neo-Thomist, is only a kind of "edging toward" or "sidling up to" truth. Analytical, self-evident truth is the real article. It is epistemologically pure because, once taken hold of, it is ours forever!

Self-evidence and intuitive knowing can lead us, as we have seen in the example, to many relatively "low-order" truths, such as the mathematical proposition about equality. But this kind of knowing can also be used to carry us into the highest regions of metaphysics and into that exclusive "country club" of truths that the Neo-Thomist calls the "First Principles." A prime example of this kind of truth is the statement: *All things have a cause.* Based ultimately in experience but essentially transcending the empirical world, this principle can be asserted as true without any recourse to experiment or testing. Furthermore, this First Principle is particularly pertinent to our discussion because it opens up some illuminating territory in the psychology of knowing.

We may say that Aristotle considered this the central principle in his search for the essence or "what-ness" of things. He found in causation the clearest road to true essential knowledge and finally came to the view that *to know anything is to know its causes.* In Aristotle's thinking there are four distinct types of causes:

The Material Cause = Matter
The Formal Cause = Form
The Efficient Cause = Maker
The Final Cause = Purpose

As it turns out, we actually proceed psychologically in somewhat this order in coming to know things. We first "sense" what a thing is made of, the basic stuff of which it is constructed. We then attend to its design and form, the total plan by which the material substance is arranged. Then we come to know it still better if we understand how it came into being, what caused it to be (our modern use of the word *cause* is confined largely to this third sense). Finally, we know it fully when we comprehend the purpose or function that the thing is to serve.

Thus, in the case of a house, the lumber is the material cause, the blueprint design is the formal cause, the carpenter is the efficient cause, and the Basic Idea of the house, its role as a dwelling place, is considered the final cause. The final cause, of course, serves as the gathering point for all the other causes; it is the occasion for all the other causes to be introduced into the logical situation. It is therefore the most important. Also, we are epistemologically satisfied when—but not until—we have reached the fourth and final cause. We say we really know something when we know its purpose.

To illustrate this, let us say that I place a piston ring before a young boy. He has never seen one before, doesn't know anything about it, and hasn't the vaguest idea of its raison d'être in the world of things. But he begins by sensing its properties—shiny, hard, heavy, etc. He comes to the material cause, steel. He then notices its design: circular, sharp corners, grooves, etc., leading to the formal cause, a sharp-edged, grooved ring. He is then told that it was manufactured by a group of metalworkers in an automobile-parts factory. This helps a good deal in narrowing the possibilities. But he is essentially still outside the full knowledge of the item because he has not yet determined what it is *for*, what its final cause is.

At this point, the Aristotelian and Neo-Thomist epistemologist claims that the next step is purely intuitive. Sense perception must precede it, to be sure, and we must have the first three causes clearly in hand before proceeding. But the fourth step is exclusively a "leap of the intellect" into the realm of intuitive insight. To discover what the piston ring is *for*, what purpose it fulfills, what function it performs, is to be visited by an immediate apprehension of its ultimate essence, by an intuition.

It is in this sense that intuition is the summit and climax of all knowing, partly because it comes last, partly because it comes instantaneously, but principally because it has the effect of producing epistemological satisfaction in the knower, a kind of closure to the undertaking that represents complete knowledge. It is as if our minds had finally and ultimately fastened upon truth and, in so doing, come into touch with ultimate reality.

Of course, comprehending the final cause of piston rings is one thing and comprehending the final cause of other existent beings is quite another. The supreme test case is to apply this epistemology to Man. What is the essence of Man? Materially he is constructed of blood and bones. Formally he can be spoken of, in Platonic language, as a "featherless biped." But we are, admittedly, a long, long way from taking hold of his essence from these meager data. Ecclesiastical Thomists incline, in their epistemologies, to hold the third or efficient cause to be of vital importance. If you want to know what a thing is, ask its maker. And so, in the case of Man, the Almighty is appealed to in order to ascertain the fourth or final cause. What is Man *for?* we ask. And the Roman Catholic Church supplies the answer: to reclaim the Life of Grace lost by us through the Fall of Adam, which means to find our way back to the source of our being, namely, Being or God. This, to the Roman Catholic, is what we are *for*.

To a Lay Neo-Thomist, however, "straight" Aristotelianism, without St. Thomas's theological overtones, is sufficient. According to this doctrine, to understand the essence of Man does not require any theological commitments, Christian or otherwise. All it requires is a steady gaze at the question of the Final Cause of Man until intuition is ours. And we have not long to wait if we are willing to return to Aristotelian thinking on this question. For in Aristotle's system Man's Final Cause was clear: "The specifically human function, the reason why [Man] exists, what he is 'for,' is the development of his rationality, both in practical and intellectual affairs." [15]

INTUITION AND REVELATION

We must now make explicit what has been implicit in the above discussion, namely, that, while Lay and Ecclesiastical Neo-Thomists share intimately in their Aristotelian heritage and in the logic of Aristotle's thought, they part company today on epistemological questions by virtue of their slight metaphysical divergencies. As noted both in Chapter 3 and in the above analysis, the Lay Neo-Thomist is willing to adopt the Aristotelian frame of things insofar as philosophical matters are concerned. It is not mandatory that there be a God, a spiritual headwaters of human reality to which we must defer. There is only a logic to reality that we must yield to. However, Lay Neo-Thomists could defensibly accept St. Thomas's philosophical system as long as they stayed on the side of (capital-*B*) Being, a purely philosophical concept, without drifting over the line into the theological concept of God; for in making the shift Lay Neo-Thomists would be adding more to their understanding than unaided reason will provide. That is to say, one can proceed logically from Matter to Form to Essence to Existence to existing beings to Pure Being. By sheer intellectual force this progression can be run. But it is an extrarational lurch to make the final step of saying that Being is the same as God. One *need not* worship Being; one *must* worship God. The two ideas are quite different.

For these and other, more sophisticated reasons, the Lay Neo-Thomists confine their epistemology to synthetic or scientific knowing capped by the highest form of knowing, analytic or intuitive knowing. If they are rationally rigorous, they will not try to claim too much or go beyond the limits set by these two methods.

[15] R. Brumbaugh and N. Lawrence, Jr., "Aristotle's Philosophy of Education," *Educational Theory* 9, no. 1 (January 1959): 8.

Ecclesiastical Neo-Thomists, on the other hand, because they hold to a theistic metaphysics, find a still higher dimension to their epistemological activity: revelation. God reveals himself to us through the intellect. Admittedly, intuition and revelation are closely related concepts; semantically they are practically touching each other. But technically they are distinct. For intuition is, metaphorically, a "reaching out" to seize upon a truth already resident in an independent reality, whereas revelation is a "receiving in" of truths from an outside source. Intuition, therefore, is active, while revelation is passive; indeed, the former is usually expressed in the active voice (I *had* an intuition; I *intuited* something) while the latter is expressed in the passive voice (It *was revealed* to me; I *was made to see* something).

Notwithstanding this distinction, the Ecclesiastical Neo-Thomist holds that revelation is one way of knowing. It is a way of knowing, moreover, that has been authenticated down through history and that therefore claims as much right to epistemological attention as any other. Furthermore, since the author of such knowledge is God himself, this is the highest and supreme category of epistemological activity known to Man. Therefore, if there is conflict between revealed and intuitive knowledge, or between revealed and scientific knowledge, revelation shall carry the day. We are, then, in Ecclesiastical Neo-Thomism, dealing not only with three varieties of knowing: scientific, intuitive, and revelatory. We are dealing also with a *hierarchy* of knowing, by which the varieties are ordered. When there is tension in the hierarchical ranks the higher form must prevail.

This hierarchy of knowing is misconstrued by many commentators on Thomism to mean that revelation and faith actually supplant and take the place of other kinds of knowing. Especially in philosophical matters, it is said, Neo-Thomists begin with spiritual commitments that they then attempt to justify in reason. This is not accurate. What the Neo-Thomist insists on is the *complementary* nature of various kinds of knowing, that is, that faith confirms and backs up what we have already achieved by reason or, conversely, that reason properly applied will lead us independently to truths already revealed to us. Moses learned the "Name" of God ("I am Who Am") through revelation. But a couple of milleniums later, St. Thomas arrived at the concept of "Being" through rational procedures exclusively. St. Thomas therefore demonstrated *rationally* what Moses had received through *revelation* from God.[16]

[16] The presumed autonomous independence of rational truth and revelatory truth is, in more sophisticated circles, still argued. Even Catholic philosophers have been known to yield some ground here. For instance, Étienne Gilson, one of the leading Ecclesiastical Neo-Thomists, says, in his *The Spirit of Medieval Philosophy* (New York: Scribner's, 1936): "It is a fact that between ourselves and the Greeks the Christian revelation has intervened, and has profoundly modified the conditions under which reason has to work. Once you are in possession of that revelation how can you possibly philosophize as though you had never heard of it? The errors of Plato and Aristotle are precisely the errors into which pure reason falls, and every philosophy which sets out to be self-sufficing will fall into them again. . . ." (Page 5.)

The Roman Catholic insistence on separate and autonomous episte-mological realms has its practical application in political and social affairs. In these matters it is held that separate realms are inhabited by church and state and that each is sovereign in its own sphere. The difficulty with this view (as developed in greater detail in Chapter 11) is the segregation of religious principles from ordinary day-to-day affairs. If religious matters are sealed off in their own compartment, then they can have little to say about how we are to live out our lives. If, on the other hand, religious prin-ciples are applied to everyday concerns, they must expect to encounter com-pelling secular and scientific ideas, with which they will occasionally collide head on. In collision, what then? Which principles—the ecclesiastical or the secular—shall prevail?

This is by way of suggesting that the Ecclesiastical Neo-Thomist epis-temology is quite obviously destined to run into a good deal of trouble in a scientific and secular America unless carefully boxed in and confined to Roman Catholic churches and schools and insulated from the wider affairs of civil society. The mood of modern America is increasingly inclined toward the scientific and empirical; and when some religious or philo-sophical group claims that its spiritual or metaphysical or merely intuitive visions contradict what the scientists can see in plain daylight to be the truth of the matter, the American temper is likely to give the final nod of approval to the scientist.[17]

This temper is the result of a new intellectual outlook that has swept the Western world within just the last couple of centuries and that has taken the modern (especially the American) mind by storm. Serving as both the storm troopers and the occupation forces for this intellectual revo-lution have been the Experimentalists, to whose epistemology we now turn.

Experimentalism: Truth as What Works

HISTORICAL PERSPECTIVES

By all measures, the philosophical colossus of our age is the scientific philosophy of Experimentalism, variously called Pragmatism or Instru-mentalism. As a philosophy it is relatively young, stretching back less than a hundred years. It is, however, the systematic expression of a move-ment that began much earlier. Customarily Galileo is considered the father of the scientific tradition. Although it is difficult to locate the origin of so nebulous a thing as an intellectual movement, there does seem to have been an epoch in time when human minds took a new turn. This epoch,

---

[17] "Humanist Manifesto—II," updating a 1933 document, "Humanist Manifesto—I," appeared in mid-1973 to restate the secular position. This statement, drafted by Paul Kurtz, editor of *The Humanist* and signed by 120 religious leaders, philosophers, scientists, writers, and social scientists from around the world, asserts that humans alone must solve the problems that threaten their existence on earth. "No deity will save us, we must save ourselves."

the latter sixteenth and early seventeenth centuries, serves in retrospect somewhat as a "Great Divide" or intellectual watershed in the historic course of human thought: on the other side, the reliance on logical, self-evident, and *a priori* truth; on this side, the reliance on experience and overt phenomena. Through the words of a brilliant commentator on the history of science, Herbert Dingle, we may begin to assess the magnitude of this shift in intellectual orientation. In an article on "Cosmology and Science," Dingle writes:

> To appreciate what kind of thinking created the cosmology of the Greek pioneers, beginning, as it inevitably had to in early times, from the natural assumption that the earth was the center of the universe, we must understand a fundamental characteristic of Greek thought—which is at variance with the scientific outlook. They presupposed certain *principles*, which were assumed to be inviolable and were accepted without question. If appearances seemed to contradict them, then the appearances were deceptive. . . . For example, they asserted that the only activity possible to heavenly bodies was perfectly uniform and circular movement, and that apart from such eternal circulations no change of any kind could take place in the heavens. . . . Since the planets appeared not to move in circles at uniform speed, the apparently erratic movements of each planet must be the resultant of a set of circular movements.
>
> The aim of Greek cosmology was to arrive at the complex system of interlocking spheres in motion that made up the universe. . . . Geometers of genius such as the Greeks produced were able to represent the observed movements of the planets with an accuracy equal to that of their imperfect observations at any given time, but as time went on the discrepancies between the geometrical requirements and the observed positions of planets increased, and so more spheres were introduced to annul them. This went on throughout the Middle Ages, until by the sixteenth century more than eighty spheres were necessary to account for the observed movements, and even that number did it very imperfectly.
>
> . . . by the sixteenth century the cosmic machinery of spheres had become so unwieldy that Copernicus, a man dominated by the mathematician's passion for simple generalization, ventured to make what seemed to him the very slight change of transferring the center of the universe from the earth to the sun. By this device he was able to reduce the number of cosmic spheres by more than half.
>
> He made no other change, nor did he realize that any other was necessary. He clung as firmly as the most orthodox medieval philosopher to the machinery of spheres and to the Aristotelian principles of perfect celestial substances and uniform circular motions. . . . By the time of Galileo, some three quarters of a century later, it had become clear that there was no need for any spheres at all, and the simple change that we would now describe as no more than choosing a different origin of coordinates had generated a conflict of world views such as the world had never before seen.[18]

[18] From "Cosmology and Science" by Herbert Dingle, *Scientific American*, 95, no. 3 (September 1956): 224–230. Copyright © 1956 by Scientific American, Inc. All rights reserved.

This, then, was the Aristotelian epistemology at work: starting with presupposed and "self-evident" principles and then attempting to make the observations of natural phenomena conform to them. In contrast to this procedure was the method of science:

> The Galilean-Newtonian philosophy, on the contrary, brought knowledge in apparently boundless measure but was logically [from the Aristotelian standpoint] outrageous. From a few phenomena, or experiments, it proposed to derive principles to be applied universally. Some bodies attract one another; this is a body; therefore it attracts every other body in the universe. No more patently invalid syllogism could be imagined; it was an error in Aristotelian logic of which even the youngest scholastic child could hardly have been capable. But it worked. And not only so, but similar generalizations later in other fields were found to work, and they go on working. We have never known heat to flow by itself from a colder to a hotter body, and we take it that it never has nor ever will anywhere in space. The brightness of a lamp in our laboratory falls off as the square of the distance as we walk away from it; hence we infer what the brightness of a distant galaxy must be. That is science. Its assertions about the universe are unlimited generalizations from a few momentary observations at a point in space.
>
> From a purely logical point of view scientific cosmology would appear to have no justification, to be a gigantic impertinence. It is saved from this by a frank recognition by scientists of what it is and what its limitations are. The work of three centuries has shown that the scientific approach is on unassailable ground when it declares itself to be the best prescription yet devised for obtaining knowledge of the relations between phenomena. Whether or not its generalizations have any right to be regarded as the *truth*, they lead to further knowledge—which, so far as we can see, would be quite unobtainable otherwise. But they do this only on the condition that we abandon them the moment we see that they cease to hold. They originate in phenomena and they are at the mercy of phenomena.
>
> The Aristotelian general principles, on the other hand, were conceived *a priori*, independently of phenomena, and phenomena were distorted at liberty so as to exemplify them. The problem was to "save the phenomena." The basic principles themselves could not be threatened; it was the phenomena that stood in need of salvation.[19]

METAPHYSICAL BACKGROUND

We noted in Chapter 3 that the Experimentalist's reality is the moving, changing, "process-in-flux" event spoken of as experience. Experience is the ultimate ground for human existence. It is both the originator and the supreme court of whatever we do or say. To put it bluntly once again, whatever reality is is what we say it is, and what we say it is is founded in ordinary experience. Experience is as close as we can get to the "name" of reality. As exasperatingly nonsubstantive as this may be, it is the best we can do.

[19] Ibid., pp. 230–234.

Knowing, then, must take on a quite different notation in this philosophy, for we are immediately confronted by the necessity to settle for something much less than fixed and permanent truth as the end point of our epistemological labors. Since our reality is characterized by flux and movement and change, certainly our knowledge cannot be otherwise. We must therefore initially retrain ourselves to recognize that whatever knowledge is possible is temporary and tentative in character. If our conception of truth (knowledge) is ultimately "at the mercy of phenomena" as we experience them, as Dingle has said, then we must be willing to alter our truth and our knowledge as new and variable phenomena come into view.

Furthermore, in Experimentalist epistemology we must rid ourselves of the subjective-objective dualism so characteristic of the three positions already discussed. Both Idealism and Realism (and, with minor qualification, Neo-Thomism) are what we have called essentially "objective" doctrines, holding to an epistemology that considers the knower as one agent and the reality-to-be-known as the alteragent in the entire knowing process. In these doctrines epistemology is the explanation of how the two substantive agents are brought together. This, to an Experimentalist, is all wrong. It presupposes, in the first place, a metaphysical dualism between the knower and his world. This presupposition is both unwarranted in metaphysical thought and obstructive to the epistemological enterprise. What it does is to *create* an epistemological problem where none exists.

Man is, after all, part of the world he is knowing. Furthermore, he is integrally *one* with it in a state of constant interaction. To extricate him from Nature and to assign him the role of spectator (ideational spectator in Idealism; perceptual spectator in Realism; logical spectator in Neo-Thomism) is to do irreconcilable violence to his true condition. He is both *in* and *of* his cosmos. He never can look at it—ideationally, perceptually, or logically—as an outsider. He is inevitably, inexorably, irreconcilably "plugged in" to his world.

When Experimentalists suggest Experience as their name for reality, they are not merely thinking up a new category. Rather, they are pointing to an already existential but hitherto unrecognized and unappreciated feature of the epistemological situation, namely, the *dynamic relationship between* the knower and his world. What Experimentalism does is to render truly existential what the other philosophies consider only superficially phenomenal, namely, the interactive relationship itself. Granted, this is not a substantive existent in the classical sense. It is a process-existent, what we may now refer to, recalling Chapter 3, as a "verb-al" or "event-ual" existent. There is no reason why events and processes cannot be as truly existential as substantive entities.[20]

[20] In the more technical discussions of ontology, the Experimentalists attempt to demonstrate that even existential *things* are really *events occurring* rather than *substantives existing*. Indeed, the very word *exist* means, in Experimentalist ontology, *to occur*. See Van Cleve Morris, "An Experimentalist on Being," *The Modern Schoolman*, 35, no. 2 (January 1958) : 125–133.

So, therefore, the Experimentalist's *Experience* is the name for an inter-active relationship, the relationship of *transaction*, of *doing-and-under-going*, which is moved to the center of the stage and given the lead role in Experimentalist epistemology. Unlike previous views, the new interest will be in interaction, in relation, in the nature of the "connectedness" *between* things, rather than in some underlying "idea" or "essence" or "logical substance" which metaphysically inheres in things.

THE NATURE OF TRUTH

Following up on these metaphysical considerations, we may now investi-gate more carefully the knowledge-problem before us. In such a meta-physics, what kind of truth is possible? As we have indicated, all knowledge to an Experimentalist must be considered temporary and con-ditional. Indeed, the word *truth* is an equivocal term that is hazardous to use in Experimentalist theory. So heavily laden is this word with the traditional meaning of permanent and unchanging statements of fact about an existential reality that it often tends to jar rather than facilitate under-standing of the Experimentalist position. To overcome this hazard, the qualifying adjective *tentative* is customarily placed before the word *truth* to designate more precisely what Experimentalists really mean in this context.

This point is labored at some length here because it is a crucial feature of experimentalist epistemology. The analogue of the scientist in the laboratory perhaps illustrates this point. Let us say that a scientist in her investigation comes upon a discovery of some kind. In the histrionics of science she is supposed to exclaim, "Eureka!" (I have found it!) But no scientist, if such a thing is ever said, really means that a permanent and immutable truth has been discovered. The scientist simply means that a new way to understand certain phenomena has been found. This discovery, like every other, is subject to change or repeal tomorrow morning if the phenomena then seem to require it. Taken literally, the statement "I have found it" is not a scientific statement but more in the nature of a theo-logical one. Realist scientists, thinking they had peered into the ultimate nature of the physical world, might possibly be caught saying such a thing, but Experimentalist scientists never. All they say is that they have come upon an idea that will serve as truth until something better comes along.

KNOWING AS PROCESS

With this caveat in hand, we may now proceed to another epistemolog-ical implication from Experimentalist metaphysics. We referred above to the "transactional" character of experience. In the enterprise called know-ing, what we are actually engaged in is a kind of dialectic with the cosmos. As we experience, various ideas occur to us as to the way things are.

We may speak of these as hunches, guesses, hypotheses, intuitions,[21] or insights; basically, all these terms designate the same genera of assertion. At this point, they have no epistemological status except that they have occurred to us; they are, as it were, "candidates" for truth.

At this point we begin to redirect our behavior and to act *as if* such and such were true. That is, we enter the *do-ing* phase of knowing; we *act on* the cosmos. Then we receive the reaction of the cosmos; we *undergo* the consequences of our doing. In simpler language, we see how things turn out. In the turning-out of things, we have a chance to see how well our original hunch or hypothesis stands up. If things turn out the way we expect we say our hunch was correct, that is, true. If things turn out some other way, we discard that hunch and try another. If the consequences provide phenomena that we have not expected or imagined, we return to our original hunch and integrate these findings into another, more sophisticated hunch.

Then, taking this new hunch, we again act upon the cosmos to see if we have come any closer to true knowledge. And we continue the doing-undergoing procedure until we arrive at a view of things that seems to satisfy the requirements of the conditions under which we are working. If the conditions change, then the consequences we undergo will change, and our original hypotheses will have to be reworked, thus directing us to engage in new *do-ings* and, hence, new *undergoings*. Furthermore, every new experience, every new set of consequences, has the effect of suggesting to us new hunches, new guesses, new intuitions of the way the world works, and we are led on into an endless array of hypotheses, which we then attempt to test out in action.

This endless progression, this open-ended series of doing-undergoing-doing-undergoing, etc., is the process by which Experimentalists engage in epistemological activity. It is what they call "reflective thinking." This is not to be confused with "reflection" in the classical sense of sitting quietly in one's study and contemplating the universe. It is, rather, literally re-flective, a "bending back again" of thought, from experienced consequences to tentative hunch. In more general terms, it is a reorganization of our hypotheses resulting from experiencing the consequences of our acts, a criticism of what we *think* by virtue of *acting on* what we think and seeing what happens. In its most general expression it is what Dewey called "the reconstruction of experience." This single phrase sums up the entire sense and meaning of scientific Experimentalist epistemology.

We may see then that knowing is an activity that never reaches a terminus; we never know something once and for all. Knowing is always open-

[21] Here is a vital and illuminating distinction in connection with intuition: In Neo-Thomism (and, to a lesser extent, in Idealism) intuitions are the *end point* of knowing; once had, they represent the termination of epistemological activity. In Experimentalism, however, they are the *starting point* for knowing; once had, they become hypotheses for inquiry—they invite investigation. That is, they provoke epistemological activity.

ended. To know some *thing* is to hold it only temporarily, until new phenomena upset it. Meanwhile, we hold it as know*ledge*—the suffix *-ledge* signifying the substantive aggregate of our knowing activity—but we hold it only "on trial," never ceasing to retest it, to question it, to inquire into it again to see if it is still relevant to the circumstances before us.

The Scientific Method

What we have been describing above in quite ordinary and pedestrian terms turns out to be the very same procedure as that used by the sophisticated scientist in the research laboratory. Contrary to popular belief, there is nothing fundamentally mysterious about how scientists work. Their procedures, which are essentially the procedures of the ordinary individual trying to reach intelligent decisions, can be abstracted and set down into five fairly distinct steps:

1. First, there occurs what Dewey called "an indeterminate situation," a situation in which there is some rupture, great or small, to the smooth on-flowing of life's affairs. To ordinary citizens it may be only a feeling or disposition, a tension that is set up in their routine. To research scientists it may be an idle puzzlement, an inchoate curiosity, or a gap somewhere in their scientific knowledge that they want to close.

2. There then occurs a refinement of the difficulty into more particular problematic form; steps are taken by the individual to diagnose the situation, to see more precisely what the problem is. To the ordinary citizen this may turn out to be only a matter of how to get to work while one's car is in the repair shop. To the scientist it may be the more sophisticated problem of locating the cause of polio.

3. At this stage, the individual sets out in search of every conceivable potential solution to the problem. The imagination is permitted to run free; any guess, any hunch, any intuition is admissible. Indeed, the doctrine of "freedom of thought" has its epistemological as well as its political root at precisely this point. For no hypothesis can be tested unless it is *thought of*; no possible solution can be introduced into a problem situation until it is objectified and admitted as a candidate for the final answer. Hence, scientists defend their freedom with a passion, for freedom of thought—the freedom to consider anything, no matter how unorthodox— is absolutely essential to the scientific procedure. Riding a bicycle to work may strike the ordinary citizen as preposterous, but it is one possibility to be examined. That a tiny living organism is the culprit in polio may seem unlikely, but it must be considered as a possibility.

4. The fourth stage consists in projecting these possible solutions in the mind so as to consider the consequences each would be likely to lead to. We think through what would happen if we adopted one or another plan of action. Dewey called this the stage of reasoning, reasoning in the sense of associating ideas—hypotheses and conjectured consequences—

in a purposeful, meaningful way. (This is in contrast with the kind of reasoning characteristic of the older philosophies, especially Neo-Thomism, in which reason is exercised on abstract syllogisms having little to do with practical affairs.) If Step 3 could be called the "inventory of possible solutions" (what Dewey called "guiding ideas"), then this Step 4 can be called the "inventory of conjectured consequences." Riding a bicycle to work will wrinkle the clothing, be somewhat tiring, and strike the neighbors as undignified, but it will be cheap. To suggest a living organism as the cause of polio infection will involve "catching" and identifying a moving object somewhere in the body; but if a vaccine can be administered that will either kill or neutralize the organism, then a decrease in infection will follow.

5. Finally, the fifth stage is that of testing. We consult experience directly to see if the conjectured consequences do in fact occur. We try walking, taking the bus, riding with a neighbor, riding the bicycle. We test out each solution individually; that is, we act on each proposal *as if* it were the answer; we literally act it out, so as to experience the consequences to which it leads. With the consequences for all alternatives in hand, we are then in a position to evaluate and judge. Likewise, scientists test out each of their hunches. They design experiments, prepare medicines, control some groups of organisms, and arrange the variables systematically among other organisms, and they do all these things so as to witness the consequences that flow from each of their separate acts in the laboratory. That is, they *act on* each hypothesis developed in Step 3 to get at the consequences, to see what happens.

The issue of consequences is especially labored at this point, and for very good reason: Here, within the texture of *consequences*, lies the heart of Experimentalist epistemology. It is the consequences of acts that contain the raw material for making epistemological decisions. We decide on the bicycle, possibly because riding in the open air turns out to be more pleasant than we had anticipated. The scientist chooses the virus hypothesis and develops a vaccine to control the polio virus in the body.

We may now present the Experimentalist epistemological system schematically. Figure 8 shows the five steps:

1. An indeterminate situation, a feeling of tension, a "felt difficulty"
2. The diagnosis and definition of the difficulty or specification of the problem (P)
3. An inventory of possible solutions (1, 2, 3, 4, 5)
4. The conjecturing of consequences (C)
5. The test for consequences (T)

It is the Experimentalist's view that all knowing takes this form, whether the knowing is in science, art, engineering, sociology, or whatever. In some subject matters, it is true, the procedure may be somewhat obscured. In the social sciences, for instance, we are not permitted to test out each

STEPS

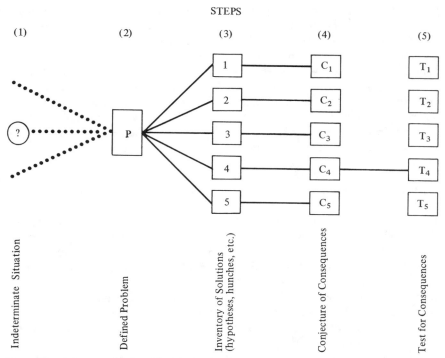

Figure 8   *Schema of Scientific Method*

suggestion in direct experience; we are required to project our imagina-
tions to assess what the consequences will probably be. In the matter of
a national health policy, for instance, we are not permitted to test out first
voluntary health insurance plans, then compulsory health insurance plans,
complete socialization of the medical profession, and whatever other
notions may occur to us. Rather, we are required to stop at Step 4 to make
an educated guess as to what the consequences are likely to be. And, to
be sure, the status quo is always one of the choices in social questions,
and its consequences must stand before the bar of judgment like any
others. But the point is that even in social questions the scientific procedure, in its most general form as described here, is the procedure most
commonly used. In social problems we do not trust to luck or appeal to a
benign deity or consult an astrologer. We try, instead, to reduce the whole
circumstance to intelligent and systematic control by defining the problem,
testing out various solutions (either directly or imaginatively), and seeing
which solution yields the most socially profitable consequences.

This procedure, so celebrated in Experimentalist literature, is also called
"The Complete Act of Thought," a name that designates the manner in

which reason is introduced into human experience. Except for Dewey's original use of the term, however, Experimentalists rarely employ the word *reason* because of its substantive overtones in classical thought. Reason or rationality is not some kind of mental entity contained in the brain, as the Greeks held. Better to speak of *intelligence,* which is a label for the *activity* of reason in life's affairs. *Intelligence* is a dynamic term, signifying not a substantive entity of mental "stuff" but an activity, a process, a form of behavior. To possess intelligence, then, in Experimentalist terms, is not to possess some *thing* but *to be able to do* something, namely, to handle life's affairs in the scientific manner just prescribed.

Truth as What Works

We may now generalize by noting that the ultimate test of truth is whether the hunch or hypothesis that is tried out and acted upon really "works." Does it, that is, explain the situation, rationalize the disparate phenomena that have been observed, solve the problem? *In the degree that it performs this duty* it is said to be true. Hence, truths in Experimentalism are always true *in degrees,* always true contingently or relatively. That is, they may seem to work better in some circumstances than in others. The wave theory of light works in one instance, but the particle theory is invoked to understand another.

Whether a hunch does indeed solve a problem or rationalize an indeterminate situation may be assessed, in part, by whether the conclusion leads on somewhere. Is more thought, more doing, more undergoing, signaled and prompted by the conclusion? If not, perhaps it has not resolved the indeterminacy. If so, and if new inquiries are forthwith suggested, then *to that degree* it may be said to be a solution.

The test of workability, then, is quite as open-ended as the test of that for which workability is itself the test: truth. We are led on and on, epistemologically, in a flowing and ongoing knowing event, tentatively stopping and holding to certain things as true, but true only insofar as they help us manage the world. To manage the world is the general empirical problem facing humanity. Knowledge and truth are but the instrumentalities for carrying on this work.

As we shall see in Chapter 9, the principle of "workability" is, according to the Experimentalists, applicable also to aesthetic and moral questions. What has originated and been found spectacularly successful in the physical sciences, and is now being increasingly applied to the social sciences, may one day, say the Experimentalists, take over in the moral and ethical sphere as well. When this occurs, our values will cease being valuable merely by heredity and tradition. Our values will become subject to the same procedure as our truths, namely, criticism and test. What this may mean for us today we shall see in later chapters.

In summary of Experimentalist epistemology, we may say that the entire knowing process is an open-ended, ongoing, and restless activity of human beings. By this time you may begin to appreciate why such an epistemology is exasperating to many people. It has no "anchor to windward," no absolutes to tie to, no quiet harbor of truth where testing can be permanently halted. There is no resting place where a person can say, once and for all, "I know this for sure." The element of contingency and relativity so pervasive in this doctrine is emotionally unacceptable to a great many individuals. They cannot stand the strain of open-endedness in the sphere of thought and belief. And their rejection of this philosophy is in a sense understandable, for Experimentalism *is* a "tough-minded" outlook. One has to have a thick intellectual and moral skin to manage it. But Experimentalism, like any other philosophic point of view, is interested not necessarily in what is comfortable but in the actual situation in which people live: To retreat to more secure doctrines is, as William James put it, "a failure of nerve."

The great advantage of Experimentalism is that it is a *public* epistemology; it is a method of knowing that is out in the open, available to all. Experimentalists do not deny private experience; all they say is that it does not produce knowledge. The sort of experience that is common to everyone, testable, and warranted is the only kind of experience that is capable of yielding what we call knowledge.

For this reason "community" plays an important role in Experimentalist epistemology. Indeed, many Experimentalists speak of the "uncoerced community of persuasion" as the central criterion of truth. Science, you will note, is of this general character; it is an open, public knowing procedure to which many people, in communication with one another, contribute. And there must exist some common persuasion among them before anything can be labeled as knowledge.

Existentialism: Truth as Existential Choice

EXISTENTIAL REQUIREMENTS

The best way to undertake our examination of Existentialist epistemology is to take another look at the metaphysics of this position discussed in Chapter 3. At the very least, this procedure helps us see better what we need in the way of knowledge, even if it does not actually ascertain what kinds of knowledge will be possible.

As the earlier discussion has shown, the central metaphysical principle in Existentialism is the priority of existence over essence. Man arrives on the scene devoid of "what-ness." His essence is not given. The individual is, so to speak, an open question. One is committed, then, to something not asked for, namely, existence. One is "locked in," as it were, to a condition from which there is no escape. In making choices one reveals *what* he or she thinks Man is. Hence, even in suicide, in attempting to "resign from existence," one has made a choice. Or, more commonly, in burying oneself in one's society—in letting society guide the choices—one has made one's choice. There is no escape from this unutterable freedom.[22] (We see in Chapter 12 the many variations this idea acquires when applied to education.)

Now when we use the word *choice* it is to be understood in its fullest meaning. Making a choice is not confined to deciding to *do* something. It also includes deciding to *believe* something, to accept something as true. Hence, we are confronted at the outset with the epistemological significance of the Existentialist metaphysics, namely, the existential freedom of choosing one's own truth. Each person is his or her own supreme court of epistemological judgment and is, therefore, in an ultimate sense, absolutely on his or her own when it comes to deciding between candidates for truth.

This is sometimes interpreted, incorrectly, to mean that Existentialist Man is driven by passion and impulse through all of existence, that he is the complete expression of hedonism in modern life in believing only what he *wants* to believe, or that he doesn't really *care* what is true. On the contrary, Existentialists care very much about knowing the truth. They are especially interested in the truth about themselves, about what they are. But since what they *are* depends on their choices of truth lying outside themselves, they are equally earnest about these also. To know that $E = mc^2$, to know that *Hamlet* is a great work of Western letters, to know that biological forms are evolutionary, is to say something about what one is. Especially in religion: When an individual speaks of knowing that there is a personal God, something is really being said about the self, about what one thinks one is. Personal choices make the individual and thereby reveal what he or she is.

Concerning wanting to believe anything, we are all guilty. What we individually believe to be the truth is what we *want* to believe. How else could it be? I believe the world is round; it does not appear that way but I have it on good authority that it is. So I believe it. But I don't *have to* believe it if I choose not to. Nobody is insisting that I do; no one is forcing this belief on me. I actively choose it as one of my beliefs. If this be impulse, then we are all impulsive. This, however, is not the usual sense in which we use the word *impulsive*.

All this suggests that the Existentialists have little to offer in the way of a method of knowing, a systematic epistemology. Rather, they are concerned with pointing out that in all knowing—sense perception, logical demonstration, scientific proof, intuition, revelation—it is the individual self that must make the ultimate decision as to what is, as a matter of fact, true. As we live out our lives, believing our histories, our literary insights, our multiple gods, our sense perceptions, we make the grand

[22] See Erich Fromm, *Escape from Freedom* (New York: Farrar and Rinehart, 1941).

mistake of thinking that these truths are in some way forced on us, either by an external and objective reality (Realism and Idealism) or by a necessary and insistent logic (Lay Neo-Thomism) or by an Absolute Being who can have it no other way (Ecclesiastical Neo-Thomism). Even the Experimentalists have led us down the primrose path to self-delusion, for there is nothing in science that makes ultimate epistemological demands on me. If a scientific truth doesn't seem to make sense to me, I can call it false, and who can contradict me?

Existentialists, however, do not spend all their time in such carping dialectic. What they are interested in is simply reminding us that there is an element of *personal appropriation* in all knowing. When all the data are in, each individual must make a personal choice to believe something. Indeed, we must each make our own personal appropriation of an epistemology. Nothing could illustrate this better than to point to the present chapter on comparative epistemologies and to recognize that, as individuals, we must make our personal selection from among these (and other) epistemological theories on the basis of which seems to be the most acceptable explanation of how knowing takes place. Each individual involved in this chapter, authors and readers, must make a personal commitment to some theory of knowledge. Each individual is, then, not only the final court of truth but the final court of how truth is arrived at—the ultimate point of origin for every epistemological program. We see this subjective conception of truth spelled out more fully in Chapter 12, especially in connection with Carl Rogers's view of teaching.

THE MODES OF KNOWING

Having said all these things, we are now in a position to approach more technically the problem of Existentialist knowing. If the prime metaphysical concept in Existentialism is the priority of existence over essence, the prime epistemological concept is the division of knowing into two *modes*, for which, unfortunately, no handy labels are available. Let us simply call them Mode One and Mode Two.

Preliminary to this analysis is Jean Paul Sartre's distinction between two modes of being: "being-in-itself" and "being-for-itself." I see a tree outside my window: I am, that is, perceptually conscious of a tree. The tree possesses "being-in-itself." Like other objects, it just *is*. My perceptual knowledge of it (Mode One) is of a brute fact of existence. However, I am conscious not only of the tree but of my consciousness of the tree; that is, I am cognitively aware of my cognition. Ultimately this means that I am conscious of my own being as well as that of the tree, but not in the same way, not perceptually. Rather, I have epistemological access to my own being through quite a different route, an internal, subjective awareness that we are calling Mode Two. I feel myself in existence, as an existential center of knowing. But *how* I know this is quite at variance with the "how-I-know" that the tree is a similar sort of existential center of other qualities. In an immediate kind of way, I feel my own being, a self-conscious, self-returning being—"being-for-itself"—that the tree does not share with me.

To put this in plain language, we can say that in Mode One I am conscious of an existential world (somewhat in the manner of the Realist; see pages 130–137), and that in Mode Two I am also conscious of my consciousness of this world. I somehow know my own existentiality.

Now, this may seem a trifle in a treatment of so recondite a subject as epistemology, but its far-reaching significance can be recognized if we extend it beyond the regions of simple sense perception into the realm of science. For science is the Mode One of knowing in its most elaborate and sophisticated form; science seeks to know the existential reality we humans inhabit.

As an epistemology, science initially took as its subject matter the physical world about us. As everyone knows, it has enjoyed spectacular success as a method of Mode One knowing. Gradually it took up and developed more and more subject matters[23]—astronomy, physics, chemistry, biology—until, about 1900, it stumbled on Man. Here, astonishingly, was some open territory that had been overlooked. What has happened since is history—an explosive proliferation of human sciences, beginning with the *social* sciences of economics, political science, and sociology, which were later augmented and in some cases overshadowed by the so-called *behavioral* sciences, such as psychology, social psychology, and cultural anthropology.

The important point to note, however, is that in this application of Mode One or scientific knowing to the study of Man there has been a gathering presumption that Man can be ultimately understood in the same manner that we have come to understand atoms, frogs, and machines, namely through the scientific method. In short, the feeling has grown that Man, the last unknown, is about to yield his secret to himself. This has not happened, of course, and the Existentialist claims that it never can happen, because an absolute chasm separates "being-in-itself" from "being-for-itself," and, therefore, a similar chasm separates Mode One from Mode Two knowing.

Psychology is an apt illustration in the above list because it began, as its name implies, as the study of the "psyche." It originated, if you will, as an attempt to employ Mode One knowing to get at and understand the Mode Two knowing of the self. It was an attempt to see whether science could unlock the doors of the selfhood's center, of the Mode Two consciousness of consciousness. The fact that psychology has given up on this and has turned instead to the study of *overt behavior* is a clue that science simply cannot penetrate the human self. Mode Two is scientifically out of reach.

---

[23] In this discussion it would be more apt to call them "object matters."

At this point two things must be said. First, the above analysis is not meant to imply that psychology is a fraudulent discipline. On the contrary, the application of Mode One knowing to human behavior, an unheard-of thing only a century ago, is a "technological," methodological invention of the very first magnitude. All we are saying here is that, so far as Existentialist Mode Two knowing is concerned, psychology has not made a dent in it. The second thing to say is that this last sentence must be qualified by the partial successes of depth psychology and psychiatry. To be sure, insofar as these are scientific—in the objective, hypothesis-forming, data-gathering, problem-solving sense of the term—it may safely be said that they have added very little to the understanding of the "being-for-itself" of the human person. But insofar as they have sought to awaken the patient's selfhood, insofar as they have quickened his consciousness of his consciousness, in that degree we can say that they have served the Existentialist cause. Too often, however, psychiatry has been the vehicle merely for dredging up from the bottom of a person's life the "objective," empirical "cause" of the emotional turbulence on the surface. Laudable as this is as therapy, it has nothing to do with the awakening of the self's inner powers of choice, as the Existentialist sees it. In fact, what this type of psychotherapy does is just the reverse: it relieves the patient from making choices. He leaves the doctor's office no larger in selfhood but only muttering, "So *that's* why I'm so neurotic! I'm really not responsible for my neurosis, after all. I couldn't help being this way." This attitude, it may plainly be seen, is the ultimate contradiction of the meaning of Mode Two knowing: it is the denial of consciousness of consciousness.

In regard to the so-called human sciences, therefore, we are forced to observe that Mode Two has remained largely untouched. It is a much deeper and more complicated dimension of human experience than science is apparently equipped to handle. What is more, there is a kind of moral paradox in even trying to understand it: Man would destroy himself if he did! To explain this, Sartre reminds us that Man is trying to know everything; he hungers after complete and absolute knowledge. Now that he is within reach of complete knowledge of his environment he has turned upon himself. But he has turned upon himself necessarily, as an *object* of knowing, as a "being-in-itself." To study Man this way is perhaps necessary and fruitful, but if we were ever to come to know him completely this way we would have driven out his "being-for-itself," his individual selfhood. There would be nothing left to do. We would have passed from a state of "being-for-itself" into the state of "being-in-itself." We would just exist, like trees, as objects but not as subjects.

It is because of this, say the Existentialists, that we really don't want to know ourselves completely. We never wish to discover that we are nothing but objects. We wish to retain our subjective base. But nevertheless we go on trying, because we have to know more and more. So we are, in Sartre's terms, *"une passion inutile,"* "a futile passion."

Mode Two and the Scientific Method

The prime epistemological task of the Existentialist, as may be surmised from the above, is to comprehend and understand what is here labeled Mode Two knowing. This turns out to be a sizable project, because this mode of knowing almost defies description and definition. About as close as we can come to it in nontechnical language is *awareness*, a kind of total feeling-tone that is simply *had* by the individual. As George Kneller puts it:

> The existentialist epistemology (if such it may be termed!) assumes that the individual is responsible for his own knowledge. Existentialist knowledge is "intuitive." It is "human." It originates in, and is composed of, what exists in the individual's consciousness and feelings as a result of his experiences and the projects he adopts in the course of his life.[24]

Furthermore, when we say, as Kneller does, that the individual is "responsible" for personal knowledge, we mean that he or she ultimately *must* be, because this knowledge belongs only to that individual, who is thereby responsible for it because it is *private* knowledge that no one else has.

Kneller continues by saying that ". . . the validity of knowledge is determined by its value to the individual."[25] What this means may be vividly illustrated by comparing this kind of private knowledge with the open, public procedure of the scientific method of the Experimentalist. If we attend closely to the analysis of the Experimentalist method (see pages 143–153 and the schema of it presented in Figure 8 (page 151) we notice that Mode Two knowing can be found implicitly residing in Step 5, which, incidentally, is also the crucial step in Experimentalist epistemology.

It is easy enough for the Experimentalist to explain that alternative hypotheses should be judged by whether they do or do not work, that is, by an appeal to the consequences to which they lead when acted upon. But the Experimentalist never explains how it is that alternative *consequences* are sorted out by those undergoing them. It is more or less assumed that when all the alternative hypotheses are acted out, and the consequences are thus set in motion and "undergone," the rest of the epistemological action will take care of itself. That is, the individual will make up his or her mind on the hypothesis that works. This is all very true, but how, asks the Existentialist, does the individual choose among the *consequences*? In terms of Step 5 in Figure 8, how do we decide between Consequence of Hypothesis 1 (T_1) and Consequence of Hypothesis 2 (T_2)? How (in this illustration) did Consequence 4 (T_4) happen to be chosen as best? What are the conditions required for deciding that something "works"? What is the measure of "workability" as it is understood in Experimentalist terms?

At this point the Experimentalist is likely to invoke a kind of sophisticated epistemological democracy of majority rule: the "uncoerced community of persuasion." But, says the Existentialist, there can be no

[24] *Existentialism and Education* (New York: Philosophical Library, 1959), p. 59.
[25] Ibid.

community of persuasion until there is individual persuasion. Each individual must cast a personal vote on certain consequences before there can be any community decision on those consequences, let alone a community decision on the hypotheses. Each individual must be heard from *as an individual* before the community can get into epistemological action. Hence, no knowing can occur until there is first "feeling." Or, more accurately, no Mode One knowing can occur until there is Mode Two knowing (awareness, "feeling," and so on).

Another way of looking at this is to recognize that scientific knowledge is ultimately contingent upon the scientific method. In discussing Karl Jaspers, Kneller states:

> . . . scientific knowledge is universally valid, once established as true; and agreement may be expected from all who possess the necessary qualifications for understanding the truth of a given scientific proposition. But the meaning of any such truth is necessarily limited, since it is relative to the methods and assumptions that have been used to obtain it.[26]

In all fairness to the Experimentalists, it must be said that they are quite willing to settle for this limitation on scientific knowledge. All they assert is that experience is all we have to go on, and that, therefore, scientific knowledge, as incomplete and contingent as it is, is the best we can do. And, in light of what it has accomplished, it is no mean achievement. Any quixotic adventure into Mode Two knowing, they say, is just a retreat into mysticism or, at the very best, into "poetry."

Nevertheless the Existentialist insists on the validity, indeed the primacy, of Mode Two knowing. Each one of us recognizes this knowing within our own selves. Although we cannot report on it concerning other people, we certainly cannot deny its existential presence within our own being. If this is poetry, let it stand. For there is a kind of knowing in poetry, after all. Poetry is not sterile of epistemological content. Quite the contrary, poetry is the vehicle of feeling and awareness; it is the vehicle for the expression of "being-for-itself." So, likewise, are the drama, the novel, the arts generally, and philosophy—particularly the last, because here we can begin to generalize our awareness, to engage in "meta-awareness" by becoming self-conscious of our self-consciousness.[27]

MODE TWO AND PHENOMENOLOGY

Over the past several decades, as Existentialism has gradually joined the family of formal philosophy, it has, like other views, been required to be more explicit concerning its epistemology and, in particular, to extend it into a metaphysics that would show more clearly just how Existential

---

[26] Ibid., pp. 59–60.

[27] A reminder of Pascal's dictum: "The last proceeding of reason is to recognize that there is an infinity of things which are beyond it." For another advocacy of the primacy of Mode Two knowledge, see Paul Roubiczek, *Existentialism For and Against* (Cambridge University Press, 1964), pp. 181–182.

knowledge is possible. Recently, efforts to this end have come to be called exercises in *phenomenology,* a jaw-breaking term that seems to conjure up unexplored territory even more impenetrable and inscrutable than that which we have already discussed.

In the first fifty pages of Jean Paul Sartre's *Being and Nothingness*[28] we get a primitive glimpse of this region. In these pages, Sartre leans heavily on the work of Edmund Husserl, generally regarded as the original explorer of this very dark continent. Husserl's writing borders on the opaque, but with Sartre's assistance, we believe he is saying something like the following:

> Philosophers can never be sure that either the world exists or that they, as human beings, exist. It would be very difficult, however, to fault the claim that in our "natural attitude" of encountering the world, something called consciousness occurs. But consciousness is always intentional; that is, it is always consciousness *of* something. Consider, then, these two terms: "consciousness" and "something." Consciousness without intentionality, that is, without the "somethings," is the province of psychology. On the other hand, the "somethings" without the presence of consciousness is the province of traditional metaphysics. What we are after is a reality lying somewhere between psychology and traditional metaphysics, somewhere between non-intentional consciousness and the world which we are conscious of. We shall call this region *phenomena,* an admittedly elusive term which is derived from a Greek word meaning "that which presents itself." Hence, the best we can do is to say that phenomena are the primitive features of the world which present themselves to our consciousness.[29]

Mode Two knowing thus has its origin in what we have earlier called being-for-itself. Knowledge comes into existence when consciousness (being-for-itself) apprehends the qualities of the world (being-in-itself) through phenomena. Meanings are not in and of the aboriginal world; Man puts them there. In short, Man *creates* meanings. In what Sartre calls Man's "lived world" or "human reality," Man endows a meaningless world with meanings. In the process, he gives meaning to his own existence. Phenomenology is the study of this undertaking and is the most general term now used to refer to an Existentialist epistemology.[30]

We have, then, in a manner of speaking, come full circle. Beginning with the Self in Idealism, we posited an Absolute Mind of which the indi-

---

[28] Trans. Hazel Barnes (New York: Philosophical Library, 1956).

[29] Van Cleve Morris, "Is There a Metaphysics of Education?" *Educational Theory* 17, no. 2 (April 1967): 145.

[30] One of the most lucid elaborations of this idea is found in Chapter 6, on "Meaning Making," of Neil Postman and Charles Weingartner's *Teaching as a Subversive Activity* (New York: Delacorte, 1969), among the more readable and penetrating books on education published during the late 1960s. To see how phenomenology as an epistemology affects the higher learning, take a look at Van Cleve Morris's "Phenomenology and Urban Teacher Education" in *Rethinking Urban Education,* Herbert J. Walberg and Andrew T. Kopan, eds. (San Francisco: Jossey-Bass, 1972).

vidual, microcosmic mind partakes. Knowing, in this tradition, is the increasing identification of the microcosmic with the macrocosmic mind. In Realism, however, the act of knowing is a far simpler operation. Working within a physical reality, the individual simply witnesses, perceptually and organically, a regulated, machine-like Nature, which is then *known* by reducing its structure and motion to facts and formulas. The Neo-Thomist attempts to combine the Idealist and Realist outlooks by laying a *logical* form upon all Being and by assigning the knowing process to the enterprise of introducing this logic into the human mind—which, fortunately, is already disposed, because of its inherent structure, to receive it. Experimentalists, of course, dismiss all the above as archaic and old-fashioned mumbo jumbo. All knowledge, they say, is contingent on experience; and it is in social and collectivized experiencing that we can come to some highly effective working truths. Finally, the Existentialist brings us once again to the individual self, insisting that all knowing, all intuiting, all experiencing, are certified within the private awareness of the human person.

Thus, from the "Imitation of the Absolute Mind" of Idealism to the "Spectation of Nature" of Realism to the "Logical Apprehension of Being" of the Neo-Thomist to the "Scientific Doing and Undergoing in Experience" of the Experimentalist to the "Phenomenology" of the Existentialist, we have come to see what a variety of ways there are for human beings to know.

The Analytic Movement

Before passing on to Chapter 7 to see how these theories affect the educative process, we must take account of a major demurrer in modern philosophy that challenges much of what we have discussed in this lengthy chapter on epistemology. This demurrer comes from those who represent a recent movement in philosophy variously called Logical Empiricism or Linguistic Analysis.

Stated very briefly, the Logical Empiricists defer questions of *truth* in favor of questions of *meaning*. In epistemology one cannot ask whether a proposition about the world is true or not true until one knows what it means. If a proposition has no meaning, it is foolish to ask whether or not it is true. This interest in meaning is characteristic of the related discipline of *semantics*, which may be defined as the study of the meaning of meaning. But whereas semantics deals primarily with the meaning carried by single words, Logical Empiricism has chosen to investigate the meaning carried by sentences. Hence, because it deals with whole propositions rather than single word-symbols, Logical Empiricism is essentially an exercise in logic or an exercise in the analysis of the language we use to utter our ideas.

Although the term *Linguistic Analysis* may appear rather imposing, the argument is relatively simple and runs somewhat as follows:

All knowledge is carried in language; an idea, to be thought of, communicated, and believed in, must first of all be rendered in linguistic form. Epistemological language, although perhaps more sophisticated, is essentially the same as ordinary language: it is constructed of sentences. A sentence is a group of words divided into a subject and a predicate. The subject presents some substantive (a thing, a process, an event, an idea), and the predicate tells us something about the substantive (what it is like, what it does, how it behaves).

Our first problem arises at this point. Suppose that for a given subject, say, an apple, we were to compose *all* the possible predicates that could be attached to it—all the adjectives ("An apple is red, round, juicy, edible, succulent. . . .") and all the predicates ("An apple grows on trees, contains seeds, taken daily keeps the doctor away. . . ."). Other philosophies have troubled themselves over such questions as these: Is the existence of the subject (apple) independent of all the possible predicates we could attach to it? Or, on the other hand, is our subject nothing more than all its possible predicates?

As we have seen earlier in this chapter, Aristotelian and Neo-Thomist logic lay great stress on the inner essence or "what-ness" of things. For this reason, these philosophies hold that the subject of a sentence is always more than all the possible predicates one could attach to it. There is an *essence* to which all predicates are attached. The Experimentalists, on the other hand, dispute this claim to essences and assert instead that processes and behaviors in our experience are to be emphasized. Hence, Experimentalists contend that subjects are known through their predicates and are nothing more than their predicates. In the shorthand of some Experimentalists: "A thing *is* what it *does*."

The difficulty with the Experimentalist position, the Logical Empiricist explains, is that it must be couched in language forms that originated in an Aristotelian tradition and that are no longer adequate to the accurate expression of ideas.

> It happens to be the case that we cannot, in our language, refer to the sensible properties of a thing without introducing a word or phrase which appears to stand for the thing itself as opposed to anything which may be said about it.[31]

The Experimentalist difficulty, then, is not an intellectual fault, says the Logical Empiricist, but a fault of language itself. At any rate, what the Experimentalist has already hinted at Logical Empiricism now affirms forthrightly, namely, that *predicates* are the key to the philosophical problem, for they give us the basic data about the world. Subjects are

[31] A. J. Ayer, *Language, Truth, and Logic*, rev. ed. (London: Victor Gollancz, 1950), p. 42.

nothing but "condensed" predicates, linguistic conventions we use to stand for a host of predicates that relate to one another, rather than to some "inner essence." In this office, subjects are merely convenient handles by which to manipulate and order our predicates. It is to predicates, therefore, and to the linguistic relationship they bear to their subjects that the Logical Empiricist turns the analysis.

This subject-predicate relationship is found in every sentence (or, in precise terminology, in every *proposition*) and holds the key to the understanding of meaning. Propositions are statements that can be shown to be true or false, valid or invalid. Hence, there can be both logical and empirical propositions. Logical propositions are intended to indicate the ways in which terms or other propositions are related to each other, while empirical propositions purport to tell us about reality, about matters of fact. When their subject-predicate relationships are under scrutiny, these two forms are called *analytic* and *synthetic* propositions. An analytic proposition is one whose predicate is analyzed out of the subject. A synthetic proposition is one whose predicate is attached to the subject on the basis of empirical evidence. In other words, in an analytic proposition, the predicate term repeats what is already contained in the subject term, as in "AB is AB" or "A black cat is black." In a synthetic proposition, such "repetition" does not occur, because the predicate term is said to contain something other (more) than what is in the subject term, as in "AB is XY" or "The black cat is fierce."

We met these two terms, *analytic* and *synthetic*, in the section on Neo-Thomist epistemology.[32] To the Neo-Thomist, an analytic proposition is absolutely true because it is intuited by the intellect to be true, everywhere and always. But to the Logical Empiricist, an analytic proposition is absolutely true because it is a tautology; that is, the predicate is contained in the *meaning* of the subject. Thus the proposition "Two things equal to the same thing are equal to each other" is held by the Neo-Thomist to be absolutely true because the intellect apprehends it intuitively; but the same proposition is held by the Logical Empiricist to be absolutely true because the predicate "equal to each other," is contained in the meaning of the subject, "two things equal to the same thing." Hence, the proposition is true by definition or, as the Logical Empiricist sometimes says, "by legislation."

Consider a simpler series of examples. The statement "A equals A" is absolutely true. But it tells us nothing about the world; it is a tautology. Now consider the proposition "Two plus two equals four." This also is absolutely true. And it appears to be saying something. It turns out, however, on closer analysis, that the predicate can be found in the meaning of the subject. "Four" is one of the *meanings* of "two plus two." Hence, another tautology. The Logical Empiricist claims that every analytic

[32] These two classes correspond roughly to *a priori* and *a posteriori* knowledge, discussed in Chapter 5.

proposition is of this character. The predicate of such a proposition tells us nothing we didn't already know; all it does is elaborate on the *meaning* of the subject.

You should not get the impression from this discussion that tautologies are completely useless. They serve, in fact, a very helpful function, that of recording "our determination to use symbols in a certain fashion," as A. J. Ayer has put it. They have meaning but they cannot produce knowledge.

As for synthetic propositions, all philosophies agree that they are not absolutely true; their predicates depend on empirical evidence. Consider, for example, "The distance from New York to Chicago is so many miles," or "The federal government is organized into three branches." What the Logical Empiricist claims is that these are the only propositions that are capable of producing knowledge.

There are a good many propositions that are not analytic tautologies and that bear a superficial grammatical resemblance to synthetic statements. Examples would include "The world is all mind," or "God is love," or, one that Ayer quotes from Bradley's *Appearance and Reality*, "The Absolute enters into, but is itself incapable of, evolution and progress." The trouble with these examples, and other propositions like them, says the Logical Empiricist, is that there is no evidence one could conceivably gather to determine their truth or falsity. They are therefore without any meaning. In order to have meaning a proposition must either be true by definition (as in the case of analytic tautologies) or there must be some possible sense experience that would be relevant to the determination of its truth or falsity.

> If a putative proposition fails to satisfy this principle, and is not a tautology, then I hold that it is metaphysical, and that, being metaphysical, it is neither true nor false but literally senseless.[33]

This line of argument eventually leads to the Logical Empiricist's main thesis: The meaning of a proposition is to be found in its method of verification. If it has no method of verification, it has no meaning.

A loose application of this so-called Verifiability Principle has led many skeptics to declare that the great bulk of philosophical literature is nonsense. However, to say that philosophical literature is nonsense is not totally to defame it or render it ridiculous. It means that philosophical statements do not carry cognitive meaning or convey information about matters of fact, although they may have emotive content and convey recommendations or express preferences of one kind or another.

Nevertheless, we are required to take a much tougher line in evaluating philosophical language, if only because the major philosophies have claimed so much more of it than the Verifiability Principle would seem to allow. In terms of the present chapter, Idealism, Realism, Neo-Thomism, *and* Existentialism all rest upon what the Logical Empiricist would call

[33] Ayer, *Language, Truth, and Logic*, p. 31.

pseudopropositions, propositions that grammatically resemble synthetic propositions but that have no method of verification. When an Idealist says that "Reality is mind"; when a Realist says that "Nature contains moral law"; when a Neo-Thomist says that "The intellect naturally tends to know"; or when an Existentialist says that "Existence precedes essence," they are all talking nonsense. Even the Experimentalist, while trying to avoid it and speak in a meaningful way, sometimes slips into nonsense with such phrases as "Reality is experience" or "Experience is the ultimate ground of knowing."

With this in mind, says the Logical Empiricist, and recognizing the linguistic nature of our problem, we may conclude that all philosophical disputes are quite fruitless. They are fruitless because they originate in language, in how we form our sentences and in how our sentences acquire meaning. Since many sentences in philosophy cannot pass the Logical Empiricist's test for meaning, it is little wonder that there is so much disagreement about matters of truth. And disagreement will continue as long as philosophers persist in using sentences of this sort. When all is said and done, says Ayer, the task of philosophy is not to build grand systems of the mind but merely "to elicit the consequences of our linguistic usage."

Notwithstanding this general judgment, we step back to our philosophical task and continue the argument. In Chapter 7 we shall examine how our several epistemologies make themselves felt in the conduct of the educative process.

Questions

1. "For ye shall know the truth and the truth shall make ye free." What is the epistemological significance of this epigram? What epistemology is suggested? In what way does truth set one "free"?

2. Some of the antonyms for *truth* are *lie, error, inaccuracy, deception, falsehood, misconception, mere opinion.* Which of these is (are) appropriate for use in epistemological discussions? Why?

3. Pick out an expository tract (a selection from an encyclopedia) or an emotive selection (the Declaration of Independence or the Gettysburg Address) and examine the kinds of statements made therein. What epistemologies apply to these statements? That is, how would their authors defend their validity?

4. Compare the concepts of *hypothesis* and *intuition.* In what way might it be said that they are the same thing?

5. A "closed-universe" metaphysics usually suggests a "closed epistemology," that is, a sum total of knowledge in the cosmos that humanity may, theoretically at least, ultimately comprehend. What would each of our five epistemological positions have to say about this?

6. Construct a series of analytic and synthetic propositions in the form of educational objectives. Which ones are easiest to translate into practice?

Further Reading

Comparative Epistemologies

Montague, William P. *The Ways of Knowing*. London: George Allen and Unwin, 1925. For the serious student of epistemology, this is a classic, standard work. In it, Montague takes up six methods of *logic:* authoritarianism, mysticism, rationalism and empiricism, pragmatism, and skepticism. Then he examines the three generic methods of *epistemology:* objectivism, dualism, and subjectivism. Finally, he attempts a reconciliation of these three in a unified epistemology, closing with an imaginary quadrilogue among an Objectivist, a Subjectivist, a Dualist, and—as reconciler—a Realist.

Idealism

Butler, J. Donald. *Four Philosophies and Their Practice in Education and Religion*, rev. ed. New York: Harper, 1957. In one of the best syntheses of Idealist thought, Butler has in Chapter 8 drawn together the metaphysics, epistemology, logic, and axiology of Idealism. The first three of these sections are particularly relevant to the epistemological development in the present chapter.

Greene, Theodore M. "A Liberal Christian Idealist Philosophy of Education," Chapter 4 in *Modern Philosophies and Education*, Fifty-fourth Yearbook of the National Society for the Study of Education, ed. N. B. Henry. Part I. Chicago: the Society, 1955. A leading contemporary Idealist here brings his insight to bear on the educative process. In the early part of the essay he sets down "My Basic Philosophical Presuppositions," the third and fourth of these being directed to epistemological and metaphysical matters. Here the Idealist Platform is clearly and concisely stated. The remainder of the chapter "fleshes out" these fundamental propositions.

Realism

Montague, William P. "A Realistic Theory of Truth and Error," in E. B. Holt, et al., *The New Realism*. New York: Macmillan, 1912. In an authoritative and somewhat technical essay, Montague sets forth the systematic outlines of Realist epistemology. He says, "Physical objects send forth waves of energy in various directions and of various kinds. . . . These energies impinge upon the organism, and the sensory end-organs and the nerve fibers then transmit to the brain the kinds of energy to which they are severally adjusted or attuned." (Page 286.) From this he shows how knowing is accomplished.

———. *The Ways of Things*. New York: Prentice-Hall, 1940. In this later (and somewhat less technical) book, Montague develops in Chapter 5 of Part 2 a systematic treatment of Realism's theory of knowing. Then he shows its relation to Idealism and Pragmatism. A lively and informative essay.

Neo-Thomism

Adler, Mortimer J. "In Defense of the Philosophy of Education," Chapter 5 in *Philosophies of Education*, Forty-first Yearbook of the National Society for the Study of Education, ed. N. B. Henry. Part I. Chicago: the Society, 1942. This chapter in the widely read Forty-first Yearbook is essentially not an essay on education but a systematic exegesis of Lay Neo-Thomist logic couched in the language of education. After a brief introduction, Adler takes up the problems of education having philosophic dimensions and then shows how the First Principles may be utilized to resolve these problems. Adler's style—and, indeed, the singular "Philosophy" in his title—bears out his fundamental belief: There is but one Truth, and if you will but pay attention and think hard you will see it. Then we can stop writing yearbooks on philosophies of education.

Maritain, Jacques. *The Range of Reason*. New York: Scribner's, 1952. In this technical and authoritative volume, the leading Catholic philosopher of the twentieth century develops the Ecclesiastical Thomist's epistemological thesis. Chapter 1, "On Human Knowledge," and Chapter 3, "On Knowledge through Connaturality," are the most directly relevant to the treatment in the present chapter.

Experimentalism

Childs, John L. *American Pragmatism and Education*. New York: Henry Holt, 1956. One of the most cogent of Dewey's interpreters, Childs here develops, in Chapter 2, on "Experimental Method and the Nurture of the Young," a working idea of how epistemological activity is undertaken in an Experimentalist frame. Beginning with the fundamental ideas of Charles Peirce, he describes the characteristics of experimental inquiry, then considers some alternative methods of certain knowing, and, finally, develops a systematic "Pragmatic Theory of Experimental Inquiry." Here, in clear and concise language, is the Experimentalist position on epistemological method.

Dewey, John. *How We Think*, rev. ed. Boston: D. C. Heath, 1933. The classic work on Experimentalist knowing theory. The word *know* was never comfortable to Dewey; rather, he thought we must search for "knowing in action," or thinking. Chapter 1 examines the question, "What is Thinking?" Chapter 7 analyzes the reflective thought process, the so-called Complete Act of Thought, or, in terms of the present chapter, the scientific method in its most generalized setting.

Existentialism

Morris, Van Cleve. *Existentialism in Education*. New York: Harper & Row, 1966. In Part 1 of this paperback, the author develops the underlying philosophical thesis of Existentialism, with discussions of Paradox and the Existential Encounter; Baseless Choice: the Cost of Freedom; The Problem of "The Other"; and Existentialism and the Scientific Philosophies. The epistemological predicament, the so-called knowledge problem, is boxed and analyzed.

Smith, Huston. *Condemned to Meaning*. New York: Harper & Row, 1965. This John Dewey Lecture brings forward in one place what might be labeled an

Existential epistemology. Smith first examines the analytic approach to Existential meaning and then explores the "constructive" character of knowledge. He closes with some comments on the import of these ideas for education.

The Analytic Movement

Archambault, Reginald D., ed. *Philosophical Analysis and Education.* New York: Humanities, 1965. Here is a collection of essays by leading British philosophers of education on the meaning of schooling from the viewpoint of the analytic school of philosophy. After discussing the nature and function of educational theory and the context of educational discussion, the authors examine several conceptions of teaching and, finally, the essence of education.

Quine, W. V., and J. S. Ullian. *The Web of Belief.* New York: Random House, 1970. In this readable volume, the authors explore an inner texture of belief: observation, self-evidence, testimony, hypothesis, intuition, explanation, persuasion—all central to the education process.

Smith, B. O., and Robert H. Ennis. *Language and Concepts in Education.* Chicago: Rand McNally, 1961. The application of the analytic method to educational discourse is well exemplified in these thirteen essays by leading educational theorists. Some of the educational profession's favorite clichés—learning by experience, meeting the needs of the child, neutrality in the schools, equality of opportunity—are here subjected to penetrating examination and criticism.

Comparative Epistemology and the Educative Process

Epistemology and Education

KNOWING THEORIES AND THE NATURE OF LEARNING

If philosophy has anything to do with education, we should expect to find this relationship at the very juncture where we now find ourselves: the juncture between a theory of knowing and a theory of teaching. Our present situation can be contrasted with that in which we found ourselves at the beginning of Chapter 4. On account of the technical and abstract nature of metaphysical problems, it could perhaps be argued that the study of *metaphysics* should be left to the philosophers, that it is too far removed from the professional concerns of teachers. But this could never be said of epistemology—our present concern—for epistemology is an active and fertile breeding ground for some very important educational ideas. This is so for a variety of reasons.

First, whatever the world is metaphysically, it must somehow be "gotten at" by ordinary human beings, by individuals who have neither the sophistication nor the specialized terminology of the trained philosopher, if it is to have any human use to them. That is, while metaphysics is essentially a study of the cosmos, epistemology is the study of how human beings take hold of their cosmos. Epistemology, as it were, introduces the human element for the first time. And since education is, if nothing else, a supremely *human* undertaking, the attention of the educator is likely to be much more readily aroused by studies in knowing than by studies in reality.

In the second place, as we saw in Chapter 5, epistemology is not only a necessary check on the credibility of our knowledge—a kind of "intellectual Pure Food and Drug Act"—but a body of fundamental theory that underlies the nature of the mind and how it works. Just as anatomy and physiology are the basic sciences underlying the study of medicine or pharmacy, so in somewhat like fashion is epistemology the basic subject matter underlying the study of psychology and learning theory.[1] That is, we must have some grasp of the general epistemological setting in which human beings find themselves before we can study in greater detail how they go about knowing and behaving intelligently. Or, to put it another way, we must understand humanity's epistemological circumstance before we can even begin to ask the right questions for psychology and learning theory to investigate.

Third, and certainly most pertinent, is the matter of sheer relevance: Theories of knowing are, in a sense, direct pointers to theories of learning. And since learning theory is at the very heart of the educative enterprise, we should not be astonished to find the various epistemologies having very relevant things to say about what goes on in the classroom.

The Methods of Learning

ABSORBING IDEAS

Children go to school, ultimately, for one fundamental reason: to be inducted systematically, efficiently, and deliberately into a way of life. Whatever else education is—and it may be more—it is certainly this. To a nonliterate society, maintaining an establishment where a quarter of their number did nothing all day long but learn things would be an outlandish luxury; but to a modern, technological society this sort of thing makes the greatest of sense. The patterns of behaving, thinking, and feeling that are necessary to people in these societies are simply too vast in number and too complex in nature to be assimilated by the normal procedures of enculturation. Some place is required where induction into the patterns of conduct can be carried on without interference and interruption.

Symbols What is more, modern people are much less dependent than nonliterates on direct experience for their learning. They have learned to abstract their experience into a vast array of symbols, which they then manipulate and refashion into "reproductions" of experience for others to have "vicariously." Indeed, it is this power to symbolize experience that makes education—as we understand it today—possible. It is The Symbol that makes it possible for boys and girls to spend the whole day inside a school building learning about the world outside.

So remarkable is the symbol in the eyes of people that it has sometimes been declared the first existent: "In the beginning was the Word"—a bit of Scripture, incidentally, that fits rather well the Idealist metaphysics

---

[1] The analogy is admittedly weak in that the former set of terms refers to empirical and scientific subject matters, while the latter set does not. If we are alert to the qualifications required by this difference, we can still find some warrant in the comparison.

discussed in previous chapters. Robert Frost, the famed American poet, celebrated this view in some of his lectures. His own philosophy of education, he says, can be reduced to what he thinks is the shortest poem on record:

A B C

1 2 3

This—word and number—is all there really is, says Frost, to learning; and he believes this couplet, itself a symbol of symbols, should appear on the coat of arms and above the entry gate of every school and university in the country.

At the very base of every program of education, then, is the task of equipping the child with symbols, almost literally the tools of learning. Although the quaint and lilting "Readin', 'Ritin', an' 'Rithmetic" may no longer be in vogue as a condensed summary of the elementary curriculum, these three subjects still remain the first business of every elementary school.

Symbols and Mind   We cannot therefore escape the fact that, whatever else education is, it is and must be first of all a symbolic activity. And it turns out, epistemologically speaking, that symbols take on a higher rank than mere tools of learning. For they are the instruments of the mind itself. They are the medium through which mind operates. And in this office they become the vehicle by which the mind comes into union with ultimate reality, the reality of Ideas. Ideas, as the Idealist sees them, are the real existents behind the sensory screen; they are thus barred from our perceptions. But fortunately, because we are human, we have access to this reality through mind, that is, through symbolic forms. For ideas have no existential expression except through symbols; we are absolutely dependent upon symbols to reach this reality.

For this reason, it is imperative, says the Idealist, to make symbols the very medium of the child's educational life, the medium of the pedagogical "environment." Learning is primarily a continuous activity in symbols— principally reading books and listening to the teacher, but also writing and reciting. It is a graded and systematic introduction to the life of words, for words, the Idealist maintains, are the keys to truth and reality.

Idealist School Practice   What this means in concrete terms may now be suggested by the generalization that Idealist educators tend to consider the library the hub of all educational activity. The classroom is, in a sense, a kind of operating arm of the library. It is the place where the symbols are explained, vitalized, brought to the life of the learner in a vibrant and meaningful way. But the classroom is also an environment of symbols, in the form of the teacher's lectures and questions and, of course, the students' responses.

It is because of this centrality of classroom and library that the Idealist is lukewarm about other, out-of-school learning experiences: field trips, use of community resources, or home projects. If there is a choice between a field trip and a day in the library, the Idealist will tend to favor the latter. Especially at the college level this preference will be unequivocal. College students, it is held, are not so dependent upon direct experience for their learning; they can learn through books. So time taken from books, while perhaps valuable, actually costs too much in deductions from the student's symbolic experience.

Colleges and universities are sometimes accused of being "ivory towers," enclaves of thought removed from the realities of life and therefore of questionable value in an "activist," materialist society. Idealists would make no apology for this whatsoever. They would insist that ivory towers are precisely what colleges and universities most certainly should be! Ordinary life is too ridden with action, they say, too saturated moment by moment with problems and requirements to *do* something. People will never find truth *there*; indeed, they will never find reality there. For to say that the realities of life are "down in the street" is merely to express a Realist sentiment. Reality is truly "up in the tower"; every society must maintain places of retreat where the mind can think and know. This is what colleges and universities are for.

IMITATING THE ABSOLUTE MIND AND ABSOLUTE SELF

We are now in a position to examine another educational outgrowth of Idealist theory: the task of bringing the learner into a more vital and fuller identification with the Absolute Mind and Absolute Self. Granted, specifications for how this is to be done may be vague and imprecise; nevertheless there is a way in which we can see the learning process in distinctive Idealist terms.

Learner and Mind[2]   To refer to our systematic treatment of Idealism in the previous chapter, we may say that the individual human mind exists as a microcosm of the Ultimate or Absolute Mind. Learning in Idealist thinking is the process of learners coming into a gradually larger and larger expression of mental awareness; and since this can be done most efficaciously through reading and study, learners shall, as we have seen, spend most of their time with books and teachers. The learners' ultimate aim, however, is not just a grinding mastery of factual content, but a broad and general understanding of the world in which they live, that is, an understanding that to some degree approximates the omnipotent understanding of the Absolute Mind. Learners are, in a manner of speaking,

[2] For a thorough discussion of the mind-body problem and the teaching-learning process, see Young Pai, *Teaching, Learning, and the Mind* (Boston: Houghton Mifflin, 1973).

attempting to expand both quantitatively and qualitatively, to imitate the fullness of the Absolute and Universal Mind, insofar as their mental capacity permits.

Learner and Self   This means, among other things, that Idealist students will be expected to respond *to* their world as well as to learn *about* it— which is to say that they will be involved as well in an expansion of microcosmic selfhood in imitation of the macrocosmic Absolute Self. Besides Mind, that is, they are attempting also to approximate the fullness of the Universal *Person*.

This idea is very much in line with modern democratic educational practice, for one of the ways to expand one's *self* is to attach oneself to other "selves," to have friends, to know people, to respond to them, and to be responded to. Another way is to identify with a self "larger" than one's own, for example, to join a club, to adopt a religion, to take an active part in one's community or national life through self-conscious (and nation-conscious) citizenship. The "Group," then—whether it be the neighborhood gang, or the family, or the Republican Party, or the First Methodist Church, or the American People, or World Judaism, or simply Mankind— is the "instrumentality" for enlarging the sense of self.

And since the classroom is potentially a "medium of enlargement" of this genre, the Idealist will encourage the beings in it to respond to one another and develop a sense of group *esprit*. For the classroom is, in Idealist language, a "community of selves." Youngsters grow in selfhood in proportion to the contact they have with other selves. And a large part of learning, we have lately discovered, is this intangible "communion of selves" in the classroom, the interchange of feeling and response that individual human beings have to their world. The teacher also, as we shall see later in the chapter, is a special case, a self individually "larger" than any of the students. And thus it is his or her job not only to facilitate the "communion-of-selves" process but to serve in an exemplary capacity with respect to the growth of selfhood on the part of the students.

One of the ways to make this point even more concretely recognizable is to refer to what is sometimes called the "psychological climate" of the school. A school, it has often been pointed out, is not just a pile of bricks; it is primarily an intimate, institutionalized association of human beings. In Idealist thinking, it is "Mark Hopkins on one end of a log and a pupil on the other"[3]—meaning that learning requires the active involvement of the selfhood and personality of the participants if it is to be successful.

---

[3] A popular corruption of a remark made by President James A. Garfield on the occasion of a Williams College alumni dinner at Delmonico's in New York on December 28, 1871: "A pine bench, with Mark Hopkins at one end of it and me at the other, is a good enough college for me." (Stevenson, *The Home Book of Quotations*.) Mark Hopkins, serving at the time as the fourth president of Williams, was disdainful of all educational apparatus, even books, and was widely known for his emphasis at Williams on the personal and uncluttered relationship between teacher and student.

Therefore the "tone," the "psychic climate" of the classroom and the entire school, is a vital concern of the Idealist educator. If rapport is not established between teacher and student, if there is no feeling of mutual respect and warmth between adult and youngster, then by so much is genuine learning prevented from taking place.

At the college level this "climate" is perhaps more actively cultivated. Colleges sometimes make a deliberate and overt attempt to create an "image" of the quality of their campus environment, and will seek to "stamp" that image upon their students prior to graduation. This "fourth dimension" of what we might call institutional "ethos" is very much a matter of educational concern among Idealists, for it is through this nebulous but nevertheless very real quality of an educational institution that young people really learn.

Absorbing Facts and Information

Just living in a stimulating human environment, however, is not all there is to learning. One must take hold of some bodies of knowledge; one must assimilate facts and master information about the world; one must, in short, confront the world with the realization that there are definite things about it that can be known and that one is in school to know them.

To return to an earlier point, symbols are indeed the medium of our epistemological work, but—and here the Realist may be heard speaking— it is not the symbol itself we are interested in but, rather, the objective existent for which the symbol stands. To become enamored of symbols for their own sake is to lose sight, says the Realist, of the real purpose of symbols, which is to stand for a real world we can perceive day by day and which, with the help of these symbols, we can turn to our own account. Granted, then, that we need symbols, but only as instruments to get at a physical reality that is existentially present in our lives every day.

Realist Pedagogy We are reminded here that Realists base their epistemology in sense perception. Nothing can be known save through being worked up from the raw material of sensation. And if this is the case the child's learning in school should be organized as much as possible around the "sensate" (as opposed to the purely intellectual or ideational) activities of learning. The Realists, therefore, though they will certainly insist on a good deal of reading and study, are likely to favor direct experience with what the symbols stand for. This means that demonstrations in the classroom, either by the teacher or by a fellow student, will become a vital pedagogical tool. Comenius, the seventeenth-century Moravian bishop and educator, became famous for his books, *Orbis Pictus* and *Didactica Magna*, in which he astonished the educational world by suggesting that visual aids—pictures—be used in instructing boys and girls in the schools! A century or so later Pestalozzi went Comenius one better. Why have just pictures? he asked in his quaintly titled *How Gertrude Teaches Her Children*. Let's have the real thing! Thus was the so-called object lesson installed in educational theory: literally, a lesson built around a physical object either brought into the classroom or observed outside the school by the class. Comenius and Pestalozzi thus stand at the head of a long line of educational Realists who want to place the learner in direct sensory contact with the world.

It goes without saying that the Realist will tend to favor field trips as pedagogically sound and desirable. If, to cite the Chinese proverb, "a picture is worth a thousand words," then perhaps direct and immediate contact with what the picture depicts might be conservatively estimated to be worth a million. This is probably saying too much, but Realist sentiment is consistent with the direction, if not the full extent, of this line of thinking. Certainly a day at the United Nations or in the Senate gallery in Washington could never be duplicated by any number of words in a civics textbook.

We have already, in Chapter 4, noted that Realist educators would favor the sciences as the primary materials in their curriculum. Quite obviously the tactical (that is, pedagogical) application of the Correspondence Theory (see pages 135–137) of knowing comes to bear most directly in this kind of learning material. Both the demonstration and the field trip are concrete examples of how the Correspondence Theory may be activated in the school's work.

But beyond these purely tactical, sensate learning procedures the Realist will employ the Correspondence Theory, in a semidirect way, through the medium of so-called audio-visual aids. Pictures, filmstrips, tape recordings, motion pictures, and television presentations are all means of simulating the real world in nonsymbolic but still vicarious forms. Hence, to the Realist these channels of contact with the real world represent a happy compromise between removing students from the school environment for a trip outside it and holding them in the library or classroom to read or hear, only in words, about the world outside. It is this middle position that audio-visual aids occupy in the pedagogical spectrum that makes them so important to Realist teaching.

Realism and Symbols　　If we are eventually driven back to symbols in our pedagogy—and we frequently are, of course—then let us, says the Realist, emphasize the existential situation these symbols may reveal. In history, for instance, we should not permit symbols to assume more stature than they really deserve. They are merely the vehicles for telling us what happened, the sequence in which things happened, and the causes and effects of historical events. When Realists include history in their curriculum, as they are in most cases obligated to do, it will be as a systematic study of concrete fact; what happened is what happened! History "stands there" as a given "past." And we may learn it—albeit through symbols—

in somewhat the same way as we may learn mathematics or chemistry, by learning the factual content of it.

This is not so severe as it may sound, for the Realist reminds us that one of the prime purposes of studying history should be to get a sense of historical time, and we study history because the chronological unfolding of events can be reduced to a series of facts all linked together in a temporal series. It is among the powers of the human mind, says the Realist, to absorb and assimilate these serial facts and to discern from them the regularities of a natural social order, a historical unfolding of events that reveals the laws and regularities of human nature.

Realism and Idealism   At this point we are not so far distant from the Idealist doctrine of the transcendent *meaning* of history—the thoughts of a Universal Mind as they are being thought out through the vehicle of human history. But there is, nevertheless, a difference in emphasis, for the Realist is more inclined to consider history as the *chronicle* of human doings, which reveals a regular and lawful cosmos, whereas the Idealist is more inclined to view history as the *interpretation* of human doings, which reveals an Ultimate Mind at work. In the one case the child is introduced to a mechanistic and "cause-effect" social tradition; in the other, to an intelligent, personalized, "friendly" cosmic design.

Although this may be embellishing what actually goes on in history classrooms, it is nevertheless indicative of the subtle motivations behind certain types of assignments as they are given. If students are asked to prepare an outline of the causes and effects of the Civil War, they are likely to get a different historical sense of this event from the "sense" they would be likely to get if they were asked to write an essay on what the Civil War was all about. Generally the former assignment is harmonious with Realist thinking, while the latter is harmonious with Idealist thinking.

Realism and S-R Learning   Realists, as this analysis suggests, are more interested in the precise and definitive types of subject matters and in the precise and definitive methods by which they may be conveyed to the learner. The development of various skills is particularly consistent with Realist practice. Learning to typewrite, play volleyball, drive an automobile, compose compound and complex sentences, or solve quadratic equations—all are examples of educational situations of which the Realists feel themselves capable of taking direct hold. Drill, practice, habit formation, and conditioning are all apt methods for these situations. Indeed, perhaps the concept of "conditioning," in its largest and most inclusive sense, best represents Realist pedagogy.

The "conditioning" theory goes back to the Russian physiologist Pavlov (1849–1936), who startled the scientific world by artificially creating a new kind of dog: a dog that would salivate at the sound of a bell! In this now famous experiment, Pavlov simultaneously offered food to the dog and rang a bell. After repeated trials he stopped offering the food—and discovered the astonishing phenomenon of salivary action "outliving" its natural stimulus. By substituting an artificial for a natural stimulus and getting the same response, he thus revealed a new "frontier" of behavior control.

What Pavlov did for physiology the psychologists picked up, early in the twentieth century, and turned into a full-blown theory, which in its clinical setting came to be known as "Stimulus-Response"—or simply S-R—psychology. In its wider application it assumed the institutionalized label of Behaviorism. This school of thought, which turned into something resembling a missionary movement led by John B. Watson, held that human personality and character are totally the product of experience. Theoretically, if the totality of the experiential environment of the child were artificially specified and controlled, then the behavioral and character-ological outcome in the child could be predicted. Every thought or move-ment has a cause; or, in psychological terms, every response has a causal stimulus. If we can specify the stimuli we can predict—hence, specify—the responses; it was as simple as that. If one were given charge of a child at birth, Watson claimed, it would be theoretically possible to turn out any adult form—gangster, musician, financial wizard, scientist, writer, gambler—by ordering the child's experiences.

No one, of course, has been able to test this hypothesis in a rigorously controlled experiment, although there is some limited evidence in its favor. As hypothesis, of course, it still stands; but since the 1930s interest in it has moderated somewhat, partly as a result of later advances (such as Gestalt theories) in psychology. However, recent developments, which we shall examine in Chapter 11, seem to give some new support to Behaviorist concepts. The implications of these new findings for educational theory are both profound and exciting.

But the point here is that Watson was operating within the Realist frame in considering the human being a kind of mechanistic responder and reactor to an equally mechanistic world. If, somehow, people could inter-vene, that is, *intelligently interfere*, with the stimulus-response "history" of human beings, they might be able to produce future generations more nearly to their desire.

Among the more spectacular practical accomplishments coming out of this curiosity in mechanistic psychology is the movement generally known as *programed instruction*, sometimes instrumented through a "teaching machine" but more generally developed in programed materials in book or pamphlet form that learners can carry around with them. One of the pioneer models of the "teaching machine" was developed by Professor B. F. Skinner, a Harvard psychologist in the Pavlovian mold who is generally regarded as the prime mover of modern Behaviorism. Skinner's original device was capable of leading an individual systematically through a prescribed body of subject matter with a question-and-answer format. In Chapter 11, we review the current state of the art in educational machinery and its use in programed and performance-based instruction.

The research behind this development occasioned, among other things, Skinner's discovery that it is possible to teach extremely complicated physical-movement patterns to animals by the mere expedient of precise and planned reinforcement procedures. Skinner, for example, has demonstrated that it is possible to set a pigeon in the middle of a bare floor and in five minutes "teach" it to walk a figure eight just by making signals with a hand clicker and tossing food pellets to it at precisely the right times and places. Reinforcements designed for human use are equally effective, Skinner maintains, in teaching human subject matters.

Whatever human beings are, Skinner believes them to be *primarily* "machines" of some kind. And human beings *are* that, undeniably. They are, at least in part, machines. But whether they are this primarily or exclusively is more a philosophic than a scientific judgment. And because this judgment finds expression in psychological experiments like the above, we say it has an affinity with Realist tendencies in epistemology and pedagogical theory.[4]

THE RECEPTACLE THEORY OF LEARNING

We may now draw together our discussion of both the Idealist and Realist doctrines concerning the relationship between epistemology and learning theory by showing how these two otherwise quite different points of view do share a common platform in educational thinking. You will recall from Chapter 3 (see pages 44–55) the argument that Idealism and Realism share an *objective* metaphysics. We saw in Chapter 6 that, insofar as they remain objective, the "Spectator Theory" of epistemology may be said to apply to both, almost literally in the case of Realism, somewhat figuratively in the case of Idealism (for instance, "seeing" with the "mind's eye").

If they share in some measure the "Spectator Theory," then both of these doctrines will consider education as the gradual introduction to the young of knowledge of an external world—in the case of Idealism, a knowledge of mind and idea; in the case of Realism, a knowledge of fact and habituated response. In both cases the learner may be likened to a receptacle into which adults "pour" knowledge. Indeed, we often speak of the "capacity" of the learner, revealing by the very use of this term an inclination to view the learner as a receptacle. Our schoolrooms are built in accord with this principle, with the teacher facing the learners, as in an

---

[4] Chapter 11 is given over to an analysis of educational strategies that have developed out of the Realist epistemology and metaphysics. These ideas represent a highly visible movement in contemporary education, with a strong and voluble advocacy led, for the most part, by Professor Skinner himself.

auditorium. Indeed, the schoolroom is literally an "audit-orium," where pupils sit and listen and *receive* knowledge.[5]

Or, to use another metaphor, some educators have likened the mind to a kind of giant psychological warehouse that is capable, by means of the learning process, of receiving and holding in "cold storage" a multitude of facts, theories, formulas, concepts, feelings, attitudes, habits, skills, and so on. Then, when occasion calls for one or another of these articles of learning, the mind delivers it to the stage of action, that is, to the "foreground" of our conscious behavioral lives. The most spectacular example of this is, of course, the high school and college quiz contestants who appear on television. In their on-camera agonies they seem almost literally to be reaching back into the dark and dingy recesses of their minds for bits of information the quiz master is ready to give them a small fortune for. But all of us, in varying degrees, are capable of this process, and it is part, at least, of how we learn.

Now if we were to view this metaphorical theory of learning—the Receptacle or "Cold-Storage Warehouse" Theory—in the most generous light, we should be close to a generalized pedagogical doctrine harmonious and consistent with the so-called Spectator Theory and, hence, with Realist and Idealist epistemological views. Where subject matter is descriptive of the world—either a physical or an ideational world—and where its function is to explain the world to the learner, then we have Idealist and Realist tendencies at work. Wherever subject matter is prepared in advance, wherever it is set out before the learner to be learned, and wherever the quantitative assimilation of such subject matter through paper-and-pencil tests and examinations is thought to be the basis for measuring the effect of an educational experience, we may suspect that we are in the presence of either an Idealist or a Realist educator.

TRAINING THE MIND

Teaching the mind ideas, facts, and habit patterns represents, certainly, a large part of education. But, to some, this is but the "anteroom" of more basic things going on inside. Perhaps the most traditionally popular and persistent of all pedagogies is that of "training the mind." And it is this so-called entity called "mind" or "intellect" that is the ultimate object of all these "lesser" educational measures. What the intellect does "inside," so to speak, is the primary question of education.

The Rational Faculty To a Neo-Thomist the Idealist's "imitation of the Absolute Mind" is too vague a pedagogical theory, and the Realist's "learning of factual knowledge" is relatively superficial. What we must do, says

---

[5] Some particularly bitter critics like to refer to this as the "Two-Gallon Jug" Theory of education.

the Neo-Thomist, is to drive to the very core of human nature—the faculty of Reason—and devise educational measures for developing it. Once this is done, then the intellect will be able to take care of itself, including the management of its own continued learning.

In the previous chapter Neo-Thomist epistemology was described principally in terms of *logic*. Knowing, according to this outlook, is primarily an exercise in logical activity. This is true because the metaphysical base of Neo-Thomism is itself a logical one. That is, Aristotelian and Thomistic metaphysics represents a reality of logical form.

If logic is the ground of our reality and the medium of action in the knowing process, obviously we must look to the training of the instrument of logic—the intellect—in educating boys and girls. At the base, therefore, of Neo-Thomist educational doctrine stands a theory of mind or intellect that has come to be known as Faculty Psychology, or the psychology of the mental faculties.

Down through the centuries there has been an abiding temptation on the part of human beings to compare mental activity with physical activity, that is, to find some analogue between mind and body. It is easy enough to see that the body is made up of a variety of parts—organs, limbs, and so on—that operate in a kind of federated system. That is, they each perform a distinct function, but they all exist together in a living union of organism. We know that it is possible by exercise to train each of these physical components. Each part has a particular potential that can be cultivated by calisthenics and drill. We can increase the power of muscles through lifting, we can increase the endurance of the lungs through running, we can improve and refine the coordination between eye and limb through repeated drill and practice. Engaging in this kind of thing may be dull and monotonous—indeed, downright unpleasant—but it works; any athlete knows it.

Now, then, if this is true of the body, might it not also be true of the mind? We know the mind has certain powers that may be said to originate in and be the function of certain mental "parts," or faculties. Customarily and traditionally these faculties are three in number: Reason, Memory, and Will. Although there are subdivisions and elaborations of these three faculties, they represent the central powers of the intellect. Of the three, of course, Reason is the dominant faculty; the rational faculty is the core and center of logical activity. But the other two are necessary adjuncts. And when all three are tuned and sharpened to their highest performance, they collectively make possible the highest kind of mental activity: the apprehension of self-evident and absolute truth, or Intuition.

Neo-Thomist Pedagogy   The primacy of the intuitive power is obvious: Intuition leads to ultimate truth. And so Neo-Thomist pedagogy centers its theory on procedures for developing this highest human faculty. If perfect health may be said to represent not only freedom from disease but also the perfection of all the bodily processes, we know that we can reach this highest bodily state by careful nutrition and physical training. So likewise with the intellect: we must "feed" it the proper materials and engage it in specially designed mental "calisthenics."

In the case of Reason this is done most effectively with what is known as "formal discipline." The term *formal* is not meant to connote a rigid or ritualistic procedure; rather, the term is used in its literal Aristotelian meaning of discipline in the *forms* of thought. Hence, Neo-Thomists are interested in the subject matters that are the most characterized by given forms—that is, the most "form-al" of subject matters. These are, at the top of the list, mathematics, which according to classical thinking is uncontaminated by irregularity or exception and completely endowed with logical forms and necessities, and language, which is somewhat less regularized but still endowed with formal structure. Languages are never planned in advance, never thought up anew and then put to use. Rather, they simply emerge in the course of human history. The fact that grammars develop signifies to Neo-Thomists that the mind naturally tends toward logical structure; the intellect by its own nature evolves in the direction of logical organization. Language is the expression of this logic; and philology, if one were to study it seriously, would be revealed as the epitomized history of the intrinsic and necessary logic upon which the human mind is built.

Training in formal discipline, then, in mathematics, in the languages, in the Latin Trivium of Grammar, Rhetoric, and Logic, is the way to develop the rational powers.

In the case of Memory (another of the prime faculties) the pedagogy is already suggested. Practice and drill in memorizing things—"Thanatopsis," or the Gettysburg Address, or the Binomial Theorem, or any other "memorable" artifact—will serve to exercise the memory. Here again the *form* rather than the *content* of the learning experience is of uppermost importance. While the Gettysburg Address is perhaps better than an equal amount of nonsense syllables by virtue of its idealistic, affective content, nevertheless in strict Faculty Theory the nonsense syllables would do as well in training the memory. Except for their other interests, it does not matter to earnest athletes developing their biceps whether they lift a barbell or a Saint Bernard, each weighing 120 pounds. So also is the rational faculty ultimately indifferent; the strategic question is that of the "discipline of form."

In the case of the faculty of Will (our third mental component) Neo-Thomist pedagogy leans in the direction of situations in which the learners are required to exercise will power by forcing themselves through tasks that they find somewhat distasteful. Physical calisthenics are, after all, something less than pure pleasure to most of us. There is no reason to expect that mental calisthenics will be much different. But just as athletes of truly top-rate caliber force themselves in training so that they may later force themselves to win a race, so does the incipient intellect force itself through mental exercises in order to be able later to force itself to the full application of its mental powers to the problems of life. Thus Will is the constant ally of Reason, and it must be trained alongside. Learners must expect to be forced through exercises they find unpleasant. One's will is tested and thereby strengthened by sticking to a task until it is done.

The Victorian exhortations to perseverance and "stick-to-it-ive-ness" have been common companions of school children for a good many decades. Even before the nineteenth century, when these virtues flowered, there was open talk of "breaking the will" of the child (in colonial Calvinism, for instance) and resetting it along more socially acceptable lines. In any event, the Will is seen as a developable faculty in the human person. It is supposedly the base of "character." Insofar as education makes attempts at so-called "character building," it will have to take some kind of stand on the Will. And the Neo-Thomist position, being the most unequivocal of all, is consequently the simplest: The Will is a human faculty that is capable of development through controlled didactic measures.

Realism, Idealism, and the Faculty Theory   Realists, generally speaking, do not often have much to say about the Will, just as they do not look at the mind from the standpoint of faculties. The Idealists, however, while disinclined to the Faculty Theory, are nevertheless emotionally drawn to the idea of Will because of their subjective, internalized notion of the Self. Thus an Idealist, while close to a Realist on the "Spectator" and "Receptacle" Theories, is in close touch with Neo-Thomists in their emphasis on discipline, mental training, and the development of will in the human self.

Lay and Ecclesiastical Neo-Thomism   In the field of pedagogical theory there is never much "open territory" between the Lay and the Ecclesiastical Wings of Neo-Thomism. Both, generally speaking, hold to a disciplinary approach to teaching; both place the rigorous subject matters of mathematics and languages high on their curricular list; and both give top priority to training the intellect.[6] But whereas the Lay representatives of this position are in search of Truth in their educational program, the Ecclesiastics are in search of God, and this variance in ends will necessarily influence the educational means. For instance, because Latin is the language of the Roman church, it is important in the language study in Catholic schools. A Lay Neo-Thomist, while approving Latin, might prefer

---

[6] In this connection it is interesting to note that some Ecclesiastical Neo-Thomists complain that their Lay compatriots have turned intellectual training into not just one of the ends of education but the *only* end of education, ignoring physical education, the creative arts, and the social development of the learner. Indeed, Catholic parochial schools remain dedicated to the so-called "whole" child even though placing the intellectual and spiritual in a primary position, whereas Lay Thomists theory would leave nonintellectual sectors of development to nonschool agencies, namely, home, church, community.

Greek or perhaps would settle for a modern language—a little more chaotic in grammar, but suitable to the purpose.

Or, again, since the Ecclesiastics have for centuries employed the Catechism in their doctrinal rites, the catechetical method is widely employed in their schools. In this procedure the learners commit to memory specific and standard answers to a list of specific and standard questions. When they are asked questions in the classroom, the "recitation" consists in giving the precise standardized answer. Here again the "form-al" principle is exemplified. By shaping the child's mind to the "form" of doctrine, the Church organizes the mind's powers in orientation to the Church's conception of Truth.[7] The Lay Neo-Thomists, on the other hand, are not particularly partial to the catechetical method. Rather, they are concerned with having the learner see and understand logical connections—between, say, grammatical forms in language study or propositions in geometry.

Finally—and one would normally expect this—the Ecclesiastical Neo-Thomists, with a primary metaphysical and epistemological interest in Being and God, will include in their educational program a considerable amount of out-and-out religious material. There will be not only doctrinal lessons and ceremonial rites but also prayer and devotions. Prayer, in a manner of speaking, is a direct approach to intuition. It is, as it were, a deliberate invitation to be visited by spiritual truth. As such it holds a pedagogical place in Ecclesiastical Neo-Thomist schools. Lay Neo-Thomists, on the other hand, do not choose to make such an open bid for intuition. Intuition becomes possible on the base of intellect. Therefore, intellectual training must precede intuition. That is, if the circumstances are favorable, intellectual development will culminate in intuitive powers. Of course, insofar as the Aristotelian or Platonic kind of "contemplation" approximates devotional prayer, one might say that Lay Theory would go along. But generally speaking the Lay Neo-Thomist will settle for rigorous and disciplined training of the Reason, leaving meditation, prayer, and contemplation to the individual.

Realist and Idealist Reactions   The relationship of Neo-Thomism to Realism and Idealism is certainly not difficult to see. Realists, being materialistically and naturalistically inclined, will put no great stock in any of the Neo-Thomist interests—language, catechism, or prayer. To be sure, there is an ancestral linkage between Realism and Neo-Thomism (especially the Lay variety) in their common appreciation of the orderliness and regularity of the cosmos. Insofar as Latin exhibits a similar orderliness—albeit in symbolic subject matter—Realists might choose it also. They probably would not choose it for its supposed disciplinary value, however, because their theory of mind development is more one of external environmental conditioning than of internal exercise of incipient faculties. As for the

---

[7] If this be indoctrination, Ecclesiastical Neo-Thomists make no apologies for it. What is wrong, they say, with indoctrinating the child with what is absolutely true?

catechetical method, Realists might be ambivalent. They like precise and definite answers to things; but prepared, "canned," unscientific answers, no. Skinner's "teaching machine" might be considered as a variant of this, somewhat of an "automated catechism," but the program fed into the machine can, after all, be altered to suit the situation. This sort of flexibility obviously would not be possible in Neo-Thomism. Certainly, being the Naturalists that they are, Realists would have little use for prayer, meditation, or contemplation in their pedagogy.

The Idealist, to review the list again, would value language study. But not Latin. It is dead. Linguistically, perhaps, it is useful in learning other, modern languages, including English, but as symbolic vehicle for the Living Mind—microcosmic or Universal—it is deficient. If we must have Latin, let it be through literature—Cicero, Vergil, et al.—but not too much grinding on grammar. The catechetical method, as a kind of mental conditioning, is somewhat alien to Idealist tendencies. It is something of a repudiation of the self to impose something on it from the outside in so uncompromising a manner. Of course, the "Spectator Theory" is sympathetic with this general "impositionist" approach, but Idealists would prefer a more personalized procedure. Understanding is what they are after, more than "answer-chopping" in catechetical "question-and-response" periods.

It is in connection with the meditational part of learning that the Idealist has the greatest contact with Neo-Thomism. For the process of coming into identification with the Absolute Mind and Self is a meditative and prayerful kind of activity. Idealists in America are often associated with religious bodies, particularly the Protestant churches, and they are eager to infuse into school life—even on a secular basis—some quality that will remind the children of their spiritual origins. Prayer as such is not possible in the secular school in America, but identification with a school's spirit or with a college's "ethos" is perhaps one way to get a sense of one's heritage. From this base, the study of all Western civilization can become a bridge to understanding the wider, universal bearings from which one springs. Further, the Idealist shares with the Neo-Thomist an abiding interest in the so-called humanities (as against the physical or social sciences), for the humanities are the special province of Mind and Intellect.

These are admittedly tenuous points of contact. Nonetheless, the Idealist and the Neo-Thomist do enjoy a certain amount of intellectual companionship.

Solving Problems

At this point in our analysis there must be a discrete break in mood, for it should become increasingly clear, if it has not already, that Experimentalism is the "Great Break with Tradition" in philosophic thinking. Its metaphysics is a repudiation of the whole long chronicle of "out-thereness" and the resultant dualism between Man and reality. Its epistemology is a repudiation of "spectator-itis" and "logic-chopping." And so its pedagogy too represents a clean separation from antecedent conceptions of the learning process.

Drawing directly upon their unified metaphysics of experience and their epistemology of "testing for consequences" (the scientific method), the Experimentalists have found the locus of learning in *problems*. "Problematic situations" is perhaps a better term, as we saw in Chapter 6, for it connotes a much wider sphere of application. And this is precisely what is intended, for we are now in a position to see, says the Experimentalist, that all situations—all experience—have an educative potential, that is, they have the potential power to *teach*, to initiate growth in us, to quicken our awareness of our world, and to lead us on to more mature use of our world for human ends. To put it simply and bluntly, *all experience educates.*

But, as simple as this may sound, it is only part of our conceptual base of understanding; for, while all experience educates, it doesn't all educate equally well. Some experience has more educative potential than other experience. That is, some circumstances call forth more concern, some situations elicit more activity—to wit, those circumstances and situations that are *problematic* in character. And it is in this type of experience that true and genuine learning takes place.

There is only one general qualification we must lay upon this principle, says the Experimentalist, and that is that the problematic character of the situation must be recognized by the learners as individuals. They must see the situation as *their* situation, the problem as *their* problem. They can, of course, be placed in other people's situations and handed other people's problems—in school, for instance, the teacher can prepare problems for them—but to that degree their growth becomes artificial, linked to motivations and promptings that are generically external to their own being.

At the very base, then, of Experimentalist pedagogical theory is the identification by the learners of their interests, the sectors of the world seen from where they stand to be most problematic. If this identification can be made honestly, if the teacher can elicit some genuine curiosities in the learners, then learning is truly under way.

Learner-Centered Learning   What this means, in more concrete terms, is that the educative process must begin with the learners' identification of their own curiosities and concerns. What should eventuate in the classroom is the evolutionary expansion of questions in the children's own minds: Why do leaves fall off the trees in the fall? Why doesn't the moon ever go away? Why do people join labor unions? How is the cost-of-living index computed? Why doesn't Puerto Rico become an independent nation? Somehow, the learners must be awakened to their own scholastic needs. Any teacher who has tried teaching in this fashion will recognize this as one of the most difficult of all pedagogical enterprises; but the

Experimentalist maintains that, while difficult, it is absolutely central to the educative process.

This has come to be known as the "learner-centered" or "child-centered" concept in teaching. It has, of course, been the object of much ridicule among educational critics. One is immediately reminded of the famous cartoon of a small boy confronting his first-grade teacher on a given morning with the wistful lament: "Do we *have* to do what we *want* to do today?" But such ridicule misses the essential point, says the Experimentalist, for it turns the principle into a license for mere entertainment, fun, and play in the classroom, when the real meaning of the principle is quite the opposite, namely, to awaken the *interest* of the learners, as a prior condition of motivation, to get them to learn what we as a society want them to learn.

Learning While Using Knowledge Presuming that this initial task has been accomplished, the procedure of learning then follows the general plan outlined in Chapter 6 in the discussion of the scientific method and the "Complete Act of Thought." That is, the learners are encouraged and helped to specify and narrow their curiosity to a workable and study-able "project"; to investigate and research the object of their curiosity, to locate possible answers to the question or possible resolutions of what we may generally call "an indeterminate situation"; to test their findings for adequacy by way of explaining or resolving the "problem"; and, finally, to set down their conclusions.

In this sequence of activities the learners will obviously require a great deal in the way of information. They will require skill in organizing and reporting this information. And they will require a degree of intelligence in explaining what they have found out to other people. Thus they have need to learn *content*: factual information, background history, current knowledge concerning the problem. They need to learn *how to analyze a situation*: the application of intelligence to the understanding of a situation. They need to learn *how to communicate*: reading skills, writing skills, speaking skills.

There are many other things they must learn, of course, but the point is that they learn content—so dear to the hearts of traditional methodologists —in the process of using that content to solve a problem or answer a question. The knowledge thus accumulated is learned not in some limbo of contrived necessity—a teacher's assignment, for instance—but within the very context of situations in the learners' own lives. The learners *use* their knowledge—and *by using learn it.*

The Logical and the Psychological John Dewey abstracted and clarified this principle of learning-through-use by pointing to the distinction between the "logical" and the "psychological" methods of teaching. The logical method is characterized by the presentation in systematic, organized, logical form of a body of material that has been especially arranged for learners—"intellectually predigested," one might say. In commenting on this well-known procedure, Dewey says:

> There is a strong temptation to assume that presenting subject matter in its perfected form provides a royal road to learning. What more natural than to suppose that the immature can be saved time and energy, and be protected from needless error by commencing where competent inquirers have left off? The outcome is written large in the history of education.[8]

This may be, Dewey contends, the *logical* way of doing things, but pedagogically it is not the most effective way. For learning does not proceed in so neat and convenient a way as this. Learning originates in a life situation, not in a book. It originates in some circumstance where what is already known is recognized by the learner as inadequate; it begins, ultimately, in a state of *dissatisfaction* with one's own condition. From this seemingly unpromising, sometimes confused, perhaps chaotic condition, the learners advance by inquiry to a larger and wider grasp of the situation with which they began. All learning, says Dewey—whatever the subject matter and whoever the individual learner—proceeds basically in this way.

We may, of course, tell the learners exactly what to learn by presenting it to them in books and lectures and requiring them to master it. That is to say, we can have learners "go through the motions" of learning. But in contriving what appear to be learning situations, we are often disappointed, for what appears to have been learned is quickly forgotten and dismissed by the learners from their own lives. What really stays with the learners is the learning that they have engaged in as the result of genuine interest. Of this, Dewey says:

> The apparent loss of time involved is more than made up for by the superior understanding and vital interest secured. What the pupil learns he at least understands. Moreover, by following, in connection with problems selected from the material of ordinary acquaintance, the method by which scientific men have reached their perfected knowledge, he gains independent power to deal with material within his range, and avoids the mental confusion and intellectual distaste attendant upon studying matter whose meaning is only symbolic.[9]

A good example of this contrast in procedures is geography. The logical method of teaching this material would begin with the earth as a planet, noting its revolutions and its circulations about the sun. From these general facts an understanding could be gained of the seasons and of certain geographical characteristics of the globe entire. Then the water areas would be distinguished from the land areas, the northern from the southern hemisphere, and the eastern from the western hemisphere. The major

[8] *Democracy and Education* (New York: Macmillan, 1916), p. 257.
[9] Ibid., p. 258.

topographical characteristics of the continents would then be examined, whereupon an American school would probably select North America for special study. After this continent had been examined, the study would arrive at the United States, its land and mineral resources, its flora and fauna, its major waterways, its crops, its weather. Then, depending on the location of the school, a particular region would be studied, and the home state would be geographically analyzed, with possibly a day or two devoted to the home town itself. Certainly this is the way most geography texts are written, and it would seem to be a not unlikely description of how such material would be presented.

It so happens, however, that the learners naturally grow in geographical understanding in quite the other direction, starting with as immediate a surrounding as the schoolyard itself. To employ the psychological procedure would be to move from this base of direct understanding to the progressively wider spheres of neighborhood, community, state, region, nation, continent, and globe. This gradual expansion to larger geographical entities is ideally made, says the Experimentalist, by awakening in the children certain curiosities as the material unfolds—why their schoolhouse is built of brick, why their mothers pay so much for oranges, why industries move away or come to town, why American foreign policy is tied to oil, and so on. But such curiosities should be aroused *before* the presentation of the material, not after, for this is the way the experience of the learner customarily unfolds. And it is only when genuine curiosity precedes learning that the learning will be permanent.

Another instance is that of history. Customarily history is taught logically, that is, *chrono*logically. We begin American history with the Vikings and Columbus, proceeding down the years to the present. When we do this, says the Experimentalist, we start at the point that is most remote—both in time and in interest—from the learner. We start, that is, with the material in which it is most difficult to evoke the interest of the learner. Thus from the outset we deplete the fund of motivation on which we may draw, trusting instead that applications to the learner's present knowledge can be made as we take up one historical situation after another. The Experimentalist reminds us that history courses taught this way and history books written this way (and almost all of them are) have had a sorry record of appeal to school children down through the decades, making history one of the least interesting—and therefore least enjoyed—subject matters.

To the Experimentalist, this unhappiness is traceable to Realist, Idealist, and, in some small measure, Neo-Thomist influences. For history taught by the logical procedure is the same as history taught from the basis of the "Spectator Theory," that is, by setting out a specified and codified body of subject matter to be mastered by the students. The students acquire learning by mastering this content, and if they balk or wonder why, they are told that the content is to be mastered for its own sake.

To reverse this, to quicken (instead of deaden) concern with the vitality of the past, is to turn the pedagogical procedure entirely around, so that we once again—as with geography—*begin with the experience of the learner.* For it is here, not in the remote past, that we are most likely to find problematic situations, curiosities, and interests on which the learning of history can be built. As Dewey has put it:

> . . . past events cannot be separated from the living present and retain meaning. The true starting point of history is always some present situation with its problems.[10]

Acting on this advice, the Experimentalist educator would attempt to arouse in the learner an interest in some present problem having historical antecedents necessary to its understanding: the energy crisis, the Watergate scandal, inflation, pollution, unemployment, drug abuse, black separatism. Consider the last named, for example.[11] Here the teacher could direct the learners, especially urban youngsters, to an examination of their own families and neighborhood, to prejudice and racism as they are currently manifest in American attitudes, to the civil rights movement, Martin Luther King, Jr., the bus boycotts, the lunch counter sit-ins, and further back to other historical materials relevant to the study of this problem: the 1954 Supreme Court decision, the *Plessey* v. *Ferguson* "separate-but-equal" doctrine of 1897, the Reconstruction Period, the Fourteenth Amendment, the Civil War, the Emancipation Proclamation, the Missouri Compromise, slavery, the Declaration of Independence (and perhaps even Aristotle's views on the political legitimacy of a slave class in Greek society).

It is evident that a teacher proceeding in this way might not "touch all the bases" that the logical, forward-working teacher would touch, but only those that would be relevant and illuminating to the problem under view. The difference lies in (1) the point of origin for study, *the present*, and (2) the criterion for the selection of materials to be studied, namely, *relevance.*

To learn best, according to Experimentalist thinking, is to engage in problem solving and inquiry and to initiate such activity from the ground of a genuine life interest. In making the recommendation to *start where the child is* (to employ a standard professional cliché), Experimentalists, it may now be noted, are doing no more than making a special application of their general theory of knowing—the scientific method. For inquiry and problem solving are pre-eminently what scientists do when they are trying to find things out. They employ, in short, what we are here calling the "psychological" method, that is, starting with their own understanding, singling out a specific curiosity, and then investigating their "problem" to find the answer. It is only *after* they have found them out that they organize their new findings into what may be called "logical" form, in the

---

[10] Ibid., p. 251.
[11] Black separatism is a paradigm of the issues confronted by a society of cultural pluralism, the main focus of discussion in Chapter 13.

books they write and the lectures they deliver to their classes in the university.[12]

The way the teacher looks at subject matter is quite different from the way the students look at it, for the teacher already knows the material and has it logically organized both mentally and in the textbooks selected for use. But the learners do not learn it in the same way; they must advance upon it from the base of their own interests and curiosities, considering the knowledge of the teacher and the textbook as resource material for the investigation of their topic. The "project" method, then, as against the lecture, "tell-it-to-them" method, is a favorite Experimentalist procedure, for the *project* method is the learner's version of the research scholar's *scientific* method. Although the magnitude and level of sophistication of the two are, of course, quite different, they are cut from the same epistemological cloth.

Basically, argues the Experimentalist, children in the first grade learn the same way research scientists do—by the problem-solving procedure. All learning follows this pattern, and hence the pedagogy of the school should be shaped to it.

Idealism, Realism, and Neo-Thomism Dissent   It goes without saying that advocates of the other methodologies bridle somewhat at this supposedly universal dictum of the Experimentalists. To place all learning in a problem-solving context is to deny a well-known feature of human education, namely, that it is both possible and feasible to introduce knowledge into an individual with no problem whatsoever being present. Certainly the Realist's conditioning does not depend on problems; and the Idealist's absorption in the Universal Self does not depend on problems; and the Neo-Thomist's mental discipline does not depend on problems. In fact, as the advocates of these positions would contend, one must be taught some things about one's world before problems can even be entertained, let alone solved. Problems grow out of knowledge, not the other way around. If we are going to teach boys and girls to live intelligently, if we mean to teach them "how to think," as the old saying goes, then we must first give them something to think about and not expect them to wallow about in problems until something strikes their little curiosities.

Much of the current controversy over education, as you may already have surmised, centers on this focal topic of "substantive content" versus "problem solving" in learning theory. This is not so much a matter of which of the two theories is correct, since each side recognizes that both factors are involved in the educative process; it is more a question of which

[12] The book you hold in your hands, incidentally, is an open violation of the "psychological" principle to begin where the learners are. Take a look at the Table of Contents. You will recognize the material as having been organized from the most intellectually remote (metaphysical theory) to the more immediately practical (educational practice). This is true not only within each of the substantive Parts Two, Three, and Four, but within the book as a whole.

factor is primary, which represents the initiating point of genuine growth on the part of the young.

Finding the Self

Finally we pass into the comparatively uncharted territory of the Existentialist. As it has been pointed out, the Existentialist has not had much to say about education, most particularly about the practical and technical questions of pedagogical method. But we can, nonetheless, begin to see the outline features and the general mood of an Existentialist approach to the education of the young.

The Existential Moment   One of the central doctrines of Existentialist thought, as you will recall from Chapter 3 (see pages 68–69), is that of the primacy of human existence. It is when we wake up to discover that our existence is the ineluctable fact of the human condition that we begin to see the meaning of the companion doctrine that moral choice is inescapable. Because we are "thrown into existence," because we "turn up on the scene" and find ourselves here, we are inescapably "locked in" a circumstance of choice. We have to choose; even to choose not to choose is a choice; even suicide is a choice.

It may be said that in macrocosmic terms humanity has begun to awaken to this moral predicament; but we also know that in microcosmic terms each individual must awaken to it in his or her own life. What has happened to the race is seen to take place in each individual. About the age of puberty there is a more or less abrupt awakening to the fact of one's own existence. We somehow become existentially awake; we discover ourselves for the first time. Prior to this moment—which we might here designate The Existential Moment—we have been aware of the existence only of things beyond our own skin; but once seized by this new idea of *self* we can never retreat to an infantile, childlike state of existential innocence. We have passed The Existential Moment.

This "moment," which generally occurs while the youngster is in the later elementary and junior high school grades, is not an easy time, since it includes the first, agonizing recognition of being responsible for what one does and how one behaves. Frequently, as we noted in Chapter 3, children will try to postpone or forestall the full impact of The Moment by disavowing responsibility for their having come into existence. But children soon realize that they cannot live out the rest of their lives upon this thesis, refusing responsibility for what they do and are. Each of us must, once we pass this "moment," take on the heavy moral burden of our every thought and move.

The Education of Choice   Educationally, of course, this means that we as individuals must become awake not only to our own existential condition and the responsibility it entails but awake to the alternatives before us from which our choices shall be made. To choose in ignorance of any alternative is to choose unfreely; therefore one must be given—in the classroom and outside—every conceivable latitude to find for oneself all the possibilities open to the individual. This means that any subject matter is "fair game" for the school, and that boys and girls must be perfectly free to follow their own inclinations in learning. To hem them in with required assignments, to codify and channel their growth along narrow lines, to suppress their individual reactions to life and learning on the grounds of some preconceived notion of propriety, is to insulate them from the truly *real* world of choice. And since *choice* in the Existential setting is fundamentally *moral* choice, the learner must be given opportunities for genuine moral choice in the learning process.

If one were to put it in Neo-Thomist terms, learners should exercise their "choice-making" power; or, better, they should be awakened to their possession of that power and the necessity for them to use it. To an Existentialist, modern education is noticeably "antiseptic" in this regard. Boys and girls are rarely asked to make choices, moral or otherwise. Experimentalist pedagogy comes the closest, perhaps, in specifying that youngsters should be led to solve problems by selecting from among alternative solutions. But here the "community of consensus," not the individual self, is the true "engine" of choice. And the traditional philosophies are even worse, since they set children in a context—in Mind (Idealism), or in Nature (Realism), or in Being (Neo-Thomism)—in which their basic choices are for the most part already made for them.

The Emotions   We must extricate the learner from this predicament, says the Existentialist; and one of the most promising places to look for the key is in the emotions. Here the choice-making function of the individual is most active, and, therefore, here we can most efficaciously gain access to the self and incite it to existential action. Indeed, Robert Ulich, an expositor of Existentialist tendencies, says that the school of tomorrow must find the thesis for its general education in the emotions.[13] This is said with the understanding that in the special subject matters of the emotions—the arts, most particularly—the most fertile ground for human growth will be found. Chapter 12's discussion of self-actualization explores the emotional, affective side of learning.

In Chapter 5, in a section devoted to subjective and objective knowledge, we pointed out (see pages 108–109) that an "in-here" metaphysics—which is how Existentialism has been characterized—calls for an "in here" kind of knowing. And this would mean, pedagogically speaking, that learners should be provided more scope for "in-here" subjective knowing. They should be offered assignments in reacting to the world—in creative writing, in drama, in responding to literature. They should be more often asked to respond to the other "selves" around them—not in a *social* way,

[13] *Crisis and Hope in American Education* (Boston: Beacon, 1951), Chap. 3.

but in a subjectivist, individualistic way. There is today, says the Existentialist, too much "Group Think" in schools, not enough "Individual Think." Learners should be quickened to respond affectively and emotionally to their world, to the people in it, to the things it makes possible, and to the things, among those it makes possible, that are genuinely worth doing.

In short, the learner must become *involved* in the world, involved in the value questions of life:

—We are by far the richest nation on earth. And yet we permit squalor, disease, and grinding poverty to demolish the spirit of millions of our own people. How about this? Isn't something dreadfully wrong here?

—After a generation of "depression" farm policy, we still pay farmers *not* to plant beans, corn or wheat. Meanwhile, millions go underfed in the world. What are the civil rights of a hungry person?

—Cigarettes kill people. Yet we continue to permit their sale and consumption, because millions of jobs depend on it. Must the economic welfare of North Carolina depend on disease and death in the remainder of the population?

—We try to find our way in an "open" cosmos, where the little questions of home and work get solved but the big questions of life and destiny go unanswered. In such a cosmos as this can there be a God? In such a cosmos, is God really necessary? If he really were to exist, what difference would it make?

This conversational cadenza is inserted simply to show that there is an emotive content to Existentialism that suffuses the entire educative process.[14] And this content, originating in the individual-as-subject, belongs to no one but the subject alone. For the subject, ultimately alone and friendless in the moral universe, must find his or her own way. Boys and girls may live superficially in a social setting in the school, just as their elders do in the wider adult society. But existentially they must remain alone, and to shield them from this lonely moral existence is to shield them from what is truly human in them.

The Teaching Method   This whole pedagogical model that we have been discussing is the complete obverse of the "Spectator Theory." Existentialism has been described as "philosophizing from the standpoint of the actor instead of, as has been customary, from that of the spectator."[15] As such, it turns inside out the whole enterprise of educating the young. Learning begins with the self, not with knowledge. The learner must be set in the very "eye" of the entire proceedings. The moral self must become the ultimate object of pedagogic attention. (See Chapter 12.)

---

14 For a similar set of questions, strong enough to jar even the most complacent of teachers, see pages 62–65 of Neil Postman and Charles Weingartner's *Teaching as a Subversive Activity* (New York: Delacorte, 1969).

15 E. L. Allen, *Existentialism from Within* (London: Routledge & Kegan Paul, 1953), p. 10. Quoted in George F. Kneller, *Existentialism and Education* (New York: Philosophical Library, 1958), p. 147.

Kneller suggests that perhaps the most available access route to the moral self is through a revival of the famed Socratic method. "In methodology, there is no question that the existentialist favor [*sic*] the Socratic approach." [16] This method, says Kneller, implies that teachers—and Socrates used it this way—have no knowledge to begin with: They are interested in eliciting knowledge from the learner. The only kind of knowledge that can be elicited from the learner without prior study and inquiry is moral knowledge, the subjective response of the individual to the world. It is this kind of knowledge, says the Existentialist, that we must revive in our schools. For this kind of knowledge will tell us again what Man is trying to become. We have forgotten who we are, and therefore what we might make of ourselves, because we have forgotten what it means to exist. We have forgotten it because we have forgotten what Socrates was all about. But Socrates is no distant saint. He is a living tradition—and, most fortunately, a *pedagogical* tradition of methodology by which we can revive the existential sense of the young.

The Teacher

What has been said in the several sections above concerning the nature of the learning process has provided ample occasion for glancing references to the role of the teacher and the methods the teacher uses as an initiator and guide to learning. There are, however, a few special notes that can be added concerning this particular role, for the role itself—in the literal sense of *role* in theatrical talk—does take on different characterological nuances from philosophy to philosophy.

THE TEACHER AS PARADIGMATIC SELF

The Idealist is looking for those qualities in the teacher that will provide for the learners a "working model" of selfhood. Since teachers are older and more mature, they stand somewhat as "liaison agents" or "middlemen" between the microcosmic self and the Absolute Self. They should also represent the same sort of middle position with respect to Mind. They are more knowledgeable than their charges. By continued study and growth in their field they should attempt to approximate the Absolute Mind more and more closely. And by so presenting themselves to their students they should draw the students toward them, constantly seeking from the students fuller microcosmic expressions of selfhood and mind.

This signifies that the personality of the teacher is crucial in Idealist theory. It is on constant display, and it should be, for through identification with this personality students should grow in the qualities of per-

---

[16] Kneller, *Existentialism and Education*, p. 133. For other views of Existential teaching strategy see Martin Buber's *I and Thou* (New York: Scribner's, 1970) and Herman Hesse's *Siddhartha* (New York: New Directions, 1951).

sonality. The lecture method is not especially singled out by Idealists, but it is obvious that this method provides the greatest "exposure time" for the selfhood of the teacher. Wherever and however the selfhood of the teacher—through enthusiasm, feeling for the subject, warmth as a person—can be brought to bear on the learners, there will the teacher be fulfilling the proper role in the school.

THE TEACHER AS DEMONSTRATOR

Realists look for different qualities. They want their teachers to be precise and businesslike explainers of the world. These teachers might be likened, to use another comparison, to guides in a national park; they are essentially "show-ers," tellers, expositors, and demonstrators of how the world works. They of course employ the lecture and the recitation to dispense and to measure, respectively, the information with which they are concerned.

They are dealing, ultimately, with a pre-existent reality of which both they and the students are spectators. The task is to cause the learners to know this reality, to produce in them an adjustment to its requirements, and thus prepare them to build further upon the established knowledge of it. Teachers, thus, are a kind of "liaison agent" between the learner and Nature. Their function is to know Nature in all its many faces and to introduce this Nature systematically to the students.

Generally speaking, the personality of the teacher is not crucial in this activity. Indeed, the Realist would prefer that the selfhood (the personality) of the teacher be muted and screened from the learners in order that the *content* of education assume the "front-and-center" position. The personality of the teacher tends to divert the attention of the child from what is to be learned; hence it is best to make the teacher as neutral as possible, at least insofar as personality is concerned. Stand aside, then, O Teacher, and let the factual knowledge of the cosmos come across the desk, straight and true.

THE TEACHER AS MENTAL DISCIPLINARIAN

The concept of mental discipline and the entire Faculty Psychology Theory have been empirically weakened over the course of the last half century by continuing studies in the possibility of "transfer of training." To discipline the mind to learn so-called intellectual habits, which are then transferable to various subject matters, is now seen to be something less than the relatively direct and systematic procedure it was once thought to be. Psychologists who study learning are generally of the view that the mind is not made up of so many faculties that can be exercised, like muscles, in isolation one from another and then transferred to other tasks unconnected with the context of learning. Transfer does take place, we are told, but only in the degree to which the learning situation and the transfer situation are similar.

The Faculty Theory of mind dies hard, however, notwithstanding mounting scientific evidence[17] against it, and there are many educators who persist in the belief that certain studies and certain disciplinary teaching procedures train and harden the mental faculties for life activities after the young leave school. The teacher, in this frame of thinking, should assume the role of a rigorous though benign "taskmaster of the intellect." Or perhaps a better, if somewhat ungenerous, figure would be that of a "director of mental calisthenics." If intellectual training is principally a development of rational powers by exercise and practice in logical procedures, then the teacher should become the chief officiator of the proceedings: not so much a model of personal selfhood; not so much a neutral dispenser of factual information; but a benignly demanding developer of mental powers.

Obviously, such teachers should themselves be possessed of well-developed logical powers. They should have a good memory, a strong will, and, above all, be capable of straight and clear reasoning. They must exhibit these qualities as teachers, but, what is even more important, they must be the developers of these incipient powers in the youngsters in their classes. Teachers in Neo-Thomist thinking should be the exercisers and conditioners of the natural unfolding of prior powers with which the child is born. They are, to use still another metaphor, "intellectual horticulturists," nurturing, feeding, and "fertilizing" the young intellect as it unfolds and develops its rational powers.

THE TEACHER AS RESEARCH-PROJECT DIRECTOR

Someone has described Experimentalist educational theory as considering the teacher as "chair of the board of directors" of a learning "industry." The figure is not inaccurate, for the teacher in "problem-solving" pedagogy, while still chief-in-charge, nevertheless solicits and utilizes the energies and resources of the learners in a very active way. That is, the learners are not—as in the previous three conceptions—passive recipients of learning. Rather they are, in Experimentalist thinking, active participants in the business of learning—investigating, inquiring, reading, thinking, testing, and so on. Furthermore, they are constantly enmeshed in the active participation of other students. They are engaged in an essentially *social* undertaking.

Hence the teacher must be a director of a social, corporate enterprise, maintaining harmony and morale, provoking from each member of the group full powers of participation, and serving as manager of the learning

---

[17] The article on "Transfer of Training" in the 1950 edition of the *Encyclopedia of Educational Research* reviews the research on this question all the way back to 1890. Little in the way of affirmative evidence is reported. Transfer *does* take place, it is true, but only when (1) the learning and applying situations are similar, (2) the learner sees the similarity, and (3) the learner is given practice in making the transfer. Under these conditions almost any subject matter, from auto shop to zoology, can be disciplinary.

project so that genuine growth takes place in the group and in each individual. An understanding on the part of the teacher of human motivation, of the psychic backgrounds to behavior, of the theory of emotional balance, and of all the other facets of human psychology begins to assume a new and decisive importance. The teacher must not only know the subject matter, but also must know the *students*. To borrow a phrase from Dewey:

> When engaged in the direct act of teaching, the instructor needs to have subject matter at his fingers' ends; his attention should be upon the attitude and response of the pupil.[18]

And to have one's attention fastened on the "attitude and response" of the pupils is to attempt to see there unique and individual personalities reacting to, or "transacting with," their world. And since this world is a world of experience, the teacher is in some ways engaged in transactional activity *with* the learner. The teacher is learning along with the student. Indeed, in carrying out projects in which the teacher learns as much as the students, we have an ideal model for teaching skill in Experimentalist terms.

Teachers then, are an integral part of the process. They do not stand outside it as "liaison agents" between the self and the Absolute Self, or as conveyor belts of factual information between the encyclopedia and the receptacle of the child's mind, or as mental calisthenicists trying to train the mind like a muscle. Rather, they are partners, *senior* partners, in the carrying out of meaningful student projects.

THE TEACHER AS PROVOCATEUR OF THE SELF

There is a good deal of puzzlement over what might be said concerning an Existentialist teacher. At the very least the matter is ambiguous, because of the overriding concern in Existenialism for individualism and the primacy of the choosing self. What use at all, one may ask, is a teacher in this context? The very presence of a second person immediately "socializes" the learner's condition and thereby compromises the possibility of developing one's own individualistic view of things.

This difficulty may account for the relative silence of Existentialism on so social an undertaking as education has turned out to be in the modern world. But it need not necessarily block us from surmising certain things that the teacher could and might do in the educational process.

The issue is joined in the concern for moral judgment in Existentialism. A second person—the teacher—can awaken the child to the moral dimension of life without prescribing the moral decisions the child must make. Teachers can pose moral as well as intellectual questions in the classroom; they can raise questions of metaphysical import, so that the youngsters may occasionally confront the root issues of being human. Who am I? What am I *for* in the world? I have maybe seventy years to live; what am

---

[18] Dewey, *Democracy and Education*, p. 215.

I going to do with it? These and a few other probes should open up the raw nerve of "metaphysical conscience," and the teacher should constantly keep this conscience agitated and alive as the child grows.

However this may be done, teachers will certainly not assume the role of paradigmatic self, or conveyor-belt explainer, or mental disciplinarian, or corporate problem solver. Rather, they will, via the Socratic model, jar and stir maturing youngsters into a recognition of their moral selfhood, so that there will never be any question as the years pass that the students will genuinely take charge of their own lives and take responsibility for how they live it day by day. (See Chapter 12.)

All the other philosophies, says the Existentialist, tend to place individuals in some kind of ready-made system where they don't have to take responsibility for their lives. The three traditional outlooks, as we have mentioned, provide external systems—ideational, natural, or logical—in which the moral content of a person's life may presumably be discovered and adopted. And in Experimentalism the social group represents an external gathering point for moral decision; though the social group never locates Absolute Truth and Right, it does serve as an external "system" to which the individual may refer moral questions.

This is all wrong, says the Existentialist. We have socialized education so much in the modern school that children have no "moral sense" left. We have, it is true, extricated them in the secular American school from the moralities of transcendentalism (Idealism), naturalism (Realism), and Aristotelian spiritualism (Neo-Thomism), but we have now become the prisoners of a new moral tyrant: the social group (Experimentalism).

The teacher's job, says the Existentialist, is to break this bond and to set the individual once again in the very center of moral commitment.

The task for this chapter has been to show the operating relationship between epistemological theory and pedagogical procedure. The business of knowing is essentially the business of coming into some kind of human touch with reality. This business is complicated, of course, by the fact that our conceptions of reality are many and various, as Part Two has attempted to show. But it is complicated further by the "internal" difficulties of epistemology as they relate to the nature of Man—his perceptual apparatus, his psychology, his powers of symbolization and ideation, and his "feedback" application of those powers on the reality in which he finds himself and which he is trying to know.

It has been the secondary task of this chapter to show that the difficulties in epistemology are visited in turn upon pedagogical theory. They create confusion and disagreement on how youngsters actually learn. This suggests—to borrow a phrase from modern technology—that "the state of the art" of epistemology, or of philosophy as a whole, is not sufficient to support a unified conception of the learning process. This sentence probably breaks some kind of record for understatement, but it is offered here as one more reminder that as far as educational theory and practice are concerned we are obligated in our utterances to maintain a humble posture.

Eventually, though, there wells up within each of us a desire to single out *one* of the many pedagogical theories as the most suitable one to "believe in." Even though it is conceivable that there is more than one "true" epistemology, nevertheless there must be some that are more adequate, more "true," than others. And there seems to be a normal and natural tendency in us to seek out the more adequate theories for use in our own lives and work.

When we launch upon this undertaking, we are brought face to face with the whole universe of value judgment. To choose among pedagogies, to choose among epistemologies, even to choose among metaphysics, is to enter upon a judgment of worth and value. To make choices among these high-minded and relatively sophisticated regions of philosophical theory may require more study than this book or your course can provide. But we certainly ought to study the question of choosing, even if at a lower level of discourse.

For, whatever else Man may be, he is certainly a "valuer." He prefers some things to others, whether they be apples in a basket, people in a room, behavior patterns in a social system, or Gods in a cosmos. And to find out how he makes such value decisions we must examine the whole complex of factors that are involved in his judgments.

It is to this region of value—axiology—we now turn in Part Four.

Questions

1. One of the "battle cries" of the twentieth century in education has been the "education of the whole child." From the standpoint of the various pedagogies discussed in this chapter, would you say they would be equally proficient in fulfilling this requirement in the work of the school? Explain.

2. One of the logical extensions of Realist "conditioning" theory is the belief that any educable dimension of the human person is subject to conditioning and habituation. This includes not only motor skills, such as typewriting, but also intellectual behavior, like the multiplication table; social behavior, like cooperation or respecting others; and even moral conduct, like telling the truth or paying the proper amount of income tax. The conditioning theory holds that we can turn any behavior—verbal or physical—into habituated response. What do you think of this as an educational theory? What would you think the other four philosophies would say about it?

3. One of the standard clichés of the modern educational age is that "the learner learns to do by doing." Precisely what function does *doing* have in the five pedagogies? Is *doing* necessary to *learning*? What represents genuine *doing*? What doesn't?

4. The so-called "open classroom" is a radical departure from conventional education. How would each of the five pedagogies evaluate its effectiveness?

5. At the end of every learning experience there is some necessity to measure the effect of the experience on the child, that is, to give tests and assign grades. How would each of the pedagogies go about this? What would they be looking for? What would they wish to test.

Further Reading

Idealism

The Harvard Committee. *General Education in a Free Society.* Cambridge: Harvard University Press, 1948. Although this famous "Harvard Report" was not written as a philosophical testament, it nevertheless reveals strong Idealist sentiments. And because it deals with educational realities rather than philosophical speculations as such (and, one might add, because it is a beautiful piece of writing), you should find it helpful in seeing how Idealists think about education in America. Chapter 2, on the "Theory of General Education," and Chapter 4, on "Areas of General Education," are the two most relevant sections for study.

Butler, J. D. *Idealism in Education.* New York: Harper & Row, 1966. In Chapter 3 in this small volume, Professor Butler explains the Idealist's conception of the school as a social institution, the pupil's role, the objectives of education, and the educative process.

Realism

Breed, F. S. "Education and the Realistic Outlook," Chapter 3 in *Philosophies of Education*, Forty-first Yearbook of the National Society for the Study of Education, ed. N. B. Henry, Part I. Chicago: the Society, 1942. The contributions to the Forty-first Yearbook were, for the most part, dialectical arguments against Experimentalism. This essay, both sharply polemic and generous in tone, explains clearly and without complication where the Realists stand, what they think is important in the educational program, and how they go about the business of teaching. As a "straight-from-the-shoulder" statement of position, this article has few equals.

Wild, John. "Education and Human Society: A Realistic View," Chapter 2 in *Modern Philosophies and Education*, Fifty-fourth Yearbook of the National Society for the Study of Education, ed. N. B. Henry, Part I. Chicago: the Society, 1955. Wild is not primarily an "educational" philosopher but a so-called "pure" philosopher, in the academic sense of the term. As one of several such individuals contributing to this yearbook, he has put together an interesting and readable treatise on how an "academic" Realist looks at education. Here he presents his thesis that "the school is the home of Pure Theory," from which he develops the Realist's position on "The Educational Process and Curriculum," "The School and Society," "The School and the Individual," and "The School and Religion."

Neo-Thomism

Brumbaugh, R. S., and N. M. Lawrence, Jr. "Aristotle's Philosophy of Education." *Educational Theory*, 9, no. 1 (January 1959): 1–15. In a splendid summation of Aristotelian thought on education, drawn from a number of places in his works, these two Yale professors have provided a magnificent service for students of educational philosophy. Here is set down in clear and unmistakable language the Aristotelian logical system of causes, the procedure by which the human being knows, and the patterns of pedagogy implicit in Aristotle's thinking. An illuminating presentation of the bases of the Lay position in Neo-Thomism.

Hutchins, Robert M. *The Higher Learning in America*. New Haven: Yale University Press, 1948. Throughout Hutchins's writings there runs a strong and strident tone of disgust and despair concerning the deterioration of education in the United States. In this most popular of his many works, he speaks with expressive sharpness about higher education, the topic, incidentally, on which he has had the most to say. Here the Lay Neo-Thomist (or, more accurately, the Neo-Aristotelian) is in full flight and at his polemic best. No student's education is complete until he has read something of Hutchins.

Redden, J. D., and F. A. Ryan. *A Catholic Philosophy of Education*, rev. ed. Milwaukee: Bruce, 1956. In Chapter 5 these two Fordham professors develop the Ecclesiastical Neo-Thomist position concerning "The Intellect and Its Function" (the nature of knowledge, truth, belief, and certitude). Then they proceed to a systematic account of educational theory by way of a section entitled "The Intellect: Its Education" (the act of learning and the acquisition, preservation, and modification of knowledge).

Experimentalism

Dewey, John. *Democracy and Education*. New York: Macmillan, 1916. Certainly the most authentic source to which one can turn on Experimentalism is John Dewey. Some of his "commentators" may have explained him better than he explained himself; but in this famous book, in Chapters 13 and 14, dealing with "The Nature of Method" and "The Nature of Subject Matter," Professor Dewey sets down in clear and concise language how the Experimentalist scientific epistemology takes on pedagogical "life" in the classroom. Later on, in the chapters on geography, history, and science in the course of study, he spells out more precisely his pedagogical ideas, including the "logical-psychological" problem in the arrangement and presentation of subject matter.

Pai, Young. *Teaching, Learning, and the Mind*. Boston: Houghton Mifflin, 1973. After a thorough examination of the classical theories of mind—the substantive, the "Bundle-Theory," Behaviorism, analytic, and materialistic theories—one of the present authors devotes a major section of this volume to "Cognitive Teaching, the Field Theory, and the Functional Concept of Mind." Here we see an updated analysis of the Experimentalist's pedagogy.

Existentialism

Morris, Van Cleve. *Existentialism in Education*. New York: Harper & Row, 1966. The concluding chapters of this small volume take up the systematic analysis of "An Educational Theory" and "An Existentialist Pedagogy." We see here the Socratic paradigm dismantled and re-explained as a vehicle for Existentialist teaching.

Neill, A. S. *Summerhill—A Radical Approach to Child Rearing*. New York: Hart, 1960. Neill says, "We have no new methods of teaching, because we do not consider that teaching itself matters very much." If you read this book, you'll find out what *does* matter.

PART FOUR

Axiology:
What is Good

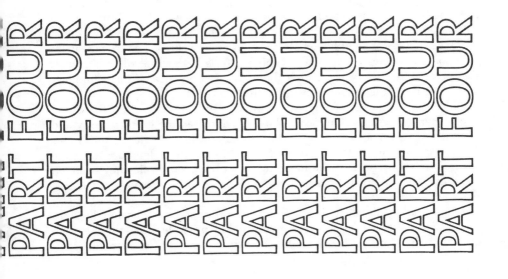

PART FOUR PART FOUR PART FOUR PART FOUR PART FOUR PART FOUR PART FOUR PART FOUR PART FOUR PART FOUR

8

Axiology:
The Question of Value

The School and Values

We pass at last into our third and final set of philosophic problems, those that collect about the pole of what people have come to call "value." Man is not only a "knowing" organism; he is also a "valuing" organism—he likes some things more than others, that is, he has preferences. Man's valuing, moreover, is perhaps an even more decisive characteristic of his behavior than his knowing. This is the view, for instance, of many people who believe that the *quality* of a person's life, that is, what we cherish, what we truly want out of life, is a better measure of our humanness than the "quantity" of our lives, that is, how *much* we know, how widely read we are, or how knowledgeable or learned we may be. We all know people who are highly educated and conversant on a great many topics but whose life values leave them, in our eyes, short of attainment of the humane and cultivated life.

So, likewise, do we judge whole societies and cultures. The true measure of a society, or even of a whole civilization, is better looked for in what the society basically *wants*, rather than in how sophisticated its technology may be or how efficient its political institutions are.

This is a particularly poignant reminder in our own time, for many Westerners, especially Americans, having witnessed the extraordinary and astonishing advances of science—into the atom, into medicine, into outer space—are beginning to wonder what exactly all this splendid knowledge is for. They contend that the meaning of our civilization lies not so much in atomic energy but in *what we do with it*, not so much in heart transplants but in *the use to which we put* the fuller and longer lives we thereby purchase, not so much in the conquest of the moon as such but in *what human ends* the conquest of the moon makes possible. And the meaning of our civilization, rather than its gadgetry, its glitter, or even its many wonderful and marvelous accomplishments, strikes us as the central question we must ponder if we are to be worthy of inclusion in the history textbooks of future ages.

What a civilization ultimately "means" is in part determined by what it *wants* to "mean" in the big record book of history. And since those "wantings" and preferences—as well as knowledge itself—will most certainly die out if not perpetuated generation by generation, we get a sense of the importance of education in enabling a civilization to express itself down through the ages.

It is the thesis here in Part Four that this sense of the importance of education is not a delusion. Educators are not only in the business of transmitting knowledge and developing trained intelligence. They are also in the business of recommending to the young a value system, a look at life, an "environment of preferences," which it is their concern as adults to make live anew in the experience of the young.

Whether or not it is the educator's privilege or duty to go beyond the perpetuation of a value system to the criticizing of it, or, further, to the encouragement of his students' criticizing the society's values, is the kind of question that is answered differently by different schools of axiological thought. This will be taken up in Chapter 9. But for the moment we are concerned with the theory of value, what the problem really amounts to, and what considerations enter into its study.

Value Defined

First of all, the word *value* is a difficult and elusive symbol. It is, as the philosopher Charles Morris says, "one of the Great Words, and, like other such words ('science,' 'religion,' 'art,' 'morality,' 'philosophy'), its meaning is multiple and complex." [1]

One of the most troublesome complexities, for instance, lies in the location of a person's values. How do you tell what people value—from what they say or from what they do? Morris points out that one type of values, called "conceived" values, represents what people believe in and openly profess but do not necessarily act on. A cigarette smoker may believe that she really ought to quit, but she doesn't "act accordingly." But her conceived, symbolic preference—and who can deny her it?— is for a state of nonsmoking. Her continued smoking, however, reveals another kind of value, a behavioral or, as Morris labels it, an "operative" value. Our overt behavior, in this sense, is a clue to our values. The old epigram, "Your actions speak so loudly I cannot hear what you say," is a popular expression of this distinction.

Put in a slightly different way, in the field of ethics, we can ask whether a person's intent—what he or she "means to do"—is a better measure of personal values than a person's observable conduct and the practical effect

[1] *Varieties of Human Value* (Chicago: University of Chicago Press, 1956), p. 9.

of that conduct. We sometimes excuse an act if a person can establish that he or she "did not mean to do it." There is a legal graduation of penalty, for instance, which distinguishes among "premeditated," "unpremeditated," and "unintentional" murder. A Catholic priest in confession can excuse sinful acts if the suppliant can prove that his or her intentions were good. We sometimes say, in other connections, that such-and-such a person is mean, or greedy, or rude, but that "his heart is in the right place" or "she means well." What this suggests is that what a person *does* is not so reliable a measure of that person's values as what is believed "down deep inside."

In the field of aesthetics we must ask whether people's tastes are revealed better by what they say they like in the way of art, music, poetry, literature, cuisine, or by what they actually surround themselves with, day by day: the kinds of clothes they wear, the automobile they buy, what they order for lunch, the way they decorate the interior of their homes, the records in their stereo cabinets, the magazines and books an unannounced guest might find on the coffee table.

At the outset, then, we are confronted with a basic difficulty, and it has serious educational implications, because when we get to the education of the young we must have in hand a reasonably well-based criterion for determining when a youngster has and when he or she has not come to accept a certain value judgment.

But, for all its importance, this may be said to be only a "tactical" difficulty compared to a still more serious and "strategic" matter, namely, not what we prefer or what we *say* we prefer, but what we *ought* to prefer. This is the familiar distinction between the preferred and the preferable, between the desired and the desirable. For all human beings, whatever their tastes, do desire and prefer things, either in their overt behavior or by symbolic profession, but the truly axiological question is whether their desires are really desirable, whether they ought to desire what they in fact do desire. Put in blunt and somewhat cryptic shorthand, we may ask: What *ought* people to ought?

EDUCATION: THE DEVELOPMENT OF PREFERENCES

This may be said to be the ultimate question in axiology, and it has a central place in educational theory by virtue of the peculiar function of the educator, the function of serving as the instrumentality of a social system that means to perpetuate itself through its young. For whether educators are skillful or not in teaching values, whether they use the "operative" or the "conceived" criterion for judging the growth of their students, their position requires them to defend the values that make up the subject matter of their teaching as representing those values that people— and therefore their students—*ought* to value. Furthermore, and this is in a way more crucial, they must be able to defend the values that make up the subject matter of *their own lives*, which are, after all, on display, before the young every day and which the teachers, because of their position, implicitly recommend to the students to imitate. No matter how they try, teachers cannot "turn off" their moral self during teaching hours. Whether they like it or not, they are on constant view as the paradigmatic model of mature adults.

This predicament is, in a sense, the microcosmic version of the larger problem facing the school, the problem of bearing ultimate responsibility for what may be generally called the "moral integrity" (*integrity* in its connotation both of *integratedness* and firm *commitment*) of the social system. We attempted to characterize the nature of this responsibility at the outset of the book. In Chapter 1 (see page 18–19) we saw that one of the primary reasons for studying educational theory is what John L. Childs has called "the moral nature" of the educational enterprise. (The term *moral* here is considered in its largest meaning of *making value judgments*.) When a society becomes "conscious of its own experience," says Childs, it reveals a concern for the management of that experience toward its own future. Hence, says Childs, "the organization of a system of schools signifies the deliberate attempt of a human group to control the pattern of its own evolution." [2]

The importance of value theory for education is most readily seen, then, in this "moral" characteristic of education. If, as Childs intimates, we are deliberately attempting to make the future "come out" the way we want it to—either for an individual or for a whole society—then we are engaging in an unmistakably value-oriented enterprise. And since the school is the "caretaker" of the future by virtue of its contact with the young, the heart of the moral enterprise of society in recreating its moral self resides in the school.

Educators, as a rule, do not wax overly self-conscious or reflective about this phase of their work. But they are engaged in it constantly. When we teach boys and girls to take turns on the swings on the playground, when we encourage cooperation with their classmates in organized study projects, when we ask for quiet in the library so that others can study, when we punish cheating on examinations, when we attempt to control drug use among adolescents, when we pipe Toscanini by Muzak into the lunchroom, we are making individually minuscule but collectively significant selections of what we want boys and girls to prefer. And such preferences, from the ridiculous to the sublime in life, represent what kinds of citizens they will become in the days ahead.

EDUCATION AND ULTIMATE VALUES

There is another and more sophisticated point of contact, however, between the study of axiology and the education of the young. It has to do with the values we exhibit and proclaim not just for our own future but for the future of all humanity. Childs's theory of "the moral nature" of

[2] *Education and Morals* (New York: Appleton-Century-Crofts, 1950), p. 6.

education is principally a social or culturological concept. That is, it relates to the choices and decisions that societies and civilizations make for their own perpetuation. While not selfish in spirit, these choices are nevertheless to some extent parochial and limited in scope; while such choices—like freedom and democracy and private property—may possibly be recommended for adoption by people everywhere, they are still expressions of a given culture, of a particular society living in a given time and occupying a given geographical space. Professor Childs reminds us that all moral decisions must be understood in this sociocultural context.

But there is another, wider sphere in which it may be said that people value. They value not just for this or that civilization, not just for "the free world" or "the Communist world," not just for "the West" or "the East" or for an ill-defined "Third World." They value for Man, and when we spell it with a capital M we are designating here a level of valuing that refers to what we think we ultimately are as the only valuing inhabitants of this spinning planet. Experimentalism, from which Childs speaks, does not customarily have much to say about this mode of valuing, leaving such comment to the other four philosophies we have taken up. There is nevertheless a way in which we can employ a famous remark by a leading Experimentalist, John Dewey, to get a grip on the meaning of this kind of valuing.

To lead up to it, we are reminded that when we deal with valuing at this level—what we might speak of as the "metaphysical" rather than the "culturological" level—we are not asking the question, "What values for our time?" We are not asking, "What can we make of twentieth-century humanity?" We are asking, rather, "What can we make of Man?" Seen in this light, the moral dimension of human preference is practically without limit, and in asking what we can make of Man we are, in a manner of speaking, asking what programs of reform and enlightenment can be wrought upon humanity to achieve the true "human spirit." And this, at bottom, is an educational question; it is to ask what kinds of educational programs can be invented to bring human beings to a higher expression of themselves.

And so, in the brilliance of his insight, John Dewey uttered one of his most famous and oft-quoted dicta: "If we are willing to conceive education as the process of forming fundamental dispositions, intellectual and emotional, toward nature and fellow men, philosophy may even be defined *as the general theory of education.*" [3]

At long last, then, after having traversed the fields of metaphysics and epistemology, we come in axiology to an ultimate reunion between philosophy, as the study of the universe and Man's place in it, and education, as the study of human beings and how they grow to fuller stature in their world. For philosophy and education are really two versions of the same activity. They both ask, "What can we make of man?" Philosophy asks

[3] *Democracy and Education* (New York: Macmillan, 1916), p. 383. (Author's italics.)

it in macrocosm—"Man." Education asks it in microcosm—"men." So philosophy is indeed "the generalized theory of education." And conversely, education may be termed "the specialized practice of philosophy." It is, one might say, the "testing laboratory" for our philosophies. For if some value, some program, some life choice is seen to be good for *Man*, it must be good for individual *men and women*. Philosophy, most especially the study of axiology, examines, analyzes, and suggests values; education "tries them out" on individuals.

THE BRANCHES OF VALUE

Having said these things, we can now set down a few ground rules concerning the discussion of the kinds of problems that are met in the study of axiology. As we have already pointed out, the field of value theory, or axiology, is customarily divided into the two branches of ethics and aesthetics. Ethics is that sphere of concern that deals with conduct, with what people do; aesthetics deals with what they consider beautiful, with what they enjoy.

Terminologically, we have in the preceding discussion permitted ourselves the license of using the word *moral* to cover all valuing, including, by implication, aesthetics. In the passages that follow, however, we shall employ the term *moral* to refer principally to ethical considerations. This is likewise true of such words as *right, wrong, good, bad*—words that also may have a wider sphere of application. In aesthetics these words shall be avoided as much as possible. Instead, we shall have need of such terms as *lovely, beautiful, enjoyable, ugly,* and so on.

This admittedly arbitrary distinction is made only to assist in the understanding of the value problem. It is conceivable, indeed rather common, to speak of "good" art or "good" music (although we never hear of a "good" sunset or a "good" flower garden) but this is merely a linguistic convention; certainly *good* in this context does not refer to moral "rightness." So we shall reserve *good* for ethical matters. Conversely, it is sometimes fitting, for the sake of emphasis or hyperbole, to speak of a "truly beautiful act," or a "really beautiful person" (referring to something other than an individual's physical features). But this is just the point; by noting such exceptions we can see the warrant for making the distinction in language because there is a different mode of value being explored in the two cases.

Ethics: The Question of Conduct

MORALS

At the base of all ethical considerations lies the question of morals. The term itself stems from the Latin *mos, moris,* meaning custom or manner. Our pluralized *mores* is the more familiar term. But while *morals* and *mores* stem from the same root they differ in meaning in a rather decisive way. The former term refers to a reflectively considered custom or procedure, whereas the latter term denotes some kind of blind or unthinking habit we have fallen into. One might say that we begin with mores but that when mores become reflective and deliberately singled out as interests they become morals. Thus, when through cultural circumstances we fall into the practice of collective action and "organization" in modern life, it may be designated a reflection of American mores. But when collective action and "organization" are singled out for special comment, either pro or con, we may speak of them as having attained some kind of moral stature.

Also involved in the term *morals* is the concern for decisions in conduct. As pointed out previously, ethics and morals refer to the direction of conduct, to the guidance of the human act. The central question in all ethical situations is: What should I do?[4] The question may include a prior question or two: What *may* I do? That is, what are the possibilities open? Or what *can* I do? That is, how many alternative courses of action am I capable of? But, aside from these special, circumstantial questions, the moral issue is resolved in deciding, either symbolically or actually, on some course of action.[5]

It is in this sense that we speak of honesty, adultery, murder, abortion, forgery, embezzlement, charity, loyalty, fairness, justice, or slavery as *moral* problems: they have to do with our conduct. There is a qualification to this definition, however, in segments of religious doctrine; for instance, Christian moral theory holds that a person's *thoughts* are quite as morally culpable as his or her *deeds*. For example, "he who looks in lust upon a woman" has, in Jesus' sense of the term, committed adultery.

In secular life this interpretation generally does not hold. It is only *conduct* that becomes subject to the moral criterion. Insofar as we codify our morals in our law, it may be said that the distinction between thought and deed is all the more definitive. A person cannot be convicted for private thoughts or opinions, only for overt acts and deeds. Of course, morality extends considerably beyond civil law, but generally speaking modern people think of morals in terms of conduct.

---

[4] Dewey has pointed out somewhere that the traditional moral systems, such as the Decalogue, center more on the negative "What *shouldn't* I do?" This "accentuation on the negative" in most inherited moral codes has had the unfortunate effect not only of deflecting people's interest from more positive concerns but also, more seriously, of discouraging people from considering moral problems in general for fear that the resolution of such problems would issue in yet another negative injunction. It was in this spirit that Alexander Woollcott uttered his famous lament: "Everything I like to do is either illegal, immoral, or fattening!"

[5] The question "What *must* I do?" is sometimes suggested as another possibility here. To some moralists this is a forbidden question, because it removes the element of choice and, therefore, the element of "should-ness" or "ought-ness." Individuals cannot, they say, really *choose* something that is forced on them. Other moralists, however, insist that morals are those patterns of action which people must follow if they would be human beings. In this sense they are "forced" on us as ways of acting. This problem will have fuller treatment in Chapter 9.

THE GOOD AND THE GOOD

To find morals in conduct, however, does not tell us much about them. Given the range of conduct in which human beings operate, and given the particular situations in which the proper course of action appears problematic—which is what we may call moral situations—how is one to go about the discovery or determination of that specific course of action considered right and good? At the base of disputes in moral theory is the issue of *absolutes*. Are there patterns of human conduct that are always right or always wrong, considered everywhere and throughout all time as morally good or bad, without regard to circumstance?

This question seems reasonable enough. And it seems worth our while to investigate, especially because it has potential educational significance. For if there are absolute goods—what we here designate with the upper-case *G* in "Good"—then the educator's function, among other things, is to locate them and teach them in the school. The problem is almost identical to that of Absolute Truth discussed in Part Three. You should be able to detect by now that the issue of axiological absolutes is very much tied up, as is the issue of epistemological absolutes, with the metaphysical questions of a static, objective, existential reality as opposed to a dynamic, evolutionary, "becoming" reality. Many of these interlocking considerations you should now be able to supply yourself out of your study of the previous sections of this book. But in any case we shall have to review them briefly at the outset of Chapter 9.

The question of absolutes, on its surface, seems reasonable because there are many human behavior patterns that are quite generally and universally held to be good—such things as charity and succor to others, for instance, and other behaviors that are quite generally condemned—injury and murder, for instance. Common sense would suggest that such things would surely classify as unqualifiedly "good" or "bad." But for a moral value to achieve the status of an absolute it must be shown to hold in *every* situation confrontable by anyone. If there is but one qualification or one instance to which it is relevant but inapplicable, then it cannot be an absolute principle. It is this rather stringent requirement that has disallowed so many candidates for absolute status. Even the principle "Thou shalt not kill," perhaps one of the strongest candidates for absolute status, is seen by many moralists as a circumstantially qualifiable principle. In the circumstance of defending oneself, for instance, one may justifiably take the view that "Thou shalt not kill" does not hold.[6]

---

[6] The most thoroughgoing development of this principle of "circumstantial qualifiability" is Joseph Fletcher's *Situation Ethics*, a book that had a wide readership in the late 1960s (Philadelphia: Westminster, 1966). In this argument, Fletcher startles us by the answer to a simple question: "If the end does not justify the means, what does?" The answer, he asserts, is "Nothing." There are no absolutely pre-eminent values. The means we employ in our daily lives to realize the good life are inevitably tied to the many ends we seek. Out of these ends, all we have are situations, each one requiring its own analysis and moral decision making.

The problem is considerably more complex than this, of course, but this is the type of axiological problem that arises in considering "the good" and "the Good." Educationally speaking, there is a world of difference between these views; for if there is no absolute company of *Goods*, but only a circumstantial company of *goods*—in specific situations or, at most, in certain classes or types of situations—then the training of the child in making moral judgments must take on a whole new texture and direction in the school.

Whatever else happens, the moral training of the young will become considerably more difficult under this view. Teaching prescribed (literally "pre-scribed," written down beforehand) moral rules to youngsters, notwithstanding the difficulty of getting rules to flow into behavior, is far simpler than teaching youngsters how to develop their moral dispositions as they go along from one new situation to another. But the relative difficulty or simplicity of a procedure is not in itself a measure of its soundness, so we must take into consideration other problems as well.

MEANS AND ENDS

One of these other problems is the old standby of means and ends. It is most commonly phrased by the question, "Does the end justify the means?" Is the theft of a loaf of bread to feed a hungry child a defensible act? Is a man morally justified in exploiting other people in order to make a fortune that he then gives to these people? Is the federal government morally justified in infringing on the civil rights of a few individuals (by breaking into their homes and offices) in order to protect the national security of 200 million other individuals?

These are the kinds of moral conundrums that most people try desperately to avoid, partly because competing values are here seen to be in conflict, partly because one of the competitors (end) has traditionally been thought to outrank the other (means) in importance (thus complicating an already complex problem), but mostly because there is no real answer to the puzzle. We moderns are less sure than the ancients that ends outrank means. Generally speaking, it could be argued that we therefore do not support the view that "the end justifies the means." But there were few Americans who did not embrace this principle when they realized in 1941 that the defeat of Nazi Germany was about to require the slaughter of millions of people and in August of 1945 that the final defeat of Japan was worth the price of almost 100,000 human beings exterminated in a microsecond at Hiroshima.

When things are going right we feel we can afford to strike a pose of insouciance about this whole matter of means and ends. But when the chips are down we reveal by our behavior where our genuine sentiments lie—which is, by the way, to express a bias in favor of "operative" as compared with "conceived" values as being the more authentic (see pages 205–206).

MORALITY AND ETHICAL RELATIVITY

Another problem, of somewhat more recent vintage in moral theory, has to do with the variability of values—both operative and conceived—throughout the world and down through history. People have long been aware, of course, that they believed in and acted upon different principles. What they have not generally known until the invention of scientific, "intercultural" anthropology is that these differences of belief and practice do not seem to be judicable by any higher standard.

When people disagree on matters of law, there are courts to which they can go. But when people disagree as to the Rule of Law itself, that is, when they disagree on whether to be lawful or not, then there is no arbiter of reference. A central issue of the Watergate scandal of the Nixon administration in the early 1970s was whether the President of the United States did or did not have the right to break the law in "the national interest," and whether this right did or did not supersede any judgment of a court.

As scientific and cultural anthropologists have roamed the earth within the last fifty to seventy-five years, their summary findings have seemed to indicate that the values people live by are so different and ultimately so arbitrary that the only sensible conclusion is that, depending on circumstance and history, people simply believe in different values, and that is that. What is more, each culture defends its ways as vigorously and aggressively as any other, usually proclaiming some divine sanction for this or that practice, which sometimes may seem to others to be the crudest and most uncivilized of habits. No amount of argument seems to have any effect. People go on believing in the same things and acting on their beliefs, sure and certain that they alone have the truth. And this trait is just as evident among Western civilized people as it is among the Trobrianders or the Navajo Indians.[7]

One of the liveliest and most succinct discussions of this point is found in W. T. Stace's *The Concept of Morals.* Although Stace will have none of ethical relativity himself, he states its central idea thus:

> . . . the whole notion of *progress* is a sheer delusion. Progress means an advance from lower to higher, from worse to better. But on the basis of ethical relativity it has no meaning to say that the standards of this age are better (or worse) than those of a previous age. For there is no common standard by which both can be measured. Thus it is nonsense to say that the morality of the New Testament is higher than that of the Old. And Jesus Christ, if he imagined that he was introducing into the world a higher ethical standard than existed before his time, was merely deluded.
>
> . . . on this view Jesus Christ can only have been led to the quite absurd belief that his ethical precepts were better than those of Moses by his personal vanity. If only he had read Westermarck and Dewey he would have understood that, so long as people continued to believe in the doctrine of

---

[7] For a typical treatment of this problem, see Ruth Benedict, *Patterns of Culture* (Boston: Houghton Mifflin, 1934).

an eye for an eye and a tooth for a tooth, that doctrine was morally *right*; and that there could not be any point whatever in trying to make them believe in his new-fangled theory of loving one's enemies. True, the new morality would *become* right as soon as people came to believe in it, for it would then be the accepted standard. And what people think right is right. But then, if only Jesus Christ and persons with similar ideas had kept these ideas to themselves, people might have gone on believing that the old morality was right. And in that case it would have *been* right, and would have remained so till this day. And that would have saved a lot of useless trouble. For the change which Jesus Christ actually brought about was merely a change from one set of moral ideas to another.[8]

In this admittedly broad language, Stace puts the thesis of the ethical relativist, albeit somewhat sarcastically. But this relativism is not merely nihilistic in spirit, for out of it have come numerous attempts to catalogue human values and reduce them by combination to a few major value-complexes. This work, the province of the social psychologists, has gone on apace as the anthropologists have brought in their data. Charles W. Morris in his book *Paths of Life* developed the thesis that there are three distinguishable types of value systems: (1) the Dionysian, in which the primary principle is self-indulgence, (2) the Promethean, in which the controlling value is to manipulate the world, and (3) the Buddhistic, in which the moving idea is the regulation of the self. By a kind of terminological shorthand, Morris felt that these three positions could be described respectively as ones of (1) dependence, (2) dominance, and (3) detachment. Moreover, there seemed to be some congruity, he thought, between these "paths of life" and the three temperament categories identified and studied by the psychologist W. H. Sheldon, namely, viscerotonia, somatotonia, and cerebrotonia.[9]

In addition to these attempts at value classification are many other arrangements. Karen Horney, for instance, in her book *Our Inner Conflicts* seeks to classify all temperaments within a triad of "tendencies": "toward," "against," and "away from" people. All value judgments, she thinks, collect about one or another of these "poles of choice." David Riesman in his astute and provocative *The Lonely Crowd* suggests still another set of character categories, with a certain historical twist: "tradition-directed," "inner-directed," and "other-directed." Americans are, he says, moving into the last of these stages in almost every area of life.

There are, of course, many provocative insights in all these attempts at cataloguing and "polarizing" human values. What they all seem to say is that, while value constellations may be reduceable to three or some other convenient number of categories, there persists a plurality of value positions people can take and, more important, there appears to be no method

---

[8] W. T. Stace, *The Concept of Morals*, pp. 48–49. Copyright, 1937, by The Macmillan Company, New York.
[9] Charles W. Morris, *Paths of Life* (New York: Braziller, 1956), p. 28.

by which we can adjudicate among value positions to find which is best or axiologically of highest rank.

If we are dealing with genuinely primary values, and these studies are of that sort, then we must recognize that when we reach this level of discourse we are traveling in unmarked territory. There are no ultimate reference points in which we may train our "moral sextants" to find out where we are and where we ought to be headed. In education it would not appear morally sound for a teacher to rebuke a child for being too "Buddhistic," that is, too contemplative and withdrawn. Likewise, a teacher should not reward a child for being gregarious and outgoing in manifestations of cooperation, helpfulness, and getting along well with others. For who is to stand in judgment and say that the Buddhistic, "away-from-others" individual is not to be preferred to the Promethean or Dionysian, "toward-others" creature so prevalent in America today? The American people, to be sure, eschew "Buddhistic" tendencies, but there is no final method by which we can say we are morally right in doing so.

On the other hand, teachers are not genuine guides to the young unless they assist their students in developing a sense of values. This means that choices must be made somehow, somewhere. And the classroom is the place where the teacher has some jurisdiction over the quality of such choices. Hence it is in the classroom that the teacher must somehow make a selection among competing life patterns and proceed to recommend a given pattern for adoption by his or her students. The fact that, beyond social convention, there is no Supreme Court of moral judgment is the very crux of the moral predicament of every educator.

MORALITY AND RELIGION

Of course, many say that there *is* a Supreme Court of morals: God. If we follow his way, our moral teaching will be anchored to something sure and right. In this view there is an Author of morals, to whose judgments we may refer.

It is common knowledge, of course, that one of the predominant concerns of organized religions has been this area of ethics. Perhaps more than any other single area of human life, that of ethics and right conduct has been taken over—almost monopolized—by organized religions as their special province of discourse and prescription. What theologians have seemed to say, thus, is that there is some inevitable and necessary connection between religious commitment and right conduct. So long as this connection is held to exist, then moral training cannot be effective outside the context of religion.

You may recognize that this theological position on morals bears close relationship to the absolutist position on morals spoken of in the section on "The good and the Good." If there is a God to prescribe our morals for us, certainly his prescriptions must be perfect, hence definable as *The*

Good.[10] In this line of thought, the educator's task is to locate God's Good and teach the young to follow it.

With the rise of the scientific, objective study of human behavior and value, there has developed an attendant skepticism of the notion of Absolute Good. If people value so many different things, and if competing conceptions of how life should be lived appear to be injudicable and hence impossible of collection under a single rubric of value, then how can we say that there is a single Good to which all other goods eventually refer? Especially is this question asked when theologians themselves differ on the nature of this Good, and when competing religions throughout the world prescribe variant programs for living the Good Life. Under these circumstances, the determination of the Good, let alone its successful propagation, is put in question.

At this stage the question may be raised whether this marriage between morals and religion is really necessary. Is there an ineluctable bond between one's views on conduct and one's views on the supernatural? Increasingly, the position has been taken that there is not. While the two deal with generally the same subject matter, and while they have historically been found together, there is no necessary connection, this position holds, between the moral question, "What should I do?" and the religious question, "Who is God?"

Hence, the question of right and wrong has been at least partially removed from religious jurisdictions, and secular methods have come to be applied to moral questions. It is not an altogether recent development, either. An age-old maxim like "Honesty is the best policy," while stemming from a Puritan tradition, is nevertheless wholly secular. In fact, it is downright pragmatic: Honesty is recommended not because it is morally right but because it is "the best policy"; that is, it works out.

In summary, then, it is becoming increasingly apparent that some moral questions—perhaps all, says the Experimentalist—can be resolved or at least examined outside the reach of supernatural considerations. *Moral* and *spiritual* values, it is held, are not the same thing, and therefore need not be treated together in the school. There can perhaps be a "division of labor," in which the secular school takes charge of the *moral* values and the various organized religions the *spiritual* values. The practice of "released time" (releasing children to their churches an hour each week for religious instruction) is, in effect, founded on this principle.

This whole question, as you can readily see, is at the center of a rather widespread controversy in American education; for there are many of the "inseparability-of-moral-and-spiritual-values" position who believe that the modern American school, so splendidly boastful of its secular character,

---

[10] It is important to note that the reverse connection does not necessarily follow. That is, the concept of "God" implies capital-G "Good," but the concept of an Absolute Good in the universe does not require a God to author or dispense it. Good could exist just as another existential feature of the cosmos, along with Mind, Cause, and Essence.

has thrown out not only God but good as well. That is, even if morals can be taught without religion, the secular American school is simply not doing it. These people remain to be convinced of the position that the two are not indissolubly linked. The secularists, on the other hand, remain firm in their view of the ultimately secular nature of moral judgments. We shall wish to examine both of these competing positions in Chapter 9.

There are, admittedly, many other features of the "problem of conduct" that might be discussed here. What, for instance, is the role of the "will" in moral judgment? This raises the issue of the will itself, whether it is genuinely free or whether all our behavior is in some sense "caused." If human behavior is thought of as a "natural phenomenon" and if it is stipulated that "all natural phenomena are caused," then there seems no escape from the view that our moral judgments are quite as circumstantially dictated as water running downhill. On the other hand, we all have an inner sense of freedom of action. We think we can arbitrarily and "causelessly" make things happen. Hence, even if we are not existentially free, we live our lives *as if* we were. And, when you come right down to it, what is the practical difference between these two?

Other matters as well might concern us. The problem of morals is virtually endless in scope. But the function of this chapter is not so much to analyze questions as merely to raise them as a prelude to the systematic treatment of the value question in Chapter 9. We pass on now to a brief look at the question of aesthetics before taking up the separate axiological theories.

Aesthetics: The Question of Enjoyment

Taste

At the very outset it must be stated that the problem of aesthetics is here put in a slightly unorthodox way. The word *enjoyment,* rather than the more familiar and orthodox word *beauty,* has been designated as the theme for this discussion, because of its more universal connotations.

There is unfortunately a kind of snobbish cultism often surrounding discussions of aesthetics that tends to take art away from the ordinary citizen. But all those who find beauty in their lives, who want to increase its presence in their experience, eventually want to develop some kind of judgment for what they like (aesthetics) as well as for what they know (epistemology) and for what they believe to be right conduct (ethics). That is to say, aesthetics is just as human and prosaically oriented an area of discourse as any other in philosophy. It treats of how ordinary human beings respond to their world. And since the word *enjoyment* seems to provide more ready access to this idea than the somewhat more specialized word *beauty,* we choose to use it here.

While ethics centers about the question, "What should I *do?*" aesthetics centers about the question, "What should I *like*?" In formal language, we usually speak of this as "taste." What tastes does a person exhibit by making aesthetic selections throughout every day? What do we appreciate and favor in what we see, hear, touch, smell, and taste? What, in short, do we *like* in life? This is, to begin with, the widest and most generalized meaning of aesthetics as it is to be discussed here.

This should not signify that all things that people like, from peanut brittle to Gauguin, must be taken up and examined. It is only to say that all things that people like represent the ground for our discussion. And since some things *ought* to be liked more than others—just as in ethics some conduct *ought to be valued* over other conduct—we are confronted with the aesthetic problem of singling out those things that people *ought* to like from the welter of things that they indeed *do* like. If people actually like what they ought to like, we say they have taste.

THE NATURE OF AESTHETIC EXPERIENCE

Taste, however, is a term that refers to the behavior of individuals as they confront alternative candidates for their enjoyment and appreciation. It is by what individuals *select* from the world of beauty that we measure their taste. What they surround themselves with, what they choose to experience, what they actively seek out to enjoy, is the measure by which we judge their taste. The question now before us is the nature and quality of these experiences of enjoyment that are selected and therefore become the attributes of taste. What are these experiences like? What features do they exhibit? What can we say of all of them, taken together?

In order to deal with these questions, we are here using the phrase "aesthetic experience" to refer to the "episode of enjoyment." Something takes place in aesthetics, something occurs in the individual who says, "That is beautiful." It is the business of aesthetics to get some kind of idea of what that "something" is and to make it occur increasingly in our lives. And, obviously, the educator's function is to make it occur, at increasingly sophisticated levels of response, in the lives of the young.

To explain our concern with "aesthetic experience" it is necessary to note that the primary problem in aesthetics has to do with what may be referred to as the *artificial production of beauty*: music, painting, dance, sculpture, architecture, poetry, literature. These are the standard and customary "arts." We know, of course, that there is beauty in nature and that response to it is possibly as variable as the response to man-made products of art. We shall wish to concern ourselves later with this natural mode of aesthetic experience. But for the moment our concern is with the artificial, man-made stimulants to aesthetic response.

One of the things that all the arts have in common is their appeal to the senses. Of the five senses, of course, sight and hearing predominate in the arts. But the question is legitimately raised whether the other three senses may be said to be capable of what is here designated as aesthetic experience. Is the enjoyment of a fine perfume an aesthetic experience? Is the tasting of exotic wine and delicate cuisine an aesthetic experience? And as far as the sense of touch—in some ways the bluntest of our senses —is concerned, is it possible to include a hot bath, a massage, a roller coaster ride, or the tactical sensation of a fine stroke at golf or tennis within the category of aesthetics?

And, more important, is the artificial production of these experiences an artistic activity? Is the perfume-maker an artist? Is the chef who prepares fine food for the gourmet engaged in aesthetic production? Is the masseur or the roller coaster engineer classifiable as an artist? None of these questions has an easy answer, for the line between a truly aesthetic experience and a merely sensory experience has never been accurately drawn.

The confusion becomes perhaps even more troublesome in the other branch of aesthetics, the nonartificial or natural realm of enjoyment. We are all familiar, of course, with the intense response we have to certain sensory experiences in nature—to a striking sunset, to a special bit of scenery, to the sound of a bird on wing, to the smell of flowers in the field, to the taste of wild blackberries, to the feel of warm sunshine or cool water. And again, concerning our sense of touch, where are we to place the ultimate in tactical sensations—sexual play and intercourse? Is sexual orgasm an aesthetic experience?

Of course, sex is so confounded with other, extra-aesthetic factors that it is a wonder we can even raise the question at all. Perhaps by its very intensity it has ruled itself out of aesthetic consideration. People have feared the sexual drive so much that they could not admit they valued it. They have been so terrified of its power that they could not see its legitimate place in the scheme of human desires. Even to this day, virtually the entire legal discussion of what is *obscene* is confined to the narrow subject of human sex. But the overpowering presence of sex in our lives cannot be denied; no other experience can come close to it. It was not with facetiousness that Hemingway had his characters declare that "the earth moved." Certainly no sunset has been capable of this.

What we mean to suggest here is that every axiological theory must somehow stake out the areas of discussion before proceeding with value analysis. Since aesthetics is the study of the "beauty dimension" of life, we must not arbitrarily restrict the *enjoyment* of beauty (here employed as the central principle) to the standard categories of traditional upperclass taste, unless of course we are willing to rationalize such a restriction with some axiological principle. To use a few examples, opera, symphonic music, ballet, poetry, painting, and sculpture are not the only things of beauty in the world. To consider them so is to render aesthetics a recondite genteel subject matter accessible only to a restricted elite. It is also to remove art from the experienced world. As Ralph Barton Perry has so pithily put it:

It is a common and not unjustified complaint that the esthetic interest which was once associated with every form of utility and with the common experience of common men, has through the obsession of its devotees lost its proper place in life, at a loss both to itself and to the life from which it has been abstracted. Celibacy, here as elsewhere, may purchase concentration at the cost of barrenness.[11]

On the contrary, we must affirm that aesthetics is just as much every person's subject matter as ethics or politics. Especially is this admonition aptly pointed at educators, for if they claim to be in the business of educating *all* American youth, then they must not turn away from aesthetics merely because historically we have allowed it to become the private plaything of aesthetes.

ART FOR ART'S SAKE

This brings us to a couple of seemingly incompatible dimensions of aesthetic experience, namely art (its production and enjoyment) for its own sake versus art as a means to other experiences. This may at first seem to be a rather needless puzzle to get into. Perhaps it is. But it nevertheless stands at the bottom of much educational controversy today, and an understanding of it may help our thinking.

In the section on epistemology we saw that some philosophies hold truth to be independent of human beings and their affairs and that people come to know it for its own sake, simply because they want to know. In contrast, other philosophies, most notably Experimentalism, hold that truth always comes to be known in a circumstance of *use*. That is, we learn things when we need to learn them and, in this sense, truth is never to be considered or sought after solely for its own sake but always in terms of its function or use in some affair of life.

In the aesthetic sphere there is the same sort of dispute. Some philosophies consider values to be existentially equivalent to knowledge and truth, namely, independent of human beings, an *a priori* feature of the cosmos, embedded and woven into the very texture of reality. People come to have values when they discern them in the world and adopt them. Most particularly for our case here, they come to have certain appreciations and likings because those preferences are somehow authenticated and confirmed in the real world. The paintings on the ceiling of the Sistine Chapel seem timeless in their appeal because they evoke a universal sense of the cosmos in the beholder. Handel's *Messiah* is treasured because Handel testified that, as he was composing it, he saw "the Great God Himself," and his listeners seem to see him too.

From this point of view, art must be considered an end in itself. A career in art is to be pursued for the intrinsic enjoyment there may be in simply painting pictures or arranging sounds or making graceful move-

[11] *Realms of Value* (Cambridge: Harvard University Press, 1954), p. 325.

ments. There is no motive to sell anything or to improve the beholder's morale or state of mind. In fact, in the purest sense, there is not even the motive to arouse others. There is only the motive to create beauty and communicate it, whether others agree or not. The art collector, the connoisseur, the critic—as consumers, rather than producers, of art—engage in their activities not for gain or prestige or fame but for the intrinsic joy of engaging in aesthetic experience for its own sake.

The art that is produced or consumed, according to this view, is not to be *used* for anything else, not to be the means to any end or object outside itself. This is what we mean when we speak of some arts as being *fine* arts. They stand alone, unattached to any other interest. To refer to an earlier comment concerning the catholicity of art, this view would hold that the chef, the dress designer, or the architect can never achieve membership in the fraternity of the fine arts because they work their art on a basically useful object. The *fine* arts are, in an absolute sense, unnecessary. That is, they are not indispensable to the survival of humanity. But food, clothing, and shelter most certainly are. And any art worked upon such materials is "contaminated" by the principle of *use*, hence not *fine*.

In this tradition, then, the subject matter of aesthetics can be narrowed to consider just the fine arts. Of course, there are also aesthetic considerations in the so-called practical or applied arts. There is balance to be achieved in automobile design or in the facade of a skyscraper, there is a certain "poetry of motion" in athletes—baseball players, basketball players, pole vaulters—as they go about their games, there is a grace of line achieved by Parisian clothing designers. But in none of these cases is there a pure and solitary concern for the aesthetic in and for itself. Therefore, these arts, while important, are nevertheless secondary. Whatever aesthetic interests they provoke must be judged by criteria established in the primary or fine arts.

In terms of education the relevance of this view is obvious. A school orchestra will be held more valuable to the musical interests of the students than a school band because the latter is, in at least some measure, a means to a nonmusical end, namely, the emotional arousal of fans at a football game. Courses in the fine arts—sketching or water-color painting, say—will be held in higher place than projects in landscaping the school grounds, because the latter is tied to the prudential and practical interests of the physical school plant. In these and many other ways, as we shall point out in Chapter 10, the *"Ars gratia artis"* position bears upon educational policy.

Art for Our Sake

There is an alternate position, however, that may be intimated from the previous discussion. It considers art, in its most general connotation, to be an instrument for the elevation and improvement of human experience.

To speak of art as an "instrument," some say, is to demean art to a lower position, but this is claimed to be merely a vestigial residue of the classical position developed in the preceding section.

For if art is to be considered for its own sake alone, then there is a temptation to fence it off from the ordinary concerns of life. It is to imply that art is to be found only in art galleries and that artistic discussions cannot be legitimate in the things people do every day—in planning cities, in building houses, in designing and marketing a multitude of products all the way from paper clips to airliners. If aesthetic considerations are held irrelevant to these concerns, then we lose the whole sense and meaning of art in life, namely, the improvement of taste wherever it is capable of improvement.

Art, after all, like the Sabbath, was invented to serve people, and not the other way around. Therefore, if beauty is to enter our lives in increasing measure, say the "Instrumentalists," it must do so within the context of use. And to use art—to design graceful buildings, to shape our automobiles, to decorate our homes—is not to demean it but to ennoble it, for art becomes a human discipline when it can be made to enter into our lives in ever more meaningful ways. To hang a picture on a wall is to *use* it, in the best sense of the term. But if it does not create the desired mood, if it jangles when it should soothe, or if it soothes when it should jangle, depending on the context, then it must be replaced, no matter who the artist.

This general position, most closely associated with Experimentalism, will obviously call for a different approach to art in the school. It will value the learning of artistic concepts in the context of utility and function. It will concern itself with the aesthetic environment of the school itself, with its location, its architecture, its landscaping, its interiors, the colors on the walls, the design of the furniture—in short, it will seek to engage the total sensibilities of the learner. Even the good looks of the teacher will assume a new importance, for the looks of the teacher are not irrelevant to the learning morale of the child.

Aesthetics and the Relativity of Taste

We are confronted in aesthetics with the same difficulty encountered in morals, namely, the variability of what people like throughout all human societies. It is an implicit obligation of aestheticians and of educators in general to expose us to all the preferences people exhibit as a prelude to the study of what they *ought* to prefer. And, as they are practiced, the arts already are more international and intercultural than moral judgments or philosophic truths. This means, of course, that the universal subject matter of aesthetics is more readily accessible and more hospitably looked upon than other subject matters.

But this is not to say that the ultimate axiological question—what people *ought to like*—is any easier of resolution. For different cultures and civilizations are equally insistent that their aesthetic sensibilities are more noble and mature than those of their neighbors. What constitutes genuine nobility and maturity in aesthetic preferences is the kind of question, therefore, that various philosophies will wish to consider, and their ultimate purpose in this endeavor will be to recommend a "principle of evaluation" by which all human preferences can be not only understood but also judged and measured. It is this theme that will dominate the discussion in Chapter 9.

The Axiological Situation

All the attention we give to human valuing would be merely an "academic" question (in the narrowest sense of the term) if it were not for the fact that we live in an age some writers have described as one of moral crisis. The old patterns of conduct and choice increasingly seem to be not only irrelevant to the requirements of our time but outright obstructive to human purposes. It is not just a popular cliché that we live in a time when our beliefs are undergoing something on the order of a revolution. It is a fact.

It is in the political and ideological sphere that this revolution is most readily recognized. We seem to be passing, for instance, from an era of individualism, sometimes garnished with the adjective *rugged*, to an as yet undefined era of collective action. In America, particularly, the incentives to individual endeavor, hard work, and quality performance are gradually yielding to the incentives of group effort, organization, social adaptability, and human relations. We are passing, as some social analysts have explained, from the era of *production*, in which people have strained to work upon their physical world to reshape it more to their hearts' desire, to the era of *consumption*, in which people find that they have solved the "problem of production" and now turn their attention to the enjoyment of the world they have so mightily brought into being.

During the early years of World War II, as America girded for total military effort, the question was repeatedly asked: "Shall it be guns or butter?" To a nation in crisis this had the ring of a rather ominous question. But the historic irony of it was that, far from being ominous, it did not seem even to be relevant. For Americans, with their special brand of arrogant optimism, decided to have both. And they did! Having just emerged from a serious depression, we had no chance to realize that during those dark years we had developed a technological know-how which, for all practical purposes, had solved once and for all the problem of producing all the wealth, in both goods and services, that we required as a people. So fantastic was our production during the war years that we not only had both "guns" *and* "butter," but we supplied most of the free world with their requirements of both as well.

Indeed, we have succeeded so well at this in this country that we have not been able to "turn it off." Our technological skills and productive energies over the last two decades have been so great that we have been producing more than we can consume. The problem now is how to get rid of the stuff! And "getting rid of the stuff" is essentially a human problem of social organization, politicoeconomics, and psychological "soapboxing," that is, creating in people, through advertising, wants and needs they never realized they had! In short, the problem is manipulating demand to match the cornucopia of supply. The energy crisis is certain to change all this, but in what ways we are not yet sure. New energy technology may be part of the answer, but the major response to the crisis will be in the modification of human behavior and the change of our living habits.

The new importance of the social sciences in our public affairs, in our social criticism, and in our schools can be traced directly to this virtual "completion" of the technological revolution. Furthermore, as we have turned from the physical to the human world, we have had time to develop new sciences, the so-called sciences of human behavior: psychology, anthropology, social psychology, and psychiatry. "People" are now the problem. And the persistence of turmoil and strife in the world, the grinding, grueling legacy of hate and fear in Southeast Asia, the Middle East, and here at home should be enough to remind us that people shall remain the problem for some time to come.

But to say that people are the problem is to say that the values they live by is the central issue of our time. And this is the message of the axiologist: that, of all the branches of inquiry in philosophy, the inquiry into human values is the most urgent for modern peoples. If freedom seems so vulnerable a good in modern times, if human liberties can be so easily violated in an epoch of crisis, if plain human decency is something we must become self-conscious about and actively work for instead of merely assume and expect, then we can conclude nothing else but that something has gone wrong with the human world.

There are, of course, many dimensions to this crisis, some more strategic than others. Even on the domestic front we recognize a kind of disintegration of values. *Disintegration* is used here not in its sense of decay or degradation but in its technical, etymological meaning of "dis-integration," of a "coming apart," of taking apart our sense of life and putting it together anew in some humane way.

We are, to cite one illustration, passing to a new morality in the field of sexual conduct, certainly the most sensitive if not ultimately the most important sector of moral affairs. We are moving from a Victorian, puritanical prudishness, in which human animality has been considered a kind of embarrassment to be endured and where sex has been considered mean and dirty and evil, to a new and as yet unspecified libertarianism in which our animality is celebrated and glamorized in advertising and public life and in which sexual freedoms are increasingly considered positive signs of maturity in social behavior. The moral crisis, however, does not consist in a mere change of behavior; it consists, rather, in a widening gap between such behavior and the quasi-Victorian values still insisted upon by otherwise modern adults. The popularity of widely available literature on sexual performance and the surprisingly large demand for hard-core pornography somehow do not square with the daily newspaper's holier-than-thou editorials on obscenity, the police department's periodic crack-downs on X-rated movie houses, and the Supreme Court's high-minded rulings on public morals. These contradictions only confirm an already sensed truth that in this sphere we profess one thing and do another. To employ our earlier terminology, there is a frightening gap opening up between our "operative" (behavioral) values and our "conceived" (pro-fessed) values. Herein lies the true moral tragedy of our sexual predicament.

We are, to cite another example, passing from a morality of work to a morality of play. As Max Lerner has put it in his monumental *The American Civilization*, America is increasingly dedicating itself to "the morality of fun." This is only a specialized illustration of the previous observation that we are passing from an epoch of production to one of consumption. But when consumption becomes the central activity it brings with it a change in moral outlook. Adaptability to others holds precedence over self-direction. Gregariousness has now been lifted to a moral deter-minant. We are exhorted to "get along," to mix well, to join, to engage increasingly in the public and socialized dimension of life. Privacy is a new and somewhat suspect immorality. One is not supposed to prefer solitude in "the coffee-break culture." If Greta Garbo's "I vant to be alone" was a news item a generation ago, it is a fanaticism today.

On the other hand, there are symptoms of a growing disaffection with "socialization" and "adjustment" as the prime moral counters in modern life. The "organization man" is, it is true, a phenomenal invention of our time, and he does make for harmony and lubrication of the social machine —but at a price. The price is nothing less than the loss of his own soul. Business executives are shaped to the will of their corporations. Teachers are hired and fired on how well they "relate," rather than on how effec-tively they teach. And all of us bend to convention, in neighborhood and nation, in search of a more serene existence. But somehow serenity is not enough; beneath it all each of us yearns to be heard from. What we seem to need is a new individualism, a new statement of the authentic self, in a world of *others*. Just what form this new autonomy will take is, of course, very much an open question. The only thing we are reasonably sure of is that it will *not* be merely a retread of the "rugged individualism" of the nineteenth century. The point is simply that we have not found a suitable moral position in "organization" life. We may soon be moving on to something else.

Or, to cite a final instance, we seem to be passing to a kind of "structure-lessness" in aesthetic taste. Modern art has escaped from inherited form. There is an opening up of possibilities, a free, deliberately experimental scattering of drops and blobs on canvas. In modern music the older harmonies are eschewed and a new and unplotted region of discord and plain noise is being explored for tonal effect. In the field of poetry and writing, "nonsense" seems to have a beguiling kind of sense all its own; it can move, even if it cannot always explain. Finally, amidst this clatter of experiment, arises a primitivism in popular music that carries us back to the savage beat. Passion is heralded in ballads with wordless words, driven through loudspeakers at decibel levels never before reached, even in the thundering, ear-splitting din of the proverbial "boiler factory."

Revolt from established patterns seems to many people impious. But impiety is the nominal price we pay for human invention and creativity. We may not yet be ready to comprehend, much less appreciate, what the new arts are attempting to say. But there is no gainsaying the excitement found there. If excitement is prelude to idea, then something seems to be on its way.

There is, to be sure, a constant temptation to consider the new always a little outrageous. Oldsters ask constantly, and not a little plaintively, "What is the younger generation coming to?" And the young, unmindful of coming to anything in particular, shrug at such anguish. But the point is that as we raise our young today there are new and uncodified preferences increasingly making themselves available to us. Moral choice and aesthetic taste now swim in an ocean of possibilities. And axiologically we are in search of a rudder. But rudders are for pointing, and, without stars or landmarks to steer by, to have a rudder is not much better than having none.

It is to the consideration of the stars or the landmarks, whichever you may prefer, but at any rate to the question of what people "ought to ought" and "ought to like," that we now turn.

Questions

1. Take the "Ways to Live" preference test on pages 15–19 of Charles W. Morris's *Varieties of Human Value* (see Further Reading below). Then write out a defense of your selections. That is, explain why you think your selections are preferable to the other alternatives.

2. In what other areas beside sex is there a noticeable difference between people's "operative" and "conceived" values? In these spheres, which is closer to what you think people *ought* to value—their behavior or their professed beliefs? Why?

3. One of the implicit themes of this chapter has been the distinction between absolute and relative values. Another theme has been the distinction between art as end and art as means. What connection, if any, is there between these concepts? Explain.

4. Can a gas station be made architecturally aesthetic? How would you design one?

5. Make a list of the things you like in the field of the arts. Then make a list of what you think you *ought* to like in the arts. Is there a difference in the two lists? If so, explain the discrepancies. That is, explain why you think you should like the things that did not appear in the first list.

6. Make a list of things you like to do. (Consider it private and confidential.) How many of these activities were encouraged by your teachers? Should the school encourage all the activities you have listed?

Further Reading

Edman, Irwin. *Arts and the Man.* New York: W. W. Norton, 1939. In this warm and friendly essay Edman isolates the role of art in experience and its function in civilization. Then, in separate sections, he considers the literary, the plastic, and the musical arts, concluding with a discussion of art and philosophy. An interesting and readable introduction to the field of aesthetics.

Fletcher, Joseph. *Situation Ethics.* Philadelphia: Westminster, 1966. After describing three approaches to ethical considerations and some presuppositions necessary to his argument, Fletcher proceeds to limn the outlines of an ethic whose only permanent mooring, and this a fragile one, is *love*. Otherwise, all ethics is an examination of each individual situation we find ourselves in and the tracing of each hypothetical response to that situation to see what its total consequences would be. Only then, says Fletcher, can we determine what is good to do.

Macquarrie, John. *Three Issues in Ethics.* New York: Harper & Row, 1970. In this discussion, oriented to a theological underpinning, the author approaches ethics by rethinking natural law, conscience, sin, and grace.

Morris, Charles W. *Varieties of Human Value.* Chicago: University of Chicago Press, 1956. In this sequel to his previous *Paths of Life,* Morris considers the possibility of applying the scientific method to the study of values. Having isolated thirteen relatively distinct and discrete "ways to live," he analyzes the social, psychological, and biological determinants of value from questionnaires administered to hundreds of individuals throughout the world.

Parker, DeWitt H. *The Philosophy of Value.* Ann Arbor: University of Michigan Press, 1957. In this posthumously published book Parker considers rival theories of value and then the expression, analysis, organization, and evaluation of values. His first chapter, on "The Definition of Value," which poses the seemingly simple but actually complex problem of human preference, is a provocative opener for the study of axiology.

Perry, Ralph Barton. *Realms of Value.* Cambridge: Harvard University Press, 1954. This is a monumental sequel to Perry's earlier volume, *General Theory of Value.* Having defined *value* as relating to the "interests" of human beings, he proceeds to work through the implications of this definition in social organization, cultural science, conscience, politics, law, economics, science, art, history, education, and religion. Chapter 1, on the definition of value, Chapter 6, on the moral theory, and Chapter 18, on aesthetics, are the most relevant for the present chapter.

Peters, R. S. *Ethics and Education*. Chicago: Scott, Foresman, 1967. Peters, as one of the contemporary leaders in the analytic movement, here turns the analytic instrument on ethics and value, eventually coming up with "a positive theory of justification" for our actions.

Rader, Melvin M., ed. *A Modern Book of Esthetics*, rev. ed. New York. Henry Holt, 1952. In this splendid anthology Rader has brought together some of the best statements of students of aesthetics. In his own editorial Introduction, which would be of the most immediate help, he attempts a definition of art. Then he considers four alternative approaches to art that provide the context of the several selections, and finally takes up "meaning and truth" in the arts and "isolationist and contextualist theories" in aesthetics. The remainder of the book, a treasury of different expert views on aesthetic theory, may profitably be referred to in connection with Chapter 9.

Comparative Axiologies

Axiology and Philosophical Theory

VALUING AND THE THEORY OF REALITY

At the outset of Part Three on Epistemology, we took time to explore the connections between metaphysical theory, discussed in Part Two, and the theories of knowing about to be brought under discussion. The burden of this discourse was simply that to hold a theory of reality is, in itself, to say something about the knowing process, if no more than to set the limits of knowing or to prescribe the "ground" in which knowing is to be carried on. That is to say, a metaphysical position suggests, even if it does not insist upon, a particular approach to epistemological matters. And the kind or kinds of knowing that are considered worthy of examination are in a measure the "products" of—that is, the kinds of knowing made possible by—a particular metaphysical theory. Later in this discussion, in Chapter 5, we brought the argument full circle by noting the fact that one's metaphysics, in turn, depends on one's epistemology. That is, what one says about reality is true only by virtue of a previously stipulated theory of how truth is found out and uttered. In these reciprocal ways there is an intimate logical and psychological relationship between metaphysical and epistemological theory.

The same relationship, generally speaking, prevails between metaphysics and value theory. The fundamental question in ethics, as we have said, is, What ought I to ought? Now, if our metaphysical position has already been set out and delineated, there is every reason to believe that this position will implicitly favor some courses of action over others. For an immediate example, Idealists are likely to consider the "life of the mind," the life lived in books and with ideas, to be a *higher*, a *better* kind of life to live than other kinds. Experimentalists are likely to consider "sharing with others" to be *good* by virtue of the metaphysical and epistemological position they have chosen for themselves. Thus, what they say about the reality they consider themselves to be inhabiting is suggestive of what they find in it to merit and consider worthy.

In like manner, one's metaphysics makes some implicit prescriptions concerning aesthetics. If the central question is, What ought I to like? then the character and quality of one's world—as set out in one's metaphysical position—provide the ground for what is to be enjoyed. In this office, a metaphysics "sets the tone," one might say, for the identification of beauty and the enjoyment of beauty. If, let us say, we hold with the Realist to a mechanistic metaphysics, in which the world is a giant machine, we are likely to appreciate and enjoy works of art that exhibit the principles of order, balance, and thought-out design, whereas if our metaphysics consists in an undefined, open-ended, essence-less condition of existing, as in Existentialism, it is probable that enjoyment will be had in arts of a more irregular, self-expressionist character. In both ethics and aesthetics, then, there is a kinship between our estimate of ultimate reality and our judgment of what we find in it to value.

There is another consideration, also found analogically in our previous discussions of metaphysics and epistemology, that may occasion more trouble. This is the notion that the linkage between our reality and our values is one of necessity, rather than the more incidental relationship suggested in the previous paragraphs. As in epistemology, some philosophies hold that there is a moral dimension to the cosmos that has ultimate sanction over us. That is, there is a "capital-G" Good (like the "capital-T" Truth) that may be said to inhabit reality absolutely and that therefore prescribes certain values for people to hold everywhere and always. The business of the axiologist, according to these outlooks, is to determine in detail what this Good consists in and what it prescribes. Then the educator can get busy helping young people learn the prescriptions and adjust their behavior to them. Generally speaking, our first three philosophies tend in this direction. In one way or another, Idealism, Realism, and Neo-Thomism all hold to the possibility of locating, defining, and applying values that the cosmos contains irrespective of the wishes or purposes of human beings.

Our other two philosophies, however, take quite a different view of the matter. Values are "man-made." Like truth, say the Experimentalist and the Existentialist, values are what people say they are—in Experimentalism through an examination of consequences, in Existentialism through choice. Our attention to metaphysics, they say, is justified primarily because our metaphysics, too, is "man-made." Furthermore, in the matter of values, especially in ethics, we cannot look outside ourselves for moral prescriptions, because to do so is to eliminate the possibility of choice. And without choice between competing courses of action, in either "What should I do?" or "What should I like?," there can be no genuine *valuing*.

As was mentioned in Footnote 5 of Chapter 8 (see page 210), I cannot simultaneously say that something is forced on me and that I freely choose to prefer (value) it. That would be a contradiction.

Thus Experimentalism and Existentialism never consider legitimate the questions, What *must* I do? What *must* I like? Such questions remove the logical ground on which all axiology stands.

The question of whether values are "cosmos-made" or "man-made" is a troublesome one. It is raised here not for explication but, rather, to show that on this issue our five theories may be said to divide into two camps. But there is a puzzling irony to the whole issue: Which side one takes in the argument is a matter of preference; the choice an individual makes at this juncture is itself a value judgment! It represents the way one *wants* to think about the world.

This brings us to our final note on metaphysics and axiology, which is, briefly, that our metaphysical outlooks depend ultimately upon our axiologies, for our outlooks are ultimately statements of what we prefer to think the cosmos is like. This may appear an inconsequential point, but not so. For every metaphysics—with the possible exception of Existentialism—arrives at a view of the cosmos that shows it hospitable to humanity. That is, almost every philosophy so far concocted by human beings has found itself, at the end of its investigations, possessed of a view of the cosmos that makes human life and human purposing possible and that, moreover, provides a certain measure of assistance in the human undertaking.

To put it in more homely language, we can say that every philosophy, except possibly Existentialism, holds that the cosmos is "on our side." Idealism posits a realm of ultimates that give us guidance. Realism posits a rational and ordered nature that provides direction. Neo-Thomism gives us Absolute Truth or God to "hold the lamp" and point the way. Even Experimentalism posits a hospitable reality, a reality that supports the scientific method: problems do, after all, get solved. In this minimum sense, the cosmos is "on our side," in that it makes scientific hypothesizing something more than just idle fantasying and renders scientific experimentation a worthwhile pursuit. In short, it makes problem solving possible.

Not only possible, but *probable* as well. Our latter-day creation of a "problem-solving" labor force—research scientists and investigators—is final proof that we believe deliberate problem solving, intentionally undertaken and consciously institutionalized in research centers, will probably and very likely lead to solutions. And by this institutionalization of problem solving we reveal a new trust in our environment, a trust that reality will yield to human intelligence.

And this trust, at bottom, is a value judgment! It is something we choose to believe—an "article of faith," if the Experimentalist will pardon the expression. And, therefore, all metaphysics (at least the traditional ones) finally boil down to a preferential "leaning" in this direction or that, to a *desired* view of the world that we want very much to be the metaphysical case if, as, or when all the data are eventually brought in.

The point of all this is simply that the idea of the cosmos being "on our side" may tell us more about ourselves than it does about the cosmos. There is really no certain warrant for believing it to be true: we should all, therefore, be a little more cautious of what our metaphysics proclaim— for oftentimes our axiologies are "showing." Not that there is necessarily anything wrong with our axiologies; but we should be awake to the possibility that, metaphysically speaking, we may be permitting "the wish to be father to the thought," and, hence, subconsciously saying that our wishes and preferences are prior to and therefore more metaphysically real, more existentially authentic, than the reality we are presumably speaking of.

Valuing and Knowing

We also, in Part Three, examined the particular function of epistemology as it relates to the ordinary business of living and the specialized business of educating. At that point we saw that the criticism of our knowledge, the checking and rechecking of what we think to be true, is the continuous task of epistemology. In this connection we likened the school to a retail establishment, in which we were pleased to authenticate the knowledge "on the shelf" before retailing it to the young. This metaphor, as was pointed out in another setting in Chapter 8, applies also to value theory. For we are obviously concerned to test and judge the values "on the shelf" of the school before transmitting them to the young. The following five axiological theories are, of course, quite different, but they each provide a procedure by which we may check our values and test our preferences for adequacy.

There was with epistemology, and there is with axiology, however, a more practical consideration. We commented in Chapter 5 that a theory of knowing can give direct assistance to the theory of education, because knowing is the principal activity in which a school child is engaged. Therefore, how human beings, in general, know is thought to have some bearing upon how boys and girls know. The same is true in axiology. For if knowing is the principal activity of youngsters in school, then valuing is certainly the next most important thing they do. And if this is so, then a theory of value may be expected to bear directly upon an educational theory of valuing on the part of the child.

We cannot, at this point, show this intimate connection. That is the business of Chapter 10. It is mentioned here only to remind you that as you study the five axiologies to follow you should be anticipating Chapter 10 by surmising how these axiologies would go about the value training— sometimes called the "character-building"—of the child.

Before we move on, a brief procedural note. When we discussed comparative epistemologies in Chapter 6, the method was to recall the metaphysical theory of each position and then develop its corresponding theory of knowing. We repeat this procedure here, but this time only very casually. By this time in this book you should be able to do some of your own "back thinking." Procedurally, it is not very difficult. All you are invited to do is to refer to the appropriate sections of Chapter 3, "Comparative Metaphysics," as background to the understanding and comprehension of the axiologies to follow.

You may wish to refer to the appropriate sections of Chapter 6, "Comparative Epistemologies," as well. This is said in anticipation of your discovery of a similarity between epistemological procedures and axiological procedures. Because they are both procedures for the attainment and authentication of some object—in the one case, a truth, in the other, a preference—you should not be too surprised to find a certain consonance of method in the two spheres. This, as you are intended to see in the remainder of the chapter, turns out to be the case.

Idealism

The Idealist's reality is Absolute Mind inhabiting the cosmos. Epistemologically, the business of knowing is the approximation of this Mind through the absorption of ideas and the "enlargement" of the microcosmic mind in increasing imitation of the Absolute Mind through symbolic learning. This Absolute Mind of which we partake may also be thought of as an Absolute Self; it is on the order of a human being extended to the limits of perfectibility in every conceivable direction, a human person—a personality—magnified to infinity and written across the reach of all existence.

Ethics: The Imitation of the Absolute Self

If we may use the metaphor of the Infinite Person, we are immediately put in touch with the Idealist's notion of how the value question is handled. For if our individual selfhoods do somehow participate in an Ultimate Selfhood, and if we consider ourselves "morally oriented," that is, capable of seeking and doing right, then by extension we can say that the Ultimate Selfhood, or Infinite Person, contains this same capability absolutely and with none of the doubts and uncertainties of ordinary human beings.[1]

---

[1] We have already commented on the bias to rule out doubt and uncertainty as basically not a part of reality. Experimentalists have never been able to figure out why all the meaner and uglier qualities of human beings do not have *their* infinity as well. Why, they ask, is infinity always toward Good and not toward Evil? Infinity is, after all, a mathematical notion that goes down as well as up. The only attempt at the "Infinity of Evil" is the Puritan's Satan, who to put it mildly does not figure very largely in modern thinking.

The Infinite Person contains the ethical directions we are looking for, in somewhat the same way that the Absolute Mind is thinking the ultimate ideas that constitute reality.

So, then, our axiological task is set out for us: We must go in search of the Infinite Person and the moral prescriptions contained therein. One of the ways to initiate this search is to proceed from individual persons to the study of *groups* of persons. That is, a group of human beings, each individually making moral decisions, but acting in concert for a larger end, will reveal a larger "personhood" and hence a larger and more dependable morality. It is as if we could find a larger "selfhood" inhabiting a community of selves.

Many moralists and political writers of the Enlightenment worked this theme by insisting that there was a kind of "Popular Will" or "Sense of the Community" that expressed itself in history. In colonial Puritanism the chief magistrate was permitted to be absolute in power precisely *because* he was popularly elected. The will of the body politic, expressed through the ballot (of the landed only, to be sure), produced a larger selfhood, a new existential entity, the State. God works his will not through a monarch but through the individual, and when aggregates of God-driven individuals express their individual wills, they bring into being a larger, communal will that then, in the person of the magistrate, assumes absolute power over them.

In more benign, more democratic circumstances, the same principle may be said to hold. When people live freely together, an Idealist might contend, they gradually gravitate to a "group mind" on how they want to live. When this pattern of living is written down we call it law; when it remains unwritten we call it custom. In either case it is the expression of the "larger selfhood" of the group, whether the group be a street gang, a garden club, a labor union, a national society, or a whole civilization. And this "larger selfhood" represents a "way station" on the long axiological journey from an individual self to the Infinite Person.

But this method is really not very satisfactory, for we know that the "Popular Will" or "group mind" often changes; and the Idealist is looking for something much more steady and reliable. What we want is a rule of conduct that applies everywhere and always, one that can always recommend itself no matter what situation comes up and that, furthermore, is not too vague to be applied to concrete affairs of everyday.

A strong candidate for such a status is the famous Golden Rule: "Do unto others as you would have them do unto you." Although the rule is usually associated with Christian teachings, it is not a religious rule. On the contrary, it is wholly secular in spirit and content. And it appears to satisfy our conditions, that is, to apply in every circumstance. And, since it is "anchored" in the individual person who is hypothetically asking "What should I do?," there is no chance of misapplication. More mystically, it could be said to be the kind of thing that the Infinite Person might say.

It turns out, however, that this rule will not qualify. Precisely because it is "anchored" in the individual person, it produces an essentially selfish and egocentric value judgment. That is, I begin with my own selfhood. How do *I* want to be treated? What is the best for *me?* What is good for me, this rule says, is good for everybody!

Obviously, this is not much of a moral principle. Immanuel Kant was particularly distressed by it. "It cannot be a universal law," he said, "for it does not contain the basis of duties toward oneself; nor of the duties out of love for others; nor, finally, of the bounden duties to others (for many a person would gladly agree that others should not help him, if only he could be relieved of doing good to them)." [2]

Furthermore, it is doubtful if the rule really works. In international politics, for instance, we should very much like the Soviets to "do unto us" by ceasing and desisting in their efforts to extend their influence throughout the world. But if this were reversed to become our policy toward the Soviets, we should be expected to cease and desist in our efforts to extend freedom everywhere—certainly a questionable kind of surrender.

It is to Kant, as a matter of fact, that we may turn for the most authentic expression of the Idealist position. Kant insisted that in making moral choices we must separate ourselves absolutely from our individual selves and from the individual exercise of the will. Furthermore, we must remove ourselves from the empirical, that is, the day-to-day moral experiences we confront, to find what we are looking for. This is because ". . . examination of moral values does not depend upon the actions that one sees, but upon their inner principles, which one does not see." [3]

The empirical realm, which we can see, calls for what he called "hypothetical imperatives," or rules that apply to this or that circumstance to achieve this or that result. But the "inner principles" of all moral actions will lead us eventually to a "categorical imperative," or an imperative that not only serves in every circumstance but, moreover, serves to validate and authenticate our several "hypothetical" imperatives.

In keeping with the "microcosm-macrocosm" model of Idealist metaphysics, Kant makes the following comment:

> Now as we look back upon all attempts that have been made in the past to discover the principle of morality, we can see why they had to fail. They saw man bound by his duties to laws, but it never occurred to anyone to see that man is subject *only to his own* and yet to universal legislation, and that he is obligated to act only in accordance with his own will which, however, in view of the end of nature is a universally legislating will.[4]

This individual will carries on its "universal legislating" in what Kant called a "realm of ends," by which he meant "the systematic union of

[2] *The Fundamental Principles of the Metaphysic of Ethics*, trans. Otto Manthey-Zorn (New York: Appleton-Century, 1938), fn. p. 48. Quoted by permission of Appleton-Century-Crofts, Inc.

[3] Ibid., p. 22.

[4] Ibid., pp. 50–51. (Author's italics.)

different rational beings by means of common laws."[5] In this "realm of ends" were to be found the universal laws of conduct. And Kant's famed Categorical Imperative is, like most great ideas, really quite simple: *Act only on that maxim which will enable you at the same time to will that it be a universal law.*

So we come at last to an essentially straightforward ethic: Do unto others not as you would have them do unto you but as you would have all people do unto all other people in keeping with a universal law. It is our apprehension of the universal law, sometimes seen only darkly, that provides the assurance that we know the Good. In answer to critics of this Platonic, other-world doctrine of morality, Kant concludes his treatise:

> . . . the idea of a pure world of reasoning as a totality of all intelligences, to which we ourselves as rational beings belong (although we are at the same time members of the world of senses also), still remains a useful and proper idea for the purposes of a rational faith. Even though knowledge ends at the border of this idea, this faith still is useful to awaken in us a lively interest in the moral law by means of the splendid ideal of a universal realm of *ends in themselves* (of rational beings), of which we can be members only if we conduct ourselves painstakingly according to the maxims of freedom as if they were laws of nature.[6]

AESTHETICS: THE REFLECTION OF THE IDEAL

We may now abstract from this moral theory a companion aesthetic theory. In short, it is the search for the "idea" of the work of art. What is the ultimate and universal quality that a work of art is expressing? Here is the locus of the aesthetic criterion.

At the outset of our discussion of Idealism a linguistic distinction was made between the words *idea* and *ideal*. This was done to insure a purely intellectual and unemotional approach to metaphysics and epistemology. In both these branches of discourse it is more proper to speak of this school of thought as "Idea-ism."

In axiology, however, we are permitted the use of the word *Idealism* in its more literal sense, for in aesthetics *idea* and *ideal* are convertible expressions. Or, in other words, the aesthetic universals, which correspond to the moral and epistemological universals, may be thought of as whatever is *ideal* in life, in the common, everyday use of that word.

We also employ the common expression "to idealize" something. A portrait painter will remove the *real* blemishes from a face to render it more proximate to the ideal face. The sculptor will attempt to "capture" the true, or idealized, person in shaping a bust or statue of a leader.

Tchaikovsky romanticizes and idealizes the world of love, making it more pure and splendid than it really is. Anne Lindbergh in *A Gift from*

[5] Ibid., p. 51.
[6] Ibid., p. 83.

the Sea idealizes a loneliness at the seashore to find in the coils of various seashells the inner symbols for the meaning of life. The French nation proclaims with a monumental statue its great love and admiration for the American idea of liberty; and poet Emma Lazarus has this great lady say: "Give me your tired, your poor,/Your huddled masses yearning to breathe free,/The wretched refuse of your teeming shore,/Send these, the homeless, tempest-tost to me:/I lift my lamp beside the Golden Door." A finer testament to an idea—an idea that is true and good and beautiful—could hardly be imagined.

Turning to other quarters, an Idealist would say that photography cannot be considered a true art form because its business is to depict things the way they happen to be in our experience. But occasionally, says the Idealist, photography can, let us say in the hands of a "Karsh of Ottawa," arrest the inner person, can seize upon the true person in the flick of the shutter to reveal to us the true Churchill or Eisenhower or John Kennedy within![7]

The function of the artist is not to represent, literally "re-present," the world to our sensibilities, but to portray the world as the Infinite Person sees it, that is, in its perfect form. A work of art is recommended for our appreciation, and for the developing appreciation of the young as they grow in taste, in the degree to which it cuts through the imperfections and blemishes of the empirical world, through the crudity and ugliness and baseness of ordinary experience, to reveal true loveliness transcendent.

Realism

We may let a leading contemporary Realist summarize our prior discussion of Realist doctrine:

> Our "common sense" tells us, first, that we inhabit a world consisting of many things which are what they are, independent of any human opinions and desires; second, that by the use of reason we can know something about these things as they actually are; and third, that such knowledge is the safest guide to human action. . . .
>
> These basic beliefs of mankind are also the three basic doctrines of realistic philosophy: (1) There is a world of real existence which men have not made or constructed; (2) this real existence can be known by the human mind; and (3) such knowledge is the only reliable guide to human conduct, individual and social.[8]

These three doctrines correspond, of course, to the trio of philosophical

---

[7] In *Portraits of Greatness* (New York: Nelson, 1959), containing ninety-six of his most famous photographic portraits, Yousuf Karsh offers a most articulate Idealist sentiment: "[I am striving to reveal] an inward power . . . the mind and the soul behind the human face."

[8] John Wild, *Introduction to Realistic Philosophy* (New York: Harper, 1948), p. 6.

questions raised in this book: What is real? What is true? What is good? It is to the third of these questions that we now want the Realist's answer.

ETHICS: THE LAW OF NATURE

We are directed first of all to the natural world, which, being ultimately real and existential, is therefore the ground of value. To approach the problem of right and wrong by way of nature may strike you as none too promising. Nature, when we look at it out our front window, does not seem to have much value in it. It is just existentially *there* to be looked at and known. The burden of the argument, then, is quite clearly on the shoulders of the "naturalists."

But there really is no burden, they say. As a matter of fact, the call to nature is very much a part of our moral tradition. We say, "Just be yourself; be *natural*." By this we mean to suggest a *desired* and *preferred* pattern of action. To act *un*naturally is *not* to act well; an *un*natural person is usually considered someone to be avoided. He or she is phony, putting up a front. The phrase, "Doing what comes naturally," is not only an erotically suggestive title to a song, but a moral prescription covering the remainder of human affairs.

But we should not infer that to follow nature is pleasure-seeking hedonism. That was the mistake of the Puritans, who considered pleasure to be inherently evil. To follow nature is merely to abide by the conditions that nature sets—indeed, to conform to them. And conformity in this sense is the highest kind of virtue, for it is conformity to that which is existentially real and, therefore, existentially good.

Another way of getting at this notion is to speak of "natural law." We have used this phrase before, in Chapter 6, concerning the Realist's conception of truth. We may now speak of a nature-borne law of conduct that controls us quite as insistently and absolutely as does natural and ultimate truth. Natural law in ethical theory is usually called "moral law," and by this term we mean a law of right and wrong that is embedded in the very structure of nature. Nature contains not just laws of gravity, thermodynamics, energy, and metabolism—that is, laws of the behavior of completely material, subhuman entities; it contains laws of *human* behavior as well.

In speaking of *group* behavior, we can cite economic and political laws, like the oft-cited Law of Supply and Demand or Lord Acton's famous law of political life: "Power corrupts; absolute power corrupts absolutely." Likewise in *individual* behavior, says the Realist, there is a moral law intrinsic to the real, natural world that we must obey if we choose to be human beings. Injunctions against taking human life, lying, and cheating are the kinds of moral taboos that may go unwritten, even unspoken, in human societies; but they are nevertheless constantly operative in our lives, for they persist in time-space and exert their force on the conduct of all people in as immanent a way as the law of gravity. Furthermore, everyone *knows* these laws, whether we can utter them or not. We live "within" them, if not always "by" them.

We meet this kind of valuing explicitly in the Declaration of Independence, in which Jefferson wrote of people being "endowed . . . with certain inalienable rights . . ."—meaning that they live in a world that contains human rights just as really and existentially as it contains trees and muskrats and oceans. Human rights are "built in" to reality and cannot be alienated by some human beings against others. Hence, Jefferson went on, we have no alternative. We must fight! This is the way things are. We cannot be true to our own nature by tolerating this evil one moment longer. We are "victims," one might say, of a benign reality that *demands* that we fight! We can choose no other course. In this curious but powerful Enlightenment logic, Jefferson stirred the colonial heart to revolution.

In Chapter 6 we devoted a full section to the Realist's notion of "pure theory." Pure theory is the kind of truth that is sought solely for its own sake. It has no necessary utility in our lives. It is simply to be known, in and for itself. Sometimes, of course, purely theoretical concepts come to have application in human affairs, but that is not why they are sought. They are hunted for simply because human beings like to know what their world is and how it works; they like to *know*.

Now, pure theory in epistemology is the analogue of natural or moral law in ethical discourse. Moral law is that law of behavior which is beyond human utility, which is unconnected with our human interests or desires, and which consists merely in a statement of what the universe requires in the way of conduct. Moralists search for these laws for the same reason scholars search for truth: just to *know* them. These laws may have no immediate application, but because they are laws of the cosmos we desire to know and hold them for their own sake. If they are seen to apply to this or that circumstance, so much the better; we make use of them. But the first and primary business of ethics is to know and commit oneself to natural and moral value.

On first glance it may appear that the Realist's "moral law" coincides with Kant's Categorical Imperative. It comes extremely close, of course, but as things turn out the Realist will have none of it. Perhaps the best spokesman for this view is John Wild, leading contemporary apostle of the Realist cause. In his *Introduction to Realistic Philosophy*, he discusses "Subjective Alternatives to Natural Law," and in particular the famous Kantian dictum. Criticizing it first in terms of Kant's other doctrines, he asks how it is possible for Kant to believe simultaneously (1) that we *cannot* ever know anything as it really is in itself but only the way it appears and behaves in our experience[9] and (2) that we *can* know what is

---

[9] A central and primary feature of Kantian philosophy.

really good in itself, without qualification. If not one, why the other? asks Wild.

This is admittedly an internal doctrinal dispute and one that Kant unfortunately is not alive to answer. Of greater consequence is Wild's distress at the barrenness of the Categorical Imperative. It is so splendidly theoretical that it neglects to tell us how to act. "How," he says, "can any concrete, moral duties be deduced from a categorical imperative which contains nothing but the empty form of logical universality?" [10]

Take the case of lying, an illustration used frequently by Kant. Employing the Categorical Imperative, Kant suggests that one should not lie because one cannot simultaneously "will the universal law" to lie, that is, one cannot will that lying be a universally applied law of conduct. Wild asks, Why not? There is nothing to stop me; there is no *formal* reason preventing me from willing the universality of lying. What stops me from universalizing such a thing is my concrete observations of natural Man behaving in natural circumstance.

> Men are, as a matter of fact, rational beings, capable of learning from experience. They will soon detect a liar and distrust him. Hence it is easy to see that universal lying would bring forth universal distrust and render rational communication, and hence human life, impossible.[11]

So, Herr Kant, says Wild, your "will to universal law" is itself grounded in the plain and ordinary sensory perception had every day by ordinary people. Your Imperative, therefore, is no more categorical, or ultimate, than the categoricity or ultimacy of my observations. And since the ultimacy of my observations resides in nature, it is nature that contains what I am looking for.

In furtherance of this theme of concrete experience, Wild develops the companion idea that we learn our values by "conditioning," by voluntarily adopting prescribed and partially automatic behavior. Rejecting the clinical psychologists' mode of conditioning—what he lightly calls the "white rat theory" of conditioning—Wild says he prefers the model established by Aristotle, namely, the mode of conditioning conceived as the *cultivation of the intellectual and moral virtues.*

As a case in point, children are not born generous; but they are not born stingy either. "Our original nature is neutral in this as in all other specific moral respects." [12] But nature itself is not neutral. Nature calls for a pattern of action toward others that we can discern through social observation. The Law of Generosity (the proper balance between generosity and stinginess) is embedded in reality, and the conduct of human beings in

[10] Wild, *Realistic Philosophy*, p. 50.
[11] Ibid.
[12] Ibid., p. 72.

their natural behavior will reveal it to us. Once it is revealed, it is our task to condition the young to follow it, not like blindly led white rats in a cage but as human beings who freely adopt this pattern of action as they grow to see *why* it is good. Rats never can know "why"; human beings can. This is the difference. Virtue is found in the *rational comprehension of natural necessity*.

As a final exhibit of the Realists' penchant for materialist, naturalist analogues for their moral theory, we may cite William P. Montague's argument on "The Geometry of the Good Life," [13] which runs somewhat as follows: Good and bad are scattered through life in "amounts." Furthermore, individual "goods" and "bads" are distributed discontinuously, that is, in units and clumps that can be singled out for analysis and manipulation, just like geometric figures. The manipulation of clumps of good and bad is governed by "The Law of Increasing Returns." This law is the counterequivalent of the economic "Law of Diminishing Returns." In economics, returns legally diminish (in a natural kind of way, of course) with increasing concentration of effort. But in human values the situation is reversed; namely, each increment of input (concentration of effort) will yield geometrically compounded profits. A philanthropy of a million dollars concentrated among, say, twenty people will evoke a yield of good—happiness, gladness, joy, and so on—far greater than a million dollars "pulverized" down to a dime for each of 10,000,000 persons.[14]

So, says Montague, individual goods should be concentrated to maximize their yield. But since the same law holds with evil—tragedy, misfortune, pain, and so on—such "bads" should not be concentrated, but, rather, spread out evenly among the population by means of insurance, mutual assistance plans, and welfare legislation. In this way we weaken the social and individual impact of evil and at the same time fortify and accentuate the impact of good. And all this becomes possible when we recognize the essentially *natural* base of morals and attend to the laws governing human conduct in valuational situations.

AESTHETICS: THE REFLECTION OF NATURE

As with Idealism, we may now abstract and extrapolate from the above ethical theory a companion notion of aesthetics. Such a notion must be looked for, obviously, somewhere within the context of what the Realist understands by the word *nature*.

One of the things human beings like most about nature is its order—"a place for everything and everything in its place." The art in which

---

[13] *The Ways of Things* (New York: Prentice-Hall, 1940), Chapter 23.
[14] This illustration of Montague's is rather spurious, because it has nothing to do with the Law of Diminishing Returns; but it's interesting, anyway.

this kind of order can most immediately be perceived is music. Music has consistently been esteemed as a carefully organized, regulated, and ordered art form. Indeed, in classical thought, music, logic, and geometry were all closely related members of the Seven Liberal arts.[15] There is, moreover, a close similarity between the emotional reactions to a piece of music and to a difficult and involved mathematical problem successfully solved. We all have experienced this latter kind of rapture, which, according to Montague, is "not exactly sensuous yet very intense and bright." [16] With this analogue to work from, perhaps we might even say that music can be defined as mathematics rendered in sound. In this connection, Montague wonders, not altogether facetiously, whether the Binomial Theorem could be given a musical "incarnation," possibly comparable to the *Doxology*.[17]

Perhaps this is as far as we can carry the mathematical simile. The point is that aesthetic quality is the kind of thing that nature already contains, and it contains it in somewhat the same way that it contains algebraic symmetry and geometric pattern. Art, therefore, should attempt to approximate the order and regularity of nature in its expressions in color, sound, and movement. It should represent, in the literal sense of "re-presenting," or presenting anew, the rationality of nature as that rationality is revealed in pattern, balance, line, and form.

The George Washington Bridge is not just a means of getting across the Hudson River: it is a work of art. Without aiming principally at doing so, the engineers produced structural loveliness, a truly beautiful thing to behold; and they did it by submitting to natural laws and to what nature fundamentally requires.

In painting, the artistic endeavour should be to render faithfully what one sees in the world, to re-create it *realistically*, so as to accentuate *pattern* and *order* and *design*, whether in a seascape, a still life, or a portrait of a human face. Portraits are works of art when they reflect what truly is, rather than what ideally ought to be, for there is a real beauty in what truly is. For this reason photography definitely qualifies for aesthetic production, says the Realist. The camera can catch and hold moments when nature is splendidly triumphant—as it always ultimately is—over the gross and chaotic clumsiness of humanity.

Taking all these ideas together, we may say that the central Realist theme is "the celebration of the orderliness and rationality of nature." It is this continuing celebration that the Realist calls Art.

---

[15] Grammar, Rhetoric, and Logic (the Trivium) and Arithmetic, Geometry, Astronomy, and Music (the Quadrivium), a curriculum fixed and codified by Martianus Capella in the late fourth century A.D.

[16] Montague, *The Ways of Things*, p. 124.

[17] Ibid., p. 125. See also G. D. Birkhoff, *Aesthetic Measure* (Cambridge: Harvard University Press, 1933), for an elaborate and very serious theory on reducing art to mathematical formulas.

Neo-Thomism

In discussions of value it is really but a short step from Realism to Neo-Thomism. We have already seen, in Chapter 3, the common ancestry of both these views in Aristotle. In Chapter 6 this congruity of approach turned up again in the theories of knowing. We should not be too surprised, then, to recognize a kind of affinity of temper between the two schools in the consideration of the problem of value. For what the Realist sees to be the *natural* requirements of the axiological situation the Neo-Thomist sees, similarly, to be the *logical* requirements of that situation.

Thus, by way of review, the Neo-Thomist looks at the world as a *logical* system, to which the human intellect is "tuned" and oriented. In this logical system the monumental Principle of Potentiality-and-Actuality is seen to govern all being and change, whether it be applied (in Aristotelian terms) to Matter and Form or (in Thomistic terms) to Essence and Existence.

Out of this metaphysical model comes a second important principle, the Principle of the Hierarchy of Being, by which some things (existents, or beings) exercise the act of "to be" in greater degree than others. In a manner of speaking, some things *are* or *exist* more than others.

In epistemology the Principle of Potentiality-and-Actuality reappears as the explanation for our natural tendency *to know*, that is, the propensity of the intellect to actualize its inherent potentialities through the apprehension of ultimate truths. And the Principle of Hierarchy reappears as the ground for saying that there is a hierarchy of knowing: at the lowest level, scientific or synthetic knowing; at the next level, analytic or intuitive knowing; and at the third and highest level, mystical or revelatory knowing.

Now we must take these two ideas—Potentiality-Actuality and Hierarchy—to see how they apply to the value situation; for they clearly do apply, and, indeed, govern as supremely in ethics and aesthetics as in metaphysics and epistemology.

ETHICS: THE RATIONAL ACT

The first thing we must say is that goodness follows from reason. The good act is that which is controlled by our rational faculty. In keeping with classical Greek thinking, the Neo-Thomist believes that ignorance is the source and core of evil. If people do not *know* what is right, they cannot be expected to *do* what is right, except by accident or chance. On the other hand, if people *do* know what is right, they can be held responsible for what they do. They may not always follow the right, but this will be due only to the fact that they have not been habituated to it. With the assistance of habituation, human beings may both *know* and *do* right.

All this is built upon an essentially benign theory of human poten- tiality. In applying the first of our two ideas, the Potentiality-Actuality doctrine, the Neo-Thomist affirms that people *naturally tend toward the good*. Just as, in the case of knowledge, people *naturally tend to know* (see the discussion on the quotation from Adler in Chapter 6, page 138), so do they naturally tend toward goodness. To be sure, this does not mean that all human beings are good, any more than all acorns are destined to become oak trees. It means only that everyone inclines toward good, just as acorns incline toward becoming oak trees. Human beings are, to use a homely expression, "given to" that sort of thing, and given to it by their very natures.

Therefore, the axiological enterprise, as the Neo-Thomist sees it, can be begun without any special prompting or stimulus because it is initi- ated and carried on under the general aegis of nature, that is, it is founded in a natural tendency. As in the case of knowing, people *cooperate* with nature in the achievement of moral values.

The simile is vastly imperfect, but the moral enterprise is something like paddling a canoe downstream. Forward direction is already a "given," a prior and assumed condition of the paddling. Man's task is to watch where he is going, avoid shoals and hazards (both natural temptations and "man-made" diversions), and contribute to the forward motion of the canoe by paddling (training himself in good habits), so as to hasten and expedite the achievement of what would eventuate in any case but not so promptly or economically, namely, the terminus of the canoe trip, or, meta- phorically, the desired moral end.

The pilot in charge of this expedition is the human will. The will is a companion instrument to the intellect, in Neo-Thomist thinking, and, although it must always be held subservient to the intellect (since the true essence of Man is reason), it must, like the intellect, be trained and developed by special instruction. By "special instruction" is meant the habituation of the will to virtue, that is, to good habits. And since the formation of good habits is nothing more nor less than the perfecting of the will's own powers—what we commonly call "will power"—we may say that the moral enterprise boils down, essentially, to the business of bringing to perfected actuality, through the agency of moral virtue (that is, the forming of good habits), the incipient and potential capacities and tendencies of the human will.

The central problem here, of course, is to determine what constitutes a "good," as against a "bad," habit. But this is easily taken care of by noting our prior requirement that the will must be subservient to the reason. As Adler puts it:

> In the case of every human power, other than the intellect itself, the natural tendency of the power is toward that actualization of itself which conforms to reason. This follows from the subordination of all human powers, in their exercised act, to reason itself. Hence, in the case of every

power there is a natural tendency which habit can violate or to which it can conform; and in conforming, the habit is good; in violating, it is bad.[18, 19]

Thus we have in hand a ready and workable criterion for conduct, both habituated and unhabituated, namely: Does it advance the power of reason or does it fulfill the requirements of reason in the lives of human beings?

Now, it is a commonplace that most people do not always do right even when they know what they ought to do. But the test of true character in Thomist thinking is not what people do but what they know in their reason they ought to do, the "conceived values" referred to on p. 205. It is on this count that Ecclesiastical Thomists in the Roman Catholic church are willing to cleanse individuals of sin at confession if the penitents honestly and sincerely demonstrate that their intentions were other than what their overt behavior turned out to be. That is, there are occasions in which our overt behavior slips loose from the moorings of reason and is led instead by undisciplined emotion—which is another way of saying that the will temporarily breaks away from its subservience to the reason and runs wild on its own. When reason reclaims will—when conscience feels the twinges of guilt—then it is time to confess.

If a man does not know any better, if he does not know his actions were wrong, he obviously cannot be held morally responsible for them. But if he *does* know better, that is, if he knows his actions were wrong, then he *can* be held responsible—unless it can be shown that he was not in rational control of himself at the moment he entered into those actions. In such fashion the Neo-Thomist explains the moral situation of the individual.

---

18 Mortimer J. Adler, "In Defense of the Philosophy of Education," Chapter 5 in *Philosophies of Education*, Forty-first Yearbook of the National Society for the Study of Education, ed. N. B. Henry, Part I (Chicago: the Society, 1942), p. 243.

19 There is a kind of nagging and bothersome circularity to statements like this, not alone from Adler but from other Aristotelian Thomists as well, and it is difficult to resist the temptation to remark on it.

Every human being, we are told, is equipped with a set of natural powers that tend to actualize themselves in conformity with reason. And reason is itself a natural power said to actualize itself in terms of itself. A habit is good to get into, then, if it helps to actualize either the power of reason or any of the other powers seeking fulfillment in terms of reason.

Now let us say that a human being is equipped with the power, i.e., the perfectible potentiality, of steadfastness and persistence; this is a reasonable and *reason*-able type of power. Now if we were to actualize the full potential of such a power by habituation, we would wind up with stubbornness and a closed mind. When does the tendency toward rational steadfastness veer off into irrational stubbornness?

Or take some other illustrations:

Will not boldness and courage, good traits both, turn eventually, if heightened and improved, into recklessness? And what is rational about recklessness?

Will not the noble habit of suspending judgment, brought to full being in a person, turn into ignoble indecisiveness?

Will not the habit of charity, begun at home but actualized abroad to its fullest and most complete limit, turn into a senseless, self-imposed penury?

But all of this so far has served only to develop the inner psychology of morality. It is quite as important to attend to the ground of values itself, for it is in this ground—the ground of reason—that ultimate values are found. And the notion of ultimate values, values that are not contingent upon the whims or preferences of human beings, is as central to Neo-Thomism as it is to Idealism and Realism, if not more so. As it has been put by Willam McGucken, a spokesman for Ecclesiastical Neo-Thomism:

> There are certain human acts which are of their very nature good and deserving of praise, and therefore independent of all human law; other actions are of their very nature, that is, intrinsically, bad and deserving of blame.[20]

If it weren't for this objective moral "map" by which Man can measure his way, Man would be but a "weathercock, carried now in this direction, now in another, according as whim or the influence of his fellows or his environment is most prevalent."[21]

The general rule to follow, McGucken reminds us, is reason. But within reason there is a tripartite division of moral obligation. For one has duties (1) to oneself, (2) to fellow human beings, and (3) to God.

> He must so live his life that the higher part of him, the spiritual, be not made subordinate to the organic. Consequently, drunkenness is in itself evil, because it is not in conformity with man's rational nature, rather it places the soul and its powers in a subordinate position to the animal appetites. Secondly, he has duties to his fellow man. Certain of these duties are in conformity with his social nature, as a member of domestic society, the family; as a member of civil society; as a member of world society. Therefore, assisting one's neighbor, playing the good Samaritan, supporting one's children, and obeying parents are things good in themselves because in conformity with man's social nature. On the other hand, dishonesty, lying, stealing, and murder are intrinsically wrong because they run counter to man's social nature. Thirdly, man's contingent nature indicates clearly man's duties to God. Therefore blasphemy, irreverence toward God are things bad in themselves. Worship and service of God are good because in accord with the contingent nature of man. Suicide is an evil thing in itself because man, as a contingent being, has no dominion over his own life.[22]

We are now in a position to introduce our second strategic principle—the Principle of Hierarchy. For these three divisions of obligation, says McGucken, represent an ascending order of duty in moral choice.

> . . . there is a hierarchy of values. If there be a conflict between man's duties to God and to his neighbor, the inferior right must cede to the superior. First things come first. Charity is a good thing, but if giving away one's possessions means impoverishment of one's dependents, right

---

[20] "The Philosophy of Catholic Education," Chapter 6 in *Philosophies of Education*, Part I, p. 254.
[21] Ibid.
[22] Ibid., pp. 254–255.

order would show that this was not a good thing. Man's duties are first to his own household.[23]

We shall wish to comment on this moral theory in greater detail later, but for now it is enough to say that the Neo-Thomist answer to our question is clear. If the question is raised, "What should I do?" the answer should ring out loud and clear: "Let Reason reign." And it is fitting and proper to close on this note, for the exercise of reason, in and for itself, is considered by Neo-Thomists to be the highest good of all. Happiness as the ultimate moral condition of humanity can be reached, said Aristotle, not through the pursuit of instruments outside ourselves—money, power, fame. Genuine happiness, the highest good, can be ours only by actualizing our own inner nature. And, since reason is at the center of this nature, it is to the exercise of our own minds that we must repair to find the truly Good Life.

Aesthetics: Creative Intuition

It is not easy to abstract an aesthetic theory from the above moral theory. Such heavy stress on reason and the rational nature of the individual may appear to compromise the issue from the outset. We do not usually associate art with reason. Indeed, it is with the subservient faculties of will and emotion that we customarily connect the world of art. It is partly for this reason that Neo-Thomist aesthetics is considerably more difficult of lucid presentation than some of its other features.

Our first major concept is that of creativity. Aesthetics is concerned not with what is to be done, which is the sphere of ethics, but with what is to be made, or brought into being. We have already seen that people by nature tend toward knowledge and truth and also toward goodness. The surmise at this point would be that people naturally tend also toward the creation of beauty. This turns out to be the case:

> Creativity, or the power of engendering, does not belong only to material organisms, it is a mark and privilege of life in spiritual things also. . . . The intellect in us strives to engender. It is anxious to produce, not only the inner word, the concept, which remains inside us, but a work at once material and spiritual, like ourselves, and into which something of our soul overflows. Through a natural super-abundance the intellect tends to express and utter *outward*, it tends to sing, to manifest itself in a work.[24]

Now this creativity is manifested in two spheres: what we usually call the fine arts and the practical arts. The fine arts are those in which beauty is created for its own sake, "cleared," as Maritain remarks, "of all adventitious elements." This mode of art is, of course, the more noble, for "it is not extraneous to the intellect," as utilitarian art tends to be, but "one with

---

[23] Ibid.
[24] Jacques Maritain, *Creative Intuition in Art and Poetry*, Bollingen Series 35, No. 1 (New York: Pantheon Books, 1953), pp. 54–55.

the intellect." "For beauty, which is of no use, is radiant with intelligence and is as transcendental and infinite as the universe of the intellect." [25] Symphonies, paintings, and ballets, for instance, are superior to love songs, illustrations, and calisthenics because they are an attempt of the intellect to express itself outwardly into the sensory regions of experience, with no other recommendation than that they are pleasing to perceive.

But it is in the practical arts that most art originates. Here we are concerned with tools, ornaments, dwellings, clothing. Our creative tendencies are worked upon existent materials so as to combine utility with enjoyment. Here the work is partially extraneous to the intellect: hence inferior.

In either the fine or the practical arts, however, the intellect plays the ultimately decisive role, and true art is controlled by what the Neo-Thomist calls "creative intuition," a somewhat mystical, probing lurch of the intellect beyond itself in the direction of Being. In this lurch it appears to be trying to escape from itself, that is, art gives the appearance of trying to escape from reason, as in modern art and poetry. But in actuality the intellect is attempting to lay hold of its preconscious self, what Jacques Maritain describes as "intuitive reason." When it succeeds in this, modern art may be said to have achieved true aesthetic dimension. When it fails and wobbles around in nonsense or buffoonery, then obviously it cannot qualify.

Because the intellect is the ultimate producer of art, we must look to it to understand the manner in which we consume, that is, appreciate and judge, art. We do this through the agency of intelligence, which serves as the headquarters for the three essential constituents of art and which, therefore, provides us a firm set of criteria in aesthetic judgment. Maritain expresses it this way:

> Now, that which knows, in the full sense of this word, is intelligence. Intelligence, then, is the proper perceiving power, the sense, as it were, of the beautiful. If beauty delights the intellect, it is because it essentially means a certain excellence in the proportion of things to the intellect. Hence the three essential characteristics or integral elements traditionally recognized in beauty: *integrity*, because the intellect is pleased in fullness of Being; *proportion or consonance*, because the intellect is pleased in order and unity; and *radiance or clarity*, because the intellect is pleased in light, or in that which, emanating from things, causes intelligence to see.[26]

Experimentalism

Experimentalism, of all the philosophies considered in this book, has spent by far the most time and energy on the problem of value. The philosophies previously considered have concerned themselves principally

---

[25] Ibid.
[26] Ibid., p. 161.

with ontology and metaphysics, spinning out from those bases their associated doctrines in epistemology and ethics. For Experimentalism, however, it has been somewhat the other way around. As the philosophical historian Edward H. Reisner has written, the Experimentalist "has been indifferent to the problems of being or metaphysics and has confined his interests to the analysis and description of experience, particularly to the problems of knowing and conduct—to the conceptions of truth and goodness." [27]

We have already seen, in Part Three on Epistemology, how Experimentalism handles "truth." We now ask Experimentalists to discuss how they go about the business of "goodness."

In asking this, there may be some surprise at the Experimentalists' deep and loving interest in the question. How, one might ask, can so scientifically oriented a philosophy address itself systematically to value, the age-old "renegade" from science? Science can tell us what is true, but can it tell us anything about what is good? Science can give us knowledge, but can it tell us what we ought to do or what we ought to like? These are fair and appropriate questions, and answering them has become a central passion of Experimentalism because it is in the field of values—the prickliest and most troublesome of all areas—that a philosophy runs its ultimate test. If Experimentation can set forth a scientific value theory and "make it stick," then Experimentalism as a whole must be accounted a mature philosophy.

As Experimentalists have attempted to do this they have found the task far from easy; for the application of a scientific methodology to ethical and aesthetic questions is admittedly somewhat novel and unorthodox. Besides, they contend, it takes time to explain and defend it in comprehensible and acceptable terms to the ordinary citizen, who has been conditioned by something like 2,000 years of rationalistic, absolutistic system building and doctrinaire theological metaphysics.

ETHICS: THE PUBLIC TEST

As in our discussions of comparative metaphysics and epistemologies, we must recognize a sharp break in continuity between the traditional philosophies just covered and the newer members of the philosophical community. The first to venture a systematic break with the inherited ethical doctrines was Experimentalism; for it repudiates the whole thesis of the earlier points of view—the thesis that we must search for ultimate and changeless values in some reality outside of, beyond the control of, human beings. It makes no difference whether this objective realm of values is the nebulous "archive of moral universals" of Idealism, or the equally mystical "natural law" of Realism, or the immanent "reason," both beyond and within human beings, of Neo-Thomism. In adventuring into

[27] "Philosophy and Science in the Western World: A Historical Overview," Chapter 1 in *Philosophies of Education*, Part I, p. 30.

any of these regions to search for value, the Experimentalist contends, we misconstrue the whole point of our searching and wind up doing our exploring in the wrong place—that is, beyond the boundaries of experience, within which, after all, people do their valuing.

There is a kind of delusory aspect to all this adventuring, the Experimentalist continues, a hankering to concoct imaginary worlds where things are neater and nicer than here. It is a common temptation to become disgruntled at the way things go in this life, for so often we see our noble intentions come to nothing and a perverse destiny frustrate our hopes and cravings.

> Under such conditions, men take revenge, as it were, upon the alien and hostile environment by cultivating contempt for it, by giving it a bad name. They seek refuge and consolation within their own states of mind, their own imaginings and wishes, which they compliment by calling both more real and more ideal than the despised . . . world [they live in].[28]

This repair to other, morally nicer and neater worlds is nothing more, says the Experimentalist, than "a failure of nerve." We relinquish a certain amount of our human dignity when we cravenly slink off to put our lives and fortunes under the protection of an absolute. For once we do this we must give up thinking about our values. Absolutes are not inquirable. They cannot be questioned or looked into. They can only be obeyed.

But we are the constructors of our values, just as we are the constructors of our truth. The reason we can risk this construction on our own, without transcendental help, is simply that we test our value claims in experience and are modest, therefore, in what we say of our values, namely, that they are only tentative and temporary statements of what ought to be done. Furthermore, such statements are never to be considered universal. They always apply to this or that situation, insofar as the situation can be blocked out for ethical analysis.

To explain this, the Experimentalist reminds us that every ethical situation arises from a desire to improve some state of affairs. Every value judgment stems from a prior longing of some kind to rearrange in more desirable fashion a specific sector of experience (the Experimentalist's reality).

Hence, the question "What should I do?" can never be thought of as having come down out of the blue somewhere, that is, as an ultimate question. It must always be considered in some human context. If I ask "What should I do?" the only sensible answer is the familiar qualifying counter, "It all depends." It depends on what ends I have in view, on what circumstances I wish to have prevail in this corner of reality. What rearrangement of the situation would be an improvement on what I have at this moment? What results do I wish when I make up my mind and go ahead and do something? All these are antecedent questions to "What shall I do?"

---

[28] John Dewey, *Democracy and Education* (New York: Macmillan, 1916), p. 405.

It should be apparent that the famous Experimentalist "Doctrine of Consequences" finds splendid application at this point. For, just as in epistemology, the principle of "What works?" is also valid here. A good act, an ethical act, is measured by the results it yields. An ethical principle is measured by what happens when one acts on it: which is by way of saying that if a Kantian universal or a naturalistic moral law or a rationalistic dictum prescribes some course of action, people will *try it out* in their lives before really putting their stamp of approval on it. If such a prescription—absolute or otherwise—consistently leads to unwanted consequences, people will eventually get rid of it.

This has happened, too, in history. The "divine right" of kings was once considered an absolute truth, and absolute obedience to the king or magistrate was therefore an absolute good: It was what God expected of you. We finally got rid of this notion, not because God repealed it but because it did not yield the kind of life we wanted to live.

Divorce was once considered evil, the breaking of a divine covenant. We are changing our minds about this; our moral values are undergoing revision, and, again, not because some heavenly universal has been legislated out of existence but, rather, because human beings in their wisdom can see the concrete effects of alternative moral policies on the institution of marriage. And they gravitate to a policy that when acted upon leads to the most beneficent experiential results.

This attention to consequences is nothing more than the scientific method applied to ethical questions. As in epistemology, we are confronted with a situation that is indeterminate; that is, how it will come out depends on what actions we take. We "try out" various policies. And that policy which when acted upon yields desirable consequences we isolate and identify as an ethical principle, or a "good." We make no claims, in keeping with the scientific method, that we have found some "absolute." We simply say that, generally speaking, in situations like this the preferred course of action is such and such.

Now obviously we cannot engage in this procedure with quite the same neat control that a physical scientist enjoys in the laboratory. In the social sciences and in moral problems we must deal much more slowly and deliberately with our variables. Human beings cannot be manipulated like test tubes, and so our "testing for consequences" must be carried on over the long stretch of history, unmanaged, for the most part, by deliberate efforts at experimentation. But this does not disqualify the theory; for the same procedure is followed, if not formally and systematically, then informally and merely "historically." For people *do* make up their minds on moral questions, in terms of the kind of life that ensues from their application in ordinary affairs. If history may be thought of as a kind of giant, humanistic "test tube," then values are quite as scientifically arrived at in human experience as is any biological or chemical truth in a laboratory.

To say that "what works is good" [29] bothers many people because it has the ring of a scandalous, licentious form of hedonism—a kind of "what-works-is-good-and-what-works-is-what-works-for-me" doctrine. While Experimentalists do not object to defending the scandalous, if by *scandalous* is meant a break with tradition, nonetheless they mean to set their theory into wider context to quiet such anxieties.

The wider context is simply the community. What "works" is not just what works for me but what works for all. It is what we might call the "pebble theory" of the act. Just as a pebble thrown into a pond produces wider and wider concentric circles of effect on the pond's surface, so likewise does a human act produce wider and wider effects as the products of this act flow into the community.

Hence, a thief may be excused for saying—according to this morality —that thievery is good because it produces desirable consequences, namely, wealth. If it didn't yield such satisfactions he probably wouldn't thieve. But the thief's private corner of experience is not the whole of the context of his act. His conduct has public consequences as well, quite beyond his own life. When those consequences are measured in the larger context, we say his conduct is bad.

The scope and intensity of public consequences are what help us to measure the morality or immorality of the act. But the point is that we do not have to go outside the public arena of consequences to find our ethical principles. Indeed, to do so is to create axiological problems where none exist. To insist, for instance, that there are some absolutes that govern in all circumstances for everyone, no matter where or when, is immediately to put ourselves in the position of defending exceptions. There can be moments, after all (indeed there are), when people must steal to feed a hungry child, when they must lie to protect another's safety, when they must take a life to save their own.

Thievery, lying, and murder cannot therefore be absolutely taboo. They each have their human context, which means they each have a variety of consequences to which they lead. And since not all such consequences are undesirable, we cannot say that this kind of conduct is absolutely undesirable. In the context of the act, that is, in the totality of public effects, moral right may be found.

To turn to the positive side of the case for a brief illustration, we can say that a value like "equality" or "brotherhood" is held to be good by virtue of the quality of social consequences to which it leads. The notion that "all men are equal" is a *good* notion, a defensible political ethic to work from, not because it is self-evident, as Jefferson insisted. There is nothing self-evident about it at all. It is a *good* notion because it *works*. Life lived according to it is preferred by us to life lived according to other

---

[29] There is an interesting logical conundrum here: The traditional philosophies prefer the reverse order, "What is good works," or, epistemologically, "What is true works." To which the Experimentalist replies, "Well, yes, but how do we find out 'what is true (good)'?" Answer: We have to try it out and see!

notions. The political and social consequences that flow from it are the kind of consequences we want.

But what, to ask the final question, *ought* we to *want*? To this the Experimentalist has no answer, for it is an ultimate question, and ultimate questions have no answers. Since values are to be found in the context of experience, we will have to find out what we *ought* to want in this selfsame, relativistic circumstance of ordinary experiencing. There simply is no absolute answer.

The only kind of sensible answer one can give is that people *ought* to want what they in fact *do* want when presented with all the alternatives and the knowledge of their consequences—which is no more than saying that a community of human beings, employing a kind of public sharing of preferences and values and being intelligent about the whole business, can come to a working notion of the kind of civilization they would like to build, that is to say, the values that they would like to work for and attain. But in the working for and attaining of these values, other values have a tendency to suggest themselves. Humanity's valuing becomes, then, a constant creation of and accommodation to the changing moral environment about it. As the consequences that flow from humanity's principles change, the principles themselves change.

This public sharing of values, incidentally, comes close to qualifying as an "ultimate" in Experimentalist moral theory. The very "public-ity" of experience, its public and open character, tacitly requires an open and public procedure by which morality can be questioned, challenged, and constantly tested in our lives.

But the "ongoing-ness" of moral experience is perhaps an even stronger candidate for ultimacy in Experimentalist value theory. For the *process* of shaping values is more often emphasized than the *substantive values* that are shaped. The Good Life to the Experimentalist is not some describable state of affairs, some Utopian content to human circumstance. It is, rather, the *process of valuing* itself. Or, to employ a bit of epigrammatic shorthand: The Good Life is *seeking* the Good Life! If anything could possibly qualify as an absolute Experimentalist value, this might.

AESTHETICS: THE PUBLIC TASTE

If the application of a scientific temper to ethical considerations is difficult, we find the aesthetic application even more so. All right, then, you may say, we test our value judgments in a scientific, consequence-oriented way! How can this possibly apply to art, and music, and poetry, and the dance?

For our edification or bedevilment (however it may strike you) John Dewey wrote a long, difficult, monumental book on the subject.[30] For clues to an Experimentalist aesthetic we could hardly go to a better source.

30 John Dewey, *Art as Experience* (New York: Minton-Balch, 1934).

In the first place, said Dewey, we must repudiate the substantive concept that we have traditionally assigned to a work of art, the notion that a painting or a symphony or a poem is a special type of entity to which we must assign certain existential qualities to account for the work's aesthetic effect on us.

Rather, said Dewey, the work of art is really the "working" of the work of art in our lives. That is to say, "the work of art is what the product does with and in experience." [31] Here again we are face to face with the primacy of "consequences." The operating, experiential consequences of a so-called work of art are the measure of its aesthetic value.

In contrast to the earlier philosophies, which find aesthetic determinants in some objective standard beyond the world of human beings, Experimentalism insists that aesthetic judgment must ultimately rest on what we respond to in our world—what we feel, what we sense, in the presence of things that claim to be beautiful. Is Beethoven's *Ninth Symphony* beautiful? The answer does not lie in some transcendent realm of criticism, or in the verdict of the musicologist, or in some inherited criteria. The answer lies in how people feel when they hear it! It is as simple as this.

We must have our critics, of course, to help us discover our tastes. But in the long run the appreciating public tells the critics what to applaud and what to scorn. If the critics consistently repudiated our preferences we would soon cease reading them.

By way of further contrast, we may also say that the earlier doctrines have held that the function of art is to idealize, reproduce, or rationalize the objective reality of which we are spectators, that is, to celebrate the inherent qualities of what ultimately *is*. To an Experimentalist this is so much nonsense. The function of art is to communicate; "the work of art tells something to those who enjoy it about the the nature of their own experience of the world: . . . it presents the world in a new experience which they undergo." [32]

The purpose of the artist, then, is not to behold ultimate reality and depict it for us in form, color, or sound. It is, rather, for the artist to have new insights, new feelings, new experiences, and to see how skillful he or she can become in enabling the rest of us to experience them too.

> Every art communicates because it expresses. It enables us to share vividly and deeply in meaning to which we had been dumb, or for which we had but the ear that permits what is said to pass through in transit to overt action. For communication is not announcing things, even if they are said with the emphasis of great sonority. Communication is the process of creating participation, of making common what had been isolated and singular; and part of the miracle it achieves is that, in being communicated, the conveyance of meaning gives body and definiteness to the experience of the one who utters as well as to that of those who listen.[33]

[31] Ibid., p. 3.
[32] Ibid., p. 83.
[33] Ibid., p. 244. Quoted by permission of G. P. Putnam's Sons.

We see, then, that aesthetic taste, as well as moral judgment, is grounded in what we may call *public experience.* We are concerned first of all with the consequences of art objects, what they do in and with our experience, what they cause to be aroused in ourselves. But then we wish to share those arousals, to test and compare, to see if the artist has shared well his or her inner experiential feelings.

What, then, am I to like? The answer can be given in the kind of terms intelligible to the ordinary citizen as well as the aesthete: If in the presence of a work I see new meanings in my life, if new dimensions of feeling come into my experience, and if by these novelties of meaning and feeling I make better emotional contact with other people, then I am experiencing a work of true art.

Existentialism

We come finally to the most recent and, in a sense, the least orthodox of all our axiologies. If Experimentalism has given over a lion's share of its time to value theory, we may safely say that Existentialism is almost obsessed with it. For Existentialism is principally a value theory, a philosophy according to which everything must pass through the funnel of choice. And since choice is fundamentally an exercise in valuing, the entirety of philosophical content in Existentialism may be described as axiological.

The only—and single—thing that escapes this classification is human existence. We did not choose that; we had no domain over coming into being. We just "turned up" and discovered ourselves in being. This single and singular nonaxiological doctrine of *existence* is, of course, better located in metaphysics or ontology. And it should be plain to you by now that it is the central principle of Existentialism.

But everything that flows from it, as we have said, is axiological. For existence necessitates choice; we cannot get out of it. Indeed, to exist means to be in a condition of forced choice. The troublesome infinitive *to be* has finally been given a definition: *To be* means to be engaged in choosing. There is no escaping the making of choices. The two terms *to be* and *to be engaged in choosing,* are synonymous and mutually convertible.

ETHICS: THE ANGUISH OF FREEDOM

What, then, can we say about the question, What should I do? Obviously, this question must now be looked at in a somewhat different light. For at the outset we must realize, as the other philosophies sometimes do not, that ethical situations absolutely require *doing something.* Even doing nothing is to do something! We cannot step back from an ethical problem and calmly decide whether we are going to enter it or not. We are already *in it.* Even by retreating from it, refusing to take part in it, refusing to choose a course of action out of it—even by these seemingly neutral behaviors we are actually asserting a positive choice.

The problem of ethics, therefore, is not just an entertaining indoor sport of moralists and philosophers. It is a serious and important activity we engage in every moment of our waking days. Every move we make, every word we utter, every feeling we show is a small but significant "building block" of choice in our definition of Man. For it is by these tiny "building blocks," these axiological "votes" we cast in the metaphysical "election," that we construct over the years of our lives our definition of the essence of Man. This is, of course, what the Existentialist considers to be the business of our lives: to define Man. And since, by reason of our existence, we cannot get out of it, we might as well make the most of it.

To make the very most of it, we must first own up to a lavish egotism: We want to be God! We want to be like him, to imitate him. Epistemologically, we want to know everything, to be absolute in our knowledge of truth (see the discussion on the two "modes of knowing" in Chapter 6, pages 155–157). But axiologically, which is more important, we want to know and do the right, the *absolute* right. We want to value absolutely, with absolute certainty. We want our conduct to be *divine*, not in a facetious but in a thoroughly earnest sense of that word.

But we have already seen, in Chapter 6, that this program in the "imitation of God" can lead only to a very mixed blessing, namely, ultimate union with God. The blessing is mixed because we really do not want to reach it, for to come to absolute and perfect union with God is to pass from becoming to being. It is to pass out of the zone of choosing, for there is no more choosing in God. God, by definition, has no ethical problems, no indeterminate moral situations. God makes no choices: he simply is.[34]

If we were to succeed, therefore, in this grand adventure, or any adventure in coming into perfect union with Absolute Good, we would lose our capacity to choose, and hence to choose ourselves, our own essence. Ethics, as a philosophical subject matter, would pass into uselessness.

---

[34] If, as mentioned earlier, to be engaged in choosing is equivalent to existing, this statement would appear confusing. A terminological difficulty is encountered here: We have no word for the "existing" of God, who does no choosing. We have to coin one arbitrarily.

You will recall that in Chapter 6 a distinction was made between "being-in-itself" and "being-for-itself." In Existentialist lexicography, the former is usually rendered simply as *being*, and the latter is customarily rendered as *existing* or *existence*. The former describes the mode of being exhibited by God, a mode that is a being without choice because it is complete and final. The latter describes the condition of Man, a condition of constant choosing because it is not complete and final. God, one Existentialist explains, entered the "zone of existence," that is, the "for-itself," the "choosing realm," in the form of Jesus Christ. Whether this was itself a "choice" of God presents, of course, an extremely troublesome metaphysical problem to Christian Existentialists.

The problem is, in fact, so troublesome that the atheistic Existentialists seize upon it as the clincher for their atheism. Their argument is that God is the combination of the "in-itself" and the "for-itself," but because this combination is impossible there is no God.

There would be no more decisions to make. And without decisions humanity would pass from existence.

The Existentialist therefore repudiates all absolutes, for to tangle with even a "little" absolute is to compromise one's essential humanity, the freedom to choose. As we have pointed out earlier, to tangle with an absolute is to surrender moral autonomy. To embrace an absolute is to place oneself within its mandatory dominion. If we do this, then we forfeit our freedom to choose.

> [If] certain values exist prior to me, it is self-contradictory for me to want them and at the same [time] state that they are imposed on me.[35]

But if I find no absolutes to rely on, how am I to value? The Experimentalist, as we have seen, answers this by saying that I should test my values for their consequences, share the results, and, by conjoint activity with others, develop some working situational values as ethical guides. This is good advice, says the Existentialist, as far as it goes. The trouble with it is—as we pointed out in similar circumstances in discussing epistemology in Chapter 6—that it creates a new absolute, the social group, to take the place of the earlier, doctrinaire absolutes. And the dominion of the group can be even more pernicious than the dominion of some transcendental ultimate.

> To battle against princes and popes—and the nearer we come to our own times the truer this is—is easy compared with struggling against the masses, the tyranny of equality, against the grin of shallowness, nonsense, baseness, and bestiality.[36]

Let us, says the Existentialist, go the whole way in ethical theory and simply say what we *must* say, namely, that our values consist of our own choices. In choosing we make our values *out of nothing*. No God, no pope, no society can tell me what I must value. They can try, of course, to insist on something, but there is never a case in which I *have* to value anything. I am never "locked in" to this or that value commitment. I am free.

If I simply *had* to do something, if there were no other choice than to cherish some one end or value in life, then I couldn't call myself a human being. I would just be another lowly existent, a determined creature, like an insect, taking up space in the cosmos. There would be nothing distinctive about me. If I have any dignity at all, if I really believe myself to be a human being, then I must remain free of "entangling alliances" with everything outside myself that pretends to help me in my valuing enterprise. It doesn't matter what the external thing is—a God, a Nature, a doctrine, or even the "uncoerced community of persuasion" of a scientific morality. In all cases, I must be the final arbiter of what is good; even to delegate my

[35] Jean Paul Sartre, *Existentialism*, trans. B. Frechtman (New York: Philosophical Library, 1947), p. 53.
[36] Sören Kierkegaard, *The Journals*, ed. A. Dru (London: Oxford University Press, 1938), p. 502 (from page 1317 of the original *Journals* set down in 1854).

responsibility for valuing to an external agent is a choice for which I am responsible.

And this is precisely where the anguish comes in. For when I wake up to discover that I am on my own—not just on my own as one person among others, as Experimentalism holds, but on my own in a complete and ultimate kind of way—I begin to see that this business of choosing is really baseless.

> My freedom is the unique foundation of values. And since I am the being by virtue of whom values exist, nothing—absolutely nothing—can justify me in adopting this or that value or scale of values. As the unique basis of the existence of values, I am totally unjustifiable. And my freedom is in anguish at finding that it is the baseless basis of values.[37]

I am therefore ultimately responsible for my own choices. I am the author of my own goods. I can make myself accountable to no other moral force or factor. I must take responsibility for what I believe and for what I do. If there is anything for which I am not responsible, then to that degree I am not fully existing.

With this logic, the Existentialists looks with abiding scorn on the Catholic confession. For a suppliant to say "I didn't mean to do it" is to say "I couldn't help it; I was being carried along by forces beyond my control; and so I am not responsible." What kind of morality is this? asks the Existentialist. This is no morality at all. Unfortunately, it has been taken over by secular men and women as well in explaining their excessive materialism, their conformity-ridden lives, their aimlessness: "I can't help it; I am conditioned by my culture to be this way; I am a prisoner of circumstance!"

You can take this stand if you wish. But if you do you have voluntarily withdrawn from human status. You are an "insect"! You are driven along like a self-less organism, required by necessity to do the things you do and, therefore, to be what you are. If you are willing to accept this condition, this surrender, however partial, to "insect-like" determinism, you are of course under no obligation to accept the Existentialist message. It is your choice to make; you are still free. But if you choose to believe that you are not in charge of your choices, then you cannot be held responsible for them. And if you cannot be held responsible for them, then you cannot qualify as a human being.

This admittedly is pretty hard advice. But to the Existentialist there is no moral escape from this logic. It represents the "human predicament" in all its simple anguish, and we turn from it only at the prohibitive cost of relinquishing our aspiration to be human beings.

People do turn from it from time to time, of course, as history so often shows. Systematic philosophies are a case in point. They start off in search of the universe, but their abiding concern is the nature of Man. If the nature of Man—his essence or definition—can somehow be fashioned out

---

[37] H. J. Blackham, *Six Existentialist Thinkers* (London: Routledge & Kegan Paul, 1952), pp. 155–156. Quoted by permission of the Macmillan Co.

of a systematic construction of the nature of the cosmos, then philosophy has succeeded in its primary function. But the quest to define Man, says the Existentialist, is completely wrongheaded. For in defining Man we limit him. We specify what he is and therefore what he must be. He cannot pass beyond this definition because this is his essence. To box Man in thus is to destroy him.

> Classical philosophy comes to an end in Hegel, because it has become folly to construct intellectual totalitarian systems in which everything is taken up, harmonized, rationalized, and justified. Such palaces are still marvelous, but nobody can live in them. The savour and reality of human existence, its perils and triumphs, its bitterness and sweetness, are outside in the street.[38]

Even the more modern views, such as Experimentalism, fall into this error. They studiously avoid the question of Man's essence, it is true, but they persist in attempting to place people in some *context*—either the context of sociality and community[39] or the context of some ultimate Method that assumes the office of final criterion for all that shall pass as human.

In either case, what is sought after is a "ground" of some kind in which human beings are to be understood. But contexts are just as much penitentiaries as definitions. They specify the boundaries of our essence even if they do not specify the essence itself. Philosophic systems of all kinds, therefore, have the effect of satisfying our quest for essence; but when they do this they unwittingly provide an escape from the anguish of our ultimate freedom, thus reducing us as human beings.

Religion is another example of human beings' turning from their "awful freedom" to find comfort in the embrace of an authority to which they may submit their choices. Man is necessary to the cosmos, we are told; indeed, he is not only necessary but specifically singled out for special care and attention by an Ultimate Being. As a finite creature, endowed by the Higher Being with certain attributes and qualities, he is enjoined to yield to certain moral canons of thought and conduct—hence, to submit to some *a priori* essence.

People forget, however, that to view Man as either central or necessary to the cosmos is in the very beginning a prodigious "as if" that we place beneath our theological scaffolding before proceeding to build our systems. In the office of an "as if," such a notion has no ultimate justifiability or warrant as a statement of truth. It is completely unjustified. It is merely a hypothesis, and a rather subconsciously uncritical one at that. As such, it reflects a choice people make about themselves, not something that is embedded in reality or forced on them from on high.

It is in this context that we may understand the distinction between the "theistic" and "atheistic" wings of Existentialism. To the theistic wing,

---

[38] Ibid., p. 44.
[39] See Van Cleve Morris, "Freedom and Choice in the Educative Process," *Educational Theory 3*, No. 4 (October 1958): pp. 231–238.

represented principally by Christian Existentialists, the "as if" itself is enough to build on. Man has a longing for an ultimate being, for God. This longing, in and of itself, is no verification of the existence of God, but at least it points to the possibility of God. So we accept it as an "as if" and let it work in our lives. We live our lives *as if* there was a God. The "as if" has the effect of reminding us of our responsibility without at the same time specifying what our choices should be. Working in this way, the "as if" levies its ethical pressure on us while leaving us free. To paraphrase the Spanish philosopher Miguel de Unamuno: "Let life be lived in such a way, with such dedication to goodness and the highest values, that if, after all, it is annihilation which finally awaits us, that will be an injustice."

To the athiest Existentialist, however, it is hazardous to assign too much stature to the "as if" simply because of our temptations as human beings to distort it from what it is—an "as if"—into a substantive and credible truth, which it is not. Furthermore, to recommend it as providing "moral pressure" is simply another instance of our weakness as human beings. If we claim to be human beings, then we should not have to depend on "as ifs" as reminders to do our duty. A sense of responsibility is not achieved by entertaining a fantasy. It is achieved by awakening to one's existential condition. Finally, the "as if" has the effect of deflecting our concern from our choices—which are, after all, the real business of existing —to the secondary concern of the possibility of divine recognition. To be interested in recognition is to be interested in currying favor or, at best—remembering Unamuno's remark—in wresting justice from the hands of a God.

But, says the atheistic Existentialist, this is not what we ought to be doing around here. We are not seeking favors. Nor are we seeking justice from an Ultimate Being. We are trying to be human beings, in the noblest sense of the term, and we can get about this business more directly if we do not worry too much about what is going to happen to us. Therefore, the being or nonbeing of God is an irrelevancy in moral theory. As Jean Paul Sartre has so splendidly put it:

> Existentialism isn't so atheistic that it wears itself out showing that God doesn't exist. Rather, it declares that even if God did exist, that would change nothing. . . . Not that we believe that God exists, but we think that the problem of His existence is not the issue.[40]

Aesthetics: The Revolt from the Public Norm

A theory of aesthetics is almost directly derivative from the above ethical theory. When in Existentialist thinking we encounter the question, "What should I like?" the answer can be given only in terms of what each individual chooses for himself. Indeed, it is in the active selection of what we like, in our preferences, our appreciations, our day-by-day takings and rejectings. But this is not to say that what *is* preferred and rejected, day

[40] Sartre, *Existentialism*, p. 61.

by day, is therefore what *ought* to be preferred and rejected. For there is no external criterion to which we can refer. When it comes to aesthetic choices we are ultimately on our own.

Once again, we have the beginnings—but only the beginnings—of the Existentialist position in Experimentalist aesthetics, discussed in the preceding section. Aesthetic quality is not what works of art contain. It is, rather, what works of art do to and for us. It is, in a manner of speaking, the "having of feelings" within us. And the having of feelings constitutes the focus of our inquiry in aesthetic judgments.

Thus, what Dewey and the Experimentalists so splendidly set out to do was to expand the theme of "operationalism" in aesthetic judgment by making much of the response and private feelings of the "consumers" of art. But, according to Existentialism, they take away with their left hand what they have just offered with their right by saying that one's private aesthetic feelings must ultimately be authenticated and validated in the open territory of public experience. When this territory is systematically explored, says the Experimentalist, certain commonly held criteria can now and then be identified and thought of as the "public standard of taste." The Experimentalist goes on to say that, while this public standard is by no means absolute or unchanging—in art, music, architecture, and so on—it nevertheless assumes a stature superior to that of the private standard of any given individual, and, hence, recommends itself as something to which individual aesthetic consumers may refer when they wish to "check" their taste.

The only trouble with this aesthetic doctrine is that it finds outside the individual's own feelings the standard by which personal feelings are to be certified. And this is precisely our old difficulty, says the Existentialist. For there are no standards outside ourselves in the setting of taste. We are as unjustifiable in this sphere as we were seen to be in the field of ethics. We are a baseless base of taste. Existentially we are suspended in midair, choosing our way to beauty and loveliness with never any assurance that we have selected rightly. This baselessness is admittedly exasperating and annoying, but it is the price we pay for aesthetic freedom. For if we were *not* baseless, but instead had a base for our aesthetic preferences, then we would *have* to choose some things over others. Our choices would be given, hence unfree. Under those conditions we could not claim to be human beings.

It is no accident that Existentialism finds the field of aesthetics so congenial to its message, for aesthetics is perhaps the one domain of life in which the ordinary person is not easily forced into line. It is that sphere of experience in which neither the canons of inherited judgment nor the views of contemporary experts seem to have much effect on the individual. Toscanini used to insist that Beethoven's *Ninth* was "the greatest piece of music ever written." Considering the source, this judgment is the kind of thing one is likely to pay attention to. But actually it reduces simply to an interesting but otherwise insignificant statement of preference.

Aesthetic pronouncements, even those of a great artist or critic, appear to have precious little lateral impact on others in the establishment of their tastes.

The common citizen is, of course, famously conservative when it comes to painting or sculpture. But he or she is also just as splendidly independent of the judgments of others. The common cliché in superficial discussions of art, "I know what I like," illustrates the deceptive simplicity of our problem. For this cliché, as ingenuous as it may sound, is as good a description as any of our aesthetic situation as the Existentialist sees it. It simply says: I have a knowledge of beauty and loveliness, a knowledge that is utterly baseless, absolutely nonreferable to any final criteria, but authentic just the same. For better or worse, I shall have to find my aesthetic answers here, and thus contribute my share to the aesthetic essence of Man.

Questions

1. Is rock music art, or only lively entertainment?

2. Now that we have examined five ethical doctrines, are there any moral prescriptions that are common to all these moralities? Does this make them *absolute*? Explain.

3. Do intelligence and reason apply to aesthetics? Is art in any way rational, as the Neo-Thomists say, or is it all emotional, nonrational, and glandular?

4. Would you say that the more intelligent individuals are, the more sensitive they are in the field of aesthetics? Are intellectuals better judges of art than nonintellectuals? How about moral questions? Are intellectuals better qualified to discuss them?

5. Consider a contemporary moral issue—racism, drug abuse, capital punishment—and examine it from the standpoint of the five ethical systems. Do they all come to the same conclusions as to what is right?

6. Consider the tallest building in your home town. Is it beautiful? How do you decide?

7. "Ought" implies that there are better reasons for acting in one way than for acting in another. What principles would you invoke in determining how "better reasons" differ from reasons?

Further Reading

Idealism

Greene, Theodore M. *The Arts and the Art of Criticism.* Princeton, N.J.: Princeton University Press, 1940. In Chapter 20, on "The Nature and Criteria of Criticism," Greene develops the thesis that style, as a historical concept, and perfection, truth, and greatness, as normative concepts, are the four ultimate criteria for the judgment and criticism of art. In succeeding chapters he analyzes these four concepts more fully.

Kant, Immanuel. *The Fundamental Principles of the Metaphysic of Ethics.* Translated by Otto Manthey-Zorn. New York: Appleton-Century, 1938. This essay, which first appeared in 1785, was Kant's first attempt at a systematic moral theory. In some ways it still stands as the core thesis of Idealist ethics. Kant examines the transition from rational to philosophical knowledge of morality, from popular morals to metaphysics, and from the metaphysic of ethics to the critique of pure practical reason. It is a relatively short book and not so difficult as it sounds.

Realism

Montague, William P. *The Ways of Things.* New York: Prentice-Hall, 1940. In an essay entitled "Beauty Is Not Enough," Montague argues for a broadening of aesthetic endeavors to include not only pleasurable sensations but *all* emotional response—the sad, the terrible, and even the horrible—so as to "set off" more singularly that which is to be called beautiful.

Wild, John. *Introduction to Realist Philosophy.* New York: Harper, 1948. In Part 1 of this very readable book, Wild examines the Realist approach to ethics under the heading "The Perfection of Human Nature." In this discussion he considers the basic moral facts of life, how people make themselves happy or miserable, intellectual and moral virtue, and the rational guidance of appetite and action.

Neo-Thomism

Huxley, Aldous. *The Perennial Philosophy.* New York: Harper, 1945. With a liberal anthological use of quotations from other writers, Huxley spells out the many-faceted design of philosophical thought in the tradition of Aristotle and St. Thomas. The short chapter on "Good and Evil" is particularly pertinent to the discussion of Neo-Thomist ethics in the present chapter. Here we see that, for the Perennial Philosophy, "good is the separate self's conformity to, and finally annihilation in, the divine Ground which gives it being; evil, the intensification of separateness, the refusal to know that the Ground exists."

Maritain, Jacques. *Creative Intuition in Art and Poetry,* Bollingen Series 35, No. 1 (The A. W. Mellon Lectures in the Fine Arts, National Gallery of Art, Washington, D.C.). New York: Pantheon Books, 1953. In this handsome volume, a leading Neo-Thomist considers art as a virtue of the practical intellect, the nature of the preconscious life of the intellect, and the phenomenon of creative intuition in all artistic activity. Constantly stressing the part played by the intellect, Maritain develops what might be called a rationalist theory of aesthetics.

Experimentalism

Dewey, John. *Art as Experience.* New York: Minton-Balch, 1934. This lengthy and relatively difficult book is the most frequently cited source for Dewey's theory of aesthetics. The first chapter, on "The Live Creature," and the concluding chapter, on "Art and Civilization," are suitable preludes to the study of the entire volume and will provide a glimpse of the Experimentalist approach to aesthetics.

——— and James H. Tufts. *Ethics*, rev. ed. New York: Henry Holt, 1936. This as a whole is a historical and systematic analysis of the entire problem of morals. Part 2, "Theory of the Moral Life," considers the nature of moral theory, ends as they relate to good and wisdom, moral judgment and knowledge, and the moral self.

Existentialism

Sartre, Jean Paul. *What Is Literature?* Translated by B. Frechtman. New York: Philosophical Library, 1949. After suffering considerable abuse from literary critics, Sartre says, he decided to strike back by examining the title's question via the subordinate questions: What is writing? Why write? For whom does one write? Chapter 1, on the first of these questions, stresses the "engagement" of the artist and the "in-the-situation" character of all truly creative endeavor.

Tillich, Paul. *The Courage To Be*. New Haven: Yale University Press, 1952. In this powerful little volume, a leading Christian Existentialist poses the problems of "Being and Courage" and "Non-Being and Anxiety," and then proceeds to an analysis of the courage to be in group participation, the courage to be as oneself, and, finally, the courage to be in the transcedent divine encounter.

10

Comparative Axiology and the Educative Process

Axiology and Education

EDUCATION AS A MORAL ENTERPRISE

Now that we have completed a tour through some of the major theories of ethical and aesthetic valuation, it is time to address ourselves to the more important question of what these axiological theories have to say about the management of the learning process. In Chapter 1 we considered the argument that education is at bottom a value enterprise. We are now in a position to see the meaning of this idea in a more sophisticated setting.

For instance, to some philosophies, most particularly Neo-Thomism, as well as most theistic systems of belief, the school is a value enterprise in the sense that it inducts the young into a scheme of belief and commitment that is ultimately certified in the cosmos by a super being or a transcendent, transempirical authority. The content of these values and preferences is of course found in social life, in our daily circumstances of ethical and aesthetic choosing, but the standards for such choices have their ultimate origin and locus somewhere beyond the historical traditions of the race. In schools of this persuasion, there is a certain surety of mood, a confidence that the values and tastes being recommended to children need not be questioned for adequacy but may be inculcated and indoctrinated in the young without argument.

To other philosophies, most notably Idealism, Realism, and Experimentalism, an educational system is a social device that civilized societies have invented to induct their young into the outlooks and preferences implicit in the living and working patterns of the community. In this context the educational enterprise is, in the best sense of the metaphor, a "tradition-transmitting mechanism," a social and cultural instrument for the perpetuation of a cherished heritage. In the case of Idealism and

Realism, this cumulation of belief and tradition, by virtue of its slow assimilation and long tenure in the annals and archives of humanity, is an approximation of what is ultimately and finally true and good and is, therefore, necessarily includable in the experience of the young.

In the case of Experimentalism, however, one of the indigenous ingredients of this American tradition of ours—in contrast to other traditions—is a certain skepticism of tradition itself, a drifting away from the idea that the past is true and good merely because it *is* the past, which in turn inclines to a certain reluctance to look backward instead of forward in the planning and shaping of human experience. But this is itself a value that is lodged in the mind of the community, a value that to the Experimentalist is actually more genuinely "tradition-al," more authentic a reflection of our cultural spirit and national character, than some of the other things we have merely inherited from an increasingly irrelevant past. Hence, it most certainly belongs in the value structure of the school and deserves to be introduced into the working patterns of the young as they grow to maturity.

But this mood of skepticism is still a value judgment, a position taken, a preference objectified—in short, a plank in the argument for a certain way of living and of life. And Experimentalism, which espouses this value, must be looked at as just as partisan a philosophy of life as any other and its schools as much dedicated to its point of view as other schools are to theirs.

When we examine the anatomy of commitment and partisanship itself we confront a peculiar paradox of all educational programs: They can sometimes argue too well for a set of values. "Nothing succeeds like success," we sometimes say. But in the case of the axiological and ideological base of modern education, it is perhaps the other way around: "Nothing fails like too much success." Take the case of twentieth-century nationalistic educational programs. A Fascist education in Germany succeeds beyond telling and brings a world to arms. A Communist education in the Soviet Union, seized by purpose and fired by ideological energy, enslaves and intimidates a people, their artists, writers, and scholars. Or, to return to our more immediate references, Idealist, Realist, and Neo-Thomist schools glorify and venerate what is past and absolute and ill prepare today's youngster for the fast-moving, relativistic present. Experimentalism and its schools concentrate on current experience and lay themselves open to the criticism of "an obsession with Present-ism," with the thinness and superficiality that such an obsession implies.

All of this is reminiscent of a remark once made by Ralph Harper: "There is nothing worse than a good idea insisted on too much." This brings us to a very troublesome feature of education—indeed, its fundamental dilemma—namely, the equivocal character of ends. Ralph Barton Perry explains it thus:

> To define in advance an end result and then to seek by all possible means to achieve it, is held to be too narrowing, too repressive, too authoritarian.

But if, on the other hand, there is no end in view, educational activity is confused and incoherent. Its various parts and successive phases do not add up to anything. Without a definition of the end there is no test by which means can be selected, and no standard by which practice can be criticized and improved.[1]

Perry goes on to say, in an Experimentalist moment, that there is an escape from this dilemma if we not only proclaim ourselves *against* narrowness, rigidity, and authoritarianism of all sorts but also proclaim ourselves *for* their opposites: breadth, flexibility, and freedom. "These opposites," he says, "and other kindred ideas themselves define an end—an end that can be methodically and constantly pursued, and that must be methodically and consistently pursued if it is to be realized." [2]

What this ideology reduces to, obviously, is an affirmative commitment to openness, to unfettered inquiry, to freedom. It is, in short, the "commitment to noncommitment," a value judgment both logically outrageous and superlatively coherent. Is freedom, really, an idea that could ever conceivably be "insisted on too much"?

Maybe we have our hands here on something that may qualify as an ultimate value: freedom. But if it is to be ultimate, then it must indeed be ULTIMATE, supremely unqualified by and unreferable to any other principle. It is this message of absolute and unqualified freedom that is the axiological "bomb" exploding over the mass societies of the twentieth century in the form of Existentialism. Existence in our time has increasingly come to be seen as axiologically absurd, totally without moral content except for what we place in it by our choices. We have come to see ourselves as completely unjustified in these choices, finally and utterly baseless in taste and judgment. Not even the Experimentalist's presumably ultimate method of science can ever certainly justify a moral choice; all it can do is render it objective, systematic, and public.

Therefore, what the Existentialist school does with tradition is even more subtle than what Experimentalism does. It provides the children with a knowledge and awareness of all the ideological choices people have ever made; it includes in this heritage the Experimentalist's value commitment to open inquiry, public sharing, scientific procedures, and freedom of thought, association, and expression. But, finally, it returns the children to themselves; it awakens the children to the final knowledge that each one of them is alone, completely and beautifully alone, in the value enterprise.

VALUES AND THE SCHOOL

What this extended analysis is intended to show is that the school is universally considered to be a place where a "value sense" is to be

[1] Ralph Barton Perry, *Realms of Value* (Cambridge: Harvard University Press, 1954), p. 426.
[2] Ibid., p. 427.

acquired by the young. To some, this "sense" has a foundation: in ultimate Mind, in objective Nature, in transcendent Being, or in social experience (as our first four theories would hold). To others, it has no foundation whatsoever, but is completely baseless (as our final theory would hold). But it is still correct to say that to all of these positions the school is at bottom an axiological institution.

The above distinction will begin to be felt almost immediately in our discussion, for it will necessitate a new division in our ranks, a division that will increasingly set Existentialism off from the others. But for the time being we may permit ourselves the further (though not altogether accurate) observation that the school is a value enterprise, not so much by virtue of the values that are taught didactically or by inference in the presentation of subject matter, but by virtue of the selection of subject matter to be presented, in the procedures employed by the principal and the teachers in dealing with the young, in the climate prevailing in the classrooms, in the art works hung on the walls and displayed in the lobby. Regardless of the way one views the axiological enterprise itself, in education, Professor John L. Childs reminds us, "The moral factor appears whenever the school, or the individual teacher or supervisor, is *for* certain things and *against* other things."

It appears, for example, in the affairs of the playground—in the kind of sports that are favored and opposed, and in the code of sportsmanship by which the young are taught to govern their behavior in the actual play of various games. It appears in the social life of the school—in all of the behaviors that are approved or disapproved as the young are taught the manners—the conventional or minor morals—of their society. It appears in the school's definition of the delinquent and in its mode of dealing with him. It appears in the way children are taught to treat those of different racial, religious, occupational, economic or national backgrounds. It appears in the department of science: in the methods the young are expected to adopt in conducting their experiments, in their reports of what actually happened during the course of their experiments, as well as in the regard of the teachers of science for accuracy, for precision, and for conclusions that are based on objective data rather than on wishful thinking. It appears in the department of social studies: in the problems that are chosen to be discussed, in the manner in which they are discussed, in the historical documents and events that are emphasized, as well as in the leaders that are chosen to illustrate the important and the worthy and the unimportant and the unworthy in the affairs of man. It appears in the department of literature: in the novels, the poems, the dramas that are chosen for study, in what is considered good and what is considered bad in the various forms and styles of human conduct and expression. It appears in the organization and the government of the school: in the part that superintendent, supervisors, teachers, pupils are expected to play in the making and the maintenance of the regulations of the school. It appears in the methods of grading, promoting, and distributing honors among the children of the school. It appears in the celebration of national holidays: in the particular events that are celebrated as well as in the historical and contemporary personalities who are chosen to exemplify the qualities of citizenship and worthy community service. It appears in the program for the general assemblies of the schools: in the various leaders from the community who are brought in to speak to the children. It appears in the way teachers are treated: the amount of freedom and initiative they enjoy, in the extent to which teachers are permitted to take part in the life of their community, and the degree to which the young believe that they are studying under leaders who are more than docile, routine drill-masters in assigned subjects. It appears in the way the community organizes to conduct its schools: in the provision it makes in its schoolgrounds, buildings, and equipment, in the kind of people it chooses to serve on the school board, and in the relation of the members of the board to the administrative and teaching staff.[3]

We are, therefore, not dealing with anything trivial when we view the school in an axiological way. We are, on the contrary, dealing with the most strategic and crucial side of the school's work—indeed, with the very medium within which teaching and learning are carried on. In the pages to follow, therefore, we cannot confine ourselves simply to the "value" dimension of education as it is popularly thought of in what we sometimes call "character-building," or even in the more inclusive sense of the development of "moral and spiritual values." What we are dealing with is the *total* life of the young, what they are taught to cherish and desire, what they are taught to reject and avoid. These decisions inhere in practically everything the school does.

Learning to Live the Ethical Life

How does an individual learn right conduct? Probably more than any other single question in learning theory, this one continues to evade our understanding in the training of the young. And so long as theoretical understanding escapes us, our classroom practice will probably continue to be confused and incoherent. In a sense, this is what we find in the typical American school today; very little deliberate moral instruction, surprisingly enough, is actually being given there. In spite of what has been said in the previous section concerning the value choices implicit in the practical functioning of educational programs, very few of these choices are made deliberately by teachers and principals with the express idea of bringing about some preferential attitude on the part of the young. They are made, rather, in a subconscious, routine way as the daily patterns of teaching and learning regularize themselves.

Such choices fail of their full axiological impact on youngsters in the degree to which they pass from conscious attention into the habitual routine of the school. For example, when a high school principal, through

[3] John L. Childs, *Education and Morals*, © 1950. Reprinted by permission of Prentice-Hall, Inc., Englewood Cliffs, New Jersey.

the magic of his "Big Brother" public-address system, leads the entire school in the flag salute, the ostensible object of this exercise is to arouse healthy instincts of national feeling, that is, to reinforce certain attitudes that are thought to be good. But such an impersonalized procedure, especially if it becomes through repetition merely another ritual in the morning homeroom period to satisfy a state law, will obviously lose its power to move youngsters to a value commitment. And so such practices become useless and empty in the moral training of boys and girls.

As the value practices of the school cease being intentional and deliberate and become increasingly more routine and automatic, there is a tendency for the school as a whole to take on the appearance of being morally neutral, perhaps even uninterested, in the entire question of ethical training. As a matter of fact, there is in contemporary educational circles a certain pseudosophisticated embarrassment concerning this whole matter. Morals, we have come to think, are old-fashioned things. There is a Victorian ring to the very word itself. For the modern, glass-front, ranch-style high school, the idea of deliberate thought being given to ethics and conduct seems inappropriate. Or perhaps, as some say, a secular public school necessarily must leave value training to some other agency, be it home, church, or neighborhood.

It is generally true that as we proceed up the educational ladder, from nursery to elementary to secondary to collegiate to graduate and professional education, we can recognize a gradual reduction of deliberate and intentional moral instruction. Whether this is as it should be is another question. In light of our growing commitment to the lifelong, "learning-has-no-age-limit" conception of education actualized in vast adult-education projects, it is noteworthy that training in belief and conduct in ethical matters is thought *not* to be lifelong but confined to the standard years of public school instruction.

At any rate, the resultant absence of deliberate moral instruction at the college level is now pretty much a matter of fact. It must be said, of course, that perhaps colleges do teach their students values and ethical norms by the more indirect methods of association. Perhaps the academic life itself and the living of it have a kind of absorptive, "osmosis" effect with respect to desired ethical traits. Operating on this hunch, Dr. Philip E. Jacob of the University of Pennsylvania a few years ago attempted to measure the changes in the value orientations of college students from the freshman to the senior year.[4] To his dismay and the consternation of a large segment of the educational community, he found precious little change in outlook on the part of his subjects, even in those particular spheres—politics, social relations, and personal morality itself—which have traditionally been thought to be most responsive to the influence of the liberal college in America.

[4] *Changing Values in College* (New York: Harper, 1957).

Why, one might ask, is deliberate education in ethical values and right conduct so ineffective? Part of the answer may lie in our ignorance of educational psychology or of pedagogy itself, that is, how to teach values. It may be due also to the grosser fact that American education only reflects a larger trouble in the adult community—indeed, in the total culture. There is a moral confusion in contemporary America; we are not sure of our values. This is not necessarily to say that American civilization is beginning its "decline and fall" in the Roman tradition, as some moralists contend. It is only to say that there are many areas of uncertainty as to what we ourselves believe and what we therefore wish to teach our children.

Social life is always a going contest between the good and the bad, however one defines these two poles of the moral life. And certainly there is no shortage of the latter to point to as symptomatic of some deficiency among Americans in taking proper care of their public morality. Crime advances, gangland violence spreads, hoodlums infiltrate our business and labor groups, presidential agents burglarize offices of the opposition party, drugs abound, dope addicts fill our hospitals, unwed and deserted mothers expand our relief rolls, divorce increases, and homes are broken. And let us not forget the transgressions closer to home. Petty pilfering from offices and plants by workers has become a major industrial expense, banks annually lose six times as much from their own employees as from armed robbers, traffic tickets get "fixed" by individuals who otherwise appear keenly sensitive to what is right, and income tax evasion—piecemeal, retail, or wholesale—grows into a major indoor sport as common citizens fondle their guide manuals like touts their racing forms and corporation lawyers think up new loopholes to outwit and outflank the Internal Revenue Service.

What all this means is simply that both within and beyond the working sphere of the school in America there is plenty of work to be done in public ethics. What our five axiologies have to suggest in this concern has obvious and immediate reference to major public problems in America today.

IDEAS, EXAMPLES, AND CONDUCT

To an Idealist the moral problem in education is by no means an easy one, but it can perhaps be best understood by viewing ethical conduct as growing out of a social tradition. "Social conventions are the wisdom of the past functioning in the present," says Herman Harrell Horne, a leading spokesman for the Idealist position. "For most persons," he says, "only bad characters come from the indulgence of appetite contrary to social usage." [5]

5 *This New Education* (New York: Abingdon, 1931), p. 182.

It then obviously becomes necessary to transmit the social conventions to the young in the school, and since this can best be accomplished through the medium of words and symbols, it is recommended that in all those subject matters having to do with convention and social ideals, teachers should lay particular stress on such values and teach them didactically. It is evident that such subject matters as history and literature afford the best vehicles for this kind of instruction. In historical legends and documents there is a lavish abundance of this type of material. At the elementary school level, for instance, the legend of George Washington and the cherry tree seems to have a hardy endurance. It does not matter too much whether it is true or not; it suffices as a paradigmatic example of the moral life that is being recommended to the young. As youngsters proceed through school they will increasingly confront more substantial representations of our moral past: the *Areopagitica*, the Magna Charta, the defense of Peter Zenger, the Declaration of Independence, the speeches of Patrick Henry, Émile Zola's appeal for Captain Dreyfus, the Constitution of the United States, the Gettysburg Address, Woodrow Wilson's "make the world safe for democracy," the 1954 Supreme Court decision on racial segregation, Martin Luther King, Jr.'s, "I have a dream."

These are the containers of our moral tradition. They speak the conscience of the Western mind and the American ethic. As such they stand for an inherited sense of the right, and, closely studied and emotionally absorbed, they and other materials like them become the base upon which an Idealist morality can be built in the child.

In the field of literature it is also true that moral content is persistently present. The famous "Little Red Hen" is not just a trivial tale; it has a "hard" message, the virtue of self-reliance, to deliver to the child. "The Three Little Pigs" is a more powerful document than adults sometimes think; it brings home the moral principle that a sturdy house not only deflects the predatory tendencies of the wolf but is itself the mark of a sturdy character. Fairy tales, Aesop's fables, stories like *Hansel and Gretel* —all contribute to the growing moral sense of the elementary school child.

Later on, the student may be introduced to King Arthur and his court, to the Arabian Nights, to *Beowulf*, the *Song of Roland*, perhaps to Homer's *Iliad*. Not only are these works examples of masterly writing, but they contain a message that we hope is not wasted on the adolescent. After school hours, the young are provided more moral incentives. Horatio Alger may be out of date, as the exemplar of a middle-class Victorian ethic of striving and succeeding by hard work, and Tom Swift's gadgeteering now seems, in the age of rockets, somewhat puerile; they have been replaced by other, more sophisticated heroes like Buckminster Fuller or the space astronauts. These continue to represent the adventurous, "frontiersmanship" morality for which America has always stood.

The fictional hero has, in a scientific age, somewhat subsided in favor of the historic and contemporary hero: Benjamin Franklin, Abraham Lincoln, Henry Ford, Babe Ruth, Eleanor Roosevelt, Henry Aaron. Here, through biography or autobiography, the youngster is brought into the presence of the "larger self" that occupied our attention in Idealist axiology in Chapter 9. These individuals, through persistence, hard work, excellence of performance, and sometimes raw courage, have shown us the way to a higher life. These are the heroic carriers of our moral tradition. They are human approximations of the Infinite Person. And, as such, they are recommended to the young for imitation.

NATURE AND CONDUCT

To a Realist the Idealist approach might appear a trifle sentimental. Sentimentalism is a very real and genuine part of our lives, and it may indeed be celebrated in historical legend and through the fictional or real hero. But this is not enough for shaping the conduct of the child to the moral dimension of a real world. If looked at carefully, the real world, the world of events and occurrences, the world of an observable Nature, can bring the child nearer to right conduct.

Perhaps the most trivial, but then again not so trivial, instance of this is a direct look at Nature to find there a moral content. We show to the child the habits of robins and sparrows, show them feeding their young and helping them learn to fly. We encourage animal pets in the home and promote small "zoos" of hamsters, turtles, and goldfish in the elementary classroom. Finally, we illustrate biological reproduction by representing this delicate subject matter in the litter of kittens brought to the classroom. In all these ways, we are, whether we are aware of it or not, implicitly sensitizing the child to the wonderful manner in which Nature tends to support and sustain life. We are sensitizing the child to the morality of life itself. These are vastly oversimplified but nonetheless authentic instances of implanting in the minds of small children the notion that there is something sacred about life. With the small kernel of this idea as a beginning, they are then brought stage by stage to a higher ethical application of it to humankind. It is, in a sense, the proper starting point for so noble an ethical principle as Albert Schweitzer's "reverence for life," which he adopted as his own ultimate value. And Schweitzer actually acted this value out in his role of physician and missionary in Lambaréné, Gabon. One does not have to take the Idealist detour through fictional legend or human heroes to get the child to feel an intense and vivid love for life; it can be found directly by observing the procedures of Nature.[6]

[6] We shall not inquire of the Realist at this point why Nature's exhibit of tenderness and concern for life is singled out and set axiologically above Nature's equivalent exhibit of violence and concern for death. If Nature is the model, should not a child be exposed to a spider eating a fly or, better yet, to a really wild and bloody dog-and-cat fight? There is certainly some moral content there.

Realists will admit that looking for morals in Nature does, of course, have its limits. As children grow older they will become more sophisticated and skeptical about the presumed moralities of Nature, particularly if they are represented in the romanticized fashion of the animal world. However, they are not through with "natural morality" even when they study biology, chemistry, and physics in high school. For these subjects, so widely thought to be value-free, still aim, as one of their underlying motifs, to portray the supreme *order* of nature to the adolescent. And what is order but a particular value that we wish to implant in the behavior patterns of the young?

It is perhaps a little too precious to intimate that the child's sense of orderly routine and self-discipline can be extracted from the economy and "single-mindedness" of a chemical reaction or an electrical circuit, but the overall effect of systematic study of nature's ways, if pointed to specifically and related to life's affairs, may conceivably contribute to the child's ethical growth. Patience, as a case in point, was found during World War II to be a human value with its analogue in nature; William Knudsen, as the nation's production chief, responded to his critics concerning the delay in mass production of bombers by alluding to similar difficulties in biology: "Gentlemen, no matter what you may desire in the matter, it still takes nine months!"

We often say that nature has its own "rhythm," that "letting nature take its course" quite often results in problems' solving themselves. "Early to bed and early to rise," while of doubtful value in the production of health, wealth, and wisdom, still contains a residual flavor of virtue. This aphorism, coming down to us as it does from Franklin's agrarian-minded, "rule-of-thumb" way of life, sounds a little quaint in our time, but it nevertheless describes, albeit somewhat obliquely, how nature actually comports herself in the rhythmic dialectic between night and day, rest and activity. We are advised to discipline ourselves to the schedule of nature in the search for the good life. In contrast to Idealism, Realism tends to look for moral exemplars not so much in human persons as in natural processes.

Concerning pedagogy itself, Realism cannot be said to have any hard and fast prescriptions. The only tendencies that seem consistent with the above have to do with the possibility of conditioning the youngsters to certain behavior patterns as a prelude to later, more mature understanding of their dominion over each human being. Reference was made in Chapter 9 to the underlying thesis of Professor Wild's axiology: "the rational comprehension of natural necessity." Standing behind this psychological dictum is the belief that:

> . . . all men share certain essential tendencies which require that certain moral principles be obeyed by all men if they are to live authentic human lives. . . . The realist believes that men are free within limits to act as they

choose in the light of what they understand. Thus, they may violate the moral law if they so decide.[7]

Hence, putting these ideas together when we come to the moral instruction of the young, we must set the limits to behavior by explaining to the children the moral laws involved and enforce certain behavior until the children can grow into a rational understanding of the laws on their own.

We must point out here that the Realist shares with the Idealist the willingness to appeal to the accumulated sense of the community as to what these moral laws may be. As Professor Harry Broudy puts it:

> Ask a representative body of citizens what they want in the way of moral education, and the answer will be somewhat as follows:
> We want our children to develop reliable tendencies to tell the truth, to respect the codes of right and wrong of the community, to be courageous, to be persevering in the face of obstacles, to withstand the temptations of disapproved pleasures, to be able to sacrifice present pleasures in favor of more remote ones, to have a sense of justice and fair play.
> Parents do not expect a guarantee that their child will do this or that at any given time in the future. What they are after are character traits, i.e., reliable tendencies or dispositions to react in certain ways in the presence of difficulties, duties, and conflicts.[8]

We are therefore dealing with tendencies and dispositions that comply with natural and moral law and that the community feels it has a right to insist on. It proceeds to insist on these tendencies by what Professor Broudy calls "moral training."

> We call it training because that is what it is. Through the constant approval and disapproval of others we form these dispositions. By living with others and feeling their pleasure and displeasure, we introject these moral attitudes so that we expect them from ourselves with the same force that others expect them from us.[9]

The Realist may possibly object to calling this procedure "conditioning" in the narrow Pavlovian or, as Wild says, "white rat" sense. But it is certainly drawn from the understanding that behavior in morals is conditionable and that it is legitimate to condition it *in advance of* children's understanding of what they are doing and why, notwithstanding the importance of such understanding to the mature moral life. It is this feature of behavioral enforcement *prior to* (even if not independent of) genuine rational understanding that marks the Realist position. As

[7] John Wild, "Education and Human Society: A Realistic View," Chapter 2 in *Modern Philosophies and Education*, Fifty-fourth Yearbook of the National Society for the Study of Education, ed. N. B. Henry, Part I (Chicago: the Society, 1955), p. 23.
[8] *Building a Philosophy of Education* (Englewood Cliffs, N.J.: Prentice-Hall, 1954), p. 405.
[9] Ibid., p. 406.

indicated earlier, we shall examine this educational approach in depth in Chapter 11.

THE HIERARCHY OF VALUES AND THE RATIONAL ACT

There is much in the Neo-Thomist position on moral training that co-incides with and supports what has been described in Realism. This is true for the same generic reason given in earlier sections of the book where the affinity between these two schools has already been noted, namely, that modern Realism and contemporary Neo-Thomism have a common ancestry in Aristotle. What Neo-Thomism does, in a sense, is to clarify and intensify the Realist pedagogy and to supply it with a power-ful ally, the training of the human will.

We may recall at this point the paramount concern in Neo-Thomist axiology (see Chapter 9) for Reason as the ultimate criterion of the good act. It would appear to follow that the training of the Reason, the full development of its powers, is a major pedagogical objective throughout the moral instruction of the young. This should not be considered to compromise or pre-empt the conditioning of the young to certain be-havior patterns by the approval-disapproval, or enforcement, procedure advocated by the Realist. Indeed, the Neo-Thomist would be likely to be even more earnest and rigorous in this phase of teaching. What the Neo-Thomist insists on with perhaps greater vigor than the Realist is that this training of the Reason is a precondition of the rational comprehension of moral law and certainly of the understanding of any specific moral dictum.

Hence, the first pedagogical prescription of the Neo-Thomist would appear to be a thorough training of the Reason through the discipline of the subject matters discussed in Chapter 7 (see pages 180–183). It is through these subject matters that the rational faculties of the mind are brought to peak power and, consequently, to a potential understanding of the rightness or wrongness of certain acts. Insofar as the rational test can be applied to specific ethical precepts—for example, to continence, charity, honesty—so much will a teacher's instruction become more mean-ingful. But the essential condition is the preparedness of the youngster to see the distinction between right and wrong on purely rational grounds.

Coming, then, to more tactical (as against strategic) considerations in moral education, the Neo-Thomist addresses the teacher's attention to the will. Here is more precisely where the moral enterprise has its origin. Now, the will is quite like the intellect in that it exists in the child but only in a state of potentiality. It is present incipiently in the young but needs training and development in order to be of use to the individual in his or her other moral life.

The will may be very weak, of course, but this is due primarily to the unfortunate events that followed its original endowment upon human nature. According to Ecclesiastical Neo-Thomists, after the so-called Fall of Man at the hands of Adam, Man's supernature was withdrawn, but his intellect and will were left standing, albeit in a weakened condition. Pope Pius XI, after tracing the Fall and Man's Redemption, says: "There remain, therefore, in human nature the effects of original sin, the chief of which are weakness of will and disorderly inclinations." [10]

The second job of the teacher, then, after the strategic training of the Reason, is the more immediate matter of the training of the will. This may be done in a variety of ways, the most familiar and traditional method being that which accords with similar procedures with the intellect, namely, discipline. To discipline the will is to exercise it, to give it tasks that will strengthen those potentialities of will power that reside in every child in the classroom.

According to a strict rendering of this methodology it might be suggested that, just as they are given difficult subject matter in language or mathematics to train their Reason, children in school should also be given difficult and distasteful tasks, which they would be enjoined to stick to until the tasks were completed. In the enforced application of will power to see an unpleasant job through, children would be given a chance to strengthen their will in preparation for more strenuous moral undertakings in the future.[11] We see, then, that the development of the will is also a strategic instead of a purely tactical affair, because we have not yet reached the particular method by which specific moral prescriptions are learned by the child.

We come to this final step in Ecclesiastical Neo-Thomism in the form of the *catechism*. The catechism is, of course, the method of instruction by which standard questions together with specific and unchanging answers are taught to the child by memory and rote, and are then tested in catechetical recitations. Once the answers to the questions have been learned, as we say, "by heart" (which itself has poetic overtones of the mystical nature of such knowledge), then the child may be said to have learned moral truth.

This procedure is defended on the supremely simple assertion that

---

[10] *Christian Education of Youth*, Encyclical Letter of His Holiness Pope Pius XI (Washington, D.C.: National Catholic Welfare Conference, 1936), p. 23.

[11] In an overzealous and somewhat ridiculous application of this principle, some educators, particularly in the latter nineteenth century, insisted that so important was the training of the will that unpleasantness should be made a regular feature of the educational program: If we develop character through the sharpening and toughening of our powers of self-discipline, then whatever is unpleasant to do in the school can be turned by the teacher into the vehicle of moral training. This eventually led to the view that if children found some task unpleasant it must be good for them. Finally, this was turned into a general educational theory—what may be called the "Spinach Theory" of education—that placed educational experiences and materials in a descending order of difficulty and distastefulness. If the subject with its attendant assignments day by day proved difficult and/or distasteful (preferably both) it must be of high educational value and therefore should be placed at the head of the list of subjects. As we all know, mathematics and languages—particularly grammar—have consistently met such qualifications.

indoctrination of ultimate truth can by no stretch of the imagination be considered illegitimate. A Catholic layman says:

> The Church does not say that morality belongs purely, in the sense of exclusively, to her; but that it belongs wholly to her. She has never maintained that outside her fold and apart from her teaching, man cannot arrive at any moral truth. . . . She does, however, say, has said, and will ever say, that because of her institution by Jesus Christ, because of the Holy Ghost sent her in His name by the Father, she alone possesses what she has had immediately from God and can never lose, the whole of moral truth, *omnem veritatem*, in which all individual moral truths are included, as well as those which man may learn by the help of reason, as those which form part of revelation or which may be deduced from it.[12]

All moral truth, therefore, and *all particular* moral truths and prescriptions are now in hand and secured safely in the "safe-deposit boxes" of the Church's dogma. If these truths can be rendered in question-and-answer form and committed to the memory, it can then be said that the child has received moral education.

In support of the training of reason and will and the subsequent instruction in the Catechism, the Ecclesiastical Neo-Thomist customarily adds certain curricular instructions to educators that bear upon the ethical problem. A typical trouble spot is sex education, certainly in any school a very delicate topic but in a Neo-Thomist school almost a traumatic matter. Says Pope Pius XI in another passage:

> Far too common is the error of those who with dangerous assurance and under an ugly term propagate a so-called sex education, falsely imagining they can forearm youth against the dangers of sensuality by means purely natural, such as a foolhardy initiation and precautionary instruction for all indiscriminately, even in public; and, worse still, by exposing them at an early age to the occasions, in order to accustom them, so it is argued, and as it were to harden them against such dangers.[13]

The danger is very real, says the Pope, that in taking remedies against sin we expose the child to occasions of and inducements to sin. Considering the faltering weakness of human nature, then, we should be wise to leave instruction to agencies outside the school or, if instruction is necessary of inclusion, to handle it with the very greatest of care.

This concern with instruction in sex is indicative of a general repugnance toward what may generally be labeled "the carnal" in life, and of the demotion of all those human pursuits of a purely physical sort. It has its application, although somewhat indirectly, in the elimination of football from the educational program of the University of Chicago during the regime of Chancellor Hutchins, perhaps the most famous twentieth-century Lay Neo-Thomist. Hutchins, it is only fair to say, never

---

[12] A. Manzoni, *Osservazioni sulla Morale Cattolica*, Chapter 3, quoted in Pope Pius XI, *Christian Education of Youth*, pp. 8–9.

[13] Ibid., p. 25.

repudiated football itself. He merely repudiated football as education; it is simply a physical recreation, and, while this is legitimate enough, it is not what education is properly concerned with.[14]

Perhaps an even more relevant example is found again on the Ecclesiastical side:

> False also and harmful to Christian education is the so-called method of "coeducation." This too, by many of its supporters, is founded upon naturalism and the denial of original sin; but by all, upon a deplorable confusion of ideas that mistakes a leveling promiscuity and equality for the legitimate association of the sexes. The Creator has ordained and disposed perfect union of the sexes only in matrimony, and, with varying degrees of contact, in the family and in society. Besides, there is not in nature itself . . . anything to suggest that there can be or ought to be promiscuity, and much less equality, in the training of the two sexes.[15]

In keeping with this papal requirement, most Catholic schools until just recently provided for the separation of the sexes as much as possible. There was usually a separate door for each sex. Preferably, if the student population was large enough, there were separate schools altogether. This policy is no longer universally observed, but it used to be the clear desire of the Church.

In all these many ways, instructional and administrative, the Neo-Thomist school intends to shape the moral tendencies of the young along preferred lines. By the nature of the case, this moral program is more consistent and unequivocal about its aims than perhaps any other we are here discussing. This constitutes, of course, both a strength and a weakness, for moral certainty is always purchased at the price of a certain moral rigidity, and in modern America there may be some question as to how much of the latter the twentieth century will stand.

The Relativity of Values and Learning through Living

This last remark is perhaps most likely to be made by Experimentalists, standing as they do at the opposite end of the axiological spectrum from the Neo-Thomists. Rigidity is only one of the unfortunate by-products, they say, of the Neo-Thomist value theory. Its fundamental difficulty is not that it is rigid but, rather, that when put to use in human affairs it produces dispute and disagreement in the area of moral judgment. For human beings, even when exercising their reason, do often come to alternative conceptions of what is good, and the Neo-Thomists have no method beyond reason to settle moral disputes.

[14] In expanding on his position concerning football, Chancellor Hutchins is supposed to have once joked about physical endeavors in general. On being asked whether he did not think it wise for persons of thought also to "keep in trim," he is reported to have said: "Whenever I get the feeling that I need some exercise, I lie down till the feeling goes away."

[15] Pope Pius XI, *Christian Education of Youth*, p. 26.

This phenomenon points to a peculiar difference between science on the one hand and classical philosophy and organized religion on the other. The latter—the philosophies and the religions—magnanimously set out on the search for a unified conception of Man and a universal and catholic sense of brotherhood among all people. But nothing is more divisive and fractured into small, well-guarded citadels of thought than the systematic philosophies (the schools discussed in this book), unless one considers the even more divisive and warring factions of sectarian religion. Organized religions have historically been the vehicles for perhaps more rancor and bloodshed in the world than any other single institution. And the reason for this, according to the Experimentalists, is that they are founded on metaphysical, hence inaccessible, grounds of judgment. One person's metaphysic is another's nonsense, and when there is dispute among metaphysicians or theologians, particularly on moral concerns, there is no court of appeal to which we may repair to settle the question.

Science, on the contrary, begins its work with no particular pretensions whatsoever about bringing people together into a moral unity or a social brotherhood. It is simply a modest methodological procedure for increasing our knowledge. Ironically, however, science has succeeded, quite unintentionally, in producing the only true international, intercultural brotherhood—what we sometimes call the "scientific community"—that the world has ever seen. Even the arts cannot match it for finding a truly global language of discourse. Whatever else may be the limitations of science, it certainly is a method that has the capacity to resolve the disparate views that people entertain about their conduct.

If the fact of *agreement* on the matters of life, therefore, has any utility as a criterion of adequacy—that is, if there is some feeling that we are closer to the good in ethics and conduct when we freely join hands and, *without* coercion, agree on something—then science is a method worth trying. It is this possibility of a kind of nonmetaphysical, nontheistic, wholly secular brotherhood that some people feel is most nearly realized in the free, universal, secular public school in America. It is the "melting pot" idea expanded to include not only language and custom and style of dress but basic beliefs and life values. Since a teeming America could not hope to find any unity in such diversity on purely metaphysical, cultural, or religious grounds, it decided to try to find it on practical, empirical grounds.

We are not as sanguine as we once were about the possibility of pulling this off. American society has discovered diversities in itself that go much deeper than we suspected and that do not seem to yield to the "melting pot" ethic. Indeed, the "melting pot" idea itself is under challenge, and the quest for unity has become a far more dubious ideal than we have traditionally been taught. Separatism and withdrawal of minority groups are now applauded and encouraged, and the fracturing and polarization of the American polity into white, black, Chicano, Puerto Rican, native

American, and other ethnic identities is in what just a generation ago we would have considered a dangerously advanced stage. The new paradigm is "cultural pluralism," a state of social organization still undergoing description and definition. We undertake a thorough examination of this new social ethic in Chapter 13, intending there to explore its possible impact on teaching and learning for America's youth.

The Experimentalists, like the rest of us, are witness to this major shift in a new definition of "E Pluribus Unum." But their response is predictable: Even though the diversities are sharper and more pronounced, the scientific mode of bringing social cohesion is still our best chance for survival. In America, we have stumbled on two great moral inventions: the open society and the universal public school, both of which are officially free of dogma and yet capable of forming moral dispositions in the individual person.

In the society at large the forming of moral dispositions is generally accomplished through politics, law, and neighborhood life, but in the more microcosmic society of the school it is done through a methodology that the Experimentalist considers capable of application to almost all moral questions. This methodology is simply the arrangement of learning situations so that children learn the morality and the patterns of conduct the society wishes them to follow by actually *living* those patterns while they are in school. This pedagogy is drawn directly from the "theory of consequences" spelled out in Chapters 6 and 9. For it is quite obvious that if children can be made to experience the consequences of their actions, in as lifelike and direct a way as it is possible to create, then they will learn the rightness or wrongness of those actions far more quickly, efficiently, and permanently than if they are merely offered some remote heroic exemplar to emulate (Idealism) or some naturalistic moral law to be conditioned to (Realism) or some rational principle or catechetical dictum to master (Neo-Thomism).

To the Experimentalist educator, moral instruction is based on the general notion that "we learn what we live." This thesis has perhaps been explained best by one of John Dewey's most faithful disciples and interpreters, William Heard Kilpatrick.

Let us, says Kilpatrick, consider a specific, concrete, and limited instance of a moral value that we wish to be adopted by the young: "taking turns." This, by way of reduction, can be said to be the child's equivalent of the American principle of "equality of opportunity." Now there are four swings on a playground. During recess a class of twenty youngsters comes to the playground; ten want to swing. At this point a problem situation is apparent: How will the allotments of swinging be distributed? Several alternative solutions present themselves. First, an undirected situation may produce the "law-of-the-jungle" alternative, in which the stronger wrest the swings from the weaker pupils. This laissez-faire policy would certainly be in the American tradition (more accurately, our nineteenth-century tradition), but it would tend to produce effects and consequences unwanted by the group, namely, acrimony, fighting, conflict, and at the very least lowered morale. It would, that is, produce the very consequences that occasioned the decline of laissez-faire morality in American life. Sensing the futility of this solution, the teacher might suggest and execute a second, the "complete-embargo," alternative, in which a fiat is issued under which *no* child shall swing. This would have the effect of restoring order but also of producing some of the same consequences as the earlier policy: frustration, rancor, and impaired morale.

The Experimentalist teacher, having deliberately permitted the youngsters to "live," that is, undergo and experience, the consequences of the above possibilities, would at this point suggest—or maybe one of the group would suggest—the possibility of taking turns, so that all the youngsters could swing. This would then be tried, and if the consequences that issued from this trial were seen to be superior to the former sets of consequences, then a moral disposition in favor of taking turns would be planted in the child's moral self.

The point here is that children do not learn the morality of taking turns because it is drawn from the Judeo-Christian ethic, or because Jefferson said it is self-evident that all people are created equal, or because reason insists on it. They learn the morality of this item of conduct by using it in their lives, by living through its application in real circumstances formulated at their level of behavior and comprehension—in short, by seeing that *it works*. Kilpatrick has repeated this theme in many of his writings, but his most explicit pronunciamento on the matter appears in his essay on "Philosophy of Education from the Experimentalist Outlook." Here he says:

> . . . we see (1) that each child learns what he lives; (2) that he learns it as he accepts it in his own heart to act on; (3) that he learns it in the degree that it is important to him and in the degree that it has meaningful connections with what he already knows; and, finally, (4) that what he learns he builds at once into character.[16]

Select, then, the moral dispositions you wish the children to have, not only in their thoughts but in their overt conduct. Then contrive real, lifelike situations where those dispositions may be tested at the youngsters' level of experience, where they can recognize through the living of a situation that there are alternative solutions to moral problems and that some alternatives are better than others, because they lead to better consequences.

If this procedure cannot be directly rendered in concrete experience—as in the case of sex education—then at least the child should be given an opportunity to examine vicariously and reflectively what different

[16] Chapter 2 in *Philosophies of Education*, Forty-first Yearbook of the National Society for the Study of Education, ed. N. B. Henry, Part I (Chicago: the Society, 1942), p. 69.

moralities produce in society and what variant recommendations can be made for them in terms of their historical social consequences. If what is found to be the most humane morality disagrees with the public morality in force at the moment regarding any sensitive area of social experience, then a larger study should be made of the matter. If disagreement still persists, then it is possible to suggest that the society itself is in need of moral reform, and that individual youngsters should anticipate the acceptance of personal responsibility to help reform it when they grow to maturity.

In the long run, says the Experimentalist, the public standard is the result of this selfsame procedure, namely, the testing of alternative ways of living to see what consequences ensue. In certain sectors of life—sex and religion in particular—there is a tendency for the public standard *as expressed in professions of belief* to change more slowly and to lag behind adjustments in the public standard *as expressed in concrete behavior.* The latter—the behavioral standard—is perhaps the more authentic expression of the society's morality, because it is through concrete behavior that real, living consequences are produced. If these consequences continue to be pernicious and mean, it is doubtful whether the behavior will continue.

The school, then, says the Experimentalist, has a larger moral duty than merely the inculcation of this or that ethical practice. Its function is the intelligent criticism of the public standard, wherever that standard is expressed in the words and deeds of people in day-to-day life.

The Baselessness of Values and Individual Choice

It is at this point that the Existentialist notices a flaw in the Experimentalist's moral theory. If the ultimate reference for moral training is to be "the public standard," we are immediately cast in a pedagogical circumstance of working *from* that standard as our point of departure in the classroom. Whether we embrace or repudiate the standard makes no difference. In either case we are using the Experimentalist's method, *itself committed to the morality of public decision,* the assumed morality of what has earlier been spoken of as "the uncoerced community of persuasion."

Nothing is said in the Experimentalist doctrine about the kind of persuasion that affects the individual when he or she is viewing the consequences of moral choice. This kind of persuasion must, by the very nature of the case, be individual rather than social. Each individual must speak out on what consequences he or she prefers. Then the community can establish its public standard in favor of this or that choice.

Hence, says the Existentialist, what we do with children in school is more than to supply them a method of valuing; it encompasses much more than providing them lifelike situations in which they can undergo the consequences of their acts. The school's job pre-eminently is to awaken each child to the ultimate responsibility he or she must bear for the selections made between alternative sets of consequences. And since this is a supremely private enterprise, assisted but never determined by the community, moral instruction can never be merely communal or social in the classroom if it is to produce authentic responsibility in the child as he or she matures. We expand on this thesis in Chapter 12.

At this point we should remind ourselves of a comment earlier in this chapter to the effect that in axiological matters Existentialism may be said to separate itself from the other four philosophies in a sharper and more uncompromising way than in the other branches of philosophy. It shares much, of course, with Experimentalism, in that it agrees that Man is the author of his morality and not the compliant creature that the other three positions would make him out to be. Furthermore, Existentialism might be said to applaud Experimentalism's concern with the open and doctrine-free procedure of science in arriving at truths and goods.

But the Existentialist insists that the scientific method itself may be said to assume certain doctrinal tendencies. Specifically, there is the growing feeling that science is the ultimate method and that scientific propositions and scientifically validated values have some kind of dominion over us. We are turned, that is, into creatures with a new mode of compliance—compliance to a social method. In the school, this proclivity of Experimentalism to consider the scientific method as ultimate leads to group-determined rules in the classroom, to group-validated ethical choices (as exemplified in the playground situation in the previous section), and, indeed, to the socialized character of learning in all its many phases.

But this pedagogy, says the Existentialist, is merely the result of another philosophic *system* replacing an earlier *system*. Experimentalism places the child in the context of the group-working-scientifically instead of the context of the Absolute Self or Nature or Reason or God. It is a new context, to be sure, and a radical and well-intentioned departure from the older contexts. But it is still context; it is still an ultimate medium in which the child is presumed to grow. Anything outside this context—the content of the private self or the proclamations of private conscience, for instance —is not considered proper for educators to pay any attention to. Indeed, private, lone individuals are not allowed to exist in an Experimentalist school. They are flushed out from their back-row seats, their reticence and detachment are taken as signs of emotional imbalance, and as soon as possible they are turned into public, gregarious social products.

To an Existentialist, this is perhaps the greatest fault in so-called Progressive Education, namely, its loving attention to the sharable in life and its consequent obsession with group dynamics, social development, and public morality in the life of the school.

> Problem-centered methodology the existentialist would consider to be impersonal and unproductive, largely because the problems are usually

socially oriented; they are of immediate concern to the individual only in his social obligations.[17]

What we must do, says the Existentialist, is to find a pedagogy that will reawaken the individual child's sense of identity, that will help the child rediscover that he or she is the ultimate base of all valuation and that when the group has completed its project or the committee its investigation the child still must find his or her own way through life. No group's conclusion and no committee's recommendation has final domain over an individual's choices. In an Experimentalist school the individual usually strings along, having been taught that scientifically group-processed choices are the best and that one would be a dunce to repudiate them. But by doing this the individual is merely consenting to a new moral imperium, whether the learner or teacher realizes it or not.

So the search for an Existentialist pedagogy may be said to originate in the desire for the release of the individual—his or her absolute release from all moral doctrines, both *systematic,* as in the case of Idealism, Realism, and Neo-Thomism, and *methodological-social,* as in the case of Experimentalism. The teaching procedure we are looking for is one that will apply to children in *physical* groups, since that is the way they are found in the school, without treating them simultaneously as *psychological* or *social* groups. That is, it is a pedagogy that can rise above the physical sociality of the typical classroom to affirm the psychic identity of each of the several human beings located there.

Much can be borrowed from the older pedagogies to satisfy these conditions. It is true, for instance, that despite their doctrinal shortcomings the traditional pedagogies of either the intellectual-discipline or the knowledge-transmission sort do give the child more time to work alone than is provided in modern Experimentalist schools. The private effort of the learner would certainly be given new attention in Existentialist classrooms, especially in ethical concerns, because of the obvious necessity for some old-fashioned soul-searching before being able to make up one's mind on the tougher sort of moral problems. But there is no intimation here that the child is to be left alone to come by dint of private effort into harmony with some external moral frame. The individual is left to do his or her own moral reflection because each child is the author of value! By this tactic alone the teacher imposes responsibility on the child for coming to personal views on the matter in question. And by this tactic the teacher also suggests that genuine self-discovery can be accomplished neither through an external moral system nor through a public exposure to group dynamics in ethical questions but, instead, in the quietude of the self's inner chamber of decision and the attendant responsibility the individual is existentially committed to assume for the decisions he or she reaches. First of all, then, the Existentialist recommends more time for private

[17] G. F. Kneller, *Existentialism and Education* (New York: Philosophical Library, 1958), p. 135.

reflection and more assignments that call for moral decisions, which in turn call for more privacy of judgment in the child's in-school and out-of-school life. And it goes without saying that the Existentialist teacher will honor the need for privacy wherever and whenever the learner petitions for it.

This approach requires a heavy emphasis on the Socratic method of instruction, which—as it was pointed out in Chapter 7—is the most prominent type of Existentialist pedagogy; for the kind of knowledge that the Socratic method is pre-eminently successful in producing is self-knowledge, and this kind of knowledge—if, indeed, it be knowledge—is primarily of the moral sort: feelings, dispositions, attitudes, commitments, beliefs, awareness.

The Socratic method, far removed from its Platonic origins in this context, will not be employed to trigger some "reminiscence" in the learners' "soul" but, rather, to awaken them to the moral difficulties that must be encountered in human existence, the alternatives those difficulties suggest, and the real meaning of ultimate responsibility for private choice. The youngsters will be asked to think over their own choices—to reflect on what they are going to do with their lives, not just in the narrow career sense but in the larger, value sense. What values are they going to live by, and with what purpose? What gods—both theistic and secular—will they worship, and why? What, in short, do they think their lives on this planet, their unique selves in this cosmos, are *for*?

It is in this vein that Ralph Harper reopens the question of religious values in the school. We must remember, he says, that the *need* for religion, the *need for recognition* by some ultimate agency, is a need every human being experiences. But:

> The religious need is not necessarily a need to which there is a religious answer. It is simply the human need of ultimate recognition. The individual . . . wants above everything some evidence that at least his need is recognized by others as the most important thing about him. He wants the universe itself to give some evidence, if possible, that it, too, recognizes this need as legitimate and appeasable. But there is no logical necessity which says that if there is a need for the universe to recognize and appease, the universe will oblige.[18]

No logical necessity, indeed. It is just because Man has historically insisted that the universe appease him in this way that he has concocted so many competing religions. And the basic difficulty with the religion-in-education issue, in its customary formulation, lies in the notion that the *need for appeasement* cannot be separated from the variety of *answers* that organized religions have, down through the centuries, given to this

---

[18] "Significance of Existence and Recognition for Education," Chapter 7 in *Modern Philosophies and Education,* Fifty-fourth Yearbook of the National Society for the Study of Education, ed. N. B. Henry, Part I (Chicago: the Society, 1955), p. 245.

need. Operating on this notion, we have felt in America that to confound the school's curriculum with sectarian "answers" to the need would serve only to promote division and contention. And so we have secularized the school by driving sectarianism out of it.

But secularizing the school has unthinkingly been interpreted to mean wholly eliminating consideration of this need we all experience. And if there is one thing that boys and girls desperately require somewhere in their maturing process, it is a reflective concern for the types of questions that the "need for recognition" provokes—questions concerning who they are, what they are doing around here in existence, and why. This set of questions simply cannot be brought under study outside the scope of the so-called religious need.

But to study the need, the Existentialist reminds us, does not require specifying any answers. Merely to state the religious need of human beings in the classroom is not the same thing as "appeasing"—to use Harper's word—the children with this or that comfortable religious solution to their need. It is, on the contrary, to awaken them to the problem of ultimate recognition and to what this problem signifies in our lonely search for ourselves.

Existentialists complain that Experimentalists have so thoroughly secularized the school that they have not only eliminated from it all sectarianism, and even any mention of God, but have been guilty of the complete expungement of any ultimate questions whatsoever from the child's experience. But the ultimate questions of life—quite unlike their answers—belong to all people. This is not because they are religious or metaphysical; it is because they are existential. That is, they reside at the very base of our being. Hence, every child in the school has a right to be assisted in viewing these questions and in considering what they mean for a human self. The Existentialist educator can be expected to put these questions back into the school's program.

Refining Aesthetic Taste

If the development of right conduct is a puzzling and perplexing educational task, the development of taste is perhaps more so. The field of aesthetics itself is difficult of compass and rational analysis; as a result it is not clearly plotted and mapped. Even well-trained and scholarly philosophers have difficulty in taking their readers through it with the same facility they exhibit in other branches of their discipline. The reason for this may be that art, itself a symbol system, resists translation into the more literal, matter-of-fact symbolism of ordinary language. Can we really reduce aesthetic feeling to verbal terms? Can the experience of enjoyment be rendered in subjects and predicates? To raise the question is to imply the possibility of a negative reply. In any event, educational theorists have generally had little to say about instruction in aesthetics in their books on teaching and learning.

It is unnecessary, therefore, to apologize for what may at first appear an altogether too brief treatment of so important a matter as aesthetics in general and the arts in particular as they influence teaching and learning. There is no intention here to diminish or depreciate the importance of the arts in education, only an effort to be realistic about the level and intensity of discourse that can be maintained concerning it.

With this rather hesitant beginning, we may proceed to say a few things about the way educators in the various schools of philosophy go about the business of refining taste.

MASTERWORKS AND THE IDEA OF BEAUTY

Certainly if Idealists were cornered on the question they would be likely to repair to their general theory of aesthetics for clues. There, as we have seen, the label of *ideal* can be taken in its common-sense and more or less literal meaning, namely, the idealization of the world we see about us. If, then, art is to be measured by the degree to which the work of art succeeds in capturing the idealized representation of that which may look commonplace in our day-to-day lives, the Idealist will wish to use such works as the stimulants to aesthetic feelings in the young. Just as the ethical training of youngsters in Idealism is built upon imitation of heroic exemplars of history or contemporary life, so likewise will their aesthetic sense be quickened by exposure to those great works of art— like the "Mona Lisa," the "Emperor Concerto," the *Swan Lake* ballet, *Hamlet*—which have aroused human sensibilities down through time. In the Idealistic aesthetic catalogue such works are the true objects of civilized taste. If we mean to bring children to like and enjoy them, then certainly the very first business of the school is to bring youngsters into direct exposure to them.

What follows is of course not necessarily peculiar to Idealism: These works are exhibited or performed for the child, and it is hoped and expected that there will be an emotional response. But the object of the Idealist teacher is never to settle only for such a response but to expect and require *understanding* of the work as well. That is, the "exposure phase" should be followed by the "understanding phase," in which the child studies the characteristics and symbolic meanings of the works under view, the artists and their lives and times, and the cultural origin of the style and mode of what they have done.

This suggests once more the primacy of Mind to the Idealists. Their metaphysics, as we have seen, is of the Infinite Mind; their epistemology sets forth the "approximation" of that Mind through the absorption of knowledge and wisdom. Now again, in aesthetics, the mind becomes the constant companion of "the feelings" in the child's growth toward cultivated taste. Indeed, it might even be said by an Idealist that we can never truly develop a taste for anything *until* we understand it. It is possibly for this reason that in most schools and colleges the courses in art appreciation or music appreciation are really nothing more than attempts at (1) exposing the learner to great works and, more importantly, (2) building *understanding* of those master-works through a study of them in much the same manner as we would study wars or historical movements or natural phenomena—that is, with the aim of objective mastery of information concerning them. Aesthetic feeling and emotional response are the end object of all this, but in order to be truly mature such responses must be built upon thorough comprehension of what has been done in the work of art. Once you understand a work of art you can then proceed to a genuinely cultivated aesthetic enjoyment of it.[19]

Beauty in Nature: Form, Balance, and Structure

The Realists certainly would not dismiss the above approach; indeed, they might adopt part or even all of it. But their interest in the *understanding* of art works would take a decidedly more mechanistic and structural turn. They would wish the learner to witness masterpieces, of course. Their abiding belief in the primacy of sensation would require that we begin here in aesthetic training. But in the study of masterpieces their *construction* would assume first pedagogical interest. Beethoven's patterns of A-A-B-A in symphonic design, the intricacy of Bach's fugues and mathematically precise polyphonies, Leonardo da Vinci's structural symbolism in "The Last Supper," Shakespeare's genius at exposition-development-climax-denouement would be singled out for special emphasis.

It is, you will remember, the *design* and *order* of nature that the Realists wish to see celebrated in art, and for this reason they want the learner in art to attend first of all to these particular qualities. Later on, of course, the learner can be shown the other things art contains—symbolisms, meanings, an underlying mystique—and perhaps experience the emotional impact it is presumed to have on others. A grasp of structural principles in the arts, however, comes first.

There is also, to be sure, a persistent theme in Realism—one that runs somewhat counter to Idealist tendencies—elevating the physical and sensuous to first rank in human experience. It is to be presumed, then, that the Realist would wish art students to take hold of the medium itself, even if only briefly, to get the feel, literally, of what the artist is working with. Studio contact with art media—playing an instrument, shaping a clay figure, painting a still life, producing a play, learning a dance—such

---

[19] Vincent Price, Hollywood actor and art collector, has published a book with this theme as its title: *I Like What I Know* (Garden City, N.Y.: Doubleday, 1959).

kinesthetic, tactile experiences must somehow be included before the learner can be said to have received instruction in the arts.

When, through this method, the learners begin to see the nature of technique and the importance of the physical control that the artist must bring to the medium, they will then begin to develop a mature appreciation and, following this, a more cultured taste for what constitutes greatness in aesthetic production.

BEAUTY THROUGH INTUITION AND REVELATION

By all measures, the most obscure of the several educational theories in aesthetics is that of the Neo-Thomist. This is due partly to the apparent lack of relationship between the arts generally, which quicken our feelings and arouse our emotions, and Reason, which, as we have seen, is the governing principle for most if not all Neo-Thomist thought. However, a more likely reason for the obscurity of Neo-Thomist educational prescriptions in the arts is that a very specialized and abstruse type of Reason is involved, namely, intuition.

Intuition is one of those notions on which, unless one is a Maritain, it is difficult to discourse. And when we are asked to apply such a notion to the training of boys and girls in aesthetic judgment and artistic taste, it is not an easy business.

Presumably, as in the case of ethics and morals, the training of the Reason would be a necessary prerequisite to any successful pedagogy in the arts. Intellectually children must be brought to a point of clarity and sharpness, via the customary disciplinary subject matters, before they can be expected to achieve anything on the order of genuinely rational taste. Once this point has been reached, it is the purpose of the Neo-Thomist instructor to single out for special cultivation intuitive "perceptions" of great works of art. In ordinary language we usually speak of this as *inspiration,* and when we fix the child's attention on that specific quality of art—that thing we might describe as a "lurch" of the artist into a completely new but essentially private vision of the ultimate nature of things —we recommend that quality to the child as the most important thing to look for.

Maritain frequently speaks of the "contemplative tendencies" of the child and suggests that we encourage those tendencies by providing occasions for them to emerge. The child's confrontation of truly great works of art, especially if their theme is Christian, will provide at least the raw materials for such occasions, and if the teacher can somehow infuse the atmosphere of the learning situation with a contemplative mood, then the learner may be drawn to this mode of activity.

It would not be altogether irrelevant to comment also on the more immediate but less spiritual kinds of enjoyment that we find in pure reason. The Neo-Thomist often points out that mathematics has its own aesthetic satisfactions; there is a transport and delight in taking intellectual hold of complicated abstractions in the calculus, or of the beautiful intricacies of conic sections and parabolas in geometry. The utter rationality of mathematics is a pleasure to behold, and it is presumed that Neo-Thomists would not allow this pleasure to be lost on their students.

The Neo-Thomists' constant emphasis on the intuitive nature of creative endeavor and their location of aesthetic delight in the pure abstractions of mathematics may help to explain why the *"Ars gratia artis"* point of view in aesthetics, discussed in Chapter 8 (see pages 220–221), has found so ready a champion in this particular school of thought. Art for its own sake is splendidly consistent with a view that holds the intellect aloof from the concerns of life. The intellect is trained to see Truth, not to solve problems; and so the aesthetic powers of the individual are developed to love Beauty-in-abstract, not to render our own experience more lovely. To solve problems and to render the conditions of life more aesthetically satisfying are certainly noble activities, but in Neo-Thomist thought they are essentially secondary to pure intellection and pure creative intuition in and for themselves. The school's task is to make this distinction between the pure and the applied clear to the learner, and to insist that the former is always of higher rank than the latter.

Aesthetic Experience as the Widening of Meanings

Experimentalists, as one may expect, begin to balk rather vigorously at this line of argument. In the first place, intuition has no public dimensions. It cannot become an object of philosophic discussion, because it is essentially private and solitary in nature. Since Experimentalists value so highly the socialized approach to life and learning, it is little wonder that they have slight confidence in the "private intuitions" of the Neo-Thomist educator. Furthermore, to set art off in a pure and uncontaminated region of its own is to demolish the very purpose of teaching it in school, namely, to arouse new meanings and new feelings in the children, to suggest to them a new and somewhat keener dimension to life, and, in the end, to bring more beauty to the affairs of human beings and to equip them to feel it and enjoy it in their daily occupations.

From this platform, the Experimentalists recall their generalized pedagogy of "learning through living" and simply apply it to the aesthetic field. If we want boys and girls to develop taste we must present to them situations in which certain objects are seen to produce aesthetic effects or consequences of a higher order than what they have hitherto given their attention to. If the school wishes to awaken taste, then the place to begin is in the experience of the learner.

Start with their taste in clothes, or rock music, or automobile design. Or, better still, start with the school. A project in the beautification of the classroom or the aesthetic improvement of the grounds would be a genuine living situation in which all kinds of aesthetic learnings could take place. Maybe it would be a project in making the cafeteria more pleasant, or in piping music to the lunchroom, or a project in which the students are given responsibility to select paintings for the hallways. Let the consequences of the youngsters' own choices be felt and undergone. Let them, that is, take hold of their own experience at the aesthetic level to see what they can make of it.

It would be hopelessly naive to think that what they would come up with would be altogether lovely—paintings in the hallways or Muzak in the cafeteria. But that is just the point: They are in school to learn. And we shall never get boys and girls to appreciate anything, whether that thing is among the so-called finer things of life or not, simply by exposing them to it or having them study the life and times of its author or having them master the laws of construction the artist followed in composing or painting or writing it, or advising them to find pure delight in the so-called intuitions it reveals. We get boys and girls to appreciate what we want them to appreciate by introducing that thing into their lives and allowing its aesthetic impact to do its own work on their sensibilities. If it does not do its work, that is, if they do not respond to it, there is not much sense in haranguing them or trying to intellectualize the whole business as if it were just another subject in the school.

Taste is a delicate and fragile trait, to be sure, requiring steady cultivation. Most of us spend precious little time trying to develop it. We go through life letting our likes and dislikes stand without criticism. But this is because we permit art to be enclosed and isolated in concert halls, art galleries, and museums. Once we get art back into life—most particularly, into the lives of the children in school as they live it day by day—then we shall be in a position to manage their aesthetic growth effectively.

It is partly for this reason that the Experimentalist educators in art have so energetically championed the child's direct participation in artistic endeavor. Like the Realists, the Experimentalists want the learners to get their hands on the medium—to try blowing a horn or carving a piece of soap or creating a dramatic character. But they want this for motives beyond that of merely involving the senses of the child, as the Realist would say. Experimentalists want it because they wish to involve the total child—not only the senses, but imagination, feelings, and the need to communicate to others. Hence in Experimentalist schools one is likely to find much more learner participation in art and music classes than in other schools. Through direct and living experience the learners acquire their tastes and an understanding of why they have acquired them.

ART AS THE STATEMENT OF THE SELF

We are, at this point, in the general vicinity of the Existentialist view of the matter. Of all that goes on in an Experimentalist school, the art and music departments look like the most likely beachheads for an Existentialist. This is because they, alone among all the departments in the school, are avowedly militant in their concern for the individuality of the child. This individuality, as we have seen, is given room for growth when the Experimentalist involves the learner directly in the artistic enterprise, and it is applauded, both theoretically and practically, in the desire to have youngsters release their feelings and express their sentiments about the world in such a way as to communicate them to their classmates.

So far, so good, says the Existentialist. We will accept this program as the base of our operations. However, we will begin to lose interest in the child's artistic productions in the degree that they are supposed to be socially consumed, that is, enjoyed and fawned over by other people. If the child is given rein to paint or sing or act in order to arouse a peer interest in what he or she is doing, then we have begun to compromise the entire pedagogy. Rather should we concern ourselves with the child's aesthetic production as a statement about selfhood and how he or she conceives this selfhood to be existing in the world. It does not matter whether a water color is to be put up on the bulletin board. What matters is that the water color be in some way the child's very own, a *particular* statement of the world as he or she sees it.

This theme is, we say, already in the ascendancy in Experimentalist thinking. It needs only a firmer and more aggressive statement to make it acceptable to Existentialism. For it is worth noting that the place in the Experimentalist's school where group dynamics has the least effect is the art room. Here, finally, is a subject matter that does not yield to the "committee approach."

So, once the children are set free from the inherited traditions of study and criticism in the arts and, *more important*, once they are set free from the heavy pressure of the group and from its dominion over them, they can finally set out in the Existentialist mode to make their own artistic statements about life.

It is not possible to set down any particular criteria as to what shall or shall not be acceptable in the way of aesthetic productions—paintings, statues, dramatic skits, music. But the Existentialist teacher will insist on two things. First, the productions must be authentic; that is, they must emanate directly from the existential consciousness of the individual child, without having the customary feeling that he or she is to paint this or that or draw in this way or in that way to satisfy some prior condition laid down by the teacher. Each child must be completely free to portray a situation as he or she sees it.

Second, and this follows from the insistence on authenticity, the learner must take responsibility for what has been produced. The child must not be permitted to escape the personal commitment to what has been created, even if others upon viewing it do not like it. There will always be temptations for the child to do this, to repudiate personal artistic products and to

SCHEMATIC SUMMARY OF VIEWS

COMPARATIVE PHILOSOPHIES

		Definition	Idealism	Realism	Neo-Thomism	Experi-mentalism	Existen-tialism
METAPHYSICS		The study of reality: What is real?	A world of mind	A world of things	A world of Reason and Being/God	A world of experience	A world of existing
EPISTEMOLOGY		The study of knowing and knowledge: What is true?	Seeing with the "mind's eye"— consistency of ideas	Spectator Theory: sensation and cor-respondence	Intuition, logical reasoning, and revelation	Testing to see what works	Subjective choice, personal appropria-tion
AXIOLOGY	Ethics	The study of valuing and values: What is good?	The imitation of the Absolute Self	The law of nature	The rational act	The public test	The anguish of freedom
	Aesthetics	What is beautiful?	Reflection of the Ideal	Reflection of nature	Creative intuition	The public taste	Revolt from the public norm

EDUCATIONAL IMPLICATIONS

	Idealism	**Realism**	**Neo-Thomism**	**Experimentalism**	**Existentialism**
Curricular Emphasis	Subject matter of the mind: literature, intellectual history, philosophy, religion	Subject matter of the physical world: mathematics and science	Subject matter of intellect and spirit: disciplinary subjects: mathematics and language and Doctrine	Subject matter of social experience: the social studies	Subject matter of choice: art, ethics, moral philosophy, religion
Preferred Method	Teaching for the handling of ideas: lecture, discussion	Teaching for mastery of factual information and basic skills: demonstration, recitation	Disciplining the mind: formal drill— readying the spirit: Catechism	Problem solving: project method	Arousing personal response: Socratic questioning
Character Education	Imitating exemplars, heroes	Training in rules of conduct	Disciplining behavior to reason	Making group decisions in light of consequences	Awakening the self to responsibility
Developing Taste	Studying the masterworks	Studying design in nature	Finding beauty in reason	Participating in art projects	Composing a personal art work

try to undo them. But, of course they can never be undone. And the teacher must help the child see this. If, however, the child's products are personally unsatisfactory not because they fail to be popular with classmates but because they have not said what he or she wanted to say with painter's brush or sculptor's knife or dancer's body, then the child should be encouraged to improve upon them, to transcend them, in a similar or perhaps more elaborate assignment. In this way the teacher can help the child reaffirm personal aesthetic selfhood at a continuously higher and higher level.

Continuous involvement is the key. To yearn constantly for expression is to be en rapport with the Existentialist frame of mind in aesthetic instruction. And if the learner is infused with this yearning for expression, not for its social effect but solely for its private effect on personal selfhood, then the Existentialist teacher has truly succeeded in this educational undertaking.

With the present chapter, we have completed our analytical tour of the major philosophies. We have examined their theories of reality, knowledge, and value and how they relate to the educative process. A schematic summary of these views is presented on pages 294–295. To the left of this chart are the three primary questions that philosophy attempts to answer. What is real? What is true? What is good? In the left half of the chart are the short answers that each of our five philosophies gives to these questions. In the right half of the chart are the applications of these answers to the educative process.

In Part Five, we "change the subject," and turn to description, analysis, and evaluation of three major educational movements in contemporary America: education as behavior engineering, education as self-actualization, and education and cultural pluralism. Here are three major "philosophies of action" currently recommended for adoption in American education. We shall see where their ideas come from, what their philosophic origins are, and, most important, what they lead to when put into practice in the American school.

Questions

1. In Catholic parochial schools, there has been a trend away from segregation of the sexes. How do you explain this departure from the traditional Catholic position, and what effect will it have on schooling?

2. In Chapter 8 there appeared a discussion of the discrepancy between what people say and what they do in the field of morals and conduct. Which of the theories of pedagogy presented here would be most likely to narrow this gap in the course of the next generation of school children? Explain.

3. The distinctions in axiological theory and practice between Experimentalism and the three traditional philosophies are relatively clear. The distinctions between Experimentalism and Existentialism, however, appear to be still in a state of flux and formulation. What can you add to the preceding analysis by way of specifying more particularly how these positions differ? In doing this, you will certainly wish to consult the earlier segments of the book and some of the reference readings.

4. Cleanliness, as a traditional value, has lost some ground to the "counter-culture" during the sixties and seventies. Should the teacher ever tell Janie to wash her hands?

5. One of the ways to test these alternative pedagogies is to single out a field of aesthetics with which you are not very familiar—say, ballet or Elizabethan poetry—and then describe the educational program you think would be pre-pared for you by an avid disciple of each of the five positions. Try it and see what results.

6. Presumably architecture has something to do with the function and purpose of a building. Suppose that exponents of the five theories discussed in this chapter were each to design a school building for construction in your com-munity. What features would you expect each to emphasize in his design? Illustrate, either graphically or verbally, how these school buildings would be different, if you think they would.

Further Reading

Idealism

Berkson, I. B. *The Ideal and the Community*. New York: Harper, 1958. Berkson's point of departure is Dewey-Kilpatrick Experimentalism, but the general thesis of the entire volume consists in a revision of this conception of education in the general direction of Idealism. In Chapter 14 he considers the matter of intelli-gence and character and whether they stem from idea and belief or experience and inquiry. He inclines toward the former source, and in effect restates the case for community ideals as they are found in history, tradition, and con-science.

Horne, Herman Harrell. *This New Education*. New York: Abingdon, 1931. Pro-fessor Horne, the "Mr. Idealism" of the educational world, in this book de-velops a cogent rebuttal to the Progressives. In Chapter 10 he considers "How Character Is Created," presenting in careful progression the steps by which the Idealist teacher would shape the conduct of the child.

Realism

Broudy, Harry S. *Building a Philosophy of Education*. New York: Prentice-Hall, 1954. Professor Broudy classifies himself as a Classical Realist. Here, in Chap-ter 13, he examines how aesthetic values are taught in the school. Then, in Chapter 14, he considers the companion problem of how moral values are in-troduced into the experience of the young by Realist teachers. He concludes with some moral criteria: self-determination, self-realization, self-integration, and democracy.

Perry, Ralph Barton. *Realms of Value.* Cambridge: Harvard University Press, 1954. Perry is a Realist with Experimentalist tendencies. In Chapter 21, on "Education and the Science of Education," he considers the general meaning of education; the curriculum; the explanatory, normative, and technological methods; indoctrination; moral education; and liberal and humane education. This is not so much a partisan prescription as it is a thematic review of major value questions as they are met in educational practice.

Neo-Thomism

Maritain, Jacques. "Thomist Views on Education," Chapter 3 in *Modern Philosophies and Education,* Fifty-fourth Yearbook of the National Society for the Study of Education, ed. N. B. Henry, Part I. Chicago: the Society, 1955. Most of Maritain's writings have an axiological flavor even when they deal with other matters, and this one is no exception. Here he treats of the aims of education, the hierarchy of values, moral education and religion, and the teaching of theology. In this essay the Thomist position is put clearly and persuasively.

Pope Pius XI. *Christian Education of Youth.* Washington: National Catholic Welfare Conference, 1936. When Pius XI spoke, it was well to listen, not only because he was as Pope the one authentic voice on doctrinal matters but also because as a man of deep feeling he spoke eloquently and well on the position of the Church. This little pamphlet places you in direct contact with a moral tradition of enormous consequence in the Western world; and it says with beautiful yet simple persuasion what the Catholic educator is obligated to do for the proper training of the child.

Experimentalism

Mason, Robert E. *Moral Values and Secular Education.* New York: Columbia University Press, 1950. Mason is an Experimentalist, but he prefers to speak of his own moral theory as "evolutionary naturalism," to which two chapters are devoted. This volume also contains an axiological discussion of Essentialism, Traditionalism, and Individualism.

Raths, Louis, Merrill Harmin, and Sidney B. Simon. *Values and Teaching.* Columbus: Merrill, 1966. Professor Raths and his colleagues examine the value dimension in the classroom and how the learner absorbs the preferences of the wider culture through the medium of the teacher's daily conduct.

Existentialism

Greene, Maxine. *Teacher as Stranger.* Belmont, Calif.: Wadsworth, 1973. Professor Greene, one of the most imaginative explorers of Existential understandings and feelings in the educational medium, here ranges widely across a broad landscape: being and learning, science and subjectivity, dilemmas and commitments. She concludes with her view of the teacher as a homecoming stranger.

Lloyd, Robert A. *Images of Survival.* New York: Dodd, Mead, 1973. This fascinating book fits into no convenient category. It is phenomenological adventuring, autobiography, imaginary dialogue, and a little actual correspondence between Lloyd, an instructor of art at Phillips Academy, and his students and friends. It is a kind of diary of the moving spirit in the lively and loving situation where people are teaching and learning.

General

Smith, Philip G. *Theories of Value and Problems of Education.* Urbana: University of Illinois Press, 1970. These special essays are arranged not by "isms" but by educational concerns: "Value Theory and Education," "Educational Objectives and the Conduct of Schooling," and "Moral Education." Here we see axiology at work in educational decision making.

Wirsing, Marie. *Teaching and Philosophy: A Synthesis.* Boston: Houghton Mifflin, 1972. One of philosophy's prime tasks is the examination of values. Values are often in conflict, sometimes in the schoolroom, where boys and girls are taught to believe contradictory things. Take a look at Chapter 2, "Transmitting the Core Values: A Dilemma," where Professor Wirsing gives us a vivid glimpse of values in collision.

We move now to educational practice.

The material in Parts One, Two, Three, and Four has been devoted to a systematic analysis of philosophical concepts and how they guide educational thinking. We wish now to expand on how educational planning is conducted in this country and how the foregoing concepts and ideas eventually find their way into the nation's classrooms.

The vehicle we have chosen for this demonstration consists of three philosophical models for educational design:

Education as Behavior Engineering: The Technological Model
Education as Self-Actualization: The Humanistic Model
Education and Cultural Pluralism: The Social Dimension

We consider these three designs in Chapters 11, 12, and 13, respectively.

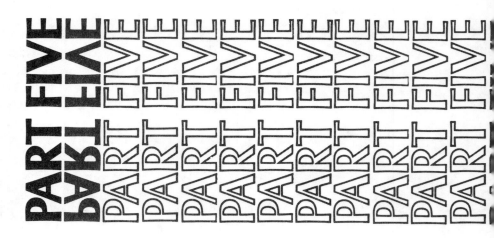

Philosophical
Models for
Educational
Practice

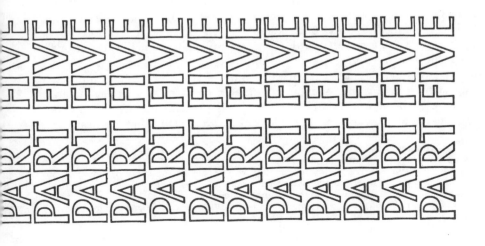

11

Education as Behavior Engineering: A Technological Model

Philosophical Basis of Education as Behavior Engineering

WHAT IS BEHAVIOR ENGINEERING?

To the advocates of education as behavior engineering,[1] "education is the establishing of behavior which will be of advantage to the individual and to others at some future time."[2] This task of modifying human behavior is to be accomplished by finding and arranging the conditions for learning by applying principles of both physical and behavioral sciences and also by utilizing mechanical and electronic devices. Such a model of education then must be based on sound empirical knowledge about human behavior and rely heavily on what B. F. Skinner calls the technology of behavior. Hence, the supporters of this technological concept of education insist that we can dispense with such time-honored ideas as cultivation of the intellect, learning by discovery, self-initiated learning, and intrinsic motivation and that the actual business of educating our children can be better accomplished if we deal only with the behaviors that are directly observable, hence controllable and measurable or quantifiable.

They go on to argue that, at least in principle, all attainable educational aims can be defined in terms of specifically observable responses. Accordingly, any educational or instructional goal that, in principle, cannot be translated into statements about observable overt acts is irrelevant and immaterial. If we understand this view, it is not difficult to see why the proponents of the engineering model of education claim that the best way

---

[1] In this chapter the expression *technology of education* will be used interchangeably with *education as behavior engineering*. However, *technology of education* is not to be confused with what is now commonly known as instructional or educational technology, which refers to the use of electronic and mechanical devices and other audiovisual materials and equipment as instructional aids.

[2] B. F. Skinner, *Science and Human Behavior*, © 1953, p. 402. Reprinted by permission of Macmillan Publishing Company, New York.

to determine the success or failure of our schools and teachers is to measure the frequency with which certain desired responses occur.

In spite of its radical departure from traditional education emphasizing the intellect, the self, the mind, and the will, this approach to education is drawing increased national attention, producing a profound impact on the development and implementation of educational policies and programs in this country. For example, the rapidly growing professional interest in behavioral objectives, teacher accountability, performance-based teacher education, and programed instruction can be traced directly to this educational theory.

PHILOSOPHICAL FOUNDATIONS

The behavior engineering model of education is supported by some of the metaphysical, epistemological, and axiological beliefs we have discussed in the earlier chapters. As noted in Chapters 4, 7, and 10, there is an inextricable relationship between our practical conduct in education and the fundamental beliefs we have about reality, knowledge, and value. In the following pages we examine the philosophical basis of education as behavior engineering.

For reasons that will become apparent, we shall henceforth call the behavior engineering model of education the behaviorist model, for it is founded on methodological (radical or descriptive) behaviorism. It is true that in general the term behaviorism is associated with a school of psychology, but it also stands for a world view, a metaphysics, or a conceptual scheme through which we see the world and everything in it, and to which we assign special meanings. Although there are several versions of behaviorism, in this chapter we shall deal mainly with B. F. Skinner's philosophical, psychological, and educational views, since his work is commonly thought to represent the behaviorist model of education.

According to methodological or Skinnerean behaviorism, reality or the universe is nonteleological in nature. The universe is neither created by a special being for a unique purpose nor moving toward a preordained goal. Although it does not have any predetermined destiny to fulfill, it is believed to have an order that is governed by certain laws of nature. These laws, being rooted in the assumption that all events are caused, govern all things in the universe. Through *publicly shareable* experiences, we can know about the universe as well as our behavior. This kind of metaphysics makes a science of behavior possible, but one of its "side effects" is to dispose of our freedom and autonomy, because we become the product of environmental causes over which we have no real control. Hence, the doctrine of free will turns into a myth, a consequence of muddled thinking, for in a causally determined world, freedom as uncaused action is not possible. As Skinner remarked:

Man's struggle for freedom is not due to a will to be free, but to certain behavioral processes characteristic of the human organism, the effect of which is the avoidance of or escape from so-called "aversive" features of the environment.[3]

Humanity's search for freedom is then synonymous with its desire to escape from pain and unpleasant conditions, and what we can become rests, to a large extent, with our environment.

Metaphysically, Skinner is a realist in that he is convinced that reality exists independent of its knower. In other words, what is real is real whether anyone knows about it or not. But more precisely, his position lies somewhere between naive Realism and scientific Realism (see Chapter 3, pages 53–54, 63). Skinner may be called a naive Realist because he holds that our uninterpreted and unedited sense data can reveal the nature of reality. He believes that observation without judgment or interpretation is possible, and if we can only observe our world objectively and describe our experiences systematically, we can discover the order in the universe and in human behavior. He is naive in the same sense as people who believe that what one sees and hears exists precisely as one perceives it. They do not suspect the possibility that what they see and hear may not exist at all or that it may exist in a very different way.

But Skinner can also be called a scientific Realist, because he accepts our shareable, intersubjective experiences as the best source of human knowledge and sees our observation and experimentation as the most reliable means of knowing the universe. In short, for him, public verifiability separates knowledge from fiction. (For further discussion of Realist metaphysics and epistemology refer to Chapter 3, pages 50–55, and to Chapter 6, pages 130–137.) As we shall see later, it is his metaphysics and epistemology that led Skinner to his radical behaviorism, which in turn resulted in the view that what is not directly observable is irrelevant in the scientific explanation of human behavior. We shall also see that it is this belief that brings the advocates of methodological behaviorism to the conclusion that we can disregard any educational consequences or goals that cannot be identified with observable responses.

Since Skinner sees reality as being nonteleological and morally neutral, he does not regard anything as being inherently good or bad. For "things are good . . . or bad . . . presumably because of the contingencies of survival under which the species evolved." [4] Behavior which enables us to survive is good, and that which hinders our survival is bad to that extent. Similarly, those cultural practices that make the survival of a society difficult are bad. Hence, a culture should be judged in terms of its survival value. Skinner goes on to point out that since a science of behavior deals with demonstrating the consequences of cultural practices, a culture that

---

[3] B. F. Skinner, *Beyond Freedom and Dignity* (New York: Knopf, 1971), p. 42.
[4] Ibid., p. 104.

makes the most efficient use of the methods of science in solving its problems is the most likely to survive.[5]

What people need today is not less control but more control; they need to make better use of the technology of behavior to create a world in which they can live together in peace, producing what they need but consuming only a reasonable part of the resources of the world, enjoying art, music, and literature, and contributing to others' enjoyment of them, adding as little as possible to the pollution of their environment, bearing no more children than can be raised decently, and constantly looking for a more efficient means of managing their lives.[6] All this can be accomplished through education, that is, behavior engineering. Such, then, is the ultimate end of behaviorist education.

Psychological Basis of Education as Behavior Engineering

Skinner is very much against theorizing, for he firmly believes that knowledge about reality can be obtained through objective and systematic observation and description. Consequently, his main interest in education lies in the development of a technology rather than a *theory* of education. He sees education and instruction as the expediting of learning rather than as a direct transmission of something to the learner.

Skinner regards the learning of all voluntary responses as a process of conditioning in which the probability of a response is increased by manipulation of certain conditions outside the organism. This concept of learning is based solely on a description of the ways in which responses and their causes (reinforcements) are related to each other. Accordingly, mental faculties, consciousness, and such other mentalistic terms as motives, insight, understanding, aspiration, intention, love, hate, and anger are thought to have only metaphorical meanings at best. Yet, most of us will find it difficult, if not impossible, to deny that we have vivid experiences of understanding, planning, aspiring, loving, hating, and being angry. Further, we often explain the actions of others as well as our own by referring to various mental and emotional states. For example, we might say that John spanked his child because he was angry or that he brought home a gift because he was in a generous mood.

But, if it is true that most people have clear and distinct experiences of undergoing mental and emotional states, why does Skinner choose to ignore them by dealing with the immediately observable responses only? On what grounds does he assert that our inner states, mental or physical, are irrelevant in explaining human behavior? These are important questions, because to a large extent the answers to them give us the basis for assessing the validity and the adequacy of the behaviorist view of education as

[5] Skinner, *Science and Human Behavior*, p. 446.
[6] Skinner, *Beyond Freedom and Dignity*, p. 214.

behavior engineering. In considering these queries, we need to examine Skinner's conception of the nature and function of science, for his ideas on the subject matter and methods of psychology are an integral part of his philosophy of science and subsequently of his account of learning.

PSYCHOLOGY: A SCIENCE OF BEHAVIOR

Etymologically, psychology is the study (logos) of mind or soul (psyche). Historically, psychology has been concerned with the analysis of mental powers and various forms of conscious states as a means of understanding the nature of the mind, which was believed to be the cause of all our overt actions. Moreover, since the term *mind* stood for an unobservable entity, it was not amenable to scientific investigation as we understand the expression today. Skinner states:

> If psychology is a science of mental life—of the mind, of conscious experience—then it must develop and defend a special methodology, which it has not yet done successfully. If it is, on the other hand, a science of the behavior of organisms, human or otherwise, then it is part of biology, a natural science for which tested and highly successful methods are available.[7]

Consequently, neither the term *mind* nor *self* has any defensible place in a science of behavior, for these invented notions together with their special characteristics provide false explanations. Furthermore, since the mind or psychic events are said to lack physical dimensions, we have additional grounds for rejecting them. Skinner goes on to argue that a science of behavior can gain nothing by using mentalistic terms. Hence, to speak of a person's mind is not to speak of some immaterial entity or self but to refer to a "device for representing a functionally unified system of responses." This means that psychology as a science of the human mind must become an empirical and experimental science devoted to studying the functional relationship between responses (dependent variables) and their causes (independent variables).

The expression "functional analysis" refers to the investigation of the cause-effect relationship between dependent variables and independent variables, which will enable us to predict and control the behavior of organisms. However, the term *cause* as used by Skinner does not imply any mysterious power of a variable (cause) to produce another event (effect), for a cause is simply a change in the independent variable and an effect is a change in the dependent variable. Therefore, when Skinner asserts that "A caused B," he means that A is followed by B, or that B is preceded by A. Like Hume, Skinner does not assume any metaphysical glue that is supposed to connect a cause with its effect, because he regards the cause-effect relationship as a conjunction between two events, cause and effect. (See

[7] B. F. Skinner, "Behaviorism at Fifty," in *Behaviorism and Phenomenology*, T. W. Wann, ed. (Chicago: University of Chicago Press, 1964), p. 79.

Chapter 6, page 131). This makes it possible to say, "If A, then always (or probably) B," rather than "A makes B happen." Through a functional analysis of human behavior we gain information about its causal relationships, and by synthesizing these facts in quantitative terms we come to have a comprehensive picture of the organism as a behaving system. But such analysis requires that we confine ourselves to the description of responses. In addition, the concepts used to describe the responses must be defined in terms of immediate observations without assigning them either mental or psychological properties. In other words, any concept that does not have an observable referent should not be used in a science of human behavior.

INNER STATES

It appears that many of our overt actions are caused by certain neurophysiological mental processes. If so, would we not do better to study the relationship between these inner states and overt responses? To this Skinner firmly replies that knowledge of inner states is of little value to a science of behavior because inner states are not directly observable. Because they are not observable, it is easy to assign properties to them without justification and to invent spurious explanations.

Neurophysiological States   Skinner opposes the use of neural or physiological conditions as explanations of human behavior not only because direct observation of the nervous system (or physiological change) has never been made, but also because these conditions can only be inferred from overt behavior. Even if these physical processes could be directly observed, they could not justifiably be used to explain the very behavior upon which they were based. In any case, we do not yet have neurophysiological knowledge based on direct observation about the conditions that precede an instance of verbal behavior (for instance, saying "No, thank you,") and the "causes" that preceded those conditions. The difficulty with this neurological approach is that the causes of saying "No, thank you" ultimately lie outside, not inside, the organism.[8] Consequently, Skinner is extremely skeptical about the usefulness of neurophysiological findings in predicting and controlling human behavior. Of course, this attitude is to be expected, since his psychology is based on the assumption that human behavior is a function of external variables. By his definition of behavior the so-called inner causes, physical or mental, become unnecessary for a scientific investigation of behavior.

Mental States   The usual practice among laypeople and perhaps some psychologists is to explain the behavior of others by attributing it to certain mental or emotional conditions. Thus Theresa is said to play the piano

[8] Skinner, *Science and Human Behavior*, p. 28.

well because she has musical ability, or Bob is said to smoke a great deal because he has a smoking habit. But if "having musical ability" means "playing the piano well" and "having a smoking habit" is equivalent by definition to "smoking a great deal," do these statements explain anything at all? Skinner inquires:

> To what extent is it helpful to be told, "He drinks because he is thirsty?" If to be thirsty means nothing more than to have a tendency to drink, this is mere redundancy. If it means that he drinks because of a state of thirst, an inner causal event is invoked. If this state is purely inferential—if no dimensions are assigned to it which would make direct observation possible —it cannot serve as an explanation. But if it has physiological or psychic properties, what role can it play in a science of behavior?[9]

In short, the inner causes, whether they are intentions, ambitions, hunger, fatigue, or thirst, are not explanatory concepts, because they are either tautologies or they are not immediately observable. Therefore, they are only, in Skinner's phrase, "explanatory fictions"!

In opposing the use of inner states as explanations of observable behavior, Skinner carefully points out that he does not deny the existence of inner states, because "an adequate science of human behavior must consider events taking place within the skin of the organism . . . as part of behavior itself." [10] But he cautions us against treating inner states as having a special nature to be known by special methods, for "the skin is not that important as a boundary. Private and public events both have the same kinds of physical dimensions." [11] In other words, we must deal with events taking place both inside and outside the skin of the organism in exactly the same way. But to demand that the method used in studying the observable events be applied to the investigation of inner states is to suggest that we disregard the latter. And if inner states are as much a part of human behavior as overt responses, how can they be considered irrelevant in a scientific analysis of human behavior?

The Value of Theories

By now it should be clear that for Skinner the only proper role for psychology is to analyze human behavior by accurately describing the conditions under which responses occur. He stubbornly insists that in carrying out such a scientific inquiry, we should be concerned with reporting directly observable variables without theorizing about them. Skinner is adamantly antagonistic toward theories (1) that refer to "any explanation of an observed fact which appeals to events taking place somewhere else at some other level of observation, described in different terms, and

[9] Ibid., p. 33.
[10] Skinner, "Behaviorism at Fifty," p. 84.
[11] B. F. Skinner, "Are Theories of Learning Necessary?" *Psychological Review 57*, No. 4 (July 1950): 193.

measured, if at all, in different dimensions," and (2) that include "explanatory events [which] are not directly observed. . . ."[12] He is opposed to the first kind of theory because it contains either physiological or mentalistic expressions, that is, unobservable inner states. The second type of theory is unacceptable to Skinner because it stresses the formulation and testing of hypotheses based on postulates, constructs, or other theoretical entities without any directly observable referents. He goes on to point out that the emphasis we place on validating hypotheses is futile and extravagant because the result of scientific investigation is a described functional relationship demonstrated in data. Describing his own approach to scientific investigation, he wrote:

> I never faced a problem which was more than the eternal problem of finding order. I never attacked a problem by constructing a Hypothesis. I never deduced theorems or submitted them to Experimental Check. So far as I can see, I had no preconceived Mode of Behavior—certainly not a physiological or mentalistic one, and I believe not a conceptual one. . . . Of course, I was working on a basic assumption—that there was order in behavior if I could only discover it—but such an assumption is not to be confused with the hypothesis of deductive theory. It is also true that I exercised a certain selection of facts, not because of relevance to theory but because one fact was more orderly than another. If I engaged in experimental design at all, it was simply to complete or extend some evidence of order already observed.[13]

Because the ends sought by both theoretical and descriptive investigations are the same, the only point at issue is which method of investigation more efficiently directs the inquiry. Skinner is firmly convinced that purely behavioral definitions of terms are much more efficient and advantageous than conceptual definitions, for they avoid the difficulty of explaining how mental causes bring about physical effects or vice versa.

Despite his strong antitheoretical stance, Skinner is not opposed to the kind of theory that summarizes lawful relationships among the collected data. Consequently, for Skinner, one of the steps in conducting a scientific inquiry, after lawful relationships have been discovered and an appreciable quantity of data collected, is to represent the data in the form of a shorthand summary, using a minimal number of terms and mathematical representations. He thinks that this sort of theoretical construction is legitimate, for it gives us greater generality than a mere collection of individual facts. Indeed, it is curious that in spite of his overwhelmingly descriptive approach to psychology, he maintains that "science is more than mere description of events as they occur. . . . It is an attempt to discover order, to show that certain events stand in lawful relations to other events."[14] (See Chapter 3, pages 53–55). Skinner is clearly consistent with this view

---

[12] Ibid., pp. 193–194.
[13] B. F. Skinner, "A Case History in Scientific Method," in *Psychology: A Study of a Science,* S. S. Koch, ed. (New York: McGraw-Hill 1959), vol. 1, p. 369.
[14] Skinner, *Science and Human Behavior,* p. 6.

when he claims that he only looks for lawful process in the behavior of the organism, and nothing more.

Thus Skinner contends that the objective order in the behavior of an organism can be discovered as it exists apart from human judgment and interpretation. He further asserts that with sufficient observation of responses the order becomes self-evident, for once the data are in order, the theories tend to become unnecessary. In other words, a set of observation statements about some aspect of human behavior will reveal an inherent and objective order without the observer's having to interpret or arrange the data according to some conceptual scheme—a scheme that is not itself a product of observation.

METHODOLOGICAL BEHAVIORISM AND THE VERIFIABILITY PRINCIPLE

Skinner's view of science makes it abundantly clear that methodological behaviorism as a behavioral science is founded on the verifiability principle. In brief, this principle asserts that for any factual statement to be meaningful, it must be empirically verifiable. Hence, all statements, psychological or otherwise, that purport to inform us about matters of fact must be publicly verifiable. But what does the term verifiable mean? Originally, its supporters, logical empiricists, interpreted verification to mean conclusive verification, which entails perception (direct and immediate observation) of whatever is being verified. According to this interpretation, all statements about matters of fact must have physical dimensions that are directly observable. Mentalistic and neurophysiological terms, as well as reports of private experiences, do not, of course, meet this requirement. Therefore, they are not accepted as legitimate parts of a scientific explanation.

In recent years a much broader interpretation has been given to the principle, so that the term verifiable is now generally understood as indirect verification or empirical confirmation, which requires that empirical statements must be confirmable by competent observers. That is, "to say that a statement is empirically confirmable is to say that possible observations can be described that would, if they were made, bestow some degree of probability on the statement." [15]

In this broader interpretation of the principle, the emphasis falls more on the consequence of a statement. For example, if we say that when a rat is deprived of food until it reaches 85 percent of its normal body weight, there will be a corresponding increase in tension within the rat, and this increase will motivate the organism to act in a certain way so as to reduce tension and restore equilibrium, this statement can be empirically confirmed, if rats do in fact behave as predicted following food deprivation. However, an assertion of this type is never conclusively verifiable, because

[15] Arthur Pap, *An Introduction to the Philosophy of Science* (New York: The Free Press of Glencoe, 1962), p. 17.

the terms *tension, equilibrium,* and *motivate* are not amenable to direct observation. But within the context of the broader conception of the verifiability principle, inference and constructs may become useful parts of scientific inquiry. It is important to note here that unless verifiability had been understood as empirical confirmation, it would not have been possible to formulate the laws of gravitation, thermodynamics, and heredity, for we can only observe the consequences of the assumed existence of gravitation, thermodynamics, and genes.

Returning to Skinner's position, from all he has said about the proper subject matter and method of psychology, there is little doubt that he stands firmly committed to the original version of the verifiability principle. And because he demands all factual statements to be conclusively verifiable, he has no alternative but to dismiss everything except immediately observable facts as irrelevant to a science of behavior. It is for this reason that Skinner sees human behavior as a series of individual responses that are related to each other in time only. And on the same grounds he maintains that statements about evidently meaningful private and mental experiences are nothing more than explanatory fictions.

In sum, Skinner and his followers are unwilling to deal with anything other than what is directly observable and measurable in human behavior. We may now ask, What kind of scientific account of human behavior and learning comes from this perspective, and how can such knowledge be applied to the business of educating our children?

OPERANT CONDITIONING

According to Skinner there are two basically different classes of behavior, respondent and operant. Respondent behavior is elicited by known, specific stimuli. These responses are reflexive and, therefore, involuntary. Given the stimulus, the response occurs automatically. Bright light and pupillary constriction, a blow on the patellar tendon and the knee jerk, are familiar examples of the connections between stimulus and respondent behavior or reflexes. Some of our reflexes are present at the time of birth, while others are acquired later through conditioning. Conditioning is the process by which an originally inadequate stimulus becomes capable of producing a response after it has been paired with a stimulus adequate in eliciting that specific response. The adequate stimulus and the response to it are called unconditioned stimulus and unconditioned response, respectively. The inadequate stimulus is known as a conditioned stimulus, while a response to it is referred to as a conditioned response. For example, Ivan Pavlov (1849–1936), a Russian physiologist, found in a now famous experiment that when food (an unconditioned stimulus) is presented to a dog, it leads to salivation (an unconditioned response). He also discovered that by presenting food (an unconditioned stimulus) with a tone (a conditioned stimulus), the latter became capable of causing salivation (a conditioned response) without food being present. Skinner calls this Type S conditioning. In Type S conditioning a specific stimulus is presented to induce a response, and therefore the stimulus always precedes the response. It is to this type of conditioning process that John B. Watson (1878–1958), a leading exponent of early behaviorism, attributed the learning of all responses.

Unlike Watson, Skinner maintains that operant responses account for most of human behavior. Operant responses are emitted by but not elicited from the organism, and since they are not induced by stimuli they are voluntary in nature. The term operant is used to emphasize the fact that the behavior operates upon the environment to generate responses. In an experiment, a rat's lever-pressing response may be made to occur more often by rewarding the rat with food after a correct response. Thus the response is strengthened or reinforced by the consequence following it. In this Type R conditioning, as it is called, reinforcement cannot occur unless a response occurs first. Therefore, reinforcement is said to be contingent upon responses. The learning of an operant response is called operant or instrumental conditioning, and it differs from Type S or classical conditioning. In operant conditioning, it is the consequence following a response that increases the rate at which an operant response is emitted, and the operant strength is indicated by this change in the probability of an operant. The following brief account of a Skinner experiment further illustrates the essentials of operant conditioning:

> A hungry rat [is placed in an] experimental space which contains a food dispenser. A horizontal bar at the end of a lever projects from one wall. Depression of the lever operates a switch. When the switch is connected with the food dispenser, any behavior on the part of the rat which depresses the lever is, as we say, "reinforced with food." The apparatus simply makes the appearance of food contingent upon the occurrence of an arbitrary bit of behavior. Under such circumstances, the probability that a response to the lever will occur again is increased.[16]

What we have here is Skinner's own reformulation of Edward L. Thorndike's Law of Effect, according to which the connection between a response and stimulus is strengthened when the former is followed by a satisfying state of affairs, while the strength of the stimulus-response bond is decreased when the response is followed by an annoying state of affairs.[17] A major difference between Thorndike and Skinner is that the latter is unwilling to use such mentalistic terms as "satisfying" and "annoying" in his explanations, because he holds that a scientific study of human behavior should only describe the observable responses. Therefore, Skinner's version of the Law of Effect simply states that when a response is followed by certain consequences the response tends to appear more frequently.

[16] B. F. Skinner, *The Technology of Teaching* (New York: Appleton-Century-Crofts, 1968), p. 62.
[17] Ibid.

But since not all consequences of a response are reinforcing, should we not attempt to find out why some consequences do and others do not strengthen a response? Here Skinner cautions us against speculating about the "whys" of behavior, because

> the only way to tell whether or not a given event is reinforcing to a given organism under given conditions is to make a direct test. We observe the frequency of a selected response, then make an event contingent upon it and observe any change in frequency. If there is a change, we classify the event as reinforcing to the organism under the existing conditions.[18]

In other words, a reinforcer is whatever increases the probability of a response. For example, verbal praises, grades, or gold stars given for reading, or even the teacher's smiles that make the learner behave in a desired way more frequently may be called reinforcers. But we do not know why a reinforcer strengthens a response. We only know that some events are reinforcing.

Skinner's reluctance to deal with the "why" questions stems from his belief that explanations of an observed fact, that is, human behavior, should not appeal to "events taking place somewhere else, at some other level of observation, described in different terms, if at all, in different dimensions." [19] Therefore, our knowledge about learning should be based solely on a descriptive study of the variables under which learning occurs, without relying on mental or physiological processes, because neither of them is accessible to direct observation. It is this kind of empirical knowledge that will enable us to actually shape behavior as a sculptor shapes a lump of clay. And by arranging appropriate contingencies of reinforcement, or the sequence in which responses are followed by reinforcing events, we can maintain the shaped behavior for a long period of time. Similarly, a complex behavior can be shaped by following a carefully designed program of gradually changing contingencies of reinforcement that will form small units of behavior successively approximating the desired response.

Now that we have examined the role of reinforcement in operant conditioning generally, we are ready to take a more detailed look at the ways in which various types of reinforcements and punishments affect the teaching-learning process.

REINFORCEMENT

Positive and Negative Reinforcements   As we pointed out earlier, Skinner found no useful answers to the question, "Why is a reinforcer reinforcing?" But we do know that some things are reinforcing when they are present in a situation, while others strengthen an operant response when they are withdrawn. A positive reinforcer is, then, a stimulus that, when added to a situation, increases the probability of a response, while a nega-

---

[18] Skinner, *Science and Human Behavior*, pp. 72–73.
[19] Skinner, "Are Theories of Learning Necessary?" p. 193.

tive reinforcer is any event that, when withdrawn, produces the same effect. For instance, the increased rate of the rat's lever-pressing response as a result of the presentation of food following the response is a case of positive reinforcement. Withdrawal of electric shocks that results in the increased performance of a pigeon's pecking activity illustrates negative reinforcement. What we must remember about these reinforcers is that whether positive or negative, both are defined in terms of their effect: the strengthening of a response. Hence, we must not confuse negative reinforcement with punishment, which is a basically different process from reinforcement. What is commonly called punishment involves either withdrawal of a positive stimulus such as food, or presentation of a negative stimulus such as an electric shock.

Conditioned Reinforcement   When a stimulus, let us say a dinner plate, which originally does not have any reinforcing power, is paired with a reinforcing (primary) stimulus such as food, the former frequently acquires the same reinforcing property as the primary stimulus. This process is called conditioned reinforcement, and the plate, in this case, is called a conditioned reinforcer. Conditioned reinforcers are often the result of natural contingencies; for example, food is usually presented on a plate. Now, when conditioned reinforcers are paired with more than one primary reinforcer, the conditioned reinforcers are said to be generalized. Money is a good example of a generalized reinforcer, for it enables us to secure food, clothing, shelter, and entertainment. Students behave or study for grades, scholarships, or diplomas, which are not as readily exchanged for other primary reinforcers as money is. But they are indeed exchangeable for high-paying jobs and prestige.

The practice of tokenism as seen in our schools today is an excellent example of the use of generalized reinforcers. The term tokenism refers to the practice of giving tokens to children for certain acts and/or achievements and allowing them to cash in the tokens for extra recess periods or other activities of their choice. Attention, affection, approval, and permissiveness are examples of other kinds of generalized reinforcers. The teacher's attention is reinforcing, because it is a necessary condition for other reinforcement that comes from the teacher. And the child cannot receive any reinforcement from the teacher unless he or she can attract the teacher's attention. This suggests that anything that attracts the attention of teachers and parents, who are likely to supply other rewards, will be reinforced. Of course, attention alone is not enough, because the teacher tends to reinforce only those acts that merit approval. Consequently, the responses, such as submissiveness, that lead to such signs of approval as a smile or verbal praise will be strengthened.

Generalization of reinforcement is particularly important in teaching because stimulus induction or transfer of learning takes place through this process. Transfer of learning is said to have occurred when "the reinforcement of a response increases the probability of all responses containing the same elements." [20] As an illustration, if we reinforce a pigeon's response of pecking a yellow round spot one square inch in area, the effects of this reinforcement will spread so that the pigeon will peck a red spot of the same size and shape because of the common properties of size and shape. The pigeon will also respond to a yellow square spot of one square inch in area because of its color and size, and to a yellow round spot two square inches in area because of similar elements of color and shape. What all this means is that, for transfer of learning to occur, the learner must be able to perceive similarities between the original and the new stimulus situations. Though Skinner might not agree with this statement—because an organism's perception of similarity is not an observable event—people often behave inappropriately because they perceive two different situations as similar.

Schedules of Reinforcement   Much of human behavior is shaped through operant conditioning. But the ways in which operant responses are shaped in everyday life are slow and inefficient, mainly because reinforcements of these responses do not occur in either a regular or a uniform manner. Thus, if we are to be effective and efficient in shaping and maintaining desired responses, we must construct schedules of reinforcement. Such schedules are especially important in forming a complex behavior, which must be shaped gradually through selective reinforcement of certain responses but not others.

The schedule in which reinforcement follows every response is called continuous reinforcement. This schedule is generally used in getting an organism to emit the desired response. But very rarely are we reinforced continuously. We do not win every time we play a game of chess, nor do we catch fish every time we go fishing. "The reinforcements characteristic of industry and education are almost always intermittent because it is not feasible to control behavior by reinforcing every response." [21] Hence, in intermittent reinforcements, only some of the responses are followed by reinforcing events. In this schedule the rate of responding is determined by the frequency of reinforcement. If we reinforce a response every two minutes, the response occurs more frequently than if reinforcements are presented every five minutes. Another kind of intermittent schedule is ratio reinforcement, in which the frequency of reinforcement depends on the rate at which operant responses are emitted. So, if we decide to reinforce every third response, it is called reinforcement at a fixed ratio. Students' receiving grades upon completion of a paper, a salesperson's selling on commission, and a worker's piecework pay are all examples of fixed ratio reinforcement. Of course, interval and ratio schedules can be combined so that responses can be strengthened according to the passage of

[20] Skinner, *Science and Human Behavior*, p. 94.
[21] Ibid.

time as well as the number of unreinforced responses emitted. Skinner reports that there are sufficient experimental data to suggest that generally the organism gives back a certain number of responses for each response reinforced, implying that there is a direct relationship between the frequency of response and the frequency of reinforcement. But now what happens if they are not reinforced?

The effect of a nonreinforcing situation is called operant extinction. In other words, if a response is not followed by any reinforcement for a period, the response becomes less and less frequent until eventually it completely ceases. Thus unrewarded acts of children often cease to occur, and though operant extinction takes place much more slowly than operant conditioning, it is an effective means of removing an unwanted behavior from the organism's repertoire. However, extinction should not be confused with forgetting, because in forgetting the effect of conditioning is lost as time passes, whereas extinction requires that the response be emitted without reinforcement.

Drives and Emotions

In explaining human behavior we often attribute one's actions to certain drives one is supposed to have. We might say that John ate a lot of food to satisfy his hunger drive, or that he drank a quart of lemonade to quench his thirst. But Skinner does not regard drives as stimuli that causally affect the rate at which responses are emitted. Only in a metaphorical sense do drives cause our actions. As Ernest R. Hilgard, a contemporary American learning theorist, reiterates, "the word drive is used [by Skinner] only to acknowledge certain classes of operations which affect behavior in ways other than the ways by which reinforcement affects it." [22] Hence, drive is simply a convenient way of referring to the effects of deprivation and satiation. Deprivation or the hunger drive can be defined operationally by withholding food from an organism, say a rat, to the point where the rat reaches about 80 percent of its normal weight, while satiation can be demonstrated by feeding the rat until it no longer takes any food. In terms of their effects, deprivation usually strengthens a response, but satiation decreases the rate of response. These operations can be applied to practical situations, for instance by prohibiting a child from having snacks so she will eat well at the regular meal time, or by serving large portions of salad and bread before the main course so that a rather skimpy dinner can be served without complaint. Skinner believes that drives should not be treated as special inner states causing overt responses, nor does he see emotions as inner causes of behavior. Rather, he insists that the terms *anger, love,* and *hate* are different ways of talking about a person's predispositions to act in certain ways, because

[22] Ernest R. Hilgard, *Theories of Learning* (New York: Appleton-Century-Crofts, 1956), p. 97.

the names of the so-called emotions serve to classify behavior with respect to various circumstances which affect its probability. The safest practice is to hold to the adjectival form. Just as the hungry organism can be accounted for without too much difficulty, . . . so by describing behavior as fearful, affectionate, timid, and so on, we are not led to look for things called emotions. The common idioms, "in love," "in fear," and "in anger" suggest a definition of an emotion as a conceptual state, in which a special response is a function of circumstances in the history of the individual.[23]

In consonance with Skinner's account of drives and emotions, one should not interpret motivation as an inner force propelling an organism to action. It is merely an expression that conveniently covers deprivation and satisfaction.

PUNISHMENT

The use of punishment as a means of controlling human behavior is as old as the human race. In school we use various punishments to influence children's behavior. Poor academic work is punished with failing grades, while recess periods are often taken away to make children less noisy. Unfortunately, punishment as a technique of controlling human behavior does not always work effectively. Children are rarely quiet for any significant length of time if they lose recess periods, and evidence fails to indicate that imprisonment reduces criminal behavior. Certainly, failing grades do not cause children to do better academic work. But if punishment is not an effective means of facilitating learning, what role does it play in shaping and maintaining behavior?

In the process of learning, reinforcement builds up responses but punishment tears them down. Punishment weakens a response in the sense that it decreases the rate of an operant, but it does not permanently reduce the organism's tendency to respond. That is, the effect of punishment is nothing more than temporary suppression of the behavior, not a reduction in the total number of responses. According to Skinner, even after the severest and most prolonged punishment, the rate of response rose when punishment was discontinued. In other words, the occurrence of the punished behavior is simply postponed rather than permanently eliminated. Moreover, since suppression of unwanted behavior does not either specify or reinforce desirable behavior, punishment is an ineffective means of correcting a child's misbehavior. In punishing a child all we are doing is arranging conditions under which acceptable behavior could be strengthened without clarifying what behaviors are acceptable. In contrast, withholding reinforcement is a much more effective means of extinguishing unwanted responses.

Punishment leads to unfortunate by-products, especially for teachers, because it often becomes the source of conditioned stimuli evoking incom-

23 Skinner, *Science and Human Behavior*, pp. 162–163.

patible behavior from students. That is, anything associated with the punished act can become a conditioned stimulus. Frequently, unwanted emotional reactions such as fear and anxiety result from punishment. Therefore, if Danny is punished for eating noodles with his fingers, he may stop eating noodles or cease to eat altogether. If certain sexual activities before marriage are punished, such acts, though socially approved after marriage, may become associated with such emotional predispositions as guilt, shame, or even a sense of sin. Such emotional by-products make it extremely difficult for teachers to establish a productive relationship with their pupils. Understandably, Skinner suggests that we avoid using punishment and find other means of weakening undesirable responses. Briefly, unwanted behavior can be weakened or controlled by modifying the circumstances. Certain behavior of your children may be allowed to pass, according to a developmental schedule, and the children may be allowed to "grow out" of their behavior naturally. Often conditioned responses can be weakened and eliminated by simply letting time pass. Of course, the most effective means of weakening responses is extinction. For example, if Mary throws objects to attract the teacher's attention, she may be allowed to continue her deed without the reinforcement of attention. Another technique is strengthening incompatible behavior through positive reinforcement. If Tom attempts to gain his teacher's attention by leaving his seat and disturbing others, the teacher may pay attention to him only when he remains in his seat, thereby strengthening the desirable behavior that is incompatible with his earlier undesirable behavior. In short, direct positive reinforcement is preferable to punishment, because this approach seems to have fewer of the objectionable by-products usually associated with punishment.

In general, punishment is a poor means of controlling pupil behavior. While punishments often temporarily postpone unwanted behavior, students can and do act to avoid aversive stimulation, namely, punishment. They may find many different ways of escaping; they may daydream or become inattentive or stay away from school altogether. Another unfortunate result of punishment is that the students may counterattack; they may attack openly or they may simply become rude, defiant, and impertinent. Today, physical attacks against the teacher are not an impossibility. If the severity of punishment is increased, counterattacks become more frequent and one party withdraws or dominates the scene. Vandalism and unresponsiveness are other consequences of punishment. Usually the reactions to punishment are accompanied by such emotional responses as fear, anxiety, anger, and resentment, so that establishment of an educationally productive teacher-pupil relationship becomes almost impossible. Therefore, Skinner recommends that teachers minimize or eliminate the use of punishment as a means of controlling pupil behavior. One way of accomplishing this is to eliminate the conditions that give rise to punishable behavior. For instance, we can separate children who cannot get along with each other, furniture can be made rugged enough so that children cannot damage it, and other means of lighting can be substituted for windows, thereby doing away with the possibility that children may break them or become distracted by the activities they see outside. In other words, we should provide conditions in which punishable behavior is not likely to occur. At the same time we should construct programs in which children will be able to succeed most of the time.

The Technology of Teaching, Programed Instruction, Performance-Based Instruction, and Accountability

With this examination of the philosophical and psychological bases of education as behavior engineering, we are ready to turn our attention to the ways in which the behaviorist model of education is translated into concrete educational procedures and stategies. Currently, there are many allegedly behavioristic programs, procedures, and techniques in education, but the technology of teaching, performance-based instruction, and educational accountability most vividly illustrate the application of behavior engineering in education. In examining these innovations, we shall also see why the use of programed instruction, teaching machines, computers, and behavioral objectives are so essential to the technology of education.

OPERANT CONDITIONING AND THE TECHNOLOGY OF TEACHING

Teaching and the Problem of the First Instance   As Skinner himself has put it so explicitly, the application of the principles of operant conditioning to teaching is simple and direct, for teaching is a matter of arranging contingencies of reinforcement under which students learn. They do, of course, learn without being taught, but by providing appropriate learning conditions we can speed up the occurrence of behavior that would have either appeared very slowly or not appeared at all. In this sense, teachers do not actually pass along some of their own behavior. They build or help construct the behavior of the students who are induced to engage in forms of behavior appropriate to certain occasions. And since operant conditioning is the process by which we learn all of our voluntary behavior, the technology of teaching becomes a matter of providing and arranging the necessary conditions with the help of mechanical devices, electronic instruments, and schedules of reinforcement so that desired learning can occur efficiently. Teachers must then help their students reach an appropriate instructional objective by progressive approximation. This means using reinforcement to form small units of desired terminal behavior. In operant conditioning, reinforcement cannot be presented unless the responses have actually occurred. In other words, we must wait until a desired response or a response similar to it appears, so that it can be strengthened. But in education many complex terminal behaviors must be established within a limited period of time. Therefore, it would be tedious and inefficient for teachers to wait for desired responses to appear. In fact, some responses may never take place without some form of deliberate inducement. How to bring about the wanted behavior without simply waiting for it thus becomes "the problem of the first instance."

Skinner indicates a number of possible solutions to the problem of the first instance. One is to force a behavior physically, as we often squeeze a child's hand around a pencil and move it to form letters. Unfortunately, the child is not writing in a real sense, and if he or she does learn to write, there are probably other variables at work. Another possibility is to evoke a response by some stimulus. For example, teachers may raise their hands or wave an object conspicuously to induce their students to pay attention to their story telling. This technique, too, has a weakness in that the elicited attention is not the attention the students eventually learn. Consequently, these two measures are useful only in a small range of teaching-learning situations. A more effective technique is to prime certain desired responses.

Shaping Behavior According to Skinner there are at least three priming procedures. One is *movement duplication*, a technique of utilizing the learner's tendency toward imitative behavior by reinforcing those responses that resemble the responses of a model, who is often the teacher. This priming procedure is possible because when students act as others do, they are naturally reinforced. Examples of movement duplication can be found in drama, physical education, and dancing courses, where students are made to "copy" the teacher's gestures and movements. Another priming procedure is *product duplication*. When the effects of a model's movements are duplicated by the learner without necessarily imitating the model's movements, the responses are said to have been primed by product duplication. For example, we can learn to pronounce certain words, deliver a line in a play, or paint a picture by imitating a model, the teacher, without actually seeing how the model has performed these acts. The modern language laboratory is an excellent example of mechanical devices that help improve product duplication. As Skinner suggests, a behavior may also be primed by utilizing already established repertoire responses. This procedure is called *nonduplicative repertoires*. To put it simply, we can tell the students what to do or how to act and then reinforce them when they act according to our instruction. What we are doing is giving a verbal instruction to evoke a certain response with the help of behavior patterns that have already been established. The evoked response is different from the established responses, but through the latter's help we can give the students a "picture" of what they must do.

Although priming techniques are useful, they do not replace other means of shaping behavior. But they do help us with the initial stages of establishing desired behavior and hence they are useful tools in the early phase of teaching. Skinner cautions us that we should not mistake simple execution of behavior as learning. Teachers often become satisfied merely if their students repeat after them, because the student's imitative behavior is often reinforcing for the teacher. In other words, learning takes place because behavior is reinforced, but not merely because it has been primed. Learning can be said to have occurred only if the learners can make similar responses on their own.

The reinforcers used in most formal learning situations to establish desired behaviors are artificial, in the sense that they are deliberately contrived. Therefore, in school, grades and praise are used to reinforce those responses that make up our teaching objectives. Such artificial reinforcers are necessary because natural reinforcers take too long a time to be effective. For example, Jennifer does not learn to think critically because she can immediately win in a debating contest, nor does Terry learn to plant seeds because he is promptly reinforced by the resulting harvest. On the contrary, any teacher who relies solely on natural contingencies of reinforcement has given up his or her role as a teacher, for to expose the students to their environment gives us no guarantee that their behavior will be followed by any reinforcing event. Therefore, contrived reinforcers, whether they be grades, gold stars, or plastic tokens, are essential in learning and the work of arranging an effective sequence of such reinforcers should make up much of our teaching activity.

PROGRAMED INSTRUCTION AND TEACHING MACHINES

If by using priming techniques we have been successful in getting our students to execute certain behavior, we have begun the process of shaping terminal behavior, namely, our teaching objectives. We must then arrange a great many contingencies of reinforcement so that the students can perform the same act on their own and maintain it. Clearly, teaching in the context of schooling involves many extremely complex terminal behaviors. Even at the elementary school level most instructional objectives go far beyond such relatively simple tasks as making letters or coloring pictures. As we go up the educational ladder, objectives become increasingly subtle and involved. Behaviors of such great complexity cannot be learned all at once but must be formed through programed instruction. Programed instruction is a process of successively or progressively approximating teaching objectives by making an efficient use of reinforcers to establish, maintain, and strengthen desired responses.

As Skinner cautions us, in programing it is important that the learners "understand" each step before they move on to the next. This means the learners stay in one stage until they master what they have to learn to move onto the next stage. In principle, however, programed instruction is more than a matter of shaping terminal behavior simply by dividing it into smaller units and reinforcing them one by one. A subject, or a skill such as critical thinking, is more than a mere aggregate of individual responses, for the smaller units are related to each other in such a way that they, as a whole, possess varying degrees of coherence and consistency. Moreover, in programed instruction each new unit of learned behavior should add to already established behaviors in a cumulative way so that terminal behavior can be reached progressively.

As Skinner reports in his *Cumulative Record*, he has recorded many millions of responses from a single organism during thousands of experimental hours.[24] In *Schedule of Reinforcement*, published in 1957, Skinner summarized about 70,000 hours of the continuously recorded behavior of individual pigeons, consisting of approximately one quarter of a billion responses. These data were presented in 921 separate charts and tables with almost no interpretive or summarizing comments. The sheer number of responses that make up behavior makes clear that any personal attempt at an effective arrangement of contingencies without some sort of mechanical device is unthinkable. If the control of animal behavior requires an elaborate mechanical arrangement, the contingencies of reinforcement for shaping and maintaining human behavior would certainly necessitate mechanical help, because human beings are much more sensitive to precise contingencies than are lower organisms. The so-called teaching machines are such instruments. They can help the teacher to apply the latest advances in the experimental analysis of learning from teaching. Skinner's description of the machine concisely explains the ways in which it functions.

> The device consists of a box about the size of a small record player. On the top surface is a glazed window through which a question or problem printed on a paper tape may be seen. The child answers the question by moving one or more sliders upon which the digits through 9 are printed. The answer appears in square holes punched in the paper upon which the question is printed. When the answer has been set, the child turns a knob. The operation is as simple as adjusting a television set. If the answer is right, the knob turns freely and can be made to ring a bell or provide some other conditioned reinforcement. If the answer is wrong, the knob will not turn. A counter may be added to tally wrong answers. The knob must then be reversed slightly and a second attempt at a right answer made. . . . When the answer is right, a further turn of the knob engages a clutch which moves the next problem into place in window. This movement cannot be completed, however, until the sliders have been returned to zero.[25]

There are many different versions of the machine with various features to make its operation more automatic and sophisticated, but the basic function they perform in facilitating learning conditions is essentially the same.

One of the advantages in utilizing teaching machines as an instructional aid is that right answers can be immediately reinforced. Often manipula-

[24] B. F. Skinner, *Cumulative Record* (New York: Appleton-Century-Crofts, 1959), p. 154.
[25] Ibid.

tion of the machine will be reinforcing enough to keep the child at work. Also, a single teacher can supervise an entire class working with such machines and at the same time help each child move at his or her own rate. In this way gifted as well as slow children can learn without being deterred by the fact that one teacher cannot individually supervise children of such diverse capacities and needs. Furthermore, the machines make it possible to present subject matter so that the solution of one problem depends on the answer to the preceding problem. The student can eventually progress to a more complex repertoire of behaviors. There are still other benefits from teaching machines. Like a good tutor the machine carries on a continuous interchange with the learner and induces constant activity to keep the learner alert. The machine also "demands" that a given point be completely understood before moving on to the next because it presents only those materials for which the student is ready. Like a skillful tutor the machine helps the student come up with the right answer and thus shapes, maintains, and strengthens correct responses by reinforcing them promptly. Moreover, it is possible to present programs through the machines when appropriate courses or teachers are not available. And individuals who cannot be in school for various reasons can "teach" themselves with the machine.

If teaching machines can indeed function as effectively as teachers, will they eventually replace teachers? As Skinner rightly points out, teaching machines do not teach in any literal sense at all. They are labor-saving devices and, therefore, only the mechanized aspects of teaching have been given to them. This arrangement leaves more time for the teachers to carry on those relationships with pupils that cannot be duplicated by an instrument. Teaching machines enable teachers to work with more children than they could ever hope to without instrumental aid. Of course, the use of these machines will change some time-honored but threadbare practices. For example, traditional grades or classes will cease to be significant indicators of the child's academic growth. Since the machine's instruction makes sure that every step is mastered, grades or marks will be important only as a means of indicating how far a child has advanced. Most of all, A, B, C, D, and F will no longer serve as motivators in the traditional sense, and the fact that each child is permitted to work at his or her own rate may lessen if not eliminate the social stigma that usually comes with being a slow learner or an underachiever.

It is indeed possible that teaching machines and the techniques of programing can be misused to produce submissive individuals who lack both initiative and creativity. On the other hand, the technology of teaching can help us maximize the development of human potential of those attributes that can make the greatest possible contribution to humanity. Skinner correctly insists that the harm or the benefit coming from the use of teaching machines and programed learning is not inherent in the technology of teaching. People must decide which goals are most worthy of pursuing both for the individual and for society. The technology of teaching is only one means of achieving an educational end, and machines and programs should not dictate the direction of our education.

BEHAVIORAL OBJECTIVES

In establishing behaviors that will be beneficial to the learner and to society, behavior engineers are most concerned with reaching target behaviors (aims of education) by gradually and systematically modifying "old" behaviors and/or shaping new responses. In other words, overall aims of education are first translated into specific objectives involving competencies in various disciplines and other areas of the learner's life, such as learning the three Rs, responsible citizenship, and so on. These objectives in turn are formulated into specific programs, courses, and learning activities, the purposes of which are also defined in terms of specific behavioral changes. Each of these competencies are then analyzed into still smaller and simpler behaviors, so that by learning them the child can eventually reach the target behavior. Hence, educational goals must be stated in terms of specific and directly observable behaviors.

It is for this reason that the use of behavioral objectives in instructional and curricular planning is indispensable to education as behavior engineering, because these objectives serve not only as clear guides to learning activities but also as standards by which the teaching-learning processes can be evaluated. Our subsequent discussion of a performance-based teacher education program will serve as an apt illustration of the ways in which behavioral objectives are incorporated into an elementary teacher education program.

As the expression *behavioral objective* suggests, statements of objectives must refer to directly observable behaviors of the learner. That is, "a properly stated behavioral objective must describe without ambiguity the nature of learner behavior or product to be measured, . . . and the nature of learner behavior change which the instructor hopes to bring about is clearly delineated." [26] Accordingly, such cognitive (intellectual) terms as *knowing* and *believing*, and affective (emotional) expressions such as *feeling* and *empathizing*, must be behaviorally explained, because, as the behavior engineers argue, observable acts are the only tangible evidence of cognitive and affective states. Hence, *knowing, believing,* and *feeling* are metaphorical ways of talking about certain kinds of overt behaviors. However, there are others who insist that overt acts are only partial indications of certain inner states or processes, and therefore outward behaviors cannot exhaustively explain *knowing, believing,* and *feeling.* From this point of view behaviorists are mistaken in maintaining that educational

[26] W. Popham, "Objectives and Instruction," in *AERA Monograph Series on Curriculum Evaluation*, vol. 3, *Instructional Objectives* (Chicago: Rand McNally, 1969), p. 37.

goals that are not behaviorally definable are irrelevant. There are several other views on the use of behavioral objectives in education, but we shall consider those in a later section (see page 343).

PERFORMANCE-BASED TEACHER EDUCATION

Performance-based teacher education (PBTE), also known as competency-based teacher education (CBTE), is an excellent example of the ways in which behavior engineering is applied to education, for it attempts to build an extremely complex behavior, effective teaching, through the use of behavioral objectives and programed instruction. Though there are many different kinds of PBTE, we shall focus our discussion on the comprehensive elementary teacher education models funded by the United States Office of Education and developed by a group of major universities in this country. While all these models have certain unique aspects, they are all "behavioral" in their approach to teacher education. Each of the ten models is divided into a number of major areas of study, which are in turn divided into subareas. The instructional objectives of these areas are then stated in behavioral terms, and *program modules*, or instructional units, are planned to achieve these objectives by progressive approximation. For example, the Michigan State University model has six major areas of study constituting the entire elementary teacher education program. They are: (1) Clinical Experience, (2) General-Liberal Education, (3) Scholarly Modes of Knowledge, (4) Professional Use of Knowledge, (5) Human Learning, and (6) Continued Professional Development.[27] The modules are computer-coded, and each student can complete them at his or her own rate. In the Michigan State model there are 3,000 or more modules. The sections on "Scholarly Modes of Knowledge" and "Professional Use of Knowledge" contain approximately 1,200 and 600 modules, respectively. In order to complete an elementary teacher education program of this type, a prospective teacher must study individual modules, which are the smallest instructional units. The nature and function of the module taken from "Scholarly Modes of Knowledge" (see Figure 9) are almost self-explanatory.[28]

We can, of course, view our educational and instructional goals as involving a number of specific actions, but this does not mean that these objectives are mere aggregates of separate and observable acts. To use a trite phrase, the whole is greater than the sum of its parts; for critical thinking requires (1) knowledge of the rules of formal logic, (2) the ability to apply the rules, (3) the detection of hidden assumptions, and (4) identification of fallacious uses of language. Yet thinking critically means more than executing these individual acts separately, for when we say that

[27] Michigan State University, *Behavioral Science Elementary Teacher Education Program*, Final Report, Project No. 8-9025, vols. 1, 2, and 3 (Washington: U.S. Government Printing Office, October 1961).

[28] Ibid., vol. 2, pp. vi–39.

●OBJECTIVES	GIVEN HYPOTHETICAL DIAGNOSIS OF MIDDLE SCHOOL PUPIL'S WORD	00485017
	RECOGNITION SKILLS, LEARNER WRITES APPROPRIATE	00485018
	INSTRUCTIONAL PLAN	00485019
●PREREQUISITE	SUCCESSFUL COMPLETION OF PREVIOUS MODULES, PARTICULARLY	00485020
	481	00485021
●EXPERIENCE	CANDIDATES FOR MIDDLE SCHOOL TEACHING LISTEN TO AND	00485012
	DISCUSS WITH INSTRUCTOR PARTICULAR TECHNIQUES FOR TEACHING	00485013
	WORD RECOGNITION SKILLS IN MIDDLE SCHOOL. EMPHASIS IS ON	00485014
	TECHNIQUES FOR TEACHING STRUCTURAL ANALYSIS, DICTIONARY,	00485015
	ETC.	00485016
●SETTING	SMALL GROUP (1-12 STUDENTS), COLLEGE	00485011
●MATERIALS	RESULTS OF HYPOTHETICAL DIAGNOSIS OF WORD RECOGNITION	00485005
	SKILLS OF MIDDLE GRADE PUPILS	00485006
●LEVEL	GRADES 5-8	00485009
●GENERAL	GENERALIST	00485008
●HOURS	1/4	00485007
●EVALUATION	LEARNER CORRECTLY WRITES APPROPRIATE INSTRUCTIONAL PLAN	00485022
	FOR DEVELOPING WORD RECOGNITION SKILLS OF HYPOTHETICAL	00485023
	MIDDLE SCHOOL PUPILS	00485024
●FILE	WORD RECOGNITION INSTRUCTIONAL TECHNIQUES MIDDLE SCHOOL	00485010

Figure 9   *A Sample Module*

a child can think critically we usually mean he or she can deal with a problematic situation by relating it to past events, the present context, and also future possibilities. Hence, this kind of thinking requires the use of the individual's total experience and knowledge of the ways in which it is related to an indeterminate situation.

Let us illustrate further. In an elementary science program prepared for the early grades by the American Association for the Advancement of Science the steps necessary in teaching scientific thinking were listed as (1) observing, (2) using space/time relationships, (3) using numbers, (4) measuring, (5) classifying, (6) communicating, (7) predicting, (8) inferring. But "observing" is not separable from "using space/time relationships" or "using numbers." In a real sense "observing" involves all these steps with the possible exception of (7), yet it would be incorrect to maintain that scientific thinking is nothing more than observing, using space/time relationships, using numbers, and so on. We can, of course, work with a child so that he or she becomes skillful in using space/time relationships and numbers in measuring, in classifying, and in communicating. But we must go beyond exercises and drills to show the learner that all these are inextricably related to each other.

In general, PBTE programs, or for that matter any performance-based instructional programs, are characterized by (1) precise learning objectives behaviorally defined, (2) the expectation that the learner will be able to meet specific performance criteria upon completion of the learning activities, and (3) the mastery of instructional modules by each learner at his or her own pace without competing with others or some general norm. In addition, PBTE programs frequently use programed instruction, computers, and particularly a "systems approach."

The systems approach in education is an application of the management procedures developed and used by industry and the Department of Defense in which goals for the entire organization and its subunits are explicitly stated and the plans for achieving them are designed. These procedures include periodic assessment of the extent to which each unit of the organization is moving toward the final goal, for the purpose of holding it accountable for its success or failure. Also, new and better devices are developed to deal with whatever gets in the way of attaining the ultimate goal. In industry, the products themselves are judged at frequent intervals, according to quality control standards. If we see education through the systems perspective and the industrial model, the schools are plants where the administrators direct the operation and the teachers engage in engineering. The pupils are then the raw materials to be processed according to the product specifications demanded by the consumer, the public. To be consistent with this view, teaching effectiveness should be evaluated according to the quality of the product, that is, the extent to which a child can perform certain specified acts according to performance standards.

As with the use of technology in teacher education, the systems approach is only a means by which PBTE can be better planned and implemented. Today more and more institutions of teacher education are being attracted to PBTE by its supposed economic efficiency, procedural clarity, and explicit accountability measures. Yet others maintain that PBTE and the systems approach in education treat human beings as objects to be manipulated in producing docile, mechanical, and inflexible teachers. We shall have more to say about this and other arguments a bit later.

ACCOUNTABILITY IN EDUCATION

As many current critics of American public education point out, too many of our children leave school without either minimal competence in the basic skills or a desire for learning. Yet greater and greater portions of the average family's income are required for public education. Consequently, the public (particularly minority groups) is becoming insistent in demanding that the schools do a better job of teaching the basic skills necessary for survival in our society—and at less public cost. In other words, our schools are asked to justify their requests for more money by showing their productivity. They are told that they will be held accountable for their success or failure and that no more funds will be made available unless the schools can guarantee each child's progress.

The accountability movement in education, then, stems from a need to develop more efficient ways of managing the present educational system and its fiscal resources so that the school can be more productive. That is, the school needs to produce results that are equivalent to the amount of money spent. This means that our educational system is expected to develop what Professor Leon M. Lessinger, a foremost advocate of accountability and professor of urban education at Georgia State University, calls a "zero reject system," [29] in which all children can become proficient in the basic skills so that they can reap the greatest amount of benefit from their chosen vocations. To make such a guarantee, the zero reject system requires that our educational goals be explicitly and behaviorally stated, the designs of attaining them planned, and the precise means devised for measuring progress and diagnosing difficulties. And when discrepancies are found between the amount of money spent (input) and student performance (output), then administrators, teachers, and other personnel are to be held accountable. In concrete terms, "to be held accountable" means to be ready to revise programs, modify procedures, promote and demote personnel, raise salaries, and even dismiss responsible individuals.

Performance Contracting   As a means of guaranteeing student performance and year-by-year progress, a managerial tool known as "performance contracting" is often used in accountability programs. The performance contract is an agreement between a business firm and a school, agreeing that the firm will deliver specific results for specific payment. The contract usually includes programs based on an analysis of learning difficulties, the achievement outcome to be expected, and the number of students involved. It guarantees that each child shall be brought up to specified levels of performance in designated areas such as reading and writing. The firm is paid according to the actual outcome of the program. According to Professor Lessinger, "performance contracting is a capability-creating resource for public education." [30]

For example, Behavioral Research Laboratories of Palo Alto, California, entered into a contract in 1971 with the public school system of Gary, Indiana, also known as "School City." This performance contract provided for the Behavioral Research Laboratories (BRL) to take over and operate Banneker Elementary School, an inner-city school of about 850 students. In the contract, Gary agreed to pay its average cost per student to BRL, which in turn guaranteed to raise the achievement level of Banneker's students. The contract further stipulated that BRL would return its fee for any student who fails. In short, BRL was to be held *accountable* for its performance. This performance contract was believed to have involved more responsibility, a longer period of time, and more money than any other contract written in education up to that time. BRL was to manage an entire school for four years with over $2,000,000 in financial transac-

[29] Leon M. Lessinger, "Accountability for Results: A Basic Challenge for America's Schools," in *Accountability in Education*, Leon M. Lessinger and Ralph W. Tyler, eds. (Worthington, Ohio: Jones, 1971), p. 8.

[30] Ibid., p. 31.

tions. As part of the contract, BRL also promised Gary an extensive community relations program and an advisory council of well-known educators and local figures.

In order to implement the contract, which is an excellent example of the systems approach to schooling, BRL provided a "systems man" as center manager and Gary appointed a learning director responsible for supervising the academic components of the system. In addition, five curriculum specialists were given responsibility for managing the major curriculum areas: language arts, mathematics, science, social studies, and foreign language. They were also responsible for arts and crafts, music, drama, and physical education as enrichment areas. To help these specialists, seventeen assistant curriculum managers carried out the major instruction. Twenty-seven additional learning supervisors were then recruited from the parents of Banneker students to work with the assistant managers.

The project began with heavy concentration on reading and mathematics; other areas were gradually phased into the project as the children's performance improved. The materials for programed instruction developed by BRL—*Project Read*, *Project Math*, and *Project Learn*—served as the basic teaching materials. Consultants from outside Gary supplemented the teaching resources and provided in-service staff training.

The staff assessed pupil progress by maintaining a profile of each child's mastery in reading, writing, mathematics, and other areas. The profile was given to the child and his parents monthly. In addition to making these evaluations, the staff used teaching materials structured in such a way that each child's day-to-day progress was noted. For long-range evaluation of each student's performance, Bernard Donovan's Center for Urban Redevelopment and Education (CURE) from New York administered the *Metropolitan Achievement Test* periodically. CURE also carried on monthly monitoring to see that BRL and Gary were conforming to the terms of the contract. Yet another firm was to audit CURE's evaluation of the entire project. For a more detailed description and discussion of the contract and some of the related problems, see "The Performance Contract in Gary," by James A. Mechlenburger and John A. Wilson in *Phi Delta Kappan*, March 1971, pages 406–410.

Who Is Accountable?   From the layperson's point of view, public schools and their personnel should be held responsible (accountable) for their results. Since schools are supported with public money, they should be able to guarantee that every child will master the basic skills of the three Rs and make a year's progress each year. Yet many teachers and administrators seriously question the layperson's demand for an accounting of the professional's work. They point out that the accountability programs in education tend to evaluate results in only a few fields of instruction, neglecting the school's role in socialization and moral education. Furthermore, if the child's learning is affected by such nonschool factors as parents, peers, family backgrounds, socioeconomic and political conditions of the community, who should be held responsible for the child's learning outcome? Since schooling is only one aspect of the child's education, why should only the school and its personnel be held accountable for the child's education?

Indeed, what are the objectives of American education? Can we measure the progress of our schools toward them on behavioral terms? For example, let us say that the primary goal of American education is the development of sound moral character and cultivation of intellectual and vocational competence. What kinds of directly observable responses would indicate that this goal had been reached? These are critical questions for both the public and the educators if they are to work toward a responsible account-ability in American education.

A Critical Estimate

PHILOSOPHICAL FOUNDATIONS

The earlier chapters of this book have examined both common-sense (naive) and scientific Realism, to which methodological Behaviorism owes its philosophical allegiance. Essential to Skinner's conceptions of science and psychology is the belief that reality exists as it is perceived by human beings. Hence, accurate description of our experience is believed to reveal the nature of reality as it exists in itself. In other words, the universe is unaffected by our perceptions of or judgment about our external world.

Unfortunately, there is neither logical nor empirical evidence for such a conclusion. The fact that we perceive what is in the external world does not necessarily imply that what we perceive exists as we "see" it. About the only defensible assertion we can make is that there must be something out there that causally contributes to our perceptual experi-ences. Our knowledge of the universe depends not on conclusive veri-fication of our sense data, but rather on the consequences of ideas we hold and assertions we make. Hence, as we shall soon see, theorizing and inference drawing are perfectly legitimate parts of our inquiry into the nature of reality.

Skinner's belief that all events are caused is a sound and necessary assumption, for it makes science possible and renders the universe, in-cluding human behavior, accessible to us. But although causality is in-dispensable to knowledge and science, it compromises the existence of free will as an uncaused state or act. If all events are thought to have causes, a belief in freedom as uncaused action is unintelligible. Skinner's reasoning thus far is quite correct, but his conclusion that freedom is noth-ing more than our attempt to avoid aversive stimuli is inadequate, because our desire to escape from unpleasant and painful situations is only a small part of what we mean by freedom, that is, moral freedom. For example, in what sense can we say that Socrates' willingness to take the poison, in his belief that people ought to obey the law, was an attempt to avoid aversive stimuli? In other words, Skinner's conception of freedom cannot account for the kind of free act stemming from the individual's moral commitment, which often leads to both pleasure and pain.

The kind of moral freedom we have just mentioned is left out of Skinner's system of values, since his primary axiological concern is the survival of the human species. He is probably correct in asserting that a society that employs the scientific method in dealing with its problems is likely to reduce pollution, control population growth, eliminate sickness and famine, and make more pleasures possible—in short, survive. But such a society will not necessarily regard humanity as an end in itself, nor will it be likely to consider every person as potentially capable of deciding what is good for humanity and how to achieve it. The society that Skinner envisions may be an efficient society in which there is more pleasure than pain, but it is not a society in which every individual can exercise freedom and accept the responsibility for the consequences of his choice.

METHODOLOGICAL BEHAVIORISM

In defending the view that a science of behavior must remain purely descriptive and atheoretical, Skinner assumes that objective order and lawfulness of behavior of organisms are discoverable if we make observations of specific responses as they occur. If we accept this premise, we have no need for theorizing; nor do we have to be concerned about inner states, physical or mental. What Skinner does not seem to realize is that empirical observation is almost never a matter of just "seeing," for we always "see" events or objects as this or that. When we say that we heard a sour note at a concert we are not implying that we first perceived (observed) a tone that we later judged (interpreted) to be sour. Quite to the contrary, we heard a sour note, because we perceived the tone in relation to other tones as well as to our own mental conception of what that particular piece of music should have sounded like.

Observation that does not contain any degree of interpretive judgment is impossible. If it were possible, there would not be any difference between Skinner and Edwin R. Guthrie, a non-Skinnerean behaviorist, for both men are strong proponents of a strictly descriptive and atheoretical science of behavior. They could observe the order in human behavior as it exists, apart from the observer's bias and interpretation. Yet Skinner claims that learning usually requires more than one pairing of a response and a reinforcer, while Guthrie attaches little significance to reinforcement, because he maintains that learning takes place at the first pairing of a stimulus and a response. Whose account accurately describes the order in human behavior as it exists independently of human judgment? This, of course, is an unanswerable question, since we cannot observe (know) things as they are in themselves. Skinner is naive if he seriously believes that pure observation of world phenomena is possible, for there is much more to scientific observation than merely standing alert with sense organs "at the ready," because it is all interest-directed and context-dependent." [31] Hence, the only way in which two individuals with different philosophical and theoretical perspectives can be said to make the same observation is in describing their perceptions in terms of immediate sense data. In other words, to observe is not to have a mass of sense data but to have an experience. Even scientific observation is never pure in the sense of not involving the observer's judgment, for the meaning of what one observes is determined by perspective as well as the context in which one makes the observation. If three individuals witnessed an automobile accident, their accounts of the event would vary because they would have seen the accident from different locations (perspectives) and in different physical and/or emotional states. It would be absurd to speak of the accident as it *really* happened apart from anyone's observation. To observe is not to have a mass of sense data about something but to have an experience, arranging and relating of the sense data in a particular way so that they become meaningful. Scientific observation is not a matter of separating sensations from what they mean to the observer, for observation necessarily involves both. In sum, observation is inseparable from judgment. Therefore, "slicing the incoming signals of sensation from an appreciating of the significance of these signals would destroy what we know as scientific observation." [32]

Mental States and Private Experiences   Skinner is at least partially correct in pointing out that statements such as "Bob smokes a great deal because he has the smoking habit" and "Theresa plays the piano well because she has musical ability" do not explain anything. Because if, by definition, "the smoking habit" and "having musical ability" imply "smoking a great deal" and "playing the piano well," respectively, they are only circular or redundant statements. But Skinner is mistaken if he takes a dispositional statement such as "He drinks because he is thirsty" as a redundant statement in the same sense in which the above-mentioned statements are circular. Everyone has the capacity to become thirsty or to have a tendency to drink. But a tendency to drink can be caused by many variables. We can come to have a tendency to drink because of a twenty-mile hike without any water, or our disposition to drink can be induced by a certain type of brain operation. Or we can be made to drink by threats or rewards. Moreover, when we offer "He drinks because he is

[31] Norwood Russell Hanson, "Observation and Interpretation," in *Philosophy of Science Today*, Sidney Morgenbesser, ed. (New York: Basic Books, 1967), p. 91.
[32] Ibid., p. 89.

thirsty" as an explanation of a particular individual's behavior, it is almost always given within a specific context in which information about relevant factors is given. That is, in the context of a twenty-mile hike the statement, "He drinks because he is thirsty," would probably mean, "He went on a twenty-mile hike when the temperature was 105° F without any water, and these conditions induced his disposition to drink; therefore he drank a lot of water." No doubt additional physiological explanations can be given. The main point here is that whenever we say, "He drinks because he is thirsty," as an explanation we usually have information about the variables that led to the individual's tendency to drink at that particular time and place. The context will also tell us something about the factors that had nothing to do with the act in question. In other words, if a person drinks because he became thirsty as a result of taking a twenty-mile hike, we would know with reasonable certainty that his act of drinking was not caused by a threat of some sort. The point that Skinner misses in his discussion is the fact that no one ever offers "He drinks because he is thirsty" as an explanation without providing at least some additional information, directly or contextually. Michael Scriven made a similar observation when he remarked:

> Even if "to be thirsty" means nothing more than to have a tendency to drink, it is by no means merely redundant to be told that on this occasion he drank because of that tendency rather than under compulsion or because of a tendency to eat. . . . To have a tendency is to have a certain disposition, and everyone has some disposition to drink, but it is not always that disposition which explains our drinking. When we are satiated, for example, we have a short term disposition not to drink; and, in such a case, the statement that we drank because we were thirsty would not, even on Skinner's first analysis, be redundant; it would be false. [Thus,] to chastise the ordinary explanations of individual events by reference to dispositions, on the grounds that some explanations of patterns of behavior by reference to dispositions are redundant, is manifestly unfair.[33]

There is no doubt that private experiences and neurophysiological states are not directly observable; therefore, what we say about them is subject to error and misunderstanding. But statements about observable events too are fallible, perhaps to a lesser degree. Therefore,

> to maintain that planning, deliberating, preference, choice, volition, pleasure, pain, displeasure, love, hatred, . . . etc. are not among the causal factors which determine human behavior, is to fly in the face of the commonest of evidence, or else to deviate in a strange and unjustifiable way from the ordinary use of language. The task is neither to repudiate these obvious facts, nor to rule out this manner of describing them. The task is

[33] Michael Scriven, "A Study of Radical Behaviorism," in *Minnesota Studies in the Philosophy of Science*, vol. 1, *The Foundations of Science and the Concepts of Psychology and Psycholanalysis*, Herbert Feigl and Michael Scriven, eds. (Minneapolis: University of Minnesota Press, 1963), p. 121.

rather to analyze the logical status of this sort of description in its relation to behavioral and/or neurophysiological descriptions.[34]

The mental and the neurophysiological states of other persons are clearly not verifiable in any conclusive sense. But occurrences of such states are empirically confirmable. In other words, since each of us can verify the occurrence of certain mental states within ourselves we can empirically confirm or disconfirm that a particular mental state has or has not taken place in another person by the use of analogical argument (for instance, when I am in a sad mood, there are observable symptoms X, Y, and Z; when I observe another person exhibiting these outward symptoms I can reasonably say that that person is in a sad mood. It is logically impossible for us to conclusively verify another person's toothache, for we would have to perceive that person's toothache. Yet, if we have reliable information about the kinds of overt symptoms usually associated with "having a toothache," it is possible to confirm whether the person in question has a toothache. This is the way we usually communicate with others.

An adequate science of behavior must deal with events taking place both inside and outside of the behaving organism. This does not mean that inner happenings should be known in the same way we come to know the observable responses. To demand that the "inner states" be known as we know the external, immediately observable, variables is to dismiss the former as being useless with insufficient warrant. Benjamin Wolman reminds us that "the task of scientific inquiry is to seek truth, be it visible and observable or private. If there are private events, we must study them. We shall study them as objectively as possible. . . . Science has to study things as they are and cannot reject things because they do not fit into one's intellectual preference or modes of thinking." [35] But Skinner does reject inner states, mental and physical, because they do not fit into his particular mode of thinking; that is, inner states are not conclusively verifiable. In one sense Skinner is similar to a man looking for his ring under a street lamp because there is more light there than in the dark alley where he lost the ring.

As we have seen, Skinner explains the learning of all voluntary actions in terms of operant conditioning. In other words, our voluntary responses occur because they are reinforced. Even verbal behavior such as giving a lecture on behaviorism and the technology of teaching is thought of as behavior reinforced through the mediation of others who, as listeners, respond to the speaker in such a way as to strengthen the lecturer's behavior. And because of his antitheoretical bias, Skinner is unwilling to

---

[34] Herbert Feigl, "The Mental and the Physical," in *Minnesota Studies in the Philosophy of Science*, vol. 2, *Concepts, Theories, and the Mind-Body Problem*, Herbert Feigl, Michael Scriven, and Grover Maxwell, eds. (Minneapolis: University of Minnesota Press, 1956), p. 389.

[35] Benjamin B. Wolman, ed., "Toward a Science of Psychological Science," *Scientific Psychology* (New York: Basic Books, 1965), p. 12.

deal with the question, "Why do reinforcers reinforce?" other than to say that they do in fact increase the probability of a response. There is little doubt that in an analysis of animal behavior or simple human responses this reinforcement view is adequate. Moreover, if all our educational and instructional objectives dealt with relatively simple responses, Skinner's operant conditioning might be sufficient. But our instructional objectives have to do with complex skills, attitudes, and beliefs that cannot be expressed completely in terms of directly observable responses.

Questions about the child's purpose and intention almost always arise in dealing with teaching-learning situations. Our own purposes and intentions as well as our interpretation of other people's aspirations and motives affect our conduct. For example, if you are hit by a baseball, your reaction to the incident depends upon how you understand the intentions of the person who threw the ball. If you decide that the ball accidentally hit you, you might walk away, but if you conclude that the ball was deliberately thrown at you, you might take a considerably different course of action. We are not, of course, suggesting that there is a world of intentions that is distinct from the world of physical events. But we are suggesting that Skinner's reinforcement language cannot adequately deal with the kinds of phenomena usually called mental.

For Skinner the term *motivation* refers to deprivation, which can be operationally defined. This means that whatever we say about the motives behind a person's decision to join the Peace Corps, study the philosophy of science, or deliver a lecture on behaviorism, they must be regarded as deprivation of some sort. But what kinds of deprivation? Deprivation of affection, attention, success, recognition, and so on are not acceptable to Skinner as explanatory terms because they are not observable behavior. It would certainly be strange to say that Skinner wrote the book *Verbal Behavior* because he had been deprived of something. Similarly, only in a trivial sense can we say that the utterances of a philosopher or of Skinner himself are nothing more than reinforced responses.

If we take Skinner's account of verbal behavior seriously, we must conclude that his own statements regarding the validity of behaviorism are nothing more than emitted verbal responses reinforced through the mediation of other persons. In other words, Skinner says that behaviorism is valid because the act of saying is reinforced by others. Whatever he says about descriptive behaviorism amounts to no more than emitted responses reinforced by others. But this hardly demonstrates the validity of his or any other point of view, for the properties that make a judgment valid are something other than reinforcement from others. The statement "Behaviorism is valid" no more makes behaviorism valid than the statement "Behaviorism is false" makes it false. If behaviorism is valid, there must be at least one exception to its basic principle that all voluntary human behaviors are nothing more than reinforced responses. The assertion "Behaviorism is valid" must be based on something more than reinforcement from other persons. Skinner would no doubt persist in saying, "Behaviorism is valid" even if his audience, or perhaps the entire world population, disagreed with him, precisely because his saying so was not brought about by concurrence (reinforcement) from others. In a paper delivered at the meeting of the American Psychological Association in September 1968, Skinner admitted that, at present, experimental analysis could not give an adequate account of complex verbal behavior. He also indicated that, in the future, behaviorism will give us an adequate explanation of such complex behavior. But can descriptive behaviorism do what Skinner promises? We think not, because Skinner's behaviorism is based on a very narrow and rigid positivistic philosophy of science.

Is a Purely Descriptive Science of Behavior Possible? After hearing so much about the antitheoretical attitude and descriptive approach to science, it is something of a surprise to learn that Skinner thinks of science as "more than mere description of events as they occur." [36] But he is correct in regarding science as "an attempt to discover order, to show that certain events stand in lawful relations to other events." [37] Contrary to Skinner's own assumption, discovering such order and lawfulness requires more than just a pile of facts, because facts alone do not reveal order. In brief, facts do not speak for themselves! We must interpret the data and bridge gaps in our observation with constructs (theoretical entities) and postulates. Drawing inferences and testing hypotheses are other essential aspects of an empirical science.

Scientific explanations are never absolutely true, nor are they always conclusively verifiable. For example, physicists claim that atoms exist, although they are never directly observed. They also assert that tremendous energy can be produced by "splitting" an atom (nuclear fission), but physicists do not directly observe the "splitting." The fact of nuclear fission is inferred (and confirmed) by an actual production of energy, e.g., an atomic explosion. Even the laws of physics, chemistry, and astronomy are accepted as highly confirmed hypotheses that "are all universal propositions, stating that under specified conditions such and such happens always and everywhere." [38] Even as fundamental a law of science as Newton's Law of Motion, according to which every body persists in a state of rest or of uniform motion in a straight line unless compelled by external force to change that state, is not based on direct observation of every body under the stated condition.

Within this conception of science, constructs (theoretical entities or the terms referring to inferred states) are useful tools insofar as they have observable consequences that help us to explain a phenomenon under investigation. Hence, theoretical constructs such as motive, drive, ego, and

[36] Skinner, *Science and Human Behavior*, p. 6.
[37] Ibid.
[38] Pap, p. 17.

so on, are said to exist when their specified consequences eventuate. If we assert that the learner will acquire "expectancies" (a construct) through associating a new stimulus and a second stimulus that has an already established meaning, the construct "expectancy" can be said to exist if what is asserted results in an observable consequence. For example, if Tim has always purchased popsicles from a white jeep with a colorful canopy and jingling bell, and if he expects the jeep and/or the popsicles whenever he hears the sound of the bell, he can be said to have acquired an "expectancy." The constructs, therefore, need not be directly observable effects. And we should regard them as "real in such-and-such a respect, but unreal . . . in such-and-such another respect." [39] Constructs may be used not only as a legitimate part of scientific explanation but often as necessary concepts in explaining why certain phenomena take place.

Even Skinner himself has not been successful in avoiding terms that have no observable referents. For example, it is usually assumed that the term "conditioning" merely describes a particular kind of relationship between stimulus and response, and that it applies to both classical and operant conditioning. But does the term refer to a directly observable stimulus-response relationship? The answer is a resounding no, for all we can "see" directly in a conditioning process is merely that one event follows another. Hence, something more than mere temporal sequence is tacitly presupposed, for the term "conditioning" is not applied to all instances of one behavioral event following another. That is, if Pat always twitches her nose before scratching her head, we would not necessarily say that the scratching was a conditioned response to twitching unless the association between them is of a certain kind. Such a relationship implies that a stimulus "can make a response happen." Skinner himself uses the term "reinforcement" to mean that which increases the probability of a response. Indeed, there are many situations in which a response following a stimulus would not be called either conditioning or reinforcement. Without assuming some sort of connection, neurological or otherwise, between stimulus and response, the concept of conditioning would not be distinguishable from mere temporal sequence.

Another example of Skinner's inability to follow his own methodological dictum is his view of the Law of Effect. In his article "Are Theories of Learning Necessary?" Skinner states that, "anyone who has seen such a demonstration knows that the Law of Effect is no theory." [40] He is, of course, referring to those situations in which a reinforcing event following a response increases the probability of that response. What Skinner is suggesting is that the expression *Law of Effect* does in fact stand for a directly observable variable, i.e., the event in which a reinforcer *does in fact increase* the probability of that response. However, Skinner cannot see such an event. What he does observe is an event following another

[39] Scriven, p. 117.
[40] Skinner, "Are Theories of Learning Necessary?" p. 200.

event. But in what way does this observation differ from Newton's observation of a falling apple? Is not the Law of Effect or the notion of reinforcement as much a theoretical concept as the term *gravitation*?

The difficulty with Skinner's position is that any system that claims to be based solely on the observation of specific responses and the frequency of their occurrences can only speculate about the probability of a particular response on the basis of the observation of prior occurrences. Hence, without making other assumptions, we cannot formulate a law covering all responses and their reinforcers. In quoting Henri Poincaré, a nineteenth-century French mathematical physicist, Benjamin Wolman reminds us that "pure empiricism does not make science more rigorous; rather it makes it less adequate. A mere collection of facts is no more a science than a pile of bricks is a house." [41]

A basic flaw of Skinner's behaviorism lies in its inability to explain adequately such complex phases of human behavior as language learning, abstract thinking, and other high-level cognitive processes. This weakness is due primarily to the behaviorists' insistence that all empirical statements must be verified through direct observation. Once the verifiability principle had been interpreted so narrowly, it was unavoidable that methodological behaviorists would disregard mental processes and neurophysiological conditions as irrelevant because they are not accessible to direct observation. In a sense methodological behaviorists can be likened to Zeno and Parmenides, who denied human beings' immediate experience of motion because the concept did not fit into their scheme of logic and assumptions. What Skinnereans need to do is to broaden their conception of verification and also to "strengthen its [methodological behaviorism's] core by admitting the contributions which other disciplines within psychology are making and by usefully incorporating and improving them whenever they are relevant." [42] As Pribram continues:

> The problem to which operant behaviorism is addressed is reinforcement. Reinforcement is a central problem in psychology "by whatever name it is called: outcome, consequence, law of effect, feedback, stamping in, etc." Thus operant behaviorism pervades psychology. But the converse also holds or should hold—psychology must pervade operant behaviorism if either is to remain viable. [43]

Finally, we need to examine Skinner's reinforcement theory, because it is so central to his psychology that any weakness in it will raise serious doubts about the validity and adequacy of his account of learning and teaching. Quite consistent with Skinner's antitheoretical perspective, his reinforcement theory is based on direct observation of the functional relationship between operant responses (dependent variables) and their

[41] Wolman, p. 11.
[42] Karl H. Pribram, "Comment," in *Explanation in the Behavioral Sciences*, Robert Borger and Frank Cioffi, eds. (Cambridge University Press, 1970), p. 380.
[43] Ibid.

causes (independent variables). Hence, it is not an inferred but a descriptive theory. However, as an empirical explanation its validity depends upon its verifiability. In other words, are there instances that confirm the claim that a response does occur more frequently when followed by reinforcement? Furthermore, can this proposition be shown to be false if appropriate evidence can be found? Though the second of the two questions may appear strange to some readers, it is as important as the first.

> All tests can be interpreted as attempts to weed out false theories—to find the weak points of a theory in order to reject it if it is falsified by the test. . . . because it is our aim to establish theories as well as we can, we must test them as severely as we can; that is, we must try to falsify them. Only if we cannot falsify them in spite of our best efforts can we say that they stood up to severe tests. This is the reason why the discovery of instances which confirm a theory means very little if we have not tried, and failed, to discover refutations.[44]

In other words, to validate an empirical theory we must not only look for the kinds of events that support the theory but also know and search for the sorts of evidence that, if found, would refute the theory. A theory is said to be valid if we find a sufficient number of confirming instances without also discovering events that could falsify it. For example, consider the statement "The sound of a buzzer that consistently follows the flashing of a bright light causing a child to blink his eyes will later induce the same response in the child without being paired with the flashing of a bright light." This general statement would be true if (1) we found supporting evidence and (2) if we did not discover instances in which the buzzer did not produce the blinking response.

Now, returning to Skinner's view of reinforcement, we can indeed find numerous cases that can confirm the assertion that an operant response increases in its probability when followed by a reinforcing situation. Children's increased interest in reading resulting from receiving gold stars or tokens of some sort from their teacher is only one of many such instances. But what sorts of evidence would refute the reinforcement theory? That is, could there be some situations in which a response followed by a reinforcer would not occur more frequently? The answer here is an emphatic no, because a reinforcer is explained in terms of its effect. Since a reinforcer is seen as whatever increases the probability of a response, there cannot be reinforcement without an increase in the occurrence of an operant. In short, Skinner's reinforcement theory is not falsifiable. When a supposedly empirical explanation turns out to be irrefutable, its validity and adequacy become suspect, for no empirical knowledge can go beyond its probable and tentative nature.

For the sake of further clarification, let us say an educational psychologist claims that a child who is given a proper instruction in spelling

---

[44] Karl Popper, *The Poverty of Historicism* (London: Routledge and Kegan Paul, 1957), pp. 133–134.

will never make any spelling mistakes. The expression "proper instruction," is explained, of course, as whatever enables the child to spell correctly at all times. Now, we should have no difficulty in finding children who always spell correctly and have received some instruction in spelling. The fact that they make no spelling errors makes whatever instruction they received the "proper" sort. But could we falsify the claim by discovering children who, in spite of proper instruction in spelling, continue to misspell? Of course not, because "proper instruction" is defined in terms of its effect. Hence, if children continue to misspell, we must conclude that the instruction they received was not of a "proper" kind. And since the properties of the so-called proper instruction that promote correct spelling have not been specified, the assertion cannot be falsified and, therefore, it cannot be thoroughly tested.

Because of this irrefutable nature of Skinner's reinforcement theory we must suspect its validity as an adequate explanation of human behavior and the teaching-learning process. It is probably this irrefutability that makes Skinner and his followers act as if the reinforcement theory were a certain truth. This attitude seems to be reflected in the Skinnereans' reluctance to consider the possibility that other perspectives in psychology may have substantive contributions to make in understanding human behavior.

THE TECHNOLOGY OF TEACHING

As Skinner pointed out several times, the most important task of the teacher is to arrange conditions under which desired learning can occur. Considering the fact that teachers are expected to bring about changes in extremely complex behavior, they should be specialists in human behavior. Effective and efficient manipulation of the multitude of variables affecting children's intellectual and social behaviors cannot be accomplished by trial and error alone, nor should such work be based solely on the personal experiences of the teacher, since this covers only a limited range of circumstances. Consequently, a scientific study of human behavior is vital in the improvement of teaching, because it provides us with accurate and reliable knowledge about learning and leads to the development of new instructional materials, methods, and techniques. Similarly, an empirical analysis of the teaching process is essential, for it clarifies the teacher's responsibility through a series of small and progressive approximations. This approach makes teaching practices more specific, thereby facilitating a more effective evaluation.

More important, the introduction of technology to teaching enables teachers to act like human beings. That is, programed instruction and teaching machines free teachers from routine chores and also from the need to maintain the learner's behavior by aversive control. Teachers can relate to the students not merely as taskmasters but as guides and advisors who are concerned about the students' present interests and future goals. Furthermore, technology makes it possible for teachers to teach more than they know, because it allows them to arrange the necessary contingencies, even when they have never been exposed to them. To sum up the value of technology in teaching, Skinner remarks that

> in the long run a technology of teaching helps most by increasing the teacher's productivity. It simply permits him to teach more—more of a given subject, in more subjects, and more students . . . . We cannot improve education simply by increasing its support, changing its policies, or reorganizing its administrative structure. We must improve teaching itself. Nothing short of an effective technology will solve that problem.[45]

As we have pointed out, the development and use of programed instruction and of teaching machines are essential to the technology of teaching. Notwithstanding Skinner's claim that programed instruction will enable teachers to teach more things to more students in a more efficient and effective way, numerous objections have been raised against these developments in education. One of the more frequent complaints is that the use of teaching machines and programed materials is tantamount to treating children like animals, because the procedures and devices used in programing instructions were originally employed in studying animal behavior. The critics go on to insist that what works for rats and pigeons will not necessarily work for human beings. However, Skinner retorts by saying that "what is common to pigeons and man is a world in which certain contingencies of reinforcement prevail."[46] Hence, regardless of how the devices and programs were developed, if they produce desired consequences there should be no objections to them just because they are also used in working with animals.

Programed instruction is also criticized for its use of contrived (artificial) contingencies of reinforcement. It is argued that in real life we do not do everything for reinforcements (rewards), and when we receive rewards they are usually natural consequences. But Skinner points out that teachers who wait for natural contingencies (reinforcements) will be ineffective, for their responsibility is to arrange necessary contingencies so that a behavior can be learned and made useful later. For example, a mother reinforces her child in learning to talk so that the child's verbal behavior will become useful in the future. At first, the child's efforts are reinforced with such contrived reinforcers as kisses, praises, and cookies. Only later is the child's verbal behavior naturally reinforced. Even adults do not learn responses because they are naturally reinforced. As a matter of fact, much of what is learned in school is due to contrived, not natural, contingencies: students study for grades, honors, and diplomas.

Programed instruction is condemned by some as a means of regimentation, which is inconsistent with democratic education. While programed

---

[45] Skinner, *The Technology of Teaching*, p. 258.
[46] Ibid., p. 84.

instruction can be used to produce submissive individuals, it is not inherently regimenting. Skinner agrees that technology can be used unwisely to produce docile people, but he also observes that it can be utilized to "maximize the genetic endowment of each student; it could make him as skillful, competent, and informed as possible; it could build the greatest diversity of interests; it could lead him to make the greatest possible contribution to the survival and development of his culture."[47] This is a slightly exaggerated estimate of what technology can accomplish, but Skinner rightly insists that the regimenting or liberating consequences of programed instruction depend not so much on the concept of programing as on the values that we hold to be worthwhile ends of education. In other words, regimentation does not necessarily follow from the use of programed instruction. In the end, our own decision of how a technology of teaching ought to be used determines its consequences.

To the cry that teaching machines will replace teachers, Skinner replies that mechanical devices will free teachers from routine and allow them to devote more time to advising and counseling students. In a sense any teacher who does not see his or her responsibility as broader than the mechanical functionings of a teaching machine deserves to be replaced by it. Education is as much a moral and cultural process as an intellectual affair, and therefore its aims must go beyond developing skills and imparting information. This means that education must go on in a social, moral, and intellectual climate in which children can learn to maintain all sorts of relationships with others and become increasingly capable of dealing with various problematic situations. Hence, programed instruction and teaching machines should be regarded as helpful teaching aids and nothing more. Someone once said, "Any teacher who fears being replaced by a machine, should be."

A frequently mentioned benefit of programed instruction is that it can provide individualized instruction for children with varying capacities and rates of achievement. Indeed, the use of programed materials and teaching machines can help a child learn at his or her own rate without hindering others of greater or lesser abilities and levels of attainment. But this is only one aspect of individualized instruction. Truly individualized teaching should make it possible for each child not only to complete the learning materials at his or her own rate but also to pursue and develop individual interests and perspectives. Since what is learned through the programed approach is predetermined, instruction becomes individualized only in the sense of permitting a child to work at his or her own rate. Moreover, this kind of teaching interferes with the spontaneous and creative aspects of certain learning processes, because it is not possible to prepare programed materials that can individually accommodate the unique interests of each child in a classroom, let alone in an entire school.

[47] Ibid., p. 91.

Because programed materials usually provide a limited number of answers to the questions posed, the child may be restricted in the variety of perspectives from which an issue can be examined. In addition, since working with teaching machines usually requires mechanically choosing one right answer from several possible answers already provided, the child is given little opportunity to develop the skills of written and oral communication, particularly in an aesthetic and creative sense.

BEHAVIORAL OBJECTIVES AND PERFORMANCE-BASED INSTRUCTION

As we have already seen, the use of behavioral objectives in curricular planning and performance-based instruction are based on the supposition that (1) learning complex behavior, such as critical thinking, can be accomplished by progressively mastering the smaller and simpler components of the target behavior and (2) all attainable education goals can be explicitly and behaviorally stated. What these assumptions imply is that the objectives not definable in behavorial terms are either unattainable or irrelevant. Because performance-based instruction and the use of behavioral objectives are so closely tied to each other, they must be examined together.

Today there is general agreement that in certain areas of learning where mastery of factual knowledge and specific skills is required the use of behavioral objectives is quite useful and even necessary. However, there is no such consensus regarding the criterion by which we can decide the number of smaller behaviors and behavioral objectives into which a target behavior can be broken down. For example, the elementary teacher education model developed by Michigan State University has over 3,000 behavioral objectives and corresponding instructional modules. But a similar model, The Toledo Model, constructed by a group of universities in Ohio, has only about 1,600 behavioral objectives. We need not, of course, stop here. We can develop a teacher education program with fewer or more behavioral goals than in these two models. In other words, we could have a model with only 500 behavioral objectives or with 6,000 or more. Our dilemma is that we have no standard by which we can say, "Now we have exactly the right number of behavioral objectives for our elementary teacher education program." In other words, since a complex target behavior such as effective elementary school teaching can be divided into almost any number of component behavior units, when should we stop formulating the behavioral objectives? Or when should we stop analyzing the target behavior into smaller units? Professor W. James Popham suggests that we "explicate to the point where explication drives [us] away from explication." [48] That is, we

---

[48] "Discussion of the Popham Chapter," in *AERA Monograph Series on Curriculum Evaluation*, vol. 3, *Instructional Objectives* (Chicago: Rand McNally 1969), p. 54.

. . . should operationalize as precisely as [we] can to the point where it becomes overwork, to the point where [we say], "Well, this is just too blasted much trouble." At this point [we] should stop.[49]

This means that one instructor may develop 50 behavioral objectives for a one-semester course in philosophy of education, while another may have 500, and still others may have 5 or 5,000, depending on their temperament and on how minutely they want to atomize their overall course objectives. While there is some truth to the argument that having 100 objectives is better than having 1, a course or program may simply die of its own weight if behavioral objectives become too numerous. But again, how should we decide whether the objectives are too numerous? Since performance-based teacher education (PBTE) requires that we be clear and specific about our educational objectives, and the more explicit we become in stating our objectives the more behavioral objectives we must develop, how can we avoid the problem of having too many of them?

The so-called merit rating (or merit pay) that was popular in the 1950s was based on a similar belief that the most efficient means of measuring teaching effectiveness is to assess the ways in which each teacher is successful in carrying out various teaching acts. Some merit rating programs used instruments with a dozen or so items to be checked by supervisors or principals, while others developed lengthy volumes containing hundreds of items to be evaluated by appropriate administrative personnel. There were neither logical nor empirical criteria for deciding how many acts constituted effective teaching. The death of merit rating plans was due not only to the excessive number of items to be evaluated but also to the fact that there was no consensus as to the nature of effective teaching. But this should have been expected, for education is so value-laden that what one means by "effective," "right," or "good" depends largely on one's conception of education, which in turn stems from one's view of reality, Man, knowledge, and values. The factors responsible for the failure of the merit-rating movement are likely to bring about the eventual demise of performance-based instruction, such as PBTE.

While factual knowledge and specific skills can be learned by mastering smaller units of the target behavior, this type of mastery learning does not enable the child to effectively handle the unexpected or attain certain higher cognitive and affective goals. For example, learning right answers to a given set of questions does not help Nancy deal with views that challenge the answers she has learned; similarly, her skills in reading and identifying the main theme of an essay will not help her understand the author's hidden message or what he has failed to express. And Ralph's ability to identify and analyze the structure of the sonata form will not result in his appreciation of Beethoven's early symphonies. Moreover, we must keep in mind that children learn not only the specified objectives but other sorts of intellectual and emotional attitudes, skills, and values

[49] Ibid.

from the kinds of learning processes they undergo. That is, they learn how to think and how to learn from the ways in which they are taught. Hence, *how* we learn is at least as important as *what* we learn. Some educational anthropologists even argue that the students' values and attitudes are influenced more by the ways in which they are taught than by what they are taught. Consequently, critical and creative thinking and self-initiated learning are not likely to come from the sort of learning process that reinforces only the correct answers.

The disagreement between the advocates and the critics of behavioral objectives is more than a dispute about the techniques of developing educational objectives. It is a dispute on basic conceptions of education. Those who support education as behavior engineering and, consequently, the use of behavioral objectives, see educational goals as product specifications that the learner should achieve after being properly processed. Hence, behavioral objectives are prescriptions to be attained by the learner. On the other hand, many critics of this view see education as a creative process wherein the learner can realize his or her own potential. From this perspective, educational goals have considerably different meanings because

> if . . . education is viewed as a form of experience that has something to do with the quality of an individual's life, if it involves helping him to learn to make authentic choices, choices that are a result of his own reflection and which depend upon the exercise of free will, then the problem of educational objectives takes a different turn.[50]

In other words, educational objectives are to be seen as the kinds of experiences the learner should encounter. The learning outcome is neither prescribed nor guaranteed, for much of what happens to the learner depends upon external conditions as well as his or her own initiative and effort.

Accountable Teaching

To review briefly, the supporters of the accountability movement insist that our schools and their personnel should be held accountable for their success and failure in enabling our children to acquire the basic skills necessary for productive life in our complex and technologically oriented society. One of the main reasons for their exclusive concern with the basic skills is that such educational goals as open-mindedness, creative thinking, appreciation, understanding, and so on, are thought to be irrelevant because they are intangible and hence neither definable nor measurable in behavioral terms. They go on to suggest that we can achieve genuine accountability in education if schools adopt the techniques of management

---

[50] E. W. Eisner, "Instructional and Expressive Educational Objectives: Their Formulation and Use in Curriculum," in *AERA Monograph Series on Curriculum Evaluation*, vol. 3, *Instructional Objectives* (Chicago: Rand McNally 1969), p. 8.

science being used in industry and the military. Accordingly, many accountability programs include such measures as performance specifications, systems analysis, program budgeting, cost effectiveness, performance contracting, and performance-based instruction. The main goal of the accountability people is to deliver tangible and quantifiable goods to our educational consumers so as to restore their confidence in school and win greater financial support.

Both educators and laypeople have always been interested in finding new ways of making our schools more effective and efficient. Therefore, there can be no argument against the view that America's schools should be made more productive and responsible. Yet the accountability movement is objectionable to many teachers, for it is exclusively concerned with the acquisition of basic skills, while completely ignoring the purposes for which these skills are to be used. Consequently, the quality of living and the kind of society we hope to achieve through the use of skills, jobs, and earnings are left out as irrelevant aspirations. But education is inevitably a moral enterprise and, therefore, it necessarily involves values that constitute our concept of the Good Life. Moreover, regardless of our intentions, what we do as teachers and administrators affects the values and attitudes of our students. As we pointed out earlier, even the ways in which instructional technology is used in our schools influence children's manner of learning, thinking, and behavior. And if it is true that we cannot avoid influencing our students, then we as teachers ought to make certain that the influence we have on our students is the result of careful and reflective deliberations of sociopolitical and moral questions related to the kind of world we wish to build and perpetuate.

As educational psychologists, sociologists, and anthropologists remind us, learning is almost always multidimensional. Hence, children acquire much more than what is specified in any given set of learning objectives. Anthropologist Jules Henry points out in his book *Culture Against Man* that children become docile and submissive if they are constantly required to give back the answers their teacher wants. In almost every teaching-learning situation this kind of concomitant learning is likely to occur. Moreover, the causes of the child's learning are so complex that what our schools and their personnel do contributes only partially to children's academic achievement.

The Coleman Report indicates that children's competencies in the basic skills are affected very little by the kinds and amount of facilities, buildings, and equipment available to the school. The report goes on to suggest that such sociocultural factors as family background, social class, and peer groups have more to do with how much and how well children learn in school.[51] In other words, the failure of our schools is not attributable to

[51] James S. Coleman et al., *Equality of Educational Opportunity* (Washington: Office of Education, Department of Health, Education and Welfare, 1969).

ineffective teaching alone, for schools reflect the culture and the socio-economic and political conditions of the society in which they exist. Hence, any radical change in schooling requires equally radical sociopolitical and economic reforms. As we shall see in Chapter 13, one of the major reasons for the failure of compensatory education programs is that the responsible individuals were preoccupied with developing skills rather than providing significant changes in the sociocultural environment where so-called deprived or disadvantaged children live.

In many accountability programs utilizing performance contracting, the level of children's academic achievement is measured primarily by their scores on standardized tests. And it is on such scores that teachers' promotion and salary raises often depend. In this way, accountable teaching often becomes nothing more than test-teaching, which tends to foster competitiveness and docility, qualities inimical to democratic society, wherein cooperation, compassion, love, and kindness are at least as important as individualism and a search for personal success. As Professor Martin Levit cautions us, accountability based solely on mastery of basic skills is "geared to the production of functionaries within a technological society rather than to the development of independent people who are social critics and constructors."[52] Hence, if we are to make our schools more effective, we need to give them a new orientation. Radical educational and sociocultural reforms are necessary to produce teachers and students who are not only the transmitters of our values but also their critics. Accordingly, our choice of procedures, techniques, and programs such as accountability measures, PBTE, and programed instruction should be made in terms of much broader educational goals, social ideals, and moral concerns than mere economic efficiency, political expediency, or immediate utility.

Conclusion

In spite of our criticisms, methodological behaviorism has made significant contributions in the experimental analysis of learning and has introduced a radically different way of studying human behavior. The technology of behavior too has had and will continue to have profound influence in American education. Consequently, if we are to improve our schools we must examine critically the implications of the evaluations of contemporary American education made by such individuals as B. F. Skinner. We must also scrutinize the ways in which the use of behavior engineering may help or hinder our work as educators.

[52] Martin Levit, "The Ideology of Accountability in Schooling," in *Philosophers Speak on Accountability in Education*, Robert L. Leight, ed. (Danville, Ill.: Interstate, 1973), p. 45.

As Skinner correctly observes, education today is too dominated by aversive stimuli. Children work to avoid or escape from a series of punishments, which may come in the form of the teacher's criticism or ridicule, being sent to the principal, suspension, or even "paddling." "In this welter of aversive consequences getting the right answer is in itself an insignificant event, any effect of which is lost amid the anxieties, the boredom, and the aggressions which are the inevitable by-products of aversive control." [53] In addition to this predominantly punitive atmosphere, the contingencies of reinforcement are far too few, and whatever contingencies we have arranged are loose and unsystematic. Our schools not only lack carefully planned schedules of reinforcement but allow too much time to elapse between reinforcements given to children. Not infrequently, days and even weeks pass before assignments and tests are returned to students with grades. We are also without carefully planned programs to help children advance through a series of progressive approximation to the terminal behavior desired. Thus Skinner persistently argues that the failure of our schools and the incompetencies of America's children can be reduced or even eliminated if we make more efficient use of available reinforcement contingencies and provide less punitive learning conditions.

As if to follow Skinner's recommendation, today many educational institutions have adopted or are experimenting with such innovations as programed instruction, performance-based instruction, a systems approach to education, and educational accountability. And these developments have "forced" many administrators and teachers to be more clear and precise about their goals, methods, and materials. Furthermore, these new measures, particularly the systems approach to education and the accountability movement, have pointed out the value of developing coherent and comprehensive plans and strategies as efficient means of achieving our educational goals. In other areas, the techniques of behavior modification have helped numerous children with a wide variety of learning difficulties to become more proficient in various tasks. In psychopathology, evidence for even more dramatic accomplishments of the technology of behavior can be found. For example, many autistic individuals were "treated" to develop normal speech and behavioral patterns through behavior modification techniques. In one instance, a rejected and ridiculed boy was helped to win back parental affection and peer acceptance by extinguishing his abnormally effeminate traits and building more masculine behaviors when reinforcement contingencies and mild punishments were systematically arranged and used.[54]

It appears that there is ample evidence to substantiate the effectiveness of operant conditioning in modifying our overt behavior. But does this fact justify making education a process of operant conditioning? We may

[53] Skinner, *Cumulative Record*, p. 150.
[54] Wayne Sage, "The Case of Deviant Gender," *Human Behavior*, September 1973, pp. 59–62.

grant that it is socially desirable to alter the behavior of autistic individuals who cannot think for themselves by utilizing the techniques of behavior engineering to make them more acceptable to themselves and others. But are we ethically justified in changing the behavior of rational and intelligent people according to some predetermined norm? How can we reconcile our concern for self-initiated learning, learning by discovery, and creativity with the view that all learning objectives must be preplanned and behaviorally specified by someone other than the learner? In other words, are the tenets underlying the technological model of education consonant with the ideals of a society wherein freedom and every person's right to exercise it are the highest values? These are difficult but important questions raised by many humanistic educators today. In the following chapter, we turn our attention to a humanistic model of education—education as a process of self-actualization—as an alternative to the behavior engineering model.

Questions

1. Is education as behavior engineering inherently totalitarian? Or is it merely a more efficient way of "getting our job done"?

2. According to *Education USA* (November 12, 1973), the independent weekly education newsletter published by National School Public Relations Association, more than thirty states in this country are either seriously studying or actively involved in developing some form of PBTE and performance-based teacher certification. In the state of Texas, the state education agency is said to have made it mandatory that all teacher training institutions must adopt PBTE programs by September 1, 1977.

   (a) If all institutions involved in teacher education were to follow Texas, would they produce a new breed of teachers? Would these teachers in turn produce a new generation of children?

   (b) If all forms of education were to become performance based, what possible social, cultural, and even moral consequences would be likely to come from such an approach to education?

   (c) Are there moral questions involved when a state agency requires educational institutions to follow PBTE or any other particular approach to teacher education?

3. List what you think are the primary goals of American education and attempt to restate them in terms of directly observable responses. What are some possible problems and benefits that may come from this approach?

4. If Skinner were to interpret "verifiablilty" to mean empirical confirmation rather than conclusive verification (which must involve direct observation of that which one attempts to verify), what differences might you find in his views of Man, learning, teaching, and psychology?

Further Reading

Houston, W. Robert, and Robert B. Howsam, eds. *Competency-Based Teacher Education.* Chicago: Science Research Associates, 1972. Houston and Howsam provide useful insights concerning pertinent concepts, emphasizing that competency and accountability go hand in hand.

Lessinger, Leon M. *Every Kid a Winner.* New York: Simon and Schuster, 1970. Lessinger argues that accountability is necessary if public schools are to reach and raise the achievement levels of those children now left behind.

Mason, Robert E. *Contemporary Educational Theory.* New York: David McKay, 1972. Mason examines nearly two centuries of Western educational theory in 265 pages.

Milhollan, Frank, and Bill E. Forisha. *From Skinner to Rogers: Contrasting Approaches to Education.* Lincoln, Nebraska: Professional Educators Publications, 1972. Humanist Carl Rogers is contrasted with Behaviorist B. F. Skinner in their two divergent approaches to psychology and education.

National Society for the Study of Education. *Behavior Modification in Education.* Chicago: University of Chicago Press, 1973. Accountability and competence-based modification are addressed from a variety of perspectives in this volume.

Stucker, J. P. *The Performance Contracting Concept in Education.* (Rand Report R-699/2-HEW, 1971). A highly technical and statistical analysis of the economics of education, particularly related to performance-contract instruction.

12

Education as Self-Actualization: A Humanistic Model

Philosophical Basis of Education as Self-Actualization

SELF-ACTUALIZATION AND HUMANISTIC EDUCATION

For more than a decade the American school has been under one of the severest attacks it has ever encountered in its history. This assault is focused, in part, on the school's alleged inability and inefficiency in help-ing our children master the knowledge and skills they need to live in a highly technological and constantly changing society. The technological model of education we discussed in Chapter 11 is an attempt to make our schools more productive through an efficient use of behavior engineering and management technology.

But another part of this attack is coming from the so-called humanistic educators,[1] who claim that today's schools are not only repressive but mindless and inhumane. These critics argue that the schools have become intellectually impotent and psychologically destructive because they are preoccupied with order, discipline, and punishment for failure. The works of such writers as John Holt, Herbert Kohl, Jonathan Kozol, William Glasser, and Charles Silberman charge that our schools have destroyed children's spontaneity, inquisitiveness, and creativity. These critics con-tend that the American school has mutilated children's joy of learning and self-esteem by making the school a dreadful and fearful place, where students are "forced" to play "games" to avoid punishment by making teachers think that they are learning something worthwhile.[2]

If the traditional schools have caused this damage, the new technology

---

[1] For a discussion of humanism, in its general sense and in education, refer to "A Critical Estimate" in this chapter.

[2] For further discussion see John Holt, *How Children Fail* (New York: New American Library, 1967); William Glasser, *Schools Without Failure* (New York: Harper & Row, 1969); Jonathan Kozol, *Death at an Early Age* (Boston: Houghton Mifflin, 1967); and Charles E. Silberman, *Crisis in the Classroom* (New York: Random House, 1970).

of education has not brought much new hope, for behavior engineers see children as raw materials to be processed through impersonal and mechanical procedures, to be molded according to predetermined specifications over which neither the children nor their parents have any choice. Humanistic educators go on to point out that this efficiency-oriented view of education not only neglects human dignity but denies our personal freedom. In other words, the traditional approach to education is demeaning to children, while the recent technological movement in education has taken away their worth as unique individuals by objectifying them and treating them as objects.

Though there are some differences in their strategies, humanistic educators generally agree that education can be made more meaningful to the learner's life if it is "humanized." That is, we should make our schools direct their efforts to "the development within each human being of intelligence, self-esteem, and personal dignity."[3] All children must be helped to become the best of what they are able to become through both cognitive (intellectual) and affective (emotional) growth. Hence, in humanistic education, fostering good attitudes and feelings is as important as imparting intellectual skills and knowledge. This means that education should be a matter of "learning to grow, learning what to grow toward, learning what is good and bad, learning what is desirable and undesirable, learning what to choose and what not to choose."[4] As humanistic psychologist Abraham Maslow states, in this kind of education the child's self-knowledge and introspective ability are more important than what he or she can acquire through associative learning, or operant conditioning. To be sure, there are many useful skills and knowledge one can gain through associative learning. But such learning is deemed insignificant, because the most important purpose of education is to become a better person.[5]

But what is significant learning? According to another humanistic psychologist-educator, Carl R. Rogers, learning becomes significant only when it has a quality of *personal involvement*. Hence, the "whole" person, that is, both the learner's feelings and mind, is involved in the learning process. Psychologists George Isaac Brown and Richard M. Jones point out that the kind of education that is predominantly concerned with cognitive learning is not adequate, for "there is no intellectual learning without some sort of feeling, and there are no feelings without the mind being somehow involved."[6] Consequently, we should find ways of guiding not

[3] Roland S. Barth, *Open Education and the American School* (New York: Agathon, 1972), p. 1.
[4] Abraham H. Maslow, *The Farther Reaches of Human Nature* (New York: Viking, 1971), p. 178.
[5] Ibid., p. 169.
[6] George Isaac Brown, *Human Teaching for Human Learning* (New York: Viking, 1971), p. 4.

only intellectually oriented children but also those who are predisposed to feelings and fantasies.[7] If we emphasized the cognitive skills only and left the emotional and imaginative skills to random development we are likely to encourage pedantry in the intellectually oriented child and estrangement in those who are more fantasy-oriented. Therefore, children should be taught in such a way that "the affective domain and cognitive domain flow together, like two streams merging into one river, and are thus integrated in individual and group learning."[8] It is for this reason that humanistic education is often called *confluent* or *affective* education.

In humanistic education self-initiated and discovery learning are central because they involve the whole person, that is, the learner's thoughts and feelings. Humanistic education, seen as a process of facilitating significant learning,[9] depends on such interpersonal factors as "realness," "prizing," "accepting," "trusting," and "empathic understanding." It has less use for environmental variables such as artificial reinforcers, computers, and other instructional facilities. From this perspective, educated people are those who have learned how to learn and how to deal effectively with a world in perpetual flux. They also realize that security lies not in tenaciously holding onto supposedly absolute and eternal truths but in constantly seeking new knowledge. They are *fully functioning* and *self-actualizing* people, because they not only have good psychological health but also a "cause," a commitment. Actions of self-actualizing, fully human people do not emanate from a desire to gain rewards. They do what they do because of their commitment and for the sake of ultimate and intrinsic values.[10] Similarly, they see their vocation as a mission in life rather than as a job for making a living.

An important purpose of humanistic education is to help the learner work out the significance of what has been learned in relation to the meaning of his or her life. People who *know themselves* are people who are passionately and infinitely interested in their own existence. Hence, they go beyond mere intellectual acceptance of what has been presented to them, for they are concerned with what knowledge means for them. Like Socrates, they not only think but also act and feel. In sum, humanistic education is a process of self-actualization—becoming a fully functioning person.

PHILOSOPHICAL FOUNDATIONS

Before we turn our attention to a closer examination of the ways in which the schools and their personnel are to facilitate the conditions for self-

[7] Richard M. Jones, *Fantasy and Feeling in Education* (New York: New York University Press, 1968), p. 197.
[8] Brown, p. 19.
[9] Carl R. Rogers, *Freedom to Learn* (Columbus: Merrill, 1969), p. 5.
[10] Maslow, *The Farther Reaches of Human Nature*, p. 192.

actualization (or significant learning), we should briefly consider the metaphysical, epistemological, and axiological beliefs on which the ideals and practices of humanistic education are said to be founded. It may be helpful for the reader to review the sections dealing with Existentialism in Chapter 3 (pages 68–72), Chapter 6 (pages 153–161), and Chapter 9 (pages 255–262) in this book for a more systematic understanding of the philosophical foundations of humanistic education. Educational implications of the views treated in these chapters are found in Chapter 4 (pages 92–95), Chapter 7 (pages 197–199), and Chapter 10 (pages 283–287).

An examination of the philosophical basis of education as self-actualization suggests that humanistic educators share with Existentialists the desire to search for personal meaning in human existence. Quite consistently, they both have an overwhelming preference for the concrete, the subjective, and the personal rather than the abstract, the objective, and the social dimensions of human knowing, valuing, and acting, respectively. And these concerns are said to be at the base of humanistic educators' attempt to make education personally meaningful to the life of every student.

Like Existentialists, humanistic educators are uninterested in acquiring or imparting abstract and objective knowledge about reality, truth, and goodness, for they are primarily concerned with what a particular belief or piece of knowledge means to their existence. Their efforts are directed to answering the question, "What does it mean *to me* that this particular thing is a reality or truth?" While objective knowledge about the external world is possible, it does not explain the meaning of a concrete individual's existence, for objective knowledge is always about that which is eternal or common (generic). It ignores "the concrete and the temporal, the existential process, the predicament of the existing individual arising from his being a synthesis of the temporal and the eternal situated in existence." [11] For example, the metaphysical belief that reality is rational points to a supposedly eternal attribute belonging to all reality. Similarly, scientific knowledge of reinforcement and its effect on behavior relates to the responses of all behaving organisms, including human beings. Neither of these beliefs says anything about the personal joys and despairs that make our existence meaningful. In other words, abstractions and objective knowledge have nothing to say about an individual's predicaments and achievements. Hence, people who try to explain the meaning of their lives by thinking abstractly and objectively become comical figures, for they want to exist meaningfully by turning away from the very particularities that make their lives unique and meaningful. For this reason both metaphysics and science are existentially impotent. To borrow Kierkegaard's own words:

[11] Sören Kierkegaard, *Concluding Unscientific Postscript,* trans. David F. Swenson and Walter Lowrie (Princeton: Princeton University Press, 1944), p. 267.

The only reality that exists for an existing individual is his own ethical reality. To every other reality he stands in a cognitive relation; but true knowledge consists in translating the real into the possible.[12]

For humanistic educators and Existentialists, Man is not a determined being. That is, he is not an organism whose behaviors are elicited entirely by external conditions. If this were the case, he could not become something other than what he already is. But since his nature is not given, since he is not completed, he is an open question. He can choose his nature. Because his essence is not predetermined, he is free. It is this freedom that enables him to "make" himself. And because he can choose to be this or that, he is responsible for what he is and what he does. As noted in Chapter 3 (pages 68–72), this is what is meant by "existence precedes essence." But this kind of freedom is not freedom from causation, for "it" exists in a different dimension. It is in the subjective person. As Rogers puts it:

Freedom is essentially an inner thing, something which exists in the living person quite aside from any of the outward choices of alternatives which we so often think of as constituting freedom. . . . It is the realization that "I can live myself, here and now, by my own choice." It is the quality of courage which enables a person to step into the uncertainty of the unknown as he chooses himself. It is the discovery of meaning from within oneself, meaning which comes from listening sensitively and openly to the complexities of what one is experiencing. It is the burden of being responsible for the self one chooses to be.[13]

In this context, education is the process by which learners choose and "make" themselves. Education *is* self-actualization.

Objective thinkers, such as scientists and philosophers, are satisfied when their knowledge is found to be true by some objective (intersubjective) criterion. But existentially, the truth status of the belief is not as important as the fact that one must "truly" relate oneself to that belief. In other words, those who seek to make their existence meaningful must act according to the beliefs to which they have committed themselves. When individuals live their commitments just because they are personal commitments, they are said to be *in the truth*. This is what Kierkegaard meant when he said "Subjectivity is the truth." [14] Similarly, humanistic educators insist that intellectual acceptance of knowledge and beliefs is not enough, for significant education must make a difference in the learner's life—in personal acts, attitudes, and feelings.

---

[12] Ibid., p. 280.

[13] Carl R. Rogers, *Freedom to Learn*, © 1969, p. 269. Reprinted by permission of Charles E. Merrill Publishing Company, Columbus, Ohio.

[14] Kierkegaard, *Concluding Unscientific Postscript*, p. 197. For example, Socrates was willing to die for his belief that men ought to obey the law. Had he escaped from his prison to avoid death because of his fear of dying, he would not have been *in the truth*.

As pointed out in Chapter 9 (page 255), "the entirety of philosophical content in Existentialism may be described as axiological." Hence, neither reality nor truth (knowledge) have any objective meaning or significance. Their value and meaning are said to be relative to the ways in which they influence the individual's life and choice. Again, to recapitulate Chapter 9, Existentialism is a value "theory," a philosophy according to which everything must pass through the funnel of choice. The only given is our existence. But to exist and to be free is to engage in choosing. Values, too, must be chosen by individuals. Perhaps this brief discussion of the philosophical underpinnings of education as self-actualization can best be closed by quoting the following entry from Kierkegaard's *Journals*, which perspicaciously express the overriding concern of Existentialism and humanistic education:

> What I really lack is to be clear in my mind what I am to do, not what I am to know, except in so far as a certain understanding must precede every action. . . . The thing is to find a truth which is true for me, to find the idea for which I can live and die. What would be the use of discovering so-called objective truth, of working through all the systems of philosophy and of being able, if required, to review them all and show up the inconsistencies within each system; . . . what good would it do me if truth stood before me cold and naked, and not caring whether I recognize her or not, and producing in me a shudder of fear rather than a trusting devotion? I certainly do not deny that I still recognize an imperative of understanding and through it one can work upon man, but it must be taken up into my life, and that is what I now recognize as the most important thing. . . . One must know oneself before knowing anything else. It is only after a man has thus understood himself inwardly, and has thus seen his way that life acquires peace and significance.[15]

Unlike some of today's Existentialists, Kierkegaard was not proposing an alternative philosophical system, because he regarded his work as representing a way of life. He saw himself only as a "corrective" to the situation in which neither philosophy nor theology had any profound impact on an individual's life. To view Existentialism as a school of philosophy departs from Kierkegaard's original intent.

Psychological Basis of Education as Self-Actualization

HUMANISTIC PSYCHOLOGY: A SCIENCE OF THE PERSON

As we have just seen, humanistic educators believe that their educational ideals are rooted in Existentialism, because it represents an attempt to make the life of concrete individuals more meaningful. Further, the means

[15] Sören Kierkegaard, *The Journals of Kierkegaard*, ed. and trans. Alexander Dru (New York: Harper, 1959), pp. 44, 46.

of facilitating humanistic education are said to have been derived from and supported by humanistic psychology, which purports to make psychology a science of the person rather than of behavior. Humanistic psychology is also referred to as phenomenological or existential psychology. But in today's educational and psychological literature, it is not always clear whether these are synonyms for a single school of psychology or expressions representing different psychologies with certain common perspectives and concerns.

According to Abraham H. Maslow all empirical sciences are about classes or groups of things, but not about single unique individuals. . . .[16] In other words, the main business of science is to describe (or explain) what is common to all plants, rocks, rats, human beings, and so on. So, when scientists study a rock, they examine it as a representative of a class. They are interested in the characteristics that the rock shares with all other members of its class, say, igneous rocks. The qualities that are unique to a particular rock are ignored. Like other empirical sciences, psychology as a science of behavior is concerned with what is common to all human beings, or rather all behaving organisms. Hence, no amount of nomothetic knowledge (scientific laws and generalizations) regarding human behavior in general can help us "know" a person, because such knowledge tells us about the traits that belong to the behavior of all human beings and disregards the attributes which that individual does not share with anyone else.[17] In other words, since the logic of scientific inquiry is supposedly the same for all sciences, psychology (that is, behaviorism) is said to treat human beings as subjects to be examined. It is in this sense that today's empirical psychology is thought to dehumanize people by denying their purpose and freedom. Therefore, if we are to humanize psychology, we must develop a science of the person—a humanistic psychology. As Maslow argues, this kind of psychology will be meaningful to the individual as a unique person.

Unlike behaviorism, humanistic psychology is concerned with the existing, existential person, that is, with the content of experiences and what they mean to him or her subjectively. Moreover, humanistic or phenomenological psychologists deny that the individual's experience can be understood by studying the environmental variables or overt responses alone. They approach psychology from a Gestalt point of view, which is the notion that the way in which a person perceives a particular object or event is a function of the total field wherein the object or event is found. According to two contemporary phenomenological psychologists, Arthur W. Combs and Donald Snygg, Gestalt is the total perceptual or phenomenal field. It is the entire universe, including the individual as he

---

[16] Abraham H. Maslow, *The Psychology of Science* (Chicago: Henry Regnery, 1966), p. 9.
[17] This view is similar to Kierkegaard's observation that abstract thoughts and objective knowledge neglect the unique particularities of a concrete individual.

or she experiences it at the instant of action.[18] And, while another person's perceptual field may appear to be an interpretation of reality to us, "his phenomenal field is reality; it is the only reality he can know." [19] The concept of field was earlier developed and used by social psychologist Kurt Lewin (1890–1957) to explain human behavior in terms of the individual's personal experience and psychological world (Life Space).

For Lewin the proper function of psychology was not the formulation of a purely descriptive and classificatory account of human behavior. On the contrary, he argued that we should study human behavior (B) as a function (f) of the person's (P) total environment (E). Hence, Lewin's concept of behavior can be expressed in the formula B $= f$ (PE). This is very similar to the Experimentalist notion of transaction, discussed in Chapter 3 (pages 65–67). What Lewin's approach requires is that we develop constructs and methods that can account for the forces underlying our behavior. And since the person is always at the center of behaving and acting "the [psychological] field which influences an individual should be described not in 'objective physicalistic' terms, but in the way in which it exists for that person at that time." [20] Thus the teacher cannot give helpful guidance to a pupil if he or she cannot "see" the psychological world in which the child lives; the elements within a person's psychological world cannot be understood apart from the situation as a whole. For example, unless the teacher knows about the student's likes, dislikes, fears, and hopes, as well as what personal meanings they have for the child, the teacher cannot be genuinely helpful to the student. From Lewin's standpoint, preoccupation with specific and observable responses alone offers us an inadequate and distorted explanation of human behavior, because the individual's own perception of the world is an indispensable part of his or her behavior.

As we shall soon see, many of the concepts in Lewin's field theory, such as vector, equilibrium, Life Space, and so on have been incorporated into humanistic psychology with varying degrees of modification and elaboration.[21]

Verifiability in Humanistic Psychology   Like Lewin, humanistic psychologists hold that our knowledge of the individual's perception of his psychological world and the meaning he gives it is essential in explaining human behavior. Although an individual's perception of his world may or

---

[18] Arthur W. Combs and Donald Snygg, *Individual Behavior*, rev. ed. (New York: Harper, 1959), p. 20.

[19] Ibid., p. 21.

[20] Kurt Lewin, *Field Theory in Social Science*, Dorwing Cartwright, ed. (New York: Harper & Row, 1951), p. 62.

[21] Combs and Snygg, mentioned earlier, are regarded as representing a modified and expanded version of Lewin's field theory today.

may not agree with the real world, his experience, as perceived, determines his behavior. Such a psychology seeks pure descriptions of phenomenal experience, or raw experience, and denies that human experience is reducible to overt responses. This means that raw or unanalyzed (phenomenal) experience should become the basis of psychological science. But since the experiences as they occur to or in an individual are private and not accessible to others, how can another person know about them? For example, how can we be certain about another person's inner feelings of sadness or happiness? How can we verify the truth of an individual's assertion about his subjective experience? If scientific knowledge depends on communication of reports of what other people experience and their intersubjective (objective) verification, how can private experiences be useful in psychology?

Maslow holds that the conventional method of public verification is not possible in phenomenology, but communication of private experience is possible "through intimacy to the mystical fusion in which the two people become one in a phenomenological way." [22] That is, we can know about another person's experience by "becoming" the other, or to use Rogers's phrase, by having an empathic understanding of the other. We can know another person's experience by placing ourselves in the other person's "shoes," and this knowledge becomes a part of us. In this way we gain experiential knowledge, which is the most valuable kind of knowledge for human purposes. Hence, the best way to know about something is to move toward fusion with it (empathize with it). To move toward fusion with anyone is to care for or even love that person. To love the object to be known is to be interested in it, for it is difficult to do anything with totally boring objects. Accordingly, from a humanistic perspective, the most fruitful inquirer "is the one who talks about his 'problem' in about the same spirit as he does about the woman he loves, as an end rather than as a means to other ends." [23] We can further clarify Maslow's explanation of verification in humanistic psychology by examining Rogers's approach to the problem of knowing.

Rogers on Knowing According to Rogers all knowing is a matter of checking out hypotheses. Hence, if we are to develop a psychology of the person, we must deal with problems of testing hypotheses about another person's phenomenological experience and perceptual world. Rogers points out that there are three different modes of knowing and hence three different means of testing hypotheses about ourselves and/or another person.

The first mode of knowing is *subjective knowing*. This is a matter of checking out our own inner hypotheses "by using the ongoing flow of our

[22] Maslow, *The Psychology of Science*, p. 103.
[23] Ibid., p. 110.

preconceptual experiencing as a referent." [24] In other words, if we think we know that we like or dislike something, we may test our inner hypothesis by asking, "Do I really like or dislike this or that?" By becoming more precise and accurate about our own feelings we might find that the feeling of disliking another person may turn out to be a feeling of envy rather than hatred. Or, by differentiating our own flow of experience more sharply we may learn that we *really* like pizza because we enjoy the taste of tomato sauce with oregano. In subjective knowing, "inner hypotheses are checked and corrected by being more sharply differentiated, by becoming more precise and accurate." [25] For Rogers, this kind of knowing is fundamental to everyday living.

The second kind of knowing is *objective knowing*. In this mode of knowing, hypotheses are based upon an external frame of reference. They concern what is publicly observable, and they are tested, confirmed or rejected by other individuals who share common criteria of evidence for certain claims or assertions. In this kind of knowing we can only gain knowledge about publicly observable objects, for this mode of knowing "turns" everything, including people, into objects.

The third mode of knowing, which is somewhere between the first and second modes of knowing, applies primarily to our *knowledge of human beings*. It is through interpersonal knowing that we can learn how another person feels or thinks. The interpersonal hypotheses can be checked in a number of ways by using "whatever skill and empathic understanding is at [our] command to get at the relevant aspect of [another person's] phenomenological field, to get inside [the person's] private world of meanings, and see whether [our] understanding is correct." [26] For example, if we think that Beth feels sad, we may directly ask her to see if our understanding is correct. Or we may watch her gestures, words, inflections, and facial expressions in order to infer the accuracy of our hypothesis about her mood. We may also create an accepting, rewarding atmosphere in which Beth might feel safe enough to disclose her inner states and, in this way, allow us to share her private world. "From this knowledge generalizations can be formed which can be tested in the same manner. It provides us scientific leverage in getting at the non-observable events which go on within the individual." [27] By using these three modes of knowing in an integrated manner, humanistic psychologists claim to make psychology a science of the person, the findings of which will not be about human behavior in general but about concrete and unique individuals.

Humanistic psychology, therefore, attempts to find out what a person is like inside, both as a member of human society and as a particular

---

[24] Carl R. Rogers, "Toward a Science of the Person," in *Behaviorism and Phenomenology*, T. W. Wann, ed. (Chicago: University of Chicago Press, 1964), p. 110.
[25] Ibid., p. 111.
[26] Ibid., p. 116.
[27] Ibid.

individual. Such a view of human nature calls for the kind of education that will place the major emphasis on development of the learner's potentiality for being human, for self-understanding and understanding others, and for achieving human needs and self-actualization. Thus, sound humanistic education would require that we cultivate self-discipline, spontaneity, and creativity all at the same time and that classroom teaching be related to the learner's life situations.

HUMAN BEHAVIOR AND LEARNING

The Perceptual Field Phenomenological psychologists see human behavior as being motivated by a constant desire to reach some goal, or to self-actualize. In a word, human behavior is purposive and goal-directed. In striving to self-actualize one does what one believes to be the best at the time. Even if one's behavior may appear irrational and purposeless to others, it is relevant and effective in the situation as the person sees it. It is not the real world itself or other people's observation that determines the person's behavior; but it is rather the individual's own perception. Hence, if we are to understand the person we must observe his or her actions from his or her point of view. As Combs and Snygg point out, "all behavior, without exception, is completely determined by, and pertinent to, the perceptual field of the behaving organism." [28] This notion is indeed similar to Lewin's concept of the field.

The perceptual or psychological field (also called personal field, private world, and life space) is the contemporaneous psychological world of a person. It includes everything the person is aware of at any given time: goals, memories, anticipations, likes and dislikes, the barriers that must be overcome to achieve personal aims. And even if the contents of the perceptual field do not happen to be objectively true or real, they are likely to affect personal behavior as long as they are psychological facts to the individual. The properties of the perceptual field are thus dependent on the person's psychological, social, and emotional history. Further, the structure of the field undergoes constant change as new learning experiences accrue, while the altered conditions of the field in turn influence the person's behavior.

Properties of the Perceptual Field We live and move in our psychological world according to certain pulls and pushes coming from its various regions. Certain areas of the perceptual field pull us toward them, while other regions may push us away from them. Moreover, since the content of the field constantly changes, what was attractive to us at one time may become repulsive to us at another time. As Combs and Snygg indicate, our perceptual field is *fluid*. But in spite of this fluidity, the field has *stability* in that it is organized. Our likes, dislikes, style of thinking, and

[28] Combs and Snygg, p. 20.

so forth in the perceptual field are more or less stable. Consequently, it should be possible to predict another person's behavior if we have enough information about the stable elements in a person's perceptual field. Combs and Snygg go on to suggest that our perceptual field also has *intensity* and *direction*, that what is in the field is organized with reference to the individual's need and the ways in which he or she is attempting to meet it. It is for this reason that one physical environment may have widely diverging meanings for different individuals, because "the meaning of any event is always the result of the relationship of any item to the totality observed." [29]

Learning Unlike behaviorists, humanistic psychologists are not interested in describing conditions for learning in general (e.g., learning in rats, pigeons, and people), for their primary attention is focused on understanding what Rogers calls "significant learning." Hence, in this chapter the term *learning* should be understood in the sense of learning to become a better person. Within this context, phenomenological psychologists define learning as the process of changing the behavior of a person through progressive differentiation within his or her perceptual field.[30] That is, a person may act differently because he or she perceives the contents of the perceptual field more sharply, or the relationship between elements in the field more clearly. The person is said to have learned something when individual behavioral changes are due to restructuring of his or her private world. For example, a very young child may first draw a person by drawing a head, two long arms, and two long legs. But this child, as he or she matures and learns, may begin to add such other details as the neck, the body, and so on. Or let us say that we have just moved into a town and rented a house. Initially, we are unclear about the various ways in which our needs can be met. Yet gradually we learn about the stores, the roads, and services of all sorts from the neighbors, trial and error, newspapers, the yellow pages, and so on. In this way the town as part of our perceptual field, that is, of our psychological world, becomes more and more structured and differentiated. Our behavior too becomes increasingly more effective and efficient in meeting our needs. This process of differentiating the contents of our field and structuring and restructuring them in relation to our goals is the process of learning. Thus the "degree and direction of differentiation are always determined by the need of behavior and the opportunities for differentiation that are available." [31] To put it differently, if we do not need to go any place, or if we have no means of transporting ourselves about town, we will learn very little or nothing about the place, because there isn't very much ground for differentiation or restructuring of our perceptual field. This suggests that the rate of learning may be ac-

[29] Ibid., p. 25.
[30] Ibid., p. 190.
[31] Ibid., p. 194.

celerated by increasing the strength of the need. Yet if learning is a function of individual need, may there not also be needs that are common to all people that might serve as motivating variables in learning?

Learning and Need   Along with other humanistic psychologists, Maslow holds that everyone has the tendency to strive toward self-actualization by meeting personal needs according to individual perception of what is necessary to actualize oneself. Once people have satisfied their basic physiological needs for survival they go on to gratify the higher needs, or Being needs (also called B needs), which are the basis for self-actualization. Rogers refers to this kind of need as the desire to become a fully functioning person, while Combs and Snygg call it the need to be more adequate with life. Maslow suggests that every person has a hierarchy of needs, and the gratification of these needs is the single most important principle in human development and learning. The highest of the needs are *aesthetic needs*, followed by *desire to know and understand, need for self-actualization, need for self-esteem, need for love and belongingness, safety needs*, and finally *physiological needs*. This hierarchy of needs is present in everyone, and behavior is motivated by one's desire to satisfy them.[32]

Both Maslow and Rogers agree that while self-actualization is most likely to occur through spontaneity and in a free atmosphere, destructive consequences may follow if the individual's perception of the world is too distorted, or if there is no congruence (agreement) between the individual's perceptual field and objective reality. This implies that one of the crucial functions of teachers and administrators is to facilitate conditions under which the need for self-actualization can be freely gratified by helping students explore and experience themselves and their world so that "they may arrive at new and more adequate relationships between themselves and the world in which they operate." [33] From this perspective, "the 'best' of education would produce a person very similar to the one produced by the 'best' of [psycho] therapy." [34]

Conditions for Learning   If learning is the process of modifying the learner's behavior through progressive differentiation of his or her perceptual field, changes in the individual's perception of his or her own psychological world and the self are essential for learning. But what conditions are likely to lead to such a change? Humanistic psychologists hold that perceptual changes will occur when the person "sees" the content of the field as being related to the maintenance and enhancement of the self. In other words, since everyone has the drive to self-actualize, that which is perceived as relevant to one's self-actualization will be most

[32] These needs are discussed in detail in Abraham H. Maslow, *Toward a Psychology of Being* (Princeton: Van Nostrand, 1968).

[33] Combs and Snygg, p. 412.

[34] Rogers, *Freedom to Learn*, p. 279.

effectively learned. And as the individual's perceptions change, self-concept begins to disagree with personal experience. For example, if Dick sees himself as a failure in all areas of his endeavor, he will continue to fail in his work. His negative self-image will be strengthened, and no new learning will take place. But if he could be placed in a situation where he could experience success, his perception of himself and his behavior would be likely to change. Such experiences, however, should not be imposed on the learner, because any force that tends to threaten the self leads to resistance to change.

An effective way of facilitating significant learning is to place the learner in a problematic situation so that he or she can personally deal with the situation as effectively as possible. The problem must be such that the learner can successfully meet the challenge in order that his or her self-concept may be enhanced. This is the reason why self-initiated learning, problem solving, and learning by discovery are thought to be central to humanistic education.

As important as freedom and problem solving are to humanistic learning there are other indispensable ingredients: empathic understanding, nonpossessive warmth, and genuineness. Empathy is the "knowing" of other people from their point of view. By placing ourselves in the other person's place we can more accurately understand his or her experience and behavior. Nonpossessive warmth is the prizing of other people's feelings, opinions, and self by caring for them without any selfish motive. It involves a basic respect for the other as a person of worth without condemnation or criticism. In short, prizing, accepting, and trusting comprise nonpossessive warmth. For Carl Rogers, genuineness or realness or authenticity is perhaps the most basic of the learning conditions:

> . . . when the facilitator [of learning conditions] is a real person, being what he is, entering into a relationship with the learner without presenting a front or a facade he is much more likely to be effective. . . . It means that he comes into a direct personal encounter with the learner, meeting him on a person-to-person basis. It means that he is being himself, not denying himself.[35]

Now that we have briefly examined the basic elements of humanistic psychology and its view of learning, we are ready to consider some of the ways in which they are applied to education.

Education as Self-Actualization

THE AIM OF EDUCATION

Because education is seen as the process of self-actualization wherein the whole person must grow intellectually, emotionally, and socially, the aim of humanistic education goes beyond transmitting knowledge and de-

[35] Ibid., p. 106.

veloping technical skills. In other words, through education a person must become "a self capable of dealing effectively and efficiently with exigencies of life, both now and in the future." [36] Such a mature person not only has a positive self-image and the capacity to accept others[37] but also possesses the minimum of "ill health, neurosis, psychosis, of loss or diminution of the basic human and personal capacities." In Rogers' words:

> [He] is a person functioning freely in all the fullness of his organismic potentialities; a person who is dependable in being realistic, self-enhancing, socialized, and appropriate in his behavior; a creative person, whose specific formings of behavior are not easily predictable; a person who is everchanging, ever developing, always discovering himself and the newness in himself in each succeeding moment of time.[38]

In other words, a fully functioning person is not only physically well but also able to live with all personal feelings and reactions without being afraid of them. This individual is completely and intensely interested in life and its personal meaning. But he or she is also realistically social, realizing that self-actualization is not possible without relationships with others. A fully functioning person is, then, a reflective and creative thinker who behaves appropriately and is not afraid to accept the consequences of personal actions. This person is open-minded, constantly on the way to becoming something better than what he or she is at any given time. In addition, while recognizing his or her unique individuality, the individual is also aware of what it means to be a human animal. Such a mature person often has peak experiences, "experience[s] of awe, wonder, or of perfect completion, as the goal and reward of learning." [39] Thus by grappling with all of the joys and the problems of one's life in their full complexity, the product of humanistic education, the self-actualizing person, is said to gain intellectual illumination and emotional ecstasy.

AFFECTIVE EDUCATION

Humanistic educators agree with others that self-actualization in today's world is extremely difficult (or even impossible) if the individual is completely incompetent in the basic skills. While the fact of being gainfully employed contributes significantly by itself to a positive self-image, most jobs require some degree of mastery in the three Rs. As a matter of fact, the higher the person's aspiration, the more complex and sophisticated are the skills needed to realize his goal. Notwithstanding the importance of knowledge and skill in contemporary living, humanistic educators warn us that our current preoccupation with cognitive learning is not enough. After all, Man is a thinking, feeling, and acting being, and hence the

[36] Combs and Snygg, p. 45.
[37] Maslow, *Toward a Psychology of Being*, p. 197.
[38] Rogers, *Freedom to Learn*, p. 295.
[39] Maslow, *The Farther Reaches of Human Nature*, p. 190.

intellect without emotions is empty and meaningless.[40] Rogers, too, cautions us that learning that takes place "from the neck up" is irrelevant, because it lacks feelings and personal meaning. Hence, humanistic educators urge that we make a deliberate attempt to develop the affective (emotional), "from the neck down," aspects so that people can learn to think and feel at the same time and to maintain satisfactory interpersonal relationships with others.

The main purpose of affective education, then, is the development of the learner's self-awareness as well as awareness of others. These emotional objectives are to be reached by allowing the learner to express personal feelings and thoughts freely, so that through them he or she can become open with others and gain a clearer self-image. Affective education seeks to promote openness by nurturing the learner's emotions so that they do not become barriers to self-development. By providing a nonthreatening, nonpunitive, and unoppressive learning climate, teachers can help students develop creativity and the ability to communicate with others, as well as the ability to deal with their own problems freely and spontaneously. In order to achieve these ends, students must be real, authentic, without any facade. If they are genuine, they can then evaluate themselves; and if there is too much discrepancy between self-image and ideal-self, they may be helped to come closer to personal ideals. The most crucial factors in affective education are such interpersonal variables as empathic understanding, genuineness, trust, acceptance, love, and caring. In George Isaac Brown's book, *Human Teaching for Human Learning*, some affective techniques and sample lessons are discussed at length.[41]

One way to nurture the learner's emotions is sensitivity training, a mode of teaching designed to help individuals acquire a deeper understanding of themselves and develop deeper interpersonal relationships through intensive group experiences. Sensitivity training, also known as T-groups, encounter groups, transactional analysis, and so on, was initiated by Carl Rogers as a psychotherapeutic technique to help teachers and administrators deal with their students and their subordinates, respectively. Rogers now suggests that high school and college courses may be taught by applying the techniques of sensitivity training. As a technique, sensitivity training is a means of encouraging the participants to shed their inhibitions through talking with or listening to each other and by touching each other physically. They are asked to share their positive and negative feelings and their reactions, both past and present, with others.

The advocates of sensitivity training hold that the individual's learning can be made to grow through improved interpersonal relationships; they implicitly assume that once a person's inhibition is removed he or she will be more creative and effective. Though sensitivity training has been

[40] Harold C. Lyon, *Learning to Feel—Feeling to Learn* (Columbus: Merrill, 1971), p. 18.
[41] George Isaac Brown, *Human Teaching for Human Learning* (New York: Viking, 1971), Chaps. 3, 4, 5, and 6.

more closely associated with affective education, its advocates claim that learning by the whole person achieves affective and cognitive goals at the same time.

In spite of the possible benefits coming from sensitivity training, it is not without some risks. A training program supervised by unqualified personnel or conducted with an inappropriate choice of participants could produce harmful, aggressive attitudes. Frank expression of personal feelings or "tearing down" of defenses that enable many persons to maintain their self-image may result in breakdowns of personality for some. Another result may be that individuals become dependent on such experiences for emotional cartharsis that does not result in changed self-perception or behavior. Hence, Maslow and Rogers both point out the desirability of freedom in such training programs but advocate very careful planning and guidance.

TEACHING

For Rogers, teaching is "a relatively unimportant and vastly over-rated activity," because he is convinced that it is not possible for a person to teach anything to anyone.[42] The results of teaching as transmission of knowledge are inconsequential, because knowledge as self-appropriated truth cannot be directly communicated to others. Hence, for Rogers, teaching is a matter of facilitating conditions for self-discovered learning, that is, significant learning.[43]

But what are the conditions for such learning, and what must the teacher do to facilitate them? Like other humanistic educators, Rogers assumes that human beings have a natural potentiality for learning and curiosity. John Holt argues that this potentiality and desire for knowledge develops spontaneously unless smothered by a repressive and punitive climate. Consequently, humanistic educators seek to remove restrictions from our schools so that the child's capacity for learning can be cultivated. They attempt to provide the child with a more supportive, understanding, and nonthreatening environment for self-discovered learning. For example, if Jimmy is having serious difficulty in reading, he should not be forced to recite or read aloud in front of his peers, whose reactions may strengthen his own perception of himself as a failure. Rogers believes that significant learning can be promoted by allowing children to confront various problematic situations directly. If students choose their own direction, discover their own resources, formulate their own problems, decide their own course of action, and accept the consequences of their choice, significant learning can be maximized. This suggests that significant learning is not possible unless the learner's feelings and the intellect are both involved in the learning process.

[42] Rogers, *Freedom to Learn*, p. 103.
[43] Ibid., p. 153.

Facilitation of Learning Conditions The primary responsibility of teachers is to facilitate these learning conditions by (1) setting the initial mood of the group, (2) organizing and making available the widest range of resources, (3) regarding themselves as a flexible resource to be used by the group, (4) taking the initiative in sharing their feelings and thoughts with the group, and (5) remaining sensitive to the expression of deep or strong feelings by the individual students.[44] In the process, the teachers, too, must become participating learners, and they must maintain certain essential attitudes toward their students. Rogers advises us that effective teachers must be real or genuine to their students, while prizing or accepting the individual learners. In brief, to be genuine is not to enter into a relationship with the learner by presenting a front, but to meet the learner on a person-to-person basis, to be oneself. In this way each teacher can accept personal feelings, and therefore will have no need to impose them on students. Consequently, "he can like or dislike a student product without implying that it [the work of his student] is objectively good or bad or that the student is good or bad." [45]

The second essential attitude is prizing the student's feelings, opinions, and person. It is caring for the learner, who has worth in his or her own right. This is a nonpossessive caring (warmth) based on the assumption that the learner is trustworthy. Thus the teacher accepts the learner as an imperfect being with many feelings and potentialities. Empathic understanding, the third attitude, establishes a climate for self-initiated learning. That is, when the teacher is able to understand the student's reactions, predicaments, and aspirations by imagining what he or she would do in the learner's place, the likelihood of significant learning is also increased. Empathic understanding is not a form of evaluative understanding, which involves making judgments about the other person as good or bad, efficient or inefficient, and so on. Empathic understanding has to do with seeing things as the other person sees them, without making any evaluation or analysis. Hence, the learner is likely to feel, "Now I can blossom and grow and learn," because he or she is free from imposition and the fear of disapproval.[46]

In facilitating all these conditions and attitudes for self-initiated learning, the teacher must always remember that whatever is learned must be relevant to the child, and that this relevance is determined by the learner's perception of the relationship between what is to be learned and his or her personal purposes. As Brown puts it, we know something is relevant "when it is personally meaningful, when we have feelings about it." [47] In other words, unless a child *feels* that having a certain kind of knowledge and skill is necessary in achieving a particular goal, such knowledge and

[44] Ibid., pp. 164–166.
[45] Carl R. Rogers, *Interpersonal Relationships in the Facilitation of Learning* (Columbus: Merrill, 1961), p. 6.
[46] Ibid., p. 13.
[47] Brown, p. 10.

skill are not relevant. Thus significant learning is said to take place only when the subject matter is seen by the learner as relevant to his or her purpose.

Freedom   While all humanistic educators agree that freedom is essential to significant learning, there is no general agreement regarding the optimum amount of freedom for self-discovered and self-initiated learning. For example, Maslow contends that all individuals can make constructive use of their freedom. He found that while some individuals have a greater tendency to make decisions that are beneficial to their goals, others are more likely to make self-defeating and harmful choices. Hence, to become a self-actualizing person the learner must recognize that certain social and physical conditions limit his or her need-gratifying activities. If the learner wants to become an effective, fully functioning person, he or she must learn to appropriately control personal behavior. Here, the teacher can help the learner see and deal with the restrictions. (Both Maslow and Rogers see self-discipline as an essential part of self-actualization.)

Unlike Maslow and Rogers, John Holt insists that any structuring of learning activities or situation will lead to fear and dependency on others. He goes on to point out that since all children have natural curiosity and "a style of learning that fits their condition, and which they use naturally and well," we should adopt children's mode of learning as the model for all education.[48] He maintains that giving children complete freedom in their own educational experiences is crucial, because children's intellectual and creative capacity is destroyed by adults who make children afraid of not doing what other people want them to do, of making mistakes, of not pleasing others, and of being wrong.[49]

A. S. Neill, the founder of Summerhill School in England and the author of *Summerhill*,[50] concurs with Holt in believing that if children are left alone without adult guidance and interference they will develop to the maximum limit of their capacity, because they are innately good, wise, and realistic.[51] Neill believes children must pass through a series of developmental stages at their own pace without any external attempt to accelerate the process. For Neill, education is preparation for life, the purpose of which is to attain happiness. He sees happiness as life's natural fulfillment; it consists of a feeling of well-being, a sense of balance, and contentment with life. The evil of life is whatever limits happiness.[52] It is because of this basic outlook that both Holt and Neill regard unrestricted freedom as so indispensable to education and view cognitive development as subordinate to affective growth. The fundamental assumption underlying these views

[48] John Holt, *How Children Learn* (New York: Pitman, 1969), p. vii.
[49] John Holt, *How Children Fail* (New York: Dell, 1965), p. 208.
[50] A. S. Neill, *Summerhill: A Radical Approach to Child Rearing* (New York: Hart, 1960).
[51] Ibid., pp. 4, 12.
[52] Ibid., p. 111.

of education is the belief that if children are given complete freedom, they will automatically become creative and develop their own aspirations as well as master whatever is necessary to become effective and self-disciplined problem solvers.

Deschooling If the preceding premises concerning children's innate learning capacity and the manner in which unrestrained freedom can lead to meaningful learning were valid, then schools as learning institutions would not be essential for education. This is precisely the conclusion Holt reaches in his book *Freedom and Beyond*.[53] Holt emphatically points out that education is much more than schooling. Moreover, meaningful education does not and cannot occur in today's schools. Holt goes on to argue that since the most desirable kind of education takes place outside the school, we should provide educational resources for learners instead of for schools.[54] Ideally, there should be no schools at all.[55] Holt's main contention is that education should not be separated from the rest of life, that learning should always be informal and practical: Susan learns to avoid hot objects by touching one. This idea of deschooling is illustrated in a comment that Holt ascribes to a member of an ideally humane and life-enhancing society 500 years in the future.

> Everyone helps other people learn things. Anyone who knows something or can do something can help someone else who wants to learn more about it. Why should there be special people to do this?[56]

Most of us would agree that learning should and does involve help from someone who knows more than the learner. But does it mean that learning of all sorts can occur in the same informal way in which one learns to avoid a hot object from an accidental experience of touching a hot object? Are there, or should there be, any differences in the method, the resources, and the environment for learning such skills as fishing, constructing a rocket to reach the moon, performing brain operations, and so on? Can informal education prepare our children for a happy life in a society as complex as ours? These and other questions related to the deschooling "movement" will be discussed at a greater length in Chapter 13.

LEARNING BY DISCOVERY

As we have seen, all humanistic educators concur that learning by discovery is central to education as self-actualization, because education is not merely a process of imparting ready-made knowledge through talking and lecturing, but must necessarily involve the learner's active participation. They maintain that only through this process can learners discover

---

[53] John Holt, *Freedom and Beyond* (New York: Dell, 1972).
[54] Ibid., p. 126.
[55] Ibid., p. 117.
[56] Ibid.

personal meaning from what they have learned, that self-initiated learning and learning by discovery must go hand in hand, and that such learning occurs best in a nonauthoritarian atmosphere in which learners may freely explore areas of their own interest. Unfortunately, this general agreement does not indicate the kinds of strategies to be used in humanistic education, nor does it clarify the meanings of "freedom" and "interest." As we pointed out, Neill and Holt claim that purposeful learning occurs only if there is complete freedom, while Maslow, Rogers, Combs, and Snygg point out the desirability of some structuring in learning activities, resources, and environments. There are still others who advocate the type of free schools found in England, such as British infant schools; in these schools teachers have much more direct involvement in classroom activities.

In recent years many humanistic educators turn to the findings of a Swiss psychologist, Jean Piaget, for empirical and theoretical support, because they believe that their concept of learning by discovery is consonant with Piaget's view that children must actively construct their own knowledge. In addition to Piaget, an American psychologist, Jerome Bruner, has also made an important contribution. Therefore, it seems appropriate to turn our attention to Piaget's developmental and Bruner's cognitive views of learning. However, we should be careful to note that the use of expressions like "learning by discovery" or "active construction of knowledge" by humanistic educators like Piaget and Bruner does not necessarily imply that they are in accord as to what such expressions mean, nor does it suggest that they hold similar theoretical and/or philosophical perspectives.

Piaget's Developmental View   Central to Piaget's developmental view of learning by discovery is the premise that learning involves the active participation of the learner, whether in relation to objects or to social relationships. In other words, knowledge is not something that is transmitted verbally or otherwise; it has to be constructed and reconstructed by the individual learner. Each individual must discover his or her own knowledge. Hence, learning, the development of intelligence, is a continuous process of assimilating the external facts of experience and integrating them into the individual's internal mental (or cognitive) structure.[57] Consequently, activity is indispensable to learning. To know something is not merely to be told about it or to see it, but to act upon it, to modify and transform it. Piaget also claims that in the learning process there is no breach between the cognitive and the affective domains, for feeling is always an aspect of thought. It is Piaget's emphasis on the necessity for a child's active and constructive involvement in learning that attracted the attention of humanistic educators.

[57] See Lawrence Kohlberg and Rochelle Mayer's "Development as the Aim of Education," *Harvard Educational Review* 42, No. 4 (November 1972): 405, for a similar view.

Now, if learning and knowing involve structuring and restructuring of what has been acquired, how do they occur? For Piaget, the answer to this question lies in understanding the process of the learner's cognitive development. According to Piaget, the processes of biological development and cognitive development are essentially the same. And since biological development occurs through organization and adaptation of the organism to the environment, the same process occurs in intellectual organization and adaptation. Organization is the tendency of living organisms to integrate processes (experiences and activities) into a coherent system. Thus an organization is said to have occurred when a child is able to perform two originally separate acts (e.g., grasping and looking) together. Adaptation refers to the organism's ability to interact with its surroundings. In human beings it is this interaction that leads to the development of an increasingly complex mental organization. Here, Piaget points out that these developmental processes do not occur at random but rather follow certain invariant stages. But before we discuss these developmental stages, we should examine Piaget's concepts of schema, assimilation, accommodation, and equilibrium, for they clarify the way in which the child moves through the various stages.

Schemata (or schema) are similar to mental categories and the ways in which a person sees his or her world and personal experiences in it. They are used to categorize or classify incoming stimuli. This means that a newborn infant has very few schemata, but they become increasingly refined, broadened, and larger in number, because each time the baby sees or experiences something new an attempt is made to integrate it into already acquired schemata. This process of integration, which is called *assimilation*, goes on constantly. It is through assimilation that individuals cognitively organize and adapt themselves to their environment. However, as individuals encounter new situations that do not fit into existing schemata, they must then either modify the schemata or create new ones to fit the new stimuli. This process is called *accommodation*. In other words, the process of adaptation consists of assimilation and accommodation. The former is the process of "forcing" new stimuli into existing categories, while in the latter, a person's schemata are changed to fit the new stimuli. Hence, cognitive growth requires that assimilation and accommodation occur in balance—there should be equilibrium.[58] And since all organisms are said to seek equilibrium, disequilibrium becomes a motivating force in the child.

The notion of balance, of equilibrium between assimilation and accommodation, suggests that things are never known by themselves as completely new and separate but always in relation to what is already known.[59] Through these processes our old experiences are also reconstructed. As we

[58] Jean Piaget, *The Origins of Intelligence in Children*, trans. Margaret Cook (New York: International Universities Press, 1952), p. 7.
[59] Ibid.

indicated, assimilation and accommodation do not occur at random but rather move through certain fixed stages.

Stages of Cognitive Development According to Piaget, cognitive development through assimilation and accommodation occurs as children go through certain invariant stages. And though these stages are innate and fixed for all children in all cultures, the precise age at which a specific stage emerges varies from child to child according to individual capacities and culture. Moreover, the stages do not appear discretely but often overlap each other. Piaget indicates that there are four invariant stages of cognitive development.[60] The first is the *sensory-motor stage*, in which children learn motor behavior. In general, this first stage develops between birth and two years of age. The *preoperational stage*, wherein children acquire the ability to conceptualize and use language, develops between the ages of about two and seven. Children's ability to apply logical thought to concrete problems manifests itself in the *stage of concrete operations*. This third stage is said to appear between the years of approximately seven and eleven. The fourth is the *stage of formal operations*, taking place between the ages of eleven and fifteen. It is in this stage that children's cognitive structures reach their greatest level of development; they learn to apply logic to problems of all sorts. These stages do not occur separately and discretely, but each leads to the emergence of the subsequent one.[61] Piaget and Barbara Inhelder further characterize the stages as follows:

> (1) Their order of succession is constant, although the average ages at which they occur may vary with the individual, according to his degree of intelligence or with the social milieu. . . . (2) Each stage is characterized by an overall structure in terms of which the main behavior patterns can be explained. (3) These overall structures are integrative and noninterchangeable. Each results from the preceding one, integrating it as a subordinate structure, and prepares for the subsequent one, into which it is sooner or later itself integrated.[62]

As noted, the developmental stages are fixed and "their order of succession is constant," but the developmental process is affected by organic growth, exercise and acquired experience, social interaction and transmission, and equilibrium.[63] Organic growth refers to maturation of nervous and endocrine systems. Piaget and Inhelder both suggest that while maturation is an essential aspect of cognitive development, the influence of the child's physical and sociocultural environment becomes increas-

---

[60] For general discussion of these stages refer to Jean Piaget, *The Psychology of Intelligence* (Patterson, N.J.: Littlefield, Adams, 1963) and Jean Piaget and Barbara Inhelder, *The Psychology of the Child*, trans. Helen Weaver (New York: Basic Books, 1969).
[61] Piaget and Inhelder, p. 153.
[62] Ibid.
[63] Ibid., pp. 154–158.

ingly more important as the child grows older. Exercise and acquired experience in acting upon objects is a critically important factor in cognitive development, for neither assimilation nor accommodation can take place unless children interact with their environment.

Social interaction and transmission are particularly important in the development of concepts that cannot be gotten by the child. In other words, concepts of love, loyalty, courage, and so on, do not have physical objects as referents. Hence, children cannot construct these ideas by looking at objects alone. They must develop them through interaction with other individuals and interchange of ideas. This is what Piaget and Inhelder meant when they said that "socialization is a structuration to which the individual contributes as much as he receives from it." [64] The last factor affecting the developmental process is equilibrium. Equilibrium is not a simple balance of forces, but rather a process of self-regulation. It is an internal mechanism that regulates and integrates the roles of organic growth, exercise and acquired experience, and social interaction and transmission.[65]

Our discussion of Piaget may give the impression that Piaget's developmental theory is primarily focused on the intellectual dimension of the child, separate and different from the child's affective aspect. However, Piaget and Inhelder carefully point out that "there is no behavior, however intellectual, which does not involve affective factors as motives." [66] Similarly, there can be no emotional states unless there is a cognitive structure based on perceptions and comprehensions. Hence, "the two aspects, affective and cognitive, are at the same time inseparable and irreducible." [67]

Piaget and Education   Although there is an increasing number of writings on the educational implications of Piagetian theory, much more systematic work needs to be done even by Piaget himself to generate educational strategies. There is also an urgent need for a critical examination of the alleged relationship between Piaget's theory and so-called free schools, open education, and various forms of humanistic education. In any event, many humanistic and other educators have become interested in using Piagetian developmental patterns to work out ways to aid children's growth so that they can develop more rapidly and effectively than they would if left alone completely to their own resources and natural environment. We must note here that Piaget himself takes a rather dim view of many American educators' attempts to accelerate children's cognitive development. Moreover, he is very skeptical about the effectiveness of such attempts. But, keeping in mind what has been said about the current

[64] Ibid., p. 156.
[65] Ibid., p. 157.
[66] Ibid., p. 158.
[67] Ibid.

status of Piaget's theory and its educational implications, we may point out certain aspects of humanistic education that seem to be similar to (or perhaps even based on) Piaget's psychology.

Humanistic educators assert that significant education must present the learners with problematic situations in which they can experiment, that is, manipulate objects to see what happens, question what is already known, compare their findings with those of others, and search for their own answers. In other words, children must be given freedom to do their own learning. This suggests that humanistic teaching must be designed in such a way that all learners confront an indeterminate situation wherein the "irritation" of personal doubts and illogical thinking could challenge them to seek an answer for and by themselves. However, from a Piagetian perspective such teaching strategies must be consistent with the learner's stage of development. In other words, while we should attempt to have students confront a puzzling situation that is likely to lead to inquiry, the situation should not be so difficult that the child will simply give up. In a word, the problem and the child's stage of development should be appropriate for each other so that the child will attempt to resolve the difficulty he or she confronts in the situation. The child moves toward a more mature understanding through self-initiated inquiry in which he or she rearranges and reconstructs thought processes. Kohlberg and Mayer expressed a similar view when they wrote:

> As applied to educational intervention, the theory holds that facilitating the child's movement to the next step of development involves exposure to the next higher level of thought and conflict requiring the active application of the current level of thought to problematic situations. This implies: (1) attention to the child's mode or styles of thought, i.e., stage; (2) match of stimulation to that stage, e.g., exposure to modes of reasoning one stage above the child's own; (3) arousal, among children, of genuine cognitive and social conflict and disagreement and problematic situations; . . . and (4) exposure to stimuli toward which the child can be active. . . .[68]

According to Piaget, Inhelder, Kohlberg and Mayer, social interaction is indispensable in education, not only because through it children can develop their language and learn to cooperate with each other, but also because disagreements among children can help them to become aware of different points of view. Moreover, children at similar levels of development can help each other more effectively than adults can. For example, "cadet programs," arrangements by which children help younger students with their reading or arithmetic, are found in many elementary schools, and their benefits for both older and younger children are said to be significant. For Piaget, Kohlberg, and their supporters, the most important goal of education is thinking. And while language in the forms of reading and writing are important, we should not become preoccupied with them at the expense of learning to think.

[68] Kohlberg and Mayer, p. 459.

Humanistic educators continue to stress that freedom is important in education, because children can learn to observe and reason by playing freely. But, unlike Neill and Holt, the advocates of Piaget's theory of development suggest that some structuring or systematization in the learning environment is helpful to the child in actively constructing personal knowledge. They point out that in building one's own knowledge it is crucial to ask the right questions at the right time. But, in learning by discovery, children are not always able to raise appropriate questions at the proper time because they are often unclear about the nature of their problem or the kinds of knowledge and reasoning required to find the answer. Hence, the teacher who has clear ideas about the learner's style of reasoning and the extent of knowledge the student already possesses can help the child to self-discover his or her knowledge.

Notwithstanding the necessity for some structuring of learning activities and environment, schools should emphasize autonomy and cooperation rather than obedience and docility. In sum,

> the pedagogical implications of Piaget's theory suggest the kind of reform that makes learning truly active and encourages social interactions among pupils to cultivate a critical spirit. The teacher in a Piagetian school does not present ready-made knowledge and morality but, rather, provides opportunities for the child to construct his own knowledge and moral standards through his own reasoning. The emphasis of a Piagetian school is definitely on the child's own thinking and judgment, rather than on the use of correct language and adult logic. . . .[69]

Many of these words are reminiscent of the Experimentalist view of education discussed in previous chapters. No doubt a question looms in many a reader's mind as to whether the kind of education described above is necessarily connected with Piaget's cognitive developmental theory. In other words, can one subscribe to the same view of education without accepting Piaget's account of cognitive development? If one's answer to this question is in the negative, in what sense can we say that the so-called humanistic education movement is founded on Piagetian psychology? We leave this question for the reader to resolve with whatever help he or she can muster from peers and instructors.

Bruner on Learning by Discovery and Teaching   A special study of the relation between education and such cognitive processes as perception, memory, thinking, and learning has been undertaken by Jerome S. Bruner, codirector of the Center for Cognitive Studies at Harvard University. His views on learning by discovery and on the role of the structure of knowledge in teaching have attracted wide attention and, since they are at the heart of humanistic education, require examination.

---

[69] Constance Kamii, "Pedagogical Principles Derived from Piaget's Theory: Relevance for Educational Practice," in *Piaget in the Classroom*, Milton Schwebel and Jane Raph, eds. (New York: Basic Books, 1973), pp. 213–214.

Unlike Piaget, Bruner does not see the course of cognitive growth as a gradual accretion, nor does he think that everyone must move through a set of invariant stages. On the contrary, he maintains that mental growth occurs in spurts.[70] These spurts occur when certain capacities begin to develop, and much cognitive development depends on mastering certain contents of a culture and then reorganizing and recoding them in new forms with the help of teachers, so that children acquire a new organization of what they already know in relation to their new experiences. As Bruner states, "the heart of the educational process consists of providing aids and dialogues for translating experience into more powerful systems of notation and ordering." [71] For this reason, Bruner is convinced that a theory of cognitive development must be connected with a theory of instruction.

According to Bruner there are three rather general "stages." [72] In the first stage, knowing occurs *enactively*, that is, through acting and manipulating objects with a minimum of reflective thinking. Though the stages or spurts are not linked to age, the first stage occurs some time before the age of five. In the second stage, children begin to reflect more and gain knowledge iconically, that is, through images. This stage emerges between five and seven. Finally, around adolescence language (symbols) becomes more and more important as a medium of thought. Children can now know *symbolically*. Where Bruner differs from Piaget is that, in the former's view, mental growth does not occur by having the child go through invariant stages in orderly succession (one stage at a time) but by becoming capable of using all three "stages" or modes of knowing.[73] In other words, a mature person is someone who can fully express his or her abilities through manipulation and action, perceptual organization and imagery, and through symbolic apparatus. Here we should remember that Bruner's developmental stages are not only stages in the Piagetian sense but also modes of representing knowledge or ways of knowing. In Bruner's words, the working heuristics of discovery can be learned only by actually trying to solve problems for oneself. To put it differently, the more one tries to work out solutions to problems and figure out things for oneself, the more one gains new insights. Only by engaging in inquiry can we improve the art and the technique of problem solving and self-discovery.

For Bruner, learning by discovery has a number of beneficial effects: (1) it increases intellectual potency, (2) it causes the learner to value intrinsic rather than extrinsic rewards, and (3) it aids in conserving memory.[74] First, by emphasizing discovery, children learn to organize their

---

[70] Jerome S. Bruner, *Toward a Theory of Instruction* (Cambridge: Harvard University Press, 1966), p. 27.

[71] Ibid., p. 21.

[72] Ibid., pp. 27–28.

[73] Ibid., p. 6.

[74] Jerome S. Bruner, *On Knowing* (New York: Atheneum, 1967), pp. 87–90, 92, 94–95.

experiences in such a way as to discover regularity and relatedness, and also to distinguish relevant evidence from irrelevant facts. Furthermore, they learn a variety of ways of solving problems and also become progressively more effective and efficient in what they do. For example, a child may discover that $2 \times 3 = 6$ is another form of $2 + 2 + 2 = 6$.

Second, children often learn knowledge or skills as a result of rewards coming from the outside; extrinsic rewards are likely to conform to what is expected of them. Hence, a child who engages in learning activities for grades alone is likely to be docile and obedient to the teacher rather than spontaneous and creative on his or her own. This child becomes primarily "other-directed." Bruner hypothesizes that approaching learning as *discovering* something rather than as learning about something will lead children to act in terms of self-reward, intrinsic reward, that is, to be rewarded by discovery itself. Learning for intrinsic reward eventually frees children from immediate stimulus control, and they become competence-oriented, so that each child can be more of an "inner-directed person."

Lastly, concerning the effect of learning by discovery on the conservation of memory, since human beings seem to be able to store more information than they can spontaneously recall, the main problem in human memory is that of effective retrieval. Bruner is convinced that the key to retrieval is organization of information. He contends that there is sufficient evidence to support the assertion that, in general, any information organized around the interests and the cognitive structure of the learner can be most efficiently recalled. Hence, the only means by which we can reduce the quick rate of loss of human memory is to organize facts according to the basic principles and concepts from which they were inferred. Further, "the very attitude and activities that characterize figuring out or discovering things for oneself also seem to have the effect of conserving memory." [75] In addition to these effects, the learning experiences resulting from self-discovery give us an increased awareness of the connections and continuities between what we learn and what we do. As a result, we are likely to see our activities in a broader context and thus gain more control of our acts in relation to an end in view. In learning by discovery, knowledge already possessed by the learner is used to gain new insights, and in the process old knowledge becomes reconstructed.

Bruner regards a sound theory of teaching as essential in facilitating learning by discovery and problem solving. The elements he sees as necessary to a theory of teaching are: (1) predisposition toward learning, (2) structure of knowledge, (3) optimal sequence, and (4) reward and punishment. [76]

The first element is concerned with specifying those conditions that

[75] Jerome S. Bruner, *The Process of Education* (Cambridge: Harvard University Press, 1966), p. 96.
[76] Bruner, *Toward a Theory of Instruction*, pp. 40–42.

predispose a child to learn effectively. Bruner explains that the teaching-learning situation is a dynamic process in which two or more individuals are involved. Hence, if a child is to cope with school and engage in learning, he or she must have minimal mastery of social skills in order to maintain many different kinds of relationship with others. Among other important factors such as cultural background, social class, and sex, the way in which the child explores different alternative courses of action directly affects learning and problem solving.

Bruner names three different approaches to the regulation of the child's exploratory or search behavior: activation, maintenance, and direction. Or to put it another way, "exploration of alternatives requires something to keep it from being random." This means that the learning situation must arouse the child's curiosity enough to activate exploratory behavior. Once the search behavior has begun, it is important that the benefit from such exploration be greater than the risk involved. Learning in the presence of a teacher should minimize the risks and make the consequences of errors less painful, because the teacher guides the child's activities and also shows the child the causes of failure. But in order to make the direction of the exploratory behavior appropriate, it is necessary that the child have a clear understanding of the goal, and knowledge of the relevant means that will be helpful in attaining it. Moreover, in encouraging children to explore alternatives we must not only cultivate the attitude of healthy skepticism toward old cherished beliefs, but we must also convince children that reflective thinking and the use of their minds are important. That is, the child's own belief that people can effectively deal with their problems and perplexities by the use of their minds is an essential factor in activating the child to explore alternatives.

In clarifying the concept of the structure of knowledge, which is the second element in a theory of teaching, Bruner asserts that "any idea or problem or body of knowledge can be presented in a form simple enough so that any particular learner can understand it in a recognizable form." [77] For example, the concept of nation may be explained to children by first discussing different units in operating the school: principals, teachers, nonteaching staff, students, and their roles and responsibilities. This study can be gradually expanded to include how the city, county, state, and nation function. Or human learning as a subject matter of study can be approached by dividing human behavior into voluntary and involuntary responses and how they are influenced by various stimulus conditions. In other words, any complex problem (or discipline) can be analyzed into a set of basic elements that can be dealt with in even simpler and more elementary operations. Therefore, knowledge about anything can be divided into fundamental ideas and principles for children to grasp. The structure, fundamental concepts, principles, and form of knowledge become indispensable in Bruner's theory of teaching.

[77] Ibid., p. 44.

The third element in Bruner's theory of teaching is a matter of guiding the learner through a series of topics and problems according to the sequence most appropriate for the learner. The nature of the sequence adopted determines how effectively and how easily the learner will achieve mastery of a subject. Bruner rightly points out that there is no single sequence appropriate for all learners, for the optimum in any particular situation depends on the learner's past training, stage of development, sociocultural background, nature of the material, and on such variables as speed of learning, mode of representation, economy, and power. However, since our intellectual development goes from enactive to iconic to symbolic representations, the optimum sequence in any subject is likely to follow the same pattern. This implies that the best sequencing begins with the presentation of materials that are familiar to the learner's sensory experiences and activities and then eventually moves to more abstract materials. Accordingly, Bruner suggests that we might first give children many particular instances so that they can grasp the underlying regularity, which can be made clearer by then giving them many contrasting cases. We should avoid having children symbolize prematurely; they should not be asked to repeat words and concepts until their meanings are understood either by manipulation or images. Lastly, we should encourage children to plod and leap. That is, let them approach a particular problem by small steps, but also permit them to take leaps and big guesses, because we sometimes know by guessing.

Rewards and punishments are important in learning, for they are often children's means of knowing the results of their activities in seeking a goal. Therefore, teaching should be carried on in such a way that learners can receive corrective information at the most appropriate time and place. But in effective learning it is essential that children become independent problem solvers who reward and punish themselves on the basis of the adequacy of their efforts. By emphasizing rewards and punishments from an outside agent, we often make children think that the agents of reward and punishment are the major initiating force for learning rather than their own success or failure. In brief, the learners should be made to regard problem solving and discovery as intrinsic rewards for learning.

Though many of the concepts used by Piaget and Bruner are found in the writings of various humanistic educators, it is not always clear just how much of humanistic educational strategies have been derived directly from the theories advanced by Piaget and Bruner. We are not even certain that Piagetian and Brunerean expressions used by some humanistic educators carry the same meanings as they do when they are used by the two psychologists. For example, do humanistic educators use "learning by discovery," and "self-appropriated knowledge" in the same sense in which Piaget uses "discovery," and "active construction of one's own knowledge"? One may also wonder if there can be a single school of psychology as a basis for humanistic education, for there are so many varieties of it. Any comprehensive and systematic treatment of these and other related questions is beyond the scope of this book. But they need to be explored by individual students and anyone else who aspires to become an effective teacher.

Examples of Education as Self-Actualization

We have already suggested that there are widely diverging means of implementing the ideals of education as self-actualization. Here are a few examples of humanistic education.

HUMANISTIC EDUCATION IN ENGLAND

Summerhill and the British primary or infant schools are two very different types of humanistic (or open) education found in England. Though both schools are based on the premise that children are innately curious and that this desire to learn can develop best in a free and nonpunitive climate, they take radically disparate means of implementing their educational ideals. Hence, it is reasonable to assume that their products will also be very different from each other.

Summerhill School Summerhill was founded about fifty years ago by the late A. S. Neill, who also wrote the book *Summerhill: A Radical Approach to Child Rearing,* which describes the school's "program" and discusses its "philosophical" and "psychological" bases. Summerhill School is situated about one hundred miles from London. Students are admitted without any examination or other formal requirements. They live on the campus in groups of about forty by age groups, with a housemother assigned to each group. Though the ages of Summerhill children range from about four to eighteen, there are no rules regarding class attendance, course requirements, or tests. Neither is there any explicit moral or religious instruction. But, of course, children do "receive" moral education, because they unavoidably acquire certain views of right and wrong from the very way life is lived in this school. For Neill, this is the way education ought to occur, because children are believed to be innately wise and realistic, and these qualities emerge if they are not corrupted by adult interference.

Though the classes at Summerhill are arranged by age and/or interest, neither the activities nor instructional materials are deliberately or uniformly structured, for the school operates on the belief that the function of the child is to live his or her own life. Hence, adult guidance and control can only produce an oppressive climate inimical to creativity and learning by discovery. Accordingly, unrestrained freedom is the key to the Summerhill School. But how do Summerhill students perform academically without any restrictions or requirements? According to Neill, "every child under freedom plays most of the time for a year, but when the time comes, the bright ones will sit down and tackle the work necessary to master the subjects covered by the government regulations." [78] Thus Neill not only rejects the notion that there is an essential body of knowledge and skill that all children must learn within a specified time period, say, twelve years, but he also subordinates intellectual development to affective growth. The Summerhillean approach to education is clearly consonant with Holt's view that adult direction of any kind will make our children fearful and docile. All of this reminds us of Taoism, an ancient Chinese philosophy, which regards education as having a corrupting influence on the child's innate goodness. Jean Jacques Rousseau's assertion that Man is naturally good[79] is also congenial to the views held by Neill and Holt.

One of the major criticisms of Neill's and Holt's insistence on giving unrestrained freedom to children is that in their eagerness to provide non-authoritarian, unrestrictive, and more responsive learning conditions, they have neglected the fact that adulthood necessarily involves becoming an adequate and self-reliant person who is able to fulfill responsibilities by meeting societal demands and restrictions. Indeed, a child may function quite well in an environment like Summerhill that is built on a set of common values and freedom. But if a Summerhillean child is to cope with the larger society, he or she is likely to encounter a radically different set of standards and restrictions. The resulting conflicts may necessitate careful adult guidance. Furthermore, a child may thoroughly learn that which is personally interesting, but he or she rarely has the experience or the foresight to know the requisite skills, concepts, and knowledge to fulfill aspirations. Nor do children automatically develop sufficient self-discipline to do what is necessary to achieve their goals. For example, a child may wish to become a banker, a teacher, or a concert pianist, but seldom has enough knowledge about what is entailed in reaching his or her objective without adult guidance. Similarly, very seldom can an individual child develop sustained discipline to do what is necessary. As Charles E. Silberman points out:

> To suggest that learning evolves from the child's interest is not to propose an abdication of adult authority, only a change in the way it is exercised. . . . Since what children are interested in is a function of their environment as well as of their native endowment, it is the teacher's responsibility to structure that environment in the best possible way, and to help it change and grow in response to each child's evolving interests and needs.[80]

[78] Neill, p. 116.

[79] For Rousseau's view of education read his book *Emile*. In brief, Rousseau argues that Man's natural goodness is corrupted by the society and its institutions. This corruption can be prevented by education that follows the natural tendencies of the child.

[80] Silberman, *Crisis in the Classroom*, p. 209.

Today there is no conclusive evidence to indicate whether a school such as Summerhill can produce happy, creative, self-sufficient, and wise children. But we might glean some clues regarding the effectiveness of the Summerhillean approach to education from Emmanuel Bernstein's study of Summerhill products later in this chapter.

British Primary Schools Many American educators have been tremendously impressed with British primary schools, also known as infant or free day schools, because they seem to combine freedom, dignity, individual attention, and emotional growth without sacrificing intellectual development. In other words, to many American educators and parents, British primary schools are at once child-centered and knowledge-centered. What makes these primary schools so different from Summerhill is that they are not based on the premise that children, if left alone, will automatically learn. This means that teachers must be actively involved in the learning process. They must have clear and precise knowledge about their goals and the means of accomplishing them. That is, they must know what materials need to be introduced how and when. They must learn to intervene at the right time, but also let the children explore by themselves so that they can learn to think and discriminate. In short, the British primary school is not a place where children are let loose to do "their own thing," because teachers and administrators believe that children's interests are dependent on their environment. Consequently, the school and its personnel must provide the necessary resources and appropriate learning climate.

Unlike many American school superintendents, their counterparts in Britain give a great deal of autonomy to headmasters (principals), who in turn give teachers much more freedom and responsibility in determining their instructional programs and materials. But, while the classroom teachers are responsible for ultimate decisions regarding what they are to do with children, their headmasters also take an active part in instructional leadership, for an administrator is regarded as a "teacher among teachers." [81] In a word, headmasters are more directive than Neill and less authoritarian than American principals. As the British administrators give teachers a great deal of freedom and autonomy, teachers too give their children a considerable amount of responsibility and help. In addition, the school itself is characterized by flexible grouping, informality of classroom arrangements and procedures, easy access to materials, pupil self-direction, high standards, and de-emphasis of ability grouping and the use of textbooks.

As for the teacher-pupil relationship, there is less hostility, more respect for children's ideas, and greater flexibility in modifying what is expected from children. There is less control of pupil behavior in British primary

[81] Robert J. Fisher, *Learning How to Learn* (New York: Harcourt, Brace, Jovanovich, 1972), p. 7.

schools, but the discipline is rarely harsh and punitive. Silberman points out that the atmosphere of civility prevailing in the primary school is in part a reflection of the British culture, in which children are taught to respect their elders. In sum, "the joy is matched by an equally impressive self-discipline and relaxed self-confidence" in the British primary school.[82] This does not mean that these schools do not have emotionally disturbed children, but that individualized and more humane treatment of these children seems to lead to less disruptive behavior than is often found in American schools.[83]

The instructional material, activities, and informal classroom procedures that American educators attempt to replicate are not the most important part of the British school. The key to understanding the informal primary school in England is that administrators and teachers see childhood as something precious in its own right. It is not thought of as a preparation for adult life or a series of stages that all children must go through to reach the idealized state of existence—adulthood. In America, we not only tend to think of childhood as a stage children should pass through as rapidly as possible, but as anthropologist Solon Kimball points out, we are also inclined to judge children's behavior in terms of adult criteria, such as the desire to improve oneself constantly. In contrast to this American attitude, British teachers and administrators take seriously the belief in the dignity of the child as a unique individual and believe that learning can take place constantly in a stimulating, responsive, and nonthreatening situation.

In this country many schools have been modeled after the British primary school in varied ways. They are known by such names as "new schools," "community schools," "experimental schools," and in some places "free schools." Some examples of the schools following the British model are the Little Red Schoolhouse in Independence, Missouri, a Communal Free School in Tokoma Park, Maryland, and the Elizabeth Cleraners Street School in New York. The ideals of these schools are to make education not only child-centered and individualized, but also open-structured and unoppressive. For various reasons the students in these schools often come from homes where children and parents have difficulties, both emotional and interpersonal. Sometimes children from the so-called counter-culture groups attend them also. And, not infrequently, teachers at these schools, though well intentioned, are poorly trained. But even those who are well grounded in psychology, sociology, anthropology, and education often work for much less pay than their counterparts in public schools. Too often the teachers' dedication to the cause of humanistic education and the satisfaction they receive in serving this cause are not sufficient to enable them to continue their work of meeting an important need for a segment of our population.

[82] Silberman, p. 228.
[83] Ibid., pp. 229–230.

HUMANISTIC EDUCATION IN AMERICA

We turn now to a discussion of three major versions of humanistic education in this country. As we shall soon see, the reader may notice many practical and theoretical similarities between the British schools and the American attempts at humanistic education, but it is not always easy to determine how much of the American strategies for humanistic education has been borrowed or derived from the British schools. In any event, this is not a critical concern for our purpose.

Free Schools We shall limit our discussion to brief descriptions of four major types of free schools and their characteristics.

According to a recent study there were about twenty-five free schools (also known as new schools, alternative schools, and open schools) operating in the period from 1965 to 1967. But the number has now grown to about 600.[84] These schools are usually very small in size and for financial, curricular, personnel, and other reasons a considerable number of them (about one out of ten) close their doors before the end of the second year.[85] All these schools, despite extremely divergent organization and programs, are concerned with freedom. As ardent supporters of humanistic education, the advocates of the free school movement abhor the structured curriculum, the emphasis on discipline and order, and the demands for conformity and obedience supposedly found in American public schools. Consequently, such supporters of free schools as Paul Goodman, John Holt, Edgar Friedenberg, George Leonard, George Dennison, Herbert Kohl, and Jonathan Kozol want to release children from the authoritarian and absolute rule of administrators and teachers. Kozol insists in his book *Free Schools* that our public schools cannot provide the kind of conditions leading to humanistic education even if their personnel are inventive and passionately committed to such education, because

> they [public schools] cannot for reasons of immediate operation, finance and survival raise serious doubts about the indoctrinational and custodial function of the public education apparatus.[86]

In other words, our public schools are obliged to carry on their custodial (or baby-sitting) function by keeping children in school until they reach a certain age (usually sixteen), because every state has made schooling mandatory. Moreover, they cannot avoid teaching (indoctrinating) what is demanded by the public and required by the state departments of education, for the very existence of our public schools depends on the financial support of the local communities and the state governments. It is for this reason that any kind of public-school-affiliated operations must

[84] Allen Graubard, "The Free School Movement," *Harvard Educational Review* 42, No. 3 (August 1972): 352.
[85] Ibid., p. 355.
[86] Jonathan Kozol, *Free Schools,* © 1972, p. 14. Reprinted by permission of Houghton Mifflin Company, Boston.

continue to indoctrinate, to label and grade, and to issue credentials, as well as to develop skills and impart information.

Ideally, the kind of free school most likely to succeed should have no more than eighty to one hundred students.[87] Ironically, the small student body required for successful free schools puts such schools beyond the reach of children from moderate-income families. Moreover, this smallness also becomes a difficult barrier to overcome in securing sufficient funds to operate the free school programs effectively.

According to Allen Graubard, free schools in this country can be classified into four general categories: (1) the classical free school, (2) the parent-teacher cooperative school, (3) the free high school, and (4) the community elementary school. These schools vary tremendously not only in organization, program, and rationale, but also in their interpretation of what is meant by "free." Graubard explains that "classical" free schools are Summerhillean schools. They are small in size and have children of all ages. Many of them are also boarding schools that enroll almost exclusively white "middle-class" children paying high tuition, such as the Lewis Waldhams School in New York and the Summerhill Ranch School in California. The parent-teacher cooperative elementary schools are usually established by young, liberal, middle-class parents who strongly oppose having their children educated in the authoritarian and coercive atmosphere of the public schools. These schools are often organized and operated by sympathetic (and also disillusioned) teachers who work more for personal satisfaction than for pay. The schools are usually very loosely organized and there is a de-emphasis on professional teachers and on equipment and facilities. Moreover, the programs offered by the parent-teacher cooperative elementary schools do not seem to appeal to the poor minority groups. The free high school, which has several varieties, is often supported by white middle-class youths who represent counter-culture groups, antiwar groups, and organizations for women's liberation. These high schools are primarily concerned with unrestrained freedom and spontaneity in learning. Hence, their programs and learning activities lack any kind of adult direction or structure. An example of such a school is the community school established by Bill Ayer in Ann Arbor. Unlike the free schools we have just described, the community elementary schools are much larger and more highly organized. They represent attempts by various communities to gain control of their schools so that they can more easily experiment with and reform curricula, teaching methods, school organization, and so on.

In general, individuals support the free school movement because they believe that, by removing their children from the regimentation of the public schools, learning can be made more self-initiated, creative, and rewarding. However, there are some who are attracted to the movement not because of their interest in education itself or children, but because

[87] Ibid., p. 16.

they enjoy "a power struggle almost like a piece of raw meat." [88] There are still others who want to control their schools in such a way that the poor and powerless can gain the sort of education that will give them enough knowledge and skill to free themselves from poverty, exploitation, and human degradation. This is why Kozol prefers to call free schools "freedom schools."

As there are widely ranging motivating forces for the free school movement, there are equally diverging conceptions of freedom. Some regard freedom as completely unrestrained conditions under which the learner does whatever he or she *feels* like doing. Kozol believes that this notion of freedom often results in a climate in which children as well as their teachers make a virtue out of their ability to start and stop things in response to sudden impulse.[89] On the other hand, there are others who equate freedom with providing an enriched environment and nonthreatening guidance to help children learn to think, to inquire, and to solve their own problems. Moreover, some free schools have thoughtfully planned programs, while others simply let children loose because this approach is the opposite of what they reject in the public schools. The impression one gets from the free school movement is that beyond a general but vague agreement that our public schools need radical reforms and that freedom, ambiguously and disparately defined, is essential to such a change, there is no well-articulated philosophical, theoretical, or even empirical basis for what goes on in many of today's free schools.

The Open Classroom   While the educational goals of the open classroom are essentially the same as the concerns expressed by the supporters of the free school movement, open classroom is not a synonym for free school. The open classroom is a means of making our classrooms less authoritarian by freeing children from regimentation and punishment in the public schools. It is also a way of seeing our students as individuals of worth and respect, not as reckless, unpredictable, immoral, and dangerous enemies. An open classroom resembles a community in which both students and their teacher work together. They change and modify their plans and expectations and challenge each other by asking *why* of what they do. Hence, the open classroom approach to teaching can belong to a free school, or it can be a means for a teacher to operate the classroom in a nonauthoritarian way in an authoritarian institution. But, in any event, it is not a permissive climate in which anything and everything is permitted, because

> In an authoritarian classroom annoying behavior is legislated out of existence. In a "permissive" classroom the teacher pretends it isn't annoying. He also permits students to behave only in certain ways, thereby retaining the authority over their behavior he pretends to be giving up. In an open

[88] Ibid., p. 65.
[89] Ibid., p. 62.

situation the teacher tries to express what he feels and to deal with each situation as a communal problem.[90]

In an open classroom the teacher does not set arbitrary rules but rather regards rules and routines as necessary because they emerge from group living. This means the teacher should not have predetermined rules, nor should the rules be the same for all classes. In short, the authoritarian teacher makes and imposes rules on students more or less arbitrarily, while the rules in an open classroom are derived from the reality of the situation. This suggests that the teacher in an open classroom should act as a moderator rather than a judge and police officer. As Herbert Kohl describes it,

> In an open classroom there is considerable give and take, argument, disagreement, even conflict. There are organic elements in the life of the group, to be dealt with and resolved by the group and arbitrated by the teacher.[91]

And children's misconduct should not be treated as a breach of some absolute law but as a disruption of what the group wants to accomplish.

In order to abandon the authoritarian use of power as a teacher, one should exercise suspended judgments. As Kohl suggests, we should not meet our students with predetermined notions about their capacities for learning—expectations as to what they can or cannot do. Unfortunately, many teachers rely too heavily on previous records of their students, and as a result they do not expect their children to do any better than their previous level of performance. It is for this reason that

> teachers' expectations have a tendency to become self-fulfilling. "Bad" classes tend to act badly, and "gifted" classes tend to respond to the special consideration . . . they expect to be given to them if they perform in a superior way.[92]

But since the teacher's role in an open classroom is to help the pupils choose and pursue what interests them, he or she should suspend personal judgments and prepare diverse materials and subjects relevant to the student's own goals. By suspending judgment about students' capabilities, the teacher gives them a fresh chance to develop in new ways in the classroom. In this way the teacher is freed from the standards by which students were evaluated in the past and children are allowed to become what they wish to become. Hence, planning an open classroom must be based on the possibility of abrupt changes in plans and activities, because there is no way of knowing what new interests will develop in the classroom.

As Kohl himself points out, there is no model open classroom. But there can be as many varieties of open classrooms as there are combinations of

90 Herbert Kohl, *The Open Classroom* (New York: New York Review, 1969), p. 15.
91 Ibid., pp. 31–32.
92 Ibid., pp. 19–20.

students and teachers. And though special techniques, arrangements, and materials for the open classroom are frequently discussed, these should not be our most crucial concerns. For the open classroom is essentially a concept of education cherishing children and childhood as worthwhile in themselves. It is also an attempt to help children, within the confines of the public school, explore areas of their own interest and curiosity without fear of authority or failure, so that they can become self-actualizing persons in their own right.

Schools Without Failure According to William Glasser, a psychiatrist and the author of *Schools Without Failure*,[93] personality problems (or mental and emotional problems) occur because individuals fail to satisfy their two most basic needs, those for love and a feeling of self-worth. And though these needs may seem separate, a person who loves and is loved will usually feel that he is a worthwhile person, and one who feels worthwhile is usually someone who is loved and who can give love in return. Glasser suggests that people with problems can be helped to find their identity, or to meet their needs for love and a sense of self-worth, through *reality therapy*. Reality therapy is a process of establishing a genuine human relationship between the therapist and the client. Such a relationship helps the client satisfy these basic needs through responsible and realistic action. Thus the client may learn to choose more appropriate ways of reaching his or her purposes. To act realistically is to consider both the immediate and long-range consequences of one's action, while acting responsibly means doing things that are beneficial to oneself and others on the basis of one's decisions.[94] In the context of schooling, knowledge and the ability to think are necessary for a feeling of self-worth.[95]

As the individual's mental and emotional problems are caused by an inability to satisfy the two basic needs already mentioned, the problem of failure in school is the result of the school's inability to establish warm interpersonal relationships through which the student's need for love and a sense of self-worth can be met. From this point of view, the most crucial concern of our administrators and teachers is finding the means by which children can fulfill the two basic needs. Glasser points out that love in the context of schooling is social responsibility, caring for and helping each other. And while the schools are better suited for providing a feeling of self-worth through helping the child in acquiring knowledge and learning to think, the child's success there may contribute to meeting the need for love, because

> if a child goes to school and fails to gain knowledge, to learn to think and to learn to solve problems, it is unlikely that his family or his environment will correct this failure. In addition to learning to think and to solve prob-

[93] William Glasser, *Schools Without Failure* (New York: Harper & Row, 1969).
[94] Ibid., p. 22.
[95] Ibid., p. 13.

lems, essential to attaining a feeling of self-worth, a child may gain enough self-confidence to learn to give and receive love. . . . A person who is loved and who learns to give love also has some chance for succeeding in the world; from love, he develops motivation to succeed and to feel worthwhile.[96]

For Glasser, the major aim of education is to reduce failure by providing schools wherein our children can succeed through a reasonable use of their capacities. Unfortunately, our schools have been more concerned with failure than success. Consequently, they must direct their attention to the formulation of ways by which children can succeed more often. Such an approach to education, to schools without failure, involves (1) positive involvement by teachers, students, and administrators, (2) concentration on present behavior rather than on emotions, (3) the learner's evaluation of the ways in which his or her own behavior contributes to personal failure, (4) selection of a better course of action, (5) commitment to his choice and enactment of it, and (6) holding the learner responsible for his commitment and action.[97]

According to Glasser, in a school without failure teachers, administrators, and students should be deeply and warmly involved with each other and with the school. In this involvement the school personnel must recognize that, even though a child has failed in the past, he or she can succeed in the present situation. Moreover, students and teachers must be concerned with present behavior rather than emotions (how one feels), because emotion is the result of behavior, and only the latter can be improved. This means the child should be encouraged to evaluate the actions that are thought to be responsible for his or her failure. For example, Lisa might learn that her hostile reactions to the teacher's suggestions and requests may contribute partially to her academic problems. But along with this self-evaluation she should be allowed to choose a better, alternative course of action by seriously considering the suggestions made by the teacher and others. However, once the selection is made, Lisa should be required to commit herself to this choice and to carry it out. After all this is done, the teacher should not accept any excuse for nonperformance but should help her as often and as long as necessary so that she can finally succeed through recommitment and renewed efforts. Only by learning to fulfill her commitment can she gain maturity, respect, love, and a successful identity.[98]

Implicit in Glasser's view of education is the belief that its primary objective is the development of responsibility and a successful identity through helping children commit themselves to progressively better courses of action based on self-evaluation and to carry them out with responsibility. Such education is believed to occur best in the climate in

[96] Ibid., p. 13.
[97] Ibid., pp. 19–24.
[98] Ibid., p. 24.

which success rather than failure is emphasized. And since failure is caused by loneliness, that is, inability to meet the needs for love and a sense of self-worth, the school must become a nonpunitive and warm place where children can learn to succeed. To implement his ideals of education, Glasser suggests that the classroom meetings be used as counseling sessions in which the teacher helps students develop the social responsibility (that is, love in the context of schooling) necessary to the solution of behavioral and educational problems in the classroom. In more concrete terms, Glasser recommends the following three class "procedures": (1) The social-problem-solving meeting, (2) the open-ended meeting, and (3) the educational-diagnostic meeting.[99] The social-problem-solving meeting concerns itself with behavioral and social problems in school. Through this meeting students and their teacher take a positive rather than negative approach in resolving problems connected with such matters as interpersonal conflict, loneliness, vocational choices, and so on. This meeting should not be a fault-finding session. The open-ended meeting provides an opportunity for the members of the class to raise and discuss questions regarding their curriculum, the school policies, and so on. Its primary purpose is to stimulate the students' ability to think and apply their knowledge to whatever is being discussed. The educational-diagnostic meeting relates directly to what is being studied in the class. Its main purpose is to determine the extent to which the class understands (or does not understand) what is being studied so that further plans and changes can be made to ensure their academic success. In sum, Glasser sees the school without failure as a means of counteracting the depersonalizing and dehumanizing forces in modern society.

A Critical Estimate

HUMANISM AND HUMANISTIC EDUCATION

It is difficult to give a single concise but comprehensive definition of humanism, for there are many different types. But, basically, all forms of humanism hold that "men should place their faith in man himself—in man's infinite possibilities . . . [as well as in] a realistic recognition of man's finite limitations."[100] Humanists emphasize the power and dignity of human beings, the worth of personality, and the freedom and responsibility of developing human potentialities so that people can solve their problems with reason. The term *reason* stands for science, which is the embodiment of the rational or intelligent ways of solving problems posed by nature or by human beings.

[99] Ibid., pp. 122–144.
[100] John Herman Randall, Jr., "What Is the Temper of Humanism?" *The Humanist*, November/December 1970, p. 34.

According to "A Humanist Manifesto II" [101] (see p. 143), the ultimate goal of Man is fulfilling the potential growth of each human personality and enhancing freedom and dignity through every individual's experience of a full range of civil liberties in all societies. The document also calls for an extension of participatory democracy in the economy, the school, the family, and all other associations. It stresses human intelligence as the best means of solving human problems, and it regards religious dogmatism as inimical to humanistic morality, which is to be derived from human need and interest. The signers of the document caution that reason must be tempered by humility, since no group has a monopoly on wisdom or virtue. Further, they deplore the division of humanity into nationalistic groups and ask that world order be based on transnational federal government.

Because the core of humanism consists of these broad beliefs, humanism is congenial to and consistent with many disparate philosophical, scientific, theological, and educational perspectives. However, not all humanists would agree with the philosophical, psychological, and educational views espoused by those who see education as self-actualization, as we have discussed them in this chapter. On the contrary, there are humanists who favor a view of education that is contradictory to the ideals of humanistic education. The fact that Skinner has not only signed "Manifesto II" but has also claimed that behaviorism has the distinction of being effective humanism[102] amply illustrates this point.

PHILOSOPHICAL FOUNDATIONS

Although there is no dearth of writings on humanistic education and the possibilities that Existentialism has for education, there does not appear to be clear-cut agreement as to the nature of the Existentialism-education relationship. Some argue that the ends and means of humanistic education have been derived from Existential philosophy, while others deny that Existentialism leads to the kinds of educational ideals and strategies we have discussed in this chapter. There are still others who insist that no educational implications can come from Existentialism. But even among those who believe that Existentialism has an important educational message, there is little consensus as to which version or aspects of Existentialism should be related to education. For example, there are such questions as: "Should we rely more on Sartre, Heidegger, Buber, or Kierkegaard in formulating an Existentialist philosophy of education?" "Do the concepts of dread, anguish, and despair have more educational relevance than the 'I-Thou' relationship and 'inwardness'?"

Even in this welter of divergent opinions there is a tacit agreement that Existentialism represents a new and more meaningful alternative to older and better established philosophies, that is, to Idealism, Realism, Experi-

---

[101] *New York Times*, August 26, 1973.
[102] B. F. Skinner, "Humanistic Behaviorism," *The Humanist*, May/June 1971, p. 35.

mentalism, Logical Empiricism, and analytic philosophy, which have allegedly failed to either explain contemporary experience or make human existence more meaningful. The failure of these older philosophies for having any significant impact on human life has been attributed to the fact that they are systems of abstract thought and objective knowledge about that which is common to all reality, human existence, and values. They have ignored the unique particularities of individuals that make their lives personally meaningful. In other words, these philosophical systems are not concerned with *my life* and what is true *for me*; they are interested in human existence in general and what is true for all people. They address themselves to the questions of whether human beings are moral, rational, or irrational, while neglecting the joys, predicaments, and hopes of concrete individuals. Consequently, some thinkers, such as Sartre, have attempted to work out systematically an Existential metaphysics, epistemology, and axiology that may be more edifying to particular individuals than the established schools of philosophy. Similarly, philosophers of education who are sympathetic to this cause have also endeavored to develop a philosophy of education based on Existentialism as a new, alternative philosophy. Many claim that the humanistic model of education we have discussed in this chapter is the result of such an attempt.

The question regarding the validity and the usefulness of developing a systematic philosophy of education based on Existentialism is more complex and technical than our purpose warrants. However, it is worth noting that the more systematic we become in building an existential philosophy and philosophy of education, the farther we get from the central message of Existentialism, namely a concern for the individual's relationship with personal beliefs and commitments. So when Existentialists ask, "What does it mean to me that this particular thing is a reality, or truth?" they are not asking a metaphysical or epistemological question. They are raising personal and ethico-religious queries, whose answers are not available in systems of philosophy, theology, or science. The answer must come from the individual.

Kierkegaard rejected systematic philosophies as existentially (subjectively) irrelevant, because they are collections of abstractions and objective thoughts about existence and reality as such. Hence, if Existentialism becomes another philosophical system, it is no better than any of the established schools of philosophy. Kierkegaard did not want to become a philosopher, a mere thinker. He saw himself more as a "corrective," whose proper function is to point out a weakness, an imbalance, a lack of something.[103] Kierkegaard's corrective is subjectivity, inwardness, but his stress on subjectivity was not meant to become a basis for another philosophical system for everyone to follow. Kierkegaard "was a 'corrective,' providing the emphasis which was needed at the time." His phrase "Truth

---

[103] See Robert Bretall, ed., *A Kierkegaard Anthology* (Princeton: Princeton University Press, 1951), p. xxvi.

is subjectivity" is not an epistemological truth; rather it describes a property of a proposition. To be "in the Truth" is to live by one's commitment.

Educationally, Existentialism reminds us that what we learn must make a difference in our life. We must go beyond intellectual acceptance of knowledge and "live it." Similarly, we should not merely learn to think but to live "thinkingly." As Kierkegaard remarked in his *Journal*, we should not fall into the cup of wisdom. We must drink out of it so that what we have acquired becomes a part of us. In other words, we must educate our children to take their beliefs into their lives. As Dewey pointed out, we must build their character and

> the kind of character we hope to build up through our education is one that not only has good intentions, but that insists upon carrying them out. Any other character is wishywashy; it is goody, not good. The individual must have the power to stand up and count for something in the actual conflicts of life. He must have initiative, insistence, persistence, courage, and industry. He must in a word have all that goes under the name "force of character."[104]

Indeed the most crucial task for all those concerned with the education of America's youth is to discover and provide the most effective means of achieving the kind of education that will build the student's character and leave a profound mark upon his or her life. Such an education requires not only a supportive, noncoercive, and nonpunitive learning climate but also a self-disciplined, rigorous, and critical inquiry into various aspects of the individual's life, society, and the universe itself. Preoccupation with the self apart from its sociocultural context will not result in education as self-actualization. Nor will excessive concern with interpersonal relationships lead to these ends.

PSYCHOLOGICAL FOUNDATIONS

As we noted earlier, humanistic educators claim that their views of learning and teaching are derived from the findings of humanistic psychology, or a science of the person, which is said to be based on Existentialism and/or phenomenology. Hence, in this portion of the chapter we shall be primarily concerned with a critical examination of the possibility of a science of the person and the ways in which Existentialism and phenomenology may help or hinder the establishment of such a science.

Is a Science of the Person Possible? According to Maslow and other humanistic psychologists, behaviorism in America has not only drawn a demeaning and mechanistic image of human beings but it has rejected the personal, the most immediate, and the most meaningful aspects of human

---

[104] John Dewey, *Moral Principles in Education* (Boston: Houghton Mifflin, 1909), pp. 49–50.

experience—namely, the emotions, intentions, and aspirations—as irrelevant to understanding people. And since behaviorists refuse to deal with anything other than what is directly observable, they completely neglect those unique and private properties that make an individual what he or she is. Moreover, the findings of contemporary behaviorism always concern what is common to all members of a class or all behaving organisms, such as rats, monkeys, and human beings. Behaviorists view learning as a phenomenon of all behaving organisms. They say nothing about a specific person's problems and achievements in learning.

Humanistic psychologists argue that behaviorism is impersonal, inhumane, and inadequate because it is uninterested in the unique qualities of concrete individuals. It is for this reason that Maslow and his supporters attempt to establish a science of *the person*, a view that will take into account the private and subjective aspects of an individual. This science of the person is to focus its attention on the uniqueness of each individual rather than on what is common to all human beings. All this is reminiscent of Kierkegaard's objection against abstract thought and objective knowledge as the basis of meaningful human existence, for they are always about what is common to a class of objects or events. But Maslow wants to establish a new science, another system of explanations, while Kierkegaard rejects all systems,[105] whether philosophical or psychological, as incapable of explaining the meaning of a unique individual's life.

Generally speaking, scientific knowledge consists of generalizations about a group of objects or events. While such generalizations do not refer to a property that belongs to only a single member of the group, they can be made useful in achieving a particular task. For example, a valid learning theory should indicate the conditions under which learning occurs. And though such a theory would not consider the effects of our personal problems on learning, it could provide a means of determining certain necessary conditions missing from our learning environment. These conditions could then be provided to facilitate more effective learning. Similarly, Skinner's "theory" of operant conditioning describes how learning, that is, behavior modification, occurs without making reference to any specific person's behavior.

What makes it possible for us to apply scientific knowledge to a wide range of circumstances is the fact that it consists of generalizations about the elements common to a class of objects and events. If such generalizations were not possible, we would have to regard an object as a class in itself. Moreover, no cumulative understanding of our world could come from this kind of inquiry. Likewise, if we were to develop a psychology solely interested in the unique attributes of each individual person, our knowledge of one person would not help us understand another person.

[105] Ideally, a philosophical system is a consistent and coherent set of beliefs, assumptions, and assertions about reality, knowledge, and value. Science as a system also consists of interrelated generalizations about a class of objects or events.

Considering the number of human beings in this world, such a psychology would be impossible. In sum, Maslow's science of the person, insofar as it is a science, cannot escape from dealing with attributes that are shared by all members of a class of "things"—human beings. For example, when humanistic psychologists (Maslow, Rogers, Combs, and Snygg) assert that *all human beings* have the innate desire to self-actualize, to become a fully functioning person, or to become more adequate in life, they are clearly generalizing about what is common to all human beings.

Maslow believes that his science of the person, or humanistic psychology, can answer the question, "What is so essential to man that without it he could no longer be defined as a man?" [106] But the only possible source for an answer to this question is the individual. No adequate answer to such an existential query could come from any science (including a science of the person), because it is an ethical and not a scientific or epistemological question. But this fact should not deter us from developing a science of psychology that will inquire into the nature of our cognitive and affective processes. Indeed, humanistic psychologists are correct in pointing out that psychology must study the perceptual experiences of the individual, who is at the center of thinking, feeling, and behaving.

Humanistic Psychology and Existentialism   Frequently, the expressions *humanistic psychology* and *existential psychology* are used interchangeably. But this equation is sometimes a source of misunderstanding. Existentialism in the Kierkegaardean sense cannot lead to any psychology as a science, because it rejects all *systems* of thought as having no existential significance. In other words, Existentialism is an attempt to do away with philosophical and scientific systems as explanations of the meaning of human existence, because they objectify it—human existence is seen as an object of impersonal and analytic inquiry. From the Kierkegaardean perspective "existential psychology" as a science is a contradiction in terms.

Due to their narrow conception of verifiability, behaviorists had no choice but to dismiss inner or private experiential variables as simply irrelevant in psychology. We have already shown why Skinner's demand for conclusive verification in scientific inquiry is unreasonable. (See pages 331–340.) In view of the behaviorist indifference to private experiences, the humanistic psychologists' attempt to attain more meaningful knowledge about such experiences is not only justifiable but to be applauded. However, current emphasis on Existentialism or phenomenology as the basis for a science of the person has not served the cause of human psychology. Existentialist expressions such as "man makes himself," and "existence precedes essence" have not given us a clearer understanding of how experiential variables affect human conduct and social processes.

Since humanistic psychology treats of inner feelings and experiences as they occur in an individual, some argue that it is based on phenomenology.

[106] Maslow, *Toward a Science of Being*, p. 12.

But how can we be more clear about our "raw" and private experiences in such a way that these experiences can be communicated to others, since science is not possible without communication? If we become trapped in our own world and our own feelings but are unable to share them with others, there can be no psychology, humanistic or otherwise. Moreover, unless we have some means of knowing whether or not communication of our private experience has been successfully accomplished, no science of psychology can be established. For example, if we feel another person's "nonpossessive warmth," how can we be more clear about this experience? We can, of course restate "nonpossessive warmth" as the other person's "unselfish regard for us," but this is no clearer. Even if we redefine "unselfish regard for us" with a "genuine caring for us," we are no closer to the degree of clarity required for a science, for the meaning of these expressions varies widely from person to person and even from one time to another.

AFFECTIVE EDUCATION

The advocates of affective education allege that the traditional emphasis on the intellectual aspect of learning has destroyed children's curiosity, creativity, and imagination. These harmful consequences are said to have resulted not only from our schools' preoccupation with the cognitive dimension of the child but also from the suppressive, coercive, and punitive school environment. And since many humanistic educators are convinced that children's innate curiosity and creativity will grow and blossom if given an emotionally enhancing atmosphere, they insist that children's affective aspects be nurtured by allowing them spontaneously to express their emotions. At least in principle, the goals of affective education are necessary catalysts to make education more humane in a society wherein so many human beings are estranged from each other and the worth of a person is measured in terms of his or her efficiency and productivity.

Because affective educators attempt to make the learning environment more supportive, spontaneous, and rewarding, what children learn can be made less abstract and remote from their own experiences and interests. In addition, the learner's active participation in the learning process beyond verbal and auditory involvement makes learning more personally meaningful. This is consistent with Piaget's view that effective learning occurs when learning activities involve many different kinds of stimuli at the same time. In sum, through affective education students are said to be made more capable of working out their problems intelligently through active participation in inquiries of all sorts, because anxieties and tensions are reduced through emotional enhancement and expression.

Though affective education is believed to be indispensable in self-actualization, it has a number of potential difficulties. For example, although affective education is said to be concerned with the learner's emotional growth through free and self-initiated expression of feelings, there do not appear to be either clearly formulated programs for action or a well-developed rationale for the kinds of feelings to be nurtured. Similarly, the methods of affective education are at best ambiguous. It is this ambiguity and seeming simplicity that attract many unqualified persons to affective education. Such individuals may ultimately do more psychological harm than good. Unrestrained expression of feelings by persons who have in the past been controlled by various social means can lead to explosive and hostile situations unless they are carefully guided by a well-trained and competent leader.

One of the more serious objections to affective education is that while its advocates seek confluence of emotions and reason, they stress the former at the expense of the latter. They seem to believe that if children's emotions are nurtured, their reason will automatically grow. Yet, when affective education becomes preoccupied with encouraging children to be more conscious of their own feelings and express them freely, children are likely to conclude that expression of feelings will settle all issues and resolve all conflicts and that systematic knowledge and intelligent reasoning are unnecessary. Not infrequently we hear children say, "I don't feel like doing it" as the ultimate justification for their action or inaction. Consequently, standards for excellence become meaningless and any form of self-expression may be thought of as creativity merely because it is free self-expression. Hence, children can easily "justify [and] defend the will-to-failure by making a virtue of the capability to start and stop things in response to sudden impulses." [107]

Indeed, the aim of affective education is more than making children feel friendly or loving, for humanistic education seeks to achieve confluence of emotion and reason. As Maslow, Rogers, and even Bruner indicate, feelings are inseparable aspects of our thought and action. They are an inherent part of our reflection, imagination, problem solving, and aesthetic experiences. Even when we can conceptually separate emotions from thinking, it is not always easy to determine what specific feelings are involved in our enjoyment of solving logical puzzles, loving our children, hating our enemies, or dedicating ourselves to world peace.

In the actual moments of enjoying, loving, or dedicating we are almost never conscious of any specific feelings, for thoughts, actions, and feelings are merged into one another. For example, when we are enjoying an exquisite painting, we do not ask ourselves, "What specific feelings do I now have?" The moment we ask this question we cease to have an aesthetic experience and begin an analytical one. In this analysis we may be able to identify certain prevailing feelings and conceptually separate them from whatever thoughts we may have about the painting. However, this does not mean that by cultivating those feelings we can teach someone else to enjoy that painting. If we desire to have our children acquire

107 Kozol, Free Schools, p. 62.

the love of reading, we should not attempt to teach them to love and to read separately. Nor should we cultivate the emotion of love alone, for love of reading comes from reading itself. We should not make affective education an end in itself by attempting to make children merely feel happy and loving. But we must strive to have them read happily, play lovingly, and become enthusiastically involved in the process of inquiry.

A confluence of emotion and reason is likely to occur if we make the school a supportive, rewarding, and nonauthoritarian place wherein our children can encounter puzzling situations and various forms of artistic experience so that they can be challenged by the problems and creative possibilities in the total life of the school. In this way children are likely to become committed to active involvement in critical inquiry, to learn to respect others, to gain more self-confidence, and to "fall in love" with what they are learning. In brief, they grow affectively and cognitively at the same time. And the cause of humanistic education may be better served by this approach to education than the kind of affective education that is focused primarily on spontaneous expression and the exchange of children's private feelings about themselves with each other.

THE PROCESS OF SELF-ACTUALIZATION

Throughout this chapter we have seen that humanistic educators as a whole agree that children can become self-actualizing persons if their innate curiosity is allowed to develop creatively through learning by discovery. They further concur that freedom is indispensable to such self-initiated learning by discovery. These concepts, so central to humanistic education—curiosity, discovery, and freedom—need to be more clearly articulated.

Curiosity All humanistic educators hold that children are innately curious. They further agree that this curiosity, as intense as the hunger drive, can be developed to make children wise and creative if it is not obstructed by adults or other restrictions. Humanistic educators seem to assume that children's interest in knowing, that is, in asking questions about this or that, is necessarily an expression of their desire to have an educational experience, and that satisfaction of this desire will lead to other related questions and findings so that their learning experiences will have cumulative effect. Yet there is little ground to warrant the view that either all children have the same intensity of curiosity or that their curiosity (asking questions) is always an indication of their desire to learn.

Contrary to the humanistic educator's claim, children frequently ask questions because they want to *avoid* learning experiences! Moreover, their curiosity is easily satisfied with partially true or even false answers. For example, seven-year-old Donna asks her mother, "Where did I come from?" The flustered mother begins her response by talking about the bees and the flowers and how Mommy and Daddy love each other. But before she can finish her reply, her daughter impatiently retorts, "But, Mom, I just want to know which hospital I came from!" The relieved mother answers, "You were born at the General Hospital." The child is now satisfied. She is no longer interested in the subject and goes merrily on with other, unrelated activities. All this points out that a spontaneous expression of the child's natural (innate) curiosity by itself does not engender the kind of disciplined attention and systematic inquiry so essential to the learning of skills, knowledge, and attitudes necessary for today's world. In other words, the development of children's curiosity as a means of self-actualization requires extremely cautious guidance.[108]

Discovery Though humanistic educators, Piaget, and Bruner have all emphasized the importance of the learner's active involvement in the process of learning by discovery, the relationship between their views is not always clear. For Piaget, self-discovery is the involvement of children in the construction of their own knowledge by modifying the schemata they already possess or by creating new ones through the processes of assimilation and accommodation.

The primary motivating force behind assimilation is the innate "desire" to maintain a state of equilibrium. This concept is quite different from the notion of "innate curiosity." According to Bruner, learning by discovery is the process of finding out something that is completely new to everyone as well as obtaining "knowledge for oneself . . . by rearranging or transforming evidence in such a way that one is enabled to go beyond the evidence so reassembled to additional new insights." [109] Learning by discovery is a process of inquiry that necessitates an optimal level of puzzlement (uncertainty), so that learners will not simply give up or become anxious because they perceive the problem as too difficult for them. In this process, learning with the help of the teacher is likely to be less painful and risky than learning on one's own. Moreover, there needs to be guidance that provides the student with a goal and some idea of what must be done to reach it. The learners must also be aware of the possible consequences of alternative courses of action they are considering in relation to the goal, so that they can follow the most appropriate means of accomplishing the objective. Though there are differences between the Piagetian and the Brunerean views, both involve a process of inquiry and exploration of alternatives for problem solving.

Humanistic educators' insistence that unstructured exploration is more useful than guided learning-by-discovery seems to be based on the assumption that only discovery that results from such an exploration will lead to

---

108 For further analysis see Bernard Z. Friedlander, "A Psychologist's Second Thoughts on Concepts, Curiosity, and Discovery in Teaching and Learning," *Harvard Educational Review* (Special Issue: Breakthroughs to Better Teaching), p. 138.

109 Jerome S. Bruner, "The Act of Discovery," *Harvard Educational Review* (Special Issue: Breakthroughs to Better Teaching), p. 125.

productive findings and satisfactory resolutions of problems. They do not suspect that children, unguided, may become involved in needless and often confusing complications which might eventuate in wrong inferences, conclusions, and insights. Children often make "wrong discoveries." One of the authors of this book recalls observing an eleven-year-old Korean boy who had never seen a refrigerator before. The boy reasoned that the light within the appliance kept the food cold because he noticed the light whenever he opened the refrigerator. One day there was a power failure, and the boy was seen putting a lighted candle in the appliance. When he was asked about the reasons for his seemingly strange behavior, he replied, "This light will keep the food cold." He was very proud of the "discovery" he had made without anyone's help. But, clearly, guidance and additional information about the mechanics of refrigeration would have led to a more productive discovery.

Children, if left alone, may very easily arrive at such "discoveries" as, "if a black cat crosses your path, it is a sign of bad luck" or "if birds chirp noisily near your house you can expect a lot of company." The point here is not that unguided exploration always leads to unfruitful consequences, but that it often results in the kinds of learning that are likely to become more a hindrance than a benefit to future learning. If learning by discovery is to have its maximum impact on children's education, it should have cumulative effect—one discovery leading to a new question which in turn results in a new discovery and so on. Yet children frequently make the same discovery time after time with the same degree of satisfaction, without relating it to previous discoveries.

The process of discovery is indeed complex, for it requires individuals to be imaginative, analytic, and synthetic at the same time in their thinking, acting, and feeling. In short, a good discoverer must not only be creative in what he or she does but must also be effectively self-critical. Even for an experienced scientist and philosopher it is extremely difficult to be both creative and critical at once. When we expect children to attain significant learning from unguided exploration we are expecting them to be critical, evaluative, imaginative, and spontaneous. As Bernard Z. Friedlander so aptly points out,

> the contradiction revolves about the opposing abilities required to generate new ideas and new combinations of thought and then subject these innovations to an almost simultaneous series of tests and evaluations [so] as to accept those that fit and reject those that do not. Combining both skills is characteristic of exceptionally mature and efficient thinking that very few of us do at all well.[110]

According to David P. Ausubel, an educational psychologist, the value of learning by discovery has not only been exaggerated but its rationale has been misunderstood. He argues that the experience of learning-by-discovery through problem solving is not inherently meaningful, nor

[110] Friedlander, pp. 151–152.

does expository learning necessarily result in blindly memorized glib verbalism. On the contrary, both problem solving (discovery) and expository learning can be rote or meaningful depending upon the conditions under which learning takes place. Ausubel goes on to point out that "in both instances meaningful learning takes place if the learning task can be related in nonarbitrary, substantive fashion to what the learner already knows, and if the learner adopts a corresponding learning set to do so." [111] Ausubel further argues that the notion that children must discover every bit of knowledge for and by themselves is contrary to the very concept of culture, because

> the most unique attribute of human culture, which distinguishes it from every other kind of social organization in the animal kingdom, is precisely the fact that accumulated discoveries of millennia can be transmitted to each succeeding generation in the course of childhood and youth, and need not be discovered anew by each generation. This miracle of culture is made possible only because it is so much less time-consuming to communicate and explain an idea meaningfully to others than to require them to rediscover it by themselves.[112]

Ausubel is correct in insisting that expository verbal teaching is not inherently meaningless and authoritarian. Nor is learning by discovery necessarily effective and more desirable; the pedagogic strategies that are contrived in such a way that students are *led to discover* certain predetermined concepts or principles or to "solve" problems according to a prescribed manner are as educationally barren as verbal teaching that concentrates on rote learning of unrelated facts. On the other hand, almost all of us have seen instances in which learning by discovery or the problem-solving approach fostered critical and creative thinking and encouraged students to become autonomous learners. We have also experienced situations where expository verbal teaching proved to be effective in stimulating critical thinking and integrating knowledge with experience.

In all fairness to the proponents of discovery learning, it must be pointed out that learning-by-discovery or problem solving should not be understood as a set of specific steps guaranteed to produce certain desired educational consequences. The central concern of learning by discovery is that it should result in integrated learning experiences that will enable the learner to deal with constant change and various social, personal, and intellectual problems in a progressively effective and efficient way. The kind of education leading to these consequences may require many different activities and procedures that are both cognitive *and* affective in nature. In some areas of study, expository verbal teaching may be more suitable than the problem solving or discovery approach. In any event,

---

[111] David P. Ausubel, "Some Psychological and Educational Limitations of Learning by Discovery," in *Readings in School Learning*, David P. Ausubel, ed. (New York: Holt, Rinehart and Winston, 1969), p. 267.
[112] Ibid.

the teacher's decision to use the discovery approach or the expository approach should depend on the nature of the subject matter, the interest of the learners, and their background and capacities, as well as on the availability of time, resource materials, and even physical facilities. Above all, the most vital aspect of learning-by-discovery is the supportive, rewarding, and nonrepressive climate that allows examination and critical analyses of "old" beliefs, new ideas, and imaginative solutions to problems. It is in this sense that learning-by-discovery is so important in education, because such an experience permits children to appreciate humanity's achievements and limitations and also gives them self-confidence, respect for others, and a faith in human ability to cope with perplexities intelligently. If this sounds all too cognitively oriented, we should remember that emotions are inextricable aspects of "appreciation," "confidence," "respect," and "faith."

Freedom

> Don't say: "We are in favor of freedom," "We think every child ought to learn at his own pace," "We think that every child is unique and beautiful." This kind of idiotic jargon means so little, or perhaps so much, that nothing in the way of clear self-definition is achieved by its reiteration. Everyone who comes into the Free School, theoretically, believes that "children should be free." The real question is what we mean by freedom. This is the part that ought to be spelled out.[113]

This poignant excerpt from Kozol's *Free Schools* succinctly points out the need for humanistic educators to more clearly articulate what they mean by freedom, which is said to be so essential to self-actualization. A careful examination of writings by humanistic educators reveals that the term *freedom* is used in at least two very different senses. In the first sense, freedom is the quality of a learning climate in which threats, punishments, and regimentation are absent. In the second sense, freedom is the power of an individual to self-actualize, to fulfill personal objectives in such a way so as not only to remove oneself from poverty, exploitation, and degradation, but also to gain higher self-esteem and respect for others. Here, *freedom as a power* is seen as the product of education that makes the individual more effective personally, socially, intellectually, and vocationally. Unfortunately, the potency of this latter concept is lessened by a lack of clear delineation between the different senses in which "freedom" is used.

When the term *freedom* is used as a quality of the learning environment, some humanistic educators regard it as a euphoric state of doing nothing, or anything, in response to sudden impulse. The ways in which Bill Ayer operated his Community School were based on this conception of freedom. Neill and Holt favor unrestrained freedom, limited only by the principle that other people's freedom should not be affected by our actions. This

[113] Kozol, *Free Schools*, p. 64.

interpretation of freedom is still different from Kohl's belief that freedom is acting within communally established rules in accordance with the ways in which a group attempts to achieve its purposes.

Thus far we have no conclusive evidence regarding the effects of learning based on the Summerhillean conception of freedom. But Emmanuel Bernstein's report of his interviews with fifty former Summerhill students may give us some hints regarding probable results of unrestrained freedom in learning. According to Bernstein, most of the students he interviewed indicated that healthy attitudes toward sex, natural relationships with the opposite sex, self-confidence and ease with authority figures, and a natural development in line with their personal interests were the most important benefits derived from their experience at Summerhill.[114] On the other hand, the majority of these individuals complained about the "lack of academic opportunity and inspiration, coupled with a dearth of inspired teachers." [115] One girl, who transferred from Summerhill to a regular state school, later said of her new school:

> I love the way learning was presented! It was something new and fresh! And, you know, it was strange; I couldn't understand why all the other children stopped working when the teacher left the room.[116]

As Kozol points out, "there has to be a way to be 'free' without being maniacally and insipidly euphoric, and to be consistent, strong, effective, but not tight-assed, business-like and bureaucratic." [117] To do this is to see freedom as power to formulate our purposes not only in terms of our present concerns but also in view of our long-range plans. We must judge and evaluate our desires and their consequences intelligently as they relate to each other and then select and order appropriate means to carry out the chosen ends. This is precisely the kind of freedom Dewey spoke of in his book *Experience and Education.*[118] In the context of what Dewey said, self-actualization should be seen as the process of building the self (rather than "letting it unfold") to one's envisioned possibilities. To do this we must strive to develop in our children those attitudes, skills, and intellectual competencies essential not only to employment but also to becoming self-fulfilling and socially contributing individuals, for building of one's self must relate to the kinds of culture and society in which one lives.

We close this discussion of freedom with another cogent expression by Kozol.

> In the face of many intelligent and respected statements, writings, essays on the subject of "spontaneous" and "ecstatic" education, it is simple truth that you do not learn calculus, biochemistry, physics, Latin grammar,

[114] Emmanuel Bernstein, "What Does a Summerhill Old School Tie Look Like?" *Psychology Today*, October 1968, pp. 38–41, 70.

[115] Ibid.

[116] Ibid., 40.

[117] Kozol, *Free Schools*, p. 50.

[118] John Dewey, *Experience and Education*, (New York: Collier Books, 1938), pp. 63–65.

mathematical logic, constitutional law, brain surgery or hydraulic engineering in the same spontaneous and organic fashion that you learn to walk and talk and breathe and make love. Hours and seasons, months and years of long, involved and—let us be quite honest—sometimes non-utopian labor in the acquisition of a single unit of complex and intricate attainment go into the expertise that makes for power in this nation. The poor and black, the beaten and despised, cannot survive if they do not have this kind of expertise in their own ranks.[119]

This applies to anyone who wishes to become a self-actualizing person.

Conclusion

From the welter of views regarding humanistic education we can discern at least two rather broad points of agreement. One is the belief that every human being has an innate curiosity and that any punitive or repressive environment that threatens the self is not conducive to its development. Here, even Skinner agrees that punishment is not the most effective means of learning, because it has unfortunate emotional by-products, such as fear, that hinder learning. The other point of agreement is the premise that learning occurs more effectively if the learner is allowed to explore freely in an enriched environment where appropriate materials are sufficiently provided and made readily accessible.[120]

In this chapter we have examined several different approaches to humanistic education, which are earnest, although sometimes desperate, attempts to make our schools more effective and humane. More often than not, these efforts have been made without scrutinizing and revising our conceptions of learning, education, knowledge, and the learner. Too frequently, we fail to see innovative models of education as representing new conceptions of education, humanity, and society. Hence, we tend to become preoccupied with finding the right curriculum and procedures and the best materials and arrangement with a built-in "money-back guarantee." Thus,

we have actually analyzed and even replicated informal British classrooms as *product*—we have made a neat package of the vocabulary, the appearance, the materials, and sold it to the schools [in which]. . . . teachers unfortunately remain actors and role players in the educational production.[121]

Not having changed their views of education, and not having understood the philosophical and psychological foundations of the new approaches, administrators and teachers often depend on formulas, thereby creating

---

[119] Kozol, *Free Schools*, pp. 59–60.
[120] See David Krech's "Psychoneurobiochemeducation," *Phi Delta Kappan*, March 1969. This article suggests that there may be a neurophysiological basis for providing an enriched learning environment as an effective means of facilitating learning.
[121] Roland S. Barth, "Should We Forget About Open Education?" *Saturday Review*, November 6, 1973, p. 59.

new orthodoxies. The end result is that one set of rigid practices is replaced by another with more "mod" labels, such as "open education," and "free schools." But this way to educational reform will surely lead us to disappointment and frustration unless it is preceded or accompanied by fundamental changes in our beliefs about the nature of humanity and the kind of society we hope to build. Educational procedures, arrangements, techniques, and materials are merely the means of attempting to fulfill these ideals.

In an attempt to counteract the dehumanizing impact of the technological approach to education, humanistic educators point out the crucial need and importance of focusing our attention on individuals—their interests, needs, and aspirations. Hence, they regard education as a process of self-actualization in which "one makes oneself." Indeed, people are not merely engineering products, for they do have something to say about what they become. On the other hand, we should not see self-actualization as a project to be accomplished by the individual alone. In the following chapter we shall examine education as a cultural process and its various implications in American society, because what an individual becomes and how this goal is reached are profoundly affected by the culture in which he or she lives.

Questions

1. Why do you think that some advocates of humanism, as defined in pages 391–392 disagree with the goals and strategies of the proponents of education as self-actualization?

2. Could the view of education as self-actualization be consistent with any non-existential philosophy and/or psychology?

3. How might you support or justify the belief that all human beings are innately curious? How would you argue for the opposite view that curiosity is culturally acquired? What educational implications would your arguments have?

4. Humanistic educators agree that freedom is essential in significant learning. Would not Skinner's concept of freedom as an escape from aversive stimuli (e.g., punishment) be an adequate definition of freedom for humanistic education?

5. Since humanistic educators do not support the belief that educational goals should be precisely stated in observable behavioral terms, how would they know whether their efforts have been successful or not?

Further Reading

Barth, Roland S. *Open Education and the American School.* New York: Agathon, 1972. On the basis of his own experiences, Barth analyzes the problems related to open education and offers suggestions for making such education viable.

Bühler, Charlotte, and Melaine Allen. *Introduction to Humanistic Psychology.* Monterey, Calif.: Brooks, Slash, & Cole, 1972. The authors examine the relationship between science, culture, existentialism, and humanistic psychology. Implications of humanistic psychology for psychotherapy and contemporary education are also discussed.

Davis, David C. L. *A Model for Humanistic Education.* Columbus: Merrill, 1971. The book discusses the founding of the Danish Folk School by Bishop Nikolai F. S. Grundtvig, the high school's role in the history of the country, and its contribution to the lives of the nation's leaders and commonfolk alike. The author points out that the central concern of the Folk High School is to develop the learner's natural abilities.

Fisher, Robert J. *Learning How to Learn.* New York: Harcourt, Brace, Jovanovich, 1973. The author describes British primary schools and compares them with American schools. A discussion of the American open school concept is also included.

Greene, Maxine. *Teacher as Stranger.* Belmont, Calif.: Wadsworth, 1973. Greene urges the teacher to function as a self-conscious, autonomous, and authentic person. She challenges the teacher to know himself or herself and to recognize the complexity of the teacher's responsibilities in contemporary society. This book represents an existentialist view of education and teaching.

Lembo, John M., ed. *Learning and Teaching in Today's Schools.* Columbus: Merrill, 1972. This anthology of writings by several advocates of humanistic education suggests ways to improve what goes on in the school and the classroom.

Troost, Cornelius J., ed. *Radical School Reform.* Boston: Little, Brown, 1973. This book contains critiques of radical school reform "movements." The book may be more congenial to those who seek reforms and alternatives without revolution.

13

Education and Cultural Pluralism: The Social Dimension

Culture and American Education

As we have seen in Chapters 11 and 12, the advocates of the technological model of education attempt to achieve their goal through manipulation of external (physical) conditions only, while the proponents of humanistic education seek to accomplish their objective by facilitating significant learning through interpersonal variables such as warmth and trust. Although these two radically different perspectives regard culture as having an important role in the educative process, neither of them considers education as a means of realizing social, economic, political, and moral ideals, that is, as a major means of perpetuating their concept of the Good Life. Yet, in most societies, education is a means of realizing social, economic, political, and moral ends. In this sense, education must be seen as something more than a process of modifying a person's overt behavior, on the one hand, or as an individual project of "making oneself" on the other.

EDUCATION AND THE TRANSMISSION OF CULTURE

From a sociocultural point of view, education does not stand for any specific set of activities, such as reading and writing. Rather it signifies a deliberate attempt on the part of a group or society to transmit something worthwhile to its members. This process of transmission can be carried on informally by parents, relatives, and peers or formally through institutions specifically designed for instructional purposes, such as schools or churches. In other words, "education is the instrument through which the members of a society assure themselves that the behavior necessary to continue their culture is learned."[1] If education is a cultural process, we must, in short, first clarify the meaning of "culture."

What Is Culture?   Though many meanings have been assigned to culture, the classic definition given by the English anthropologist Edward B. Taylor is the most relevant to our discussion. According to Taylor, culture is "that complex whole which includes knowledge, beliefs, art, morals, law, custom and any other capabilities and habits acquired by man as a member of a society."[2] In other words, culture is that pattern of knowledge, skills, behaviors, attitudes, and beliefs, as well as material artifacts, that have been produced by a human society and transmitted from one generation to another. Hence, it would be absurd to speak of a culturally deprived child as if there could be a child without any culture. Culture is the whole of humanity's intellectual, social, technological, political, economic, moral, religious, and aesthetic accomplishments.

Central to the concept of culture is the fact that any culture is a goal-oriented system.

> These goals are expressed, patterned, lived out by people in their behaviors and aspirations in the form of values—objects or possessions, conditions of existence, features of personality or characters and states of mind, that are conceived as desirable, and act as motivating determinants of behaviors.[3]

Culture is more than a set of acts or beliefs; rather, it is that which gives special meanings to these acts, objects, and events. In other words, a culture is the result of our ability to "originate, determine, and bestow meaning upon things and events in the external world and the ability to comprehend such meanings."[4] Hence, an ordinary cow becomes a sacred cow and plain water becomes holy water, because human beings give them special meanings and significance. In sum, the meaning and significance of things, events, and behavioral patterns should be understood and appreciated within a specific cultural context rather than in terms of their supposed intrinsic properties.[5] As we shall see later, the process by which people bestow meanings on objects and behaviors within a specific culture has many important implications in education.

In their book *The Concept of Culture*, Leslie A. White and Beth Dillingham explain that the process of symboling occurs through thinking, feeling, and acting. The corresponding products—ideas, attitudes, acts, and

---

[1] James Guillen, "Problems and Prospects," in *Education and Culture*, George D. Spindler, ed. (New York: Holt, Rinehart and Winston, 1963), p. 50.

[2] Julius Gould and William L. Kolb, eds., *A Dictionary of the Social Sciences* (New York: Free Press, 1964), p. 166.

[3] George D. Spindler, "Education in a Transforming American Culture," in *Education and Culture*, p. 132.

[4] Leslie A. White and Beth Dillingham, *The Concept of Culture* (Minneapolis: Burgess, 1973), p. 1.

[5] Ibid., p. 27.

objects—are indigenous to a culture.[6] The patterns of beliefs and behaviors found in various societies have no intrinsic meaning apart from their cultural contexts, for such patterns are reflections of unique world views and value orientations belonging to individual societies. For example, when Navajo Indians say that "death is taking place within John," they are reflecting the belief that human beings belong to a world in which forces of nature make "things" happen to people. On the other hand, the Western world view regards the individual as an agent who causes events to occur in the world, who *does* "things" to his or her world. Hence, a person in Western society would speak of John dying as if dying were something that a person performs. Similarly, the Oriental concern for not "losing face" reveals the belief that moral principles stem from relationships between people rather than between an individual and a divine being. In dealing with different cultural beliefs and the behavioral patterns arising from them, we must always take into account the basis of their symboling process.

There is probably no definitive answer to the question as to why a particular culture assigns certain meanings and worth to a given set of events, objects, or acts. But we can reasonably assume that the dominant world view of a society is a major source of meanings and values. In turn, a prevailing world view of a culture results from certain experiences that enabled a group of people to successfully solve the problems of daily living. In a very important sense, "a culture is a conception of reality and how it works." [7] For example, Navajo Indians are said to have a passive view of Man, for they see the world as "doing things to people," while others, such as white people, are said to have an active (or aggressive) conception of Man because they regard human beings as "making things happen" in the world.

The symboling process we have just discussed occurs not only in the large society but also takes place within many subunits of society. These subunits may be social, political, intellectual, economic, educational, religious, racial, or ethnic in nature. Hence, a society can be said to have many subcultures or minority cultures, such as Mexican-American culture, Afro-American culture, the school culture, or the youth culture, each with its own value orientations. Conflicts often arise between the dominant and minority cultures because they subscribe to different or even contradictory sets of values. Violent confrontations are more likely to occur if the dominant (or mainstream) culture adopts the attitude that its own value system is the only right and proper norm for all individuals and subunits in the society.

From the fact that particular behaviors and belief patterns have been worked out by a given culture as means of dealing with its problems, we

---

[6] Ibid.

[7] Joseph Church, quoted in Mary Ellen Goodman, *The Culture of Childhood* (New York: Teachers College Press, 1970), p. 113.

should not conclude that such patterns are necessarily the best possible ways of meeting the human needs in that culture. Yet the very existence of certain cultural practices suggest that they do serve some worthwhile functions. Hence, it would be unreasonable to argue that any one set of cultural practices is universally good for all societies or is inherently superior to all other cultures. If we accept the notion that behavioral patterns and belief systems of a society should be understood and evaluated in terms of the basic value orientation of that society, then we must not regard any specific set of ideas, attitudes, acts, or objects as having fixed and absolute (hence universal) meaning and worth. For instance, we cannot support the notion that punctuality is good for all people everywhere at all times. For, when the dominant group in a society adopts the posture that its own set of values constitutes the only idealized norm in that society, the ethnic practices or traits of minority cultures are likely to be seen as deficient patterns that must be corrected either through education or coercion. In other words, the dominant culture will tend to regard the minority cultures as "sick" forms of the normal or right culture. Such terms as ethnocentrism and cultural imperialism refer to this attitude of cultural superiority, "which defines a difference as a deficit." [8] Today there are those who argue that all minority cultures in America are being evaluated by the government, by dominant institutions, and even by social scientists according to a single idealized norm of "American behavior." Further, "this norm is defined operationally in terms of the way white middle-class America is supposed to behave." [9] These same individuals also insist that it is this ethnocentrism (or social pathology model) that perpetuates institutional racism and minimizes the effectiveness of the so-called compensatory education. [10]

Core Values   Most societies attempt to perpetuate their concept of the Good Life by transmitting their most basic and dominant value orientation from one generation to another. Hence, the goal of education as a major means of cultural transmission is closely connected with the prevailing value system of the society. It is for this reason we need to examine the concept of core values in relation to education and schooling.

While attempting to deal with its daily problems, each society develops certain patterns of behavior and attitudes that are useful in meeting human needs and resolving conflicts between individuals and groups. When these patterns become well defined (and even institutionalized)

[8] Stephen S. Baratz and Joan C. Baratz, "Early Childhood Intervention: The Social Science Base of Institutional Racism," *Harvard Educational Review* 4, No. 1 (February 1970) 34.

[9] Ibid., p. 31.

[10] Refer to *Harvard Educational Review*, Vol. 40, No. 1 and 2 (February and May 1970) and Vol. 41, No. 2 (May 1971). See also *The Myth of Cultural Deprivation*, Nell Keddie, ed. (Baltimore: Penguin Books, 1973) for more discussion of this topic. Also see page 421–425 in this book.

and accepted by the dominant group within a society, they constitute what anthropologist George Spindler calls the *core values* of a culture. And though these core values are accepted by the majority of the mainstream culture, they are often surrounded by other, alternative (minority) patterns, which often challenge the validity of the core values of the dominant group. Consequently, the possibility of realizing cultural pluralism in any society depends on the extent to which the dominant group will permit the alternative patterns to exist and grow.

Historically, the primary function of the American school has been seen as the transmission of the core values of the society at large. Even today, most school personnel, as well as the public, except for some ethnic minorities, accept this as the most important role of the school. But since the core values of the so-called American culture are defined in terms of the value orientation of the White-Anglo-Saxon-Protestant (WASP) tradition, we need to reconsider seriously the proper role of the American school if cultural pluralism is to be realized in this country.

Education as a Cultural Process   As we pointed out, every culture attempts to perpetuate itself through deliberate transmission of what is considered the most worthwhile knowledge, belief, skills, behaviors, and attitudes. Anthropologist Melville J. Herskovits puts it this way:

> Education is to be thought of as that part of the enculturative experience that, through the learning process, equips an individual to take his place as an adult member of his society.[11]

In nonliterate societies this educative process is carried out in a more or less informal manner. That is, the young learn various skills, beliefs, and attitudes from their elders as well as from their peers without having a specific time or place designated for this purpose. This informal process sometimes involves certain formal rituals, for example, puberty rites. In such societies even folkways and mores serve as instructional media. However, in a complex, literate, and technological society, much of cultural transmission takes place within the confines of specially arranged environments. There the young are expected to learn certain amounts and kinds of knowledge and skills within a specified period of time from those who are specialists in these areas. This formal (and more restrictive) process of cultural transmission may be called schooling.

In sum, education is a form of enculturation, the process of learning one's own culture. When this process occurs formally in an institutional setting, it is called schooling. Thus the process of enculturation is much broader than education, because the former includes both deliberate and nondeliberate learning, such as teaching and learning through imitation,

[11] Melville J. Herskovits, "Education and the Sanctions of Custom," in *Readings in the Socio-Cultural Foundations of Education*, John H. Chilcott, Norman C. Greenberg, and Berhert B. Wilson, eds. (Belmont, Calif.: Wadsworth 1968), p. 98.

while the latter only includes deliberate teaching and learning activities. Schooling, compared to education, is a much narrower concept, for it necessarily involves specialists teaching within the institutions designed specifically for this purpose. On the other hand, education, though deliberate, need not take place in a formal and institutional setting.

In spite of the differences between enculturation, education, and schooling, "all three are to be regarded as expressions of a single process, whereby an individual masters and manipulates his culture." [12] This means that enculturation and education, at least in their informal sense, are present in all cultures and that education is only one agent of enculturation. Similarly schooling is one of many ways in which a person can become educated. All this suggests that while there is no society without enculturation and education, some societies are without schooling.

Education in a society as complex as America, wherein the individual members represent diverse cultural backgrounds, is not only *enculturative* but also *acculturative*. That is, we learn not only our own culture but other cultures as well. In a very real sense, the ghetto child learning white, middle-class values from a white, middle-class teacher, is learning an alien culture. In a multicultural society, it is important for school administrators and teachers to realize that different behavioral and belief patterns of minority children due to their ethnic backgrounds should not be treated as either a social or cognitive deficit. To most minority children, schooling in America represents a difficult and agonizing process of learning to function in an alien (WASP) culture that either rejects their own ethnic heritage or gives it a low status.

The American School as an Agent of Cultural Transmission Today various minority groups are increasingly demanding that their own cultural patterns should not only be allowed to exist but also be encouraged to develop in their own way. They ask that full civil rights be guaranteed and that social, economic, political, and educational equality be provided for all, regardless of their ethnic, religious, or racial background. These demands stem from the belief that America has consistently attempted to assimilate the minority cultures into the White-Anglo-Saxon-Protestant (WASP) culture. Moreover, socioeconomic rewards, such as social status and income, are thought to be awarded on the basis of the extent to which minorities conform to the WASP norm. To members of minority groups, perpetuation of such a cultural imperialism (ethnocentrism) that regards cultural difference as a cultural deficit is clearly contradictory to the ideals of democracy. They are also convinced that the American school, as a special agent of the society at large, plays a major role in maintaining the attitude of Anglo-superiority by teaching all children that to be American is to be white, Anglo-Saxon, and Protestant.

[12] Ibid.

AMERICANIZATION

The American School and Its Mission No nation has had more faith in education than America. As a people, we have always believed that through education not only could we produce literate, enlightened, responsible, and productive citizens but we could also establish a society wherein freedom, equality, and fraternity could be guaranteed for all regardless of their sociocultural, religious, and racial heritages. It was through free, public schools that America was to achieve these goals. The public, erroneously equating education with schooling, was convinced that through schooling even the backward, the poor, and the ill prepared could be taught to become productive, loyal, and affluent Americans. In short, schooling was seen as one of the most effective agents of socioeconomic mobility.

America's faith in education went even beyond this, because schooling was also thought to be the major means of resolving social, moral, and political problems. This American dream, based on an inadequate understanding of the role of schooling in a complex socioeconomic and political order, opened the way for a massive attack against the American school during the post-Sputnik era. Schools were blamed for being obsessed with something called "life adjustment" and were charged with the responsibility for America's being Number Two in the space race against the USSR. Even today many believe that better schooling will reduce, if not eliminate, drug abuse, unemployment, alleged sexual promiscuity, and supposed general moral decay, as well as socioeconomic inequalities.

It was this faith in American schools that prompted a noted historian of education, Lawrence Cremin, to remark:

> The common schools increased opportunity; they taught morality and citizenship; they encouraged a talented leadership; they maintained social mobility; they promoted social responsiveness to social conditions.[13]

The public school was seen as the prime process by which native sons and daughters as well as immigrants could achieve economic affluence, higher social status, political and religious freedom and thereby become patriotic and responsible citizens.

Anglo-Conformity as Americanization Because the school was seen as a primary facilitator of Americanization, its major mission was to enculturate the children of the WASP community and to acculturate the children of those who did not have the Anglo-Saxon-Protestant heritages. This involved changing not only the behavioral and belief patterns of the immigrants and their children into Anglo patterns but also having them adopt the English language as their "native" tongue. The Americanization

---

[13] Lawrence Cremin, *The Transformation of the School* (New York: Knopf, 1961), pp. vii–ix, 3–22.

of immigrants prior to 1870 did not pose a serious problem, because most of them came from the British Isles or northern European countries with Anglo-Teutonic backgrounds. But the immigrants who reached the American shores after 1870 differed markedly from their predecessors, for they came from southern and eastern European countries, Asia, and South American countries.

These newcomers, without the Anglo-Saxon heritage, had more than a little difficulty in adjusting to the English language and Protestant orthodoxy that dominated public schools. Establishment of ethnic settlements by these new immigrants and their attempts to maintain the manners, customs, observances, and languages of the "old" countries presented a new problem and a challenge to educators and government officials. But rather than rethinking their Americanization policy and the goal of education in an increasingly culturally diverse society, the nation's educators simply reaffirmed their belief in Americanization as Anglo-conformity. Thus an educational historian, Ellwood P. Cubberly, remarked:

> Our task is to break up these groups or settlements, to assimilate and amalgamate these people as a part of our American race, and to implant in their children, so far as can be done, the Anglo-Saxon conception of righteousness, law and order, and popular government, and to awaken in them a reverence for our democratic institutions and for those things in our national life which we as a people hold to be of abiding worth.[14]

As Milton M. Gordon, the author of *Assimilation in American Life,* points out, the large majority of the dominant cultural group was Anglo-Saxon in orientation and they "presumably [were] either convinced of the cultural superiority of Anglo-Saxon institutions as developed in the United States, or believed simply that, regardless of superiority or inferiority, since English culture has constituted the dominant framework for the development of institutions, newcomers should expect to adjust accordingly." [15] This meant that being American and democratic was equated with conforming to the Anglo-Saxon pattern of language, morality, and behavior, and the immigrants were to give up their own cultural forms. An implicit assumption underlying this view was that if the members of the minority groups conformed to the WASP norm, prejudice and discrimination would disappear. But, of course, rejection, segregation, and prejudice did not disappear for those nonwhite ethnics, even if they did succeed in adopting the Anglo-Saxon pattern. Hence, "the kind of life proper for America [was] regarded as a matter to be decided altogether by the Anglo-Saxon and by those who became assimilated." [16] It was felt that the members of minority groups should do all the changing. The

---

[14] Ellwood P. Cubberly, *Changing Conceptions of Education* (Boston: Houghton Mifflin, 1909), pp. 15–16.

[15] Milton M. Gordon, *Assimilation in American Life,* ©, 1964, pp. 103–104. Reprinted by permission of Oxford University Press, New York.

[16] Isaac B. Berkson, *Theories of Americanization* (New York: Arno Press and the New York *Times,* 1969), p. 55.

sooner they divested themselves of their own ethnic traits the better. Moreover, this view of Americanism as Anglo-conformity was held not only by those who came from WASP backgrounds but often by non–Anglo-Saxon immigrants.

The Melting Pot Ideal as Americanization   Following the massive influx of immigrants from all over the world between 1870 and the 1920s, both the native-born Americans and newcomers to the country realized that simple Anglo-conformity was not feasible. Hence, around the turn of the century, Americanization as Anglo-conformity took on a more liberalized form as the Melting Pot ideal. According to this view all ethnic differences of the various groups in the country were to be "melted" into a single "pot" producing a synthesis—a new homogeneous culture that was not Anglo-Saxon, Jewish, Italian, or Oriental. The Melting Pot ideal was an attempt to propose an alternative means of establishing a viable nation by challenging the belief that anything that weakened the Anglo-Saxon pattern would result in national disaster. The advocates of the Melting Pot ideal argued:

> A nation is great, not on account of the number of individuals contained within its boundaries, but through the strength begotten of common ideals and aspirations. No nation can exist and be powerful that is not homogeneous in this sense. And the great ethnic problem we have before us is to fuse these elements into one common nationality, having one language, one political practice, one patriotism and one ideal of social development.[17]

In a more dramatic vein, Israel Zangwill glorified the Melting Pot ideal in his play *Melting Pot* in the following way:

> It is in the fires of God round His Crucible. There she lies, the great Melting-Pot—listen! can't you hear the roaring and the bubbling? There gapes her mouth—her harbour where a thousand mammoth feeders come from the ends of the world to pour in their human freight. Ah, what a stirring and seething! Celt and Latin, Slav and Teuton, Greek and Syrian—black and yellow—Jew and Gentile—
> Yet, East and West, and North and South, the palm and the pine, the people and the equator, the crescent and the cross—how the great Alchemist melts and fuses them with his purging flame! Here shall they all unite to build the Republic of Man and the Kingdom of God. Ah, Vera, what is the glory of Rome and Jerusalem where all nations come to worship and look back, compared with the glory of America, where all races and nations come to labour and look forward!
> Peace, peace, to all ye millions, fated to fill this continent—the God of our children give you peace.[18]

Many poor and illiterate immigrants making fame and fortune supported the Melting Pot ideal. When we consider the number of non–Anglo-Saxon

---

[17] Richmond Mayo-Smith, *Emigration and Immigration* (New York: Scribner, 1904), p. 78.
[18] Israel Zangwill, *The Melting Pot* (New York: Macmillan, 1909), pp. 184–185.

individuals who contributed to American civilization as scholars, scientists, industrialists, philanthropists, artists, it would appear that the Melting Pot has produced a new and unique culture. Yet these individual contributions to American technology, science, art, and literature seem to have made little or no difference in what is generally accepted as the core value of American culture. As Gordon suggests, in some respects the Melting Pot was "realized," for "American cuisine includes antipasto and spaghetti, frankfurters and pumpernickel, filet mignon and french-fried potatoes, borscht, sour cream, and gefüllte fish [and even chow mein and teriyaki] on a perfect equality with fried chicken, ham and eggs, and pork and beans." [19] But he cautions us that it would be a mistake to infer from this that Americans see themselves as "a composite synthesis of widely diverging elements."

> The American's image of himself is still the Anglo-American ideal it was at the beginning of our independent existence. The national type as ideal has always been, and remains, pretty well fixed. It is the Mayflower, John Smith, Davy Crockett, George Washington, and Abraham Lincoln that define America's self image.[20]

In reality, what has happened in the Melting Pot conception of Americanization is that all varieties of ethnicities were melted into one pot, but the brew turned out to be Anglo-Saxon again. To put it more bluntly, "our cultural assimilation has taken place not in a 'melting pot' but rather in a . . . 'transmuting pot' in which all ingredients have been transformed and assimilated to an idealized 'Anglo-Saxon' model." [21]

The process of melting into the Anglo-Saxon model was not only difficult for nonwhite ethnic minorities; it was an impossibility! Because, while they were taught that to be American is to adopt the Anglo-norm, it was an unattainable goal for the blacks, the reds, and the yellows to become white. Moreover, racial discrimination made it extremely difficult, if not impossible, for these groups to participate meaningfully in the democratic process or even assimilate into the mainstream culture through intermarriage. It is indeed ironic that Americanization as Anglo-conformity and its more liberalized Melting Pot ideal resulted in the same end, that of forcing the ethnic minorities to divest themselves of the cultural elements central to their identity. In sum, the promise of a new synthesis—a unique and homogeneous American culture from the melting pot—was a myth. It was an illusion because

> given the prior arrival time of the English colonists, the numerical dominance of Anglo-Saxon institutions, the invitation extended to non-English immigrants to "melt" could only result, if thoroughly accepted, in the latter's loss of group identity, the transformation of their cultural survival

[19] Gordon, p. 128.
[20] Ibid.
[21] Ibid.

into Anglo-Saxon patterns, and the development of their descendants in the image of the Anglo-Saxon American.[22]

The Core Values of American Culture   Before we turn our attention to forces challenging the core values constituting the American conception of the Good Life, it may be helpful to examine some of these core values. According to anthropologist George D. Spindler, the traditional values that make up the core of the Anglo-American pattern fall into the following five general categories: (1) Puritan morality, (2) work-success ethic, (3) individualism, (4) achievement orientation, and (5) future-time orientation.[23]

Puritan morality stresses respectability, thrift, self-denial, duty, delayed gratification, and sexual restraints. Hence, in Spindler's words, "A Puritan is someone who can have anything he wants, as long as he does not enjoy it!"[24] The second traditional value, the so-called work-success ethic, is the belief not only that people should work hard to succeed but also that those who have not become successful are either lazy or stupid or both. Hence, people must constantly work diligently to convince themselves of their worth. Individualism, the third value, emphasizes the sacredness of the individual, which ideally should lead to self-reliance and originality. However, it often manifests itself in a form of egocentrism and disregard for other people's rights and desires. Spindler suggests that it is this individualism coupled with the work-success ethic that leads many to view welfare programs as "giveaways" to people who are lazy and unworthy of help.

The fourth value, achievement orientation, relates to the work-success ethic in that everyone should constantly try to achieve a higher goal through hard work. This means that an individual should not be satisfied with a given position but always seek something higher and better. The last and fifth traditional value, future-time orientation, is summed up in the attitude of "save today for tomorrow." Our stereotyped image of teachers as stern drillmasters who encourage children to respect their elders, work hard for tomorrow's success, and always reach for higher and higher grades reflects these traditional values.

The five values we have mentioned are only broad categories, and they can be further elaborated to indicate numerous implications for daily living. But, for our purpose, it is enough to point out that the most fundamental trait of these traditional values is that they are regarded as absolute and fixed. Hence, they are believed to constitute the idealized norm of behavior for all Americans and perhaps for all humanity. It is for this reason that we may say that the holders of these traditional values are ethnocentric.

[22] Ibid., p. 136.
[23] Spindler, "Education in a Transforming American Culture," in *Education and Culture*, pp. 136–139.
[24] Ibid., p. 139.

Though there appear to be a number of forces challenging the validity of these core values, such as youth, the women's liberation movement, and ethnic minorities, the American school appears to persist in transmitting these core values to all children as the American norm, regardless of their sociocultural and racial backgrounds. Moreover, the adult members of the mainstream culture do not appear to have moved away from the traditional values. As two noted American sociologists, Talcott Parsons and Winston White, point out, the belief in the work-success ethic and the achievement orientation are still widely held today. What seem to have changed are the ways in which "working hard" and "success" are defined and measured. Because our economic system has moved from individualistic, entrepreneurial arrangements to those of giant corporations and conglomerates, "hard work" and "success" are being defined in terms of productivity and efficiency as seen by corporations and industries.[25]

In spite of the fact that there are many alternative value orientations, such as those in youth groups and minority groups, the major institutions in this country, including the schools, continue to adhere to the traditional conception of the American way. The only discernible change seems to be that "occupational roles have become more thoroughly professionalized [and] 'success' is measured by the degree of approval one meets in carrying out the role responsibility." [26]

DEMANDS FOR SOCIAL AND EDUCATIONAL REFORM

With acceleration of the civil rights movement and President Lyndon B. Johnson's "War on Poverty" in the 1960s, special measures were developed —such as the Economic Opportunity Act and ethnic studies to encourage the growth of minority cultures and grant them full civil rights as well as to assure them of economic, social, political, and educational equality. These projects and programs were also designed to promote better understanding of the significant role played by various minority groups in the development of this country. Although there were some instances of social, economic, and educational gains, the massive War on Poverty did not achieve the promise of America's becoming a "Great Society" without poverty or injustice. Educationally, these special efforts to help the poor and ethnic minorities seem to have had little impact on the cognitive growth of minority children or on the way teachers dealt with the role of ethnic minorities in contemporary America.

One specific example of the War on Poverty was Project Head Start. The primary goal of this program, which began in the summer of 1965,

25 Talcott Parsons and Winston White, "The Link Between Culture and Society," in *Social Structure and Personality*, Talcott Parsons, ed. (London: Free Press of Glencoe, 1964), pp. 202–205.
26 George D. Spindler, "Current Anthropology," in *Education and Culture*, p. 40.

was to provide preschool education for "culturally deprived" children. It eventually involved a total of 560,000 children, their parents, 500,000 volunteers, and 37,000 teachers. The project provided "child development centers" where children of four, five, and six years of age were given the kinds of sensory and social experiences that would facilitate the development of adequate language, as well as the perceptual and attentional skills and motivations needed to succeed in school. These experiences involved field trips and the use of a wide variety of objects and books, as well as work with individual teachers and volunteers. In addition, the children were given physical examinations, dental care, and free meals. Though a high proportion of the children involved in the program were black, the project was integrated in both the North and the South in conformity with the Civil Rights Act.

Notwithstanding the worthiness of the project's goal, a comprehensive study of Head Start by the Westinghouse Learning Corporation and Ohio University[27] indicates that the program did not appear to make any significant impact on the affective (emotional) development of minority children. And though the program did have marginal effect on certain areas of the children's cognitive development, these influences were so insignificant that "it requires a heroic assumption to imagine that it is going back to improve the life chance of these children or indeed their performance in school." [28] Moreover, there do not seem to be any reliable data indicating that Project Head Start has had any influence in helping the children develop a positive self-image reflecting their own ethnic heritage.

Attempts to present a balanced picture of the minority cultures in America through "ethnic studies" and "non-Western studies" do not seem to have made any substantial change in the ways in which non-Anglo cultures are presented in the instructional materials designed for our schools. For example, Michael B. Kane's *Minorities in Textbooks* indicates that of the thirty standard textbooks in American history, American problems, and civics, a total of two history texts and eight civics texts completely omitted material on Asian-Americans.[29] Eleven American history and five social problems textbooks mentioned only Japanese Americans. Though this survey dealt with only one segment of minority groups in this country, the result indicates the extreme paucity of balanced and representative materials on ethnic groups in contemporary America.

Without regard for the outcome of these attempts to make America a genuinely democratic and culturally pluralistic society, the most important point is our failure to recognize and correct the ethnocentric assumptions

[27] Refer to *Harvard Educational Review* 40, No. 1 (February 1970), for an analysis and a reply to the analysis of the Westinghouse evaluation of Head Start program.

[28] Victor G. Ciorelli et al., "A Reply to the Report Analysis," *Harvard Educational Review* 40, No. 1 (February 1970): 124.

[29] Michael B. Kane, *Minorities in Textbooks* (Chicago: Quadrangle Books, 1970), pp. 122–139.

underlying these "projects." Our efforts to help the members of the economically lower class and culturally different communities were founded on the traditional concept of Anglo-Americanism, which defines being normal, educable, and American as conforming to the social, cognitive, and moral norms of the WASP culture. As an illustration, consider the premises underlying two recent movements: (a) compensatory education and (b) the teaching of Afro-American dialect (black English) in school.

Compensatory Education   Compensatory education, of which Head Start is only one form, was an important part of the War on Poverty because it was considered a primary means of helping the educationally disadvantaged children of the poor and ethnic minorities to acquire the necessary cognitive skills (reading, writing, and calculating skills), which will eventually lift them out of their low socioeconomic status through finding and keeping better-paying jobs. Hence, compensatory education was also central to the Johnson administration's Great Society program.

According to the proponents of compensatory education, the inability of the individuals from low socioeconomic (and culturally different) classes to free themselves from their deprivation is due primarily to their cognitive deficiency, that is, inadequate language and perceptual skills, and lack of motivation. They argue that these deficiencies, caused by sensory and cultural deprivation, force the children to start school with a serious handicap that makes them fall farther and farther behind their more "favored" peers in achievement as they move up the grades. In other words, early cognitive deficits and cultural deprivation will have cumulatively harmful effects with the passing years. "On the average, by the eighth grade, these children are about three years behind grade norms in reading and arithmetic as well as in other subjects." [30] One of the most serious consequences of this situation is that the children of low socioeconomic class are trapped in their low class status.

The advocates of compensatory education insist that the most effective means of liberating the disadvantaged from poverty and low social status is to give them the kinds of educational, social, and even sensory experiences that enable middle-class white children to acquire the skills and attitudes believed to be necessary for a successful life in American society. In sum, poor and minority children are believed to suffer from a lack of educability resulting from cultural deprivation, which in turn stems from deficient sensory and social experiences. [31]

The supporters of intervention or compensatory education further hold that since the deleterious effects of early cognitive deficiencies cannot be "remedied," or compensated for in a few weeks or months, or by educational programs alone, they should extend the program and intervene and

[30] Cole S. Brembeck, *Social Foundations of Education* (New York: Wiley, 1966), p. 468.
[31] Baratz and Baratz, p. 35.

alter the children's own sociocultural environments, for example, child-rearing practices. Project Head Start is required by law to include parental and community participation and the promotion of physical, social, emotional, and intellectual growth of the children. Thus intervention in *all* aspects of the child's life is regarded as necessary, and the earlier the intervention, the greater the benefit. In other words, nothing short of "total effort" is thought to be adequate for successful compensatory education. Now, let us examine its underlying assumptions to see why some people regard this apparently well-intentioned and worthwhile program as a basis for perpetuating Anglo-conformity and institutional racism.

Cultural Deprivation If we interpret the expression *culturally deprived children* in its literal sense, it suggests that some children are without any culture. However, the advocates of compensatory education, who attribute minority children's lack of educability to cultural deprivation, are not insisting that these children do not have a culture of their own. "It appears, therefore, that the term [cultural deprivation] becomes a euphemism for saying that working-class and ethnic groups have cultures which are at least dissonant with, if not inferior to, the 'mainstream' culture of the society at large." [32] To put it more bluntly, children from ethnic groups have been deprived of the culture possessed by all "normal" (WASP) people. This ethnocentric assumption may be said to come from a misconception of "the egalitarian principle—which asserts that all people are created equal under the law and must be treated as such from a moral and political [and intellectual] point of view. This normative view, however, wrongly equates equality with sameness." [33] Hence, all members of this society are expected to speak, believe, and act the same according to a single idealized norm—the WASP pattern. It is in this sense that compensatory education is said to perpetuate institutional racism (perhaps unintentionally) by teaching children to assimilate into the mainstream culture and abandon their own unique ethnic traits.

From this ethnocentric perspective, behaviors, beliefs, and values of minority cultures are seen as not merely different from those of the dominant WASP culture. They are regarded as deficits to be compensated for, or corrected, so that members of minority groups can acquire the mainstream culture and the corresponding socioeconomic rewards. Based on this social pathology view of ethnic minorities, compensatory education, and particularly Project Head Start, denies the strengths within an ethnic community and may unintentionally have promoted annihilation of a cultural system which is little understood by most social scientists. [34] As a result,

[32] Nell Keddie, ed., *The Myth of Cultural Deprivation* (Baltimore: Penguin Books, 1973), p. 8.
[33] Baratz and Baratz, p. 31.
[34] Ibid., p. 30.

the beliefs that to deviate from whites is to be inferior and that there is no such thing as minority culture are reinforced.

Standard English vs. Black English   As a specific example of the social pathology approach to minority culture, let us examine the way in which Afro-American dialect (black English) is often seen by the school and its personnel. In this country, most school administrators and teachers regard standard English as the only "correct" form of English to be used. Consequently, they treat the linguistic patterns of black children "as a structureless, unexpressive, 'incorrect' version of what arrogant cultural elites are pleased to call standard English."[35] Hence, these children are labeled as "nonverbal" or verbally deficient. But systematic studies[36] indicate that the so-called errors actually conform to discernible grammatical rules, different from those of the standard language but no less systematic.[37]

According to Professor Jane W. Torrey, a psychologist, statements such as "We at Jane house," "Jane makin' me a cow," and "it look like you don' brush your teeth" follow the rules of Afro-American English (black English) consistently. These rules of Afro-American English permit the deletion of the words "is" and "are" in many contexts, the possessive *s* is also optional, and the third person singular or present tense verb has no distributive *s* ending.[38] The major point is that Afro-American or black English is no less systematic in its rules and structure or more ambiguous in its expression than standard English.

The foregoing discussion suggests that the Afro-American dialect is a legitimate linguistic form both structurally and functionally. Hence, we ought not to regard it as a "corrupt" version of the right, or standard, English. This is not to suggest that children from black or any other ethnic communities should not be taught to use the "standard" form of English, but it does mean that the standard form should be taught as a second language in addition to their own linguistic patterns. In other words:

> The teaching of standard English should not have the purpose of "stamping out" the native dialect. Standard English would be a second language, or rather, a second dialect, to be available alongside the native one for special purposes such as school and contact with the standard-speaking community.[39]

[35] Charles A. Valentine, "Deficit, Difference, and Bi-cultural Models of Afro-American Behavior," *Harvard Educational Review* 41, No. 2 (May 1971): 138.

[36] Refer to a special issue entitled "Illiteracy in America," *Harvard Educational Review* 40, No. 2 (May 1970); see also J. L. Dillard, *Black English* (New York: Random House, 1972), and Nell Keddie, ed., *The Myth of Cultural Deprivation* (Baltimore: Penguin Books, 1973).

[37] Jane W. Torrey, "Illiteracy in the Ghetto," *Harvard Educational Review* 40, No. 2 (May 1970): 254.

[38] Ibid.

[39] Ibid.

It is a handicap for a French-speaking child if he has to do all of his school work in English. On the other hand, it is a disadvantage for an English-speaking child to function in a French-speaking school. Similarly, just as it is a handicap for black children to be able to speak only their own dialect in the "standard-speaking" community, it is equally disadvantageous for them to speak only standard English on the streets of Harlem. This suggests that "education for culturally different children should not attempt to destroy functionally viable processes of the subculture minority cultures. . . .The goal of such education should be to produce a bicultural [or multicultural] child who is capable of functioning both in his subculture and in the mainstream." [40]

The most pernicious effect of assimilating all minority children into a single linguistic, behavioral, and value orientation toward the WASP culture is that these children learn to regard themselves and their ethnic community as bad, ugly, and inferior. When the linguistic forms that they have learned spontaneously and that have served them so well are associated with a low-status, rejected culture, children become alienated from the teacher and his or her culture, as well as their own ethnic heritage. This then becomes a basis of hostility toward and rejection of the whole educational process and the mainstream culture as racist and culturally imperialistic.

As we have seen in the preceding analysis of the assumptions of compensatory education, these educational measures are insensitive to the unique and meaningful ethnic traits minority children bring to the classroom setting, because the school defines educability only in terms of the children's ability to perform within an alien (WASP) culture.[41] And hence the school is unable (or unwilling) to use the children's distinct cultural patterns as the means for teaching them new skills and additional cultural styles.

We should not regard ethnic minorities as worthy of our respect only to the extent that we can "melt" them into the dominant culture. We must see them as legitimate and functional patterns worthy of respect and growth on their own. To achieve this goal,

> Schools could become more flexible in their willingness to recognize and value the life experience that every child brings to school, and at the same time become more *willing* to examine and to justify what schooling could be about and what kind of life experiences children are being offered.[42]

But it would be unrealistic to expect to change the attitude of school administrators and teachers toward minority cultures without also reforming the whole educational, social, and economic system of America. Educationally, this means that "the academic world in general must broaden its cultural base beyond those subjects, methods, and media that

[40] Baratz and Baratz, pp. 42–43.
[41] Ibid., p. 42.
[42] Keddie, p. 19.

have been traditional in schools and universities, or they will continue to discriminate against the 'other' cultures and languages of the nation." [43] Cultural pluralism based on multicultural education is then essential as a broader cultural foundation of American education.

Finally, we wish to point out that in criticizing the assumptions underlying compensatory education we are not attempting to suggest that minority groups need not acquire those skills and attitudes that the dominant society requires for socioeconomic success. Rather, we hope to show that the unexamined assumptions of compensatory education, which treats minority patterns (perhaps unintentionally) as deficit forms of the WASP culture, may defeat the very purposes for which the Great Society programs were initiated.

Today, we cannot ignore the fact that most ethnic minorities seek to achieve higher social and economic status by "making it" in the mainstream society. And in order to "make it" they must learn those cognitive and social skills, behaviors, and attitudes that the dominant society regards as necessary for economic, social, and political success. Granting that some individuals may wish to remain in their own ethnic enclave forever, most members of minority cultures should become bicultural (multicultural) so that they can function optimally both in the mainstream and in their own cultures.

Demands for Cultural Pluralism

Today there are many more educational and employment opportunities for the poor and ethnic minorities than were open to them even a decade ago. But, like the Melting Pot ideal, neither the governmental measures nor educational "reforms" in the area of ethnic studies have had a significant impact on the dominant attitude that to be American is to be white and Anglo-Saxon, if not Protestant also. Americanism as Anglo-conformity persists, because "the 'model American minority' is made from a strictly majority point of view. [For example] Japanese-Americans are good because they conform—they don't 'make waves'—they work hard and are quiet and docile. As in a colonial situation, there tends to be one set of prescriptions for those in power and another for the subject people [minority cultures]." [44] In other words, the attitude of Anglo-superiority still prevails in this country, and the granting of full civil rights to all is not yet a reality.

One of the most agonizing aspects of the experiences of nonwhite ethnic minorities in this country has been that even if they do conform to the Anglo-patterns of values, behavior, and language, they continue to be subjected to prejudice and discrimination, for it is simply impossible for them

[43] Torrey, p. 259.
[44] Harry H. L. Kitano, *Japanese Americans* (Englewood Cliffs, N.J.: Prentice-Hall, 1969), p. 146.

to become white. Hence, they try to establish their identity and gain self-respect and integrity as human beings by demanding their right to exist as unique and free individuals and not to be "punished" for being different. This is clearly a demand for cultural pluralism, a social reform that will encourage cultural diversity and recognize it as an asset in American culture. Further, the ethnic minorities argue that if American society is serious about freeing individuals to function at their highest levels, then cultural pluralism is indispensable in America.

The quest for cultural pluralism through a search for freedom, equality, and identity is fervently expressed by Mari Evans, the author of *I Am a Black Woman,* when she asks the black community to build black schools, black children, black minds, black love, black impregnability, and a strong black nation.[45] Similarly, young Asian-Americans are "challenging the monocultural idea of the majority society which in their eyes causes imperialism abroad and various manifestations of racial inequality at home." [46] By seeking to establish a culturally pluralistic society, minority cultures are challenging the moral validity of the white system of domination. This challenge and the demand for sociocultural reform in America are expressed in the following words of Vincent Harding, Director of the Institute of the Black World, an independent research center belonging to the Martin Luther King, Jr., Memorial Center in Atlanta:

> Pluralism, as a next, but not ultimate, stage must be wrested from the white nationalist system of today. A new order must come to birth within the mothering belly of the old, with all the dangerous tensions involved.
>
> Release cannot come without hard, persistent, organized struggle. . . . But unless that release comes, and unless new humane systems of life and growth are developed, the identity of no man will be secured and we shall be fated to wander with Black Everyman in the sewers (bombs and pollution shelters?) of the Western world.[47]

These cries for cultural pluralism are echoed in the words of Eugene Sekaquaptewa, Education Programs Administrator for the Hopi tribe Indian Agency in Keams Canyon, Arizona, when he wrote that

> the fact cannot be overemphasized that over a hundred American Indian cultures and languages form the foundation for Indian communities; therefore, the right of the Indian community, or any other ethnic community to exist, to participate in, and to maintain its role in America must be the ultimate objective of all programs designed to initiate change in American education.[48]

[45] Mari Evans, *I Am a Black Woman* (New York: Morrow, 1970), pp. 91–92.

[46] Don Hata, Jr., "Asian Americans and Education for Cultural Pluralism," in *Cultural Pluralism in Education: A Mandate for Change,* Madelon D. Stent et al., eds. (New York: Appleton-Century-Crofts, 1973), p. 129.

[47] Vincent Harding, "Black Reflections on the Cultural Ramifications of Identity," in *Cultural Pluralism in Education,* p. 113.

[48] Eugene Sekaquaptewa, "Community as a Producer of Education for Cultural Pluralism: Conformal Education vs. Mutual Respect," in *Cultural Pluralism in Education,* p. 36.

Manuel H. Guerra, who was awarded the Presidential Citation and a bronze medal for his bilingual and bicultural studies concerning Mexican-American children, concurs with Sekaquaptewa:

> . . . until very recently, the monolingual and monocultural approach to the problems of the Indian, Chicano, and Puerto Rican at most have been good intentions with bad results, and more often a rude imposition of undemocratic concepts and practices. Lack of motivation, lack of relevancy to instruction, high dropout rates, and indifference—how else can the human being show displeasure toward education that oppresses personal dignity and self expression?
>
> Cultural pluralism in education is recognition of the facts and the truth about people and society in America. . . . It is precisely this view of America that has not predominated in our classrooms, textbooks and mass media.[49]

It is important to note here that the demand for cultural pluralism also comes from members of the mainstream culture, and their views are found in many of the sources cited in this chapter. However, we have deliberately refrained from mentioning them here, for our primary concern was to indicate the prevailing sentiments of ethnic minorities themselves.

As we shall see later, the challenges to the WASP value orientation coming from America's younger generation are very similar to those arising out of ethnic minorities. Some seriously claim that white American youth's empathy for the minority may be traced to "traumatic" encounters with parental bigotry in their childhood, when their parents forbade them to play with children of the poor and minority cultures. But, more important, the challenges of the young may be seen as revolt against "colonization" by adults who tenaciously adhere to the traditional, adult, WASP values as absolute maxims to be followed by all. In other words, adults are thought to reject the cultures of childhood and youth as legitimate systems of values. Rather, they consider them "things" to be abandoned. Consequently, the grownups demand unquestioning conformity and obedience to the norms of the adult world. We are suggesting that the basic tenets of cultural pluralism (see pages 434–438) apply not only to non-WASP ethnic groups but also to groups such as children and women.

Deschooling as a Social Reform

The so-called deschooling "movement" is not directly related to cultural pluralism. However, the advocates of deschooling and cultural pluralism seem to share a concern for social reform that will provide equal opportunities for socioeconomic, political, and educational growth for everyone regardless of background or class status.

The early impetus of the deschooling movement came from two educational reformers and social critics, Ivan Illich and Everett Reimer, at the

---

[49] Manuel H. Guerra, "Bilingual and Bicultural Education," in *Cultural Pluralism in Education*, pp. 30–31.

Center for Intercultural Documentation (CIDOC) in Cuernavaca, Mexico. The center is both a language school and a gathering place for students from all over the world who want to study and lecture on a variety of topics.

The main contention of the deschoolers is that Western technological societies have become dysfunctional, self-defeating, and people-defeating by institutionalizing and bureaucratizing the functions that once enabled individuals to interact successfully with their environment and others. In other words, the Western technological societies have lost control of their environment and the individual's ability to determine his or her own meaning and purpose. As Reimer puts it:

> The difficulty is that we are the prisoners of our institutions rather than their masters. Seldom do we consciously design them and, when we do, we can scarcely finish the process before bowing down in reverence.[50]

Because contemporary individuals are so oriented toward production efficiency and consumption, they attempt to build a world that will serve them. But they also make themselves fit the environment they have created for themselves. In other words, "man has developed the frustrating power to demand anything because he cannot visualize anything which an institution cannot do for him. Surrounded by all-powerful tools, a man is reduced to a tool of his tools."[51] The result is that institutions, industries, and bureaucracies have become the sources of normal behavior, health, and social status, so that existing institutions can be perpetuated. These institutions, of which school is one, are said to be manipulative in purpose.

Manipulative and Convivial Institutions   Institutions in our technological society are manipulative rather than convivial (Illich's term) or democratic (Reimer's term) in that they support a culture and a life style that is characterized by production and consumption, which become additive and addictive. The constantly increasing production of goods and services not only leads to greater and greater demands and more production, but it also creates new needs. Illich includes law-enforcing agencies, welfare agencies, nursing homes, jails, and schools in this category because, he says, they are obligatory and coercive by design.[52]

Convivial or democratic institutions, on the other hand, have as their main concern the needs and interests of individuals. They allow creativity and serve all individuals, while the manipulative institutions serve only those who are on the "in." This means that the rules of convivial institutions are (or should be) designed to meet individuals' basic needs and interests. Hence, a sewage system, subways, mail service, the telephone, and public markets are convivial in nature. According to Illich, a convivial

---

[50] Everett Reimer, *School Is Dead* (Garden City, N.Y.: Doubleday, 1971) pp. 96–97.
[51] Ivan Illich, *Deschooling Society* (New York: Harper & Row, Harrow Books, 1971), pp. 155, 157.
[52] Ibid., p. 140.

society is one that allows self-realization and creativity, one whose institutions allow its members autonomy and freedom.

According to the proponents of deschooling, the American school is a manipulative institution whose purpose is to perpetuate the values of Western technological culture. They argue that schools lead to the worst form of social slavery, because they make genuine social mobility impossible by keeping the poor and the middle class in their social positions.[53] Accordingly, the deschooling "movement" has as its objective a radical revolution that will release the creative potential of the economically deprived by ending their acceptance of enslavement, that is, the goodness of schooling. This task is to be accomplished by disestablishing the school. The first step toward deschooling is said to be the destruction of myths about schooling.

The Myths of Schooling   The advocates of deschooling go on to argue that the school perpetuates its manipulatory function by creating myths about itself. One such myth is the notion that all education results from teaching and schooling and that the amount of schooling one has received is the only fair means of determining one's socioeconomic status.[54]

The school is also accused of creating the illusion that educational progress is the product of moving from one grade level to another and educational achievement can be measured by the number of diplomas, grades, and certificates received. These myths and illusions have conditioned society to think that schooling is the key to success and that the more schooling one has, the more successful one is likely to be.[55] Consequently, social and economic positions are associated with the kind of schooling one has received, and the poor people cannot escape from their low status because they can only afford lesser education, which, in turn, limits their social mobility.

Deschoolers are emphatic in pointing out that, while education and learning can occur outside the school, myths created by the school lead people to believe that learning and education are not only identical with schooling but that learning and education can be packaged and sold like other goods. With this illusion goes another false belief, namely, that schooling leads to a better life. In short, the higher the level of schooling, the more intelligent and the better qualified one is to participate in the society.

Another myth about schooling is the erroneous belief that the growth of presently limited knowledge can occur only in school, and hence all meaningful research must be carried out in or with a school. Moreover, this belief is said to reinforce the illusion that knowledge of values can be

---

[53] Joel Spring, "Deschooling as a Form of Social Revolution," in *Roots of Crisis*, Clarence J. Karier, Paul Violas, and Joel Spring, eds. (Chicago: Rand McNally, 1973), p. 139.

[54] Ibid., p. 140.

[55] Illich, pp. 15–17, 35.

measured only in school and that students must learn to obey the rules, social and academic, set by the school. This docility through schooling destroys the students' creativity, uniqueness, and autonomy in choosing and organizing their own values and knowledge in the way that is most meaningful to them.[56]

Finally, the school is accused of transmitting the false notion that greater and greater outlays of funds for educational resources are necessary and justifiable, for the need for schooling is constantly rising and hence new curricular materials and skills are necessary to teach more and more people. Also, because the school has taken on the task of defining the needs of the individual and society, it is seen as creating technological elitists who are trained to do special tasks and who wish to guard their knowledge and skills. Knowledge thus becomes private property to be handled by the very few, i.e., specialists.[57] But this robs the poor of the skills necessary to free themselves from their low socioeconomic status. For example, if three-year programs in nursing are replaced more and more by four-year programs, those who do not have sufficient financial resources to attend a four-year program cannot become nurses.

Conditions for Deschooling   In order to establish a democratic or convivial society, we must take seriously the belief that everyone has the "right of maximum freedom from human constraint," so that "the right of any man to impose either truth or virtue upon another" can be denied.[58] So argues Reimer. What this means is that we must reject the right of any group or individual to monopolize anything that other people need, whether this be information, fresh air, pure water, nutrition, or skills. Reimer insists that we must abolish the school system by law if we are to build a democratic society, because if education becomes an institutional monopoly of the state, the school can no longer serve the people.[59]

In addition to this legislative prohibition of establishing the school, Reimer further suggests that "we need an extension of anti-discrimination laws to include schooling." [60] If these measures are accomplished, an individual would not be discriminated against because of race, religion, or schooling, for "where and how one has been schooled is as irrelevant to one's capacity to do a job as is race or religion." [61] Further, the deschoolers hold that we should also equalize educational opportunity by distributing educational resources (through legislation) in an inverse ratio to present privilege. In other words, more resources would be made available to those who have less wealth and fewer resources to those who are wealthy.

[56] Ibid. pp. 57–58.
[57] Ibid., pp. 128–129.
[58] Reimer, p. 179.
[59] Ibid., p. 176.
[60] Ibid., p. 177.
[61] Ibid.

What the deschoolers attempt to achieve through disestablishing our schools is to guarantee freedom in learning, with the hope that the individual will help others to grow into their own uniqueness as he or she did. This belief is based on an implicit assumption that when a person wants to learn something he or she will find some way of learning it. Thus, Illich has written:

> Learning is the human activity which least needs manipulation by others. Most learning is not the result of instruction. It is rather the result of unhampered participation in a meaningful setting. Most people learn best by being "with it." [62]

Learning Networks   But once the schools are disestablished, how should education and learning occur? Illich suggests four convivial learning networks[63] whose main objectives are to "provide all who want to learn with access to available resources at any time in their lives; empower all who want to share what they know to find those who want to learn it from them; and finally, furnish all who want to present an issue to the public with the opportunity to make their challenge known." [64] The four learning networks proposed by Illich are then the means of fulfilling these needs.

The first network is a reference service to educational objects. Things in the environment are made available to all who wish to learn about them without being isolated from the environment as students are in the classroom. This means that educational artifacts are to be found in many places —libraries, tool shops, game rooms, laboratories, and so on. Learners are given the right to choose the activities in their environment that they regard as necessary and relevant for their purposes. The second of the four networks is a skill exchange. This network includes a listing of skills by those who are willing to share them with others. Various skill centers and banks could be set up in present school buildings. They could be subsidized by different groups and the services made free to all. Students could also be given vouchers to pay business and industry to teach them desired skills. The peer matching service, whereby various individuals are matched with others who have similar interests, constitutes the third network. This service enables individuals to pursue their own special interest with others. The fourth and last network is a reference service to professional educators, who are tested to determine their merit and abilities so that they may serve as guides to parents in raising their children or as guides to learners.

The four learning networks are for all ages; learners are to participate voluntarily according to their needs. The only role of the government is to act as a guarantor and sponsor in providing various resources so that equality of educational opportunity can be assured for everyone without

[62] Illich, p. 56.
[63] Ibid., pp. 111–149.
[64] Ibid., p. 108.

discriminatory practices based on race, religion, or cultural background. In sum, the most urgent goal of the deschooling "movement" is to abolish the school as an instrument of the state and to put education into the hands of parents, businesspeople, and the individual learner.

To Deschool or Not to Deschool? The deschoolers' view that school is a manipulative institution perpetuating Western technological values and maintaining social slavery is based primarily on Reimer and Illich's experiences in Latin American countries. This image of the school is probably quite accurate in countries where education has always been a privilege of the wealthy. That is, wealthy children went to the best schools, the middle class went to mediocre schools, and the poor went to either bad schools or no school at all. For example, in many countries in Asia, a child's future career as a neurosurgeon depends on what kind of elementary and secondary schools he or she can attend. Because the child's progression from elementary and secondary schools to medical school requires attendance at first-rate (hence expensive) schools, he or she cannot otherwise hope to enter a first-class medical school. Moreover, passing entrance examinations to these schools almost always requires extra tutoring outside of the school, and children with few resources cannot afford such services to prepare themselves for entrance into better schools.

But this view of the school as an agent of "social slavery" is inconsistent with American experience. In spite of all the problems plaguing the American school, it still offers opportunities to the children of the poor to grow economically and socially. As a noted educational sociologist, Robert J. Havighurst, points out, "it [the school] has succeeded in this to some extent, as is proven by the number of poor children who have become quite successful workers, citizens, and parents at least partly with the aid of schools." [65] This is not to suggest that the American school has been successful in eradicating poverty, racism, and discrimination. But, in spite of its weaknesses and failures, the school is still a means of freeing oneself from poverty. For example, with current federal provisions in education, many students from low-income families have been able to attend expensive and prestigious institutions through student loans, grants, and work-study programs.

If the deschoolers are serious about freeing the creativity of the poor, as well as enabling them to escape from their economic deprivation, then what is needed is not deschooling but better schooling. If we are to achieve the kind of freedom and social mobility the deschoolers are envisioning, then we must help more poor and minority children become lawyers, physicians, engineers, scholars, economists, architects, and nuclear physicists. But this cannot be accomplished with the belief that these com-

---

[65] Robert J. Havighurst, "Prophets and Scientists in Education," in *Farewell to Schools???*, Daniel U. Levine and Robert J. Havighurst, eds. (Worthington, Ohio: Jones, 1971), p. 85.

plex fields can be learned by leaving the children free and making the resources more readily available to them. As Jonathan Kozol pointed out, the young children in the ghettos "need strong models in effective, bold, risk-taking, conscientious and consistent adults." [66] And a

> tough, aggressive, skeptical and inventive "skill" like beating out a tough and racist and immensely difficult examination for the civil service, for City College or for Harvard Law School, rings a good deal more of deep-down revolution than the handlooms and science gadgets and the gerbil-cages that have come.[67]

Curiously enough, the belief that the disestablishment of the school will do more for the poor than for the wealthy is likely to lead to an elitist society. If we abolish our schools and establish the four learning networks suggested by Illich, the rich will be able to educate their children well with the networks of their own private resources. But the poor, because of their illiteracy and simply the business of making a living, are not likely to make the most effective use of the networks to educate their children. "Eventually, people with a social conscience would work through political and economic measures to set up educational institutions to serve the disadvantaged people better, and a school system would emerge again." [68]

One of the more fundamental errors the deschoolers make is the notion that by disestablishing our schools, society can be remade. While the advocates of the deschooling "movement" are aware that the school must be understood and examined in terms of the sociopolitical and cultural contexts in which it functions, they seem to forget that the nature of our society and culture is not the result of schooling. Rather, the school reflects the nature of our society and culture. And even if we grant that the American school is a manipulative institution perpetuating Western technological values, it is difficult to see how "the forces which sustain the existing economic and political stratification and the structures of mass media will allow the educational resources to be used against them." [69] It would seem more realistic to hold that the school can change along with other institutions, "both helping to change them and being helped to change by their change. But education in the school cannot be the prime transformer" of the society.[70]

As Neil Postman realistically points out, "America is not going to be deschooled, tomorrow, next year, or even in the next ten years." [71] In the final analysis, the entire deschooling proposal is irrelevant to betterment

---

[66] Jonathan Kozol, *Free Schools* (Boston: Houghton Mifflin, 1972), p. 57.
[67] Ibid., p. 44.
[68] Havighurst, p. 90.
[69] Amitai Etzioni, "The Educational Mission," in *Farewell to Schools???*, p. 96.
[70] Ibid.
[71] Neil Postman, "My Ivan Illich Problem," in *After Deschooling, What?* Alan Gartner, Colin Greer, and Frank Riessman, eds. (New York: Harper & Row, 1973), p. 145.

of American education because the improvement of children's education would have to come at least partially from a more effective schooling.

Cultural Pluralism and Democracy

The demand for cultural pluralism in America is based partly on the belief that it is intrinsic to democracy. Yet its proponents have not always clearly articulated the meaning of cultural pluralism. Nor have they critically examined its social, political, and educational implications or its alleged connections with democracy. Consequently, in the following pages we shall suggest a concept of cultural pluralism consonant with the tenets of democracy, the implementation of which may help us meet the needs and interests of minority cultures in contemporary American education. We shall also briefly examine the philosophical basis of cultural pluralism.

CULTURAL PLURALISM IN AMERICA

Clearly, the kind of cultural pluralism believed to be consistent with democracy is much more than the separate or independent existence of disparate ethnic groups without any contact between institutions or individuals. Rather, it is an ideal that seeks to establish and encourage cultural diversity as well as a basis of unity so that America can become a cohesive society whose culture is enriched by sharing widely diverging ethnic experiences. According to the National Coalition for Cultural Pluralism, which was formed at the Conference on Education and Teacher Education for Cultural Pluralism in Chicago on May 12–14, 1971, cultural pluralism is

> a state of equal co-existence in a mutually supportive relationship within the boundaries or framework of one nation of people of diverse cultures with significantly different patterns of belief, behavior, color, and in many cases with different languages. To achieve cultural pluralism there must be unity with diversity. Each person must be aware of and secure in his own identity, and be willing to extend to others the same respect and rights that he expects and enjoys himself.[72]

Hence, cultural pluralism is based on the belief in equality of opportunity for all people, respect for human dignity, and the conviction that no single pattern of living is good for everyone. In this context, the traditional notion of tolerance for different cultural patterns is said to be patronizing, for it suggests an attitude in which the dominant group regards human dignity as a grant bestowed by "me" on "you" or "you" on "me."[73]

Cultural pluralism, then, must include the belief that in the coexistence of people with diverse cultural backgrounds, to be different is not to be

---

[72] William R. Hazard and Madelon D. Stent, "Cultural Pluralism and Schooling: Some Preliminary Observations," in *Cultural Pluralism in Education*, p. 14.
[73] Ibid., p. 15.

inferior. While this pluralistic view entails the acceptance of the intrinsic worth of all human beings and their unique individuality, it should not prevent one from learning new cultural patterns. On the contrary, the individual life or the culture of a group or a nation may be enriched by preserving and sharing different ethnic patterns. The possibility of changing one's life style through membership in other ethnic groups, based on mutual interest, as well as in one's own should not be restricted. For example, one can belong to and participate in the activities of racially or ethnically mixed community groups, Asian-American groups, or Mexican-American groups, yet at the same time develop a unique life style that incorporates various aspects of these groups.

In a somewhat similar vein, Horace N. Kallen, a Harvard-educated philosopher and American Jew, asserted that ethnic groups should develop a positive self-image and a pride in their respective group's cultural heritage and communal values, but still function as partially integrated political and economic entities in American society. He was convinced that America would be richer as a result of cultural diversity, for he was not persuaded that the value systems the immigrants brought to this country were inimical to American democracy. Kallen argued not only that democracy is linked with the concept of semi-independent and autonomous groups and communities interacting on the important issues of experience alone, but also that a culturally pluralistic society is a natural state, for human beings have differing needs that are so deeply rooted in their nature that they cannot be eliminated, nor should their development be deliberately suppressed. Accordingly, he conceived America as a nation consisting of a number of nationalities federated into a single nation, a Federation of Nationalities. In Kallen's words:

> The American way is the way of orchestration. As in an orchestra, the different instruments, each with its own characteristic timbre and theme, contribute distinct and recognizable parts to the composition, so in the life and culture of a nation, the different regional, ethnic, occupational, religious, and other communities compound their different activities to make up the national spirit.[74]

Thus the American national spirit would consist of the union of the different. And it will be sustained by equality of different ethnic groups and the interactions (transactions) between the "different but equal" without any single group dominating the rest.

Another advocate of cultural pluralism, Isaac B. Berkson, supervisor of schools and extension activities of the Bureau of Jewish Education and a student of John Dewey, joined in disavowing Anglo-conformity and the Melting Pot ideal as inconsistent with American democracy. Like Dewey, Berkson and Kallen both believed a democratic society has the obligation

[74] Horace N. Kallen, *The Education of Free Men* (New York: Farrar, Straus, 1949), p. 117.

to provide the opportunity for "the perfection and conservation of differences" in every individual. And because Berkson saw self-determination as the quintessence of democracy, he criticized Kallen's Federation of Nationalities for being too restrictive in allowing the members of a minority group to leave their ethnic enclave if they so desired. He argued that Kallen's model would lead to freedom of association for the various cultural groups, but not enough freedom of contact for the individual. For example, Kallen would encourage different ethnic groups to have joint activities but would discourage ethnically mixed marriages.

Unlike Kallen, Berkson was more concerned with the integrity of ethnic groups that occur naturally within the larger society. His primary concern was with reducing, if not eliminating, the forces in the large society that would pressure a minority to either dissolve or perpetuate itself. This means that if an ethnic community decides to eliminate itself, or if an individual member of the ethnic community decides to leave the group and join the dominant group, such a decision should be accepted as proper and legitimate (this is also known as the Community Model). Both Kallen and Berkson adhered to the desirability of preserving ethnic communities, but the latter argued for greater flexibility and opportunities for choice, while the former envisioned ethnic communities "as a reservoir of some specific tradition and excellence which one or another of its sons may lift into the powers and perspectives of the larger national life, making it stronger and richer." [75]

The central problem of cultural pluralism is how minority groups can maintain enough separation from the dominant culture to perpetuate and develop their own ethnic traditions without, at the same time, interfering with the execution of their standard responsibilities to the American society of which they are also members. That is, how can cultural diversity and unity be maintained simultaneously, particularly when conflicts arise between the society at large and these subunits? One suggested solution is that a

> value conflict, where it exists, is to be fought out in the arena of the ballot box and public opinion, but the goal is to keep such conflict at a minimum by emphasizing the areas of flexibility, permitted alternatives, and free choice in American life and by refraining from imposing one's own collective will as standards of enforced behavior for other groups.[76]

In other words, value conflicts between groups should be resolved according to majority rule, but society should avoid such conflicts as much as possible by giving the groups many alternatives from which to choose their own courses of action. For example, one can choose to learn the dominant language and behavior patterns and work outside of one's ethnic group, or one can choose to remain in the ethnic enclave and carry on a trade that would serve primarily the members of that community. A

[75] Ibid., pp. 117–118.
[76] Gordon, *Assimilation in American Life*, p. 159.

constantly recurring theme of cultural pluralism is the belief that no single group should impose its own pattern as the idealized norm for every other group.

To some, cultural pluralism as a social ideal to preserve each ethnic group's cultural distinctiveness within the context of American citizenship involves contradictory social practices. To maintain one's unique cultural traits, a person must maintain the most meaningful personal relationships with his or her group. But, if an individual is to achieve social, political, and economic status in the larger society, he or she must also participate in the processes of the dominant culture. Whether these practices are contradictory to each other or not is quite debatable. What seems to have happened in America is that many members of minority groups have shed much of their cultural distinctiveness. Yet they carry on only minimal interaction with other minority groups or with the dominant society. For example, a great majority of the professionals and semiprofessionals with non-Anglo backgrounds have adopted many WASP patterns, but their involvement in activities carried on by their own ethnic groups or by the mainstream community is only minimal.

On the basis of the foregoing discussion, it would be quite legitimate to ask if cultural pluralism is in fact an achievable ideal. Currently, some argue that America is approaching a so-called open society, rather than a culturally pluralistic society.[77] That is, while a pluralistic society encourages cultural differences, an open society regards cultural differences as no longer relevant in determining the worth or merit of individuals. Hence, America as an open society should emphasize individual equality and national unity rather than cultural diversity, so that each member of any given minority group can form his or her identity as a citizen of the country rather than as a member of a subculture.

While America may be approaching the state wherein the individual's position and merit are evaluated in terms of equality and competence, it is little help to tell nonwhite minority youth that their identity should be achieved in terms of their status as citizens of this country. These young people find that their status as Americans is still affected by their color and ethnic backgrounds. At the same time, they discover that they belong to neither the dominant white culture nor the culture of their parents, and consequently they see themselves as dislocated and alienated. This condition is common among today's younger generation of minority cultures, whose self-image is not intimately bound up with their legal citizenship in the United States.

The children of an ethnic minority must be helped to develop pride in their own racial and cultural heritage and to achieve their identity as unique and intrinsically worthwhile human beings by rejecting the belief that to be different is to be inferior. This kind of positive self-image and

[77] Thomas Green, "Education and Pluralism: Ideal and Reality," Twenty-sixth A. J. Richard Street Lectures, Syracuse University, School of Education, 1966, p. 25.

cultural integrity needs to be developed not only in the children of poor ethnic minorities but also in the children whose parents occupy upper-middle-class socioeconomic status, for the so-called identity crisis is no less severe among these children than among the poor.

In sum, in a multicultural society such as America, it is not enough to propose that an individual be evaluated according to merit and competence. We must also regard cultural diversity as an asset to be developed, for even a person with full civil rights cannot escape from the racial and ethnic backgrounds that inexorably govern one's view of oneself. The identity crisis experienced by most minority children *cannot* be resolved unless special efforts are made to develop a pride about the "Mexican," "Asian," or "Afro" parts of the labels "Mexican-American," "Asian-American," and "Afro-American." Cultural pluralists do not seek cultural diversity alone; they also regard unity as a basis for this nation. This unity should not come from establishing the linguistic, ethical, and behavioral patterns of the mainstream culture as the only idealized norms for all individuals. The unity should be based on the acceptance by the members of both minority and dominant cultures of the belief that all human beings are to be regarded as ends in themselves so that no person can be exploited by other individuals or institutions.

The question of whether cultural pluralism is or is not achievable in this country hinges on the meaning of "cultural pluralism" in the context of American democracy. Neither Kallen's Federation of Nationalities nor Berkson's Community Model is wholly acceptable. The concept of the open society, too, is unsatisfactory, because this model places individual equality and national unity ahead of the development of cultural diversity. The view of a society described in the preceding paragraph seems most consistent with cultural pluralism as understood by minority groups. Whether such a society is achievable in this country remains to be seen.

Democracy as a Culturally Pluralistic Society

Is cultural pluralism intrinsic to American democracy? The fundamental principles of democracy as articulated in the Declaration of Independence and the Constitution of the United States clearly indicate that the founders of this country believed that each person is to be regarded as an end. As John L. Childs, a noted philosopher of education and a student of John Dewey, pointed out, "Democracy is an attempt to embody in our social relationships the principle which regards each individual as possessing intrinsic worth or dignity." [78] It is for this reason that exploitation of any individual or group violates a democratic maxim. Institutions in our society must be made to serve the individual, not vice versa. In Dewey's words:

[78] John L. Childs, "The Educational Philosophy of John Dewey," in *The Philosophy of John Dewey*, Paul Arthur Schilpp, ed., (New York: Tudor, 1951), p. 441.

Democracy has many meanings, but if it has a moral meaning, it is found in resolving that the supreme test of all political institutions and industrial arrangements shall be the contribution they make to the all-around growth of every member of society.[79]

To regard each individual as an end is to accept the belief that there is an "intrinsic connection between the prospects of democracy and belief in the potentialities of human nature—for its own sake." [80] In building democracy we must begin with the faith that all people have the capacity to develop and exercise their own intelligence in shaping their own future.[81] It is not that these capacities are already formed and ready to be unfolded, but if given the opportunity individuals can grow socially, emotionally, and intellectually so that they can not only decide what is good for them but also find the most effective means of attaining it. Hence, democracy "denotes a state of affairs in which the interest of each in his work is uncoerced and intelligent: based upon its congeniality to his own aptitudes." [82] Consequently, freedom of all kinds is essential to democracy, and "the cause of democratic freedom is the cause of the fullest possible realization of human potentialities." [83]

A democratic society is necessarily pluralistic (culturally, politically, intellectually, and socially) because it is founded on a belief in the intrinsic worth of individuals and their unique capacities to become intelligent human beings. In this sense, the unique qualities of individuals or groups become assets rather than hindrances. Accordingly, "there is no physical acid which has the corrosive power possessed by intolerance directed against persons because they belong to a group that bears a certain name." [84] Bigotry and ethnocentrism are anathema to democracy.

A social corollary of the belief that each person should be treated as an end is that a society must provide the equality of opportunity that will enable individuals to develop their capacities to the fullest possible extent. Hence, "all individuals are entitled to equality of treatment by law and in its administration. Each one is affected equally in quality if not in quantity by the institutions under which he lives and has an equal right to express his judgment." [85] Thomas Jefferson's insistence that there be a system of education open to all youth as a necessity for democracy reflects this equal opportunity principle. The demand of ethnic minorities to preserve and develop their own cultural patterns stems from the firm belief in the democratic principle, which regards the uniqueness of individuals and equal opportunity for their development as intrinsically good.

[79] John Dewey, *Freedom and Culture* (New York: Capricorn Books, 1939), p. 127.
[80] Ibid.
[81] Dewey, *Reconstruction in Philosophy*, p. 49.
[82] John Dewey, *Democracy and Education* (New York: Macmillan, 1961), p. 316.
[83] Dewey, *Reconstruction in Philosophy*, p. 129.
[84] Dewey, *Freedom and Culture*, p. 127.
[85] John Dewey, "The Modes of Societal Life," in *Intelligence in the Modern World*, Joseph Ratner, ed. (New York: Random House, 1939), p. 403.

It is important to note that democracy requires not only an emphasis on personal needs and interests and on varied points of shared common interest, but also a recognition of mutual interest as a means of social control. In other words, a democratic society should not only encourage free interaction among individuals and groups but also changes in social habits, that is, continuous readjustment through meeting new situations produced by a wide variety of interactions with others. It is essential that the members of a democratic society recognize that the needs of others are as important to those people as their own are to them. This recognition is a necessary prerequisite for effective handling of conflicts among individuals and groups.

As Dewey recognized, conflicts in interests and values are bound to arise in a society like America that has diverse cultural elements. But since no single group is to rule over others, because of our implicit faith in the human capacity for intelligent behavior, democracy requires a method of resolving conflicts by inquiry, discussion, and persuasion rather than by violence. Hence, education that befits this kind of society must cultivate reflective thinking and critical inquiry.

Cultural Pluralism and American Education

The advocates of cultural pluralism believe that multicultural education is necessary to a democratic society. This belief is based on their implicit assumption that children's basic intellectual and emotional disposition toward nature and other people can be formed or changed through education. In other words, cultural pluralists hope to bring about a fundamental change in the attitude of American young people toward cultures that are different from their own through "establishing a *mutually supportive relationship* within the boundaries or framework of one nation of people of diverse cultures." [86] Such an education must provide a genuinely representative and balanced account of the contributions made by diverse cultural groups in the making of this country. But, more important, teachers should help children abandon the belief that there is a single style of living that befits everyone. One way to do this is by cultivating the attitude that their own modes of behavior and belief are as important and functional to them as other patterns are to others.

MULTICULTURAL EDUCATION

Recently, many minority groups, chafing under the pressure for Anglo-conformity, have demanded that our schools and their personnel become multicultural. This mounting interest in and concern for cultural pluralism in education has been given a boost by an official statement that was adopted by the board of directors of the American Association of Colleges

[86] Hazard and Stent, p. 14. Italics are ours.

for Teacher Education (AACTE) in October 1972. The fact that AACTE is one of the largest and most influential organizations of institutions involved in teacher preparation suggests the seriousness and urgency with which American educators view the problem of making our schools a major means of achieving cultural pluralism. Here are excerpts from the adopted statement.

Multicultural Education

. . . Multicultural education rejects the view that schools should seek to melt away cultural differences or the view that schools should merely tolerate cultural pluralism. Instead, multicultural education affirms that schools should be oriented toward the cultural enrichment of all children and youth through programs rooted to the preservation and extension of cultural alternatives. . . .

To endorse cultural pluralism is to endorse the principle that there is no one model American. To endorse cultural pluralism is to understand and appreciate the differences that exist among the nation's citizens. It is to see these differences as a positive force in the continuing development of a society which professes a wholesome respect for the intrinsic worth of every individual. . . .

Cultural pluralism rejects both assimilation and separatism as ultimate goals. The positive elements of a culturally pluralistic society will be realized only if there is a healthy interaction among the diverse groups which comprise the nation's citizenry. Such interaction enables all to share in the richness of America's multicultural heritage . . . and provides a means for coping with intercultural tensions that are natural and cannot be avoided in a growing, dynamic society. . . .

Education for cultural pluralism includes four major thrusts: (1) the teaching of values which support cultural diversity and individual uniqueness; (2) the encouragement of the qualitative expansion of existing ethnic cultures and their incorporation into the mainstream of American socioeconomic and political life; (3) the support of explorations in alternative and emerging life styles; and (4) the encouragement of multiculturalism, multilingualism, and multidialectism. . . .

In helping the transition to a society that values cultural pluralism, educational institutions must provide leadership for the development of individual commitment to a social system where individual worth and dignity are fundamental tenets. This provision means that schools and colleges must assure that their total educational process and educational content reflect a commitment to cultural pluralism . . . [and help] all students to understand that being different connotes neither superiority nor inferiority. . . .

If cultural pluralism is to become an integral part of the educational process, teachers and personnel must be prepared in an environment where the commitment to multicultural education is evident. Evidence of this commitment includes such factors as a faculty and staff of multiethnic and multiracial character, a student body that is representative of the culturally diverse nature of the community being served, and a culturally pluralistic curriculum that accurately represents the diverse nature of American society.

Multicultural education programs for teachers are more than special courses or special learning experiences grafted onto the standard program. The commitment to cultural pluralism must permeate all areas of the education experience provided for prospective teachers.

Multicultural education reaches beyond awareness and understanding of cultural differences. More important than the acceptance and support of these differences is the recognition of the right of these different cultures to exist. The goal of cultural pluralism can be achieved only if there is full recognition of differences and an effective educational program that makes cultural equality real and meaningful. . . .[87]

Some Recommendations for Multicultural Education On a different level and in more concrete terms, the Conference on Education and Teacher Education for Cultural Pluralism held in Chicago, May 1971, made recommendations to implement multicultural education. Over a hundred proposals were made by various groups participating in the conference.[88] These recommendations ranged from such often-heard suggestions as multiethnic staffing for schools and government positions, bilingualism, open enrollment admission policy, and the involvement of minority groups in curriculum development to stronger proposals such as boycotting the publishers who do not produce materials that are accurately representative of ethnic minorities, controlling the school district by a community body representative of the school's student population, and giving each community the authority to define the credentials for its teachers.

Though these recommendations do not represent a consistent and coherent proposal for a school reform supported by sound psychosocial and cultural theories of learning, they do suggest that multicultural education is much more than adding new courses on minority cultures, including more studies about different ethnic patterns, or even employing members of minority groups as teachers and administrators. The conference group's recommendations clearly imply that effective multicultural education cannot be achieved without social and political reforms.

The failure of our educational institutions to provide multicultural education can be attributed to such factors as the inability or unwillingness of the schools, the publishers, or the government to incorporate various ethnic elements into the standard instructional materials used in our schools. However, the most difficult aspect of implementing multicultural education for the promotion of cultural pluralism is the preparation of teachers who have in-depth understanding and appreciation of minority cultures and experiences without being patronizing and tacitly ethnocentric.

[87] *AACTE Bulletin*, October 1972. Reprinted by permission of the American Association for Colleges of Teacher Education, Washington, D.C. Since this statement was adopted by the AACTE board of directors, the Commission on Multicultural Education/Competency-based Teacher Education Project has been started under the general auspices and supervision of the board of directors, the Teacher Corps, and the University of Toledo.
[88] Madelon D. Stent et al., eds., *Cultural Pluralism in Education: A Mandate for Change* (New York: Appleton-Century-Crofts, 1973), pp. 153–158.

It appears that most teachers, save those from minority groups, lack knowledge about and experience in other cultures. Hence, their approach in teaching about other cultures often emphasizes the descriptive study of interesting cultural practices that are different from the dominant culture. For example, children learn that the Chinese write "up and down" (not left to right), Japanese eat raw fish, people from Middle Eastern countries eat with their fingers, some Africans brush their teeth with wooden sticks, and so on. Although students often go beyond these practices and learn about family structure and other social and moral customs, they rarely raise questions regarding why these seemingly strange patterns are given special meanings and significance in their respective cultures. Hence, our study of other cultures tends to reinforce American ethnocentrism, which is subtly but also deeply entrenched in almost every aspect of American life. Consequently, children may learn that alien patterns of behavior and belief are at least weird, if not inferior.

Not infrequently do we find classes deeply involved in cooking "foreign" dishes, singing ethnic folk songs, making native costumes, building native huts, and doing ritual dances in the name of understanding other cultures. Though the teacher's intention may be good, these activities are not likely to help children understand that they are only overt (physical) manifestations of each culture's unique symboling process (see pages 409–410) reflecting its unique world view and value orientation. In order to implement an effective multicultural program in any school, teachers must change from monocultural individuals into multicultural individuals by divesting themselves of Anglo-centrism. They must become serious students of culture.

The Esperanza Model for Multicultural Education   One attempt to change monocultural school programs to multicultural curriculums by assisting teachers to adopt a culturally pluralistic orientation is the Esperanza Model, developed by a number of individuals at the University of New Mexico.[89] As Figure 10 indicates, the model has three major phases dealing with (1) awareness, (2) application of awareness, and (3) logistics of implementation. The model is an attempt to show how a school can move from a monocultural to a multicultural curriculum with the purpose of providing meaningful education for the culturally different children and also enriching the life of the Anglo children.[90]

---

[89] The model, which was developed by Drs. Thomas Arciniega, John Aragon, Frank Angel, and Mari-Luci Ulibarri Jaramillo, appears in a Ph.D. dissertation written by Mari-Luci Ulibarri Jaramillo, entitled "In-Service Teacher Education in a Tri-Ethnic Community: A Participant-Observer Study," University of New Mexico, 1970. It is shown in Figure 10.

[90] More detailed explanations of the phases and their sections appear in an unpublished paper, "Public School Education in a Pluralistic Society: Problems of Program Implementation," by Mari-Luci Ulibarri Jaramillo. This paper was presented at the Cubberly Conference in Cultural Pluralism held at Stanford University in October 1973.

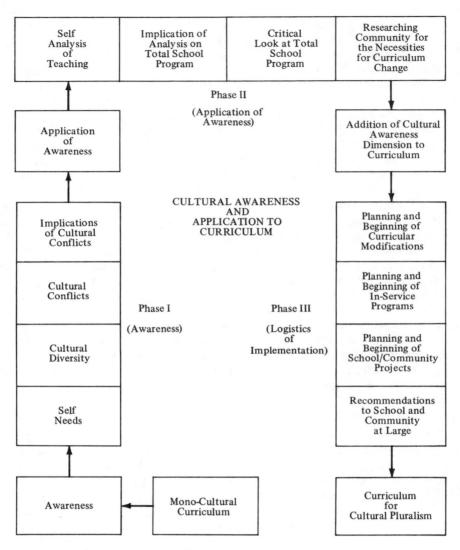

Figure 10   *The Esperanza Model*

The primary purpose of Phase 1 is to make school personnel more sensitive to different cultural elements in the school. In this phase, the personnel of the participating school are divided into groups of ten to twelve persons, and the groups meet perhaps ten times, with each session lasting from four to six hours. The main objective of this phase is to prepare the participants to accept cultural pluralism through an open discussion and examination of their own values, insecurities (complacency, tradition), and prejudices. The procedure is reminiscent of sensitivity training or the encounter group (T-group) mentioned in Chapter 12 (see pages 366–367). This phase is correctly based on the assumption that effective curricular and instructional reforms should be preceded or accompanied by changes in the teacher's own attitudes and beliefs.

It appears that at least two other benefits can arise from Phases 2 and 3 of this model, in addition to merely changing the curriculum. One is that the use of personal resources from the ethnic groups represented in the school district in analyzing and developing the new curriculum may give the members of minority groups a genuine sense of participation, thereby helping them to believe that they do belong to the community and the school. The other benefit is that the procedures outlined in the model force the school personnel and the members of the community to make comprehensive plans for implementing the new curriculum, based on a realistic and thorough understanding of the resources and the needs of the district. It is from this type of planning and community involvement that a coherent and effective curriculum consistent with the educational ideals of the community is likely to be born. Ideally, an effective application of the Esperanza Model could change the ways in which the school personnel, the members of the community, and the students relate to each other and could give them a broader basis for understanding American society and the meaning of democracy.

While these worthwhile results are, in principle, possible, the effectiveness of the model depends on how genuinely the school personnel and the community are interested in critically examining their attitudes toward minority cultures and how willing they are to make fundamental changes in their basic value orientation. Ethnocentrism, like racism, is an integral part of a person's world view and cannot be altered in one day, one week, or even in one month. Any major change in a person's fundamental disposition toward ethnocentrism or racial superiority requires a long, arduous, and often painful analysis of one's most cherished beliefs. Yet, the model (Phase 1, on awareness) appears to assume that once teachers disclose their insecurities, prejudices, and complacency, they will be ready to accept cultural pluralism. A few teachers might change, but others may simply go through the motions of change because of the external pressure for a school reform to provide multicultural education. Multicultural programs taught by ethnocentric teachers will be no better than a monocultural (WASP-centered) curriculum. Genuine surrender of ethnocentrism requires a long-term and on-going program in which the sociocultural foundations of education are seriously examined and debated in relation to the fundamental principles of American democracy.

Finally, the standard school curriculum should incorporate various cultural elements in the community. But many schools may need to provide special programs on minority cultures for the children from ethnically different groups. Such courses should help children develop a strong self-identity based on an accurate understanding of the contributions and role of their respective cultures in American society, so that they will not accept an inferior status and become defeatists even if they do encounter prejudice and discrimination. Cultural pluralism, like democracy, is not inherited but must be built.

EQUALITY OF EDUCATIONAL OPPORTUNITY

Inasmuch as cultural pluralism and democracy are both based on the premise that each individual not only has dignity and worth for his or her own sake but that all human beings have the capacity to become intelligent if given the opportunity for development, equality of educational opportunity is said to be intrinsic to a democratic society. Right or wrong, the economically disadvantaged minorities are convinced that their low socio-economic status stems from poor education due to inequality in educational opportunity based on prejudice and discrimination. Although the current debates about equality in education are primarily concerned with helping the poor rather than establishing cultural pluralism, the latter is not achievable if the social and economic growth of a minority is impeded by its color, religion, or ethnic background.

Today there is ample evidence to indicate that attending school does not necessarily constitute equality of educational opportunity. In reality, there appears to be a great deal of inequality in our schools—in the amount of money spent per pupil and the caliber of teachers available, as well as in the kinds of curriculum offered. Some argue that this inequality is the result of our outdated mode of financing public schools. Since most school districts are supported by local property taxes, the richer the district the more money it can spend on its schools. The difference between the most and the least spent on schooling is said to be at least $1,000 per student.[91] Hence, the poor insist that the resources of schools be equalized for equal opportunity through increased expenditures in the poorer school districts, because equal educational opportunity is believed to be implicitly guaranteed by the Constitution of this country.

In August 1971, the California Supreme Court—in *Serrano* v. *Priest*—ruled that the state system of financing public schools with real property taxes was unconstitutional because it "invidiously discriminates against the poor by making equality of a child's education a function of the wealth of his parents and neighbors." [92] This California decision was based on what the court believed to be implied in the rules of equal protection under

---

91 Duane J. Mattheis, *Emergency in School Finance*, Report to the School Business Officials Annual Convention (Chicago: U.S. Office of Education, 1972).
92 See *Harvard Educational Review* (November 1971): 501–534.

the Fourteenth Amendment.[93] In December of the same year, the Texas Supreme Court adopted the California ruling in a similar case. This means that if education is considered by a state as a "fundamental interest" vital to the state and the individual, any system of financing that prevents equal educational opportunity to all children violates the Fourteenth Amendment of the federal Constitution, which provides equal protection under the law for all citizens.

Those who favor the equalizing of educational opportunity through equalizing school expenditures assume that the economically disadvantaged can be freed from their condition of deprivation if they are given the same kind of schooling that white, middle-class children receive. In his book *The Cheerful Prospect*, Charles S. Benson, an economist, supports this view when he remarks that "a more generous supply of educational resources appears to be associated with greater learning on the part of the students." [94] He refers to a study conducted by J. Alan Thomas of the University of Chicago suggesting that "interdistrict differences in variables such as teachers' salaries, size of classes, size of school libraries, and experience of the teaching staff had positive relationship with scores on a battery of 18 achievement tests in 206 high schools in 46 states." [95] Thus Thomas and Benson agree that greater provision of educational resources means better schooling.

Moynihan and Jencks on Educational Equality   Contrary to Benson and Thomas, the Coleman Report indicates little relationship between available school resources and the academic achievement of children. The general conclusion of this massive governmental study on the equality of educational opportunity is supported by Frederick Mosteller and Daniel P. Moynihan, two Harvard scholars who analyzed the original report.[96] Mosteller and Moynihan further indicate that there is a significant relationship between children's social-class background and their educational achievement. Moynihan added that beyond a certain point increased

---

[93] This refers to the following parts of Section I of the Fourteenth Amendment: "No State shall make or enforce any law which shall abridge the privileges or immunities of citizens of the United States; nor shall any State deprive any person of life, liberty, or property, without due process of law; nor deny to any person within its jurisdiction the equal protection of the laws." The Serrano decision was overturned by the United States Supreme Court on March 21, 1973, in *San Antonio Independent School District* v. *Rodriquez*, because the majority opinion of the Court did not regard education as a "fundamental interest." It is important to note that in the California State Constitution, education is specifically mentioned as a "fundamental interest" of the state and its citizens. See *Saturday Review*, October 9, 1973, pp. 44–47.

[94] Charles S. Benson, *The Cheerful Prospect* (Boston: Houghton Mifflin, 1965), p. 27.

[95] Ibid.

[96] See Frederick Mosteller and Daniel P. Moynihan, eds., *On Equality of Educational Opportunity* (New York: Random House, 1972).

expenditures have no significant influence on academic achievement. In other words, the utility of extra spending

> diminishes until the exchange of input [extra spending] for output [academic achievement] is no longer equal, and finally to the point where additional input is almost totally wasted as virtually no additional output results.[97]

This means that, for Moynihan, educational spending could be reduced without seriously affecting the quality of education.

In his study of the relationship between schooling and adult success (income) Christopher Jencks, another Harvard scholar, challenges the conventional view that there is a significant relationship between educational opportunity and adult success. In his book *Inequality*, Jencks concludes that differences between schools and their resources have little effect on what happens to students after they complete schooling. Moreover, there is no evidence to indicate that school reforms can reduce cognitive inequality, for instance, differences in reading comprehension, verbal fluency, and mathematical skills.[98]

Jencks holds that the primary reason for economic inequality among adults is not inequality in cognitive skills, for differences in income are found among individuals with similar cognitive achievement. Consequently, he does not believe that economic failures can be reduced by equalizing everyone's reading scores or mathematical skills. On the contrary, he believes that

> economic success seems to depend on varieties of luck and on-the-job competence that are only moderately related to family background, schooling, or scores on standardized tests. The definition of competence varies greatly from one job to another, but it seems in most cases to depend more on personality than on technical skills.[99]

Equalizing competence or "luck" is difficult to imagine, but this does not imply that poverty cannot be reduced or even eliminated. According to Jencks, equalization of income would require at least two conditions. One is that the poor must cease to accept their condition as inevitable and must demand changes in the rules of the "game" (employment). The second condition is that some of those with high incomes must begin to feel ashamed of economic inequality. Jencks is convinced that if these changes were to occur, significant institutional changes in the machinery of income distribution would become politically feasible.[100] The distribution of wealth can be equalized through political and other institutional changes resulting from individuals' attitudes regarding their economic conditions.

---

[97] Daniel Moynihan, "On Equality: II. Equalizing Education—In Whose Benefit?" *Public Interest*, Fall 1972, p. 69.
[98] Christopher Jencks, *Inequality: A Reassessment of the Effect of Family and Schooling in America* (New York: Harper & Row, Harper Colophon Books, 1972), pp. 7–8.
[99] Ibid., p. 8.
[100] Ibid., p. 265.

But Jencks does not say how individual dispositions can be altered, nor does he suggest how schooling might affect children's attitudes.

As we have already seen, the Coleman and Jencks studies dealt with different aspects of the impact of schooling, yet their conclusions seem to dispel some of the commonplace beliefs about what schooling can or cannot do to influence children's intellectual, economic, and social achievements. In sum, these studies indicate that increased expenditures, reallocation of resources, reassignment of pupils, and curricular reforms seldom change the way teachers and students treat each other or affect children's academic or economic achievements.

Accordingly, Jencks argues that since professional educators know as little about the effects of schooling as laypeople and since the character of schooling appears to have relatively little long-term influence on a person's development, there are no good grounds for limiting the range of educational choices open to parents and students. He goes on to suggest that society should provide a wide variety of schools, for those who value the life of the mind and ideas as well as for those who favor discipline and competitive excellence or simply behaving properly.[101] And, since "the list of competing objectives is nearly endless, . . . we favor diversity and choice." [102] But would this also mean that the society must make available the kind of schooling that encourages educational and social inequality, simply because there are elitists in our society who desire such conditions?

Clearly, the issue here is what Jencks means by "diversity and choice." If Jencks believes that equal distribution of wealth is desirable, that the poor should demand social change and the wealthy must become ashamed of economic inequality, it is self-defeating for him to suggest that parents and students be provided any kind of education they desire.

IEA Study on Schooling For the past several years the International Association for the Evaluation of Educational Achievement (IEA) has studied the factors influencing students' academic achievement. This study covered some twenty countries involving approximately 258,000 students at three age levels (ten, fourteen, and eighteen), 50,000 teachers, and 9,700 schools. The study attempted to identify the variables affecting students' success in science, reading comprehension, literature, English and French as foreign languages, and civic education.

The IEA study[103] supports the Coleman Report concerning the powerful influence of the *home background* on success in the areas of reading comprehension, literature, and civic education. The data further indicate that there is a close relationship between student achievement and parents' level of education, the father's occupation, and even the number of books

---

[101] Ibid., pp. 256–257.
[102] Ibid., p. 257.
[103] Four of these reports, entitled International Studies in Evaluation, have been published by Wiley.

at home. Moreover, children appear to develop the basis for future cognitive ability, that is, verbal ability, before they enter school. However, unlike the Coleman Report, the IEA study suggests a strong relationship between schooling and academic achievement in science and in foreign languages. The "opportunity to learn," the degree of student exposure to given areas of a subject, and the amount of time a student spends on a subject are significantly related to academic performance. Teacher competence in both teaching skill and in subject matter also seem to have a positive relationship with student success in schools.

We must remember that the Coleman Report, its analysis by Mosteller and Moynihan, and the IEA study examined the relationship between the socioeconomic background of students and their academic success measured by certain standardized tests. On the other hand, Jencks' work on inequality studied the impact of schooling on adult income. But none of these studies was concerned with the impact of schooling on attitudinal or belief changes in children and how such changes may influence the image children have of themselves, of adults, of the society, and of the world in which they live. What we are suggesting is not that there is a significant relationship between schooling and students' attitudinal, belief, and affective changes, but that the apparent lack of close relationship between schooling and academic achievement and academic achievement and adult income should not lead us to conclude that schooling is unnecessary. It would indeed be wise to take seriously the following remarks made by Robert L. Thorndike, who prepared the report on *Reading Comprehension Education in Fifteen Countries*, a part of the IEA reports:

> It [lack of significant relationship between schooling and reading comprehension] may merely imply that the schools that have been studied all represent at least a basic level of competence, and that beyond that the differences between schools are either inadequately assessed by our instruments or of minor importance as far as achievement is concerned.[104]

In spite of divergent conclusions, these studies make clear that the socio-cultural background of children is a crucial factor in their growth and development. It is also evident that schooling is not and cannot be the major force in equalizing the vast differences in the socioeconomic status of individuals, for schooling, at best, is only one variable. Moreover, if we are to understand "equality of educational opportunity" to mean that all the young people in this country should get a fair chance at developing their individual potentiality, then such an equalizing process necessarily involves massive changes in the social, economic, political, and industrial sectors of our society.

Considering the relatively small amount of time that children spend at school compared to time outside school, it would be unrealistic to expect

---

[104] Robert L. Thorndike, *Reading Comprehension Education in Fifteen Countries*, International Studies in Evaluation III (New York: Wiley, Halsted Press, 1973), pp. 179–180.

the school to act as a primary force for social reform. To attribute economic inequality, political corruption, social injustice, and moral decay to our schools alone is as unreasonable as blaming the weather forecasters for floods. There is, however, an urgent need to conduct comprehensive studies on the impact of schooling on children's emotional and intellectual dispositions. Findings from such studies may indicate the means of achieving multicultural education and cultural pluralism, which require fundamental changes in our deep-seated attitudes and beliefs about all human beings and their cultures.

Cultural Pluralism and the School as a Smaller Society

The American school can be seen as a microcosm of the society at large. Consequently, the basic tenets of cultural pluralism and democracy can be applied to schools themselves and their various "subcultures": board members, administrators, teachers, and students. Moreover, the conflicts between these units could be regarded as cultural, and value conflicts could be resolved through inquiry and persuasion rather than by one group suppressing another.

THE SCHOOL AS A MICROCOSM OF THE LARGE SOCIETY

Like the larger society, the school with its simpler and smaller social form may be seen to have its own unique behavior and language patterns, assignments of roles and status, and even rites and ceremonies, for example, initiation activities and commencement ceremonies. But perhaps the most important aspect of the school as a society is the fact that its primary function, enculturation and acculturation of the young, is carried on through human interaction. Whether students acquire love or hatred for learning or become docile or creative is influenced in part by the nature of the interaction that goes on between students and school personnel.

The modes of social and personal interactions in the school are affected by the cultural conditions of the larger society. The ways in which adult members of the society deal with children are likely to be reflected in the teacher's approach to evaluating students' achievements and failures. Similarly, if a culture contains contradictory beliefs and practices these may be transmitted to students unless the school consciously and deliberately points out and reduces, or eliminates, such contradictions. For example, Americans generally believe that one should always be truthful. But many people also believe that it is all right to "cheat" a little in their income tax returns or to make campaign promises for local elections, even though they may not be able to fulfill them. Recently, a candidate for the presidency of an elementary school student council promised to put Coca Cola machines in every classroom and provide longer and more frequent recess periods if he were elected to the office. The boy was elected, but the school officials regarded the boy's tactic as merely humorous and imaginative. While the purpose of allowing a student council to function may have been to teach children the meaning of fair play and the democratic process in operation, the school actually may have helped in teaching that child that whatever means one uses to attain one's goal is justifiable.

Before we examine the school as a smaller society—the various units of its formal structure, their basic value orientations, and the conflicts that may arise between them—we must first consider some of the major contradictions in American culture and the significant impact they may have on schooling.

Contradiction in American Culture

Many aspects of American culture are in conflict with one another. Theodore Brameld, a noted philosopher of education, characterizes American culture as "schizophrenic." [105] We emphasize self-promotion and individual achievement in socioeconomic status, and reward it with civic dignity, but we also praise and encourage social concern in philanthropic work. Moreover, while our country is said to guarantee equal rights and opportunities to all, full civil rights have yet to be granted to many of its people. Further, while long-range socioeconomic planning is often regarded as un-American and socialist, there seems to be an increasing trend toward the belief that governmental plans and intervention are necessary and desirable, for example, wage, price, energy, and media controls.

There are still other inconsistencies. For example, most members of the dominant culture in America believe that moral principles are absolute and hence unchangeable, yet they also insist that one has to be flexible in making value decisions, particularly in relation to business practices, which affect other individuals. As Spindler points out, unless administrators and teachers are aware of these contradictions and how they influence teaching-learning activities in school, they may transmit qualities that are self-defeating.[106] In other words, while the school may intend to develop self-reliance, creativity, and democratic leadership, students may become docile and submissive if the school activities and climate are inconsistent with the intended objectives. More specifically, a course in social studies should not be taught in an authoritarian manner, nor should the school rules be merely repressive measures.

One of the most serious inconsistencies is that while children are evaluated according to adult criteria, the young are assumed to be incapable of dealing with their problems without massive adult intervention.

---

[105] Theodore Brameld, *Patterns of Educational Philosophy* (New York: Holt, Rinehart and Winston, 1971), pp. 24–37.
[106] George D. Spindler, "Transmission of American Culture," in *Education and Culture*, pp. 149–150.

According to anthropologist Mary Ellen Goodman, there are at least two basic and unwarranted assumptions that underlie American pedagogy and child rearing. One is the fallacy of universal age-stage linkage and the other is the underestimation fallacy.[107] The first is demonstrated in the belief that adolescence anywhere at anytime is necessarily a period of storm, stress, and confusion. Hence, we characterize adolescent behavior as confused whenever it deviates from the adult norm. The second assumption suggests that children and adolescents are incapable of appreciating interpersonal relations and unable to cope with their frustrations, tensions, and problems. Lois Barclay Murphy, a child psychologist and one of the authors of *The Widening World of Childhood*, concurs when she says "seldom do we think of the child as a small human being, carrying on his own struggle to make sense out of life, to meet his own needs, to master the challenge presented by life. . . ." When the child does not "behave" as adults demand, he is said to have behavior problems, or "symptoms." [108] Consequently, children and adolescents are thought of primarily in terms of incapacities and inabilities.

Because the notion of age-stage linkage and the underestimation fallacy are so widely held by adults, the behavior and value patterns of the young are often described as "senseless," "irrational," "confused," "irresponsible," and "insensitive." "In view of these ideas, it is not surprising that children and adolescents are usually treated with a kind of amiable tolerance; little is expected of them in the way of learning, control, or responsibility." [109] It appears that as the members of the WASP culture regard their belief and behavior pattern as the idealized norm for everyone, adult members of our society see their pattern of behavior and values as the fixed norm for both adults and children. In other words, the behavior and belief systems of children and adolescents are not seen as functionally viable means of dealing with their problems. Adults in our society have rejected the notion of the cultures of childhood and adolescence just as the WASP culture rejects minority and ethnic patterns as cultures. In a very real sense, the young have been "colonized" the way ethnic minorities have been "colonized" by the dominant culture.

As Goodman rightly points out, what the young can accomplish in the areas of cognitive, social, and even motor skills is determined not only by maturation and training but also by the level of culturally patterned expectations.[110] In a word, the lower the expectation, the less the achievement. For example, in this country we have minimal expectations with respect to the kinds of social responsibilities and cognitive skills the young are to achieve. Consequently, if children or adolescents lack "social grace" in relating to older people, they are usually "excused" because adults believe

107 Goodman, *The Culture of Childhood*, p. 2.
108 Lois Barclay Murphy et al., *The Widening World of Childhood* (New York: Basic Books, 1962), pp. 1, 3.
109 Goodman, p. 11.
110 Ibid., p. 21.

that "kids are kids and they can't be expected to behave and talk properly." Yet in many societies, adolescents and even children work and behave at a much more sophisticated level, and this is due largely to the high level of culturally patterned expectations.

While most of us would contest the caricature of the American way of life as a *pedocracy* wherein parents obey their children, only a few of us would disagree that Americans are preoccupied with and anxious about their children and uncertain about how to deal with them. Thus on the one hand we claim to respect the rights and dignity of the young as intrinsically worthwhile, but on the other hand we evaluate them according to the criteria used for adult members of the society. American adults implicitly assume that children's behavior and belief patterns are deficit forms of their adult norm. In other words:

> However rewarding the culture of childhood, that of the grown-up world is continuously and persistently presented as more rewarding and desirable, and childhood is defined as a transitory and to-be-abandoned stage of life. No matter how entrancing, the never-never world of Peter Pan turns out to be just that, a fantasy in which childhood is forever threatened by pirates symbolizing demanding adults who must eventually win in the age-old struggle between old and young.[111]

According to anthropologist Solon Kimball, grownups in America expect their children to have a strong commitment to change, to desire constant progress and improvement. Hence, children who are satisfied with the status quo are penalized.[112] Children are expected not only to acquire competence, wisdom, and maturity, but also to seek to achieve goals higher than what they have already accomplished. These requirements present to our children unresolvable contradictions and unreachable ends because in a constantly changing society "final achievement is impossible because objectives themselves are not fixed."[113] In other words, the goals are modified as conditions change within the society, and each individual contributes to the change.

In addition to committing themselves to constant improvement and self-fulfillment, children are also required to assume a posture of perpetual optimism.[114] They are expected to perform their roles in a mood of perpetual hopefulness, because "our culture demands that we maintain this euphoric facade in our own perception of the world and our place in it. Furthermore, we demand that our children exhibit the same psychological posture."[115] These three criteria of evaluation coupled with our underestimation of children's ability to deal with problems present young Amer-

---

[111] Solon Kimball, "Cultural Influences Shaping the Role of the Child," in *Socio-Cultural Foundations of Education*, John H. Chilcott, Norma C. Greenberg, and Herbert B. Wilson, eds. (Belmont, Calif: Wadsworth, 1968), p. 125.

[112] Ibid., p. 128.

[113] Ibid., p. 129.

[114] Ibid.

[115] Ibid.

icans with an unresolvable dilemma, because while they are *not expected to act like adults, they are judged by the standard* by which grownups are evaluated. This kind of contradiction widens the intergenerational rift and increases the sense of alienation and dislocation felt by the young.

Perhaps the most pernicious aspect of the contradictions we have discussed is that the behavior and beliefs of young Americans have been and are still judged according to the same social pathology model with which the dominant culture has evaluated ethnic minorities. That is, adults consider the belief and behavior patterns of the young as deficit (pathological) forms of the grown-up norm, which is thought to be the only idealized pattern for everyone. Hence, parents demand unquestioning obedience to their rules and the school expects docility and submissiveness from its students. Accordingly, nonconformity to the school rules is often treated as violation of absolute commandments requiring repentence and punishment. If our schools are to function more effectively and humanely in consonance with the principles of democracy and cultural pluralism, we must re-examine our adult conception of the nature and function of the cultures of childhood, adolescence, and young adulthood. We must also encourage students at all educational levels to become actively involved in participatory democracy as representatives of minority cultures.

CULTURAL CONFLICTS IN SCHOOL

As the dominant WASP culture should recognize and utilize the values of minority cultures in teaching culturally different children to function satisfactorily in multicultural situations, so should the adult world accept the existence of the culture of our young people and become more responsive (but not submissive) to their needs·and changing values. If the American school is to make any significant contribution in helping to educate our youth to become intelligent individuals who can successfully deal with the problems arising out of a perpetually and rapidly changing society, we must critically re-examine the basis of the goal of American education as a means of transmitting the so-called traditional core values. Moreover, since our schools must serve both the society and its children, who will later become the adult members of society, we must relate what schools do to the value systems of the younger generation.

SHIFTS IN CORE VALUES

According to a study conducted by Spindler in the early 1960s, the core values of college students had shifted considerably from those of their parents.[116] The study involved several hundred students enrolled in professional education courses and representing lower-middle-class to upper-middle-class socioeconomic status. But since Spindler's data was collected

[116] Spindler, "Education in a Transforming American Culture," p. 133.

over a period of several years, the new emerging core values he speaks of relate to college students from the mid-1950s to early 1960s. Unlike their parents, Spindler's subjects held as their core values (1) sociability, (2) a relativistic moral attitude, (3) consideration for others, (4) a hedonistic present-time orientation, and (5) conformity to the group.[117]

By sociability is meant liking people and being able to get along well with them. The second value, a relativistic moral attitude, is the belief that what is moral is relative to the group to which one belongs. To be considerate of others means being sensitive to and having tolerance for other people's feelings so that the harmony of the group is not disturbed. Hedonistic, present-time orientation is the opposite of the traditional future-time orientation that belongs to the Puritan morality. It is said to come from the notion that since no one can be certain about tomorrow, we should enjoy the present, a sort of "drink and be merry for tomorrow we die" attitude. Yet even this fourth value was to be carried out within the limits of the norm set by the group. The last value of conformity to the group emphasizes the importance of group harmony as the ultimate goal of individual members.

The following words of Spindler summarizing the data from his study clearly describe the core values of many college students from the mid-1950s to the early 1960s:

> The keynote to the character type regarded as the most desirable, and therefore constituting a complex of values, is *balance, outward-orientedness, sociability* and *conformity* for the sake of adjustment. Individuality and creativity, or even mere originality, are not stressed in this conception of values. Introspective behavior is devaluated. . . . Deviancy, it seems, is to be tolerated only within the narrow limits of sociability, of general outwardness, of conformity ("Artists are perverts"). The All-American is altogether adjusted.[118]

Conflicts between parents and school officials steeped in Puritan morality and the young people Spindler studied were unavoidable because their value orientations were contradictory. But no serious confrontations occurred between those two generations because the young were more concerned with *balance, adjustment,* and *harmony* than with individualism, spontaneity, and autonomy.

Since the completion of Spindler's study there has been increasing evidence that the value orientation of today's youth has moved even further from the value systems of their parents. Today even a casual conversation with upper grade school and junior high school children will reveal their strong belief in the individual's right to privacy and freedom. The significant change in the value commitments of young people may be partially attributable to the student activism and counterculture movement

---

[117] Ibid., pp. 136–137.
[118] Ibid., p. 135.

of the mid-1960s. But, more important, the conditions thought to have led to the youth movements of the 1960s persist today.

Although today's adolescents and college youths may tend to conform more to adult demands and norms, the flame of their doubts about the legitimacy of the traditional core values of American society continues to burn. It is to this condition that we can attribute some fundamental changes in certain areas of young people's value orientation.

The Transformation of Youth Values

THE COUNTERCULTURE MOVEMENT

The proponents of the counterculture movement in the mid-1960s argued that though America has achieved an unprecedented economic affluence through the work-success and achievement ethic, it continues to emphasize economic success and productivity. As a result of this endless search for greater and greater affluence even the worth of an individual is now said to be determined according to success and productivity as defined by corporations and industry. But to growing numbers of young people in this country the long-sought economic affluence and security became simple facts of life. They were no longer legitimate objects to be achieved. Consequently, the young were convinced that the core values of the older generation, that is, the cultural values of the industrial ethic, were outdated and irrelevant to their lives. As Theodore Roszak, a social critic, points out:

> A high-consumption, leisure-wealthy society doesn't need rigidly trained, "responsible" young workers. The middle class can afford to prolong the ease and drift of childhood, and so it does. It "spoils" its kids, meaning it influences them to believe that being human has something to do with pleasure and freedom.[119]

Once the society is able to demonstrate that it can produce enough for all its members (though this is questionable today), the society's primary concern should not be to produce more and consume more. The supporters of the counterculture movement insisted that we develop a more just and equal means of distributing the nation's wealth so that more people could live meaningfully and leisurely. In sum, the young people of the mid-1960s were not against technology but rather the worship of it, for such a culture tends to treat people as products of a technological system and subordinates human needs to industrial and technological needs. As the deschoolers argued, people had become tools of their own tools. To the advocates of the counterculture movement, the moral imperatives and urgency behind production, acquisition, materialism, and greater economic

---

[119] Theodore Roszak, "Youth and the Great Refusal," in *The Prospect of Youth*, Thomas J. Cottle, ed. (Boston, Little, Brown, 1972), p. 61.

affluence had lost their validity. At the same time, the authorities (adults) who subscribed to the traditional values had lost their legitimacy.

In his book *The Greening of America*, Charles A. Reich, another social critic, suggests that the counterculture movement was probably caused by disorder, corruption, hypocrisy, war, poverty, distorted priorities, law making by private power, uncontrolled technology, and the destruction of environment. To these he also adds decline of a sense of community and the loss of self.[120] Reich argues that the generations disagreed not only about the problems America faced but also about the solutions to them. That is, the grownups insisted that the young must work within the system to change it, while their offspring argued that they could not effect genuine changes by working in the system, because doing so meant conforming to the norms established by the system. In other words, since the very core of the system—economic rewards for technological productivity—was illegitimate, no real social reform could result from becoming subservient to the very notions the young were attempting to destroy.

For the young to believe that they had been oppressed by their elders was nothing new and perhaps to be expected in almost any period in history. "But for authority to be regarded likewise as illegitimate [was] something new." It made conflict far more disruptive. It was, in fact, the characteristic that most clearly distinguished the intergenerational conflict of the 1960s from that which commonly occurs between successive generations.[121] One of the consequences of this phenomenon was that with declining legitimacy of the authorities there was a rise in coercive violence launched by terrified authorities to maintain their threatened power. Such violence was justified as a necessary means of controlling the younger generation that had no respect for "authority" and "law and order."[122]

Contrary to the prevailing attitude of the older generation, Roszak holds that the declining legitimacy of the mainstream culture and its core values was more a symptom of default on the part of adults than of youth.[123] Roszak bases his argument on the premise that the elders had "surrendered their responsibility to make morally demanding decisions, to generate ideals, to control public authority, to safeguard the life of the community against its despoilers."[124] The older generation had been so scared off and bought off that it had become "a barrier of paralyzed complacency," rather than a catalyst in the growth of its children.[125]

Because the young were convinced of the illegitimacy of the Establish-

---

[120] Charles A. Reich, *The Greening of America* (New York: Random House, 1970), pp. 4–7.
[121] Roszak, p. 147.
[122] Edgar Z. Friedenberg, *Coming of Age in America* (New York: Random House, 1965), p. 147.
[123] Roszak, p. 63.
[124] Ibid.
[125] Ibid.

ment and its values, they struggled against institutional conformity, centralized power, and uniformity of any kind. On the other hand, they extolled

> privacy and a rich inner life at the expense of achievement and the development of social skills in manipulating and competing with others—to value these is to reject the fundamental and official attitudes of American society, to fly in the face (and perhaps up the nose) of the school system, the Little League and the core virtues of the Land of Opportunity.[126]

The demand for radical cultural revolution by the young appeared in the form of increased requests for the governed to become actively involved in the political, economic, and social processes. Students also sought an opportunity to participate in their own educational experience and planning. An idiosyncratic life style and personal grooming were said to symbolize the young's revolt against uniformity, and marijuana smoking was believed to be a ritual action by which they asserted a new moral position.

According to Edgar Z. Friedenberg, "potblowing" is ideological in that it represents the belief that people who enjoy themselves without endangering others have an inalienable right to privacy.[127] Also a drug that enables its users to turn inward upon their own experience, enriching their fantasy at the expense of their sense of the need to achieve or relate to others, is as moral as alcohol, which encourages a false gregariousness and increasingly pugnacious or competitive behavior.

The counterculture movement is no longer a potent force among America's youth. But as the results of the following surveys indicate, young people's desires for privacy, autonomy, and a greater involvement in participatory democracy have not changed. In sum, the younger generation today still questions the legitimacy of the traditional values, even though many young people are willing to conform more to the adult norm because of the current insecurities related to finding and keeping jobs and anxieties related to general political, social, and economic uncertainties of the time.

YOUTH VALUES IN THE 1970s

In 1971, the firm of Daniel Yankelovich, Inc., conducted a survey of 1,244 students on fifty college and university campuses for the John D. Rockefeller III Foundation to study the possible shifts in students' value orientation.[128] Of those interviewed, over 75 percent mentioned that they were chiefly concerned with friendship, privacy, freedom of opinion, and nature. Only about 25 percent still regarded changing society and combatting hypocrisy as their primary interest. This data seems to suggest

---

[126] Friedenberg, p. 149.
[127] Ibid.
[128] *Kansas City Times*, April 13, 1972, p. 4B.

that college students had moved away from emotional involvement in social and political causes. They appeared to be channeling their efforts to those aspects of their lives over which they could have more control.

According to the survey, these students were less willing than those in the 1960s to fight wars for any reason; 50 percent of the participants saw war as justified only if it were for counteracting aggression (a 14 percent decline from a similar study in 1968). Perhaps the greatest single erosion of relations to authority was in the "boss" relationship: only 36 percent of the students did not mind being "bossed" around on the job. Moreover, in 1971 only 39 percent held the belief that "hard work always pays off," while another survey conducted by Yankelovich for the Foundation in 1968 showed that 69 percent believed that "hard work will always pay off." This shift from the traditional work-success ideal was indeed radical. In regard to sex, the group generally sought a much greater degree of sexual freedom and its acceptance by their elders. In summing up the study, a majority of the interviewed believed that American democracy or justice does not function evenhandedly and that there is a considerable degree of inconsistency between American ideals and practice. This disillusionment about America appears to be supported by the fact that 30 percent of the participating students preferred to live in some country other than the United States. A similar figure was reported by the Gallup Poll in 1971.

A survey conducted by the University of California at Los Angeles and the American Council on Education suggested that college freshmen in 1973 tended to be more liberal and were more inclined to support greater freedom of students than their predecessors.[129] The study polled more than 318,000 freshmen at 579 institutions, and from this population 190,000 were statistically adjusted to represent the nation's 1.65 million freshmen. In regard to the question of student freedom and institutional authority, 31 percent believed that student publications should be cleared through college officials and only 23 percent agreed that college administration has the right to ban extremist speakers. This data indicates a considerable liberalization of student attitudes, for the 1968 survey by the same institutions showed that 56 percent and 32 percent believed in college censoring of student publications and banning of extremist speakers, respectively.

In other areas, only 11 percent thought colleges have a right to regulate their off-campus life (compared to 23 percent in 1968) and 48 percent supported legalization of marijuana (compared to 19 percent in 1968). In regard to the women's liberation movement, 91 percent supported the movement. This figure indicates a 10 percent increase in three years.

Although the studies conducted by Daniel Yankelovich, Inc., UCLA, and the American Council on Education dealt primarily with college students, their cumulative data since 1968 indicates a major shift in the core values of a sizable segment of American youth. The apparent increase in the desires for right to privacy, personal freedom, and autonomy, concern

129 *Kansas City Star*, February 10, 1974, p. 15A.

for people, disillusionment with American democracy, and rejection of authority revealed an even greater degree of disagreement with the grown-ups than the group interviewed by Spindler in an earlier study.

In spite of the evidence for rapid shifts in the core values of our young people, few board members, administrators, and teachers critically examine the role of the school in American society. Nor do they critically analyze the grounds for the officially prescribed norms of behavior and learning activities in relation to the changes taking place in the students' world view and belief patterns. Too many educators refuse to understand the young from their own cultural perspective. And even when they study the young, it is usually for the purpose of inducing them to abandon their "barbarism" and "irrationality" so that they can assimilate (or acculturate) the young into the idealized norm of the grown-up world.

In a very real sense, as the white middle class is ignorant about minority cultures, so too are adults ignorant about the culture of childhood, adolescence, and youth. Although understanding the young people's acts and values from their cultural perspective will not remove disagreements, it may help to make the conflicts less disruptive and alienating. If we are to treat conflicts in school and in the classroom as cultural conflicts, both school officials and students must abandon their ethnocentrism, that is, the attitude that youngsters are "senseless" and the attitude that "old fogies just don't understand." Educationally, this means that board members, administrators, and teachers must act not as royalty but as members of a society in which individuals with varied cultural (both ethnic and generational) backgrounds live together. School personnel and students should act as members of a community that creates rules as a means of effective functioning of the group and resolves conflicts through inquiry. Hence administrators and teachers should act more as "moderators" than judges.

Cultural pluralism in the larger society requires that full civil rights be granted to all ethnic minorities. Students must also be granted these rights as unique individuals representing their own minority culture in the school. And if the principles of cultural pluralism are to be applied to the American school, the behavior and value systems of our children should not be treated as deficit forms of adult behavior. Rules and practices, social or academic, must emerge out of the life of the school as a democratic society.

Conclusion

Cultural pluralism as a social ideal cannot be accomplished by improving the school alone. Nor can multicultural education be achieved through changes in school curriculum and reassignment of teaching personnel, because fundamental changes in the sociopolitical and economic systems of the country are essential to any major social reform, such as cultural pluralism. But the American school could contribute to significant social change in the long run if our students are made to see the contradictions between the supposed ideals of American democracy and social reality. We must make sure that educational reforms are not adopted simply as more effective means of transmitting the long-established and traditional values. In other words, our schools as instruments of a free society "must serve as the principal medium for developing in youth the attitude and skills of social, political, and cultural criticisms."[130]

Education for cultural pluralism and democracy must be based on reflective (critical) thinking, because such

> thinking enables us to direct our activities with foresight and to plan according to ends-in-view, or purposes of which we are aware. It enables us to act in deliberate and intentional fashion to attain future objects or to come into command of what is now distant and lacking. By putting the consequences of different ways and lines of action before the mind, it enables us to know what we are about when we act. It converts action that is merely appetitive, blind, and impulsive into intelligent action.[131]

In other words, reflective thinking gives us a better control of our present life as well as of future possibilities.

It is probably not possible to establish any necessary or logical connection between cultural pluralism and a particular school of philosophy. However, if one attempts to be consistent in one's metaphysics, epistemology, and axiology, cultural pluralism could not be derived from any philosophical perspective that insists that there is only one absolute and *a priori* norm for reality, truth, and goodness. In short, cultural pluralism is inconsistent with (or contradictory to) any philosophical system that denies human experience as its primary source of knowledge and value, because cultural pluralism implicitly assumes that the meaning and worth of any belief or value system are determined by the ways in which they help people meet their needs in dealing with other people and nature.

Cultural pluralism is based upon a pluralistic philosophy in that it regards the criteria of what is real, true, and good as culture-bound and experience-bound. This perspective is perhaps most congenial to the following words of Dewey:

> If ideas, meanings, concepts, notions, theories, systems are instrumental to an active reorganization of the given environment, to a removal of some specific trouble and perplexity, then the test of their validity and value lies in accomplishing this work. If they succeed in their office, they are reliable, sound, valid, good and true. If they fail to clear up confusion, uncertainty and evil when they are acted upon, then are they false.[132]

If a given pattern of behavior consistently helps us resolve our problems, then to that extent the pattern is true and good. But the fact that a given

---

[130] Neil Postman and Charles Weingartner, *Teaching as a Subversive Activity* (New York: Delacorte, 1969), p. 2.
[131] John Dewey, *How We Think* (Boston: D. C. Heath, 1933), p. 17.
[132] Dewey, *Reconstruction in Philosophy*, p. 156.

behavior and belief pattern has worked in the past does not necessarily imply that it will always help us in working out our perplexities, for there may be new and more effective means of solving our problems. By constantly revising our problem-solving approaches we increase our knowledge and change cultural patterns and social habits. Again, the validity and significance of what we do and what we believe is context-bound.

In closing, the reader must be reminded that no single school of philosophy necessarily leads to the basic tenets of cultural pluralism. Moreover, it is doubtful that many contemporary advocates of cultural pluralism have attempted to relate their social ideology to metaphysical, epistemological, and axiological issues. But, in terms of the philosophical perspective discussed in the first ten chapters of this book, the philosophical view most consonant with the ideals of cultural pluralism is Experimentalism.

Questions

1. Is cultural pluralism achievable in America? Are there other forms of social, political, or philosophical perspectives that may be consistent with and congenial to cultural pluralism as discussed in this chapter?

2. Develop a teaching unit in your field of specialization by incorporating what you regard as distinct ethnic traits of several minority cultures in this country.

3. Describe what you regard as the core values of several ethnic minorities in this country and indicate how they may be made an integral part of your classroom climate. If possible, try the Esperanza Model using your class as a school district.

4. Visit some schools and classes and make a list of rules and practices that, in your opinion, may transmit unintended values and attitudes, i.e., ethnocentrism. Analyze them with other students and indicate what changes could be made.

5. Is there any connection between considering the conflicts in school as cultural conflicts and the concept of the open classroom?

6. What evidence can you cite concerning discrepancies between the core values of the grown-up world (particularly the school board members, administrators, and teachers) and students? Why? Do you think there are such discrepancies in your community? If your answer is "no," how to you account for it? But, if your answer is "yes," what can you do to reduce or eliminate such discrepancies between the value orientations of adults and the young in your community?

Further Reading

Cottle, Thomas J., ed. *The Prospect of Youth*. Boston: Little, Brown, 1972. Displaying a poet's passion for his topic, Cottle blends sociology, first-person essays, and observation pieces in a lyric on youth and its culture. The book deals with conflicts that American youths encounter in moving from childhood and adolescence into young adulthood.

Dillard, J. L. *Black English*. New York: Random House, 1972. Dillard examines black language, its cultural roots, and its inherent legitimacy as a medium of communication and accommodation within the framework of American education and instruction.

Itzkoff, Seymour W. *Cultural Pluralism and American Education*. Scranton, Penn.: International Textbook, 1969. The concept of cultural pluralism is examined in terms of its philosophical basis and educational implications. The notions of Anglo-conformity and the "Melting Pot" model as different forms of assimilationism (Americanization) are also discussed. The author suggests that mass society as well as technologically oriented society erodes human values, and conformity to a single pattern of values and behavior crushes the humanizing elements of cultural pluralism. He suggests that education, while no panacea, is the best hope for maintaining and nurturing the creative and liberalizing capacities for people.

Mead, Margaret. *Culture and Commitment*. Garden City, N.Y.: National History Press, Doubleday, 1970. Mead discusses different stages of cultural development. She indicates that experiences of the past provide little guidance for the future, and hence adults cannot serve as adequate models for their children. On the contrary, we may have reached the stage in which elders must learn from their young.

Pratte, Richard. *The Public School Movement*. New York: David McKay, 1973. This book examines the failure of the public school movement in America. The author attributes much of this failure to the unrealistic, and perhaps unrealizable, expectation America placed upon its schools. The author calls for reforms rather than abandonment of our schools. The book is written from the perspective of analytic philosophy.

Stone, James C., and Donald P. De Nevi, eds. *Teaching Multi-Cultural Populations*. New York: Van Nostrand Reinhold, 1971. The articles in this anthology emphasize the belief that teaching in a culturally diverse society requires a great amount of knowledge about the cultures represented in the society. The materials deal with histories, value orientations, and problems of the five minority cultural heritages in America, namely, the Afro-American heritage, the Puerto Rican heritage, the Mexican–American heritage, the Indian heritage, and the Asian–American heritage.

Index

DATE DUE